Environment and Trade

Environment and Trade

A Guide to WTO Jurisprudence

Nathalie Bernasconi-Osterwalder, lead author, with Daniel Magraw, Maria Julia Oliva, Marcos Orellana and Elisabeth Tuerk

EARTHSCAN

London • Sterling, VA

First published by Earthscan in the UK and USA in 2006

ISBN-13: 978-1-84407-298-9
ISBN-10: 1-84407-298-3

Typesetting by JS Typesetting Ltd, Porthcawl, Mid Glamorgan
Printed and bound in the UK by Bath Press, Bath
Cover design by Andrew Corbett

For a full list of publications please contact:

Earthscan
8–12 Camden High Street
London, NW1 0JH, UK
Tel: +44 (0)20 7387 8558
Fax: +44 (0)20 7387 8998
Email: earthinfo@earthscan.co.uk
Web: **www.earthscan.co.uk**

22883 Quicksilver Drive, Sterling, VA 20166-2012, USA

Earthscan is an imprint of James and James (Science Publishers) Ltd and publishes in association with the International Institute for Environment and Development

A catalogue record for this book is available from the British Library

Library of Congress Cataloging-in-Publication Data

Environment and trade : a guide to WTO jurisprudence / Nathalie Bernasconi-Osterwalder . . . [et al.].
p. cm.
Includes bibliographical references and index.
ISBN 1-84407-298-3
1. Foreign trade regulation–Environmental aspects–Cases. 2. Foreign trade regulation–Cases. 3. Non-tariff trade barriers–Law and legislation–Environmental aspects. 4. Non-tariff trade barriers–Cases. 5. International trade–Environmental aspects. 6. Environmental policy–Economic aspects. I. Bernasconi-Osterwalder, Nathalie.
K4610.E58 2005
343′.087–dc22

2005022291

Printed on elemental chlorine-free paper

Contents

List of Contributors

Nathalie Bernasconi-Osterwalder is the managing attorney of the Geneva office of the Center for International Environmental Law (CIEL). She works primarily on issues relating to trade, investment and sustainable development. Ms Bernasconi is a former fellow of the Institute of International Economic Law in Washington, DC and has worked for the United Nations Development Programme (UNDP) in Vietnam, for the Australian law firm Phillips Fox, and for the Justice Department in Switzerland. She has an LLM from Georgetown University Law Center in Washington, DC, and a Lic.iur. from Université de Neuchatel, Switzerland; she is a member of the Bar of Basel, Switzerland.

Daniel Magraw is President of the Center for International Environmental Law (CIEL) in Washington, DC. Prior to joining CIEL, Mr Magraw was the Associate General Counsel and Director of the International Environmental Law Office at the US Environmental Protection Agency. He has also been a professor of international law at the University of Colorado in Boulder, worked in a private law practice in Washington, DC, and served as a Peace Corps volunteer in India. Mr Magraw served as Chair of the Section of International Law and Practice of the American Bar Association, as a member of the Executive Council of the American Society of International Law, on the Board of Directors of Lawyers Alliance for World Security and in other professional associations. He has published numerous books and articles and is a widely recognized expert in the field of environmental law. He has a BA in Economics (with high honours) from Harvard University and JD from the University of California, Berkeley.

María Julia Oliva is a staff attorney at the Center for International Environmental Law (CIEL), where she is Director of the Project on Intellectual Property. She earned an LLM Degree in environmental law from Northwestern School of Law at Lewis and Clark College, where she graduated *cum laude* and was awarded first place in the Davis, Wright and Tremaine International Law Writing Competition. During this time, Ms Oliva also worked at the Office of the Solicitor of the US Department of the Interior. Previously, she earned her law degree at the University of Mendoza in Argentina, where she also practised law in the civil society sector. Ms Oliva edits *Intellectual Property (IP) Quarterly Update*, a publication of the South Centre and CIEL (see www.ciel.org/Publications/pubipqu.html).

Marcos A. Orellana is senior attorney at the Center for International Environmental Law (CIEL), where he is director of the Trade and Sustainable Development programme.

Prior to joining CIEL, Mr Orellana was affiliated as a fellow to the Lauterpacht Research Centre for International Law of the University of Cambridge, UK. He also was a visiting scholar with the Environmental Law Institute in Washington, DC. Previously, Mr Orellana lectured on international law and environmental law at the Universidad de Talca, Chile, and provided legal counsel to the Chilean Ministry of Foreign Affairs. In 1997–1998, Mr Orellana completed his LLM degree at American University, during which time he also worked as an intern at the World Bank's Inspection Panel. In addition to his work at CIEL, he has lectured on the law of the sea, human rights and environment, and on international institutions and sustainable development at American University, Washington College of Law.

Elisabeth Tuerk is a former staff attorney with the Center for International Environmental Law (CIEL). She specializes in multilateral trade policy and sustainable development. She is currently staff at the United Nations Conference on Trade and Development (UNCTAD). She has a Masters degree in law, and a Masters degree in business management from the Franzens University Graz, Austria. She also has a postgraduate degree in international economics and international law from the World Trade Institute (WTI), Bern. Prior to her position in CIEL, she worked at the World Trade Organization (WTO), Geneva, the European Commission, DG Trade, Brussels and Boehler Uddeholm AG, Buenos Aires, Argentina.

Foreword

Global interdependencies, both economic and environmental are growing. The need for coherence and coordination in trade and environmental policies is more important than ever.

At the World Trade Organization (WTO) Conference in Doha 2001, Trade Ministers agreed to negotiations on a number of critical trade and environment issues, including the relationship between trade obligations in multilateral environmental agreements (MEAs) and WTO rules, procedures for information exchange and observer status in WTO bodies, as well as on the reduction of tariffs and non-tariff barriers on environmental goods. Strong language in the Doha Ministerial Declaration about the need for coherence and mutual supportiveness between trade and environment has expanded the political space at the WTO and elsewhere. After a long night of political debate in September 2002 at the Johannesburg World Summit on Sustainable Development (WSSD), heads of states and governments also reaffirmed the need for coherence and mutual supportiveness.

The knowledge of the basic facts and of the ongoing developments of discussions and decisions within WTO promotes better understanding of the issue of mutual supportiveness between trade and the environment. It also helps to ensure coherence between trade and environmental policies and to achieve a better understanding of the synergies between MEAs and the rules of the WTO, which must be further strengthened. This Guide to WTO Jurisprudence relating to Environment and Trade, elaborated by the Center for International Environmental Law (CIEL), is a very helpful instrument to these ends. The precise examination of environment-related jurisprudence in the WTO highlights recent developments in WTO cases that are relevant to a range of key trade and environment issues. The analysis focuses both on jurisprudence arising in relation to key WTO obligations, and on developments in the broader body of WTO jurisprudence.

I trust that this Guide will be of use to policy makers in the area of trade and environment to further develop their agenda and participate effectively in ongoing negotiations. It is an important contribution to all our efforts to increase mutual supportiveness between trade and environment.

Philippe Roch,
Former State Secretary, and Director of the Swiss Agency for the Environment, Forests and Landscape

Acknowledgements

In writing this book, the attorneys of the Center for International Environmental Law (CIEL) have benefited from the support and assistance of many people. CIEL is exceedingly grateful to the Swiss Agency for Environment, Forests and Landscape (SAEFL) for the grant that made the publication of this book possible. Special thanks go to Manuela Jost, our patient, wise and helpful contact at SAEFL.

Thanks are also due to the many people who assisted with the preparation of this book. CIEL expresses its deep appreciation to David Stewart Christy, Jr of The Loeffler Group for his valuable and tireless input into the chapters of this book. Erica Pencak also deserves special thanks for her very fine research and editorial assistance in preparing the book for publication. We are also grateful to Robyn Briese, Eric Dixon, Lise Johnson, Alicia Kaiser, Aman McHugh, Tiernan Mennen, Sasha Sajovic and Erin Webrick, who assisted with research in various stages. Johanna Borcic, office manager of CIEL's Geneva office, also deserves great appreciation for her support.

Finally, CIEL would like to thank Rob West and his colleagues at Earthscan for their professional and expeditious handling of the book's publication.

Nathalie Bernasconi-Osterwalder
Daniel Magraw
Maria Julia Oliva
Marcos Orellana
Elisabeth Tuerk

List of Acronyms and Abbreviations

AB	Appellate Body
BGH	bovine growth hormone
CAA	US Clean Air Act
CAFE	US Corporate Average Fuel Economy
CBD	Convention on Biological Diversity
CIEL	Center for International Environmental Law
CITES	Convention on International Trade in Endangered Species of Wild Fauna and Flora
COP	Conference of Parties
CTE	Committee on Trade and Environment
DSB	Dispute Settlement Body
DSM	Dispute Settlement Mechanism
DSU	Dispute Settlement Understanding
EC	European Communities
EEC	European Economic Community
EPA	US Environmental Protection Agency
ESA	US Endangered Species Act
ETP	Eastern Tropical Pacific Ocean
EU	European Union (officially referred to as European Communities in WTO)
FAO	Food and Agriculture Organization
FCCC	Framework Convention on Climate Change
GATS	General Agreement on Trade in Services
GATT	General Agreement on Tariffs and Trade
GMOs	genetically modified organisms
ICJ	International Court of Justice
IPRs	intellectual property rights
ISO	International Organization for Standardization
MEA	multilateral environmental agreement
MFN	most-favoured nation
MMPA	US Marine Mammal Protection Act
NAFTA	North American Free Trade Agreement
NGO	non-governmental organization
OECD	Organisation for Economic Co-operation and Development
PCIJ	Permanent Court of International Justice

PIC	prior informed consent
PPMs	processes and production methods
RICO	US Racketeer Influenced and Corrupt Organizations Act
SAEFL	Swiss Agency for Environment, Forests and Landscape
SCM Agreement	Subsidies and Countervailing Measures Agreement
S&D or SDT	special and differential treatment (for developing countries)
SPS Agreement	Agreement on Sanitary and Phytosanitary Measures
TBT Agreement	Agreement on Technical Barriers to Trade
TED	Turtle excluder device
TNC	Trade Negotiations Committee
TRIMs Agreement	Agreement on Trade-Related Investment Measures
TRIPS Agreement	Agreement on Trade-Related Aspects of Intellectual Property Rights
UN	United Nations
UNCED	United Nations Conference on Environment and Development
UNCTAD	United Nations Conference on Trade and Development
UNDP	United Nations Development Programme
UNEP	United Nations Environment Programme
USTR	US Trade Representative
WSSD	World Summit on Sustainable Development
WTI	World Trade Institute
WTO	World Trade Organization

List of Relevant GATT and WTO Disputes

Short title	**Full title and citation**
Australia – Ammonium Sulphate	Report of the Working Party on *The Australian Subsidy* on *Ammonium Sulphate*, 31 March 1950, GATT/CP.4/39-II/188, adopted 3 April, 1950
Argentina – Bovine Hides	*Argentina – Measures Affecting the Export of Bovine Hides and Import of Finished Leather* (brought by European Communities), panel report (WT/DS155/R) adopted 16 February 2001
Australia – Salmon	*Australia – Measures Affecting Importation of Salmon from Canada* (brought by Canada), Appellate Body report (WT/DS18/AB/R) and panel report as modified by Appellate Body report (WT/DS18/R) adopted 6 November 1998
Australia – Salmon 21.5	*Australia – Measures Affecting Importation of Salmon from Canada – Recourse to Article 21.5* (implementation panel requested by Canada), implementation panel report (WT/DS18/RW) adopted 17 April 2000
Belgian Family Allowances	*Belgium – Family Allowances*, panel report (BISD 1S/59) adopted 7 November 1952
Canada – Automotive Industry	*Canada – Certain Measures Affecting the Automotive Industry* (brought by Japan/European Communities), Appellate Body report (WT/DS139/AB/R and WT/DS142/R) and panel report as modified by the Appellate Body report (WT/DS139/R and WT/DS142) adopted 19 June 2000
Canada – Hormones	*Canada – Continued Suspension of Obligations in the EC – Hormones Dispute* (brought by European Communities), composition of the panel (DS320) determined 6 June 2005
Canada – Patent Protection	*Canada – Patent Protection of Pharmaceutical Products* (brought by European Communities), panel report (WT/DS114/R) adopted 7 April 2000
Canada – Periodicals	*Canada – Certain Measures Concerning Periodicals* (brought by United States), Appellate Body report (WT/DS31/AB/R) and panel report as modified by the Appellate Body report (WT/DS31/R), adopted 30 July 1997
Canada – Unprocessed	*Canada – Measures Affecting Exports of Unprocessed Herring*

Herring and Salmon	*and Salmon*, panel report (BISD 35S/98) adopted 22 March 1988
Chile – Alcoholic Beverages	*Chile – Taxes on Alcoholic Beverages* (brought by EC), Appellate Body report (WT/DS87/AB/R and WT/DS110/AB/R) and panel report as modified by the Appellate Body report (WT/DS87/R and WT/DS110/R) adopted 12 January 2000
DR – Cigarettes	*Dominican Republic – Measures affecting the importation and internal sale of cigarettes* (brought by Honduras), Appellate Body report (WT/DS302/AB/R) and panel report as modified by Appellate Body report (WT/DS302/R) adopted 19 May 2005
EC – Asbestos	*European Communities – Measures Affecting Asbestos and Products Containing Asbestos* (brought by Canada), Appellate Body report (WT/DS135/AB/R) and panel report as modified by Appellate Body report (WT/DS135/R) adopted 5 April 2001
EC – Bananas III	*European Communities – Regime for the Importation, Sale and Distribution of Bananas* (brought by Ecuador/Guatemala and Honduras/Mexico/US), Appellate Body report (WT/DS27/AB/R) and panel reports as modified by Appellate Body report (WT/DS27/R/ECU, WT/DS27/R/HND, WT/DS27/R/MEX and WT/DS27/R/USA) adopted 25 September 1997
EC – Biotech	*European Communities – Measures Affecting the Approval and Marketing of Biotech Products*, panel report pending as of 30 June 2005 (DS293)
EC – Cotton from India	*European Communities – Anti-dumping Duties on Imports of Cotton-type Bed Linen from India* (brought by India), Appellate Body report (WT/DS141/AB/R) and panel report as modified by Appellate Body report (WT/DS141/R) adopted 12 March 2001
EC – Hormones	*European Communities – Measures Concerning Meat and Meat Products* (brought by United States/Canada), Appellate Body report (WT/DS26/AB/R and WT/DS48/AB/R) panel reports as modified by Appellate Body report (WT/DS26/R/USA and WT/DS48/R/CAN) adopted 13 February 1998
EC – Sardines	*European Communities – Trade Description of Sardines*, (brought by Peru), Appellate Body report (WT/DS231/AB/R) and panel report as modified by Appellate Body report (WT/DS231/R) adopted 23 October 2002
EEC – Oilseeds and Related Animal-Feed Proteins	*European Economic Community – Payments and Subsidies Paid to Processors and Producers of Oilseeds and Related Animal-Feed Proteins*, panel report (BISD/37S/86) adopted 25 January 1990

Short title	**Full title and citation**
Indonesia – Automobile	*Indonesia – Certain Measures Affecting the Automotive Industry* (brought by European Communities/Japan/United States/Japan), panel report (WT/DS54/R, WT/DS55/R, WT/DS59/R and WT/DS64/R) adopted 23 July 1998
Japan – Alcoholic Beverages (1987)	*Japan – Customs Duties, Taxes and Labelling Practices on Imported Wines and Alcoholic Beverages*, panel report (BISD/34S/83) adopted 10 November 1987
Japan – Alcoholic Beverages (1996)	*Japan – Taxes on Alcoholic Beverages* (brought by EC/Canada/US), Appellate Body report (WT/DS8/AB/R, WT/DS10/AB/R and WT/DS11/AB/R) and panel report as modified by Appellate Body report (WT/DS8/R, WT/DS10/R and WT/DS11/R) adopted 1 November 1996
Japan – Apples	*Japan – Measures Affecting the Importation of Apples* (brought by US), Appellate Body report (WT/DS245/AB/R) and panel report as upheld by Appellate Body report (WT/DS245/R) adopted 10 December 2003
Japan – Lumber	*Japan – Tariff on Imports of Spruce, Pine, Fir (SPF) Dimension Lumber*, panel report (BISD/36S/167) adopted on 19 July 1989
Japan Varietals (also referred to as *Japan Agricultural Products II*)	*Japan – Measures Affecting Agricultural Products* (brought by US), Appellate Body report (WT/DS76/AB/R) and panel report as modified by Appellate Body report (WT/DS76/R) adopted 19 March 1999
Korea – Beef	*Korea – Measures Affecting Imports of Fresh, Chilled and Frozen Beef* (brought by US/Australia), Appellate Body report (WT/DS161/AB/R and WT/DS169/AB/R) and panel report as modified by Appellate Body report (WT/DS161/R and WT/DS169/R) adopted 10 January 2001
Spain – Unroasted Coffee	*Spain – Tariff Treatment of Unroasted Coffee*, panel report (BISD/28S/102) adopted on 11 June 1981
Thailand – Anti-dumping Duties	*Thailand – Anti-dumping Duties on Angles, Shapes and Sections of Iron or Non-alloy Steel and H-beams from Poland* (brought by Poland), Appellate Body report (WT/DS122/AB/R) and panel report as modified by Appellate Body report (WT/DS122/R) adopted 5 April 2001
Thailand – Cigarettes	*Thailand – Restrictions on Importation of and Internal Taxes on Cigarettes*, panel report (BISD 37S/200)_adopted 7 November 1990
US – Copyright	*United States – Section 110(5) of the U.S. Copyright Act* (brought by European Communities), panel report (WT/DS160/R) adopted 27 July 2000
US – Countervailing Measures on Certain EC Products	*United States – Countervailing Measures Concerning Certain Products from the European Communities* (brought by European Communities), Appellate Body report (WT/DS212/AB/R) and panel report as modified by Appellate Body report (WT/DS212/R) adopted 8 January 2003

Short title	**Full title and citation**
US – Gambling	*United States – Measures Affecting the Cross-Border Supply of Gambling and Betting Services* (brought by Antigua and Barbuda), Appellate Body report (WT/DS285/AB/R) and panel report as modified by Appellate Body report (WT/DS285/R) adopted 20 April 2005
US – Hormones	*United States – Continued Suspension of Obligations in the EC – Hormones Dispute* (brought by European Communities), composition of the panel (DS321) determined 6 June 2005
US – Lead and Bismuth Carbon Steel	*United States – Imposition of Countervailing Duties on Certain Hot-Rolled Lead and Bismuth Carbon Steel Products Originating in the United Kingdom* (brought by European Communities), Appellate Body report (WT/DS138/AB/R) and panel report as modified by Appellate Body report (WT/DS138/R) adopted 7 June 2000
US – Malt Beverages	*United States – Measures Affecting Alcoholic and Malt Beverages*, panel report (BISD 39S/206) adopted 19 June 1992
US – Petroleum	*United States – Taxes on Petroleum and Certain Imported Substances*, panel report (BISD/34S/136) adopted on 17 June 1987
US – Reformulated Gasoline	*United States – Standards for Reformulated and Conventional Gasoline* (brought by Venezuela), Appellate Body report (WT/DS2/AB/R) and panel report as modified by Appellate Body report (WT/DS2/R) adopted 20 May 1996
US – Section 337	*United States – Section 337 of the Tariff Act of 1930*, panel report (BISD 36S/345) adopted on 7 November 1989
US – Shrimp/Turtle I	*United States – Import Prohibition of Shrimp and Shrimp Products* (brought by India, Malaysia, Pakistan and Thailand), Appellate Body report (WT/DS58/R/AB) and panel report as modified by Appellate Body report (WT/DS58/R) adopted 6 November 1998
US – Shrimp/Turtle 21.5	*United States – Import Prohibition of Shrimp and Shrimp Products – Recourse to Article 21.5* (implementation panel requested by Malaysia), Appellate Body report (WT/DS58/AB/RW) and panel report as upheld by Appellate Body report (WT/DS58/RW) adopted 21 November 2001
US – Softwood Lumber (Preliminary Determinations)	*United States – Preliminary Determinations with Respect to Certain Softwood Lumber from Canada* (brought by Canada), panel report (WT/DS236/R) adopted 1 November 2002
US – Softwood Lumber (Final Determinations)	*United States – Final Countervailing Duty Determination with Respect to Certain Softwood Lumber from Canada* (brought by Canada), Appellate Body (WT/DS257/AB/R) and panel (WT/DS257/R) reports adopted 17 February 2004)
US – Taxes on Automobiles	*United States – Taxes on Automobiles*, panel report (DS31/R) circulated 11 October 1994 (NOT ADOPTED)
US – Tuna and Tuna	*United States – Prohibition of Imports of Tuna and Tuna*

Short title	**Full title and citation**
Products from Canada	*Products from Canada*, panel report (BISD 29S/91) adopted 22 February 1982
US – Tuna/Dolphin I	*United States – Restrictions on Imports of Tuna*, panel report (DS21/R) circulated 3 September 1991 (NOT ADOPTED)
US – Tuna/Dolphin II	*United States – Restrictions on Imports of Tuna*, panel report (DS29/R) circulated 16 June 1994 (NOT ADOPTED)

List of Relevant WTO Agreements

Agreement on Implementation of Article VI of the General Agreement on Tariffs and Trade 1994 ('Anti-dumping Agreement'), LT/UR/A-1A/3, 15 April 1994.

Agreement on Technical Barriers to Trade ('TBT Agreement'), LT/UR/A-1A/10, 15 April 1994.

Agreement on Subsidies and Countervailing Measures ('SCM Agreement'), LT/UR/A-1A/9, 15 April 1994.

Agreement on the Application of Sanitary and Phytosanitary Measures ('SPS Agreement'), LT/UR/A-1A/12, 15 April 1994.

Agreement on Trade-Related Aspects of Intellectual Property Rights ('TRIPS Agreement'), LT/UR/A-1C/IP/1, 15 April 1994.

General Agreement on Tariffs and Trade 1994 ('GATT 1994' or 'GATT'), LT/UR/A-1A/1/GATT/1, 15 April 1994.

General Agreement on Tariffs and Trade 1947 ('GATT 1947' or 'GATT'), LT/UR/A-1A/1/GATT/2, 15 April 1994.

General Agreement on Trade in Services ('GATS'), LT/UR/A-1B/S/1, 15 April 1994.

Marrakesh Agreement Establishing the World Trade Organization ('WTO Agreement'), LT/UR/A/2, 15 April 1994.

Understanding on Rules and Procedures Governing the Settlement of Disputes ('Dispute Settelement Understanding' or 'DSU'), LT/UR/A-2/DS/U/1, 15 April 1994.

Introduction

BACKGROUND

International trade rules significantly impact domestic policy making, including in the area of environmental law and policy. The most comprehensive set of global trade rules is established under the World Trade Organization (WTO), which, as of 30 June 2005, had 148 developed and developing country Members. WTO Members have agreed to a number of trade 'disciplines', which can sometimes overlap with other laws and policies, at the domestic, regional and global levels. If a Member believes that a measure of another Member, including environmental and health measures, is inconsistent with one or more of the WTO disciplines, the Member can challenge that measure in an institutionalized binding dispute settlement system. In the event that the WTO Dispute Settlement Body (DSB) finds that a measure violates WTO law, the challenging Member may impose trade sanctions until the challenged Member comes into compliance with the recommendations of the WTO DSB.

The role of WTO dispute settlement and its resulting jurisprudence are thus of critical importance for the environment and trade debate. WTO tribunals have addressed and continue to consider fundamental questions concerning the adequate interpretation and implementation of WTO rules vis-à-vis environmental and human health laws and regulations established by WTO Members. For instance, do WTO rules allow Members to treat products differently based on environmental considerations? Or, do they allow Members to exercise precaution when environmental and health risks are at stake? Do individuals and groups have the right to voice their environmental and health concerns in dispute settlement proceedings? These are just some of the pertinent questions. *Environment and Trade: A Guide to WTO Jurisprudence* examines how WTO jurisprudence has addressed these and many other questions. The *Guide* offers a convenient and easy-to-use tool for practitioners, civil society, academics, students and policy makers who work on environment and/or trade issues. It is intended to improve understanding of the environment and trade interface and thereby contribute to finding sustainable solutions in areas where the balance between environmental, social and economic values is being forged.

ORGANIZATION OF THE GUIDE

This Guide to environment-and-trade jurisprudence provides an overview of the major themes relevant to the environment and trade linkage and analyses how these themes have been treated in the jurisprudence under the 1947 General Agreement on Tariffs and Trade (GATT 1947) and the World Trade Organization (WTO) agreements.

The themes covered are as follows:

1 Like Products
2 General Exceptions Clauses
3 The Necessity Requirement
4 Processes and Production Methods (including eco-labelling)
5 Extraterritoriality
6 The Role of Science and the Precautionary Principle (including the relationship of trade rules and environmental agreements)
7 Intellectual Property Rights and Conservation of Biological Diversity
8 Participation in WTO Dispute Settlement – The Case of Amicus Briefs

The Guide deals with these themes in separate chapters. Cross references between the chapters indicate overlaps and inter-linkages, which are frequent. Each chapter contains two types of material. The first type consists of background information, followed by analyses of the various WTO provisions relevant to the theme covered, including how GATT and WTO tribunals have interpreted these provisions.

The second type of material in each chapter chronologically covers GATT and WTO disputes as they relate to the environment-and-trade theme covered in that chapter. Each discussion of a dispute begins with a short summary and comments, which are not exhaustive, but instead address specifically the respective theme covered. The summary and comments are followed by selected excerpts from the report of that dispute which demonstrate how the WTO Appellate Body and WTO/GATT panels have applied WTO law relating to the theme covered. The Guide has taken into account jurisprudence until 30 June 2005.

OVERVIEW OF CONTENT

Chapter 1 focuses on the cornerstone of the WTO's framework on trade: its rules on non-discrimination. The GATT – and later the WTO – established the principles of most-favoured-nation (MFN) treatment and national treatment as the basis for international trade. Under the most-favoured-nation principle, Members must extend any advantage granted to a product from one WTO Member to 'like products' from all other Members. Under the national treatment principle, internal taxes and regulations must treat imported products no less favourably than like domestic products. Similar non-discrimination rules also apply for trade in services. In the context of trade and environment, the discussions have focused primarily on the national-treatment principle and its inherent concept of 'like products'. When products are considered 'like', one product generally may not be treated more favourably than the other. If products are not considered 'like', Members may treat them differently. This distinction has been at the heart of a number of environment related cases, and arguably will come up again in the currently pending *EC – Biotech* case. In that case, the WTO panel has been called to examine the WTO consistency of the European Communities' authorization system for genetically modified products and the ban on such products adopted by individual EU members. Here, the panel might be faced with the question of whether genetically modified maize, cotton, corn or soya are 'like' conventional, non-genetically modified products. This chapter includes summaries and excerpts from a fairly large number of cases examining the concept of likeness under Article I of the GATT (most-favoured-nation treatment) and Article III of the GATT (national treatment), including, most prominently, *Japan – Alcoholic Beverages (1996)* and *EC – Asbestos*.

Chapter 2 gives an overview of the general exceptions clauses included in the GATT and the General Agreement on Trade in Services (GATS). The chapter provides insights into how these clauses have been interpreted, and points to their significance for WTO Members' ability to protect the environment and human health. The exceptions clauses allow WTO Members to derogate from their obligations under the GATT and the GATS in a number of specific instances, including to conserve exhaustible natural resources and protect human, animal or plant life or health. The analysis in Chapter 2 focuses in large part on the overall structure of the exceptions clauses, as well as some more specific interpretational aspects. However, some issues related to the exceptions clauses are treated in subsequent chapters on the 'necessity requirement' and 'extraterritoriality'; jurisprudence relating to these two topics is therefore not covered extensively in Chapter 2. With respect to jurisprudence, Chapter 2 discusses important GATT and WTO decisions, including, among others, the famous (but unadopted) *US – Tuna/Dolphin* GATT decisions, as well as *US – Reformulated Gasoline* and the two *US – Shrimp/Turtle* decisions. It also provides insights into the recent *US – Gambling*, a case brought under the GATS.

Chapter 3 provides greater detail regarding the requirement that trade-restrictive measures enacted to protect the environment and human health must be found 'necessary' if they are to be considered valid under the WTO framework agreements. The GATT, the GATS, the Agreement on Technical Barriers to Trade (TBT Agreement) and the Agreement on Sanitary and Phytosanitary Measures (SPS Agreement) each contain a variation of the so-called 'necessity test', but each test is slightly different. This chapter discusses and compares these tests, examines the 'legitimate objectives' factor of the necessity test, and discusses the topic of international standards and the presumption of necessity, as it relates to the SPS and TBT Agreements. The jurisprudence examined in Chapter 3 includes disputes regarding the necessity test under Articles XX (b) and (d) of the GATT, the TBT Agreement, the SPS Agreement and the GATS. The decisions include, *inter alia*, the pre-WTO GATT cases, such as *US – Section 337* and *Thailand – Cigarettes*, and more recent WTO cases such as *Korea – Beef*, *EC – Asbestos*, *Dominican Republic – Cigarettes*, *EC – Sardines*, *Australia – Salmon*, *Japan – Varietals* and *US – Gambling*.

Chapter 4 discusses the measures enacted and adopted in order to protect the environment and human health from the harmful effects resulting from the manner in which a product is produced, commonly referred to as processes or production methods (PPMs), and why such measures are so controversial. The chapter explains the distinctions between product related PPM-based measures and non-product related PPM-based measures, and between country-based and origin-neutral PPM-based measures. Eco-labelling is also discussed, as are PPM-based measures in the context of Articles I, III, XI and XX of the GATT, and the SPS and TBT Agreements. With respect to jurisprudence, *Belgian Family Allowances* and *Canada – Automotive Industry* are discussed in the context of Article I of the GATT; the unadopted *US – Tuna/Dolphin I* and *II* and *US – Malt Beverages* panel reports, *US – Taxes on Automobiles*, and *US – Reformulated Gasoline* are discussed in the context of Articles III and XX; and *US – Shrimp/Turtle I* and *21.5* are discussed in the context of Article XX.

Chapter 5 addresses the topic of extraterritoriality, focusing on environment and health protection measures that apply to or affect persons, property, acts, or events located or occurring outside the territory of the state attempting to adopt or enforce the measures. The chapter also points out the misleading notion that measures with extraterritorial effects are per se inconsistent with international customary law and WTO law. The chapter discusses the link between extraterritoriality and non-product related PPM-based measures, and extraterritoriality in the context of the GATT and the SPS and TBT Agreements. Relevant jurisprudence includes the unadopted *US – Tuna/Dolphin I* and *II* reports, and *US – Shrimp/Turtle I.*

Chapter 6 discusses the role of science and the precautionary principle, which calls for decision makers to take a precautionary approach when faced with incomplete knowledge and the prospect of harm to the environment or human health. The precautionary principle is an important tool for protecting the environment and human health, but WTO jurisprudence has raised the question of whether WTO rules allow governments to take trade related measures based on precaution, and if so, to what extent. The chapter addresses the ways in which the GATT and the SPS and TBT Agreements approach science and allow for or limit the use of the precautionary principle. The chapter focuses in particular on the SPS Agreement, and its requirements relating to 'sufficient scientific evidence' and risk assessment (Article 5.1). The chapter also contains a discussion of international standards, burden of proof, and precaution in the context of multilateral environmental agreements. *EC – Hormones, Australia – Salmon, Japan – Varietals* and *Japan – Apples* are discussed in the context of the SPS Agreement, and *EC – Asbestos* is discussed in the context of the GATT.

Chapter 7 examines the relationship between the Convention on Biological Diversity (CBD) and the Agreement on Trade-Related Aspects of Intellectual Property Rights (TRIPS Agreement), and the ways in which intellectual property rights (IPRs) can both support or weaken efforts to conserve biological diversity. In particular, the chapter also looks at the possible conflicts between the CBD and the TRIPS Agreement, from an inherent distinction with regards to the ownership of genetic resources – the CBD grants States sovereign rights over their genetic resources, while the TRIPS Agreement allows private rights over the same resources – to the linkages in specific areas. The chapter explores four main clusters of issues that have emerged in discussions on the relationship between the TRIPS Agreement and the CBD: (i) patentability of life forms; (ii) access to a fair and equitable sharing of benefits arising from the use of genetic resources; (iii) preservation and respect for the knowledge, innovation and practices of indigenous and local communities; and (iv) transfer of technology. The chapter also discusses recent developments at the WTO, TRIPS Council and the Committee on

Trade and Environment (CTE). Relevant jurisprudence to date is scarce. *Canada – Patent Protection* and *US – Copyright* are briefly discussed.

Chapter 8 addresses the role of public participation in WTO dispute settlement. Since the WTO dispute settlement system is limited to claims brought by governments against other governments, submission of amicus briefs is currently the *only* means through which the public, including, civil society groups, businesses, and individuals can present their views directly to the WTO's dispute settlement tribunals. Public participation in environment and public health related disputes is particularly important because the outcomes of these cases have a significant impact on the general public. The chapter discusses the provisions that give panels and the Appellate Board the legal authority to accept and consider amicus briefs, noting that this authority grants panels and the Appellate Board the *discretion* to accept and consider amicus briefs, but does not *require* them to do so. It further notes that amicus briefs are most likely to be accepted and considered if they are attached to a party's or third party's submission. Jurisprudence discussed in this chapter includes, among others: *EC – Hormones, US – Shrimp/Turtle I, US – Lead and Bismuth Carbon Steel, US – Copyright, EC – Asbestos, US – Shrimp/Turtle 21.5*, and *EC – Sardines.*

COVERED JURISPRUDENCE

The Guide covers a variety of WTO decisions. First, it includes cases that are strictly environment related (i.e. where an environmental measure is challenged). Second, the Guide also includes health related cases – given that environment and health are intrinsically linked, and the jurisprudence in one area is often relevant to the other. Finally, the Guide covers a series of cases that, while they relate to neither environment nor health, have contributed to environment and health related jurisprudence in certain areas. For example, the necessity requirement, an important concept in the trade and environment debate, has been examined and further developed in a number of cases not linked to the environment or human health.

The reports selected for this Guide include both GATT and WTO reports. Most GATT reports discussed were adopted by the GATT Council, but some were not. Generally speaking, adopted GATT reports continue to have important jurisprudential significance while the relevance of those GATT reports that were never adopted is more limited. With respect to adopted GATT panel reports, the WTO Appellate Body in *Japan – Alcoholic Beverages (1996)* stated that these 'are an important part of the GATT *acquis.* They are often considered by subsequent panels. They create legitimate expectations among WTO Members, and, therefore, should be taken into account where they are relevant to any dispute' (*Japan – Alcoholic Beverages (1996)* AB report, sec. E). With respect to unadopted reports, the Appellate Body in the same case said that 'a panel could nevertheless find useful guidance in the reasoning of an unadopted panel report that it considered to be relevant' (Ibid.).

The selection of the excerpts of the cases for this Guide has been an important challenge. Due to space constraints some excerpts had to be kept shorter than others. We have done our best to shape the summary in a way that makes the excerpts as easy to contextualize and understand as possible, while accurately reflecting the reasoning and conclusions of the dispute settlement panels.

CITATIONS AND REFERENCES

The Guide refers to the GATT and WTO disputes by their short titles. A chronological table of cases is also included. It provides the full titles of reports, including their official document symbols, and their respective short titles.

The Guide also refers to WTO Agreements either by their short titles or their acronyms. A table is included in the Guide that contains a list of the WTO Agreements referred to in this Guide, in alphabetical order according to the name of each agreement. The table sets out both the long and the short titles of the agreements, as well as their acronyms, together with citations to the instruments.

The Guide uses the abbreviation 'GATT' throughout the text to refer to both the GATT 1947 and the GATT 1994. Only occasionally does the Guide specifically refer to GATT 1947 or GATT 1994, as it is generally easy to determine which of the two is relevant from the contexts. The reader should note that GATT 1947 was terminated on 31 December 1995, one year after the WTO Agreement and the agreements annexed to it (which includes the GATT 1994) entered into force on 1 January 1995.

A very small number of references to selected books, articles and papers are included in each chapter. These deal specifically with the issue dealt with in the respective chapter, rather than with the general trade and environment linkage.

CHAPTER 1

Like Products

BACKGROUND

Introduction

The World Trade Organization's (WTO's) principles of most-favoured nation (MFN) treatment and national treatment are the cornerstones of the international trade regime. Under the most-favoured nation principle, Members must extend any advantage granted to a product from one WTO Member to 'like products' from all other Members. Under the national treatment principle, internal taxes and regulations must treat imported products no less favourably than like domestic products. Similar non-discrimination rules also apply for trade in services.

The trade and environment discussions have focused primarily on the national treatment principle and its inherent concept of 'like products'. When products are considered 'like', one product may not be treated more favourably than the other. If products are not considered 'like', Members may treat them differently. For example, a WTO Member may wish to apply lower taxes to energy-efficient automobiles and higher ones to energy-inefficient cars. If both categories of cars are viewed as 'like', they must generally be treated similarly, and preferential taxation would not be permitted, whereas, if the categories are not viewed as 'like', preferential taxation would be permitted. The question of 'like products' has most recently come up in the currently pending *EC – Biotech* case, in which the panel has been called to examine the WTO consistency of the European Communities' authorization system for genetically modified products, as well as the ban on genetically modified organisms (GMOs) adopted by individual European Union (EU) members. Here, the panel might be faced with the question of whether genetically modified products (such as maize, cotton, corn or soya) are 'like' conventional, non-genetically modified products.

The concept of like products

The concept of 'like' products is relevant to several provisions of the General Agreement on Tariffs and Trade (GATT) as well as other WTO Agreements, such as the Agreement on Technical Barriers to Trade (TBT Agreement), and the Agreement on Subsidies and Countervailing Measures (SCM Agreement). The meaning of this concept, however, is anything but uniform. As the Appellate Body described in an oft-cited paragraph:

> *[t]he concept of 'likeness' is a relative one that evokes the image of an accordion. The accordion of 'likeness' stretches and squeezes in different places as different provisions of the WTO Agreement are applied. The width of the accordion in any one of those places must be determined by the particular provision in which the term 'like' is encountered as well as by the context and the circumstances that prevail in any given case to which that provision may apply* (Japan – Alcoholic Beverages, 1996, *Appellate Body report, section H.1.a).*

Thus, 'likeness' varies amongst the agreements and their respective provisions. Furthermore, while some agreements, such as the SCM, do assign 'likeness' a specific meaning, others do not contain any such definitions. Consequently, although there has been much WTO and GATT jurisprudence addressing the concept of 'likeness', the exact meaning and parameters of the concept as well as its variations remain shrouded with uncertainty.

It is also important to note that 'likeness' is relevant to services, as well as to products. The General Agreement on Trade in Services (GATS) contains provisions addressing 'like' services and service suppliers. This section of the compendium, however, does not discuss the meaning of 'likeness' in the context of the GATS. Rather, it limits its discussion to the comparatively large body of jurisprudence on 'like products'.

The determination of what products are considered 'like' affects how wide panels and the Appellate Body will cast the WTO net to find countries in violation of its agreements' provisions. This is because a narrow interpretation of 'like products' will allow countries more leeway to differentiate between imported and domestic products in their regulatory and tax measures, while a broad interpretation of that term will necessitate further judicial scrutiny of those allegedly discriminatory measures.

That further scrutiny is an analysis of whether the challenged measure is discriminatory. It is important to note that 'likeness' is just one part of the inquiry. If products are deemed 'like', the next stage in the analysis of whether a measure violates national treatment or MFN obligations asks whether the challenged measure discriminates between the 'like' products. As with the meaning of 'likeness', the concept of discrimination also varies amongst the agreements and their respective provisions. These differences arise from variations in the actual text of the national treatment and MFN provisions in the agreements, and from WTO jurisprudence interpreting those provisions.

The relevance of like products for environmental policy making

The question of 'like' products is central to the interaction between international trade law and national environmental measures. Many domestic environmental measures, for example, differentiate between products that are – on their face or in their use – similar, but that in some aspect – in their use, in their production process or in their disposal – have different environmental or health implications. Thus, if the concept of 'likeness' is interpreted so as to consider environmentally harmful products as being different from environmentally sustainable products, then the WTO's non-discrimination obligations would grant considerable flexibility to Members enacting domestic environmental or health measures. In turn, if environmental considerations were not to play a role when determining whether two products or services are like, then the WTO's non-discrimination provisions could constrain the domestic regulatory prerogative to enact environmental or health protection measures. To date, the exact boundaries of 'likeness' (as applied in the various WTO obligations) and the precise impact of the 'likeness' determination on domestic environmental and health policy making remains unclear.

The present chapter on 'like products' attempts to give guidance as to the scope and meaning of 'likeness' under the various WTO provisions. It provides an analysis of the various considerations used to determine whether or not a product is 'like'. In this context, it also addresses the question, among many others, whether it is legitimate under WTO rules to deem 'unlike' two products which were produced in a distinct manner. In WTO parlance this issue is usually referred to as Processes and Production Methods (PPMs). Because of its primary relevance for environmental and health concerns, this issue is treated in a separate chapter of this compendium: Chapter 4, Processes and Production Methods.

DISCUSSION OF RELEVANT WTO PROVISIONS

The GATT in general

Within the GATT the phrase 'like product' appears in Articles I:1, II:2, III:2, III:4, VI:1, IX:1, XI:2(c), XIII:1, XVI:4 and XIX:1. Nowhere, however, does the GATT contain a definition of what are 'like products'. Identifying the meaning of 'like product' has been a central aspect in jurisprudence relating to the GATT. As mentioned above, the scope of what are 'like products' has important implications for the stringency of the GATT non-discrimination obligations.

As noted earlier 'likeness' determinations are but one part of the inquiry into whether a measure violates the GATT's non-discrimination obligations. An important caveat to note here, however, is that some cases examining allegations of MFN and national treatment violations have concluded that 'likeness' determinations are not always a necessary part of non-discrimination analyses. At least in cases where the challenged measure discriminates between products based on explicitly origin-related criteria, WTO tribunals have been willing to skip the first step – examining whether the affected products are 'like' – and move directly into an assessment of whether the challenged measure impermissibly treats imported products less favourably than domestic products (i.e. *Korea – Beef* or *Indonesia – Automobile*).

The following section focuses on the meaning of 'likeness' as it is incorporated in GATT Article I (MFN) and GATT Article III (national treatment). Article III is treated first because of its particular relevance in the context of domestic environmental policy making. Article I is discussed subsequently.

Article III of the GATT

In general

Article III sets forth the GATT's national treatment obligations. In essence, Article III obliges WTO Members to grant foreign products treatment at least as favourable as the treatment granted to domestic like products. Article III applies to: taxation and other internal regulatory measures.

Because it encompasses both tax and other internal regulatory measures, Article III can cover an extremely large variety of environmental and health measures. While the scope of Article III's coverage does not alone dictate the rate at which measures will be deemed inconsistent with Article III, Article III's breadth does indicate that the provision is of prime importance in the context of environmental and health policy making.

Paragraph 2 of Article III relates to taxation. Its first sentence prohibits Members from taxing 'like' imported products 'in excess of' 'like' domestic products. Its second sentence states that Members will be in violation of the GATT if, under their tax regimes, 'directly competitive or substitutable' imported and domestic products are 'not similarly taxed'. Paragraph 4 of Article III addresses other, non-tax laws and regulations, such as '. . . laws, regulations and requirements affecting [the] internal sale, offering for sale, purchase, transportation, distribution or use' of products. Specifically, Article III:4 requires Members to ensure that such internal regulatory measures accord 'treatment no less favorable [to imported products] than that accorded to like products of national origin'.

Article III jurisprudence indicates that 'likeness' determinations should be based on case-by-case analysis, and involve an 'unavoidable element of individual, discretionary judgment'. (*Japan – Alcoholic Beverages (1996)* AB report, section H.1.a.) Against that general background, several more specific approaches and tests have emerged and evolved to guide 'likeness' determinations.

The Scope and meaning of the 'likeness' concept in Articles III:2 and III:4

As mentioned above, Article III contains references to 'like products' in its paragraphs 2 and 4. WTO tribunals have pointed out that the meaning of 'like products' in Article III:2 does not necessarily have the same scope as 'like products' in Article III:4. While it is currently unclear exactly how the scope of 'like products' differs between the two provisions, the tribunals have attempted to give at least some minimal guidance.

Article III:2 sets forth two national treatment obligations. First, it requires WTO Members to ensure that 'like' imported products are not taxed 'in excess' of 'like' domestic products; second, it requires WTO Members to subject 'directly competitive or substitutable products' to similar levels of taxation. Thus, paragraph 2 of Article III covers two categories of comparable products: 'like products' and 'directly competitive or substitutable products'. In *Japan – Alcoholic Beverages (1996)*, the Appellate Body clarified that the phrase 'like products' in Article III:2 must be interpreted narrowly so as to not overshadow Article III:2's second, broader category of 'directly competitive or substitutable products' (*Japan – Alcoholic Beverages (1996)* AB report, section H.1.a.).

BOX 1.1 ARTICLE III OF THE GATT

Article III

National treatment on internal taxation and regulation

1 The contracting parties recognize that internal taxes and other internal charges, and laws, regulations and requirements affecting the internal sale, offering for sale, purchase, transportation, distribution or use of products, and internal quantitative regulations requiring the mixture, processing or use of products in specified amounts or proportions, should not be applied to imported or domestic products so as to afford protection to domestic production.

2 The products of the territory of any contracting party imported into the territory of any other contracting party shall not be subject, directly or indirectly, to internal taxes or other internal charges of any kind in excess of those applied, directly or indirectly, to like domestic products. Moreover, no contracting party shall otherwise apply internal taxes or other internal charges to imported or domestic products in a manner contrary to the principles set forth in paragraph 1.
[paragraph 3 omitted]

4 The products of the territory of any contracting party imported into the territory of any other contracting party shall be accorded treatment no less favourable than that accorded to like products of national origin in respect of all laws, regulations and requirements affecting their internal sale, offering for sale, purchase, transportation, distribution or use. The provisions of this paragraph shall not prevent the application of differential internal transportation charges which are based exclusively on the economic operation of the means of transport and not on the nationality of the product.
[paragraphs 5–10 omitted]

Ad Article III
Any internal tax or other internal charge, or any law, regulation or requirement of the kind referred to in paragraph 1 which applies to an imported product and to the like domestic product and is collected or enforced in the case of the imported product at the time or point of importation, is nevertheless to be regarded as an internal tax or other internal charge, or a law, regulation or requirement of the kind referred to in paragraph 1, and is accordingly subject to the provisions of Article III.

Ad Article III, Paragraph 2
A tax conforming to the requirements of the first sentence of paragraph 2 would be considered to be inconsistent with the provisions of the second sentence only in cases where competition was involved between, on the one hand, the taxed product and, on the other hand, a directly competitive or substitutable product which was not similarly taxed.

[Editors' note: Paragraphs 1 and 5 omitted; no Ad notes to paragraphs 3 and 4.]

In this context, it is important to keep in mind that the determination of whether or not products are 'like' or 'directly competitive or substitutable' is only the first stage in the analysis of whether a measure is consistent with that provision of the GATT. For example, once the tribunal considers products to be 'like' under Article III:2, it will then determine whether the imported products are taxed 'in excess' of the 'like' domestic products. The Appellate Body explained this two-tier approach in *Japan – Alcoholic Beverages (1996)*. In this context, the Appellate interpreted 'in excess of' strictly, holding that it is irrelevant whether the different levels of taxation are merely *de minimis.* Any level of taxation imposed on imported products that exceeds the level imposed on domestic 'like' products will likely be deemed inconsistent with the first sentence of Article III:2 (*Japan – Alcoholic Beverages (1996)* AB report, section H.1.b.)

This second stage of analysis, however, differs if the products are considered to be 'directly competitive or substitutable'. According to *Japan – Alcoholic Beverages (1996)*, the tribunals will then examine (i) whether the products are similarly taxed; and, (ii) if they are not similarly taxed, whether the different rates of taxation are applied 'so as to afford protection to domestic production'. Thus, even if the scope of 'directly competitive or substitutable products' is relatively broad, it can potentially be offset by more deferential interpretations of 'similarly taxed' and 'so as to afford protection'.

In contrast to Article III:2, Article III:4 does not address two categories of products. Rather, paragraph 4 of Article III solely refers to 'like products'. The Appellate Body in *EC – Asbestos* addressed the significance of this textual difference. It worked from the premise that, to give effect to the purpose of Article III, the combined product scope of Article III:2's two product categories should not differ significantly from the scope Article III:4's 'like products' category. The Appellate Body found that, in order for Article III:2 and Article III:4 to have a similar scope, the meaning of 'like products' must differ between the two paragraphs. It explained the parameters within which Article III:4's 'like products' must fall in order to give Article III the desired consistency: that category must be broader than Article III:2's 'like products', but not as broad as the combined scope of Article III:2's two product categories. However, exactly where in that continuum Article III:4's 'like products' lies is still unclear.

If products are found to be 'like' under Article III:4, the WTO tribunals will then examine whether the imported products are afforded treatment 'less favourable' than their domestic counterparts. Different treatment is not necessarily 'less favourable' treatment. The Appellate Body in *Korea – Beef* declared that countries' regulations may formally discriminate between imported and domestic products. Those regulations, however, must not modify the conditions of competition in the relevant market to the disadvantage of the imported product.

In *EC – Asbestos,* the Appellate Body again addressed the interpretation of 'less favourable' treatment, although the Panel's interpretation of that phrase had not been appealed. The Appellate Body explained that the meaning of 'less favourable' treatment is informed by the general principle, expressed in Article III:1, that Members should not apply their measures 'so as to afford protection to domestic production' (*EC – Asbestos* AB report, paragraphs 97–98). Commentators debate the significance of the Appellate Body's paragraph in *EC – Asbestos* on the meaning of 'less favourable' treatment. The Appellate Body's statement could be understood as a deferential stance toward national regulations distinguishing between products on an origin-neutral basis, even if those regulations disadvantage some imported goods.

Although a full examination of the contours of 'less favourable' treatment is outside the scope of this section on 'like products', it is important to keep in mind that, as the second step to analysis of a measure's consistency with Article III:4, the meaning of 'less favourable' treatment has important consequences for a Member's ability to enact environmental and health related measures.

'Likeness' criteria

An integral aspect of 'likeness' jurisprudence is the 1970 pre-WTO report of the Working Party on *Border Tax Adjustments (1970)*. That report identified three criteria, which should be examined when determining whether products are like for taxation purposes. Those criteria are: the product's end-uses in a given market; consumers' tastes and habits, which change from country to country, and the product's properties, nature and quality.

The ensuing Article III 'likeness' cases almost always referenced the three *Border Tax* criteria. Although the *Border Tax* report addressed likeness under Article III:2, subsequent tribunals utilized those *Border Tax* criteria when analysing claims under both Article III:2 *and* Article III:4. In *Japan – Alcoholic Beverages (1987)* the GATT panel added another criterion to the *Border Tax* list. That criterion involved an examination of the products' tariff classifications. Currently, when WTO tribunals refer to the *Border Tax* criteria, they are usually referring to all four of the above criteria.

In *EC – Asbestos*, the Appellate Body examined the *Border Tax* criteria and clarified what proper application of those criteria entails. In that dispute, Canada challenged a measure banning the import of highly carcinogenic asbestos fibres and asbestos-containing products, alleging that the ban was inconsistent with, among other provisions, Article III of the GATT. The European Communities defended the measure by arguing, in part, that carcinogenic asbestos fibres are not 'like' non-carcinogenic fibres. After conducting an examination of the *Border Tax* criteria, the Appellate Body agreed with the European Communities' position.

In its report, the Appellate Body stressed that the panels must look at *all evidence* relevant to a 'likeness' determination. It stated that, when examining the *Border Tax* criteria, panels must look at *each* criterion, and each criterion separately, then weigh *all* of the relevant evidence in concluding whether products are 'like products'(*EC – Asbestos* AB report, paragraphs 101–103). Therefore, even if the evidence related to one of the *Border Tax* criteria is extremely persuasive, a panel may not end its 'like products' analysis after examining only that one specific factor. Rather, it must also proceed to look at all of the evidence related to the other three criteria.

Some commentators viewed the *EC – Asbestos* dispute as providing the Appellate Body with an opportunity to add another criterion to the *Border Tax* framework – namely, a criterion based on a product's health effects. In the end, however, the Appellate Body did not expand the list of *Border Tax* criteria. Rather, it stated that analysis of the health effects of asbestos should be subsumed within the analysis of the existing criteria. One member of the Appellate Body wrote a separate concurrence questioning that approach. He argued the high carcinogenicity of asbestos fibres should have alone been sufficient to make those products not 'like' other products. Yet, although declining to create a separate health criterion, the Appellate Body did state that the *Border Tax* list was not exhaustive. Future additions to the *Border Tax* list (including criteria related to health or environmental concerns) are thus not entirely excluded.

Nevertheless, questions remain about the extent to which non-economic concerns can influence 'likeness' determinations. For example, one criticism of the *Border Tax* criteria is that they are too economically-oriented and, therefore, leave little room for Members to distinguish between products based on non-market or non-economic considerations. Furthermore, in *EC – Asbestos*, the Appellate Body emphasized 'a determination of "likeness" under Article III:4 is, fundamentally, a determination about the nature and extent of a competitive relationship between and among products' (*EC – Asbestos* AB report, paragraph 99). Some, including the concurring opinion expressed by one member of the Appellate Body, have raised concerns regarding the economic focus of that characterization of 'likeness' assessments. Whether such an economic emphasis can adequately take into account environmental or health concerns arising from trade in certain products is an unresolved issue in the trade and environment context.

It is likely that the panel in the currently pending *EC – Biotech* dispute will again be faced with having to determine the scope of likeness in the politically sensitive area of genetically modified organisms, which includes a number of non-economic dimensions, including health and environmental considerations. In this dispute, Argentina, Canada and the US challenged the European Communities' authorization system for genetically modified products as well as certain EC member states' marketing and import bans on genetically modified products. Among other things, the issue of an alleged violation of Article III:4 of the GATT has been raised. If the panel considers the challenged measure under this provision, then the question of whether or not genetically modified products and conventional products are 'like products' is likely to arise.

The 'aims and effects' test

The extent to which non-economic concerns can influence 'likeness' determinations is not a new issue. Rather, pre-WTO GATT panels already addressed that subject when developing and applying the so-called 'aims and effects' test. The 'aims and effects' test broadened the analytical strictures of a 'likeness' determination beyond the confines of the *Border Tax* framework, and allowed panels to include non-economic aspects in 'likeness' determinations.

One characterization of the 'aims and effects' test is that it is a means through which tribunals can take into consideration the general purpose of Article III when conducting their 'likeness' analyses. That general purpose, which is expressed in Article III:1, is to ensure that Members do not apply internal measures 'to imported or domestic products so as to afford protection to domestic production'. Thus, the principle behind Article III is essentially one of anti-protectionism.

Panels integrated this anti-protectionist principle into their 'likeness' analysis by examining whether the 'aims or effects' of the challenged measures was to 'afford protection to domestic production'. The first GATT case employing the 'aims and effects' test was *US – Malt Beverages*. There, the panel concluded that the overall anti-protectionist purpose of Article III must guide any interpretation of the phrase 'like products'. Thus, whether the challenged measure distinguished between imported and domestic products for valid public policy purposes, or for protectionist reasons, was relevant to the question of whether the affected products were, in fact, 'like products'.

Although some applauded the valuable role of the 'aims and effects' test in helping to strike a balance between promoting free trade and protecting other environmental and social policies, others criticized it as unworkable in that it required a difficult inquiry into 'intent'. The test also drew fire because it was seen by some to deviate too far from an ordinary meaning of the text of Article III.

Perhaps inspired by these criticisms, the Appellate Body in *Japan – Alcoholic Beverages (1996)* rejected the 'aims and effects' test – at least with respect to the first sentence of

Article III:2, which states that, '[t]he products of the territory of any contracting party imported into the territory of any other contracting party shall not be subject, directly or indirectly, to internal taxes or other internal charges of any kind in excess of those applied, directly or indirectly, to like domestic products.' Although concluding that Article III:1's general anti-protectionist principle did implicitly inform 'likeness' analysis under Article III:2, the Appellate Body held that, to demonstrate a violation of that first sentence of Article III:2, a party need not demonstrate any protective aim or application of the challenged tax.

EC – Bananas III again touched upon the 'aims and effects' test. In that case, the Appellate Body noted that it had previously rejected that test in the Article III:2 'likeness' context in *Japan – Alcoholic Beverages (1996)*. It did not, however, go so far as to conclude that the 'aims and effects' test had also been rejected in the Article III:4 context. Yet, the fact remains that, post *Japan – Alcoholic Beverages (1996)*, the 'aims and effects' test has not been used to assess 'likeness' under either paragraph 2 or 4 of Article III. Possibly, even though the WTO tribunals have not explicitly banned the 'aims and effects' test from playing a role in Article III:4 jurisprudence, the practical effect of *Japan – Alcoholic Beverages (1996)* was to eliminate that test from both Article III:2 and Article III:4 jurisprudence.

If the 'aims and effects' test has been rejected in Article III jurisprudence, it is important to ask whether and how that will affect the outcomes of WTO disputes under that provision. It could be argued that the death of the 'aims and effects' test in the Article III context will not necessarily alter the actual outcomes of WTO disputes because some of the measures it would shelter can also be protected by Article XX, the article that sets forth the exceptions to Members' obligations under the GATT. On the other hand, in practice, parties have not always been successful in invoking Article XX's exceptions to defend their measures. Some factors contributing to that lack of success could be the shift in the parties' burdens of proof under Article XX, and the requirements imposed by Article XX's necessity test and its chapeau. For a closer look at Article XX, and its relationship with Article III, see the discussion in Chapter 4: Processes and Production Methods. Article XX is also discussed in Chapter 3: The Necessity Requirement and Chapter 2: General Exceptions Clauses.

Article I of the GATT

Article I contains the GATT's MFN obligation. It requires 'any advantage, favour, privilege or immunity granted by any Member to any product originating in or destined for any other country' to be granted 'immediately and unconditionally to the *like product* originating in or destined for the territories of all other Members' (emphasis added). This provision's scope is generally understood to be broad, covering levies on goods or related payment transfers, the methods of imposing those levies, rules and formalities related to international trade, and also covering those regulatory and tax measures addressed in paragraphs 2 and 4 of Article III.

There are several similarities between Article I and Article III 'likeness' jurisprudence. One similarity between 'likeness' determinations under Articles I and III is that both have employed the *Border Tax* criteria. Second, as with 'likeness' in the context of Article III, the meaning of that concept under Article I can have important implications for a Member's power to differentiate between products. For example, in a pre-WTO case, *Japan – Lumber*, Canada argued that Japan's system of applying different tariff rates to different kinds of lumber violated Article I. The GATT panel, however, disagreed. It found that Japan could use the species of trees as a basis upon which to distinguish between lumber; in other words, lumber from one tree species was not 'like' lumber from another tree species.

Another similarity between Article I and Article III 'likeness' is that, under both provisions, determining whether products are 'like' is only one step of the analysis. If the products are deemed to be 'like', the tribunal's next step is to determine whether the country in question discriminates between its WTO trading partners. In terms of Article I, whether a tribunal finds 'discrimination' depends, in part, on the tribunal's interpretation of Article I's other two key phrases – 'immediately and unconditionally' and 'any advantage, favour, privilege or immunity'. An analysis of these two phrases is outside of the scope of this discussion on 'like products'.

Finally, when assessing the meaning of 'like products' under Article I, it is useful to keep in mind the Appellate Body's accordion metaphor for interpreting the term in *Japan – Alcoholic Beverages (1996)*. Because Article I and Article III serve different purposes, the meaning of 'likeness' will likely differ between the two provisions. Moreover, pursuant to the Appellate Body's interpretative approach, the meaning of 'like products' will vary depending on the facts of the particular case arising under Article I.

Article 2.1 of the TBT Agreement

Article 2.1 of the TBT Agreement, which sets forth Members' non-discrimination obligations, contains a 'like products' reference, similar in part, to the provision in Article III:4 of the GATT. But in addition to covering only the national treatment principle, it also covers the MFN principle. It provides:

> *Members shall ensure that in respect of technical regulations, products imported from the territory of any Member shall be* accorded treatment no less favourable than that accorded to like products *of national origin and to like products originating in any other country (emphasis added).*

The WTO tribunals, however, have yet to address the scope and meaning of the 'like products' concept within the context of the TBT Agreement. It is most important to note that, while the concept is phrased in a way similar to Article III:4, the TBT Agreement offers no (explicit) exceptions to the national and MFN treatment obligations, similar to the exceptions clause under Article XX of the GATT. It remains to be seen whether this fact will allow for a narrower reading of the term 'like', which would result in a more limited scope of products being considered 'like'. Otherwise, there would arguably be little space left for Members to distinguish products for environmental or health reasons. Related aspects of the TBT Agreement are discussed in more detail in Chapter 4: Processes and Production Methods.

Article 6.3 of the Agreement on Subsidies and Countervailing Measures (SCM Agreement)

The SCM Agreement regulates both the use of subsidies, and the actions WTO Members can take to counteract the effects of subsidies. The Agreement contains several references to 'like products'. It also, unlike the GATT, contains a definition of the phrase. That definition, set forth in footnote 46 to Article 15.1 of the SCM Agreement, provides:

> *Throughout this Agreement the term 'like product' ('produit similaire') shall be interpreted to mean a product which is identical, i.e. alike in all respects to the product under consideration, or in the absence of such a product, another product which, although not alike in all respects, has characteristics closely resembling those of the product under consideration.*

Thus, in contrast to the GATT, the SCM Agreement provides for a uniform definition that is to apply throughout the agreement. The same definition is also used in Article 2.6 of the Agreement on the Implementation of the GATT 1994, the Antidumping Agreement (not discussed here).

Until the 1998 decision in *Indonesia – Automobile*, however, no GATT or WTO tribunal had thoroughly interpreted or applied the SCM Agreement's definition of 'like products'. After noting that it was working in 'uncharted territory' the *Indonesia – Automobile* panel looked to both the purpose and meaning of the specific SCM provision, the SCM Agreement as a whole, and existing GATT jurisprudence on the 'likeness' issue when making its 'like product' determination.

An interesting issue related to 'likeness' determinations in the SCM context is whether the SCM's provisions on special and differential treatment for developing countries affect the scope of 'like products' or alter who has the burden of proving that the products at issue are, in fact, 'like'. Indonesia in *Indonesia – Automobile* argued that those special and differential treatment provisions, set forth in Article 27, should apply to impose both an especially narrow construction on the phrase 'like product', and a particularly high burden of proof on the complainants. The panel, however, essentially rejected Indonesia's argument. While it agreed that the complainants did have the burden of proving 'likeness', it did not agree 'that the complainants [should] bear a heavier than usual burden of proof in [that] dispute or that the concept of "like product" should be interpreted more narrowly than usual because Indonesia is a developing country Member' (*Indonesia – Automobile Industry* panel report, paragraph 14.169).

SELECTED LITERATURE

Choi, W.-M. (2003) *'Like Products' in International Trade Law: Towards a Consistent GATT/WTO Jurisprudence*, Oxford University Press, Oxford

Davey, W. J. and Pauwelyn, J. (2002) *MFN Unconditionality:* 'A legal analysis of the concept in view of its evolution in the GATT/WTO jurisprudence with particular reference to the issue of "Like Product"', in Cottier, T. and Mavroidis, P. C. (eds) *Regulatory*

Barriers and the Principle of Non-discrimination, University of Michigan Press, Ann Arbor, pp13–15

Ehring, L. (2002) 'De facto discrimination in world trade law, national and most-favoured-nation treatment – Or equal treatment', *Journal of World Trade*, vol 36, pp921–977

Howse, R. and Tuerk, E. (2001) 'The WTO impact on internal regulation: A case study of the Canada–EC asbestos dispute', in de Búrca, G. and Scott, J. (eds) *The EU and the WTO: Legal and Constitutional Issues*, Hart Publishing, Oxford, p283

Hudec, R. E. (1998) 'GATT/WTO constraints on national regulation: Requiem for an "aim and effects" test', *International Law*, vol 32, p619

Mattoo, A. and Subramian, A. (1998) 'Regulatory autonomy and multilateral disciplines: The dilemma and a possible resolution', *Journal of International Economic Law*, vol 1, p303

Regan, D. H. (2003) 'Further thoughts on regulatory purpose under Article III of the GATT', *Journal of World Trade*, vol 37, p737

SELECTED JURISPRUDENCE RELATING TO 'LIKE PRODUCTS' UNDER GATT ARTICLES I AND III

The following are excerpts of WTO cases that are relevant for a discussion of 'like products'. The excerpts are preceded by a short summary and commentary of the corresponding case, to put them into context. The cases are listed in chronological order, and the summaries do not encompass all the issues raised in the cases, but focus primarily on issues regarding 'likeness', and thus are not comprehensive for other purposes.

Several of the cases relating to 'like products' refer to the Report of the Working Party on *Border Tax Adjustments*, which was adopted on 2 December 1970. The report is available at http://www.worldtradelaw.net/reports/gattpanels/bordertax.pdf. Paragraph 18 of the Report provides:

> *18. With regard to the interpretation of the term '. . . like or similar products . . .', which occurs some sixteen times throughout the General Agreement, it was recalled that considerable discussion had taken place in the past, both in GATT and in other bodies, but that no further improvement of the term had been achieved. The Working Party concluded that problems arising from the interpretation of the term should be examined on a case-by-case basis. This would allow a fair assessment in each case of the different elements that constitute a 'similar' product. Some criteria were suggested for determining, on a case-by-case basis, whether a product is 'similar': the product's end-uses in a given market; consumers' tastes and habits, which change from country to country; the product's properties, nature and quality. It was observed, however, that the term '. . . like or similar products . . .' caused some uncertainty and that it would be desirable to improve on it; however, no improved term was arrived at.*

The Australian Subsidy on Ammonium Sulphate, 1950

Short summary and commentary

This dispute involved a claim by Chile that Australia violated certain provisions of the GATT when it ceased subsidizing one fertilizer (nitrate of soda), yet continued subsidizing another (ammonium sulphate). When examining whether Australia's actions violated the MFN obligation, the working party addressed the question of whether or not the two types of fertilizers were 'like products'. Based on its finding that Australia and other countries listed and/or treated the products differently for tariff purposes, the working party concluded that the products were not 'like'. At the same time, the working party stressed that it did not attempt to define the term 'like products' (Working party report, paragraph 8). Subsequently, the working party based its 'likeness' finding under Article III on its determination under Article I (*Id.* at paragraph 9).

Excerpts

Report of the Working Party on *The Australian Subsidy on Ammonium Sulphate*, 31 March 1950, GATT/CP.4/39-II/188, adopted April 3, 1950.

III. Consistency of the Australian Measures with the Provisions of the General Agreement [paras 7–11]

. . .

8 As regards the applicability of Article I to the Australian measure, the working party noted that the General Agreement made a distinction between 'like products' and 'directly competitive or substitutable products'. This distinction is clearly brought out in Article III, paragraph 2, read in conjunction with the interpretative note to that paragraph. The most-favoured-nation treatment clause in the General Agreement is limited to "like products". Without trying to give a definition of "like products", and leaving aside the question of whether the two fertilizers are directly competitive, the working party reached the conclusion that they were not to be considered as "like products" within the terms of Article I. In the Australian tariff the two products are listed as separate items and enjoy different treatment. Nitrate of soda is classified as item 403 (C) and sulphate of ammonia as item 271 (B). Whereas nitrate of soda is admitted free both in the preferential and most-favoured-nation tariff, sulphate of ammonia is admitted free only for the preferential area and is subject to a duty of 12½ per cent for the m.f.n. countries; moreover, in the case of nitrate of soda the rate is bound whereas no binding has been agreed upon for sulphate of ammonia. In the tariffs of other countries the two products are listed separately. In certain cases the rate is the same, but in others the treatment is different: for instance, in the case of the United Kingdom, nitrate of soda is admitted free, whereas a duty of £4 per ton is levied on ammonium sulphate.

9 In view of the fact that Article III, paragraph 4, applies to "like products", the provisions of that paragraph are not applicable to the present case, for the reasons set out in paragraph 8 above. As regards the provisions of paragraph 9 of the same article, the working party was informed that a maximum selling price for ammonium sulphate was no longer fixed by governmental action and, in any event, noted that Australia had considered the Chilean complaint and had made an offer within the terms of that paragraph. Since it was not found that any of the substantive provisions of Article III were applicable, the exception contained in paragraph 8 *(b)* is not relevant.

Belgian Family Allowances, 1952

A summary and excerpts can be found in Chapter 4: Processes and Production Methods.

Spain – Tariff Treatment of Unroasted Coffee ('Spain – Unroasted Coffee'), 1981

Short summary and commentary

In this dispute, Brazil argued that Spain's method of classifying unroasted coffee for tariff purposes violated the MFN clause in Article I:1 of the GATT. Specifically, Spain divided unroasted coffee into three categories: mild, unwashed Arabica and Robusta coffees. Under this classification system, unwashed Arabica and Robusta coffees were subject to higher tariff rates than mild coffee. Brazil argued that all three types of unroasted coffees were 'like products', and that by treating 'like products' differently under its tariff classification system, Spain violated Article I:1.

In response, Spain argued that the three types of unroasted coffees were not 'like products'. Spain argued that due to the different areas in which the three types of coffee were grown, the ways in which they were cultivated, and the methods by which they were prepared, the coffee beans had different tastes and aromas, and were of different qualities. Moreover, Spain argued that in its domestic market, consumer preferences supported the view that the three categories of unroasted coffees were not 'like'.

With respect to Article I:1, the panel stated that each contracting party had the right to establish its own tariff classification system, yet was obligated to provide the same tariff treatment to 'like products'. According to the panel, Spain's system violated Article I:1, in that it provided different tariff treatment to mild, unwashed Arabica and Robusta coffees. Under the panel's analysis, those products were 'like products' in terms of Article I:1. The panel found that the differences in the beans resulting from where they were produced, how they were cultivated or processed, or what type of plant they derived from, did not justify the conclusion that the three types of coffees were 'unlike'. Differences in tastes and aromas resulting from different processes and production methods did not, according to the panel, warrant different tariff treatment (Panel report, paragraph 4.6).

In addition to concluding that the coffees' product-related PPMs were not a valid basis upon which to distinguish between the products for tariff purposes, the panel also referred to two other reasons supporting its finding that the three types of coffee were 'like products'. First, it noted that all types of unroasted coffee had the same end-use – drinking (*Id.* at paragraph 4.7). Second, it pointed out that no other contracting party's tariff regime treated unroasted coffee in a similar manner as Spain's system (*Id.* at paragraph 4.8).

After the panel determined that mild, unwashed Arabica and Robusta coffees were 'like products' in terms of Article I:1, it discussed how Spain's tariff classification system related to Brazil's coffee exports. Although Brazil exported all three types of unroasted coffees, its primary exports were of the categories subject to the higher tariff duties. Thus, according to the panel, Spain's practice of distinguishing between 'like products' was discriminatory vis-à-vis coffee imports from Brazil (*Id.* at paragraph 4.10).

This report stands in contrast with the subsequent decision in *Japan – Lumber* (discussed below). While the panel in *Spain – Unroasted Coffee* did not accept Spain's reasons for distinguishing between unroasted coffees, the panel in *Japan – Lumber* appeared relatively deferential to Japan's decisions regarding how it structured its tariff regime. Another important aspect of the *Spain – Unroasted Coffee* report is the panel's dismissal of product-related PPMs as a basis upon which to distinguish between 'like' products.

Excerpts

Report of the Panel, *Spain – Tariff Treatment of Unroasted Coffee*, L/5135 – 28S/102, adopted on 11 June 1981.

IV. Findings and conclusions [paras 4.1–4.12]

. . .

4.4 The Panel found that there was no obligation under the GATT to follow any particular system for classifying goods, and that a contracting party had the right to introduce in its customs tariff new positions or sub-positions as appropriate.[1] The Panel considered, however, that, whatever the classification adopted, Article I:1 required that the same tariff treatment be applied to "like products".

[1] Provided that a reclassification subsequent to the making of a concession under the GATT would not be a violation of the basic commitment regarding that concession (Article II:5).

4.5 The Panel, therefore, in accordance with its terms of reference, focused its examination on whether the various types of unroasted coffee listed in the Royal Decree 1764/79 should be regarded as "like products" within the meaning of Article I:1. Having reviewed how the concept of "like products" had been applied by the CONTRACTING PARTIES in previous cases involving, *inter alia*, a recourse to Article I:1[2] the Panel noted that neither the General Agreement nor the settlement of previous cases gave any definition of such concept.

[2] BISD Vol II/188; BISD S1/53; BISD S25/49; L/5047.

4.6 The Panel examined all arguments that had been advanced during the proceedings for the justification of a different tariff treatment for various groups and types of unroasted coffee. It noted that these arguments mainly related to organoleptic differences resulting from geographical factors, cultivation methods, the processing of the beans, and the genetic factor. The Panel did not consider that such differences were sufficient reason to allow for a different tariff treatment. It pointed out that it was not unusual in the case of agricultural products that the taste and aroma of the end-product would differ because of one or several of the above-mentioned factors.

4.7 The Panel furthermore found relevant to its examination of the matter that unroasted coffee was mainly, if not exclusively, sold in the form of blends, combining various types of coffee, and that coffee in its end-use, was universally regarded as a well-defined and single product intended for drinking.

4.8 The Panel noted that no other contracting party applied its tariff régime in respect of unroasted, non-decaffeinated coffee in such a way that different types of coffee were subject to different tariff rates.

4.9 In the light of the foregoing, the Panel *concluded* that unroasted, non-decaffeinated coffee beans listed in the Spanish Customs Tariffs under CCCN 09.01 A.1a, as amended by the Royal Decree 1764/79, should be considered as "like products" within the meaning of Article I:1.

4.10 The Panel further noted that Brazil exported to Spain mainly "unwashed Arabica" and also Robusta coffee which were both presently charged with higher duties than that applied to "mild" coffee. Since these were considered to be "like products", the Panel concluded that the tariff régime as presently applied by Spain was discriminatory vis-à-vis unroasted coffee originating in Brazil.

Japan – Customs Duties, Taxes and Labelling Practices on Imported Wines and Alcoholic Beverages ('Japan – Alcoholic Beverages (1987)'), 1987

Short summary and commentary

Japan – Alcoholic Beverages (1987) involved a claim by the European Communities that Japan's liquor tax system violated Article III:2 of the GATT. Japan's tax system classified liquors into categories and sub-categories, and applied different rates of taxation to the products depending upon the category and sub-category to which the products belonged. Some of the factors used to classify the products were the raw materials used in producing the liquor, the manufacturing method applied to produce the liquor, and the price of the product. Although the tax system did not classify products according to whether they were of domestic or foreign origin, the European Communities argued that Japan had organized its tax classification system in such a way that it penalized imported products vis-à-vis domestic products.

Before discussing the merits of the European Communities' claims, the panel first addressed the issue of how Article III:2 should be interpreted and applied. Japan had argued that, in examining the European Communities' Article III:2 claim, the panel did not have to determine whether the products at issue were 'like' or 'directly competitive or substitutable'. According to Japan, the panel did not have to conduct this analytical first step because the relevant inquiry was not whether or not the products were 'like' or 'directly competitive or substitutable', but rather, whether or not the tax system disadvantaged the imported products. Japan argued that Article III:2 did not prohibit Members from enacting tax measures distinguishing between 'like' or 'directly competitive or substitutable' domestic and imported products, as long as the measures did not result in a heavier tax burden on the imported products than on domestic products.

The European Communities, on the other hand, advocated a different approach to the resolution of Article III:2 claims. It argued that the panel first had to determine whether the products at issue were 'like' or 'directly competitive or substitutable'. Only after this determination would the panel have to determine whether or not the imported products were taxed in excess of the 'like' domestic products, or alternatively, whether or not the imported products were subject to internal taxes affording protection to domestic directly competitive or substitutable products.

The panel determined that the correct approach to examining the conformity of internal taxation measures with Article III:2 of the GATT was the two-step approach described by the European Communities. First, the panel would determine whether the relevant imported and domestic products were 'like' or 'directly competitive or substitutable'. Then, if the products were 'like', the panel would determine whether the tax was discriminatory. If, however, the products were 'directly competitive or substitutable', the panel would have to assess whether the tax was protective (Panel report, paragraph 5.5).

The panel first discussed general notions about the scope of 'likeness'. It stated that 'like' in the context of Article III:2 had been interpreted as being broader than 'identical' or 'equal'; it had been interpreted as covering products with similar qualities (*Id.*).

Next, the panel turned to the issue of how the concept of 'likeness' should be applied in practice. It decided that the *Border Tax* criteria (the products' end-uses, consumers' tastes and habits, and the products' properties, nature and quality), and the products' tariff classifications, could be used to determine, on a product-by-product basis, whether the relevant imported and domestic products were 'like' (*Id.* at paragraph 5.6). The panel cautioned, however, that the picture produced by examining consumers' tastes and habits could be misleading It explained that where differential taxes had been used to crystallize consumer preferences for domestic products, such consumer preferences should not be a reason for products to be deemed 'unlike' (*Id.* at paragraph 5.7). Furthermore, the panel clarified that minor differences in taste, colour, and other properties were not sufficient to prevent products from qualifying as 'like products' under Article III:2, first sentence (*Id.* at paragraph 5.6).

The panel stated that also relevant to 'likeness' determinations are such 'objective' criteria as the composition and manufacturing processes of products (*Id.* at paragraph 5.7). This statement is interesting in that it suggests PPMs are relevant to 'likeness' determinations. It is unclear, however, whether the panel meant its statement to apply solely to manufacturing processes detectable or influencing the end-product (product-related PPMs), or whether its statement referred to PPMs in general.

The panel identified several categories of 'like' imported and domestic products (*Id.* at paragraph 5.6). It then concluded that Japan's tax system taxed the imported products 'in excess of' 'like' domestic products in violation of Article III:2, first sentence (*see Id.* at paragraphs 5.8–5.9 for the legal reasoning leading to this conclusion).

Next, the panel examined the products it identified to be 'directly competitive or substitutable' within the meaning of Article III:2, second sentence. Whether products were 'directly competitive or substitutable' depended, according to the panel, upon whether the products had common characteristics, and whether consumers seemed to view or use certain alcoholic beverages as alternatives or substitutes for others (*Id.* at paragraph 5.7). Some products which the panel did not conclude were 'like', were nevertheless found to be 'directly competitive or substitutable'.

After identifying various types of liquors as being 'directly competitive or substitutable', the panel concluded, for various reasons, that Japan's tax system discriminated between the imported and domestic products, in violation of Article III:2, second sentence (*Id.* at paragraphs 5.10–5.11).

This case made several important contributions to 'likeness' jurisprudence. First, it clarified that the determination of whether or not a measure covered by Article III is consistent with that provision requires a two-step analysis: first, the tribunal must make a case-by-case determination of whether the affected products are 'like' or 'directly competitive or substitutable'; then, if 'like', the panel must then assess whether the tax is discriminatory, and if 'directly competitive or substitutable', the panel must assess whether the tax is protective.

As will be discussed in the case summaries for *Canada – Periodicals, Indonesia – Automobile Argentina – Bovine Hides* and *Korea – Beef,* Article III jurisprudence has developed in such a manner that it now appears as if the two-step analysis described here in *Japan – Alcoholic Beverages* (1987), is not the only approach to assessing whether measures are consistent with Article III. Specifically, where measures are not origin-neutral, tribunals may automatically find that the 'like products' requirement has been met and move directly to assessment of whether the measures tax imported products 'in excess of' domestic products.

A second contribution made by this report is that it added a criterion to the *Border Tax* list. The *Border Tax* report had explained that products' end-uses, consumers' tastes and habits, and products' properties, natures and qualities were factors relevant to determining whether or not products at issue were 'like'. This decision also noted that products' tariff classifications were relevant to 'likeness' determinations. Subsequent decisions referring to the *Border Tax* criteria have generally referred to all four of these factors.

Excerpts

Report of the Panel, *Japan – Customs Duties, Taxes and Labelling Practices on Imported Wines and Alcoholic Beverages*, L/6216 – 37S/86, adopted on 10 November 1987.

5. Findings and conclusions [paras 5.1–5.16]

. . .

5.5 The Panel carefully examined these two divergent interpretations of Article III:2 and reached the following conclusions:

(a) The *text of the first sentence of Article III:2* clearly indicates that the comparison to be made is between internal taxes on imported products and those applied . . . to like domestic products. The wording "like" products (in the French text: "products similaires") has been used also in other GATT Articles on non-discrimination (*e.g.* Article I:1) in the sense not only of "identical" or "equal" products but covering also products with similar qualities (see, for instance, the 1981 Panel Report on Tariff Treatment by Spain of Imports of Unroasted Coffee, BISD 28S/102, 112).

(b) The *context of Article III:2* shows that Article III:2 supplements, within the system of the General Agreement, the provisions on the liberalization of customs duties and of other charges by prohibiting discriminatory or protective taxation against certain products from other GATT contracting parties. The Panel found that this context had to be taken into account in the interpretation of Article III: 2. For instance, the prohibition under GATT Article I:1 of different tariff treatment for various types of "like" products (such as unroasted coffee, see BISD 28S/102, 112) could not remain effective unless supplemented by the prohibition of different internal tax treatment for various types of "like" products. Just as Article I:1 was generally construed, in order to protect the competitive benefits accruing from reciprocal tariff bindings, as prohibiting "tariff specialization" discriminating against "like" products, only the literal interpretation of Article III:2 as prohibiting "internal tax specialization" discriminating against "like" products could ensure that the reasonable expectation, protected under GATT Article XXIII, of competitive benefits accruing under tariff concessions would not be nullified or impaired by internal tax discrimination against like products. It had therefore been correctly stated in another Panel Report recently adopted by the CONTRACTING PARTIES that "Article III:2, first sentence, obliges contracting parties to establish certain competitive conditions for imported products in relation to domestic products" (L/6175, paragraph 5.1.9). And it had been for similar reasons that, during the discussion in the GATT Council of the panel report on Spain's restrictions on the domestic sale of soyabean oil which had not been adopted by the Council, several contracting parties, including Japan, had emphasized "with regard to Article III:4 that the interpretation of the term 'like products' in the Panel Report as meaning 'more or less the same product' was too strict an interpretation" (C/M/152 at page 16).

(c) The *drafting history* confirms that Article III:2 was designed with "the intention that internal taxes on goods should not be used as a means of protection" (see: UN Conference on Trade and Employment, Reports of Committees, 1948, page 61). As stated in the 1970 Working Party Report on Border Tax Adjustments in respect of the various GATT provisions on taxation, "the philosophy behind these provisions was the ensuring of a certain trade neutrality" (BISD 18S/99). This accords with the broader objective of Article III "to provide equal conditions of competition once goods had been cleared through customs" (BISD 7S/64), and to protect thereby the benefits accruing from tariff concessions. This *object and purpose of Article III:2* of promoting non-discriminatory competition among imported and like domestic products could not be achieved if Article III:2 were construed in a manner allowing discriminatory and protective internal taxation of imported products in excess of like domestic products.

(d) *Subsequent GATT practice* in the application of Article III further shows that past GATT panel reports adopted by the CONTRACTING PARTIES have examined Article III: 2 and 4 by determining, firstly, whether the imported and domestic products concerned were "like" and, secondly, whether the internal taxation or other regulation discriminated against the imported products (see, for instance, BISD 25S/49, 63; L/6175, paragraph 5). Past GATT practice has clearly established that "like" products in terms of Article III:2 are not confined to identical products but cover also other products, for instance if they serve substantially identical end-uses (see L/6175, paragraph 5.1.1).

The Panel concluded that the ordinary meaning of Article III:2 in its context and in the light of its object and purpose supported the past GATT practice of examining the conformity of internal taxes with Article III:2 by determining, firstly, whether the taxed imported and domestic products are "like" or "directly competitive or substitutable" and, secondly, whether the taxation is discriminatory (first sentence) or protective (second sentence of Article III:2). The Panel decided to proceed accordingly also in this case.

5.6 The CONTRACTING PARTIES have never developed a general *definition of the term "like products" in Article III:2*. Past decisions on this question have been made on a case-by-case basis after examining a number of relevant factors. The working party report on border tax adjustments, adopted by the CONTRACTING PARTIES in 1970, concluded that problems arising from the interpretation of the terms "like" or "similar" products, which occurred some sixteen times throughout the General Agreement, should be examined on a case-by-case basis using, inter alia, the following criteria: the product's end-uses in a given market; consumers' tastes and habits, which change from country to country; and the product's properties, nature and quality (BISD 18S/102, paragraph 18). The GATT drafting history confirms that "the expression had different meanings in different contexts of the Draft Charter" (EPCT/C II/65, p2). Subsequent GATT practice indicates that, as stated in respect of GATT Article I:1 in the 1981 Panel Report on the Tariff Treatment applied by Spain to Imports of Unroasted Coffee, "neither the General Agreement nor the settlement of previous cases gave any definition of such concept" (BISD 28S/102, III). The Panel was aware of the more specific definition of the term "like product" in Article 2:2 of the 1979 Antidumping Agreement (BISD 26S/172) but did not consider this very narrow definition for the purpose of antidumping proceedings to be suitable for the different purpose of GATT Article III:2. The Panel decided, therefore, to examine the table of "like products" submitted by the EEC (see Annex V) on a product-by-product basis using the above-mentioned criteria as well as others recognized in previous GATT practice (see BISD 25S/49, 63), such as the Customs Cooperation Council Nomenclature (CCCN) for the classification of goods in customs tariffs which has been accepted by Japan. The Panel found that the following alcoholic beverages should be considered as "like products" in terms of Article III:2 in view of their similar properties, end-uses and usually uniform classification in tariff nomenclatures:

[HERE THE PANEL GAVE A LIST OF 'LIKE' PRODUCTS, WHICH IS NOT REPRODUCED]

. . .

The Panel agreed in this respect with the arguments submitted to it not only by the European Communities but also by other important producing countries of wines and distilled spirits that gin, vodka, whisky, grape brandy, other fruit brandy, certain "classic" liqueurs, still wine and sparkling wine, respectively, were recognized not only by governments for purposes of tariff and statistical nomenclature, but also by consumers to constitute "each in its end-use . . . a well defined and single product intended for drinking" (BISD 28S/102, 112, paragraph 4.7). The Panel also agreed in this respect with the finding of an earlier panel report adopted by the CONTRACTING PARTIES that minor differences in taste, colour and other properties did not prevent products qualifying as "like products" (BISD 28S/102, 112).

5.7 The Panel did not exclude that also other alcoholic beverages could be considered as "like" products. Thus, even though the Panel was of the view that the "likeness" of products must be examined taking into account not only objective criteria (such as composition and manufacturing processes of products) but also the more subjective consumers' viewpoint (such as consumption and use by consumers), the Panel agreed with the arguments submitted to it by the European Communities, Finland and the United States that Japanese shochu (Group A) and vodka could be considered as "like" products in terms of Article III:2 because they were both white/clean spirits, made of similar raw materials, and their end-uses were virtually identical (either as straight "schnaps" type of drinks or in various mixtures). Since consumer habits are variable in time and space and the aim of Article III:2 of ensuring neutrality of internal taxation as regards competition between imported and domestic like products could not be achieved if differential taxes could be used to crystallize consumer preferences for traditional domestic products, the Panel found that the traditional Japanese consumer habits with regard to shochu provided no reason for not considering vodka to be a "like" product. The Panel decided not to examine the "likeness" of alcoholic beverages beyond the requests specified in the complaint by the European Communities (see Annex V). The Panel felt justified in doing so also for the following reasons: Alcoholic drinks might be drunk straight, with water, or as mixes. Even if imported alcoholic beverages (e.g. vodka) were not considered to be "like" to Japanese alcoholic beverages (e.g. shochu Group A), the flexibility in the use of alcoholic drinks and their common characteristics often offered an alternative choice for consumers leading to a competitive relationship. In the view of the Panel there existed – even if not necessarily in respect of all the economic uses to which the product may be put – direct competition or substitutability among the various distilled liquors, among various liqueurs, among unsweetened and sweetened wines and among sparkling wines. The increasing imports of "Western-style" alcoholic beverages into Japan bore witness to this lasting competitive relationship and to the potential product substitution through trade among various alcoholic beverages. Since consumer habits vis-à-vis these products varied in response to their respective prices, their availability through trade and their other competitive inter-relationships, the Panel concluded that the following alcoholic beverages could be considered to be *"directly competitive or substitutable products" in terms of Article III:2, second sentence*:

[HERE THE PANEL GAVE A LIST OF DIRECTLY COMPETITIVE OR SUBSTITUTABLE PRODUCTS, WHICH IS NOT REPRODUCED]

United States – Taxes on Petroleum and Certain Imported Substances ('US – Petroleum'), 1987

Short summary and commentary

In this case Canada, the European Economic Community and Mexico requested the panel to examine whether certain taxes enacted by the US pursuant to its Superfunds Amendments and Reauthorization Act of 1986 ('Superfund Act') were consistent with Article III:2 of the GATT Under the Superfund Act, the US imposed taxes on petroleum and certain imported substances. Those taxes, among other taxes imposed by the Superfund Act, funded programmes to clean up hazardous waste sites and to run health programmes aimed at dealing with the effects of hazardous wastes.

The case raised a number of issues relating to the interpretation of Article III:2 of the GATT, including questions relating to the nullification or impairment of benefits accruing under the GATT. These aspects are not discussed here.

With respect to its 'likeness' determination, the *US – Petroleum* panel referred to the report of the Working Party on *Border Tax Adjustments*. In conducting its analysis, the panel placed particular emphasis on the *Border Tax* criterion that looks to whether or not the products have similar end-uses. Noting that the products at issue in the case were either identical or served 'substantially identical end-uses', the panel concluded that the products were 'like products' within the meaning of Article III:2 (Panel report, paragraph 5.1.1).

Excerpts

Report of the Panel, *United States – Taxes on Petroleum and Certain Imported Substances*, L/6175-34S/136, adopted on 17 June 1987.

5. Findings and conclusions

5.1 Tax on Petroleum [5.1.1–5.1.12]

5.1.1 The Panel examined the tax on petroleum in the light of the obligations the United States assumed under the General Agreement and found the following: the tax on petroleum is an excise tax levied on imported and domestic goods. Such taxes are subject to the national treatment requirement of Article III:2, first sentence, which reads:

> *"The products of the territory of any contracting party imported into the territory of any other contracting party shall not be subject, directly or indirectly, to internal taxes or other internal charges of any kind in excess of those applied, directly or indirectly, to like domestic products".*

The CONTRACTING PARTIES have not developed a definition of the term "like products" in the above provision. In the report of the Working Party on Border Tax Adjustments, adopted by the CONTRACTING PARTIES in 1970, it was suggested that the problems arising from the interpretation of this term should be examined on a case-by-case basis and that one of the possible methods for determining whether two products were like products was to compare their end-uses in a given market (BISD 18S/102). The domestic products subject to the tax are: crude oil, crude oil condensates and natural gasoline. The imported products subject to the tax are: crude oil, crude oil condensates, natural gasoline, refined and residual oil and certain other liquid hydrocarbon products. The imported and domestic products are thus either identical or, in the case of imported liquid hydrocarbon products, serve substantially identical end-uses. The imported and domestic products subject to the tax on petroleum are therefore in the view of the Panel "like products" within the meaning of Article III:2. The rate of tax applied to the imported products is 3.5 cents per barrel higher than the rate applied to the like domestic products. Article III:2, first sentence, applies whether or not the products concerned are subject to a tariff concession and whether or not adverse trade effects occurred (see paragraph 5.1.9 below). The tax on petroleum is for these reasons inconsistent with the United States obligations under Article III:2, first sentence.

Japan – Tariff Import of Spruce, Pine, Fir, (SPF) Dimension Lumber ('Japan – Lumber'), 1989

Short summary and commentary

In *Japan – Lumber*, Canada requested that the panel examine whether Japan's application of an 8 per cent tariff on spruce-pine-fir (SPF) dimension lumber imports was consistent with Article I of the GATT. Japan based its tariff rates on dimension lumber imports on the species of tree from which the dimension lumber was produced. According to its tariff system, Japan applied this 8 per cent tariff to SPF dimension lumber, but not to dimension lumber from other tree species. Canada argued that SPF dimension lumber was 'like' dimension lumber from other tree species, and that therefore, Japan violated the MFN obligation of Article I by discriminating between 'like' products. Furthermore, Canada alleged that because most of its dimension lumber exports were subject to the 8 per cent tariff, while most dimension lumber exports from the US were not, Japan's policy of using tree species as the basis for differentiating between dimension lumber imports de facto discriminated against Canadian products.

Japan defended its tariff measure by arguing that: SPF dimension lumber was not 'like' dimension lumber from other species; that Article I was concerned with prohibiting discrimination between countries, not between 'like products'; and that its measures did not discriminate between countries.

The panel began its analysis by noting the principles guiding the relationship between the GATT system and tariff classification. It found that the GATT 'left wide discretion to the contracting parties' to design their national tariff structures and goods classifications. (Panel report, paragraph 5.8.) It also noted that tariff differentiation was a legitimate means of trade policy, one which allowed nations to accomplish its protection needs and to conduct successful tariff and trade negotiations (*Id.* at paragraph 5.9). Given the importance of tariff classification as a policy tool, the panel concluded those challenging a specific tariff classification had the burden of proving that the tariff classification was being used as a means of discrimination in international trade (*Id.* at paragraph 5.10).

When examining Canada's specific claim, the panel found that Canada had erred in trying to apply its concept of dimension lumber to Japan's tariff classification scheme. According to the panel, Canada's concept of dimension lumber was 'extraneous' to Japan's tariff, and was not 'an appropriate basis for establishing "likeness" under Article I:1 (*Id.* at paragraph 5.13). The panel concluded that Japan could differentiate between dimension lumber based upon whether the lumber came from a specific tree species.

Japan – Lumber could be interpreted to contradict with the earlier *Spain – Unroasted Coffee*. In contrast to *Spain – Unroasted Coffee*, *Japan – Lumber* seems to recognize that contracting parties should be able to use their tariff systems to serve certain national interests by giving states that flexibility.

Excerpts

Report of the Panel, *Japan – Tariff Import of Spruce Pine Fir Dimension Lumber*, BISD 36S/165, adopted on 19 July 1989.

V. Findings [paragraphs 5.1–5.16]

. . .

General Most-Favoured Nation Treatment

. . .

5.8 The Panel noted in this respect that the General Agreement left wide discretion to the contracting parties in relation to the structure of national tariffs and the classification of goods in the framework of such structure (see the report of the Panel on Tariff Treatment of Unroasted Coffee, BISD 28S/102, at III, paragraph 4.4). The adoption of the Harmonized System, to which both Canada and Japan have adhered, had brought about a large measure of harmonization in the field of customs classification of goods, but this system did not entail any obligation as to the ultimate detail in the respective tariff classifications. Indeed, this nomenclature has been on purpose structured in such a way that it leaves room for further specifications.

5.9 The Panel was of the opinion that, under these conditions, a tariff classification going beyond the Harmonized System's structure is a legitimate means of adapting the tariff scheme to each contracting party's trade policy interests, comprising both its protection needs and its requirements for the purposes of tariff and trade negotiations. It must however be borne in mind that such differentiations may lend themselves to abuse, insofar as they may serve to circumscribe tariff advantages in such a way that they are conducive to discrimination among like products originating in different contracting parties. A contracting party prejudiced by such action may request therefore that its own exports be treated as "like products" in spite of the fact that they might find themselves excluded by the differentiations retained in the importing country's tariff.

5.10 Tariff differentiation being basically a legitimate means of trade policy, a contracting party which claims to be prejudiced by such practice bears the burden of establishing that such tariff arrangement has been diverted from its normal purpose so as to become a means of discrimination in international trade. Such complaints have to be examined in considering simultaneously the internal protection interest involved in a given tariff specification, as well as its actual or potential influence on the pattern of imports from different extraneous sources. The Canadian complaint and the defence of Japan will have to be viewed in the light of these requirements.

. . .

5.13 *The Panel* considered that the tariffs referred to by the General Agreement are, quite evidently, those of the individual contracting parties. This was inherent in the system of the Agreement and appeared also in the current practice of tariff negotiations, the subject matter of which were the national tariffs of the individual contracting parties. It followed that, if a claim of likeness was raised by a contracting party in relation to the tariff treatment of its goods on importation by some other contracting party, such a claim should be based on the classification of the latter, i.e. the importing country's tariff.

5.14 The Panel noted in this respect that "dimension lumber" as defined by Canada was a concept extraneous to the Japanese Tariff. It was a standard applied by the Canadian industry which appeared to have some equivalent in the United States and in Japan itself, but it could not be considered for that reason alone as a category for tariff classification purposes, nor did it belong to any internationally accepted customs classification. The Panel concluded therefore that reliance by Canada on the concept of dimension lumber was not an appropriate basis for establishing "likeness" of products under Article I:1 of the General Agreement.

European Economic Community – Payments and Subsidies Paid to Processors and Producers of Oilseeds and Related Animal-Feed Proteins ('EEC – Oilseeds and Related Animal-Feed Proteins'), 1990

Short summary and commentary

In this case, the US alleged, among other things, that the European Economic Communities' (EEC) oilseeds regime violated Article III:4, in that it granted less favourable treatment to imported oilseeds than to domestic oilseeds. The US cited the 'products' intended end-uses, commercial interchangeability, commercial value and price, purchaser preferences and physical characteristics' in support of its claim that the products were 'like' (Panel Report, paragraph 49). The EEC countered by saying that all oilseeds could not make up a single 'like product'. It also emphasized that there is a distinction between products that are 'directly competitive or substitutable' and products which are 'like' – the latter category being narrower than the former (*Id.* at paragraph 50).

The panel ultimately concluded that the EEC's challenged regime violated Article III:4 by affording less favourable treatment to imported products than to 'like' domestic products. Its report, however, did not contain a discussion of how it ultimately concluded the products at issue were 'like products', which is why the excerpts are not reproduced here (*Id.* at paragraph 141).

United States – Restrictions on Imports of Tuna ('US – Tuna/Dolphin I'), 1991

Short summary and commentary

This case, though unadopted, is significant in that it addresses whether products can be distinguished based on the processes and production methods (PPMs) that were used to produce them. The US placed import restrictions on tuna and tuna products harvested in a manner that resulted in the incidental killing of dolphins. Because the PPMs at issue (the tuna harvesting method) did not affect or were not detectable in the actual end product (tuna), these import restrictions were of the kind categorized as non-product-related PPM-based measures. When implementation of these PPM-based restrictions resulted in a ban on tuna imported from Mexico, Mexico initiated dispute settlement proceedings to challenge the consistency of the restrictions with various provisions of GATT.

The US argued that its regulations were permissible under Article III because they applied equally to 'like' domestic and imported products. The US maintained that it treated domestic tuna harvested in a way that caused the incidental killing of dolphins the same as it treated imported tuna harvested in a way that caused the incidental killing of dolphins. The panel, however, found that even if the tuna from Mexican vessels were harvested in a manner more harmful to dolphins than the tuna harvested by American vessels, Article III did not permit the US to discriminate between Mexican and American tuna *as a product* (Panel report, paragraph 5.15). The panel's ruling indicated that non-product-related PPMs were not a valid basis upon which to make 'like products' determinations under Article III. The Dispute Settlement Body (DSB), however, did not adopt the panel's report.

Interestingly, the panel addressed the likeness question *after* concluding that Article III did not apply to the US measures. Chapter 4: Processes and Production Methods addresses this aspect of the panel's ruling in more detail. Nevertheless, although finding that Article III did not apply, the panel proceeded to state that even if Article III did apply, the US measures would be in violation of that provision because they treated like domestic and imported products differently.

For additional analysis and excerpts, see Chapter 4: Processes and Production Methods.

Excerpts

Report of the Panel, *United States – Restrictions on Imports of Tuna*, DS21/R – 39S/155 (3 September 1991), NOT ADOPTED.

B. Prohibition of imports of certain yellowfin tuna and certain yellowfin tuna products from Mexico

Categorization as internal regulations (Article III) or quantitative restrictions (Article XI)

...

5.15 The Panel further concluded that, even if the provisions of the MMPA enforcing the tuna harvesting regulations (in particular those providing for the seizure of cargo as a penalty for violation of the Act) were regarded as regulating the sale of tuna as a product, the United States import prohibition would not meet the requirements of Article III. As pointed out in paragraph 5.12 above, Article III:4 calls for a comparison of the treatment of imported tuna as a product with that of domestic tuna as a product. Regulations governing the taking of dolphins incidental to the taking of tuna could not possibly affect tuna as a product. Article III:4 therefore obliges the United States to accord treatment to Mexican tuna no less favourable than that accorded to United States tuna, whether or not the incidental taking of dolphins by Mexican vessels corresponds to that of United States vessels.

United States – Measures Affecting Alcoholic and Malt Beverages ('US – Malt Beverages'), 1992

Short summary and commentary

In *US – Malt Beverages,* Canada claimed that various state and federal measures in force in the US violated, in relevant part, paragraphs 1, 2 and 4 of Article III of the GATT. Those challenged tax and regulatory measures applied to the production, wholesale distribution or retail sale of beer, wine or cider. As such, the challenged measures were diverse, and used various criteria as a basis upon which to draw distinctions between the relevant products or producers. For example, some of the challenged measures applied taxes to only those breweries producing a certain volume of beer, and other measures imposed specific regulations on beer having a certain content of alcohol. Thus, these regulations' designs presented the panel with varying scenarios under which to determine if the products at issue were 'like products'. As will be discussed more thoroughly, the panel's analysis in this case is noteworthy for two reasons: (i) it dismissed the idea that products could be differentiated based on non-product-related PPMs; and (ii) it employed an 'aims and effects' test in making the 'like products' determination.

The first 'like products' issue the panel addressed was whether or not, under Article III:2, regulations could subject beers to different treatment depending on whether or not those beers were produced in large or small breweries. The panel concluded that the size of the breweries did not affect the nature of the beer or the beer as a product (Panel report, paragraph 5.19). Thus, it found that regulations could not validly use the size of the beer producers as a basis upon which to impose discriminatory taxes (*Id.*). This holding, therefore, suggested that a country (or, more specifically, a country's states or provinces) could not rely upon non-product-related PPMs, or PPMs based on the characteristics of the producer, as a basis for discriminating between otherwise 'like products'.

The panel again addressed the 'like products' issue under Article III:2 when analysing whether or not regulations could grant more favourable treatment to a domestic wine than an imported wine, based on the fact that the domestic wine was produced using a particular, locally grown grape. The panel looked to how previous decisions had addressed the 'like products' issue. It found that past determinations had been made on a case-by-case basis, and had utilized a set of criteria such as the 'product's end-uses in a given market, consumers tastes and habits, and the product's properties, nature and quality' (*Id.* at paragraph 5.24). Next, the panel discussed its view that any interpretation of the phrase 'like products' must take into account the overall purpose of Article III – to prevent governments from protecting domestic production (*Id.* at paragraph 5.25). Thus, it opined that governments may enact laws distinguishing between 'like products' if the distinctions between the products were drawn for some valid public policy purpose, and not drawn 'so as to afford protection to domestic production' (*Id.*).

The panel pointed out that the US had not advanced a policy purpose justifying the differentiation based on the grape variety, and also took note of the fact that 'tariff nomenclatures and tax laws, including those at the US federal and state level, [did] not generally make such a distinction between still wines on the basis of the variety of grape used in their production' (*Id.*). Based on those two factors, the panel concluded that the domestic and imported wines were 'like products' and the distinction between the two had been made so as to afford protection to the domestic product (*Id.*).

Finally, when judging whether beers with different alcohol contents were 'like products' within the meaning of Article III:4, the panel again stated that any 'like product' determination had to be made in light of the overall purpose of Article III – to prevent countries from affording protection to domestic production (*Id.* at paragraph 5.71). If, for example, a regulation distinguished between foreign and domestic products for environmental or standardization purposes, such distinctions would be permissible so long as they were not made for the purpose of protecting the domestic products (*Id.* at paragraph 5.72). In judging whether the regulations distinguishing between low and high alcohol content beer were enacted so as to afford protection to domestic production, the panel considered the aims, effects and design of the regulations. It noted (i) that both Canadian and US beer manufacturers produced high and low alcohol beer; (ii) the laws and regulations did not differentiate between domestic and imported beer; (iii) the burdens did not fall more heavily on Canadian than US producers; and (iv) the policy goals and legislative background indicated that the measures were not aimed at affording protection to domestic production (*Id.* at paragraph 5.74). The panel also noted that consumer preferences suggested there was a valid basis for differentiating between high and low alcohol content beer. Based on the above factors, the panel concluded that high and low alcohol content beer were not 'like products' within the meaning of Article III:4 (*Id.* at paragraph 5.75).

US – Malt Beverages also discusses the question of what constitutes discriminatory treatment under Article III:2 and Article III:4. A comprehensive discussion of non-discrimination, however, is outside the scope of this chapter on 'like products'.

Excerpts

Report of the Panel, *United States – Measures Affecting Alcoholic and Malt Beverages*, DS23/R – 39S/206, adopted on 19 June 1992.

5. Findings [Paras 5.1–5.77]

. . .

State Excise Tax Credits Based on Annual Production [paras 5.18–5.19]

. . .

5.19 The Panel further noted that the parties disagreed as to whether or not the tax credits in Minnesota were available in the case of imported beer from small foreign breweries. The Panel considered that beer produced by large breweries is not unlike beer produced by small breweries. Indeed, the United States did not assert that the size of the breweries affected the nature of the beer produced or otherwise affected beer as a product. Therefore, in the view of the Panel, even if Minnesota were to grant the tax credits on a non-discriminatory basis to small breweries inside and outside the United States, imported beer from large breweries would be "subject . . . to internal taxes . . . in excess of those applied . . . to like domestic products" from small breweries and there would still be an inconsistency with Article III:2, first sentence. Accordingly, the Panel found that the state excise tax credits provided by Kentucky, Minnesota, Ohio and Wisconsin to domestic breweries based on annual beer production, but not to imported beer, are inconsistent with Article III:2, first sentence.

. . .

State Excise Tax on Wine Based on a Specified Variety of Grape [paras 5.23–5.26]

5.23 The Panel then examined the claim by Canada that the state of Mississippi applied a lower tax rate to wines in which a certain variety of grape was used, contrary to Articles III:1 and III:2. The Panel recalled the United States argument that the tax provision in Mississippi was applicable to all qualifying wine produced from the specified variety of grape, regardless of the point of origin.

5.24 The Panel considered that Canada's claim depends upon whether wine imported from Canada is "like" the domestic wine in Mississippi made from the specified variety of grape, within the meaning of Article III:2. In this regard, the Panel noted that the CONTRACTING PARTIES have not developed a general definition of the term "like products", either within the context of Article III or in respect of other Articles of the General Agreement. Past decisions on this question have been made on a case-by-case basis after examining a number of relevant criteria, such as the product's end-uses in a given market, consumers' tastes and habits, and the product's properties, nature and quality.[6] The Panel considered that the like product determination under Article III:2 also should have regard to the purpose of the Article.

[6] See the Report of the Panel on "Japan – Customs duties, taxes and labelling practices on imported wines and alcoholic beverages", adopted on 10 November 1987, BISD 34S/83, p115.

5.25 The basic purpose of Article III is to ensure, as emphasized in Article III:1,

> *"that internal taxes and other internal charges, and laws, regulations and requirements affecting the internal sale, purchase, transportation, distribution or use of products . . . should not be applied to imported or domestic products so as to afford protection to domestic production".*

The purpose of Article III is thus not to prevent contracting parties from using their fiscal and regulatory powers for purposes other than to afford protection to domestic production. Specifically, the purpose of Article III is not to prevent contracting parties from differentiating between different product categories for policy purposes unrelated to the protection of domestic production. The Panel considered that the limited purpose of Article III has to be taken into account in interpreting the term "like products" in this Article. Consequently, in determining whether two products subject to different treatment are like products, it is necessary to consider whether such product differentiation is being made "so as to afford protection to domestic production". While the analysis of "like products" in terms of Article III:2 must take into consideration this objective of Article III, the Panel wished to emphasize that such an analysis would be without prejudice to the "like product" concepts in other provisions of the General Agreement, which might have different objectives and which might therefore also require different interpretations.

5.26 Applying the above considerations to the Mississippi wine tax, the Panel noted that the special tax treatment accorded in the Mississippi law to wine produced from a particular type of grape, which grows only in the southeastern United States and the Mediterranean region, is a rather exceptional basis for a tax distinction. Given the limited growing range of the specific variety of grape, at least in North America, the Panel was of the view that this particular tax treatment implies a geographical distinction which affords protection to local production of wine to the disadvantage of wine produced where this type of grape cannot be grown. The Panel noted that a previous panel concerning Article III treatment of wines and alcoholic beverages found imported and Japanese unsweetened still wines to be like products.[7] The Panel agreed with the reasoning of this previous panel and was of the view that tariff nomenclatures and tax laws, including those at the United States federal and state level, do not generally make such a distinction between still wines on the basis of the variety of grape used in their production. The Panel noted that the United States did not claim any public policy purpose for this Mississippi tax provision other than to subsidize small local producers. The Panel concluded that unsweetened still wines are like products and that the particular distinction in the Mississippi law in favour of still wine of a local variety must be presumed, on the basis of the evidence submitted to the Panel, to afford protection to Mississippi vintners. Accordingly, the Panel found that the lower rate of excise tax applied by Mississippi to wine produced from the specified variety of grape, which lower rate is not available to the imported like product from Canada, is inconsistent with Article III:2, first sentence. The Panel wished to point out that even if the wine produced from the special variety of grape were considered unlike other wine, the two kinds of wine would nevertheless have to be regarded as "directly competitive" products in terms of the Interpretive Note to Article III:2, second sentence, and the imposition of a higher tax on directly competing imported wine so as to afford protection to domestic production would be inconsistent with that provision.

[7] Report of the Panel on "Japan – Customs duties, taxes and labelling practices on imported wines and alcoholic beverages", adopted on 10 November 1987, BISD 34S/83, 115–116.

. . .

Beer Alcohol Content Requirements [paras 5.70–5.77]

5.70 The Panel then examined the claim by Canada that restrictions on points of sale, distribution and labelling based on the alcohol content of beer above 3.2 per cent by weight maintained by the states of Colorado, Florida, Kansas, Minnesota, Missouri, Oklahoma and Utah, and above 5 per cent by volume in Alabama and above 4 per cent by weight in Oregon, discriminated against imported beer and contravened Articles III:1 and III:4. The Panel recalled in this regard Canada's argument that all beer, whether containing an alcohol content of above or below the particular level set by these states (hereinafter referred to as "high alcohol beer" and "low alcohol beer", respectively) were like products within the meaning of Article III:4. Canada argued that the 3.2 per cent (or 5 per cent by volume or 4 per cent by weight) level were entirely arbitrary. According to Canada, restrictions as to the location at which high alcohol beer could be sold in the states of Alabama, Colorado, Kansas, Missouri, Oklahoma, Oregon and Utah, and differential labelling requirements imposed on such beer in the states of Florida, Kansas, Minnesota and Oklahoma, discriminated against imported beer. The Panel further recalled the arguments of the United States that the beer alcohol content measures in the above-named states did not differentiate between imported and domestic beer or otherwise discriminate against imported beer; that low alcohol beer need not be considered a like product to high alcohol beer; that in any case such measures could be justified under Articles XX(a) and (b) as necessary to the protection of human life and health and public morals; and that certain of the state statutes in question were covered by the PPA.

5.71 The Panel began its examination of these beer alcohol content distinctions in the named states by considering whether, in the context of Article III:4, low alcohol beer and high alcohol beer should be considered "like products". The Panel recalled in this regard its earlier statement on like product determinations and considered that, in the context of Article III, it is essential that such determinations be made not only in the light of such criteria as the products' physical characteristics, but also in the light of the purpose of Article III, which is to ensure that internal taxes and regulations "not be applied to imported or domestic products so as to afford protection to domestic production". The purpose of Article III is not to harmonize the internal taxes and regulations of contracting parties, which differ from country to country. In light of these considerations, the Panel was of the view that the particular level at which the distinction between high alcohol and low alcohol beer is made in the various states does not affect its reasonings and findings.

5.72 The Panel recognized that the treatment of imported and domestic products as like products under Article III may have significant implications for the scope of obligations under the General Agreement and for the regulatory autonomy of contracting parties with respect to their internal tax laws and regulations: once products are designated as like products, a regulatory product differentiation, e.g. for standardization or environmental purposes, becomes inconsistent with Article III even if the regulation is not "applied . . . so as afford protection to domestic production". In the view of the Panel, therefore, it is imperative that the like product determination in the context of Article III be made in such a way that it not unnecessarily infringe upon the regulatory authority and domestic policy options of contracting parties. The Panel recalled its earlier statement that a like product determination under Article III does not prejudge like product determinations made under other Articles of the General Agreement or in other legislative contexts.

5.73 The Panel recognized that on the basis of their physical characteristics, low alcohol beer and high alcohol beer are similar. It then proceeded to examine whether, in the context of Article III, this differentiation in treatment of low alcohol beer and high alcohol beer is such "as to afford protection to domestic production". The Panel first noted that both Canadian and United States beer manufacturers produce both high and low alcohol content beer. It then noted that the laws and regulations in question in the various states do not differentiate between imported and domestic beer as such, so that where a state law limits the points of sale of high alcohol content beer or maintains different labelling requirements for such beer, that law applies to all high alcohol content beer, regardless of its origin. The burdens resulting from these regulations thus do not fall more heavily on Canadian than on United States producers. The Panel also noted that although the market for the two types of beer overlaps, there is at the same time evidence of a certain degree of market differentiation and specialization: consumers who purchase low alcohol content beer may be unlikely to purchase beer with a higher alcohol content and vice-versa, and manufacturers target these different market segments in their advertising and marketing.

5.74 The Panel then turned to a consideration of the policy goals and legislative background of the laws regulating the alcohol content of beer. In this regard, the Panel recalled the United States argument that states encouraged the consumption of low alcohol beer over beer with a higher alcohol content specifically for the purposes of protecting human life and health and upholding public morals. The Panel also recalled the Canadian position that the legislative background of laws regulating the alcohol content of beer showed that the federal and state legislatures were more concerned with raising tax revenue than with protecting human health and public morals. On the basis of the evidence submitted, the Panel noted that the relevant laws were passed against the background of the Temperance movement in the United States. It noted further that prior to the repeal of the Eighteenth Amendment of the United States Constitution authorizing Prohibition, amendments to the federal Volstead Act – the Act which implemented the Eighteenth Amendment – authorized the sale of low alcohol beer, and that the primary focus of the drafters of these amendments may have been the establishment of a brewing industry which could serve as a new source of tax revenue. However, irrespective of whether the policy background to the laws distinguishing alcohol content of beer was the protection of human health and public morals or the promotion of a new source of government revenue, both the statements of the parties and the legislative history suggest that the alcohol content of beer has not been singled out as a means of favouring domestic producers over foreign producers. The Panel recognized that the level at which the state measures distinguished between low and high alcohol content could arguably have been other than 3.2 per cent by weight. Indeed, as the Panel previously noted, Alabama and Oregon make the distinction at slightly different levels. However, there was no evidence submitted to the Panel that the choice of the particular level has the purpose or effect of affording protection to domestic production.

5.75 Thus, for the purposes of its examination under Article III, and in the context of the state legislation at issue in Alabama, Colorado, Florida, Kansas, Minnesota, Missouri, Oklahoma, Oregon and Utah, the Panel considered that low alcohol content beer and high alcohol content beer need not be considered as like products in terms of Article III:4. The Panel again emphasized that this determination is limited to this particular case and is not to be extended to other Articles or other legislative contexts.

United States – Taxes on Automobiles ('US – Taxes on Automobiles'), 1994

Short summary and commentary

In *US – Taxes on Automobiles*, the European Communities alleged that two US tax laws and a fuel efficiency regulation were inconsistent with Article III of the GATT. In its unadopted report, the panel first concluded that the 'aims and effects' of a regulation must inform the determination of whether two products are 'like products' under Article III. Elaborating upon this 'aims and effects' test, the panel stated that the aims of a legislative act were its 'desired outcome[s]', and not simply its 'incidental consequence[s]' (Panel report, paragraph 5.10). Furthermore, the aims of a regulation could not be deciphered merely by looking at statements made or the preparatory work done in drafting the legislation, but also depended upon an analysis of the 'wording of the legislation as a whole' (*Id.* at paragraph 5.12). And, in analysing whether the legislation's effects afforded protection to domestic production, the proper inquiry, according to the panel, would look at whether the effects were changes in the 'conditions of competition', as opposed to whether they simply were changes in the volume or flow of imports (*Id.*).

After outlining the 'aims and effects' test, the panel applied the test to the US' two tax laws. The first law it examined imposed a luxury tax on automobiles costing more than $30,000. The panel concluded that the measure did not afford protection to domestic production and that, consequently, the products above and below the tax's threshold could not be considered 'like products' under Article III:2 (*Id.* at paragraph 5.15).

Next, the panel applied the 'aims and effects' test to the second law, which imposed a 'gas guzzler' tax on automobiles whose fuel efficiency was less than 22.5 miles per gallon. The panel concluded that the challenged features of the gas guzzler tax did not afford protection to domestic production because they were neither intended to protect domestic products, nor did they change the conditions of competition for the imported products (*Id.* at paragraph 5.20). Because the tax and its threshold 22.5 mile per gallon fuel efficiency standard did not afford protection to domestic production, the panel found that (i) domestic automobiles above the fuel efficiency threshold and foreign automobiles below the threshold were not 'like products'; (ii) 'an individual imported automobile whose model type fuel economy was less than 22.5 mpg was not "like" an individual domestic automobile whose model type fuel economy was above 22.5 mpg, even if the fuel economy of the individual domestic automobile was below 22.5 mpg' (*Id.* at paragraph 5.32); and (iii) imported automobiles were not 'like' domestic light trucks (*Id.* at paragraph 5.35).

The panel then proceeded to examine the consistency of the fuel efficiency regulations with Article III:4. One challenged feature of the regulations was that they distinguished between foreign and domestic car fleets when calculating the fuel efficiency of those fleets. The panel found that this accounting system afforded less favourable competitive conditions to imported cars and car parts than to domestic 'like' products. As a result, it concluded that the regulations were not consistent with Article III:4 (*Id.* at paragraph 5.55).

Another challenged feature of the fuel efficiency regulations was that they employed a fleet averaging requirement, which was based on the ownership or control of the car manufacturers or importers. The panel found that this system violated Article III:4 because that article does not allow Members use factors, such as the characteristics of the producers or importers, as a basis upon which discriminate between imported and domestic 'like' products. Rather, the panel stated that to be consistent with Article III:4, any distinctions drawn between products must be drawn based upon the products as such.

Another significant aspect of the panel's likeness analysis in this case is its apparent rejection of a 'least trade restrictive alternative' test suggested by the European Communities. To support its argument that the aims of the gas guzzler tax were to afford protection to domestic production, the European Communities argued that if the US truly wanted to achieve its stated policy goal of conserving fossil fuels, it would have enacted a gasoline tax, rather than the gas guzzler tax. The panel did not accept the European Communities' argument, stating that, while a tax on fuel might be a better means of achieving the policy goal of conserving fossil fuels, that fact was not 'by itself relevant in determining obligations under Article III' (*Id.* at paragraph 5.24). If the panel had followed the European Communities' suggested approach, it could have opened up likeness determinations to inquiries into whether or not the enacting countries' measures were truly the optimal or least trade restrictive means available for achieving the desired policy objectives. Thus, this case is noteworthy in that it is deferential to the decisions of a country regarding how that country wants to achieve a stated policy goal.

Excerpts

Report of the Panel, *United States – Taxes on Automobiles*, DS31/R (11 October 1994), NOT ADOPTED.

V. Findings

A. Luxury Tax

. . .

(i) Article III:2, first sentence

(a) Treatment of like products under Article III [paras 5.5–5.10]

5.5 The Panel noted that the central issue raised by the parties was whether under Article III:2 cars selling for more than $30,000 were "like" products to domestic cars selling for less. The resolution of this issue required a preliminary analysis of the scope of Article III with respect to the treatment to be accorded to a product of foreign origin. The Panel proceeded to examine the terms of Article III. It observed that Article III deals with differences in treatment between products. These differences in treatment resulted from regulatory distinctions made by governments. If regulatory distinctions were drawn explicitly with respect to the origin of the product, or with respect to manifestly different products, then the consistency with Article III:2 or 4 could be determined in a straightforward manner. If the regulatory distinctions were not drawn explicitly with respect to origin, then it had to be determined whether the products were 'like'. The Panel recalled the EC argument that likeness of products under Article III should be based on factors such as their end use, physical characteristics and tariff classification, and that the disproportionate impact of the measure on a foreign product is relevant in determining the overall consistency of the measure with Article III. The Panel noted, on the other hand, that the United States argued that the key criterion in judging likeness under Article III was whether the measure was applied "so as to afford protection to domestic production".

. . .

5.7 In order to determine this issue, the Panel examined the object and purpose of paragraphs 2 and 4 of Article III in the context of the article as a whole and the General Agreement. The Panel noted that the purpose of Article III is set out in paragraph 1 of the article, which states:

> *"The contracting parties recognize that internal taxes and other internal charges, and laws, regulations and requirements affecting the internal sale, offering for sale, purchase, transportation, distribution or use of products, and internal quantitative regulations requiring the mixture, processing or use of products in specified amounts or proportions, should not be applied to imported or domestic products* so as to afford protection to domestic production" *(emphasis added).*

The Panel considered that paragraphs 2 and 4 of Article III had to be read in the light of this central purpose. The Panel reasoned therefore that Article III serves only to prohibit regulatory distinctions between products applied so as to afford protection to domestic production. Its purpose is not to prohibit fiscal and regulatory distinctions applied so as to achieve other policy goals. This view has been expressed in a recent panel report, which states:

> *"The purpose of Article III is . . . not to prevent contracting parties from using their fiscal and regulatory powers for purposes other than to afford protection to domestic production. Specifically, the purpose of Article III is not to prevent contracting parties from differentiating between different product categories for policy purposes unrelated to the protection of domestic production. The Panel considered that the limited purpose of Article III has to be taken into account in interpreting the term "like products" in this Article. Consequently, in determining whether two products subject to different treatment are like products, it is necessary to consider whether such product differentiation is being made "so as to afford protection to domestic production".*[128]

[128] Report of the Panel on *United States – Measures affecting alcoholic and malt beverages*, adopted 19 June 1992, DS23/R, BISD 39S/206.

5.8 The Panel noted that earlier practice of the CONTRACTING PARTIES had been to determine the permissibility of regulatory distinctions under Article III on a case-by-case basis, examining likeness in terms of factors such as "the product's end-uses in a given market, consumers' tastes and habits, which change from country to country; the product's properties, nature and quality."[129] The Panel noted that regulatory distinctions based on such factors were often, but not always, the means of implementing government policies other than the protection of domestic industry. Non-protectionist government policies might, however, require regulatory distinctions that were not based on the product's end use, its physical characteristics, or the other factors mentioned. Noting that a primary purpose of the General Agreement was to lower barriers to trade between markets, and not to harmonize the regulatory treatment of products within them, the Panel considered that Article III could not be interpreted as prohibiting government policy options, based on products, that were not taken so as to afford protection to domestic production.

[129] Report of the Working Party on *Border Tax Adjustments,* adopted on 2 December 1970, BISD 18S/97, 102.

5.9 The Panel noted that the EC had relied in its interpretation of Article III:2 on the findings of an earlier panel. That panel had stated that:

> *"the ordinary meaning of Article III:2 in its context and in the light of its object and purpose supported the past GATT practice of examining the conformity of internal taxes with Article III:2 by determining, firstly, whether the taxed imported and domestic products are "like" or "directly competitive or substitutable" and, secondly, whether the taxation is discriminatory (first sentence) or protective (second sentence of Article III:2)."*[130]

This two-step approach implied that less favourable tax treatment could not be imposed on a foreign product consistently with Article III:2 if the domestic and foreign products shared certain common features (likeness) and if the tax measure was discriminatory or protective. However, the first step of determining the relevant features common to the domestic and imported products (likeness) would in the view of the Panel, in all but the the most straightforward cases, have to include an examination of the aim and effect of the particular tax measure. Therefore the second step of determining whether the tax measure was discriminatory or protective was simply a continuation of the inquiry under the first step. The Panel concluded that its interpretation was consistent with previous ones, but made explicit that issues of likeness under Article III should be analysed primarily in terms of whether less favourable treatment was based on a regulatory distinction taken so as to afford protection to domestic production.

[130] Report of the Panel on "Japan – Customs duties, taxes and labelling practices on imported wines and alcoholic beverages", adopted on 10 November 1987 (L/6216) BISD 34S/83 at 115, para 5.5.

5.10 The Panel then proceeded to examine more closely the meaning of the phrase "so as to afford protection". The Panel noted that the term "so as to" suggested both aim and effect.[131] Thus the phrase "so as to afford protection" called for an analysis of elements including the aim of the measure and the resulting effects. A measure could be said to have the aim of affording protection if an analysis of the circumstances in which it was adopted, in particular an analysis of the instruments available to the contracting party to achieve the declared domestic policy goal, demonstrated that a change in competitive opportunities in favour of domestic products was a desired outcome and not merely an incidental consequence of the pursuit of a legitimate policy goal. A measure could be said to have the effect of affording protection to domestic production if it accorded greater competitive opportunities to domestic products than to imported products. The effect of a measure in terms of trade flows was not relevant for the purposes of Article III, since a change in the volume or proportion of imports could be due to many factors other than government measures. A previous panel had stated:

> *"Article III:2, first sentence, obliges contracting parties to establish certain competitive conditions for imported products in relation to domestic products. Unlike some other provisions in the General Agreement, it does not refer to trade effects."*[132]

The Panel observed that the central objective of the analysis remained the determination of whether the regulatory distinction was made "so as to afford protection to domestic production". The analysis of aims and effects of the measure were elements that contributed to that determination.

[131] This term "shows the logical result or purpose of an action done in a specific manner" (*Webster's Third New International Dictionary of the English Language* (Unabridged)). This meaning is also reflected in the French authentic text of Article III:1 which uses the expression "de manière à".
[132] Report of the Panel on United States – Taxes on petroleum and certain imported substances, adopted 17 June 1987 (L/6175) BISD 34S/136 at p158, para 5.1.9; referring to the Report of the Working Party on Brazilian Internal Taxes, adopted on 30 June 1949, BISD II/181 at 185, para 16; same view in Report of the Panel on United States – Measures affecting alcoholic and malt beverages adopted on 19 June 1992 (DS23/R) BISD 39S/206 at 271, para 5.6.

Japan – Taxes on Alcoholic Beverages ('Japan – Alcoholic Beverages (1996)'), 1996

Short summary and commentary

The US, Canada and the European Communities initiated this action to challenge the Japanese Liquor Tax Law (Shuzeiho), Law No 6 of 1953 as amended ('Liquor Tax Law'), alleging that it violated Article III:2 of the GATT. The complaining parties made two different legal arguments to support their claims. First, the European Communities and the US asserted that the Liquor Tax Law was inconsistent with Article III:2, first sentence, of the GATT because the Liquor Tax Law taxed imported products 'in excess of' 'like' domestic products. The European Communities and the US also argued, in the alternative, that the Liquor Tax Law violated Article III:2, second sentence, of the GATT, in that it applied a different rate of taxation to 'directly competitive or substitutable' products. Canada based its claim solely on the latter of the two arguments. On 11 July, 1996, the panel issued its report, which found that Japan's Liquor Tax Law was not consistent with either the first or second sentences of Article III:2 of the GATT.

Both Japan and the US appealed the panel's decision. In relevant part, Japan claimed that the panel had erred by (i) failing to determine whether the Liquor Tax Law was designed to afford protection to domestic production, and (ii) in determining that vodka and shochu were 'like products' within the meaning of Article III:2, first sentence. The US, although agreeing with the panel's ultimate conclusion, claimed that the panel had erred in its interpretation of Article III:2, first and second sentences, by failing to interpret those provisions in light of the general principles set forth in Article III:1. According to the US, any inquiry into the permissibility of regulatory distinctions between imported and domestic products had to consider whether such distinctions were made 'so as to afford protection to domestic production' (GATT Article III:1). Although the appellate decision affirmed the panel's overall conclusion that Japan's Liquor Tax Law violated Article III of the GATT, it modified some of the panel's legal reasoning and conclusions.

Referring to principles of treaty interpretation set forth in the *Vienna Convention*, the Appellate Body agreed with both Japan and the US that Article III:1 must inform any interpretation of Article III:2 (AB report, section G). The Appellate Body elaborated upon its conclusion that Article III:1 guides a correct interpretation of Article III:2 by stating that Article III:1 affects the meaning of the first and second sentences of Article III:2 in different ways. In considering how Article III:1 affects the meaning of the first sentence of Article III:2, the Appellate Body emphasized that that first sentence of Article III:2 does not specifically reference Article III:1. According to the Appellate Body, '[t]hat omission must have some meaning' (*Id.* at section H.1). It reasoned that the failure of the first sentence of Article III:2 to reference Article III:1 means 'simply that the presence of a protective application need not be established separately from the specific requirements that are included in the first sentence in order to show that a tax measure is inconsistent with the general principle set out in the first sentence' (*Id.*). Rather, to establish a violation of Article III:2, first sentence, a party is simply required (i) to show that the taxed imported and domestic products are 'like', and (ii) that 'the taxes applied to the imported products are "in excess of" those applied to the like domestic products' (*Id.*).

After setting forth the two-part test for establishing whether a measure is inconsistent with the first sentence of Article III:2, the Appellate Body then discussed the proper application of that test by explaining how to determine (i) whether imported and domestic products are 'like' products, and (ii) whether the imported products are taxed 'in excess of' the domestic products.

With respect to the 'like products' issue, the Appellate Body first concluded that the definition of 'like products' should be construed narrowly (*Id.* at section H.1.a). It reached this conclusion after noting that the first sentence's prohibition on measures affecting 'like' products was different from the second sentence's prohibition on measures affecting directly comparable and substitutable products. The Appellate Body reasoned that, in order to give effect to the two categories of products established by the first and second sentences of Article III:2, the definition of 'like products' must be narrowly read (*Id.*). If it were not narrowly read, the significance of the second category – directly comparable or substitutable products – would be eviscerated.

Yet, in describing how strictly the definition of 'like products' should be interpreted, the Appellate Body did not provide much specific guidance. It stated that the determination of whether products were 'like' products should be made on a case-by-case basis 'considering the various characteristics of products in individual cases' (*Id.*). Although the determination would inevitably involve 'an element of individual, discretionary judgment', it should be made based upon an evaluation of the oft-cited criteria set forth in the Report of the Working Party on *Border Tax Adjustments*, adopted by the CONTRACTING PARTIES in 1970 (*Id.*). Those criteria are 'the product's end-uses in a given market; consumers' tastes and habits, which change from country to country; [and] the product's properties, nature and quality' (*Id.*). Furthermore, the Appellate Body stated that other factors such as a product's tariff classification may also be relevant to the determination of whether products are like products (*Id.*). The Appellate Body's report then cautioned, however, that tariff bindings or concessions are likely 'not a reliable criterion for determining or confirming product "likeness" under Article III:2' (*Id.*).

This case is significant for the 'likeness' issue in several respects. First, it emphasizes that the broad purpose of Article III of the GATT, as set forth in Article III:1, is to inform and guide interpretation of the specific provisions included in Article III:2. Second, the Appellate Body report clarifies that the determination of whether or not a tax is consistent with Article III:2, first sentence, requires application of a two-part test. The first part of the test asks whether the domestic and imported products are 'like' products. If the products are, in fact, 'like' products, the second part of the test asks whether the imported products are taxed 'in excess of' the domestic products. Hence, under that two-part test as enunciated by the Appellate Body, in determining whether a measure complies with Article III:2, first sentence, there is no need for an investigation into the aims or goals behind the legislation or regulation. Finally, the Appellate Body decision clarifies that if a measure taxes imported products in excess of 'like' domestic products, it is irrelevant whether that excess level of taxation is merely a *de minimis* burden on the imported products. In other words, the actual *effect* of the measure is irrelevant to determining whether the measure is consistent with Article III:2, first sentence.

In addition to its treatment of the 'like products' issue and the first sentence of Article III:2, the Appellate Body also devoted much time in its report to elaborating upon the meaning of 'directly competitive and substitutable products' and the proper interpretation and application of the second sentence of Article III:2. Because, in contrast to the first sentence of Article III:2, the second sentence of Article III:2 references Article III:1 directly, the Appellate Body concluded that the two sentences must invoke different tests (*Id.* at section H.2). Specifically, while analysis of a measure's consistency with Article III:2, first sentence, requires two steps, an examination of (i) whether the products are 'like' products and (ii) whether the imported product is taxed in excess of the 'like' domestic product, the analysis required to determine whether a measure is inconsistent with Article III:2, second sentence, involves three steps: First, there must be a determination that the imported and domestic products are '*"directly competitive or substitutable products" which are in competition with each other*'; second, there must be a showing that '*the directly competitive or substitutable imported and domestic products are "not similarly taxed"*' and third, it must be demonstrated that the dissimilar taxation *is '"applied . . . so as to afford protection to domestic production"'* (*Id.*). The Appellate Body concluded that the third step was necessary because of the fact that Article III:2, second sentence, directly referred to Article III:1 and its prohibition of measures 'applied . . . so as to afford protection to domestic production' (*Id.*).

Although the category of 'directly competitive or substitutable products' is a broader category than that of 'like products', it is similar in two important respects. First, like the determination of whether products are 'like' products, the determination of whether they are directly competitive or substitutable is made on a case-by-case basis (*Id.* at section H.2.a). Second, analysis of whether products are 'directly competitive or substitutable' involves an examination of some of the same criteria relevant to 'like products' examinations. For example, the Appellate Body report stated that, when determining whether products fit into the broader product category of Article III:2's second sentence, it is appropriate to look at such factors as the physical characteristics of the products, the products' end-uses, and tariff classifications (*Id.*).

Yet, the Appellate Body proceeded to add that an analysis of the market place is also important in determining whether products are 'directly competitive or substitutable'. With respect to that analysis of the market place, the Appellate Body opined that looking at elasticity of substitution is *one means* of examining those relevant markets (*Id.*).

This decision has been commonly read as rejecting the 'aims and effects' test. Yet, it is important to note that much of the decision's language that is read as rejecting the 'aims and effects' test was set forth in the Appellate Body's discussion of Article III:2, first sentence. Thus, it would appear important to ask to what extent the Appellate Body's discussion of the 'aims and effects' of challenged measures is similarly applicable to Article III:2, second sentence. Along these lines, it is also important to remember that the decision addressed a claim under Article III:2, not under Article III:4. A subsequent WTO tribunal in *EC – Bananas III* noted that the *Japan – Alcoholic Beverages (1996)* decision rejected the 'aims and effects' test with respect to Article III:2. Although it is not clear how deliberately the tribunal chose its language, the tribunal say the test was rejected in the context of Article III:2; it did *not* say the text was rejected in the context of Article III, as a whole. To date, no WTO decision has explicitly rejected the 'aims and effects' with respect to Article III:4. Nevertheless, WTO tribunals since the *Japan – Alcoholic Beverages (1996)* decision have not explicitly invoked an 'aims and effects' test for claims arising under either Article III:2 or Article III:4.

Relatively recently, some commentators have questioned the accuracy of the belief that *Japan – Alcoholic Beverages (1996)* stands for a rejection of the 'aims and effects' test. The basic premise of this argument is that the decision in *Chile – Alcoholic Beverages*, which is discussed, *infra*, should prompt a reexamination of the common interpretation of the *Japan – Alcoholic Beverages (1996)* decision.

Excerpts

Report of the Appellate Body, *Japan – Taxes on Alcoholic Beverages*, WT/DS8/AB/R, adopted on 1 November 1996.

[Note: this report does not utilize paragraph numbers]

G. Article III:1

The terms of Article III must be given their ordinary meaning – in their context and in the light of the overall object and purpose of the *WTO Agreement*. Thus, the words actually used in the Article provide the basis for an interpretation that must give meaning and effect to all its terms. The proper interpretation of the Article is, first of all, a textual interpretation. Consequently, the Panel is correct in seeing a distinction between Article III:1, which "contains general principles", and Article III:2, which "provides for specific obligations regarding internal taxes and internal charges".[40] Article III:1 articulates a general principle that internal measures should not be applied so as to afford protection to domestic production. This general principle informs the rest of Article III. The purpose of Article III:1 is to establish this general principle as a guide to understanding and interpreting the specific obligations contained in Article III:2 and in the other paragraphs of Article III, while respecting, and not diminishing in any way, the meaning of the words actually used in the texts of those other paragraphs. In short, Article III:1 constitutes part of the context of Article III:2, in the same way that it constitutes part of the context of each of the other paragraphs in Article III. Any other reading of Article III would have the effect of rendering the words of Article III:1 meaningless, thereby violating the fundamental principle of effectiveness in treaty interpretation. Consistent with this principle of effectiveness, and with the textual differences in the two sentences, we believe that Article III:1 informs the first sentence and the second sentence of Article III:2 in different ways.

[40] Panel Report, para 6.12.

H. Article III:2

1 First Sentence

Article III:1 informs Article III:2, first sentence, by establishing that if imported products are taxed in excess of like domestic products, then that tax measure is inconsistent with Article III. Article III:2, first sentence does not refer specifically to Article III:1. There is no specific invocation in this first sentence of the general principle in Article III:1 that admonishes Members of the WTO not to apply measures "so as to afford protection". This omission must have some meaning. We believe the meaning is simply that the presence of a protective application need not be established separately from the specific requirements that are included in the first sentence in order to show that a tax measure is inconsistent with the general principle set out in the first sentence. However, this does not mean that the general principle of Article III:1 does not apply to this sentence. To the contrary, we believe the first sentence of Article III:2 is, in effect, an application of this general principle. The ordinary meaning of the words of Article III:2, first sentence leads inevitably to this conclusion. Read in their context and in the light of the overall object and purpose of the *WTO Agreement*, the words of the first sentence require an examination of the conformity of an internal tax measure with Article III by determining, first, whether the taxed imported and domestic products are "like" and, second, whether the taxes applied to the imported products are "in excess of" those applied to the like domestic products. If the imported and domestic products are "like products", and if the taxes applied to the imported products are "in excess of" those applied to the like domestic products, then the measure is inconsistent with Article III:2, first sentence.[41]

This approach to an examination of Article III:2, first sentence, is consistent with past practice under the GATT 1947.[42] Moreover, it is consistent with the object and purpose of Article III:2, which the panel in the predecessor to this case dealing with an earlier version of the Liquor Tax Law, *Japan – Customs Duties, Taxes and Labelling Practices on Imported Wines and Alcoholic Beverages* ("*1987 Japan – Alcohol*"), rightly stated as "promoting non-discriminatory competition among imported and like domestic products [which] could not be achieved if Article III:2 were construed in a manner allowing discriminatory and protective internal taxation of imported products in excess of like domestic products".[43]

(a) "Like Products"

Because the second sentence of Article III:2 provides for a separate and distinctive consideration of the protective aspect of a measure in examining its application to a broader category of products that are not "like products" as contemplated by the first sentence, we agree with the Panel that the first sentence of Article III:2 must be construed narrowly so as not to condemn measures that its strict terms are not meant to condemn. Consequently, we agree with the Panel also that the definition of "like products" in Article III:2, first sentence, should be construed narrowly.[44]

How narrowly is a matter that should be determined separately for each tax measure in each case. We agree with the practice under the GATT 1947 of determining whether imported and domestic products are "like" on a case-by-case basis. The Report of the Working Party on *Border Tax Adjustments*, adopted by the CONTRACTING PARTIES in 1970, set out the basic approach for interpreting "like or similar products" generally in the various provisions of the GATT 1947:

> *. . . the interpretation of the term should be examined on a case-by-case basis. This would allow a fair assessment in each case of the different elements that constitute a "similar" product. Some criteria were suggested for determining, on a case-by-case basis, whether a product is "similar": the product's end-uses in a given market; consumers' tastes and habits, which change from country to country; the product's properties, nature and quality.*[45]

This approach was followed in almost all adopted panel reports after *Border Tax Adjustments*.[46] This approach should be helpful in identifying on a case-by-case basis the range of "like products" that fall within the narrow limits of Article III:2, first sentence in the GATT 1994. Yet this approach will be most helpful if decision makers keep ever in mind how narrow the range of "like products" in Article III:2, first sentence is meant to be as opposed to the range of "like" products contemplated in some other provisions of the GATT 1994 and other Multilateral Trade Agreements of the *WTO Agreement*. In applying the criteria cited in *Border Tax Adjustments* to the facts of any particular case, and in considering other criteria that may also be relevant in certain cases, panels can only apply their best judgement in determining whether in fact products are "like". This will always involve an unavoidable element of individual, discretionary judgement. We do not agree with the Panel's observation in paragraph 6.22 of the Panel Report that distinguishing between "like products" and "directly competitive or substitutable products" under Article III:2 is "an arbitrary decision". Rather, we think it is a discretionary decision that must be made in considering the various characteristics of products in individual cases.

No one approach to exercising judgement will be appropriate for all cases. The criteria in *Border Tax Adjustments* should be examined, but there can be no one precise and absolute definition of what is "like". The concept of "likeness" is a relative one that evokes the image of an accordion. The accordion of "likeness" stretches and squeezes in different places as different provisions of the *WTO Agreement* are applied. The width of the accordion in any one of those places must be determined by the particular provision in which the term "like" is encountered as well as by the context and the circumstances that prevail in any given case to which that provision may apply. We believe that, in Article III:2, first sentence of the GATT 1994, the accordion of "likeness" is meant to be narrowly squeezed.

The Panel determined in this case that shochu and vodka are "like products" for the purposes of Article III:2, first sentence. We note that the determination of whether vodka is a "like product" to shochu under Article III:2, first sentence, or a "directly competitive or substitutable product" to shochu under Article III:2, second sentence, does not materially affect the outcome of this case.

A uniform tariff classification of products can be relevant in determining what are "like products". If sufficiently detailed, tariff classification can be a helpful sign of product similarity. Tariff classification has been used as a criterion for determining "like products" in several previous adopted panel reports.[47] For example, in the *1987 Japan – Alcohol* Panel Report, the panel examined certain wines and alcoholic beverages on a "product-by-product basis" by applying the criteria listed in the Working Party Report on *Border Tax Adjustments:*

> *. . . as well as others recognized in previous GATT practice (see BISD 25S/49, 63), such as the Customs Cooperation Council Nomenclature (CCCN) for the classification of goods in customs tariffs which has been accepted by Japan.*[48]

Uniform classification in tariff nomenclatures based on the Harmonized System (the "HS") was recognized in GATT 1947 practice as providing a useful basis for confirming "likeness" in products. However, there is a major difference between tariff classification nomenclature and tariff bindings or concessions made by Members of the WTO under Article II of the GATT 1994. There are risks in using tariff bindings that are too broad as a measure of product "likeness". Many of the least-developed country Members of the WTO submitted schedules of concessions and commitments as annexes to the GATT 1994 for the first time as required by Article XI of the *WTO Agreement*. Many of these least-developed countries, as well as other developing countries, have bindings in their schedules which include broad ranges of products that cut across several different HS tariff headings. For example, many of these countries have very broad uniform bindings on non-agricultural products.[49] This does not necessarily indicate similarity of the products covered by a binding. Rather, it represents the results of trade concessions negotiated among Members of the WTO.

It is true that there are numerous tariff bindings which are in fact extremely precise with regard to product description and which, therefore, can provide significant guidance as to the identification of "like products". Clearly enough, these determinations need to be made on a case-by-case basis. However, tariff bindings that include a wide range of products are not a reliable criterion for determining or confirming product "likeness" under Article III:2.[50]

With these modifications to the legal reasoning in the Panel Report, we affirm the legal conclusions and the findings of the Panel with respect to "like products" in all other respects.

. . .

2. Second Sentence

Article III:1 informs Article III:2, second sentence, through specific reference. Article III:2, second sentence, contains a general prohibition against "internal taxes or other internal charges" applied to "imported or domestic products in a manner contrary to the principles set forth in paragraph 1". As mentioned before, Article III:1 states that internal taxes and other internal charges "should not be applied to imported or domestic products so as to afford protection to domestic production". Again, *Ad* Article III:2 states as follows:

> *A tax conforming to the requirements of the first sentence of paragraph 2 would be considered to be inconsistent with the provisions of the second sentence only in cases where competition was involved between, on the one hand, the taxed product and, on the other hand, a directly competitive or substitutable product which was not similarly taxed.*

Article III:2, second sentence, and the accompanying *Ad* Article have equivalent legal status in that both are treaty language which was negotiated and agreed at the same time.[52] The *Ad* Article does not replace or modify the language contained in Article III:2, second sentence, but, in fact, clarifies its meaning. Accordingly, the language of the second sentence and the *Ad* Article must be read together in order to give them their proper meaning.

Unlike that of Article III:2, first sentence, the language of Article III:2, second sentence, specifically invokes Article III:1. The significance of this distinction lies in the fact that whereas Article III:1 acts implicitly in addressing the two issues that must be considered in applying the first sentence, it acts explicitly as an entirely separate issue that must be addressed along with two other issues that are raised in applying the second sentence. Giving full meaning to the text and to its context, three separate issues must be addressed to determine whether an internal tax measure is inconsistent with Article III:2, second sentence. These three issues are whether:

(1) the imported products and the domestic products *are "directly competitive or substitutable products" which are in competition with each other*;
(2) the directly competitive or substitutable imported and domestic products *are "not similarly taxed"*; and
(3) the dissimilar taxation of the directly competitive or substitutable imported domestic products *is "applied . . . so as to afford protection to domestic production"*.

Again, these are three separate issues. Each must be established separately by the complainant for a panel to find that a tax measure imposed by a Member of the WTO is inconsistent with Article III:2, second sentence.

(1) *"Directly Competitive or Substitutable Products"*

If imported and domestic products are not "like products" for the narrow purposes of Article III:2, first sentence, then they are not subject to the strictures of that sentence and there is no inconsistency with the requirements of that sentence. However, depending on their nature, and depending on the competitive conditions in the relevant market, those same products may well be among the broader category of "directly competitive or substitutable products" that fall within the domain of Article III:2, second sentence. How much broader that category of "directly competitive or substitutable products" may be in any given case is a matter for the panel to determine based on all the relevant facts in that case. As with "like products" under the first sentence, the determination of the appropriate range of "directly competitive or substitutable products" under the second sentence must be made on a case-by-case basis.

In this case, the Panel emphasized the need to look not only at such matters as physical characteristics, common end-uses and tariff classifications, but also at the "market place".[53] This seems appropriate. The GATT 1994 is a commercial agreement, and the WTO is concerned, after all, with markets. It does not seem inappropriate to look at competition in the relevant markets as one among a number of means of identifying the broader category of products that might be described as "directly competitive or substitutable".

Nor does it seem inappropriate to examine elasticity of substitution as one means of examining those relevant markets. The Panel did not say that cross-price elasticity of demand is "*the* decisive criterion"[54] for determining whether products are "directly competitive or substitutable". The Panel stated the following:

> *In the Panel's view, the decisive criterion in order to determine whether two products are directly competitive or substitutable is whether they have common end-uses,* inter alia, *as shown by elasticity of substitution.*[55]

We agree. And, we find the Panel's legal analysis of whether the products are "directly competitive or substitutable products" in paragraphs 6.28–6.32 of the Panel Report to be correct.

[41] In accordance with Article 3.8 of the *DSU*, such a violation is *prima facie* presumed to nullify or impair benefits under Article XXIII of the GATT 1994. Article 3.8 reads as follows:

> In cases where there is an infringement of the obligations assumed under a covered agreement, the action is considered *prima facie* to constitute a case of nullification or impairment. This means that there is normally a presumption that a breach of the rules has an adverse impact on other Member parties to that covered agreement, and in such cases, it shall be up to the Member against whom the complaint has been brought to rebut the charge.

[42] See *Brazilian Internal Taxes,* BISD II/181, para 14; *Japan – Customs Duties, Taxes and Labelling Practices on Imported Wines and Alcoholic Beverages,* BISD 34S/83, para 5.5(d); *United States – Taxes on Petroleum and Certain Imported Substances,* BISD 34S/136, para 5.1.1; *United States – Measures Affecting the Importation, Internal Sale and Use of Tobacco,* DS44/R, adopted on 4 October 1994.
[43] *Japan – Customs Duties, Taxes and Labelling Practices on Imported Wines and Alcoholic Beverages,* BISD 34S/83, para 5.5(c).
[44] We note the argument on appeal that the Panel suggested in paragraph 6.20 of the Panel Report that the product coverage of Article III:2 is not identical to the coverage of Article III:4. That is not what the Panel said. The Panel said the following:

> *If* the coverage of Article III:2 is identical to that of Article III:4, a different interpretation of the term "like product" would be called for in the two paragraphs. Otherwise, if the term "like product" were to be interpreted in an identical way in both instances, the scope of the two paragraphs would be different (emphasis added).

This was merely a hypothetical statement.
[45] Report of the Working Party on *Border Tax Adjustments,* BISD 18S/97, para 18.
[46] *The Australian Subsidy on Ammonium Sulphate*, BISD II/188; *EEC – Measures on Animal Feed Proteins,* BISD 25S/49; *Spain – Tariff Treatment of Unroasted Coffee*, BISD 28S/102; *Japan – Customs Duties, Taxes and Labelling Practices on Imported Wines and Alcoholic Beverages*, BISD 34S/83; *United States – Taxes on Petroleum and Certain Imported Substances*, BISD 34S/136. Also see *United States – Standards for Reformulated and Conventional Gasoline,* WT/DS2/9, adopted on 20 May 1996.
[47] *EEC – Measures on Animal Feed Proteins,* BISD 25S/49; *Japan – Customs Duties, Taxes and Labelling Practices on Imported Wines and Alcoholic Beverages,* BISD 34S/83; *United States – Standards for Reformulated and Conventional Gasoline,* WT/DS2/9, adopted on 20 May 1996.
[48] *Japan – Customs Duties, Taxes and Labelling Practices on Imported Wines and Alcoholic Beverages,* BISD 34S/83, para 5.6.
[49] For example, Jamaica has bound tariffs on the majority of non-agricultural products at 50%. Trinidad and Tobago have bound tariffs on the majority of products falling within HS Chapters 25–97 at 50%. Peru has bound all non-agricultural products at 30%, and Costa Rica, El Salvador, Guatemala, Morocco, Paraguay, Uruguay and Venezuela have broad uniform bindings on non-agricultural products, with a few listed exceptions.
[50] We believe, therefore, that statements relating to any relationship between tariff bindings and "likeness" must be made cautiously. For example, the Panel stated in paragraph 6.21 of the Panel Report that ". . . with respect to two products subject to the same tariff binding and therefore to the same maximum border tax, there is no justification, outside of those mentioned in GATT rules, to tax them in a differentiated way through internal taxation". This is incorrect.
[52] The negotiating history of Article III:2 confirms that the second sentence and the Ad Article were added during the Havana Conference, along with other provisions and interpretative notes concerning Article 18 of the draft ITO Charter. When introducing these amendments to delegates, the relevant Sub-Committee reported that: "The new form of the Article makes clearer than did the Geneva text the intention that internal taxes on goods should not be used as a means of protection. The details have been relegated to interpretative notes so that it would be easier for Members to ascertain the precise scope of their obligations under the Article" E/CONF.2/C.3/59, p8. Article 18 of the draft ITO Charter subsequently became Article III of the GATT pursuant to the Protocol Modifying Part II and Article XXVI, which entered into force on 14 December 1948.
[53] Panel Report, para 6.22.
[54] United States Appellant's Submission, dated 23 August 1996, para 98, p63 (emphasis added).
[55] Panel Report, para 6.22.

United States – Standards for Reformulated and Conventional Gasoline ('US – Reformulated Gasoline'), 1996

Short summary and commentary

Brazil and Venezuela initiated this action to challenge regulations enacted by the US pursuant to its Clean Air Act (CAA). Those regulations applied different air pollution emissions standards to foreign oil refineries than to domestic oil refineries. Brazil and Venezuela argued that, because of those different standards, the oil produced by foreign refineries was treated less favourably than 'like products' from domestic oil refineries.

The panel in this case first described the methods it would use to decipher the phrase 'like products'. At the outset of its discussion, it looked to the ordinary meaning of the word 'like', which it determined to be 'similar' or 'identical'. Then, the panel looked to subsequent practice of the CONTRACTING PARTIES by examining the *Border Tax Adjustments* report and the 1987 decision in *Japan – Alcoholic Beverages*. The *Border Tax Adjustments* report emphasized that likeness determinations were to be made on a case-by-case basis, and could refer to criteria such as the products' end-uses, consumers' tastes and habits, and the products' properties, natures and qualities. *Japan – Alcoholic Beverages* (1987) similarly referenced the *Border Tax Adjustments* report, but also stated that a panel could look at the products' tariff classifications in making likeness determinations.

Because the panel found that domestic and imported gasoline had exactly the same physical characteristics, end-uses, tariff classifications and were perfectly substitutable, it concluded that domestic and imported gasoline were 'like products' (Panel report, paragraph 6.9). In making its 'likeness' determination, the panel also rejected the US' argument that the 'situation of the parties dealing in the gasoline' should be taken into consideration when evaluating whether a regulatory distinction could be drawn between the relevant products (*Id.*). The panel concluded that, when judging likeness, only the characteristics of the products need be taken into account; the characteristics of the producers or manufacturers were not relevant to a determination of the likeness of products.

With respect to its reference to *US – Malt Beverages*, the panel noted that that decision answered the question of whether *taxation* measures could use the characteristics of producers as the basis upon which to distinguish between products (*Id.* at paragraph 6.8). Nevertheless, it found no reason to limit the *US – Malt Beverages* holding to the Article III:2 context. According to the panel in *US – Reformulated Gasoline*, the idea that producer characteristics are not a valid basis upon which to discriminate between products was an idea just as applicable to Article III:4 as it was to Article III:2 (*Id.* at paragraph 6.11).

Excerpts

Report of the Panel, *United States – Standards for Reformulated and Conventional Gasoline*, WT/DS2/R, adopted on 20 May 1996, as modified by Appellate Body Report, *United States – Standards for Reformulated and Conventional Gasoline*, WT/DS2/AB/R.

VI. Findings [paras 6.1–6.43]

. . .

B. Article III [paras 6.5–6.17]

. . .

6.6 The Panel noted the arguments of Venezuela and Brazil that imported gasoline was "like" domestic gasoline, but received treatment less favourable because imported gasoline was subjected to more demanding quality requirements than gasoline of US origin. The United States replied that gasoline from similarly-situated parties was treated in the same manner under the Gasoline Rule. Gasoline from importers was treated no less favourably than that from other domestic non-refiners such as blenders, or refiners who had only limited or no operations in 1990.

6.7 The Panel observed that Article III:4 deals with treatment to be accorded to like products. However, the text does not specify exhaustively those aspects that determine whether the products are "like". In resolving this interpretative issue the Panel referred, in conformity with Article 3.2 of the Understanding on Rules and Procedures Governing the Settlement of Disputes, to the Vienna Convention on the Law of Treaties, which states in Article 31 that "a treaty shall be interpreted in good faith in accordance with the ordinary meaning to be given to the terms of the treaty in their context and in the light of its object and purpose".[25]

[25] *Vienna Convention on the Law of Treaties, Art. 31.*

6.8 The Panel proceeded to examine this issue in the light of the ordinary meaning of the term "like". It noted that the word can mean "similar", or "identical". The Panel then examined the practice of the CONTRACTING PARTIES under the General Agreement. This practice was relevant since Article 31 of the Vienna Convention directs that "subsequent practice in the application of the treaty which establishes the agreement of the parties regarding its interpretation" is also to be considered in the interpretation of a treaty. The Panel noted that various criteria for the determination of like products under Article III had previously been applied by panels. These were summarized in the 1970 Working Party Report on Border Tax Adjustments, which had observed:

> *With regard to the interpretation of the term 'like or similar products', which occurs some sixteen times throughout the General Agreement, it was recalled that considerable discussion had taken place . . . but that no further improvement of the term had been achieved. The Working Party concluded that problems arising from the interpretation of the terms should be examined on a case-by-case basis. This would allow a fair assessment in each case of the different elements that constitute a 'similar' product. Some criteria were suggested for determining, on a case-by-case basis, whether a product is 'similar': the product's end-uses in a given market; consumers' tastes and habits, which change from country to country; the product's properties, nature and quality.*[26]

These criteria had been applied by the panel in the 1987 Japan Alcohol case in the examination under Article III:2 of internal taxation measures. That panel had proceeded on a case-by-case basis, determining whether various alcoholic beverages were "like" on the basis of "their similar properties, end-uses and usually uniform classification in tariff nomenclatures".[27] The Panel considered that those criteria were also applicable to the examination of like products under Article III:4.

[26] L/3464, adopted on 2 December 1970, BISD 18S/97, 102, para 18.

[27] "Japan – Customs Duties, Taxes and Labelling Practices on Imported Wines and Alcoholic Beverages", BISD 34S/83, 115, para 5.6 (adopted on 10 November 1987).

6.9 In light of the foregoing, the Panel proceeded to examine whether imported and domestic gasoline were like products under Article III:4. The Panel observed first that the United States did not argue that imported gasoline and domestic gasoline were not like per se. It had argued rather that with respect to the treatment of the imported and domestic products, the situation of the parties dealing in the gasoline must be taken into consideration. The Panel, recalling its previous discussion of the factors to be taken into account in the determination of like product, noted that chemically-identical imported and domestic gasoline by definition have exactly the same physical characteristics, end-uses, tariff classification and are perfectly substitutable. The Panel found therefore that chemically-identical imported and domestic gasoline are like products under Article III:4.

. . .

6.11 The Panel then examined the US argument that the requirements of Article III:4 are met because imported gasoline is treated similarly to gasoline from similarly situated domestic parties – domestic refiners with limited 1990 operations and blenders. According to the United States, the difference in treatment between imported and domestic gasoline was justified because importers, like domestic refiners with limited 1990 operations and blenders, could not reliably establish their 1990 gasoline quality, lacked consistent sources and quality of gasoline, or had the flexibility to meet a statutory baseline since they were not constrained by refinery equipment and crude supplies. The Panel observed that the distinction in the Gasoline Rule between refiners on the one hand, and importers and blenders on the other, which affected the treatment of imported gasoline with respect to domestic gasoline, was related to certain differences in the characteristics of refiners, blenders and importers, and the nature of the data held by them. However, Article III:4 of the General Agreement deals with the treatment to be accorded to like products; its wording does not allow less favourable treatment dependent on the characteristics of the producer and the nature of the data held by it. The Panel noted that in the Malt Beverages case, a tax regulation according less favourable treatment to beer on the basis of the size of the producer was rejected.[29] Although this finding was made under Article III:2 concerning fiscal measures, the Panel considered that the same principle applied to regulations under Article III:4. Accordingly, the Panel rejected the US argument that the requirements of Article III:4 are met because imported gasoline is treated similarly to gasoline from similarly situated domestic parties.

[29] "*United States – Measures Affecting Alcoholic and Malt Beverages*", BISD 39S/206, para 5.19 (adopted on 19 June 1992).

6.12 Apart from being contrary to the ordinary meaning of the terms of Article III:4, any interpretation of Article III:4 in this manner would mean that the treatment of imported and domestic goods concerned could no longer be assured on the objective basis of their likeness as products. Rather, imported goods would be exposed to a highly subjective and variable treatment according to extraneous factors. This would thereby create great instability and uncertainty in the conditions of competition as between domestic and imported goods in a manner fundamentally inconsistent with the object and purpose of Article III.

6.13 The Panel considered that the foregoing was sufficient to dispose of the US argument. It noted, however, that even if the US approach were to be followed, under any approach based on "similarly situated parties" the comparison could just as readily focus on whether imported gasoline from an identifiable foreign refiner was treated more or less favourably than gasoline from an identifiable US refiner. There were, in the Panel's view, many key respects in which these refineries could be deemed to be the relevant similarly situated parties, and the Panel could find no inherently objective criteria by means of which to distinguish which of the many factors were relevant in making a determination that any particular parties were "similarly situated". Thus, although these refineries were similarly situated, the Gasoline Rule treated the products of these refineries differently by allowing only gasoline produced by the domestic entity to benefit from the advantages of an individual baseline. This consequential uncertainty and indeterminacy of the basis of treatment underlined, in the view of the Panel, the rationale of remaining within the terms of the clear language, object and purpose of Article III:4 as outlined above in paragraph 6.12.

Canada – Certain Measures Concerning Periodicals ('Canada – Periodicals'), 1997

Short summary and commentary

In this dispute, the US challenged three Canadian measures affecting the importation, excise taxation rates and postal fees of periodicals. The panel found that each of those measures were inconsistent with various provisions of the GATT. Canada appealed, arguing, in part, that the panel had erred in finding the disparate excise taxation rates violated Article III:2 of the GATT. Specifically, Canada claimed that the panel was incorrect in concluding that the products at issue, domestic non-split-run periodicals and imported split-run periodicals, were 'like products' under Article III:2 of the GATT.

In finding that the domestic and imported products were 'like products', the panel had relied on a single hypothetical example in which it compared two editions of the same magazine. The Appellate Body approved, in general, of the panel's decision to examine hypothetical 'like products' (AB report, section V.A). The Appellate Body did not approve, however, of how the panel actually constructed its hypothetical example. The panel had based its hypothetical example on a comparison of two editions of the same magazine, 'both imported products, which could not have been in the Canadian market at the same time' (*Id.*). The Appellate Body criticized the panel's reliance on this lone, incorrect hypothetical example (*Id.*).

The Appellate Body also criticized the panel for failing to examine factors relevant to a 'likeness' analysis including (i) the products' end-uses in a given market; (ii) the consumers' tastes and habits; and (iii) the products' properties, nature and quality in determining whether the products were 'like products' within the meaning of Article III:2 (*Id.*). According to the Appellate Body, the panel's approach was not nuanced nor detailed enough to enable it to properly make the narrow, case-by-case analysis required in likeness determinations (*Id.*).

Yet, after finding that the panel had erred in 'leaping' to its conclusion that the products were 'like products', the Appellate Body declined to complete the legal analysis and make a determination of whether, in fact, those products were 'like products'. It refrained from conducting this examination by stating that the inadequate analysis at the panel stage made it impossible for the Appellate Body to conduct the 'particularly delicate' 'like products' analysis (*Id.*). Nevertheless, the Appellate Body did proceed to complete the legal analysis under the second sentence of Article III:2, which requires a determination of whether the products are directly competitive or substitutable.

The Appellate Body found that domestic non-split-run and imported split-run periodicals were, in fact, 'directly competitive or substitutable' products (*Id.* at section VI.B.1). Key to the Appellate Body's finding on this issue was its analysis of how the products competed in the Canadian market. The Appellate Body also explained for products to be 'directly competitive or substitutable' they did not have to be *perfectly* substitutable (*Id.*). Perfectly substitutable products, according to the Appellate Body, were those covered by the first sentence of Article III:2, not the second sentence (*Id.*).

In addition to finding that Canada's measures affected 'directly competitive and substitutable products', the Appellate Body also found that the measures satisfied the other two criteria necessary for a finding of a violation of Article III:2, second sentence. Specifically, the Appellate Body determined that the measures were inconsistent with the GATT in that (i) they did not similarly tax the foreign and domestic products; and (ii) that they were applied so as to afford protection to domestic production (*Id.* at section VI.B.2).

Excerpts

Report of the Appellate Body, *Canada – Certain Measures Concerning Periodicals*, WT/DS31/AB/R, adopted on 30 July 1997.

[Note: this report does not utilize paragraph numbers.]

V. Article III:2, First Sentence, of the GATT 1994

. . .

A. Like Products

We agree with the legal findings and conclusions in paragraphs 5.22–5.24 of the Panel Report.[34] In particular, the Panel correctly enunciated, in theory, the legal test for determining "like products" in the context of Article III:2, first sentence, as established in the Appellate Body Report in Japan – Alcoholic *Beverages*. We also agree with the second point made by the Panel. As Article III:2, first sentence, normally requires a comparison between imported products and like domestic products, and as there were no imports of split-run editions of periodicals because of the import prohibition in Tariff Code 9958, which the Panel found (and Canada did not contest on appeal) to be inconsistent with the provisions of Article XI of the GATT 1994, hypothetical imports of split-run periodicals have to be considered.[35] As the Panel recognized, the proper test is that a determination of "like products" for the purposes of Article III:2, first sentence, must be construed narrowly, on a case-by-case basis, by examining relevant factors including:

(i) the product's end-uses in a given market;
(ii) consumers' tastes and habits; and
(iii) the product's properties, nature and quality.[36]

However, the Panel failed to analyze these criteria in relation to imported split-run periodicals and domestic non-split-run periodicals.[37] Firstly, we note that the Panel did not base its findings on the exhibits and evidence before it, in particular, the copies of *TIME*, *TIME Canada* and *Maclean's* magazines, presented by Canada, and the magazines, *Pulp & Paper* and *Pulp & Paper Canada*, presented by the United States,[38] or the Report of the Task Force on the Canadian Magazine Industry (the "Task Force Report").[39]

Secondly, we observe that the Panel based its findings that imported split-run periodicals and domestic non-split-run periodicals "can" be like products, on a single hypothetical example constructed using a Canadian-owned magazine, Harrowsmith Country Life. However, this example involves a comparison between two editions of the same magazine, both imported products, which could not have been in the Canadian market at the same time. Thus, the discussion at paragraph 5.25 of the Panel Report is inapposite, because the example is incorrect.[40]

The Panel leapt from its discussion of an incorrect hypothetical example[41] to

> *conclude that imported "split-run" periodicals and domestic non "split-run" periodicals* can *be like products within the meaning of Article III:2 of GATT 1994. In our view, this provides sufficient grounds to answer in the affirmative the question as to whether the two products at issue* are *like because, . . . the purpose of Article III is to protect expectations of the Members as to the competitive relationship between their products and those of other Members, not to protect actual trade volumes*[42] *(emphasis added).*

It is not obvious to us how the Panel came to the conclusion that it had "sufficient grounds" to find the two products at issue are like products from an examination of an incorrect example which led to a conclusion that imported split-run periodicals and domestic non-split-run periodicals can be "like".

We therefore conclude that, as a result of the lack of proper legal reasoning based on inadequate factual analysis in paragraphs 5.25 and 5.26 of the Panel Report, the Panel could not logically arrive at the conclusion that imported split-run periodicals and domestic non-split-run periodicals are like products.

We are mindful of the limitation of our mandate in Articles 17.6 and 17.13 of the DSU. According to Article 17.6, an appeal shall be limited to issues of law covered in the Panel Report and legal interpretations developed by the Panel. The determination of whether imported and domestic products are "like products" is a process by which legal rules have to be applied to facts. In any analysis of Article III:2, first sentence, this process is particularly delicate, since "likeness" must be construed narrowly and on a case-by-case basis. We note that, due to the absence of adequate analysis in the Panel Report in this respect, it is not possible to proceed to a determination of like products.

We feel constrained, therefore, to reverse the legal findings and conclusions of the Panel on "like products". As the Panel itself stated, there are two questions which need to be answered to determine whether there is a violation of Article III:2 of the GATT 1994: (a) whether imported and domestic products are like products; and (b) whether the imported products are taxed in excess of the domestic products. If the answers to both questions are affirmative, there is a violation of Article III:2, first sentence. If the answer to one question is negative, there is a need to examine further whether the measure is consistent with Article III:2, second sentence.[43]

Having reversed the Panel's findings on "like products", we cannot answer both questions in the first sentence of Article III:2 in the affirmative as is required to demonstrate a violation of that sentence. Therefore, we need to examine the consistency of the measure with the second sentence of Article III:2 of the GATT 1994.

[34] WT/DS8/AB/R, WT/DS10/AB/R, WT/DS11/AB/R, adopted 1 November 1996, pp19–20.
[35] Panel Report, para 5.23.
[36] Appellate Body Report, *Japan – Alcoholic Beverages,* WT/DS8/AB/R, WT/DS10/AB/R, WT/DS11/AB/R, adopted 1 November 1996, p20.
[37] Panel Report, para 5.26.
[38] *TIME* and *Pulp & Paper* are non-split-run United States' magazines which are imported into Canada. *TIME Canada* is a United States' split-run magazine produced in Canada. *Maclean's* and *Pulp & Paper Canada* are Canadian non-split-run magazines.
[39] 'A Question of Balance', *Report of the Task Force on the Canadian Magazine Industry,* Canada 1994, First Submission of the United States to the Panel, 5 September 1996, Exhibit A.
[40] Both the United States and Canada agreed that the example of *Harrowsmith Country Life* was incorrect: Canada's Appellant's Submission, 12 May 1997, pp17–18, paras 64–71; United States ' Appellee's Submission, 26 May 1997, p32, para 80; Canada's Statement at the oral hearing, 2 June 1997; United States' Statement at the oral hearing, 2 June 1997.
[41] Panel Report, para 5.25.
[42] Panel Report, para 5.26.
[43] See Panel Report, para 5.21, cited with approval at page 20 herein.

VI. Article III:2, Second Sentence, of the GATT 1994

. . .

1. Directly Competitive or Substitutable Products

In *Japan – Alcoholic Beverages*, the Appellate Body stated that as with "like products' under the first sentence of Article III:2, the determination of the appropriate range of 'directly competitive or substitutable products" under the second sentence must be made on a case-by-case basis.[47] The Appellate Body also found it appropriate to look at competition in the relevant markets as one among a number of means of identifying the broader category of products that might be described as "directly competitive or substitutable", as the GATT is a commercial agreement, and the WTO is concerned, after all, with markets.

According to the Panel Report, Canada considers that split-run periodicals are not "directly competitive or substitutable" for periodicals with editorial content developed for the Canadian market. Although they may be substitutable advertising vehicles, they are not competitive or substitutable information vehicles.[48] Substitution implies interchangeability. Once the content is accepted as relevant, it seems obvious that magazines created for different markets are not interchangeable. They serve different end-uses.[49] Canada draws attention to a study by the economist, Leigh Anderson, on which the Task Force Report was at least partially-based, which notes:

> *US magazines can probably provide a reasonable substitute for Canadian magazines in their capacity as an advertising medium, although some advertisers may be better served by a Canadian vehicle. In many instances however, they would provide a very poor substitute as an entertainment and communication medium.*[50]

Canada submits that the Task Force Report characterizes the relationship as one of "imperfect substitutability" – far from the direct substitutability required by this provision. The market share of imported and domestic magazines in Canada has remained remarkably constant over the last 30-plus years. If competitive forces had been in play to the degree necessary to meet the standard of "directly competitive" goods, one would have expected some variations. All this casts serious doubt on whether the competition or substitutability between imported split-run periodicals and domestic non-split-run periodicals is sufficiently "direct" to meet the standard of Ad Article III.[51]

According to the United States, the very existence of the tax is itself proof of competition between split-run periodicals and non-split-run periodicals in the Canadian market. As Canada itself has acknowledged, split-run periodicals compete with wholly domestically-produced periodicals for advertising revenue, which demonstrates that they compete for the same readers. The only reason firms place advertisements in magazines is to reach readers. A firm would consider split-run periodicals to be an acceptable advertising alternative to non-split-run periodicals only if that firm had reason to believe that the split-run periodicals themselves would be an acceptable alternative to non-split-run periodicals in the eyes of consumers. According to the United States, Canada acknowledges that "[r]eaders attract advertisers" and that, ". . . Canadian publishers are ready to compete with magazines published all over the world in order to keep their readers, but the competition is fierce".[52]

According to the United States, the Task Force Report together with statements made by the Minister of Canadian Heritage and Canadian officials, provide further acknowledgment of the substitutability of imported split-run periodicals and domestic non-split-run periodicals in the Canadian market.[53]

We find the United States' position convincing, while Canada's assertions do not seem to us to be compatible with its own description of the Canadian market for periodicals.

. . .

We, therefore, conclude that imported split-run periodicals and domestic non-split-run periodicals are directly competitive or substitutable products in so far as they are part of the same segment of the Canadian market for periodicals.

[47] WT/DS8/AB/R, WT/DS10/AB/R, WT/DS11/AB/R, adopted 1 November 1996, p25.
[48] Panel Report, para 3.113.
[49] Panel Report, para 3.115.
[50] Panel Report, para 3.119.
[51] Panel Report, para 3.119.
[52] Panel Report, para 3.117.
[53] Panel Report, para 3.118.

European Communities – Regime for the Importation, Sale and Distribution of Bananas ('EC – Bananas III'), 1997

Short summary and commentary

EC – Bananas III was a complex dispute that raised a number of legal questions, including questions relating to Article III:4 of the GATT. At issue in that case were several aspects of the European Communities' regime for the importation, sale and distribution of bananas, including the European Communities' practice with respect to hurricane licences (pursuant to which producers, producer organizations or operators would be compensated for their losses in the event of a hurricane). The Appellate Body agreed with the panel that EC practice to issue licences exclusively to EC producers and producer organizations, or to operators including or directly representing them, could create an incentive for operators to purchase bananas of EC origin for marketing in the European Communities. Thus, the Appellate Body concluded, in accordance with the panel, that the European Communities' hurricane licensing practice affected the competitive conditions in the market in favour of EC bananas, and thus was inconsistent with Article III:4 of the GATT 1994.

However, the Appellate Body, while coming to the same conclusion as the panel, criticized and rejected the panel's interpretative approach. The panel had proposed that an interpretation of Article III:4 incorporated the 'protective application' analysis the Appellate Body had called for in *Japan – Alcoholic Beverages (1996)* according to which the general policy of Article III:1 (that internal measures should not be applied 'so as to afford protection',) informed the other provisions of Article III:2 (Panel Report, paragraphs 7.181, 7.249). The panel found that, because the European Community's practice regime had been applied so as to afford protection, it was inconsistent with Article III:4. The Appellate Body rejected this interpretation of its reasoning in *Japan – Alcoholic Beverages (1996)*. It reminded the panel that, like the first sentence of Article III:2, the text of Article III:4 contains no explicit reference to the general principles of article III:1. As a result, the Appellate Body ruled that it would be inappropriate for a panel to make any further inquiry about 'protective application' when applying the 'like product' test of Article III:4 (AB report, paragraphs 215–216).

Thus, in *EC – Bananas III* the Appellate Body fairly clearly rejected the aims and effects test with respect to Article III:4 of the GATT. For more details on the aims and effects test, see the summary and excerpts relating to *Japan – Alcoholic Beverages (1996)*.

Excerpts

Report of the Appellate Body, *European Communities – Regime for the Importation, Sale and Distribution of Bananas*, WT/DS27/AB/R, adopted 25 September 1997.

8. Article III of the GATT 1994 [paras 208–216]

. . .

212. On the second issue, the Panel found that the EC practice with respect to hurricane licences may create an incentive for operators to purchase bananas of EC origin for marketing in the European Communities, and that this practice is an advantage accorded to bananas of EC-origin that is not accorded to bananas of third-country origin. The Panel concluded, therefore, that the issuance of hurricane licences

exclusively to EC producers and producer organizations, or operators including or directly representing them, is inconsistent with the requirements of Article III:4 of the GATT 1994.

213. Hurricane licences allow for additional imports of third-country (and non-traditional ACP) bananas at the lower in-quota tariff rate. Although their issuance results in increased exports from those countries, we note that hurricane licences are issued exclusively to EC producers and producer organizations, or to operators including or directly representing them. We also note that, as a result of the EC practice relating to hurricane licences, these producers, producer organizations or operators can expect, in the event of a hurricane, to be compensated for their losses in the form of "quota rents" generated by hurricane licences. Thus, the practice of issuing hurricane licences constitutes an incentive for operators to market EC bananas to the exclusion of third-country and non-traditional ACP bananas. This practice therefore affects the competitive conditions in the market in favour of EC bananas. We do not dispute the right of WTO Members to mitigate or remedy the consequences of natural disasters. However, Members should do so in a manner consistent with their obligations under the GATT 1994 and the other covered agreements.

214. For these reasons, we agree with the Panel that the EC practice of issuing hurricane licences is inconsistent with Article III:4 of the GATT 1994.

215. We note that, in coming to this conclusion, the Panel found:

> *However, before deciding whether the practice of issuing hurricane licences is inconsistent with Article III:4, we need to consider that Article III:1 is a general principle that informs the rest of Article III, as the Appellate Body has recently stated. Since Article III:1 constitutes part of the context of Article III:4, it must be taken into account in our interpretation of the latter. Article III:1 articulates a general principle that internal measures should not be applied so as to afford protection to domestic production. According to the Appellate Body, the protective application of a measure can most often be discerned from the design, the architecture, and the revealing structure of the measure. We consider that the design, architecture and structure of the EC practice of issuing hurricane licences all indicate that the measure is applied so as to afford protection to EC (and ACP) producers.*[120]

[120] See paragraph 7.249 of the Panel Reports (footnotes deleted). See also a similar finding in paragraph 7.181 relating to the operator category rules.

216.The Panel has misinterpreted what we said in the Appellate Body Report in *Japan – Alcoholic Beverages*.[121] We were dealing in that case with allegations of inconsistencies with Article III:2, first and second sentences, of the GATT 1994. It is true that at page 18 of that Report, we stated that "Article III:1 articulates a general principle" which "informs the rest of Article III". However, we also said in that Report that Article III:1 "informs the first sentence and the second sentence of Article III:2 in different ways".[122] With respect to Article III:2, first sentence, we noted that it does not refer specifically to Article III:1. We stated:

> *This omission must have some meaning. We believe the meaning is simply that the presence of a protective application need not be established separately from the specific requirements that are included in the first sentence in order to show that a tax measure is inconsistent with the general principle set out in the first sentence.*[123]

With respect to Article III:2, second sentence, we found:

> *Unlike that of Article III:2, first sentence, the language of Article III:2, second sentence, specifically invokes Article III:1. The significance of this distinction lies in the fact that whereas Article III:1 acts implicitly in addressing the two issues that must be considered in applying the first sentence, it acts explicitly as an entirely separate issue that must be addressed along with two other issues that are raised in applying the second sentence.*[124]

The same reasoning must be applied to the interpretation of Article III:4. Article III:4 does *not* specifically refer to Article III:1. Therefore, a determination of whether there has been a violation of Article III:4 does *not* require a separate consideration of whether a measure "afford[s] protection to domestic production".

121 WT/DS8/AB/R, WT/DS10/AB/R, WT/DS11/AB/R, adopted 1 November 1996.
122 *Ibid.*, p18.
123 *Ibid.*
124 *Ibid.*, p24.

Indonesia – Certain Measures Affecting the Automobile Industry ('Indonesia – Automobile'), 1998

Short summary and commentary

In *Indonesia – Automobile*, the European Communities, the US and Japan challenged certain Indonesian measures under Articles I and III of the GATT, and Article 6.3 of the Agreement on Subsidies and Countervailing Measures (SCM Agreement). Those measures formed parts of two different programmes. The first programme, the '1993 programme', essentially subjected imported cars and car parts to different tax and tariff rates depending upon the cars' and car parts' local content. Generally, the lower the percentage of local content, the higher the tax rate. The second programme, the 'National Car Programme, involved a series of measures aimed at developing and promoting a national car industry. In simplified terms, those measures granted tax benefits and duty exemptions to Indonesian car companies meeting certain requirements, and to cars manufactured overseas if the cars had a certain amount of local content and were produced by Indonesian nationals. The 'National Car Programme' also involved a series of loans granted to one company to carry out the national car project.

With respect to Article I, the European Communities, the US and Japan claimed that Indonesia's measures violated the GATT's most-favoured nation obligation because the measures provided tax and customs duty benefits to National Cars produced in Korea, but did not provide similar benefits to 'like' imports from the complaining parties. Furthermore, Japan and the European Communities claimed that Indonesia violated Article I by according customs duty benefits to certain parts and components used for the production of National Cars in Indonesia. The panel agreed with the complaining parties that Indonesia's measures violated Article I.

This case is particularly interesting in that it highlights how panels might use 'like products' jurisprudence and findings under one trade agreement or one provision to inform their 'likeness' analyses under different agreements or provisions. The *Indonesia – Automobile*'s panel first conducted a 'like products' assessment under Article 6.3 of the SCM Agreement. In assessing whether the products at issue were 'like products' within the meaning of the SCM Agreement, the panel relied heavily on 'likeness' jurisprudence from other disputes arising under the GATT. Afterwards, the panel used its 'like products' findings under the SCM Agreement as its basis for concluding that the products were also 'like' within the meaning of Article III of the GATT. And finally, the panel concluded that because it had found the products to be 'like' under Article III of the GATT, they were also 'like' under Article I of the GATT.

After finding that certain imported cars and car parts were 'like' National Cars imported from Korea, the panel then noted that the criteria Indonesia used to discriminate between the products at issue were not based on the products per se, but were instead based on origin-related criteria. The panel hinted that such origin-based systems of differentiation could, alone, violate Article I because they could lead, *in principle*, to less favourable treatment of the same products.

Excerpts

Report of the Panel, *Indonesia – Certain Measures Affecting the Automobile Industry*, WT/DS54/R, adopted on 23 July 1998.

F. Claims of MFN Discrimination [paras 14.123–14.148]

. . .

2. Criteria for an Article 1 of the GATT violation [paras 14.137–14.148]

. . .

(b) Are these advantages offered 'unconditionally' to all 'like products'? [paras 14.140–14.148]

(i) 'like products' [paras 14.140–14.142]

14.140 The European Communities, following the same logic it used for the like product definition in its Article III claims, submit that National Cars and their parts and components imported from Korea are to be considered "like" any motor vehicle and parts and components imported from other Members. The European Communities argue that imported parts and components and motor vehicles are all like the relevant domestic products since the definition of "National Cars" and their parts and components is not based on any factor which may affect per se the physical characteristics of those cars and parts and components, or their end uses. The United States argues that cars imported in Indonesia are like the Kia Sephia from Korea. Japan argues that parts and components and cars imported from Japan, or any other country, and those imported from Korea constitute "like products".

14.141 We have found in our discussion of like products under Article III:2 that certain imported motor vehicles are like the National Car.[714] The same considerations justify a finding that such imported vehicles can be considered like National Cars imported from Korea for the purpose of Article I. We also consider that parts and components imported from the complainants are like imports from Korea. Indonesia concedes that some parts and components are exactly the same for all cars. As to the parts and components which arguably are specific to the National Car, Indonesia does not contest that they can be produced by the complainants' companies. This fact confirms that the parts and components imported for use in the National Car are not unique. As before, we note in addition that the criteria for benefiting from reduced customs duties and taxes are not based on any factor which may affect per se the physical characteristics of those cars and parts and components, or their end uses. In this regard, we note that past panels interpreting Article I have found that a legislation itself may violate that provision if it could lead in principle to less favourable treatment of the same products.[715]

14.142 We find, therefore, that for the purpose of the MFN obligation of Article I of GATT, National Cars and the parts and components thereof imported into Indonesia from Korea are to be considered "like" other similar motor vehicles and parts and components imported from other Members.

[714] We refer to our discussions in paragraphs 14.110 and 14.111 where we found that given that the Timor, Escort, 306, Optima and Corolla models are in the same market segments, there would not appear to be any relevant differences in respect of consumers' tastes and habits sufficient to render these products unlike. In our view, this evidence is also sufficient to establish a presumption of likeness between the Timor, Corolla, Escort, 306 and Optima

for purposes of Article I of GATT. Since Indonesia has submitted no evidence or argument to rebut the presumption of likeness for purposes of Article I of GATT, we find that at least these imported motor vehicles are like the National Car for purposes of Article I of GATT.

715 See, for instance, the Panel Report on *United States – Denial of Most-favoured-nation Treatment as to Non-rubber Footwear from Brazil,* adopted on 19 June 1992, BISD 39S/128, para 6.12.

Chile – Taxes on Alcoholic Beverages ('Chile – Alcoholic Beverages'), 2000

Short summary and commentary

This case involved a challenge brought by the European Communities that Chile's tax regime on alcoholic beverages was inconsistent with Article III:2. The panel determined that Chile's tax regime violated Article III:2, second sentence. In making its finding, it looked at evidence suggesting the actual existence of competition between and substitutability of the products. It also looked at evidence indicating whether the products could 'reasonably be expected to become directly competitive or substitutable in the near future' (Panel report, paragraph 7.24). The factors the panel referred to in assessing whether the products were, or could reasonably be expected to be, 'directly competitive or substitutable' were the products' end-uses, physical characteristics, channels of distribution and points of sale, cross-price elasticities and other relevant characteristics (*Id.* at paragraph 7.30).

On appeal, Chile did not challenge the panel's finding that its domestic alcohol and imported alcoholic beverages were 'directly competitive or substitutable products'. It did, however, challenge the panel's findings that the products were 'not similarly taxed' and that the tax regime was applied 'so as to afford protection to domestic production'.

In its discussion of whether a measure is applied 'so as to afford protection to domestic production', the Appellate Body stated that 'a measure's *purposes,* objectively manifested in the design, architecture and structure of the measure, are intensely pertinent to the task of evaluating whether or not the measure is applied so as to afford protection to domestic production' (Appellate Body report, paragraph 71, emphasis added). Some have noted that it is difficult to reconcile these statements from *Chile – Alcoholic Beverages* with those from *Japan – Alcoholic Beverages (1996).* More specifically, commentators have argued that *Chile – Alcoholic Beverages* raises questions regarding the accuracy of the common understanding that *Japan – Alcoholic Beverages (1996)* rejected the 'aims and effects' test. Furthermore, it has also been argued that *Chile – Alcoholic Beverages* not only reinvigorated the 'aims and effects' test in the context of the second sentence of Article III:2, but that the decision might suggest a role for the 'aims and effects' test in analysis under both sentences of Article III:2, and under Article III:4. Whether such a reading of *Chile – Alcoholic Beverages* will prove to be accurate, however, remains to be seen.

Excerpts

Report of the Panel, *Chile – Taxes on Alcoholic Beverages*, WT/DS87/R, WT/DS110/R, adopted on 12 January 2000, as modified by the Appellate Body Report, WT/DS87/AB/R, WT/DS110/AB/R.

7.24 We agree that panels should look at evidence of trends and changes in consumption patterns and make an assessment as to whether such trends and patterns lead to the conclusion that the products in question are either directly competitive or substitutable now or can reasonably be expected to become directly competitive or substitutable in the near future.

. . .

7.30 The next step is to consider the various attributes of the products at issue to determine whether these attributes support a conclusion that there is a directly competitive or substitutable relationship between the imported and domestic products. In this regard, we will examine the end-uses of the products, their physical characteristics, the channels of distribution, price relationships (including cross-price elasticities), and other relevant characteristics.[367]

[367] These are the criteria we have examined in this case. There may be other criteria more or less relevant in other situations depending on the facts available.

Report of the Appellate Body, *Chile – Taxes on Alcoholic Beverages*, WT/DS/87/AB/R, adopted on 12 January 2000.

71. We recall once more that, in *Japan – Alcoholic Beverages*, we declined to adopt an approach to the issue of "so as to afford protection" that attempts to examine "the many reasons legislators and regulators often have for what they do".[66] We called for examination of the design, architecture and structure of a tax measure precisely to permit identification of a measure's objectives or purposes as revealed or objectified in the measure itself. Thus, we consider that a measure's purposes, objectively manifested in the design, architecture and structure of the measure, are intensely pertinent to the task of evaluating whether or not that measure is applied so as to afford protection to domestic production. In the present appeal, Chile's explanations concerning the structure of the New Chilean System – including, in particular, the truncated nature of the line of progression of tax rates, which effectively consists of two levels (27 per cent ad valorem and 47 per cent ad valorem) separated by only 4 degrees of alcohol content – might have been helpful in understanding what prima facie appear to be anomalies in the progression of tax rates. The conclusion of protective application reached by the Panel becomes very difficult to resist, in the absence of countervailing explanations by Chile. The mere statement of the four objectives pursued by Chile does not constitute effective rebuttal on the part of Chile.

[66] Appellate Body Report, WT/DS8/AB/R, WT/DS10/AB/R, WT/DS11/AB/R, adopted 1 November 1996, p27.

Argentina – Measures Affecting the Export of Bovine Hides and the Import of Finished Leather ('Argentina – Bovine Hides'), 2001

Short summary and commentary

The European Communities requested a panel in this case to examine, among other claims, whether certain tax measures and methods of tax collection in force in Argentina violated Article III:2 of the GATT. Two main tax measures were at issue. The first, the 'IVA', a general value added tax system, applied, *inter alia,* to the sale of goods within, and the definitive importation of goods into the Argentine territory. The IVA's rate of taxation did not differ depending upon whether the transaction involved foreign or domestic goods. However, the method of collecting the tax did differ. The tax was collected in advance on the importation of goods and on certain internal sales of goods. Importers had to pay the IVA due on the import transaction, and also had to pay an additional amount. Where the importer was a registered taxable person, the additional amount could be credited against its final IVA liability after the imported goods had been resold in Argentina. Yet, where the importer was a non-registered taxable person, the additional amount could not be credited to the final IVA liability.

The second challenged tax, the 'IG', was an income tax levied, *inter alia*, on profits derived from the sale of domestic and imported merchandise. The tax was collected in advance on most import transactions, and was withheld in advance on certain internal sales of goods. The amount collected in advance could be credited against the taxpayer's final IG liability.

The European Communities argued that these advance payment requirements for the IVA and the IG caused importers to bear a heavier financial cost than buyers of 'like' domestic goods. In examining the European Communities' claim, the panel first had to determine whether Article III:2 covered the tax collection measures. It concluded that Article III:2 did, in fact, cover the measures. Next, the panel discussed what elements were necessary to prove a violation of that provision. Argentina and the European Communities presented conflicting views as to what analysis under Article III:2 entailed.

Argentina argued that the first step in the analysis required the panel to define which products affected by the challenged measures were 'like'. That analysis, according to Argentina, had to be done on a case-by-case basis and with 'specific reference to the well-established criteria for defining likeness' (Panel report, paragraph 11.165). Only after conducting that 'likeness' assessment could the panel then examine whether the measures at issue taxed the imported products in excess of 'like' domestic products. The European Communties, however, advocated for a very different approach. It argued that in cases such as this one where the tax collection mechanisms explicitly differentiated between imported and domestic products, no specific 'like' products had to be identified.

The panel agreed with the European Communities' suggested approach. It found that due to the origin-based nature of Argentina's measures, it was not necessary to compare specific products, or to examine the criteria identified as being relevant for 'likeness' determinations. What mattered to the panel was not the 'likeness' of the products, but the design and structure of the challenged measures. The panel concluded that the measures were designed in such a way that they distinguished between products not based on the products' physical characteristics or end-uses, but, rather, based on 'factors not relevant to the definition of likeness'. Those factors identified as being 'not relevant' to 'likeness' were factors such as whether a product was definitively imported into Argentina, and factors based on the characteristics of the seller or purchaser of the product.

The panel's chosen approach suggests that where regulations facially discriminate between imported and domestic goods, 'likeness' determinations are not necessary. This type of approach contrasts with the two-step approach, used in such cases as *Japan – Alcoholic Beverages (1987)* and *(1996)*, where the tribunals first determine whether products at issue are 'like', and then determine whether the challenged measure taxes the imported product 'in excess' of the 'like' domestic product.

Thus, *Argentina – Bovine Hides* is significant in that it appears to represent a different branch of 'likeness' jurisprudence, a branch in which the 'like products' requirement is met in the absence of any case-by-case product analysis. Another important feature of this decision is perhaps more subtle, but might have important implications for the rate at which measures will be deemed inconsistent with Article III:2. Article III:2, it should be remembered, contains two products categories: 'like' products, and 'directly competitive or substitutable' products. Argentina had argued that if the origin-based nature of its measures were to lead to any automatic determination with respect to the first step of Article III analysis, it should be a determination the measures affected 'directly competitive or substitutable' products, rather than the 'like' products. The

Argentina – Bovine Hides panel, however, found that the origin-based nature of Argentina's measures automatically satisfied the 'like' products requirement of Article III:2, first sentence.

The panel's conclusion that the origin-based nature of the measures satisfied the 'like' products requirement, rather than the 'directly competitive or substitutable' requirement, can potentially have significant implications for the rate at which challenged measures are found to be inconsistent with Article III:2. This is because if products are found to be 'like', the panel then asks whether the measure taxes imports 'in excess of' domestic products. Taxation 'in excess of' has been interpreted by WTO tribunals as including even *de minimis* tax differentials. However, if products are deemed to fall into Article III:2's 'directly competitive or substitutable' product category, the next step in the analysis looks to whether the imported and domestic products are 'similarly taxed'. WTO tribunals have interpreted 'similarly taxed' to allow some degree of variation between the taxes imposed on imported and domestic products. Thus, while 'in excess of' has been interpreted as imposing a strict requirement of equal treatment, 'similarly taxed' has been interpreted as allowing Members some latitude to discriminate between imported and domestic products.

Ultimately, the panel found that by maintaining the measure at issue, Argentina was in violation of Article III:2, first sentence (*Id.* at paragraph 11.248).

Excerpt

Report of the Panel, *Argentina – Measures Affecting the Export of Bovine Hides and the Import of Finished Leather*, WT/DS155/R, adopted on 16 February 2001 (this decision was not appealed).

XI. Findings

. . .

C. Claims Under Article III:2, First Sentence, of the GATT 1994

. . .

4. Likeness of imported and domestic products [paras 11.162–11.173]

. . .

11.169 We consider that in the specific context of a claim under Article III:2, first sentence, the quantum and nature of the evidence required for a complaining party to discharge its burden of establishing a violation is dependent, above all, on the structure and design of the measure in issue.[462] The structure and design of RG 3431 and RG 3543 and their domestic counterparts RG 3337 and RG 2784 are such that the level of tax pre-payment is not determined by the physical characteristics or end-uses of the products subject to these resolutions, but instead is determined by factors which are not relevant to the definition of likeness, such as whether a particular product is definitively imported into Argentina or sold domestically as well as the characteristics of the seller or purchaser of the product.[463] It is therefore inevitable, in our view, that like products will be subject to RG 3431 and its domestic counterpart, RG 3337. The same holds true for RG 3543 and its domestic counterpart, RG 2784.[464] The European Communities has demonstrated this to our satisfaction, and, in our view, this is all it needs to establish in the present case as far as the "like product" requirement contained in Article III:2, first sentence, is concerned.[465]

[462] As the Appellate Body has stated in *United States – Shirts and Blouses, supra, at p14:*

> In the context of the GATT 1994 and the *WTO Agreement*, precisely how much and precisely what kind of evidence will be required to establish such a presumption will necessarily vary from measure to measure, provision to provision, and case to case.

[463] In our view, the mere fact that a product is of non-Argentinean origin or that it is being definitively imported into Argentina does not, *per se*, distinguish it – in terms of its physical characteristics and end-uses – from a product of Argentinean origin or a product which is being sold inside Argentina. Nor does likeness turn on whether the sellers or purchasers of the products under comparison qualify as registered or non-registered taxable persons or as *agentes de percepción* under Argentinean tax law.

[464] This view is unaffected by the fact that, according to the Appellate Body, the term "like products", as it appears in Article III:2, first sentence, is to be construed narrowly and on a case-by-case basis. See the Appellate Body Report on *Japan – Alcoholic Beverages II, supra,* at pp19–20.

[465] We consider that the European Communities can challenge RG 3431 even if no trade involving like imported products actually exists. As the Appellate Body has noted in its report on *Japan – Alcoholic Beverages II, supra*, p16 (footnote omitted): "[Article III] protects expectations not of any particular trade volume but rather of the equal competitive relationship between imported and domestic products". Thus, Article III provides protection not only to those EC producers who are actually contesting the Argentinean internal market, but also to those who are planning on contesting it or are preparing to do so. As to whether like products can exist, we confine ourselves to noting that, in our view, the European Communities, like other Members, is a potential producer and exporter of a wide range of products which are like Argentinean products, even considering the narrow definition of likeness appropriate in the context of Article III:2, first sentence.

11.170 This view is consistent with that adopted by the panel in *Indonesia – Automobile*. That panel was of the view that:

> *an origin-based distinction in respect of internal taxes suffices in itself to violate Article III:2, without the need to demonstrate the existence of actually traded like products.*[466]

[466] Panel Report on *Indonesia – Automobile, supra*, at para 14.113. See also the Panel Reports on *Korea – Measures Affecting Imports of Fresh, Chilled and Frozen Beef*, under appeal, WT/DS161/R, WT/DS169/R, at para 627 (with respect to Article III:4 of the GATT 1994) and *United States – Import Measures on Certain Products from the European Communities*, under appeal, WT/DS165/R, at para 6.54 (with respect to Article I:1 of the GATT 1994).

11.173 It follows from the preceding considerations that like products will be subject to the resolutions referred to by the European Communities, i.e. RG 3431 and RG 3337 (with respect to collection at source of the IVA), on the one hand, and RG 3543 and RG 2784 (with respect to collection at source of the IG), on the other hand. We therefore conclude that the "like products" requirement contained in Article III:2, first sentence, is fulfilled in the present case.

European Communities – Measures Affecting Asbestos and Products Containing Asbestos ('EC – Asbestos'), 2001

Short summary and commentary

In *EC – Asbestos*, Canada asked the panel to declare that a French ban on asbestos and asbestos-containing products violated Article III:4 of the GATT. To analyse the measures' consistency with Article III:4, the panel had to inquire whether or not the domestic and imported products affected by the ban were 'like products' within the meaning of that provision. The panel utilized the approach set forth in the *Border Tax Adjustments* report and examined four general criteria in conducting its 'likeness' analysis. Those criteria are: (i) the properties, nature and quality of the products; (ii) the end-uses of the products; (iii) consumers' tastes and habits; and (iv) the tariff classification of the products. In conducting its analysis, the panel declined to expand the *Border Tax* criteria by applying a 'risk criterion', which, in this case, would examine whether the health risks posed by a product could influence a 'likeness' determination. Ultimately, the panel concluded that the imported and domestic products were 'like products' and that the measures discriminated against them in violation of Article III:4 (but were justified under the Article XX(b) exceptions clause, which provides an exception for measures necessary to protect human, animal or plant life, or health).

The European Communities appealed, arguing that the panel had erred in finding that the imported asbestos and asbestos-containing products were 'like' certain other fibres and products containing those other non-asbestos fibres. The European Communities wanted the Appellate Body to look to the health risks of the respective products in conducting its 'likeness' analysis.

In looking at the 'likeness' issue, the Appellate Body first noted that *EC – Asbestos* was its first opportunity to examine the meaning of the word 'like' in the context of Article III:4 of the GATT. It then looked at several different means by which to assess the meaning of the phrase 'like products' under Article III:4. Namely, the Appellate Body noted it could glean guidance from the interpretation given to 'like products' in other GATT and WTO provisions, and the context of Article III:4. (Appellate Body report, paragraphs 88–89).

In discussing Article III:4, the Appellate Body paid particular attention to the fact that, while Article III:2 refers both to 'like' and 'directly competitive or substitutable' products, Article III:4 applies solely to 'like products'. Based on those textual differences, the Appellate Body concluded that the phrase 'like products' as it is used in Article III:2 means something different than that phrase in Article III:4. Referring to the analogy used in *Japan – Alcoholic Beverages (1996)*, the Appellate Body stated that the '"accordion" of "likeness" stretches in . . . different way[s]' depending on which provision is at issue (*Id.* at paragraph 96). Nevertheless, as with any 'like products' determination under Article III:2, that determination under Article III:4 should also be guided by the 'general principle' set forth in Article III:1. That principle aims to prevent Members from applying internal taxes and regulations in a manner 'so as to afford protection to domestic production'.

From that discussion of the context of Article III:4, the Appellate Body concluded that 'a determination of "likeness" under Article III:4, is, fundamentally, a determination about the nature and extent of a competitive relationship between and among products' (*Id.* at paragraph 99). Yet, it proceeded to state that it was 'mindful that there is a spectrum of degrees of "competitiveness" or "substitutability" of products in the market place, and that it is difficult, if not impossible, in the abstract, to indicate precisely where on this spectrum the word "like" in Article III:4 of the GATT 1994 falls' (*Id.*). To counteract the vagueness of that statement and provide some practical guidance to the 'likeness' issue, however, the Appellate Body ultimately stated that although it did not rule 'on the precise product scope of Article III:4, [it did] conclude that the product scope of Article III:4, although broader than the *first* sentence of Article III:2, is certainly not broader than the *combined* product scope of the *two* sentences of Article III:2 of the GATT 1994' (*Id.*).

Using the principles it had just enunciated in its discussion of Article III:4 'likeness', the Appellate Body then proceeded to evaluate whether the products at issue in the case were 'like products'. The Appellate Body found that the panel had erred in its 'like products' analysis by failing to examine and weigh *all* of the evidence under *each* of the four *Border Tax* criteria. It also specified that the *Border Tax* criteria are not the only factors a panel can examine, but that panels should also look at any other evidence relevant to assessing the 'likeness' of products. Furthermore, while the Appellate Body found that a separate 'risk' criterion was not necessary to the 'likeness' determination, it did conclude that the health risks should have been evaluated *within* the context of the four *Border Tax* criteria (*Id.* at paragraph 113). For example, in the opinion of the Appellate Body, the carcinogenicity of the asbestos fibres should have affected the panel's analysis of at least two of the *Border Tax* criteria – first, because the carcinogenic asbestos fibres had different physical properties than non-carcinogenic fibres, and second, because the carcinogenicity of the asbestos fibres likely would have had a significant impact on consumers' attitudes toward the products. Yet, while the Appellate Body subsumed the risk analysis into the broader *Border Tax* framework, one member wrote a separate concurrence to explain that he would have given the 'risk' factor determinative, independent weight in this case. He would have found the asbestos fibres to be unlike the other fibres based solely on the well-established severe carcinogenicity of asbestos fibres.

Another noteworthy aspect of the Appellate Body's report is that it stated that when physical differences exist between products, as they existed between asbestos and other fibres, 'a higher burden is placed on complaining Members to establish that, despite the pronounced physical difference, there is a competitive relationship between the products such that *all* of the evidence, taken together, demonstrates that the products are "like" under Article III:4 of the GATT 1994' (*Id.* at paragraph 118). In even stronger language, the Appellate Body made it clear that where the products are 'physically very different, a panel *cannot* conclude that they are "like products" if it does not examine evidence relating to consumers' tastes and habits' (*Id.* at paragraph 121).

Finally, after reexamining the affected products under each of the *Border Tax* criteria, taking into account the carcinogenicity of the asbestos fibres, the Appellate Body found that the evidence did not justify a conclusion that the products at issue were 'like products' within the meaning of Article III:4 of the GATT.

Because the Appellate Body found that the products at issue were not 'like products', it did not have to determine whether France's ban accorded the imported products treatment less favourable than that accorded to 'like' domestic products. Nevertheless, the Appellate Body chose to insert into its report a brief discussion on the meaning of 'less favourable' treatment. It noted that the interpretation of 'less favourable' treatment was important, particularly given the potentially broad scope of Article III:4 and that, according to the Appellate Body, 'less favourable' treatment expresses the general principle set forth in Article III:1 that measures should not be applied 'so as to afford protection to domestic production'. The Appellate Body further clarified that Article III:4's prohibition on 'less favourable' treatment does not necessarily prevent Members from distinguishing between 'like' products (*Id.* at paragraph 100).

The interpretation and application of the concepts of 'less favourable' by WTO tribunals can, of course, just as with the concept of 'likeness', directly affect the degree to which the GATT limits domestic regulatory and fiscal autonomy.

Excerpts

Report of the Appellate Body, *European Communities – Measures Affecting Asbestos and Products Containing Asbestos*, WT/DS135/AB/R, adopted on 5 April 2001.

It should be noted that these excerpts include the concurring statement of a Member of the Division hearing the appeal in paras 149–154.

VI. "Like Products" in article III:4 of the GATT 1994 [paras 84–154]

. . .

B. Meaning of the Term "Like Products" in Article III:4 of the GATT 1994 [paras 87–100]

88. The European Communities' appeal on this point turns on the interpretation of the word "like" in the term "like products" in Article III:4 of the GATT 1994.[57] Thus, this appeal provides us with our first occasion to examine the meaning of the word "like" in *Article III:4* of the GATT 1994. Yet, this appeal is, of course, not the first time that the term "like products" has been addressed in GATT or WTO dispute settlement proceedings. [footnote omitted] Indeed, the term "like product" appears in many different provisions of the covered agreements, for example, in Articles I:1, II:2, III:2, III:4, VI:1, IX:1, XI:2(c), XIII:1, XVI:4 and XIX:1 of the GATT 1994.[59] The term is also a key concept in the *Agreement on Subsidies and Countervailing Measures*, the *Agreement on Implementation of Article VI of the General Agreement on Tariffs and Trade 1994* (the "*Anti-Dumping Agreement*"), the *Agreement on Safeguards* and other covered agreements. In some cases, such as in Article 2.6 of the *Anti-Dumping Agreement*, the term is given a specific meaning to be used "[t]hroughout [the] Agreement", while in others, it is not. In each of the provisions where the term "like products" is used, the term must be interpreted in light of the context, and of the object and purpose, of the provision at issue, and of the object and purpose of the covered agreement in which the provision appears. Accordingly, and as we observed in an earlier case concerning Article III:2 of the GATT 1994:

> there can be no one precise and absolute definition of what is "like". *The concept of "likeness" is a relative one that evokes the image of an accordion. The accordion of "likeness" stretches and squeezes in different places as different provisions of the WTO Agreement are applied.* The width of the accordion in any one of those places must be determined by the particular provision in which the term "like" is encountered as well as by the context and the circumstances that prevail in any given case to which that provision may apply *(emphasis added)*.[60]

[57] We have already had occasion to interpret other aspects of Article III:4 of the GATT 1994 in two other appeals, but in neither appeal were we asked to address the meaning of the term "like products" (see Appellate Body Report, *European Communities – Regime for the Importation, Sale and Distribution of Bananas,* WT/DS27/AB/R, adopted 25 September 1997, and Appellate Body Report, *Korea – Beef, supra*, footnote 49).

[59] In addition, the term "like commodity" appears in Article VI:7 and the term "like merchandise" is used in Article VII:2 of the GATT 1994.

[60] Appellate Body Report, *Japan – Alcoholic Beverages, supra*, footnote 58, at 114. We also cautioned against the automatic transposition of the interpretation of "likeness" under the first sentence of Article III:2 to other provisions where the phrase "like products" is used (p113).

89. It follows that, while the meaning attributed to the term "like products" in other provisions of the GATT 1994, or in other covered agreements, may be relevant context in interpreting Article III:4 of the GATT 1994, the interpretation of "like products" in Article III:4 need not be identical, in all respects, to those other meanings.

. . .

99. As products that are in a competitive relationship in the market place could be affected through treatment of *imports* "less favourable" than the treatment accorded to *domestic* products, it follows that the word "like" in Article III:4 is to be interpreted to apply to products that are in such a competitive relationship. Thus, a determination of "likeness" under Article III:4 is, fundamentally, a determination about the nature and extent of a competitive relationship between and among products. In saying this, we are mindful that there is a spectrum of degrees of "competitiveness" or "substitutability" of products in the market place, and that it is difficult, if not impossible, in the abstract, to indicate precisely where on this spectrum the word "like" in Article III:4 of the GATT 1994 falls. We are not saying that *all* products which are in *some* competitive relationship are "like products" under Article III:4. In ruling on the measure at issue, we also do not attempt to define the precise scope of the word "like" in Article III:4. Nor do we wish to decide if the scope of "like products" in Article III:4 is co-extensive with the combined scope of "like" and "directly competitive or substitutable" products in Article III:2. However, we recognize that the relationship between these two provisions is important, because there is no sharp distinction between fiscal regulation, covered by Article III:2, and non-fiscal regulation, covered by Article III:4. Both forms of regulation can often be used to achieve the same ends. It would be incongruous if, due to a significant difference in the product scope of these two provisions, Members were prevented from using one form of regulation – for instance, fiscal – to protect domestic production of certain products, but were able to use another form of regulation – for instance, non-fiscal – to achieve those ends. This would frustrate a consistent application of the "general principle" in Article III:1. For these reasons, we conclude that the scope of "like" in Article III:4 is broader than the scope of "like" in Article III:2, first sentence. Nonetheless, we note, once more, that Article III:2 extends not only to "like products", but also to products which are "directly competitive or substitutable", and that Article III:4 extends only to "like products". In view of this different language, and although we need not rule, and do not rule, on the precise product scope of Article III:4, we do conclude that the product scope of Article III:4, although broader than the *first* sentence of Article III:2, is certainly *not* broader than the *combined* product scope of the *two* sentences of Article III:2 of the GATT 1994.

100. We recognize that, by interpreting the term "like products" in Article III:4 in this way, we give that provision a relatively broad product scope – although no broader than the product scope of Article III:2. In so doing, we observe that there is a second element that must be established before a measure can be held to be inconsistent with Article III:4. Thus, even if two products are "like", that does not mean that a measure is inconsistent with Article III:4. A complaining Member must still establish that the measure accords to the group of "like" *imported* products "less favourable treatment" than it accords to the group of "like" *domestic* products. The term "less favourable treatment" expresses the general principle, in Article III:1, that internal regulations "should not be applied . . . so as to afford protection to domestic production". If there is "less favourable treatment" of the group of "like" imported products, there is, conversely, "protection" of the group of "like" domestic products. However, a Member may draw distinctions between products which have been found to be "like", without, for this reason alone, according to the group of "like" *imported* products "less favourable treatment" than that accorded to the group of "like" *domestic* products. In this case, we do not examine further the interpretation of the term "treatment no less favourable" in Article III:4, as the Panel's findings on this issue have not been appealed or, indeed, argued before us.

C. Examining the "Likeness" of Products under Article III:4 of the GATT 1994 [paras 101–103]

101. We turn to consideration of how a treaty interpreter should proceed in determining whether products are "like" under Article III:4. As in Article III:2, in this determination, "[n]o one approach . . . will be appropriate for all cases."[71] Rather, an assessment utilizing "an unavoidable element of individual, discretionary judgement"[72] has to be made on a case-by-case basis. The Report of the Working Party on Border Tax Adjustments outlined an approach for analyzing "likeness" that has been followed and developed since by several panels and the Appellate Body.[73] This approach has, in the main, consisted of employing four general criteria in analyzing "likeness": (i) the properties, nature and quality of the products; (ii) the end-

uses of the products; (iii) consumers' tastes and habits – more comprehensively termed consumers' perceptions and behaviour – in respect of the products; and (iv) the tariff classification of the products.[74] We note that these four criteria comprise four categories of "characteristics" that the products involved might share: (i) the physical properties of the products; (ii) the extent to which the products are capable of serving the same or similar end-uses; (iii) the extent to which consumers perceive and treat the products as alternative means of performing particular functions in order to satisfy a particular want or demand; and (iv) the international classification of the products for tariff purposes.

[71] Appellate Body Report, *Japan – Alcoholic Beverages, supra*, footnote 58, at 114.

[72] Appellate Body Report, *Japan – Alcoholic Beverages, supra*, footnote 58, at 113.

[73] See, further, Appellate Body Report, *Japan – Alcoholic Beverages, supra*, footnote 58, at 113 and, in particular, footnote 46. See, also, Panel Report, *United States – Gasoline, supra*, footnote 15, para 6.8, where the approach set forth in the *Border Tax Adjustment* case was adopted in a dispute concerning Article III:4 of the GATT 1994 by a panel. This point was not appealed in that case.

[74] The fourth criterion, tariff classification, was not mentioned by the Working Party on *Border Tax Adjustments*, but was included by subsequent panels (see, for instance, *EEC – Animal Feed, supra*, footnote 58, para 4.2, and 1987 *Japan – Alcoholic Beverages, supra*, footnote 58, para 5.6).

102. These general criteria, or groupings of potentially shared characteristics, provide a framework for analyzing the "likeness" of particular products on a case-by-case basis. These criteria are, it is well to bear in mind, simply tools to assist in the task of sorting and examining the relevant evidence. They are neither a treaty-mandated nor a closed list of criteria that will determine the legal characterization of products. More important, the adoption of a particular framework to aid in the examination of evidence does not dissolve the duty or the need to examine, in each case, all of the pertinent evidence. In addition, although each criterion addresses, in principle, a different aspect of the products involved, which should be examined separately, the different criteria are interrelated. For instance, the physical properties of a product shape and limit of the end-uses to which the products can be devoted. Consumer perceptions may similarly influence – modify or even render obsolete – traditional uses of the products. Tariff classification clearly reflects the physical properties of a product.

103. The kind of evidence to be examined in assessing the "likeness" of products will, necessarily, depend upon the particular products and the legal provision at issue. When all the relevant evidence has been examined, panels must determine whether that evidence, as a whole, indicates that the products in question are "like" in terms of the legal provision at issue. We have noted that, under Article III:4 of the GATT 1994, the term "like products" is concerned with competitive relationships between and among products. Accordingly, whether the Border Tax Adjustments framework is adopted or not, it is important under Article III:4 to take account of evidence which indicates whether, and to what extent, the products involved are – or could be – in a competitive relationship in the market place.

D. The Panel's Findings and Conclusions on "Likeness" Under Article III:5 of the GATT 1994 [paras 104–132]

. . .

109. In our analysis of this issue on appeal, we begin with the Panel's findings on the "likeness" of chrysotile asbestos and PCG fibres and, in particular, with the Panel's overall approach to examining the "likeness" of these fibres. It is our view that, having adopted an approach based on the four criteria set forth in *Border Tax Adjustments*, the Panel should have examined the evidence relating to each of those four criteria and, then, weighed all of that evidence, along with any other relevant evidence, in making an overall determination of whether the products at issue could be characterized as "like". Yet, the Panel expressed a "conclusion" that the products were "like" after examining only the first of the four criteria.[87] The Panel then repeated that conclusion under the second criterion – without further analysis – before dismissing altogether the relevance of the third criterion and also before rejecting the differing tariff classifications under the fourth criterion. In our view, it was inappropriate for the Panel to express a "conclusion" after examining only one of the four criteria. By reaching a "conclusion" without examining all

of the criteria it had decided to examine, the Panel, in reality, expressed a conclusion after examining only some of the evidence. Yet, a determination on the "likeness" of products cannot be made on the basis of a partial analysis of the evidence, after examination of just one of the criteria the Panel said it would examine. For this reason, we doubt whether the Panel's overall approach has allowed the Panel to make a proper characterization of the "likeness" of the fibres at issue.

[87] Panel report, paragraph 8.126.

. . .

113. The European Communities argues that the inquiry into the physical properties of products must include a consideration of the risks posed by the product to human health. In examining the physical properties of the product at issue in this dispute, the Panel found that "it was not appropriate to apply the 'risk' criterion proposed by the EC".[94] The Panel said that to do so "would largely nullify the effect of Article XX(b)" of the GATT 1994.[95] In reviewing this finding by the Panel, we note that neither the text of Article III:4 nor the practice of panels and the Appellate Body suggest that any evidence should be excluded a priori from a panel's examination of "likeness". Moreover, as we have said, in examining the "likeness" of products, panels must evaluate all of the relevant evidence. We are very much of the view that evidence relating to the health risks associated with a product may be pertinent in an examination of "likeness" under Article III:4 of the GATT 1994. We do not, however, consider that the evidence relating to the health risks associated with chrysotile asbestos fibres need be examined under a separate criterion, because we believe that this evidence can be evaluated under the existing criteria of physical properties, and of consumers' tastes and habits, to which we will come below.

[94] Panel Report, para 8.132.
[95] *Ibid.*, para 8.130.

114. Panels must examine fully the physical properties of products. In particular, panels must examine those physical properties of products that are likely to influence the competitive relationship between products in the market place. In the case of chrysotile asbestos fibres, their molecular structure, chemical composition and fibrillation capacity are important because the microscopic particles and filaments of chrysotile asbestos fibres are carcinogenic in humans, following inhalation. In this respect, we observe that, at paragraph 8.188 of its Report, the Panel made the following statements regarding chrysotile asbestos fibres:

> *. . . we note that the carcinogenicity of chrysotile fibres has been acknowledged for some time by international bodies. This carcinogenicity was confirmed by the experts consulted by the Panel, with respect to both lung cancers and mesotheliomas, even though the experts appear to acknowledge that chrysotile is less likely to cause mesotheliomas than amphiboles. We also note that the experts confirmed that the types of cancer concerned had a mortality rate of close to 100 per cent. We therefore consider that we have sufficient evidence that there is in fact a serious carcinogenic risk associated with the inhalation of chrysotile fibres. Moreover, in the light of the comments made by one of the experts, the doubts expressed by Canada with respect to the direct effects of chrysotile on mesotheliomas and lung cancers are not sufficient to conclude that an official responsible for public health policy would find that there was not enough evidence of the existence of a public health risk.*

This carcinogenicity, or toxicity, constitutes, as we see it, a defining aspect of the physical properties of chrysotile asbestos fibres. The evidence indicates that PCG fibres, in contrast, do not share these properties, at least to the same extent.[96] We do not see how this highly significant physical difference cannot be a consideration in examining the physical properties of a product as part of a determination of "likeness" under Article III:4 of the GATT 1994.

[96] Panel Report, para 8.220.

115. We do not agree with the Panel that considering evidence relating to the health risks associated with a product, under Article III:4, nullifies the effect of Article XX(b) of the GATT 1994. Article XX(b) allows a Member to "adopt and enforce" a measure, inter alia, necessary to protect human life or health, even though that measure is inconsistent with another provision of the GATT 1994. Article III:4 and Article XX(b) are distinct and independent provisions of the GATT 1994 each to be interpreted on its own. The scope and meaning of Article III:4 should not be broadened or restricted beyond what is required by the normal customary international law rules of treaty interpretation, simply because Article XX(b) exists and may be available to justify measures inconsistent with Article III:4. The fact that an interpretation of Article III:4, under those rules, implies a less frequent recourse to Article XX(b) does not deprive the exception in Article XX(b) of effet utile. Article XX(b) would only be deprived of effet utile if that provision could not serve to allow a Member to "adopt and enforce" measures "necessary to protect human . . . life or health". Evaluating evidence relating to the health risks arising from the physical properties of a product does not prevent a measure which is inconsistent with Article III:4 from being justified under Article XX(b). We note, in this regard, that different inquiries occur under these two very different Articles. Under Article III:4, evidence relating to health risks may be relevant in assessing the competitive relationship in the market place between allegedly "like" products. The same, or similar, evidence serves a different purpose under Article XX(b), namely, that of assessing whether a Member has a sufficient basis for "adopting or enforcing" a WTO-inconsistent measure on the grounds of human health.

116. We, therefore, find that the Panel erred, in paragraph 8.132 of the Panel Report, in excluding the health risks associated with chrysotile asbestos fibres from its examination of the physical properties of that product.

117. Before examining the Panel's findings under the second and third criteria, we note that these two criteria involve certain of the key elements relating to the competitive relationship between products: first, the extent to which products are capable of performing the same, or similar, functions (end-uses), and, second, the extent to which consumers are willing to use the products to perform these functions (consumers' tastes and habits). Evidence of this type is of particular importance under Article III of the GATT 1994, precisely because that provision is concerned with competitive relationships in the market place. If there is – or could be – no competitive relationship between products, a Member cannot intervene, through internal taxation or regulation, to protect domestic production. Thus, evidence about the extent to which products can serve the same end-uses, and the extent to which consumers are – or would be – willing to choose one product instead of another to perform those end-uses, is highly relevant evidence in assessing the 'likeness' of those products under Article III:4 of the GATT 1994.

118. We consider this to be especially so in cases where the evidence relating to properties establishes that the products at issue are physically quite different. In such cases, in order to overcome this indication that products are not "like", a higher burden is placed on complaining Members to establish that, despite the pronounced physical differences, there is a competitive relationship between the products such that all of the evidence, taken together, demonstrates that the products are "like" under Article III:4 of the GATT 1994. In this case, where it is clear that the fibres have very different properties, in particular, because chrysotile is a known carcinogen, a very heavy burden is placed on Canada to show, under the second and third criteria, that the chrysotile asbestos and PCG fibres are in such a competitive relationship.

119. With this in mind, we turn to the Panel's evaluation of the second criterion, end-uses. The Panel's evaluation of this criterion is far from comprehensive. First, as we have said, the Panel entwined its analysis of "end-uses" with its analysis of "physical properties" and, in purporting to examine "end-uses" as a distinct criterion, essentially referred to its analysis of "properties".[97] This makes it difficult to assess precisely how the Panel evaluated the end-uses criterion. Second, the Panel's analysis of end-uses is based on a "small number of applications" for which the products are substitutable. Indeed, the Panel stated that "[i]t suffices that, for a *given utilization*, the properties are the same to the extent that one product can replace the other"[98] (emphasis added). Although we agree that it is certainly relevant that products have similar end-uses for a "small number of . . . applications", or even for a "given utilization",

we think that a panel must also examine the other, different end-uses for products.[99] It is only by forming a complete picture of the various end-uses of a product that a panel can assess the significance of the fact that products share a limited number of end-uses. In this case, the Panel did not provide such a complete picture of the various end-uses of the different fibres. The Panel did not explain, or elaborate in any way on, the "small number of . . . applications" for which the various fibres have similar end-uses. Nor did the Panel examine the end-uses for these products which were not similar. In these circumstances, we believe that the Panel did not adequately examine the evidence relating to end-uses.

[97] Panel Report, para 8.136.
[98] *Ibid.*, para 8.124.
[99] *Ibid.*, paras 8.124 and 8.125.

120. The Panel declined to examine or make any findings relating to the third criterion, consumers' tastes and habits, "[b]ecause this criterion would not provide clear results".[100] There will be few situations where the evidence on the "likeness" of products will lend itself to "clear results". In many cases, the evidence will give conflicting indications, possibly within each of the four criteria. For instance, there may be some evidence of similar physical properties and some evidence of differing physical properties. Or the physical properties may differ completely, yet there may be strong evidence of similar end-uses and a high degree of substitutability of the products from the perspective of the consumer. A panel cannot decline to inquire into relevant evidence simply because it suspects that evidence may not be "clear" or, for that matter, because the parties agree that certain evidence is not relevant.[101] In any event, we have difficulty seeing how the Panel could conclude that an examination of consumers' tastes and habits "would not provide clear results", given that the Panel did not examine any evidence relating to this criterion.

[100] *Ibid.*, para 8.139.
[101] In that respect, we note that, at the oral hearing before us, Canada stated that it believed that the parties were in agreement that consideration of consumers' tastes and habits "would add nothing" to the determination of "likeness".

121. Furthermore, in a case such as this, where the fibres are physically very different, a panel cannot conclude that they are "like products" if it does not examine evidence relating to consumers' tastes and habits. In such a situation, if there is no inquiry into this aspect of the nature and extent of the competitive relationship between the products, there is no basis for overcoming the inference, drawn from the different physical properties of the products, that the products are not "like".

122. In this case especially, we are also persuaded that evidence relating to consumers' tastes and habits would establish that the health risks associated with chrysotile asbestos fibres influence consumers' behaviour with respect to the different fibres at issue.[102] We observe that, as regards chrysotile asbestos and PCG fibres, the consumer of the fibres is a manufacturer who incorporates the fibres into another product, such as cement-based products or brake linings. We do not wish to speculate on what the evidence regarding these consumers would have indicated; rather, we wish to highlight that consumers' tastes and habits regarding fibres, even in the case of commercial parties, such as manufacturers, are very likely to be shaped by the health risks associated with a product which is known to be highly carcinogenic.[103] A manufacturer cannot, for instance, ignore the preferences of the ultimate consumer of its products. If the risks posed by a particular product are sufficiently great, the ultimate consumer may simply cease to buy that product. This would, undoubtedly, affect a manufacturer's decisions in the market place. Moreover, in the case of products posing risks to human health, we think it likely that manufacturers' decisions will be influenced by other factors, such as the potential civil liability that might flow from marketing products posing a health risk to the ultimate consumer, or the additional costs associated with safety procedures required to use such products in the manufacturing process.

[102] We have already noted the health risks associated with chrysotile asbestos fibres in our consideration of properties (*supra*, para 114).

[103] We recognize that consumers' reactions to products posing a risk to human health vary considerably depending on the product, and on the consumer. Some dangerous products, such as tobacco, are widely used, despite the known health risks. The influence known dangers have on consumers' tastes and habits is, therefore, unlikely to be uniform or entirely predictable.

123. Finally, we note that, although we consider consumers' tastes and habits significant in determining "likeness" in this dispute, at the oral hearing, Canada indicated that it considers this criterion to be irrelevant, in this dispute, because the existence of the measure has disturbed normal conditions of competition between the products. In our Report in *Korea – Alcoholic Beverages*, we observed that, "[p]articularly in a market where there are regulatory barriers to trade or to competition, there may well be latent demand" for a product.[104] We noted that, in such situations, "it may be highly relevant to examine latent demand" that is suppressed by regulatory barriers.[105] In addition, we said that "evidence from other markets may be pertinent to the examination of the market at issue, particularly when demand on that market has been influenced by regulatory barriers to trade or to competition."[106] We, therefore, do not accept Canada's contention that, in markets where normal conditions of competition have been disturbed by regulatory or fiscal barriers, consumers' tastes and habits cease to be relevant. In such situations, a Member may submit evidence of latent, or suppressed, consumer demand in that market, or it may submit evidence of substitutability from some relevant third market. In making this point, we do not wish to be taken to suggest that there is latent demand for chrysotile asbestos fibres. Our point is simply that the existence of the measure does not render consumers' tastes and habits irrelevant, as Canada contends.

[104] *Supra*, footnote 58, para 115.
[105] *Ibid*., para 120. We added that "studies of cross-price elasticity . . . involve an assessment of latent demand" (para 121).
[106] *Supra*, footnote 58, para 137.

124. We observe also that the Panel did not regard as decisive the different tariff classifications of the chrysotile asbestos, PVA, cellulose and glass fibres, each of which is classified under a different tariff heading.[107] In the absence of a full analysis, by the Panel, of the other three criteria addressed, we cannot determine what importance should be attached to the different tariff classifications of the fibres.

[107] Panel Report, para 8.143.

125. In sum, in our view, the Panel reached the conclusion that chrysotile asbestos and PCG fibres are "like products" under Article III:4 of the GATT 1994 on the following basis: the Panel disregarded the quite different "properties, nature and quality" of chrysotile asbestos and PCG fibres, as well as the different tariff classification of these fibres; it considered no evidence on consumers' tastes and habits; and it found that, for a "small number" of the many applications of these fibres, they are substitutable, but it did not consider the many other end-uses for the fibres that are different. Thus, the only evidence supporting the Panel's finding of "likeness" is the "small number" of shared end-uses of the fibres.

126. For the reasons we have given, we find this insufficient to justify the conclusion that the chrysotile asbestos and PCG fibres are "like products" and we, therefore, reverse the Panel's conclusion, in paragraph 8.144 of the Panel Report, "that chrysotile fibres, on the one hand, and PVA, cellulose and glass fibres, on the other, are 'like products' within the meaning of Article III:4 of the GATT 1994."

. . .

128. As the Panel said, the primary physical difference between cement-based products containing chrysotile asbestos fibres and cement-based products containing PCG fibres lies in the particular fibre incorporated into the product. This difference is important because, as we have said in our examination of fibres, we believe that the health risks associated with a product may be relevant to the inquiry into the physical properties of a product when making a determination of "likeness" under Article III:4 of the GATT 1994.[113] This is also true for cement-based products containing the different fibres. In examining the physical properties of the two sets of cement-based products, it cannot be ignored that one set of

products contains a fibre known to be highly carcinogenic, while the other does not.[114] In this respect, we recall that the Panel concluded that "there is an undeniable public health risk in relation to chrysotile contained in high-density chrysotile-cement products."[115] We, therefore, reverse the Panel's finding, in paragraph 8.149 of the Panel Report, that these health risks are not relevant in examining the "likeness" of the cement-based products.

[113] *Supra*, para 113.
[114] *Supra*, para 114.
[115] Panel Report, para 8.203.

. . .

130. In addition, even if the cement-based products were functionally interchangeable, we consider it likely that the presence of a known carcinogen in one of the products would have an influence on consumers' tastes and habits regarding that product. We believe this to be true irrespective of whether the consumer of the cement-based products is a commercial party, such as a construction company, or is an individual, for instance, a do-it-yourself ("DIY") enthusiast or someone who owns or lives or works in a building. This influence may well vary, but the possibility of such an influence should not be overlooked by a panel when considering the "likeness" of products containing chrysotile asbestos. In the absence of an examination of consumers' tastes and habits, we do not see how the Panel could reach a conclusion on the "likeness" of the cement-based products at issue.[117]

[117] See, further, *supra*, paras 117 and 118. See, also, *supra*, paras 121 and 122.

. . .

Completing the "Like Product" Analysis Under Article III:4 of the GATT 1994 [paras 133–154]

139. As we have already stated, Canada took the view, both before the Panel and before us, that consumers' tastes and habits have no relevance to the inquiry into the "likeness" of the fibres.[127] We have already addressed, and dismissed, the arguments advanced by Canada in support of this contention.[128] We have also stated that, in a case such as this one, where the physical properties of the fibres are very different, an examination of the evidence relating to consumers' tastes and habits is an indispensable – although not, on its own, sufficient – aspect of any determination that products are "like" under Article III:4 of the GATT 1994.[129] If there is no evidence on this aspect of the nature and extent of the competitive relationship between the fibres, there is no basis for overcoming the inference, drawn from the different physical properties, that the products are not "like". However, in keeping with its argument that this criterion is irrelevant, Canada presented no evidence on consumers' tastes and habits regarding chrysotile asbestos and PCG fibres.[130]

[127] *Supra*, paras 120 and 123.
[128] *Ibid.*
[129] Our reasons for reaching this conclusion are set forth, *supra*, in paras 117, 118, 121 and 122.
[130] Canada did present evidence that the impact of the Decree was to reduce demand for chrysotile (Panel Report, paras 3.20 and 3.422). However, as Canada recognized, this is a necessary consequence of the prohibition on chrysotile and is not evidence of consumers' attitudes and choices regarding the products at issue. As we have said, regulatory measures *may* suppress latent consumer demand for a product (*supra*, para 123).

140. Finally, we note that chrysotile asbestos fibres and the various PCG fibres all have different tariff classifications. While this element is not, on its own, decisive, it does tend to indicate that chrysotile and PCG fibres are not "like products" under Article III:4 of the GATT 1994.

141. Taken together, in our view, all of this evidence is certainly far from sufficient to satisfy Canada's burden of proving that chrysotile asbestos fibres are "like" PCG fibres under Article III:4 of the GATT 1994. Indeed, this evidence rather tends to suggest that these products are not "like products" for the purposes of Article III:4 of the GATT 1994.

2. Cement-based products containing chrysotile and PCG fibres

142. We turn next to consider whether cement-based products containing chrysotile asbestos fibres are "like" cement-based products containing PCG fibres under Article III:4 of the GATT 1994. We begin, once again, with physical properties. In terms of composition, the physical properties of the different cement-based products appear to be relatively similar. Yet, there is one principal and significant difference between these products: one set of cement-based products contains a known carcinogenic fibre, while the other does not. The Panel concluded that the presence of chrysotile asbestos fibres in cement-based products poses "an undeniable public health risk".[131]

[131] Panel Report, para 8.203.

143. The Panel stated that the fibres give the cement-based products their specific function – "mechanical strength, resistance to heat, compression, etc."[132] These functions are clearly based on the physical properties of the products. There is no evidence of record to indicate whether the presence of chrysotile asbestos fibres, rather than PCG fibres, in a particular cement-based product, affects these particular physical properties of the products. For instance, a tile incorporating chrysotile asbestos fibres may be more heat resistant than a tile incorporating a PCG fibre.

[132] *Ibid.*, para 8.145.

144. In addition, there is no evidence to indicate to what extent the incorporation of one type of fibre, instead of another, affects the suitability of a particular cement-based product for a specific end-use.[133] Once again, it may be that tiles containing chrysotile asbestos fibres perform some end-uses, such as resistance to heat, more efficiently than tiles containing a PCG fibre. Thus, while we accept that the two different types of cement-based products may perform largely similar end-uses, in the absence of evidence, we cannot determine whether each type of cement-based product can perform, with equal efficiency, all of the functions performed by the other type of cement-based product.

[133] *Supra*, para 129.

145. As with the fibres, Canada contends that evidence on consumers' tastes and habits concerning cement-based products is irrelevant. Accordingly, Canada submitted no such evidence to the Panel. We have dismissed Canada's arguments in support of this contention.[134] We have also indicated that it is of particular importance, under Article III of the GATT 1994, to examine evidence relating to competitive relationships in the market place.[135] We consider it likely that the presence of a known carcinogen in one of the products will have an influence on consumers' tastes and habits regarding that product.[136] It may be, for instance, that, although cement-based products containing chrysotile asbestos fibres are capable of performing the same functions as other cement-based products, consumers are, to a greater or lesser extent, not willing to use products containing chrysotile asbestos fibres because of the health risks associated with them. Yet, this is only speculation; the point is, there is no evidence. We are of the view that a determination on the "likeness" of the cement-based products cannot be made, under Article III:4, in the absence of an examination of evidence on consumers' tastes and habits. And, in this case, no such evidence has been submitted.

[134] *Supra*, paras 120 and 123.
[135] *Supra*, para 117.
[136] *Supra*, para 130.

146. As regards tariff classification, we observe that, for any given cement-based product, the tariff classification of the product is the same.[137] However, this indication of "likeness" cannot, on its own, be decisive.

[137] *Panel Report, para 8.148.*

147. Thus, we find that, in particular, in the absence of any evidence concerning consumers' tastes and habits, Canada has not satisfied its burden of proving that cement-based products containing chrysotile asbestos fibres are "like" cement-based products containing PCG fibres, under Article III:4 of the GATT 1994.

148. As Canada has not demonstrated either that chrysotile asbestos fibres are "like" PCG fibres, or that cement-based products containing chrysotile asbestos fibres are "like" cement-based products containing PCG fibres, we conclude that Canada has not succeeded in establishing that the measure at issue is inconsistent with Article III:4 of the GATT 1994.

. . .

149. One Member of the Division hearing this appeal wishes to make a concurring statement. At the outset, I would like to make it abundantly clear that I agree with the findings and conclusions reached, and the reasoning set out in support thereof, by the Division, in: Section V (*TBT Agreement*); Section VII (Article XX(b) of the GATT 1994 and Article 11 of the DSU); Section VIII (Article XXIII: 1(b) of the GATT 1994); and Section IX (Findings and Conclusions) of the Report. This concurring statement, in other words, relates only to Section VI ("Like Products" in Article III: 4 of the GATT 1994) of the Report.

152. In the present appeal, considering the nature and quantum of the scientific evidence showing that the physical properties and qualities of chrysotile asbestos fibres include or result in carcinogenicity, my submission is that there is ample basis for a definitive characterization, on completion of the legal analysis, of such fibres as not "like" PCG fibres. PCG fibres, it may be recalled, have not been shown by Canada to have the same lethal properties as chrysotile asbestos fibres. That definitive characterization, it is further submitted, may and should be made even in the absence of evidence concerning the other two *Border Tax Adjustments* criteria (categories of "potentially shared characteristics") of end-uses and consumers' tastes and habits. It is difficult for me to imagine what evidence relating to economic competitive relationships as reflected in end-uses and consumers' tastes and habits could outweigh and set at naught the undisputed deadly nature of chrysotile asbestos fibres, compared with PCG fibres, when inhaled by humans, and thereby compel a characterization of "likeness" of chrysotile asbestos and PCG fibres.

153. The suggestion I make is not that any kind or degree of health risk, associated with a particular product, would a priori negate a finding of the "likeness" of that product with another product, under Article III:4 of the GATT 1994. The suggestion is a very narrow one, limited only to the circumstances of this case, and confined to chrysotile asbestos fibres as compared with PCG fibres. To hold that these fibres are not "like" one another in view of the undisputed carcinogenic nature of chrysotile asbestos fibres appears to me to be but a small and modest step forward from mere reversal of the Panel's ruling that chrysotile asbestos and PCG fibres are "like", especially since our holding in completing the analysis is that Canada failed to satisfy a complainant's burden of proving that PCG fibres are "like" chrysotile asbestos fibres under Article III:4. That small step, however, the other Members of the Division feel unable to take because of their conception of the "fundamental", perhaps decisive, role of economic competitive relationships in the determination of the "likeness" of products under Article III:4.

154. My second point is that the necessity or appropriateness of adopting a "fundamentally" economic interpretation of the "likeness" of products under Article III:4 of the GATT 1994 does not appear to me to be free from substantial doubt. Moreover, in future concrete contexts, the line between a "fundamentally" and "exclusively" economic view of "like products" under Article III:4 may well prove very difficult, as a practical matter, to identify. It seems to me the better part of valour to reserve one's opinion on such an important, indeed, philosophical matter, which may have unforeseeable implications, and to leave that matter for another appeal and another day, or perhaps other appeals and other days. I so reserve my opinion on this matter.

CHAPTER 2

General Exceptions Clauses

BACKGROUND

The trade and environment debate centres in large part on the question of whether or not the World Trade Organization (WTO) framework provides sufficient policy space for governments to protect the environment and human health. Specifically, the debate focuses on whether or not the use of trade-related measures to protect the environment and human health are permissible under the WTO framework. Environmentalists first began to focus on the international trading regime in the early 1990s after a General Agreement on Tariffs and Trade (GATT) panel ruled that a US import ban on tuna caught in a manner harmful to dolphins was illegal under GATT rules. The *US – Tuna/Dolphin I* ruling was never adopted. A second *US – Tuna/Dolphin II* panel reaffirmed the earlier panel's approach and also found that the US import ban violated GATT rules (although based on different reasoning). Despite the fact that this panel report (like the earlier one) was not adopted, the reports raised much concern with respect to the unbalanced approach taken by the GATT panels. Specifically, the panels rejected the application of the general exceptions clause in Article XX of the GATT, which allows measures to protect human, animal or plant life or health and to conserve natural resources. The panel's conclusion was largely based on the view that measures adopted to protect the environment would threaten the multilateral framework on trade in goods. This approach came as a surprise to many who had thus far perceived Article XX of the GATT as providing the necessary balance between domestic regulatory autonomy in the environment field and the trade liberalization disciplines set forth by the GATT, including, *inter alia*, national treatment, most-favoured nation treatment and the prohibition on quantitative restrictions. One scholar described the situation as follows:

> *Before the Tuna/Dolphin rulings, the prevailing view was that Article XX of the GATT decided any conflicts between free-trade rules and environmental norms in favor of the latter. The Tuna/Dolphin panels tried to switch the preference in favor of the latter. Worse still, they approached the question solely from the perspective of effects on liberalized trade. Traditionally, the GATT demonstrated respect for regulatory diversity and progressive government. But after Tuna/Dolphin, environmentalists – and others with concerns about how the trading system balances competing values – saw the GATT as a regime dedicated to the triumph of free trade over all other human concerns. (Howse 2002, footnotes omitted.)*

The balance or imbalance between trade and environmental consideration has depended, and still depends, in large part on the interpretation of Article XX of the GATT. Environmentalists and many scholars generally welcomed the more recent Appellate Body jurisprudence on Article XX (particularly in *US – Shrimp/Turtle I* and *21.5*), which explicitly distanced itself from the unbalanced approach applied in the two *US –Tuna/Dolphin* reports.

However, since the inception of the new international legal framework under the WTO, the trade and environment debate has centred not only on the rules of the GATT but also of other elements of the WTO framework, particularly the Agreement on Sanitary and Phytosanitary Measures (SPS Agreement) and the Agreement on Technical Barriers to Trade (TBT Agreement). These, too, contain important disciplines for the application of domestic regulation, including regulations that protect the environment and public health. For example, the discussions around the legality of restricting trade in genetically modified organisms (GMOs) have involved primarily (but not only) the SPS Agreement. Moreover, there are interpretational linkages between the various WTO Agreements. The general exceptions clause under the General Agreement on Trade in Services (GATS), for example, has been interpreted largely based on the methodologies elaborated under Article XX of the GATT.

DISCUSSION OF RELEVANT WTO PROVISIONS

Article XX of the GATT (in general)

Article XX of the GATT is a pivotal provision that addresses the tensions that can arise between trade and other legitimate policy goals listed as exceptions in paragraphs (a) to (j). The two exceptions most relevant for trade-related environmental measures are contained in paragraphs (b) and (g) of Article XX, which cover measures that are:

(b) necessary to protect human, animal, or plant life or health;

or

(g) relating to the conservation of exhaustible natural resources if such measures are made effective in conjunction with restrictions on domestic production or consumption.

However, according to the introductory clause (chapeau) of Article XX, these measures are:

> *[s]ubject to the requirement that such measures are not applied in a manner which would constitute a means of arbitrary or unjustifiable discrimination between countries where the same conditions prevail, or a disguised restriction on international trade, ...*

While Article XX affirms the legal right of WTO Members to adopt measures that address environmental issues, some environmentalists are concerned about the fact that this right is contained in clauses that are 'exceptions' to other substantive obligations. Thus, the member invoking an Article XX exception is required to prove the various elements required under paragraphs (b) or (g) of Article XX. This can include, *inter alia*, the need to show that a measure is 'necessary', or that it aims at protecting 'exhaustible natural resources'. Additionally, the right of Members to protect their environment is qualified by Article XX's chapeau, which generally aims to prevent the abuse of the rights provided in Article XX. However, while the Appellate Body has affirmed that the Member raising Article XX as an affirmative defence bears the burden of proof, it also stressed that Article XX is a right proper, which will be interpreted neither expansively nor narrowly, but according to customary principles of treaty interpretation.

This chapter provides an overview of the trade–environment linkage focusing on Article XX of the GATT, including on the meaning of Article XX(g) concerning measures relating to the conservation of exhaustible natural resources, the meaning of Article XX(b) concerning measures necessary to protect human, animal and plant life or health, and the function of Article XX's chapeau. Other chapters cover more specific issues linked to Article XX of the GATT, such as the necessity requirement, extraterritoriality, and processes and production methods.

Article XX(g) of the GATT

The architectural design of Article XX, that is a chapeau and discrete exceptions, has significantly influenced the manner in which WTO tribunals have interpreted and applied Article XX. Only those measures that satisfy the terms of one of the subparagraphs of the general exception (e.g. 'necessary to protect human, animal or plant life or health'; or 'relating to the conservation of exhaustible natural resources . . .') are scrutinized for their consistency with the chapeau. Indeed, the Appellate Body has reasoned that the interpretation of the chapeau is hardly possible where the interpreter has not first examined the specific exception (*US – Shrimp/Turtle I* Appellate Body (AB) report, paragraph 120).

The meaning of 'measures'

In *US – Reformulated Gasoline*, the first case brought under the WTO's dispute settlement system, the Appellate Body took the view that the term 'measures' in Article XX, referred to conservation measures in their entirety and not only the provisions or elements of the overall measure found to violate the core GATT provisions (*US – Reformulated Gasoline* AB report, section III.A). This interpretation introduces greater deference to environmental considerations, broadening the potential scope of application of paragraph (g) of Article XX.

'Exhaustible natural resources'

The application of Article XX (g) is restricted to measures relating to the conservation of 'exhaustible natural resources'. This term has been scrutinized by both pre-WTO panels and by the Appellate Body in cases involving biological resources such as fish stocks or endangered turtles, and in cases involving non-living resources such as clean air. The Appellate Body has interpreted the term 'exhaustible natural resources' to include living, renewable and non-renewable resources.

With respect to the treatment of biological resources in the pre-WTO jurisprudence, the adopted 1982 Panel Report on the *US – Tuna and Tuna Products from Canada* noted that 'both parties considered tuna stocks, including albacore tuna, to be an exhaustible natural resource in need of conservation management (*US – Tuna and Tuna Products from Canada* AB report, paragraph 4.9). Similarly, the adopted *Canada – Unprocessed Herring and Salmon* 1988 Panel Report 'agreed with the parties that salmon and herring stocks are "exhaustible natural resources"' (*Canada – Unprocessed Herring and Salmon* panel report, paragraph 4.4). In both these cases, all parties to the disputes agreed on the nature of fish stocks as exhaustible natural resources.

The situation was markedly different in the *US – Tuna/Dolphin I* and *US – Tuna/Dolphin II* controversies, in which the parties were not in agreement as to the meaning of 'exhaustible natural resources'. In *US – Tuna/Dolphin I*, Mexico argued that the term could not be justifiably extended to include fisheries and fishery products, nor to include any other living being. Likewise, in *US – Tuna/Dolphin II*, the European Economic Community (EEC) disputed the fact that dolphins could be considered a natural resource, on the grounds that the Convention on the International Trade in Endangered Species of Wild Fauna and Flora (CITES) ensured that there was no trade in dolphin species and that one could thus question whether dolphins were resources in any economic sense (*US – Tuna/Dolphin II* panel report, paragraph 3.52). The panels in both cases disagreed with these arguments and concluded that dolphins qualified as natural resources (*US – Tuna/Dolphin II* panel report, paragraph 5.13).

In 1996, the panel in *US – Reformulated Gasoline* also had the opportunity to discuss the exhaustible resources issue. Venezuela disputed that clean air is an exhaustible natural resource, arguing that it is rather a 'condition' of air that is renewable. The panel, however, determined first that clean air is a resource, second that such a resource is natural, and third that such a resource could be depleted (*US – Reformulated Gasoline panel report*, paragraph 6.37). The panel's reference to potential depletion followed the US arguments that Article XX(g) does not require that the natural resource be exhausted or depleted, only that the resource be *capable* of exhaustion or depletion. On this basis, the Appellate Body concluded that US measures were covered by the natural resources exception.

In *US – Shrimp/Turtle I*, India, Pakistan and Thailand argued that the phrase 'exhaustible natural resources' referred to finite resources such as minerals, rather than biological or renewable resources. The joint appellees went on to argue that if *all* natural resources were considered to be exhaustible, the term exhaustible would become superfluous. The Appellate Body dealt with these arguments with the following statement:

> *One lesson that modern biological sciences teach us is that living species, though in principle, capable of reproduction and, in that sense, 'renewable', are in certain circumstances indeed susceptible of depletion, exhaustion and extinction, frequently because of human activities. Living resources are just as 'finite' as petroleum, iron ore and other non-living resources. (US – Shrimp/Turtle I AB report, paragraph 128)*

In arriving at this interpretation, the Appellate Body noted that the words included in Article XX(g), 'must be read by a treaty interpreter in the light of contemporary concerns of the community of nations about the protection and conservation of the environment' (*Id.* at paragraph 129). Pursuant to this reasoning, the Appellate Body resorted to international environmental agreements – such as CITES, the Convention on Biological Diversity (CBD), and the UN Convention on the Law of the Sea – and to the opinions of environmental experts for the factual determination of whether turtles were exhaustible (*Id.* at paragraphs 132–133). It thus concluded that these agreements provided sufficient evidence that endangered species are 'exhaustible' despite the reproductive capacities of individual members of the species (*Id.* at paragraph 134).

The meaning of 'relating to'

The Appellate Body has made a clear distinction between the term 'necessary', used in paragraph (b), and the term 'relating to', used in paragraph (g). In *US – Reformulated Gasoline*, it explained that the two phrases are not equivalent. It also rejected the approach taken in the pre-WTO 1988 panel report on *Canada's Restrictions on Exports of Unprocessed Herring and Salmon*, which held that a 'measure had to be "primarily aimed at" the conservation of an exhaustible natural resource' to be considered within the meaning of Article XX(g) (*Canada – Unprocessed Herring and Salmon* panel report, paragraph 4.6). In *US – Reformulated Gasoline*, the Appellate Body acknowledged that the 'primarily aimed at' test does not form part of the treaty text (*US – Reformulated Gasoline* AB report, section III.B).

However, given that all participants and third-participants to the appeal considered the *Canada – Unprocessed Herring and Salmon* 'primarily aimed at' standard to be applicable, the Appellate Body went on to evaluate the measures enacted by the US accordingly.

In *US – Shrimp/Turtle I*, the Appellate Body undertook a more thorough examination of the 'relating to' standard and finally departed from the 'primarily aimed at' interpretation. In so doing, the Appellate Body offered a new test, in which the 'relationship between the measure at stake and the legitimate policy of conserving exhaustible natural resources' plays a decisive role (*US Shrimp/Turtle I* AB report, paragraph 135). Although this test may also introduce some vagueness, it overcomes the trade-above-all interpretation of the 'primarily aimed at' standard.

'Restrictions on domestic production or consumption'

Article XX(g) of GATT explicitly subjects the legality of measures relating to the conservation of exhaustible natural resources to the condition that such measures be made effective in conjunction with restrictions on domestic production or consumption. According to the Appellate Body, this requirement is one of even-handedness and impartiality, which prevents importing countries from practising unacceptable double standards in their trade relations (*See*, e.g., *US – Reformulated Gasoline* AB report, section III.C and *US – Shrimp/Turtle I* AB report, paragraph 143).

In *US – Reformulated Gasoline*, the Appellate Body further explained that the requirement that the measure be 'made effective in conjunction with restrictions on domestic production of consumption' should not be interpreted to establish an empirical 'effects test' (*US – Reformulated Gasoline* AB report, section III.C). The Appellate Body gave two main reasons for its decision: that it is generally difficult to determine causation and that a substantial period of time may have to elapse before effects of the measure can be observed (*Id.*).

Article XX(b) of the GATT

The exception under Article XX(b) of the GATT allows a WTO Member to safeguard a country's ability to adopt measures 'necessary to protect human, plant, or animal life or health'. The linkages between public health and the environment can readily be seen in areas such as air and water quality, food safety, epidemic diseases, safety in the workplace, etc. Several disputes under the GATT have dealt with the exception in Article XX(b), including the pre-WTO *Thailand – Cigarettes* in 1990 and, more recently, *EC – Asbestos.*

In *EC – Asbestos,* the Appellate Body dismissed a Canadian complaint against a health-based French ban on asbestos in construction materials. For the first time, a tribunal upheld a health measure under Article XX(b). The Appellate Body's conclusion depended in large part on its interpretation of the term 'necessary'. In its reasoning on 'necessity' and least-trade-restrictiveness, the Appellate Body placed considerable emphasis on examining 'reasonably available alternatives', in light of existing scientific evidence, as the basis for its finding on the applicability of paragraph (b) of Article XX. The Appellate Body also accepted that a country could seek to halt the spread of a highly risky product while allowing the use of less risky products. Stated differently, a country may single out a product and adopt measures to address its health risks, without first exhaustively investigating the risks posed by substitutes. The necessity requirement is dealt with comprehensively in Chapter 3: The Necessity Requirement.

Function of Article XX's chapeau

Interpretation of the chapeau's requirements

The chapeau of Article XX prohibits a measure from being applied in a manner that would constitute a means of 'arbitrary or unjustifiable discrimination between countries where the same conditions prevail' or a 'disguised restriction on international trade'. These three standards in the chapeau – arbitrary discrimination, unjustifiable discrimination and disguised restrictions – are separate and additional to requirements contained under the exceptions listed in Article XX. In *US – Reformulated Gasoline,* the Appellate Body stressed that the chapeau deals only with the application of measures, not whether or not the measures themselves are justified under Article XX (*US – Reformulated Gasoline* AB report, section IV). In *US – Shrimp/Turtle I* the Appellate Body also dismissed panel's approach inspired by pre-WTO jurisprudence that excluded a priori certain measures from justification under the chapeau, such as conditioning market access on the adoption by exporting countries of certain conservation policies (*US – Shrimp/Turtle I,* AB Report, paragraphs 121–122). On this latter aspect, see also Chapter 5: Extraterritoriality.

In interpreting the chapeau's requirements, the Appellate Body explicitly referred to the notion of sustainable development in trade policy, as reflected in the text resulting from the Uruguay Round of negotiations and in Members' prior practice (*US – Shrimp/ Turtle I* AB report, paragraph 152). It noted that the examination of the opening paragraph in the WTO Agreement's preamble confirmed that WTO negotiators departed from the original GATT language and recognized that optimal use of the world's resources should be made in accordance with the objective of sustainable development (*Id.*). According to the Appellate Body, this preambular language 'must add colour, texture and shading to the rights and obligations of Members under the *WTO Agreement*, generally, and under the GATT 1994, in particular', including under the chapeau of Article XX of the GATT (*Id.* at paragraph 155). In addition, it pointed to the decision of Ministers to establish a permanent Committee on Trade and Environment, as a reflection of Members' concerns about the environment (*Id.* at paragraph 154).

Abuse of rights

Although the GATT 1994 does not contain an explicit reference to *abus de droit*, the WTO's jurisprudence is moving towards interpreting the chapeau of Article XX as a safeguard against abusive application of the exceptions included in Article XX. The Appellate Body specifically dealt with the meaning of the chapeau in two important cases: *US – Reformulated Gasoline* and *US – Shrimp/Turtle I.*

In *US – Reformulated Gasoline* the Appellate Body noted that the essential issue under consideration was whether the *application* of a measure inconsistent with the GATT constituted an abuse or misuse of the exceptions provided by Article XX (*US – Reformulated Gasoline* AB report, section IV). Such abuse or misuse occurs when the *application* of the measure constitutes a means of arbitrary or unjustifiable discrimination between countries where the same conditions prevail, or a disguised restriction on international trade (*Id.*). The Appellate Body found that members should apply the measures falling within the particular exceptions 'reasonably, with due regard both to the legal duties of the party claiming the exception and the legal rights of the other parties concerned' (*US – Reformulated Gasoline* AB report, section IV).

In *US – Shrimp/Turtle I,* the Appellate Body reaffirmed the *abus de droit* function of the chapeau and noted that 'the Chapeau is, in fact, but one expression of the principle of *bona fide*' (*US – Shrimp/Turtle I* AB report, paragraph 158). The Appellate Body also indicated that the chapeau recognizes the need to maintain a balance between the *right* of a Member to invoke an exception and the *obligation* of that Member to respect the rights of other Members (*Id.* at paragraph 159).

Thus, the Appellate Body has consistently held that the chapeau calls for an examination of the *application* of trade-related environmental measures. In this respect, Appellate Body jurisprudence has clarified that trade restrictions should be applied in an open and transparent way, with due publication and notification. It also specified that such restrictions should be tailored to address the conservation challenge, taking into account the different environmental conditions that surface in different countries and regions. In the context of global or transboundary environmental threats, Appellate Body jurisprudence has put an emphasis on countries' willingness to cooperate and engage in serious good faith negotiations before enacting trade-restrictive measures.

All of these aspects of the Article XX chapeau are described in more detail in the following paragraphs.

Unilateralism and cooperation

It is generally agreed that international cooperation is the best strategy to address global and transboundary threats. However, most also agree that legitimate unilateral trade policy measures for environmental purposes are necessary in certain circumstances. Until the Appellate Body issued its *US – Shrimp/Turtle I* ruling, the general approach of panels had been to interpret Article XX in a way which prohibited any use of unilateral measures.

In the *US – Shrimp/Turtle I* ruling, the Appellate Body strongly rejected the panel's approach of assuming that unilateral measures that condition market access on the policies of the exporting countries are, as a matter of general principle, not justifiable under Article XX (*US – Shrimp/Turtle I* AB report, paragraph 121).

This was an important step away from the idea that Article XX sets out a blanket prohibition on unilateral measures. However, at the same time, WTO jurisprudence does not allow for unilateral measures in all circumstances, but sets out parameters under which unilateral measures are permitted. In interpreting Article XX, the Appellate Body addressed the question of unilateralism mainly from the perspective of good faith efforts to cooperate. The Appellate Body has closely linked the question of cooperation to the specific inquiry on arbitrary or unjustifiable discrimination pursuant to the chapeau of Article XX. Several questions have arisen in the assessment of what constitutes good faith efforts to cooperate and what is actually involved in cooperation (e.g. capacity building, financial assistance and technology transfer). The key cases that illuminate this discussion are: *US – Reformulated Gasoline, US – Shrimp/Turtle I,* and *US – Shrimp/Turtle 21.5.*

In *US – Reformulated Gasoline,* the Appellate Body concluded that the US approach of allowing certain US refiners to use individual baselines while denying this possibility to Venezuelan and Brazilian refiners, constituted, in its application, unjustifiable discrimination and a disguised restriction on international trade (*US – Reformulated Gasoline* AB report, section IV). It based this conclusion on the fact that the US had not adequately explored the possibility of cooperating with the governments of Venezuela and Brazil to overcome the administrative difficulties of utilizing individual baselines for their refiners (*Id.*). According to the Appellate Body, such an omission resulted in 'discrimination [that] must have been foreseen, and was not merely inadvertent or unavoidable' (*Id.*).

The Appellate Body followed this line of reasoning in *US – Shrimp/Turtle I,* in which India, Malaysia, Pakistan and Thailand challenged a US measure that prohibited imports of shrimp from any country that did not have a turtle-conservation programme comparable to that of the US. The Appellate Body inquired as to whether or not the US had made an effort to cooperate with WTO Members to address the problem of shrimp trawlers causing harm to endangered sea turtles. It found that the US had provided technical assistance to some Members but not to others, and had granted longer phase-in periods to some Members than others (*US – Shrimp/Turtle I* AB report, paragraphs 169–174). Further, the Appellate Body took note of the fact that the US had failed to engage in serious, across-the-board negotiations for the protection and conservation of sea turtles and, instead had negotiated seriously with some, but not all, of the complainants (even though the law itself contained a requirement to negotiate with *all* relevant countries) (*Id.* at paragraph 172). This, the Appellate Body concluded, amounted to discrimination that was unjustifiable and thus did not meet the requirements under the chapeau of Article XX (*Id.* at paragraph 176).

In *US – Shrimp/Turtle 21.5*, the Appellate Body had the opportunity to further clarify important issues with respect to the extent of the US obligation to pursue international cooperation. One of the *Shrimp/Turtle I* complainants, Malaysia, had challenged the measures the US had taken to implement the *Shrimp/Turtle I* Appellate Body decision. The Appellate Body rejected this challenge, concluding that the US had brought its measures into compliance with Article XX (*US – Shrimp/Turtle 21.5* AB report, paragraph 153(b)). In its decision, the Appellate Body specified that the US was expected to make good faith efforts to reach international agreements that are comparable from one forum of negotiation to the other, and concluded that the US' active participation in and financial support of the negotiations constituted such good faith efforts (*Id.* at paragraphs 132–134). The Appellate Body stressed, however, that the chapeau did not require the successful conclusion of an environmental treaty (*Id.* at paragraph 123).

Flexibility in applying trade measures

The application of the chapeau standards, particularly the prohibition of unjustifiable discrimination, has involved an inquiry on whether or not trade measures are applied with sufficient flexibility to account for the particular conditions that may occur in other countries. Underlying this interpretation and inquiry lies a fundamental point of contention in the trade and environment debate. Countries claim a sovereign right to determine their own environmental policies, which translates in the determination of their own standards and levels of protection. At the same time, the developing world opposes the inflexible imposition of standards that may not be technically or financially feasible, or that respond to environmental conditions unrelated to their specific realities. In the backdrop of these heated policy debates, the Appellate Body has placed an emphasis on policy flexibility to achieve environmental objectives.

In *US – Shrimp/Turtle I*, the Appellate Body found that 'the most conspicuous flaw' in the US measure's application related to its intended and actual coercive effect on the specific policy decisions made by foreign governments (*US – Shrimp/Turtle I* AB report, paragraph 161). The Appellate Body noted that the US measures established a 'rigid and unbending' standard, which failed to take into account other specific policies and measures that an exporting country may have adopted for the protection and conservation of sea turtles (*Id.* at paragraph 163). The Appellate Body concluded that it is 'not acceptable' to '*require* other Members to adopt essentially the same comprehensive regulatory program' (*Id.* at paragraph 164).

Later, in *Shrimp/Turtle 21.5*, the Appellate Body agreed with the panel's finding that the application of the revised US measure allowed for sufficient flexibility so as to avoid arbitrary and unjustifiable discrimination (*US – Shrimp/Turtle 21.5* AB report, paragraph 144). The Appellate Body held that the chapeau authorizes 'an importing Member to condition market access on exporting Members putting in place regulatory programmes *comparable in effectiveness* to that of the importing Member . . .' and concluded that the revised US measure allowed for certification of exporting Members with regulatory programs 'comparable in effectiveness' to that of the US (*Id.*).

Concerning flexibility, a final point debated in *US – Shrimp/Turtle 21.5* was whether or not the importing country was under an obligation to account for the specific conditions in every individual exporting Member. The Appellate Body disagreed with Malaysia and observed that 'a measure should be designed in such a manner that there is sufficient flexibility to take into account the specific conditions prevailing in *any* exporting Member, including, of course, Malaysia' (*Id.* at paragraph 149). This conclusion introduces a measure of realism, as it is hardly feasible for any country to anticipate and provide explicitly for the changing conditions in other countries. It also underscores the need for flexibility to accommodate differing and evolving circumstances.

Transparency and due process

The related issues of transparency and due process mainly involve the chapeau standard that prohibits arbitrary discrimination. This standard played an important role in *US – Shrimp/Turtle I*, where the Appellate Body criticized the absence of a transparent and predictable certification process. In particular, the Appellate Body contested: the partisan nature of the inquiries and certifications, the absence of formal opportunity for the country under investigation to be heard or to respond to any arguments made against it, the absence of formal written reasoned decision and of notice of denial, and the absence of procedure for review of, or appeal from, a denial of an application (*US – Shrimp/Turtle I* AB report, paragraphs 180–183). The Appellate Body also noted that GATT 1994 Article X:3 establishes certain minimum standards for transparency and procedural fairness in the administration of trade regulations, which were not met (*Id.*). Upon these findings, the Appellate Body concluded that the US measure was applied in a manner that amounted to a means of not only 'unjustifiable discrimination', but also of 'arbitrary discrimination', contrary to the requirements of the chapeau of Article XX (*Id.* at paragraph 184).

Article XIV of the GATS

Similar to Article XX of the GATT, the GATS also has a general exceptions clause – Article XIV. Article XIV of the GATS lists five legitimate policy goals that Members may pursue. It thus enables Members to adopt measures that are otherwise inconsistent with their obligations under the GATS, including measures:

(a) necessary to protect public morals or to maintain public order;
(b) necessary to protect human, animal or plant life or health;
(c) necessary to secure compliance with laws or regulations which are not inconsistent with the provisions of this Agreement.

Like the introductory clause of Article XX of the GATT, the chapeau of Article XIV subjects the exceptions to the requirement that measures be applied in a manner that does not constitute an arbitrary or unjustifiable discrimination between countries where like conditions prevail, or a disguised restriction on trade in services. Thus, as under

Article XX of the GATT, WTO tribunals have determined that examining a measure under Article XIV requires a two-step process. First, the challenged measure is examined to determine whether or not it is both designed to and necessary to achieve one of the listed policy goals. Second, the measure is then examined to determine if its application results in arbitrary or unjustifiable discrimination or if it is a disguised restriction on trade in services. Only if the measure is deemed necessary *and* its application does not result in arbitrary or unjustifiable discrimination *and* it is not a disguised restriction on trade, can the measure be considered valid under Article XIV.

Notably, footnote 5 to Article XIV(a) states that '[t]he public order exception may be invoked only where a genuine and sufficiently serious threat is posed to one of the fundamental interests of society'. In addition, while Article XX(g) of the GATT provides an exception for measures 'relating to the conservation of exhaustible natural resources', Article XIV of the GATS contains no such exception.

The only dispute to consider whether or not a measure was valid under Article XIV to date is *US – Gambling*. At issue in that case were several US statutes, which were claimed by Antigua and Barbuda to violate the GATS, as they constituted a prohibition of the cross-border supply of remote gambling and betting services to the US. In order to justify the statutes, the US invoked the GATS' general exceptions clause, asserting that the statutes were necessary to protect public morals or to maintain public order, under Article XIV(a), and necessary to secure compliance with other WTO-consistent US laws – in this case, the Racketeer Influenced and Corrupt Organizations Act (RICO) – under Article XIV(c).

The Appellate Body upheld the panel's finding that the statutes were designed to protect public morals and/or maintain public order and to secure compliance with other WTO-consistent US laws. It also found that the statutes were in fact necessary, therefore reversing the panel's finding that they were not. Thus, the Appellate Body found the measures fell under the scope of Articles XIV(a) and XIV(c). However, the Appellate Body concluded that they did not satisfy the requirements of the chapeau and consequently were not justified by Article XIV.

Although *US – Gambling* did not involve environmental measures, it nevertheless indicates how WTO tribunals may approach general exceptions clauses (including environmental and health exceptions), in the context of the GATS.

SELECTED LITERATURE

Howse, R. (2002) 'The Appellate Body Rulings in the Shrimp/Turtle Case: A new legal baseline for the trade and environment debate', *Columbia Journal of Environmental Law*, vol 27, p491

Marceau, G. and Trachtman, J. P. (forthcoming) *A Map of the World Trade Organization Law of Domestic Regulation of Goods: The Technical Barriers to Trade Agreement, the Sanitary and Phytosanitary Measures Agreement, and the General Agreement on Tariffs and Trade*, Columbia Law School Series on WTO Law and Policy, vol 1: Trade and Health

SELECTED JURISPRUDENCE UNDER ARTICLES XX(B) AND (G) OF THE GATT AND ARTICLE XIV OF THE GATS

The following are excerpts of GATT and WTO cases that are relevant for a discussion of general exceptions clauses, specifically GATT Articles XX(b) and XX(g) and GATS Article XIV. The excerpts are preceded by a short summary and commentary of the corresponding case, aiming to put the excerpts into context. The cases are listed in chronological order. The case summaries focus primarily on issues regarding general exceptions clauses, and thus are not comprehensive for other purposes. A number of these cases are also relevant to the discussion of the necessity requirement and/or extraterritoriality. Those aspects of the cases are not addressed in detail here, but rather in Chapters 3 and 5, respectively.

United States – Prohibition of Imports of Tuna and Tuna Products from Canada ('US – Tuna and Tuna Products from Canada'), 1982

Short summary and commentary

In *US – Tuna and Tuna Products from Canada*, the panel examined an import prohibition on tuna and tuna products imposed by the US against Canada in response to Canada's seizure of US fishing vessels in waters regarded by Canada to be under its jurisdiction. While Canada argued that the import prohibition was discriminatory and inconsistent with US obligations under the GATT, the US responded that the prohibition, enacted pursuant to the Fishery Conservation and Management Act of 1976, was instead justified under Article XX(g) of the GATT, which provides an exemption from GATT obligations for measures 'relating to the conservation of exhaustible natural resources'.

In examining the dispute, the panel determined the US prohibition to be consistent with the chapeau of Article XX, finding it to be neither necessarily discriminatory nor a disguised restriction on international trade (Panel report, paragraph 4.8). The panel also noted that both parties agreed that tuna was an 'exhaustible natural resource' (*Id.* at paragraph 4.9). However, as the panel found no equivalent restrictions on *domestic* production and consumption of tuna, it ultimately found the measure failed the requirement of Article XX(g) that such measures be 'made effective in conjunction with restrictions on domestic production or consumption' (*Id.* at paragraphs 4.10–4.12). The panel thus declined to find the US measure a valid exemption under Article XX(g), and declared the prohibition inconsistent with Article XI of the GATT (*Id.* at paragraph 4.15).

Excerpts

Report of the Panel, *United States – Prohibition of Imports of Tuna and Tuna Products from Canada*, L/5198 – 29S/91, adopted on 22 February 1982.

III. Main Arguments

. . .

(b) Justification under Article XX(g) [paras 3.7–3.20]

3.7 The representative of the United States argued that the measures imposed by the United States restricting the import of tuna and tuna products from Canada were justified under Article XX(g) and met each element necessary to constitute an action authorized under the Article.

3.8 He explained that the first element in showing the measures were justified under Article XX(g) was that the subject was an exhaustible natural resource. In this respect, there was little question that tuna stocks were potentially subject to over-exploitation and exhaustion. According to a preliminary listing by the United States National Marine Fisheries Service albacore tuna was under intensive use, as was yellowfin tuna in the Atlantic. Yellowfin tuna in the Pacific was described as being in imminent danger and both Atlantic and Pacific stocks of bluefin tuna were described as being in imminent danger and perhaps depleted.

3.9 In his view, the action taken by the United States also fully met the other requirements of Article XX(g) as it was taken in conjunction with measures aimed at restricting domestic production or consumption of tuna, although not specifically that of albacore tuna; it related to conservation of tuna in that it was taken in order to avoid and deter threats to the international management approach which the United States considered essential to conservation of the world's tuna stocks; it did not apply in a manner that arbitrarily or unjustifiably discriminated between countries where the same conditions prevailed, as shown by restrictions maintained against Peru and Costa Rica. Recalling that measures under Article XX must not be used in such a way as to constitute a disguised restriction on international trade, he pointed out that the motivation for United States action was in no way trade related. The trade effect was at most nominal. Figures for United States production and consumption of tuna are given in Table 2.

. . .

3.12 He also explained to the Panel that the embargo on tuna and tuna products from Canada had been imposed under Section 205 of the Fishery Conservation and Management Act of 1976 and should be seen in relation to laws applicable to the conservation of tuna and efforts made by the United States to promote international cooperation to conserve tuna. Section 205 of the Fishery Conservation and Management Act of 1976 stated the Congress' findings that stocks of many species of tuna were depleted, or threatened with depletion, but that proper management of such species could ensure satisfactory yield. One purpose of the provisions of Section 205 of the Fishery Conservation and Management Act of 1976 was to encourage other countries to cooperate in international conservation of tuna. The provisions imposing an embargo on imports of fish from a country seizing United States fishing vessels were intended to dissuade other countries from claiming unilaterally 200-mile jurisdiction over tuna stocks and from seizing United States tuna vessels under such claims. The United States did not itself claim jurisdiction over tuna in its 200-mile zone.

3.13 The representative of *Canada* agreed that tuna was an exhaustible natural resource. Although his authorities did not doubt that the United States had a genuine interest in the conservation of tuna stocks he denied that the measures in question were truly triggered by the United States concerns about conservation, or related in some way to measures to promote or achieve improved conservation. He argued that the specific event which triggered the import prohibition, was not a general concern on the part of the United States about Canadian policies and actions related to the conservation of tuna, but the seizure of a number of fishing vessels and the arrest by Canadian authorities of United States fishermen engaged in fishing for albacore tuna, without authorization, inside Canada's zone of fisheries jurisdiction off the West Coast of Canada. The United States and one other country were standing alone in not recognizing coastal State jurisdiction over tuna. In this regard it was noteworthy that the United States Comptroller General, in his report to Congress of December 1976, referred to Section 205 of the Fishery Conservation and Management Act of 1976. He was clearly not referring to conservation when he stated that the Act included sanctions (Section 205) designed to deal with the anticipated negative effects of the

200-mile limit on the United States tuna fishery. Conservation was not, therefore, uppermost in the minds of the original drafters of the provisions that gave rise to the dispute. Rather, it may have been the existence of domestic legislation in Canada and other countries which could have the effect of restricting United States tuna vessels from operating in coastal waters under their jurisdiction. United States legislation was intended, in effect, to be a lever to dissuade Canada and other nations from enforcing their domestic laws to the detriment of commercial interests of the United States tuna industry.

. . .

IV. Findings and conclusions [paras 4.1–4.16]

. . .

4.7 The Panel noted that the representative of the United States based his arguments concerning the justification for the action taken against imports of tuna and tuna products from Canada entirely on Article XX(g).[1] The Panel therefore proceeded to an examination of the arguments presented in respect of this Article by both the representatives of the United States and Canada.

[1] "Subject to the requirement that such measures are not applied in a manner which would constitute a means of arbitrary or unjustifiable discrimination between countries where the same conditions prevail, or a disguised restriction on international trade, nothing in this Agreement shall be construed to prevent the adoption or enforcement by any contracting party of measures:

. . .

(g) relating to the conservation of exhaustible natural resources if such measures are made effective in conjunction with restrictions on domestic production or consumption" (BISD Volume IV, pages 37 and 38).

4.8 The Panel noted the preamble to Article XX. The United States action of 31 August 1979 had been taken exclusively against imports of tuna and tuna products from Canada,[2] but similar actions had been taken against imports from Costa Rica, Ecuador, Mexico and Peru and then for similar reasons. The Panel felt that the discrimination of Canada in this case might not necessarily have been arbitrary or unjustifiable. It furthermore felt that the United States action should not be considered to be a disguised restriction on international trade, noting that the United States prohibition of imports of tuna and tuna products from Canada had been taken as a trade measure and publicly announced as such. The Panel therefore considered it appropriate to examine further the United States import prohibition of tuna and tuna products from Canada in light of the list of specific types of measures contained in Article XX, and notably in Article XX(g).

[2] United States – Federal Register, Vol. 44, No. 178 (12 September 1979).

4.9 The Panel furthermore noted that both parties considered tuna stocks, including albacore tuna, to be an exhaustible natural resource in need of conservation management and that both parties were participating in international conventions aimed, *inter alia*, at a better conservation of such stocks. However, attention was drawn to the fact that Article XX(g) contained a qualification on measures relating to the conservation if they were to be justified under that Article, namely that such measures were made effective in conjunction with restrictions on domestic production or consumption.

4.10 The Panel noted that the action taken by the United States applied to imports from Canada of all tuna and tuna products, and that the United States could at various times apply restrictions to species of tuna covered by the IATTC and the ICCAT. However, restrictions on domestic production (catch) had so far been applied only to Pacific yellowfin tuna, from July to December 1979 under the Tuna Convention Act (related to the IATTC) and to Atlantic yellowfin tuna, bluefin tuna and bigeye tuna under the Atlantic Tunas Convention Act (related to the ICCAT), and no restrictions had been applied to the catch or landings of any other species of tuna, such as for instance albacore.

4.11 The Panel also noted that the United States representative had provided no evidence that domestic consumption of tuna and tuna products had been restricted in the United States.

4.12 The Panel could therefore not accept it to be justified that the United States prohibition of imports of all tuna and tuna products from Canada as applied from 31 August 1979 to 4 September 1980, had been made effective in conjunction with restrictions on United States domestic production or consumption on all tuna and tuna products.

4.13 The Panel also noted that the United States prohibition of imports of all tuna and tuna products from Canada had been imposed in response to Canadian arrest of United States vessels fishing albacore tuna. The Panel could not find that this particular action would in itself constitute a measure of a type listed in Article XX.

. . .

4.15 In the light of the foregoing, the Panel *concluded* that the United States embargo on imports of tuna and tuna products from Canada as applied from 31 August 1979 to 4 September 1980 was not consistent with the provisions of Article XI. It *did not find* that the United States representative had provided sufficient evidence that the import prohibition on all tuna and tuna products from Canada as applied from 31 August 1979 to 4 September 1980 complied with the requirements of Article XX and notably sub-paragraph (g) of that article.

Canada – Measures Affecting Exports of Unprocessed Herring and Salmon ('Canada – Unprocessed Herring and Salmon'), 1988

Short summary and commentary

The *Canada – Unprocessed Herring and Salmon* report examined the GATT-compliance of Canadian regulations prohibiting the exportation of certain unprocessed salmon and unprocessed herring to other countries under the Canadian Fisheries Act of 1970. The US brought a complaint against Canada alleging a violation of obligations under GATT Article XI; Canada argued in its defence that the export prohibitions were justified under Article XX(g) as part of a long-standing management programme aimed at conserving fishery resources.

As in *US – Tuna and Tuna Products from Canada*, the panel recognized salmon and herring stocks as 'exhaustible natural resources' and proceeded to the other requirements of XX(g): that the measures are 'relating to' the conservation of salmon and herring stocks, and that they are made effective 'in conjunction with' restrictions on domestic production and consumption of salmon and herring (Panel report, paragraph 4.4). However, as it had not been necessary to interpret the terms 'relating to' and 'in conjunction with' in *US – Tuna Products*, the *Canada – Herring* panel had to analyse the meaning of these terms. The panel decided that a trade measure must be '*primarily aimed at* the conservation of an exhaustible natural resource' in order for the measure to be considered as 'relating to' conservation, and '*primarily aimed at* rendering effective' the domestic restrictions with which it purports to conjoin, in order for the measure to be considered as 'in conjunction with' the restriction (*Id.* at paragraph 4.6, emphasis added). Finding that the prohibitions were not *primarily aimed at* conservation or rendering effective restrictions on harvesting of salmon and herring, the panel determined that the Canadian regulations were not justified under GATT Article XX(g) and were thus contrary to GATT Article XI (*Id.* at paragraph 4.7).

Excerpts

Report of the Panel, *Canada – Measures Affecting Exports of Unprocessed Herring and Salmon*, L/6268 – 35S/98, adopted on 22 March 1988.

4. FINDINGS

(a) The issue before the Panel

4.1 The Panel noted that the basic issue before it was the following: Canada prohibits the export of sockeye and pink salmon that is not canned, salted, smoked, dried, pickled or frozen (hereinafter referred to as "certain unprocessed salmon") and of food herring, roe herring, herring roe and herring spawn on kelp that is not canned, salted, dried, smoked, pickled or frozen (hereinafter referred to as "unprocessed herring"). The parties to the dispute and the Panel agree that such prohibitions are contrary to Article XI:1 of the General Agreement according to which contracting parties shall not institute or maintain prohibitions on the exportation of any product destined for the territory of any other contracting party. Canada invokes as justifications for the prohibitions two exceptions in the General Agreement: first, Article XI:2(b) permitting "export prohibitions . . . necessary to the application of standards or regulations for the classification, grading or marketing of commodities in international trade" and, second, Article XX(g) permitting any measure "relating to the conservation of exhaustible natural resources . . . made effective in conjunction with restrictions on domestic production or consumption". The United States denies that the export prohibitions are "necessary to the application of standards or regulations" within the meaning of Article XI:2(b) and that they are "related to the conservation of exhaustible natural resources" within the meaning of Article XX(g).

. . .

(c) Article XX(g) [paras 4.4–4.7]

4.4 The Panel then turned to the question of whether Article XX(g) justified the imposition of the export prohibitions on certain unprocessed salmon and unprocessed herring. The Panel noted that both parties agreed that Canada maintains a variety of measures for the conservation of salmon and herring stocks and imposes limitations on the harvesting of salmon and herring. The Panel agreed with the parties that salmon and herring stocks are "exhaustible natural resources" and the harvest limitations "restrictions on domestic production" within the meaning of Article XX(g). Having reached this conclusion the Panel examined whether the export prohibitions on certain unprocessed salmon and unprocessed herring are "relating to" the conservation of salmon and herring stocks and whether they are made effective "in conjunction with" the restrictions on the harvesting of salmon and herring.

4.5 Article XX(g) does not state how the trade measures are to be related to the conservation and how they have to be conjoined with the production restrictions. This raises the question of whether *any* relationship with conservation and *any* conjunction with production restrictions are sufficient for a trade measure to fall under Article XX(g) or whether a *particular* relationship and conjunction are required. The Panel noted that the only previous case in which the CONTRACTING PARTIES took a decision on Article XX(g) was the case examined by the Panel on "*United States – Prohibition of Imports of Tuna and Tuna Products from Canada*" but that that Panel had found that the party invoking Article XX(g) did not maintain restrictions on the production or consumption of tuna and thus had not been required to interpret the terms "relating to" and "in conjunction with".[2] The Panel therefore decided to analyze the meaning of these terms in the light of the context in which Article XX(g) appears in the General Agreement and in the light of the purpose of that provision.

[2] *BISD 29S/91.*

4.6 The Panel noted that some of the subparagraphs of Article XX state that the measure must be "necessary" or "essential" to the achievement of the policy purpose set out in the provision (cf. subparagraphs (a), (b), (d) and (j)) while subparagraph (g) refers only to measures "relating to" the conservation of exhaustible natural resources. This suggests that Article XX(g) does not only cover measures that are necessary or essential for the conservation of exhaustible natural resources but a wider range of measures. However, as the preamble of Article XX indicates, the purpose of including Article XX(g) in the

General Agreement was not to widen the scope for measures serving trade policy purposes but merely to ensure that the commitments under the General Agreement do not hinder the pursuit of policies aimed at the conservation of exhaustive natural resources. The Panel concluded for these reasons that, while a trade measure did not have to be necessary or essential to the conservation of an exhaustible natural resource, it had to be primarily aimed at the conservation of an exhaustible natural resource to be considered as "relating to" conservation within the meaning of Article XX(g). The Panel, similarly, considered that the terms "in conjunction with" in Article XX(g) had to be interpreted in a way that ensures that the scope of possible actions under that provision corresponds to the purpose for which it was included in the General Agreement. A trade measure could therefore in the view of the Panel only be considered to be made effective "in conjunction with" production restrictions if it was primarily aimed at rendering effective these restrictions.

4.7 Having reached these conclusions the Panel examined whether the export prohibitions on certain unprocessed salmon and unprocessed herring maintained by Canada were primarily aimed at the conservation of salmon and herring stocks and rendering effective the restrictions on the harvesting of salmon and herring. The Panel noted Canada's contention that the export prohibitions were not conservation measures *per se* but had an effect on conservation because they helped provide the statistical foundation for the harvesting restrictions and increase the benefits to the Canadian economy arising from the Salmonid Enhancement Program. The Panel carefully examined this contention and noted the following: Canada collects statistical data on many different species of fish, including certain salmon species, without imposing export prohibitions on them. Canada maintains statistics on all fish exports. If certain unprocessed salmon and unprocessed herring were exported, statistics on these exports would therefore be collected. The Salmonid Enhancement Program covers salmon species for which export prohibitions apply and other species not subject to export prohibitions. The export prohibitions do not limit access to salmon and herring supplies in general but only to certain salmon and herring supplies in unprocessed form. Canada limits purchases of these unprocessed fish only by foreign processors and consumers and not by domestic processors and consumers. In light of all these factors taken together, the Panel found that these prohibitions could not be deemed to be primarily aimed at the conservation of salmon and herring stocks and at rendering effective the restrictions on the harvesting of these fish. The Panel therefore concluded that the export prohibitions were not justified by Article XX(g).

Thailand – Restrictions on Importation of and Internal Taxes on Cigarettes ('Thailand – Cigarettes'), 1990

Short summary and commentary

Thailand – Cigarettes addressed the GATT-consistency of an import prohibition instituted by Thailand on tobacco and tobacco products, while Thailand simultaneously permitted the sale of domestic cigarettes. The US complained that the import measures were inconsistent with Article XI of the General Agreement, while Thailand argued for their justification under Article XX(b), as a measure 'necessary to protect human . . . life or health'. While the panel stated that the scope of Article XX(b) encompassed measures intended to reduce consumption of cigarettes, it found that the measures taken in this case did not meet the necessity requirement of Article XX(b). Choosing to follow a recent panel interpretation of the term 'necessary' in Article XX(d), the panel determined that in order for the necessity requirement of Article XX(b) to be met, there must be no alternative measure consistent with, or less *in*consistent with, Thailand's obligations under the GATT, which Thailand could reasonably have been expected to employ to achieve the same objectives (Panel report, paragraph 75). The panel found that there *were* alternative GATT-consistent measures reasonably available to Thailand that would ensure the quality and reduce the consumption of cigarettes in Thailand (*Id.* at paragraphs 77–78). Thus, it concluded that the import ban was not 'necessary' to protect human health within the context of Article XX(b).

For excerpts of *Thailand – Cigarettes*, see Chapter 3: The Necessity Requirement.

United States – Restrictions on Imports of Tuna ('US – Tuna/Dolphin I'), 1991 (NOT ADOPTED)

Short summary and commentary

In *US – Tuna/Dolphin I*, Mexico challenged the US' import ban on certain yellowfin tuna and yellowfin tuna products as inconsistent with Articles XI, and XIII, and III of the GATT. The US Marine Mammal Protection Act (MMPA) attempted to regulate the harvesting of yellowfin tuna in the Eastern Tropical Pacific Ocean (ETP), an area where a unique association between tuna and dolphins has been observed. Under the MMPA, the US rejected tuna and tuna products that were caught within the ETP by 'purse-seine' nets and other technologies that result in the excessive incidental killing of dolphin and other ocean mammals. The MMPA subjected fishermen operating within US jurisdiction to limitations on incidental 'taking' of dolphins and other marine mammals, and also placed a direct embargo on importation of tuna or tuna products caught with technology resulting in incidental taking of ocean mammals in excess of 1.25 times the US standard. The MMPA also banned the importation of tuna and tuna products from all 'intermediary nations' unless the intermediary nation had also banned imports of tuna and tuna products from countries subject to the direct embargo.

The US defended the MMPA provisions and pursuant embargoes as consistent with the GATT 1947, and, if not, as justified by Article XX(b) and/or (g). Eleven other countries made submissions to the panel as interested third parties, all generally agreeing with Mexico's complaint. After finding the US measures to be inconsistent with Article XI, the panel examined the measures to determine if they were justified under Article XX.

Looking first at the direct embargo, the panel considered the US claim that the measure was justified under Article XX(b) as 'necessary to protect human, animal or plant life or health'. The panel noted that the central issue of this inquiry was whether or not extrajurisdictional protection of life and health fell within the scope of Article XX(b), as was asserted by the US (Panel report, paragraph 5.25). The panel found several difficulties with this assertion, and ultimately reasoned that even if Article XX(b) was interpreted in such a way, the US measures would fail to meet the necessity requirement, as the panel did not believe the US had exhausted all reasonably available alternatives to achieve its objective of ocean mammal protection (*Id.* at paragraph 5.28). The panel indicated that international cooperative arrangements, or even a differently drafted import prohibition, were reasonably available alternatives that would have been consistent with, or less inconsistent with, GATT obligations; thus the current measures were not necessary within the meaning of Article XX(b) (*Id.*).

The panel then examined the US direct embargo in the context of Article XX(g) to determine whether it was 'relating to the conservation of exhaustible natural resources', was effected 'in conjunction with restrictions on domestic production or consumption', and did not 'constitute a means of arbitrary or unjustifiable discrimination ... or a disguised restriction on international trade'. In following the *Canada – Herring* interpretation of 'in conjunction with' to mean 'primarily aimed at rendering effective', the *US – Tuna/Dolphin I* panel found that it could not regard the unpredictable conditions of the import embargo as being 'primarily aimed at' protection of dolphins as a natural resource (*Id.* at paragraph 5.33). In addition, the panel faced the same question of extrajurisdictional applicability as within the context Article XX(b), and again it rejected this notion as potentially allowing the conservation policies of one country to unilaterally determine those of others (*Id.* at paragraph 5.32).

The panel thus rejected the US' assertions that the direct embargo was justified under either Article XX(b) or (g), and the same considerations led them to reject justification of the secondary embargo on imports from 'intermediary nations' (*Id.* at paragraphs 5.38, 6.3).

This panel report, however, was never adopted.

Excerpts

[Editor's note: Excerpts regarding Article XX(b) are reproduced in Chapter 3: The Necessity Requirement and Chapter 5: Extraterritoriality.]

Report of the Panel, *United States – Restrictions on Imports of Tuna ("Tuna/Dolphin I")*, DS21/R – 39S/155 (3 September 1991), NOT ADOPTED.

5. Findings [paras 5.1–5.44]

. . .

B. Prohibition of imports of certain yellowfin tuna and certain yellowfin tuna products from Mexico [paras 5.8–5.34]

. . .

Article XX [paras 5.22–5.34]

General [paras 5.22–5.23]

5.22 The Panel noted that the United States had argued that its direct embargo under the MMPA could be justified under Article XX(b) or Article XX(g), and that Mexico had argued that a contracting party could not simultaneously argue that a measure is compatible with the general rules of the General Agreement and invoke Article XX for that measure. The Panel recalled that previous panels had established that Article XX is a limited and conditional exception from obligations under other provisions of the General Agreement, and not a positive rule establishing obligations in itself.[39] Therefore, the practice of panels has been to interpret Article XX narrowly, to place the burden on the party invoking Article XX to justify its invocation,[40] and not to examine Article XX exceptions unless invoked.[41] Nevertheless, the Panel considered that a party to a dispute could argue in the alternative that Article XX might apply, without this argument constituting *Ipso facto* an admission that the measures in question would otherwise be inconsistent with the General Agreement. Indeed, the efficient operation of the dispute settlement process required that such arguments in the alternative be possible.

[39] Panel report on *"United States – Section 337 of the Tariff Act of 1930"*, adopted 7 November 1989, BISD 36S/345, 385, para 5.9.

[40] Panel reports on *"Canada – Administration of the Foreign Investment Review Act"*, adopted 7 February 1984, BISD 30S/140, 164, para 5.20; and *"United States – Section 337 of the Tariff Act of 1930"*, adopted 7 November 1989, BISD 36S/345, 393 para 5.27.
[41] *See*, e.g., the panel report on *"EEC – Regulation of Parts and Components"*, adopted 16 May 1990, BISD 37S/132, L/6657, para 5.11.

5.23 The Panel proceeded to examine whether Article XX(b) or Article XX(g) could justify the MMPA provisions on imports of certain yellowfin tuna and yellowfin tuna products, and the import ban imposed under these provisions. The Panel noted that Article XX provides that:

> *"Subject to the requirement that such measures are not applied in a manner which would constitute a means of arbitrary or unjustifiable discrimination between countries where the same conditions prevail, or a disguised restriction on international trade, nothing in this Agreement shall be construed to prevent the adoption or enforcement by any contracting party of measures . . .*
> *(b necessary to protect human, animal or plant life or health; . . .*
> *(g) relating to the conservation of exhaustible natural resources if such measures are made effective in conjunction with restrictions on domestic production or consumption; . . ."*

. . .

Article XX(g) [paras 5.30–5.34]

5.30 The Panel proceeded to examine whether the prohibition on imports of certain yellowfin tuna and certain yellowfin tuna products from Mexico and the MMPA provisions under which it was imposed could be justified under the exception in Article XX(g). The Panel noted that the United States, in invoking Article XX(g) with respect to its direct import prohibition under the MMPA, had argued that the measures taken under the MMPA are measures primarily aimed at the conservation of dolphin, and that the import restrictions on certain tuna and tuna products under the MMPA are "primarily aimed at rendering effective restrictions on domestic production or consumption" of dolphin. The Panel also noted that Mexico had argued that the United States measures were not justified under the exception in Article XX(g) because, inter alia, this provision could not be applied extrajurisdictionally.

5.31 The Panel noted that Article XX(g) required that the measures relating to the conservation of exhaustible natural resources be taken "in conjunction with restrictions on domestic production or consumption". A previous panel had found that a measure could only be considered to have been taken "in conjunction with" production restrictions "if it was primarily aimed at rendering effective these restrictions".[44] A country can effectively control the production or consumption of an exhaustible natural resource only to the extent that the production or consumption is under its jurisdiction. This suggests that Article XX(g) was intended to permit contracting parties to take trade measures primarily aimed at rendering effective restrictions on production or consumption within their jurisdiction.

[44] Panel report on *"Canada – Measures Affecting Exports of Unprocessed Herring and Salmon"*, adopted 22 March 1988, BISD 35S/98, 114, para 4.6.

5.32 The Panel further noted that Article XX(g) allows each contracting party to adopt its own conservation policies. The conditions set out in Article XX(g) which limit resort to this exception, namely that the measures taken must be related to the conservation of exhaustible natural resources, and that they not "constitute a means of arbitrary or unjustifiable discrimination . . . or a disguised restriction on international trade" refer to the trade measure requiring justification under Article XX(g), not however to the conservation policies adopted by the contracting party. The Panel considered that if the extrajurisdictional interpretation of Article XX(g) suggested by the United States were accepted, each contracting party could unilaterally determine the conservation policies from which other contracting parties could not deviate without jeopardizing their rights under the General Agreement. The considerations that led the Panel to reject an extrajurisdictional application of Article XX(b) therefore apply also to Article XX(g).

5.33 The Panel did not consider that the United States measures, even if Article XX(g) could be applied extrajurisdictionally, would meet the conditions set out in that provision. A previous panel found that a measure could be considered as "relating to the conservation of exhaustible natural resources" within the meaning of Article XX(g) only if it was primarily aimed at such conservation.[45] The Panel recalled that the United States linked the maximum incidental dolphin-taking rate which Mexico had to meet during a particular period in order to be able to export tuna to the United States to the taking rate actually recorded for United States fishermen during the same period. Consequently, the Mexican authorities could not know whether, at a given point of time, their conservation policies conformed to the United States conservation standards. The Panel considered that a limitation on trade based on such unpredictable conditions could not be regarded as being primarily aimed at the conservation of dolphins.

[45] Panel report on *"Canada – Measures Affecting Exports of Unprocessed Herring and Salmon"*, adopted 22 March 1988, BISD 35S/98, 114, para 4.6.

5.34 On the basis of the above considerations, the Panel found that the United States direct import prohibition on certain yellowfin tuna and certain yellowfin tuna products of Mexico directly imported from Mexico, and the provisions of the MMPA under which it is imposed, could not be justified under Article XX(g).

C. Secondary embargo on imports of certain yellowfin tuna and certain yellowfin tuna products from 'intermediary nations' under the MMPA [paras 5.35–5.40]

. . .

Article XX(b) and XX(g) [para 5.38]

5.38 The Panel noted that the United States had argued that the intermediary nations embargo was justified as a measure under Articles XX(b) and XX(g) to protect and conserve dolphin, and that the intermediary country measures were necessary to protect animal life or health and related to the conservation of exhaustible natural resources. The Panel recalled its findings with regard to the consistency of the direct embargo with Articles XX(b) and XX(g) in paragraphs 5.29 and 5.34 above, and found that the considerations that led the Panel to reject the United States invocation of these provisions in that instance applied to the "intermediary nations" embargo as well.

6. Concluding remarks [paras 6.1–6.4]

. . .

6.3 The Panel further recalled its finding that the import restrictions examined in this dispute, imposed to respond to differences in environmental regulation of producers, could not be justified under the exceptions in Articles XX(b) or XX(g). These exceptions did not specify criteria limiting the range of life or health protection policies, or resource conservation policies, for the sake of which they could be invoked. It seemed evident to the Panel that, if the CONTRACTING PARTIES were to permit import restrictions in response to differences in environmental policies under the General Agreement, they would need to impose limits on the range of policy differences justifying such responses and to develop criteria so as to prevent abuse. If the CONTRACTING PARTIES were to decide to permit trade measures of this type in particular circumstances it would therefore be preferable for them to do so not by interpreting Article XX, but by amending or supplementing the provisions of the General Agreement or waiving obligations thereunder. Such an approach would enable the CONTRACTING PARTIES to impose such limits and develop such criteria.

United States – Restrictions on Imports of Tuna ('US – Tuna/Dolphin II'), 1994 (NOT ADOPTED)

Short summary and commentary

In *US – Tuna/Dolphin II,* the US again faced complaints that the import prohibitions imposed under the MMPA were inconsistent with its obligations under the GATT. In this dispute, the EEC and the Netherlands were the complainants, and the US again defended both the primary nation and intermediary nation embargoes as consistent with the GATT, or alternately, as justified under Article XX(b) and/or (g). After concluding that the US measures were not encompassed by Article III and were contrary to Article XI, the panel examined them as exceptions in the context of Article XX(b) and (g).

The panel suggested that Article XX(g) required a three-pronged inquiry: (i) 'whether the *policy* . . . fell within the range of policies to conserve exhaustible natural resources', (ii) 'whether the *measure* . . .was "related to" the conservation of exhaustible natural resources, and whether it was made effective "in conjunction" with restrictions on domestic production or consumption', and (iii) 'whether the measure was applied in conformity with the requirement set forth in the preamble to Article XX, namely that the measure not be applied in a manner which would constitute a means of arbitrary or unjustifiable discrimination . . . or . . . a disguised restriction on international trade' (Panel report, paragraph 5.12).

In considering the first criterion, the panel accepted that the conservation of dolphins qualified as a policy to conserve an exhaustible natural resource (*Id.* at paragraph 5.13). Furthermore, in contrast to *Tuna/Dolphin I,* the panel saw no reason to restrict Article XX(g)'s application to the conservation of exhaustible natural resources located within the territory of the country invoking the policy (*Id.* at paragraph 5.20). The panel instead declared that the US policy aimed at conserving dolphins in the ETP, as pursued within its jurisdiction over its nationals and vessels, fell within the scope of Article XX(g) (*Id.*).

With respect to the second criterion, the panel confirmed that the term 'relating to' should be taken to mean 'primarily aimed' at the conservation of natural resources, and that the term 'in conjunction with' should be taken to mean 'primarily aimed' at rendering effective the restrictions on domestic production or consumption (*Id.* at paragraph 5.22). It held that 'measures taken so as to force other countries to change their policies regarding persons and things within their own jurisdictions', and that were effective only if such changes occurred, could not be primarily aimed at either the conservation of an exhaustible natural resource, or at rendering effective restrictions on domestic production or consumption, in the meaning of Article XX(g) (*Id.* at paragraph 5.27). This aspect is further examined in Chapter 5: Extraterritoriality.

In reviewing the US import restrictions under Article XX(b), the panel again undertook a three-pronged inquiry: (i) 'whether the *policy* . . . fell within the range of policies . . . to protect human, animal or plant life or health'; (ii) 'whether the *measure* . . . was "necessary" to protect human, animal or plant life or health'; and (iii) 'whether the measure was applied in a manner consistent with the requirement set out in the preamble to Article XX, namely that the measure not be applied in a manner which would constitute a means of arbitrary or unjustifiable discrimination . . . or . . . a disguised restriction on trade (*Id.* at paragraph 5.29).

As in its earlier analysis in *US – Tuna/Dolphin I,* the panel again found that a policy protecting dolphin life or health in the ETP, as pursued by the US within its jurisdiction over its nationals and vessels, would fall within the scope of Article XX(b) (*Id.* at paragraph 5.33). Similarly, in its analysis of the second criterion, the panel again rejected the notion that measures considered 'necessary' under Article XX(b) could include measures requiring other countries to change their policies with respect to their own jurisdictions in order to be effective (*Id.* at paragraph 5.39). Therefore, the panel similarly found no need to examine the last requirement of Article XX(b), and concluded finally that the US trade embargoes were not justified by either Article XX(b) or (g) (*Id.* at paragraphs 5.27, 5.39).

Excerpts

[Editor's note: Further excerpts regarding Article XX(b) and (g) are reproduced in Chapter 3: The Necessity Requirement and Chapter 5: Extraterritoriality.]

Report of the Panel, *United States – Restrictions on Imports of Tuna ("Tuna/Dolphin II")*, DS29/R (16 June 1994), NOT ADOPTED.

V. Findings [paras 5.1–5.43]

. . .

C. Article XX(g) [paras 5.11–5.27]

5.11 The Panel noted the United States argument that both the primary and intermediary nation embargoes, even if inconsistent with Articles III or XI, were justified by Article XX(g) as measures relating to the conservation of dolphins, an exhaustible natural resource. The United States argued that there was no requirement in Article XX(g) for the resources to be within the territorial jurisdiction of the country taking the measure. The United States further argued that the measures were taken in conjunction with restrictions on domestic production and consumption. Finally, it argued that the measures met the requirement of the preamble to Article XX. The EEC and the Netherlands disagreed, stating that the resource to be conserved had to be within the territorial jurisdiction of the country taking the measure. The EEC and the Netherlands were further of the view that the United States measures were not related to the conservation of an exhaustible natural resource under Article XX(g), and were not taken in conjunction with domestic restrictions on production or consumption.

5.12 The Panel proceeded first to examine the text of Article XX(g), which, together with its preamble, states:

> *"Subject to the requirement that such measures are not applied in a manner which would constitute a means of arbitrary or unjustifiable discrimination between countries where the same conditions prevail, or a disguised restriction on international trade, nothing in this Agreement shall be construed to prevent the adoption or enforcement by any contracting party of measures:*
>
> . . .
>
> *(g) relating to the conservation of exhaustible natural resources if such measures are made effective in conjunction with restrictions on domestic production or consumption;"*

The Panel observed that the text of Article XX(g) suggested a three-step analysis:

- First, it had to be determined whether the policy in respect of which these provisions were invoked fell within the range of policies to conserve exhaustible natural resources.
- Second, it had to be determined whether the *measure* for which the exception was being invoked – that is the particular trade measure inconsistent with the obligations under the General Agreement – was "related to" the conservation of exhaustible natural resources, and whether it was made effective "in conjunction" with restrictions on domestic production or consumption.
- Third, it had to be determined whether the measure was applied in conformity with the requirement set out in the preamble to Article XX, namely that the measure not be applied in a manner which would constitute a means of arbitrary or unjustifiable discrimination between countries where the same conditions prevail or in a manner which would constitute a disguised restriction on international trade.

1. Conservation of an exhaustible natural resource

5.13 Concerning the first of the above three questions, the Panel noted that the United States maintained that dolphins were an exhaustible natural resource. The EEC disagreed. The Panel, noting that dolphin stocks could potentially be exhausted, and that the basis of a policy to conserve them did not depend on whether at present their stocks were depleted, accepted that a policy to conserve dolphins was a policy to conserve an exhaustible natural resource.

. . .

2. "Related to" the conservation of an exhaustible natural resource; made effective "in conjunction" with restrictions on domestic production or consumption

5.21 The Panel then examined the second of the above three questions, namely whether the primary and intermediary nation embargoes imposed by the United States on yellowfin tuna could be considered to be "related to" the conservation of an exhaustible natural resource within the meaning of Article XX(g), and whether they were made effective "in conjunction with" restrictions on domestic production or consumption. The United States argued that its measures met both requirements. The EEC disagreed, stating the measures had to be "primarily aimed" at the conservation of the exhaustible natural resource, and at rendering effective the restrictions on domestic production or consumption.

5.22 The Panel proceeded first to examine the relationship established by Article XX(g) between the trade measure and the policy of conserving an exhaustible natural resource, and between the trade measure and the restrictions on domestic production or consumption. It noted that a previous panel had stated that the scope of the terms "relating to" and "in conjunction with" had to be interpreted in a way that ensured that the scope of provisions under Article XX(g) corresponded to the purposes for which it was included in the General Agreement. That panel had stated that

> *". . . the purpose of including Article XX(g) in the General Agreement was not to widen the scope for measures serving trade policy purposes but merely to ensure that the commitments under the General Agreement do not hinder the pursuit of policies aimed at the conservation of exhaustive natural resources".*[83]

The previous panel had concluded that the term "relating to" should be taken to mean "primarily aimed" at the conservation of natural resources, and that the term "in conjunction with" should be taken to mean "primarily aimed" at rendering effective the restrictions on domestic production or consumption. The Panel agreed with the reasoning of the previous panel, on the understanding that the words "primarily aimed at" referred not only to the purpose of the measure, but also to its effect on the conservation of the natural resource.

[83] Report of the Panel in *Canada – Measures affecting the exports of unprocessed herring and salmon,* adopted 22 March 1988, 35S/98, 114, para 4.6

United States – Standards for Reformulated and Conventional Gasoline ('US – Reformulated Gasoline'), 1996

Short summary and commentary

US – Reformulated Gasoline was the first case to be decided under WTO dispute settlement procedure. The central issue in *US – Reformulated Gasoline* was whether US environmental standards were being applied in a discriminatory fashion.

The US Environmental Protection Agency (EPA) had enacted the 'Gasoline Rule' to comply with certain compositional and performance specifications for gasoline under the Clean Air Act of 1990 (CAA). As the CAA required that conventional gasoline remain at least as clean as 1990 baseline levels, the Gasoline Rule contained detailed 'baseline establishment rules' which set the baseline levels for different entities. While the Gasoline Rule assigned an *individual* baseline (established by the refiner's own gasoline quality in 1990) to any domestic refiner that was in operation for at least six months in 1990, the Gasoline Rule assigned a *statutory* baseline (established by the EPA and intended to reflect average US 1990 gasoline quality) to foreign refiners of gasoline, as well as any domestic refiners who were in business less than six months in 1990. Venezuela, later joined by Brazil, complained that the US composition rules were stricter for imported gasoline than for domestically refined gasoline, and therefore inconsistent with GATT Article III.

The dispute settlement panel found the baseline establishment methods inconsistent with Article III, and also found that the measures could not be justified under either Article XX(b) or (g). The US appealed the panel's finding on Article XX(g). In reviewing that decision, the Appellate Body first set out to determine whether or not the measures in question, the baseline establishment rules, fell under the exception of Article XX(g). The panel found that a policy to reduce air pollution was a policy to conserve an exhaustible natural resource. However, referring to the approach taken in *Canada – Unprocessed Herring and Salmon,* the panel concluded that the measures at issue were *not* sufficiently '"relating to" the conservation of exhaustible natural resources' to fall within the scope of Article XX(g), as they were not 'primarily aimed at' such conservation. Since no party to the appeal had questioned the *Canada – Unprocessed Herring and Salmon* interpretation equating the term 'relating to' to 'primarily aimed at', the Appellate Body accepted it in turn. While noting that 'the phrase "primarily aimed at" was not itself treaty language and was not designed as a simple litmus test for inclusion or exclusion from Article XX(g)', the Appellate Body came to the conclusion that the measures *were* 'primarily aimed at' conservation as they exhibited a 'substantial relationship' with, and were not 'merely incidentally or inadvertently aimed at' the conservation of natural resources (AB report, sec. III:B). The Appellate Body therefore determined that the measures qualified as sufficiently 'relating to the conservation' under Article XX(g) (*Id.*).

The Appellate Body then proceeded to the third condition of Article XX(g), that the measure be 'made effective in conjunction with restrictions on domestic production or consumption'. The Appellate Body rejected previous interpretations of this criterion, viewing it not as a requirement that the measure be 'primarily aimed at' making effective such restrictions (see *Canada – Unprocessed Herring and Salmon* panel report, paragraphs 4.6–4.7; *US – Tuna/Dolphin I* panel report, paragraph 5.31; *US – Tuna/Dolphin II* panel report, paragraph 5.22), but rather as 'a requirement of *even-handedness* in the imposition of restrictions' (*Id.* at section IV:C). Additionally noting that this requirement did *not* amount to a requirement of identical treatment, the Appellate Body found that the measures before them satisfied the third requirement because they imposed restrictions not only with respect to imported products, but also with respect to domestic ones (*Id.*).

Having determined the measures to be provisionally justified under Article XX(g), the Appellate Body then turned secondarily to an analysis of the measures under the chapeau of Article XX. The Appellate Body noted that this analysis addresses the *manner of application* of the measures and presents a heavier task than the initial inquiry, and furthermore that it is the party invoking the Article XX exception that bears the burden of demonstrating compliance with the chapeau (*Id.* at section IV). In analysing the measures under the chapeau, the Appellate Body questioned the US' failure to pursue available alternative non-discriminatory measures, such as an imposition of either statutory or individual baselines without differentiation as to domestic and imported gasoline (*Id.*). While the Appellate Body recognized the anticipated difficulties in making individual baselines available to foreign refiners, it noted that the US had failed 'to explore adequately means . . . of mitigating the administrative problems relied on as justification . . . for rejecting individual baselines for foreign refiners; and to count the costs for foreign refiners that would result from the imposition of statutory baselines' (*Id.*). For those reasons, the Appellate Body concluded that the baseline establishment rules constituted both 'unjustifiable discrimination' and a 'disguised restriction on international trade' (*Id.*). The measures thereby failed to meet the requirements of the Article XX chapeau, and ultimately, to be justified as an exception under Article XX (*Id.*).

Excerpts

Report of the Appellate Body, *United States – Standards for Reformulated and Conventional Gasoline*, WT/DS2/AB/R, adopted on 20 May 1996.

[Note: this report does not utilize numbered paragraphs.]

III. The Issue of Justification Under Article XX(g) of the General Agreement

. . .

A. "Measures"

The initial issue we are asked to look at relates to the proper meaning of the term "measures" as used both in the chapeau of Article XX and in Article XX(g). The question is whether "measures" refers to the entire Gasoline Rule or, alternatively, only to the particular provisions of the Gasoline Rule which deal with the establishment of baselines for domestic refiners, blenders and importers.

Cast in the foregoing terms, the issue does not appear to be a live one. True enough the Panel Report used differing terms, or terms of shifting reference, in designating the "measures" in different parts of the Report. The Panel Report, however, held only the baseline establishment rules of the Gasoline Rule to be inconsistent with Article III:4, to the extent that such rules provided "less favourable treatment" for imported than for domestic gasoline. These are the same provisions which the Panel evaluated, and found wanting, under the justifying provisions of Article XX(g). The Panel Report did not purport to find the Gasoline Rule itself as a whole, or any part thereof other than the baseline establishment rules, to be inconsistent with Article III:4; accordingly, there was no need at all to examine whether the whole of the Gasoline Rule or any of its other rules, was saved or justified by Article XX(g). The Panel here was following the practice of earlier panels in applying Article XX to provisions found to be inconsistent with Article III:4: the "measures" to be analyzed under Article XX are the same provisions infringing Article III:4.[28] These earlier panels had not interpreted "measures" more broadly under Article XX to include provisions not themselves found inconsistent with Article III:4. In the present appeal, no one has suggested in their final submissions that the Appellate Body should examine under Article XX any portion of the Gasoline Rule other than the baseline establishment rules held to be in conflict with Article III:4. No one has urged an interpretation of "measures" which would encompass the Gasoline Rule in its totality.[29]

At the oral hearing and in its Post-Hearing Memorandum, the United States complained about the designation of the baseline establishment rules in the Panel Report and by the Appellees Venezuela and Brazil, in such terms as "the difference in treatment", "the less favourable treatment" or "the discrimination". It is, of course, true that the baseline establishment rules had been found by the Panel to be inconsistent with Article III:4 of the *General Agreement*. The frequent designation of those provisions by the Panel in terms of its legal conclusion in respect of Article III:4, in the Appellate Body's view, did not serve the cause of clarity in analysis when it came to evaluating the same baseline establishment rules under Article XX(g).

[28] *Canada – Administration of the Foreign Investment Review Act,* BISD 30S/140, adopted 7 February 1984; *United States – Section 337 of the Tariff Act of 1930,* BISD 36S/345, adopted 7 November 1989; *United States – Taxes on Automobiles,* DS31/R (1994), unadopted.

[29] Although, in earlier submissions to the Appellate Body, the United States suggested that "the Gasoline Rule" should be examined in the context of Article XX(g), in its Post-Hearing Memorandum, dated 1 April 1996, the United States confirmed its understanding that the "measures" in issue are the baseline establishment rules contained in the Gasoline Rule.

Brazil stated, in its final submission to the Appellate Body, dated 1 April 1996, that "'the measure' with which this appeal is concerned is the baseline methodology of the Gasoline Rule, not the entire rule itself." This would suggest a position similar to that adopted by the United States. Thereafter, Brazil continued to state that "Brazil and Venezuela did not challenge all portions of the Rule; they challenged only the discriminatory methods of establishing baselines."

Venezuela stated, in its summary statement, dated 29 March 1996, that "the measure to be examined is the discriminatory measure, that is, the aspect of the Gasoline Rule that denies imported gasoline the right to use the same regulatory system of baselines applicable to US gasoline, namely, the system of individual baselines."

B. "Relating to the conservation of exhaustible natural resources"

The Panel Report took the view that clean air was a "natural resource" that could be "depleted". Accordingly, as already noted earlier, the Panel concluded that a policy to reduce the depletion of clean air was a policy to conserve an exhaustible natural resource within the meaning of Article XX(g). Shortly thereafter, however, the Panel Report also concluded that "the less favourable baseline establishments methods" were *not* primarily aimed at the conservation of exhaustible natural resources and thus fell outside the justifying scope of Article XX(g).

The Panel, addressing the task of interpreting the words "relating to", quoted with approval the following passage from the panel report in the 1987 *Herring and Salmon* case:[30]

> *as the preamble of Article XX indicates, the purpose of including Article XX:(g) in the General Agreement was not to widen the scope for measures serving trade policy purposes but merely to ensure that the commitments under the General Agreement do not hinder the pursuit of policies aimed at the conservation of exhaustive natural resources. The Panel concluded for these reasons that, while a trade measure did not have to be necessary or essential to the conservation of an exhaustible natural resource, it had to be* primarily aimed

> *at the conservation of an exhaustible natural resource to be considered as "relating to" conservation within the meaning of Article XX:(g) (emphasis added by the Panel).*

The Panel Report then went on to apply the 1987 *Herring and Salmon* reasoning and conclusion to the baseline establishment rules of the Gasoline Rule in the following manner:[31]

> *The Panel then considered whether the precise aspects of the Gasoline Rule that it had found to violate Article III – the less favourable baseline establishments methods that adversely affected the conditions of competition for imported gasoline – were primarily aimed at the conservation of natural resources. The Panel saw no direct connection between less favourable treatment of imported gasoline that was chemically identical to domestic gasoline, and the US objective of improving air quality in the United States. Indeed, in the view of the Panel, being consistent with the obligation to provide no less favourable treatment would not prevent the attainment of the desired level of conservation of natural resources under the Gasoline Rule. Accordingly, it could not be said that the baseline establishment methods that afforded less favourable treatment to imported gasoline were primarily aimed at the conservation of natural resources. In the Panel's view, the above-noted lack of connection was underscored by the fact that affording treatment of imported gasoline consistent with its Article III:4 obligations would not in any way hinder the United States in its pursuit of its conservation policies under the Gasoline Rule. Indeed, the United States remained free to regulate in order to obtain whatever air quality it wished. The Panel therefore concluded that the less favourable baseline establishments methods at issue in this case were not primarily aimed at the conservation of natural resources.*

It is not easy to follow the reasoning in the above paragraph of the Panel Report. In our view, there is a certain amount of opaqueness in that reasoning. The Panel starts with positing that there was "*no direct connection*" between the baseline establishment rules which it characterized as "less favourable treatment" of imported gasoline that was chemically identical to the domestic gasoline and "the US objective of improving air quality in the United States". Shortly thereafter, the Panel went on to conclude that "*accordingly, it could not be said that* the baseline establishment rules that afforded less favourable treatment to imported gasoline *were primarily aimed at* the conservation of natural resources" (emphasis added). The Panel did not try to clarify whether the phrase "direct connection" was being used as a synonym for "primarily aimed at" or whether a new and additional element (on top of "primarily aimed at") was being demanded.

One problem with the reasoning in that paragraph is that the Panel asked itself whether the "less favourable treatment" of imported gasoline was "primarily aimed at" the conservation of natural resources, rather than whether the "measure", i.e. the baseline establishment rules, were "primarily aimed at" conservation of clean air. In our view, the Panel here was in error in referring to its legal conclusion on Article III:4 instead of the measure in issue. The result of this analysis is to turn Article XX on its head. Obviously, there had to be a finding that the measure provided "less favourable treatment" under Article III:4 before the Panel examined the "General Exceptions" contained in Article XX. That, however, is a conclusion of law. The chapeau of Article XX makes it clear that it is the "measures" which are to be examined under Article XX(g), and not the legal finding of "less favourable treatment".

Furthermore, the Panel Report appears to have utilized a conclusion it had reached earlier in holding that the baseline establishment rules did not fall within the justifying terms of Articles XX(b); i.e. that the baseline establishment rules were not "necessary" for the protection of human, animal or plant life. The Panel Report, it will be recalled, found that the baseline establishment rules had not been shown by the United States to be "necessary" under Article XX(b) since alternative measures either consistent or less inconsistent with the *General Agreement* were reasonably available to the United States for achieving its aim of protecting human, animal or plant life.[32] In other words, the Panel Report appears to have applied the "necessary" test not only in examining the baseline establishment rules under Article XX(b), but also in the course of applying Article XX(g).

. . .

The 1987 *Herring and Salmon* report, and the Panel Report itself, gave some recognition to the foregoing considerations of principle. As earlier noted, the Panel Report quoted the following excerpt from the *Herring and Salmon* report:

> *as the preamble of Article XX indicates, the purpose of including Article XX(g) in the General Agreement was not to widen the scope for measures serving trade policy purposes but merely* to ensure that the commitments under the General Agreement do not hinder the pursuit of policies *aimed at the conservation of exhaustible natural resources*[36] *(emphasis added).*

All the participants and the third participants in this appeal accept the propriety and applicability of the view of the *Herring and Salmon* report and the Panel Report that a measure must be "primarily aimed at" the conservation of exhaustible natural resources in order to fall within the scope of Article XX(g).[37] Accordingly, we see no need to examine this point further, save, perhaps, to note that the phrase "primarily aimed at" is not itself treaty language and was not designed as a simple litmus test for inclusion or exclusion from Article XX(g).

Against this background, we turn to the specific question of whether the baseline establishment rules are appropriately regarded as "primarily aimed at" the conservation of natural resources for the purposes of Article XX(g). We consider that this question must be answered in the affirmative.

The baseline establishment rules, taken as a whole (that is, the provisions relating to establishment of baselines for domestic refiners, along with the provisions relating to baselines for blenders and importers of gasoline), need to be related to the "non-degradation" requirements set out elsewhere in the Gasoline Rule. Those provisions can scarcely be understood if scrutinized strictly by themselves, totally divorced from other sections of the Gasoline Rule which certainly constitute part of the context of these provisions. The baseline establishment rules, whether individual or statutory, were designed to permit scrutiny and monitoring of the level of compliance of refiners, importers and blenders with the "non-degradation" requirements. Without baselines of some kind, such scrutiny would not be possible and the Gasoline Rule's objective of stabilizing and preventing further deterioration of the level of air pollution prevailing in 1990, would be substantially frustrated. The relationship between the baseline establishment rules and the "non-degradation" requirements of the Gasoline Rule is not negated by the inconsistency, found by the Panel, of the baseline establishment rules, with the terms of Article III:4. We consider that, given that substantial relationship, the baseline establishment rules cannot be regarded as merely incidentally or inadvertently aimed at the conservation of clean air in the United States for the purposes of Article XX(g).

30 *Canada – Measures Affecting Exports of Unprocessed Herring and Salmon,* BISD 35S/98, para 4.6; adopted on 22 March 1988, cited in Panel Report, para 6.39.

31 Panel Report, para 6.40.

32 Panel Report, paras 6.25–6.28.

36 *Canada – Measures Affecting Exports of Unprocessed Herring and Salmon,* BISD 35S/98, para 4.6; adopted 22 March 1988, cited in Panel Report, para 6.39.

37 We note that the same interpretation has been applied in two recent unadopted panel reports: *United States – Restrictions on Imports of Tuna,* DS29/R (1994); *United States – Taxes on Automobiles,* DS31/R (1994).

C. "If such measures are made effective in conjunction with restrictions on domestic production or consumption"

The Panel did not find it necessary to deal with the issue of whether the baseline establishment rules "are made effective in conjunction with restrictions on domestic production or consumption", since it had earlier concluded that those rules had not even satisfied the preceding requirement of "relating to" in the sense of being "primarily aimed at" the conservation of clean air. Having been unable to concur with that earlier conclusion of the Panel, we must now address this second requirement of Article XX(g), the United States having, in effect, appealed from the failure of the Panel to proceed further with its inquiry into the availability of Article XX(g) as a justification for the baseline establishment rules.

The claim of the United States is that the second clause of Article XX(g) requires that the burdens entailed by regulating the level of pollutants in the air emitted in the course of combustion of gasoline, must not be imposed solely on, or in respect of, imported gasoline.

On the other hand, Venezuela and Brazil refer to prior panel reports which include statements to the effect that to be deemed as "made effective in conjunction with restrictions on domestic production or consumption", a measure must be "primarily aimed at" making effective certain restrictions on domestic production or consumption.[38] Venezuela and Brazil also argue that the United States has failed to show the existence of restrictions on domestic production or consumption of a natural resource under the Gasoline Rule since clean air was not an exhaustible natural resource within the meaning of Article XX(g). Venezuela contends, finally, that the United States has not discharged its burden of showing that the baseline establishment rules make the United States' regulatory scheme "effective". The claim of Venezuela is, in effect, that to be properly regarded as "primarily aimed at" the conservation of natural resources, the baseline establishment rules must not only "reflect a conservation purpose" but also be shown to have had "some positive conservation effect".[39]

The Appellate Body considers that the basic international law rule of treaty interpretation, discussed earlier, that the terms of a treaty are to be given their ordinary meaning, in context, so as to effectuate its object and purpose, is applicable here, too. Viewed in this light, the ordinary or natural meaning of "made effective" when used in connection with a measure – a governmental act or regulation – may be seen to refer to such measure being "operative", as "in force", or as having "come into effect".[40] Similarly, the phrase "in conjunction with" may be read quite plainly as "together with" or "jointly with".[41] Taken together, the second clause of Article XX(g) appears to us to refer to governmental measures like the baseline establishment rules being promulgated or brought into effect together with restrictions on domestic production or consumption of natural resources. Put in a slightly different manner, we believe that the clause "if such measures are made effective in conjunction with restrictions on domestic product or consumption" is appropriately read as a requirement that the measures concerned impose restrictions, not just in respect of imported gasoline but also with respect to domestic gasoline. The clause is a requirement of *even-handedness* in the imposition of restrictions, in the name of conservation, upon the production or consumption of exhaustible natural resources.

There is, of course, no textual basis for requiring identical treatment of domestic and imported products. Indeed, where there is identity of treatment – constituting real, not merely formal, equality of treatment – it is difficult to see how inconsistency with Article III:4 would have arisen in the first place. On the other hand, if *no* restrictions on domestically-produced like products are imposed at all, and all limitations are placed upon imported products *alone*, the measure cannot be accepted as primarily or even substantially designed for implementing conservationist goals.[42] The measure would simply be naked discrimination for protecting locally-produced goods.

In the present appeal, the baseline establishment rules affect both domestic gasoline and imported gasoline, providing for – generally speaking – individual baselines for domestic refiners and blenders and statutory baselines for importers. Thus, restrictions on the consumption or depletion of clean air by regulating the domestic production of "dirty" gasoline are established jointly with corresponding restrictions with respect to imported gasoline. That imported gasoline has been determined to have been accorded "less favourable treatment" than the domestic gasoline in terms of Article III:4, is not material for purposes of analysis under Article XX(g). It might also be noted that the second clause of Article XX(g) speaks disjunctively of "domestic production *or* consumption".

We do not believe, finally, that the clause "if made effective in conjunction with restrictions on domestic production or consumption" was intended to establish an empirical "effects test" for the availability of the Article XX(g) exception. In the first place, the problem of determining causation, well-known in both domestic and international law, is always a difficult one. In the second place, in the field of conservation of exhaustible natural resources, a substantial period of time, perhaps years, may have to elapse before the effects attributable to implementation of a given measure may be observable. The legal characterization of such a measure is not reasonably made contingent upon occurrence of subsequent events. We are not, however, suggesting that consideration of the predictable effects of a measure is never relevant. In a particular case, should it become clear that realistically, a specific measure cannot in any possible situation have any positive effect on conservation goals, it would very probably be because that measure was not designed as a conservation regulation to begin with. In other words, it would not have been "primarily aimed at" conservation of natural resources at all.

[38] *Canada – Measures Affecting Exports of Unprocessed Herring and Salmon,* BISD 35S/98, paras 4.6–4.7; adopted 22 March 1988. Also, *United States – Restrictions on Imports of Tuna,* DS29/R (1994), unadopted; and *United States – Taxes on Automobiles,* DS31/R (1994), unadopted.

[39] Venezuela's Appellee's Submission, dated 18 March 1996; Venezuela's Statement at the Oral Hearing, dated 27 March 1996.

[40] *The New Shorter Oxford English Dictionary on Historical Principles* (L. Brown, ed., 1993), Vol. I, p786.

[41] *Ibid.,* p481.

[42] Some illustration is offered in the *Herring and Salmon* case which involved, *inter alia,* a Canadian prohibition of exports of unprocessed herring and salmon. This prohibition effectively constituted a ban on purchase of certain unprocessed fish by foreign processors and consumers while imposing no corresponding ban on purchase of unprocessed fish by domestic processors and consumers. The prohibitions appeared to be designed to protect domestic processors by giving them exclusive access to fresh fish and at the same time denying such raw material to foreign processors. The Panel concluded that these export prohibitions were not justified by Article XX(g). BISD 35S/98, para 5.1, adopted 22 March 1988. See also the Panel Report in the *United States – Prohibition of Imports of Tuna and Tuna Products from Canada,* BISD 29S/91, paras 4.10–4.12; adopted on 22 February 1982.

IV. The Introductory Provisions of Article XX of the General Agreement: Applying the Chapeau of the General Exceptions

Having concluded, in the preceding section, that the baseline establishment rules of the Gasoline Rule fall within the terms of Article XX(g), we come to the question of whether those rules also meet the requirements of the chapeau of Article XX. In order that the justifying protection of Article XX may be extended to it, the measure at issue must not only come under one or another of the particular exceptions – paragraphs (a) to (j) – listed under Article XX; it must also satisfy the requirements imposed by the opening clauses of Article XX. The analysis is, in other words, two-tiered: first, provisional justification by reason of characterization of the measure under XX(g); second, further appraisal of the same measure under the introductory clauses of Article XX.

The chapeau by its express terms addresses, not so much the questioned measure or its specific contents as such, but rather the manner in which that measure is applied.[43] It is, accordingly, important to underscore that the purpose and object of the introductory clauses of Article XX is generally the prevention of "abuse of the exceptions of [what was later to become] Article [XX]."[44] This insight drawn from the drafting history of Article XX is a valuable one. The chapeau is animated by the principle that while the exceptions of Article XX may be invoked as a matter of legal right, they should not be so applied as to frustrate or defeat the legal obligations of the holder of the right under the substantive rules of the *General Agreement*. If those exceptions are not to be abused or misused, in other words, the measures falling within the particular exceptions must be applied reasonably, with due regard both to the legal duties of the party claiming the exception and the legal rights of the other parties concerned.

The burden of demonstrating that a measure provisionally justified as being within one of the exceptions set out in the individual paragraphs of Article XX does not, in its application, constitute abuse of such exception under the chapeau, rests on the party invoking the exception. That is, of necessity, a heavier task than that involved in showing that an exception, such as Article XX(g), encompasses the measure at issue.

The enterprise of applying Article XX would clearly be an unprofitable one if it involved no more than applying the standard used in finding that the baseline establishment rules were inconsistent with Article III:4. That would also be true if the finding were one of inconsistency with some other substantive rule of the *General Agreement*. The provisions of the chapeau cannot logically refer to the same standard(s) by which a violation of a substantive rule has been determined to have occurred. To proceed down that path would be both to empty the chapeau of its contents and to deprive the exceptions in paragraphs (a) to (j) of meaning. Such recourse would also confuse the question of whether inconsistency with a substantive rule existed, with the further and separate question arising under the chapeau of Article XX as to whether that inconsistency was nevertheless justified. One of the corollaries of the "general rule of interpretation" in the *Vienna Convention* is that interpretation must give meaning and effect to all the terms of a treaty. An interpreter is not free to adopt a reading that would result in reducing whole clauses or paragraphs of a treaty to redundancy or inutility.[45]

The chapeau, it will be seen, prohibits such application of a measure at issue (otherwise falling within the scope of Article XX(g)) as would constitute

(a) "arbitrary discrimination" (between countries where the same conditions prevail);
(b) "unjustifiable discrimination" (with the same qualifier); or
(c) "disguised restriction" on international trade.

. . .

"Arbitrary discrimination", "unjustifiable discrimination" and "disguised restriction" on international trade may, accordingly, be read side-by-side; they impart meaning to one another. It is clear to us that "disguised restriction" includes disguised *discrimination* in international trade. It is equally clear that *concealed* or *unannounced* restriction or discrimination in international trade does *not* exhaust the meaning of "disguised restriction". We consider that "disguised restriction", whatever else it covers, may properly be read as embracing restrictions amounting to arbitrary or unjustifiable discrimination in international trade taken under the guise of a measure formally within the terms of an exception listed in Article XX. Put in a somewhat different manner, the kinds of considerations pertinent in deciding whether the application of a particular measure amounts to "arbitrary or unjustifiable discrimination", may also be taken into account in determining the presence of a "disguised restriction" on international trade. The fundamental theme is to be found in the purpose and object of avoiding abuse or illegitimate use of the exceptions to substantive rules available in Article XX.

There was more than one alternative course of action available to the United States in promulgating regulations implementing the CAA. These included the imposition of statutory baselines without differentiation as between domestic and imported gasoline. This approach, if properly implemented, could have avoided any discrimination at all. Among the other options open to the United States was to make available individual baselines to foreign refiners as well as domestic refiners. The United States has put forward a series of reasons why either of these courses was not, in its view, realistically open to it and why, instead, it had to devise and apply the baseline establishment rules contained in the Gasoline Rule.

In explaining why individual baselines for foreign refiners had not been put in place, the United States laid heavy stress upon the difficulties which the EPA would have had to face. These difficulties related to anticipated administrative problems that individual baselines for foreign refiners would have generated. This argument was made succinctly by the United States in the following terms:

> *Verification on foreign soil of foreign baselines, and subsequent enforcement actions, present substantial difficulties relating to problems arising whenever a country exercises enforcement jurisdiction over foreign persons. In addition, even if individual baselines were established for several foreign refiners, the importer would be tempted to claim the refinery of origin that presented the most benefits in terms of baseline restrictions, and tracking the refinery or origin would be very difficult because gasoline is a fungible commodity. The United States should not have to prove that it cannot verify information and enforce its regulations in every*

instance in order to show that the same enforcement conditions do not prevail in the United States and other countries. . . The impracticability of verification and enforcement of foreign refiner baselines in this instance shows that the "discrimination" is based on serious, not arbitrary or unjustifiable, concerns stemming from different conditions between enforcement of its laws in the United States and abroad.[47]

Thus, according to the United States, imported gasoline was relegated to the more exacting statutory baseline requirement because of these difficulties of verification and enforcement. The United States stated that verification and enforcement of the Gasoline Rule's requirements for imported gasoline are "much easier when the statutory baseline is used" and that there would be a "dramatic difference" in the burden of administering requirements for imported gasoline if individual baselines were allowed.[48]

While the anticipated difficulties concerning verification and subsequent enforcement are doubtless real to some degree, the Panel viewed them as insufficient to justify the denial to foreign refiners of individual baselines permitted to domestic refiners. The Panel said:

While the Panel agreed that it would be necessary under such a system to ascertain the origin of gasoline, the Panel could not conclude that the United States had shown that this could not be achieved by other measures reasonably available to it and consistent or less inconsistent with the General Agreement. Indeed, the Panel noted that a determination of origin would often be feasible. The Panel examined, for instance, the case of a direct shipment to the United States. It considered that there was no reason to believe that, given the usual measures available in international trade for determination of origin and tracking of goods (including documentary evidence and third party verification) there was any particular difficulty sufficient to warrant the demands of the baseline establishment methods applied by the United States.[49]

. . .

In the view of the Panel, the United States had reasonably available to it data for, and measures of, verification and assessment which were consistent or less inconsistent with Article III:4. For instance, although foreign data may be formally less subject to complete control by US authorities, this did not amount to establishing that foreign data could not in any circumstances be sufficiently reliable to serve US purposes. This, however, was the practical effect of the application of the Gasoline Rule. In the Panel's view, the United States had not demonstrated that data available from foreign refiners was inherently less susceptible to established techniques of checking, verification, assessment and enforcement than data for other trade in goods subject to US regulation. The nature of the data in this case was similar to data relied upon by the United States in other contexts, including, for example, under the application of antidumping laws. In an antidumping case, only when the information was not supplied or deemed unverifiable did the United States turn to other information. If a similar practice were to be applied in the case of the Gasoline Rule, then importers could, for instance, be permitted to use the individual baselines of foreign refiners for imported gasoline from those refiners, with the statutory baseline being applied only when the source of imported gasoline could not be determined or a baseline could not be established because of an absence of data.[50]

We agree with the finding above made in the Panel Report. There are, as the Panel Report found, established techniques for checking, verification, assessment and enforcement of data relating to imported goods, techniques which in many contexts are accepted as adequate to permit international trade – trade between territorial sovereigns – to go on and grow. The United States must have been aware that for these established techniques and procedures to work, cooperative arrangements with both foreign refiners and the foreign governments concerned would have been necessary and appropriate. At the oral hearing, in the course of responding to an enquiry as to whether the EPA could have adapted, for purposes of establishing individual refinery baselines for foreign refiners, procedures for verification of information found in US antidumping laws, the United States said that "in the absence of refinery cooperation and the possible absence of foreign government cooperation as well", it was unlikely that the EPA auditors would be able to conduct the on-site audit reviews necessary to establish even the overall quality of refineries' 1990 gasoline.[51] From this statement, there arises a strong implication, it appears to the Appellate Body, that the United States had not pursued the possibility of entering into cooperative arrangements with the governments of Venezuela and Brazil or, if it had, not to the point where it encountered governments that were unwilling to cooperate. The record of this case sets out the detailed justifications put forward by the United States. But it does not reveal what, if any, efforts had been taken by the United States to enter into appropriate procedures in cooperation with the governments of Venezuela and Brazil so as to mitigate the administrative problems pleaded by the United States.[52] The fact that the United States Congress might have intervened, as it did later intervene, in the process by denying funding, is beside the point: the United States, of course, carries responsibility for actions of both the executive and legislative departments of government.

In its submissions, the United States also explained why the statutory baseline requirement was not imposed on domestic refiners as well. Here, the United States stressed the problems that domestic refineries would have faced had they been required to comply with the statutory baseline. The Panel Report summarized the United States' argument in the following terms:

> *The United States concluded that, contrary to Venezuela's and Brazil's claim, Article XX did not require adoption of the statutory baseline as a national standard even if the difficulties associated with the establishment of individual baselines for importers were insurmountable. Application of the statutory baseline to domestic producers of reformulated and conventional gasoline in 1995 would have been* physically and financially impossible because of the magnitude of the changes required in almost all US refineries; it thus would have caused a substantial delay in the programme. *Weighing the feasibility of policy options in economic or technical terms in order to meet an environmental objective was a legitimate consideration, and did not, in itself, constitute protectionism, as alleged by Venezuela and Brazil. Article XX did not require a government to choose the most expensive possible way to regulate its environment*[53] *(emphasis added).*

Clearly, the United States did not feel it feasible to require its domestic refiners to incur the physical and financial costs and burdens entailed by immediate compliance with a statutory baseline. The United States wished to give domestic refiners time to restructure their operations and adjust to the requirements in the Gasoline Rule. This may very well have constituted sound domestic policy from the viewpoint of the EPA and US refiners. At the same time we are bound to note that, while the United States counted the costs for its domestic refiners of statutory baselines, there is nothing in the record to indicate that it did other than disregard that kind of consideration when it came to foreign refiners.

We have above located two omissions on the part of the United States: to explore adequately means, including in particular cooperation with the governments of Venezuela and Brazil, of mitigating the administrative problems relied on as justification by the United States for rejecting individual baselines for foreign refiners; and to count the costs for foreign refiners that would result from the imposition of statutory baselines. In our view, these two omissions go well beyond what was necessary for the Panel to determine that a violation of Article III:4 had occurred in the first place. The resulting discrimination must have been foreseen, and was not merely inadvertent or unavoidable. In the light of the foregoing, our conclusion is that the baseline establishment rules in the Gasoline Rule, in their application, constitute "unjustifiable discrimination" and a "disguised restriction on international trade". We hold, in sum, that the baseline establishment rules, although within the terms of Article XX(g), are not entitled to the justifying protection afforded by Article XX as a whole.

[43] This was noted in the Panel Report on *United States – Imports of Certain Automotive Spring Assemblies,* BISD 30S/107, para 56; adopted on 26 May 1983.

[44] EPCT/C.11/50, p7; quoted in *Analytical Index: Guide to GATT Law and Practice,* Vol. I, p564 (1995).

[45] E.g. *Corfu Channel Case* (1949) *I.C.J. Reports,* p24 (International Court of Justice); Territorial Dispute Case (Libyan Arab Jamahiriya v. Chad) (1994) *I.C.J. Reports,* p23 (International Court of Justice); 1966 *Yearbook of the International Law Commission,* Vol. II at p219; *Oppenheim's International Law* (9th ed, Jennings and Watts eds., 1992), Vol. 1, pp1280–1281; P. Dallier and A. Pellet, *Droit International Public,* 5è ed. (1994) para 17.2); D. Carreau, *Droit International,* (1994) para 369.
[47] Para 55 of the Appellant's Submission, dated 4 March 1996. The United States was in effect making the same point when, at pages 11 and 12 of its Post-Hearing Memorandum, it argued that the conditions were not the same as between the United States, on the one hand, and Venezuela and Brazil on the other.
[48] Supplementary responses by the United States to certain questions of the Appellate Body, dated 1 April 1996.
[49] Panel Report, para 6.26.
[50] Panel Report, para 6.28.
[51] Supplementary responses by the United States to certain questions of the Appellate Body, dated 1 April 1996.
[52] While it is not for the Appellate Body to speculate where the limits of effective international cooperation are to be found, reference may be made to a number of precedents that the United States (and other countries) have considered it prudent to use to help overcome problems confronting enforcement agencies by virtue of the fact that the relevant law and the authority of the enforcement of the agency does not hold sway beyond national borders. During the course of the oral hearing, attention was drawn to the fact that in addition to the antidumping law referred to by the Panel in the passage cited above, there were other US regulatory laws of this kind, e.g., in the field of anti-trust law, securities exchange law and tax law. There are cooperative agreements entered into by the US and other governments to help enforce regulatory laws of the kind mentioned and to obtain data from abroad. There are such agreements, *inter alia,* in the anti-trust and tax areas. There are also, within the framework of the WTO, the *Agreement on the Implementation of Article VI of GATT 1994,* (the "Antidumping Agreement"), *the Agreement on Subsidies and Countervailing Measures (*the *"SCM Agreement")* and the *Agreement on Pre-Shipment Inspection,* all of which constitute recognition of the frequency and significance of international cooperation of this sort.
[53] Panel Report, para 3.52.

V. Findings and conclusions

. . .

It is of some importance that the Appellate Body point out what this does *not* mean. It does not mean, or imply, that the ability of any WTO Member to take measures to control air pollution or, more generally, to protect the environment, is at issue. That would be to ignore the fact that Article XX of the *General Agreement* contains provisions designed to permit important state interests – including the protection of human health, as well as the conservation of exhaustible natural resources – to find expression. The provisions of Article XX were not changed as a result of the Uruguay Round of Multilateral Trade Negotiations. Indeed, in the preamble to the *WTO Agreement* and in the *Decision on Trade and Environment,*[54] there is specific acknowledgement to be found about the importance of coordinating policies on trade and the environment. WTO Members have a large measure of autonomy to determine their own policies on the environment (including its relationship with trade), their environmental objectives and the environmental legislation they enact and implement. So far as concerns the WTO, that autonomy is circumscribed only by the need to respect the requirements of the *General Agreement* and the other covered agreements.

[54] Adopted by Ministers at the Meeting of the Trade Negotiations Committee in Marrakesh on 14 April 1994.

United States – Import Prohibition of Certain Shrimp and Shrimp Products ('US – Shrimp/Turtle I'), 1998

Short summary and commentary

US – Shrimp/Turtle I presents another case in which environmental measures were found unjustified under Article XX. Four countries – India, Malaysia, Pakistan and Thailand – complained that a US import ban on shrimp and shrimp products harvested with technology that posed risks to sea turtles was inconsistent with Article XI of the GATT.

The US defended the import ban as justified under Article XX(g). Enacted under the Endangered Species Act of 1973 (ESA), the import ban was coupled with a requirement that all US shrimp trawl vessels use turtle excluder devices (TEDs) in times and areas where interaction with sea turtles was likely. The regulations under the Act also exempted from the ban 'certified' nations who adopted a comparable regulatory programme governing the incidental taking of sea turtles, and who achieved an average rate of incidental taking comparable to that of US vessels.

After a panel report concluded that the US measure was inconsistent with GATT Article XI as well as unjustified under Article XX, the US appealed the Article XX finding. In reviewing this finding, the Appellate Body found the panel had erred in its Article XX appraisal by reversing the sequence of the two-tiered analysis set out in *US – Gasoline* (AB report, paragraphs 117–119). The Appellate Body opined that by examining the validity of the measure in the context of the chapeau *before* considering whether it fell within any particular exception, the panel had rendered 'the task of interpreting the chapeau so as to prevent the abuse or misuse of the specific exemptions . . . very difficult, if . . . possible at all . . .' (*Id.* at paragraph 120). The Appellate Body accordingly reversed the panel's finding that the US measure did not fall 'within the scope of measures permitted under the chapeau', and proceeded with an analysis of the measure under Article XX(g) (*Id.* at paragraphs 122–123).

In following with the *US – Gasoline* approach, the Appellate Body first sought to determine whether the measure was provisionally justified under Article XX(g). Beginning with the term 'exhaustible natural resources', the Appellate Body found that Article XX(g) referred not only to the conservation of exhaustible mineral or other non-living natural resources but also to living resources, and concluded that sea turtles were both a 'natural resource' and 'exhaustible' within the meaning of Article XX(g) (*Id.* at paragraph 134).

The Appellate Body next considered whether the US measure was 'related to' the conservation of sea turtles. Finding the US measure not a 'simple, blanket prohibition', but instead 'narrowly focused', the Appellate Body declared that the relationship between the US measure and its conservation goal was 'every bit as substantial as that which we found in *US – Gasoline* . . .' (*Id.* at paragraph 141). The Appellate Body thus found the measure fulfilled the 'related to' requirement (*Id.* at paragraph 142).

Finally, the Appellate Body cited its *US – Gasoline* interpretation of the 'made effective in conjunction with restrictions on domestic production or consumption' element as a requirement of 'even-handedness' (*Id.* at paragraph 143). As the measure's restrictions applied domestically as well as abroad, the Appellate Body determined that the US measure therefore qualified as 'even-handed' and met this final requirement of Article XX(g) (*Id.* at paragraph 144).

As the Appellate Body found the measure provisionally justified under Article XX(g), it then proceeded with a secondary analysis under the Article XX chapeau to determine whether the particular *application* of the measure constituted 'an abuse or misuse of the provisional justification made available by Article XX(g)' (*Id.* at paragraph 160). In so doing, the Appellate Body examined whether the measure's application resulted in 'arbitrary or unjustifiable discrimination between countries where the same conditions prevail', as specified by the chapeau. First addressing the element of 'discrimination', the Appellate Body recalled its findings in *US – Gasoline* that discrimination could occur not only between exporting members, but also between exporting and importing members, and also that discrimination under the Article XX chapeau necessarily differed from that which might have already been found under other GATT provisions (*Id.* at paragraph 150).

The Appellate Body found that the US measure, although itself justified under Article XX(g), was applied in a manner that constituted unjustifiable discrimination (*Id.* at paragraph 176). Finding that the measure had an 'intended and actual coercive effect on . . . foreign governments' to adopt '*essentially the same* policies and enforcement practices as the US', the Appellate Body held that 'discrimination results not only when countries in which the same conditions prevail are differently treated, but also when the application of the measure at issue does not allow for any inquiry into the appropriateness of the regulatory program for the conditions prevailing in those exporting countries' (*Id.* at paragraphs 161, 165).

The Appellate Body found that the US' failure to pursue the conservation of sea turtles through bilateral or multilateral agreements with the complaining countries before resorting to a unilateral import ban constituted an additional incident of unjustifiable discrimination (*Id.* at paragraph 166). Several factors contributed to this finding, but perhaps weighing heaviest among them was the US' collaboration with certain countries from the Caribbean/Western Atlantic region in the Inter-American Convention for the Protection and Conservation of Sea Turtles (*Id.* at paragraph 169). The US' participation in this convention demonstrated not only 'that an alternative course of action was reasonably open to the US for securing the legitimate policy goal of its measure', but also that the US *had pursued* such alternative means with certain countries, but not with the complainants (*Id.* at paragraphs 171–172). The Appellate Body characterized these uneven negotiation efforts, as well as differential treatment in terms of technical assistance and lengths of 'phase-in' periods, as unjustifiable discrimination (*Id.* at paragraphs 172–176).

The Appellate Body also found that the application of the US measure constituted *arbitrary* discrimination. In the Appellate Body's view, the measure's 'rigidity and inflexibility' allowed for 'little or no flexibility in how officials make the determination for certification pursuant to these provisions' (*Id.* at paragraph 177). Furthermore, finding the US certification process to be informal and casual, and neither transparent nor predictable, the Appellate Body declared that 'exporting Members applying for certification whose applications are rejected are denied basic fairness and due process, and are discriminated against, vis-à-vis those Members that are granted certification' (*Id.* at paragraph 181).

Ultimately, although the US measure was provisionally justified under Article XX(g) as serving a legitimate environmental goal, its application was found to constitute arbitrary and unjustifiable discrimination between Members of the WTO under the chapeau, thus failing to be justified under Article XX (*Id.* at paragraph 186).

Excerpts

Report of the Appellate Body, *United States – Import Prohibition of Certain Shrimp and Shrimp Products ("Shrimp/Turtle I")*, WT/DS58/AB/R, adopted on 6 November 1998.

VI. Appraising Section 609 Under Article XX of the GATT 1994 [paras 111–186]

111. We turn to the second issue raised by the appellant, the United States, which is whether the Panel erred in finding that the measure at issue 76 constitutes unjustifiable discrimination between countries where the same conditions prevail and, thus, is not within the scope of measures permitted under Article XX of the GATT 1994.

A. The Panel's Findings and Interpretative Analysis [paras 112–124]

. . .

115. In the present case, the Panel did not expressly examine the ordinary meaning of the words of Article XX. The Panel disregarded the fact that the introductory clauses of Article XX speak of the "manner" in which measures sought to be justified are "applied". In *United States – Gasoline*, we pointed out that the chapeau of Article XX "by its express terms addresses, not so much the questioned measure or its specific contents as such, *but rather the manner in which that measure is applied*"[84] (emphasis added). The Panel did not inquire specifically into how the *application* of Section 609 constitutes "a means of arbitrary or unjustifiable discrimination between countries where the same conditions prevail, or a disguised restriction on international trade". What the Panel did, in purporting to examine the consistency of the measure with the chapeau of Article XX, was to focus repeatedly on the *design of the measure itself*. For instance, the Panel stressed that it was addressing "a particular situation where a Member has taken unilateral measures which, *by their nature*, could put the multilateral trading system at risk"[85] (emphasis added).

[84] Adopted 20 May 1996, WT/DS2/AB/R, p22.

[85] Panel Report, para 7.60. The Panel also stated, in paras 7.33–7.34 of the Panel Report:

> Pursuant to the chapeau of Article XX, a measure may discriminate, but not in an 'arbitrary' or 'unjustifiable' manner.
>
> We therefore move to consider *whether the US measure* conditioning market access on the adoption of certain conservation policies by the exporting Member *could be considered as 'unjustifiable' discrimination* . . . (emphasis added).

116. The general design of a measure, as distinguished from its application, is, however, to be examined in the course of determining whether that measure falls within one or another of the paragraphs of Article XX following the chapeau. The Panel failed to scrutinize the *immediate* context of the chapeau: i.e., paragraphs (a) to (j) of Article XX. Moreover, the Panel did not look into the object and purpose of the *chapeau of Article XX*. Rather, the Panel looked into the object and purpose of the *whole of the GATT 1994 and the WTO Agreement*, which object and purpose it described in an overly broad manner. Thus, the Panel arrived at the very broad formulation that measures which "undermine the WTO multilateral trading system"[86] must be regarded as "not within the scope of measures permitted under the chapeau of Article XX".[87] Maintaining, rather than undermining, the multilateral trading system is necessarily a fundamental and pervasive premise underlying the *WTO Agreement*; but it is not a right or an obligation, nor is it an interpretative rule which can be employed in the appraisal of a given measure under the chapeau of Article XX. In *United States – Gasoline*, we stated that it is "important to underscore that the purpose and object of the introductory clauses of Article XX is generally the prevention of '*abuse of the exceptions of [Article XX]*'"[88] (emphasis added). The Panel did not attempt to inquire into how the measure at stake was being *applied in such a manner* as to constitute *abuse or misuse of a given kind of exception*.

[86] See, for example, Panel Report, para 7.44.

[87] Panel Report, para 7.62.

[88] Adopted 20 May 1996, WT/DS2/AB/R, p22.

117. The above flaws in the Panel's analysis and findings flow almost naturally from the fact that the Panel disregarded the sequence of steps essential for carrying out such an analysis. The Panel defined its approach as first "determin[ing] whether the measure at issue satisfies the conditions contained in the chapeau."[89] If the Panel found that to be the case, it said that it "shall then examine whether the US measure is covered by the terms of Article XX(b) or (g)."[90] The Panel attempted to justify its interpretative approach in the following manner:

> *As mentioned by the Appellate Body in its report in the* Gasoline *case, in order for the justification of Article XX to be extended to a given measure, it must not only come under one or another of the particular exceptions – paragraphs (a) to (j) – listed under Article XX; it must also satisfy the requirements imposed by the opening clause of Article XX. We note that panels have in the past considered the specific paragraphs of Article XX before reviewing the applicability of the conditions contained in the chapeau. However,* as the conditions contained in the introductory provision apply to any of the paragraphs of Article XX, it seems equally appropriate to analyse first the introductory provision of Article XX[91] *(emphasis added).*

. . .

[89] Panel Report, para 7.29.
[90] *Ibid.*
[91] Panel Report, para 7.28.

118. In *United States – Gasoline*, we enunciated the appropriate method for applying Article XX of the GATT 1994:

> *In order that the justifying protection of Article XX may be extended to it, the measure at issue must not only come under one or another of the particular exceptions – paragraphs (a) to (j) – listed under Article XX; it must also satisfy the requirements imposed by the opening clauses of Article XX.* The analysis is, *in other words,* two-tiered: first, provisional justification by reason of characterization of the measure under XX(g); second, further appraisal of the same measure under the introductory clauses of Article XX[92] *(emphasis added).*

[92] Adopted 20 May 1996, WT/DS2/AB/R, p22.

119. The sequence of steps indicated above in the analysis of a claim of justification under Article XX reflects, not inadvertence or random choice, but rather the fundamental structure and logic of Article XX. The Panel appears to suggest, albeit indirectly, that following the indicated sequence of steps, or the inverse thereof, does not make any difference. To the Panel, reversing the sequence set out in *United States – Gasoline* "seems equally appropriate".[93] We do not agree.

[93] Panel Report, para 7.28.

120. The task of interpreting the chapeau so as to prevent the abuse or misuse of the specific exemptions provided for in Article XX is rendered very difficult, if indeed it remains possible at all, where the interpreter (like the Panel in this case) has not first identified and examined the specific exception threatened with abuse. The standards established in the chapeau are, moreover, necessarily broad in scope and reach: the prohibition of the *application* of a measure "in a manner which would constitute a means of *arbitrary* or *unjustifiable discrimination* between countries where the same conditions prevail" or "a *disguised restriction* on international trade" (emphasis added). When applied in a particular case, the actual contours and contents of these standards will vary as the kind of measure under examination varies. What is appropriately characterizable as "arbitrary discrimination" or "unjustifiable discrimination", or as a "disguised restriction on international trade" in respect of one category of measures, need not be so with respect to

another group or type of measures. The standard of "arbitrary discrimination", for example, under the chapeau may be different for a measure that purports to be necessary to protect public morals than for one relating to the products of prison labour.

121. The consequences of the interpretative approach adopted by the Panel are apparent in its findings. The Panel formulated a broad standard and a test for appraising measures sought to be justified under the chapeau; it is a standard or a test that finds no basis either in the text of the chapeau or in that of either of the two specific exceptions claimed by the United States. The Panel, in effect, constructed an *a priori* test that purports to define a category of measures which, *ratione materiae*, fall outside the justifying protection of Article XX's chapeau.[94] In the present case, the Panel found that the United States measure at stake fell within that class of excluded measures because Section 609 conditions access to the domestic shrimp market of the United States on the adoption by exporting countries of certain conservation policies prescribed by the United States. It appears to us, however, that conditioning access to a Member's domestic market on whether exporting Members comply with, or adopt, a policy or policies unilaterally prescribed by the importing Member may, to some degree, be a common aspect of measures falling within the scope of one or another of the exceptions (a) to (j) of Article XX. Paragraphs (a) to (j) comprise measures that are recognized as *exceptions to substantive obligations* established in the GATT 1994, because the domestic policies embodied in such measures have been recognized as important and legitimate in character. It is not necessary to assume that requiring from exporting countries compliance with, or adoption of, certain policies (although covered in principle by one or another of the exceptions) prescribed by the importing country, renders a measure *a priori* incapable of justification under Article XX. Such an interpretation renders most, if not all, of the specific exceptions of Article XX inutile, a result abhorrent to the principles of interpretation we are bound to apply.

[94] See, for example, Panel Report, para 7.50.

122. We hold that the findings of the Panel quoted in paragraph 112 above, and the interpretative analysis embodied therein, constitute error in legal interpretation and accordingly reverse them.

123. Having reversed the Panel's legal conclusion that the United States measure at issue "is not within the scope of measures permitted under the chapeau of Article XX",[95] we believe that it is our duty and our responsibility to complete the legal analysis in this case in order to determine whether Section 609 qualifies for justification under Article XX.

. . .

[95] Panel Report, para 7.62.

B. Article XX(g): Provisional Justification of Section 609 [paras 125–145]

125. In claiming justification for its measure, the United States primarily invokes Article XX(g). Justification under Article XX(b) is claimed only in the alternative; that is, the United States suggests that we should look at Article XX(b) only if we find that Section 609 does not fall within the ambit of Article XX(g).[99] We proceed, therefore, to the first tier of the analysis of Section 609 and to our consideration of whether it may be characterized as provisionally justified under the terms of Article XX(g).

[99] Additional submission of the United States, dated 17 August, 1998, para 5.

126. Paragraph (g) of Article XX covers measures:

> *relating to the conservation of exhaustible natural resources if such measures are made effective in conjunction with restrictions on domestic production or consumption;*

1. "Exhaustible Natural Resources"

127. We begin with the threshold question of whether Section 609 is a measure concerned with the conservation of "exhaustible natural resources" within the meaning of Article XX(g). The Panel, of course, with its "chapeau-down" approach, did not make a finding on whether the sea turtles that Section 609 is designed to conserve constitute "exhaustible natural resources" for purposes of Article XX(g). In the proceedings before the Panel, however, the parties to the dispute argued this issue vigorously and extensively. India, Pakistan and Thailand contended that a "reasonable interpretation" of the term "exhaustible" is that the term refers to "finite resources such as minerals, rather than biological or renewable resources".[100] In their view, such finite resources were exhaustible "because there was a limited supply which could and would be depleted unit for unit as the resources were consumed".[101] Moreover, they argued, if "all" natural resources were considered to be exhaustible, the term "exhaustible" would become superfluous.[102] They also referred to the drafting history of Article XX(g), and, in particular, to the mention of minerals, such as manganese, in the context of arguments made by some delegations that "export restrictions" should be permitted for the preservation of scarce natural resources.[103] For its part, Malaysia added that sea turtles, being living creatures, could only be considered under Article XX(b), since Article XX(g) was meant for "nonliving exhaustible natural resources".[104] It followed, according to Malaysia, that the United States cannot invoke both the Article XX(b) and the Article XX(g) exceptions simultaneously.[105]

[100] Panel Report, para 3.237.
[101] *Ibid.*
[102] *Ibid.*
[103] Panel Report, para 3.238. India, Pakistan and Thailand referred, *inter alia,* to E/PC/T/C.II/QR/PV/5, 18 November 1946, p79.
[104] Panel Report, para 3.240.
[105] *Ibid.*

128. We are not convinced by these arguments. Textually, Article XX(g) is *not* limited to the conservation of "mineral" or "non-living" natural resources. The complainants' principal argument is rooted in the notion that "living" natural resources are "renewable" and therefore cannot be "exhaustible" natural resources. We do not believe that "exhaustible" natural resources and "renewable" natural resources are mutually exclusive. One lesson that modern biological sciences teach us is that living species, though in principle, capable of reproduction and, in that sense, "renewable", are in certain circumstances indeed susceptible of depletion, exhaustion and extinction, frequently because of human activities. Living resources are just as "finite" as petroleum, iron ore and other non-living resources.[106]

[106] We note, for example, that the World Commission on Environment and Development stated: "The planet's species are under stress. There is growing scientific consensus that species are disappearing at rates never before witnessed on the planet." World Commission on Environment and Development, *Our Common Future* (Oxford University Press, 1987), p13.

. . .

132. We turn next to the issue of whether the living natural resources sought to be conserved by the measure are "exhaustible" under Article XX(g). That this element is present in respect of the five species of sea turtles here involved appears to be conceded by all the participants and third participants in this case. The exhaustibility of sea turtles would in fact have been very difficult to controvert since all of the seven recognized species of sea turtles are today listed in Appendix 1 of the Convention on International Trade in Endangered Species of Wild Fauna and Flora ("CITES"). The list in Appendix 1 includes "all species *threatened with extinction* which are or may be affected by trade"[117] (emphasis added).

[117] CITES, Article II.1.

133. Finally, we observe that sea turtles are highly migratory animals, passing in and out of waters subject to the rights of jurisdiction of various coastal states and the high seas. . . The sea turtle species here at stake, i.e., covered by Section 609, are all known to occur in waters over which the United States exercises jurisdiction.[119] Of course, it is not claimed that *all* populations of these species migrate to, or traverse, at one time or another, waters subject to United States jurisdiction. Neither the appellant nor any of the appellees claims any rights of exclusive ownership over the sea turtles, at least not while they are swimming freely in their natural habitat – the oceans. We do not pass upon the question of whether there is an implied jurisdictional limitation in Article XX(g), and if so, the nature or extent of that limitation. We note only that in the specific circumstances of the case before us, there is a sufficient nexus between the migratory and endangered marine populations involved and the United States for purposes of Article XX(g).

[119] See Panel Report, para 2.6. The 1987 Regulations, 52 Fed. Reg. 24244, 29 June 1987, identified five species of sea turtles as occurring within the areas concerned and thus falling under the regulations: loggerhead (Caretta caretta), Kemp's ridley (*Lepidochelys kempi*), green (*Chelonia mydas*), leatherback (*Dermochelys coriacea*) and hawksbill (*Eretmochelys imbricata*). Section 609 refers to "those species of sea turtles the conservation of which is the subject of regulations promulgated by the Secretary of Commerce on 29 June, 1987."

134. For all the foregoing reasons, we find that the sea turtles here involved constitute "exhaustible natural resources" for purposes of Article XX(g) of the GATT 1994.

. . .

2. "Relating to the Conservation of [Exhaustible Natural Resources]"

137. In the present case, we must examine the relationship between the general structure and design of the measure here at stake, Section 609, and the policy goal it purports to serve, that is, the conservation of sea turtles.

138. Section 609(b)(1) imposes an import ban on shrimp that have been harvested with commercial fishing technology which may adversely affect sea turtles. This provision is designed to influence countries to adopt national regulatory programs requiring the use of TEDs by their shrimp fishermen. In this connection, it is important to note that the general structure and design of Section 609 *cum* implementing guidelines is fairly narrowly focused. There are two basic exemptions from the import ban, both of which relate clearly and directly to the policy goal of conserving sea turtles. First, Section 609, as elaborated in the 1996 Guidelines, excludes from the import ban shrimp harvested "under conditions that do not adversely affect sea turtles". Thus, the measure, by its terms, excludes from the import ban: aquaculture shrimp; shrimp species (such as *pandalid* shrimp) harvested in water areas where sea turtles do not normally occur; and shrimp harvested exclusively by artisanal methods, even from non-certified countries.[124] The harvesting of such shrimp clearly does not affect sea turtles. Second, under Section 609(b)(2), the measure exempts from the import ban shrimp caught in waters subject to the jurisdiction of certified countries.

[124] See the 1996 Guidelines, p17343.

139. There are two types of certification for countries under Section 609(b)(2). First, under Section 609(b)(2)(C), a country may be certified as having a fishing environment that does not pose a threat of incidental taking of sea turtles in the course of commercial shrimp trawl harvesting. There is no risk, or only a negligible risk, that sea turtles will be harmed by shrimp trawling in such an environment.

140. The second type of certification is provided by Section 609(b)(2)(A) and (B). Under these provisions, as further elaborated in the 1996 Guidelines, a country wishing to export shrimp to the United States is required to adopt a regulatory program that is comparable to that of the United States program and to have a rate of incidental take of sea turtles that is comparable to the average rate of United States' vessels. This is, essentially, a requirement that a country adopt a regulatory program requiring the use of

TEDs by commercial shrimp trawling vessels in areas where there is a likelihood of intercepting sea turtles.[125] This requirement is, in our view, directly connected with the policy of conservation of sea turtles. It is undisputed among the participants, and recognized by the experts consulted by the Panel,[126] that the harvesting of shrimp by commercial shrimp trawling vessels with mechanical retrieval devices in waters where shrimp and sea turtles coincide is a significant cause of sea turtle mortality. Moreover, the Panel did "not question . . . the fact generally acknowledged by the experts that TEDs, when properly installed and adapted to the local area, would be an effective tool for the preservation of sea turtles."[127]

[125] See the 1996 Guidelines, p17343.
[126] For example, Panel Report, paras 5.91–5.118.
[127] Panel Report, para 7.60, footnote 674.

141. In its general design and structure, therefore, Section 609 is not a simple, blanket prohibition of the importation of shrimp imposed without regard to the consequences (or lack thereof) of the mode of harvesting employed upon the incidental capture and mortality of sea turtles. Focusing on the design of the measure here at stake,[128] it appears to us that Section 609, *cum* implementing guidelines, is not disproportionately wide in its scope and reach in relation to the policy objective of protection and conservation of sea turtle species. The means are, in principle, reasonably related to the ends. The means and ends relationship between Section 609 and the legitimate policy of conserving an exhaustible, and, in fact, endangered species, is observably a close and real one, a relationship that is every bit as substantial as that which we found in *United States – Gasoline* between the EPA baseline establishment rules and the conservation of clean air in the United States.

[128] We focus on the *application* of the measure below, in Section VI.C of this Report.

142. In our view, therefore, Section 609 is a measure "relating to" the conservation of an exhaustible natural resource within the meaning of Article XX(g) of the GATT 1994.

3. "If Such Measures are Made Effective in conjunction with Restrictions on Domestic Production or Consumption"

143. In *United States – Gasoline*, we held that the above-captioned clause of Article XX(g),

> *. . . is appropriately read as a requirement that the measures concerned impose restrictions, not just in respect of imported gasoline but also with respect to domestic gasoline. The clause is a requirement of* even-handedness *in the imposition of restrictions, in the name of conservation, upon the production or consumption of exhaustible natural resources.*[129]

In this case, we need to examine whether the restrictions imposed by Section 609 with respect to imported shrimp are also imposed in respect of shrimp caught by United States shrimp trawl vessels.

[129] Adopted 20 May 1996, WT/DS2/AB/R, pp20–21.

144. We earlier noted that Section 609, enacted in 1989, addresses the mode of harvesting of imported shrimp only. However, two years earlier, in 1987, the United States issued regulations pursuant to the Endangered Species Act requiring all United States shrimp trawl vessels to use approved TEDs, or to restrict the duration of tow-times, in specified areas where there was significant incidental mortality of sea turtles in shrimp trawls.[130] These regulations became fully effective in 1990 and were later modified. They now require United States shrimp trawlers to use approved TEDs "in areas and at times when there is a likelihood of intercepting sea turtles",[131] with certain limited exceptions.[132] Penalties for violation of the Endangered Species Act, or the regulations issued thereunder, include civil and criminal sanctions.[133]

The United States government currently relies on monetary sanctions and civil penalties for enforcement.[134] The government has the ability to seize shrimp catch from trawl vessels fishing in United States waters and has done so in cases of egregious violations.[135] We believe that, in principle, Section 609 is an even-handed measure.

[130] 52 Fed. Reg. 24244, 29 June 1987.
[131] See the 1996 Guidelines, p17343.
[132] According to the 1996 Guidelines, p17343, the exceptions are: vessels equipped exclusively with certain special types of gear; vessels whose nets are retrieved exclusively by manual rather than mechanical means; and, in exceptional circumstances, where the National Marine Fisheries Service determines that the use of TEDs would be impracticable because of special environmental conditions, vessels are permitted to restrict tow-times instead of using TEDs.
[133] Endangered Species Act, Section 11.
[134] Statement by the United States at the oral hearing.
[135] Statement by the United States at the oral hearing.

145. Accordingly, we hold that Section 609 is a measure made effective in conjunction with the restrictions on domestic harvesting of shrimp, as required by Article XX(g).

C. The Introductory Clauses of Article XX: Characterizing Section 609 under the Chapeau's Standards [paras 146–186]

146. As noted earlier, the United States invokes Article XX(b) only if and to the extent that we hold that Section 609 falls outside the scope of Article XX(g). Having found that Section 609 does come within the terms of Article XX(g), it is not, therefore, necessary to analyze the measure in terms of Article XX(b).

147. Although provisionally justified under Article XX(g), Section 609, if it is ultimately to be justified as an exception under Article XX, must also satisfy the requirements of the introductory clauses – the "chapeau" – of Article XX, that is,

Article XX

General Exceptions

> *Subject to the requirement that such measures are* not applied in a manner which would constitute a means of arbitrary or unjustifiable discrimination between countries where the same conditions prevail, *or* a disguised restriction on international trade, *nothing in this Agreement shall be construed to prevent the adoption or enforcement by any Member of measures (emphasis added).*
>
> *We turn, hence, to the task of appraising Section 609, and specifically the manner in which it is applied under the chapeau of Article XX; that is, to the second part of the two-tier analysis required under Article XX.*

1. General Considerations

. . .

150. We commence the second tier of our analysis with an examination of the ordinary meaning of the words of the chapeau. The precise language of the chapeau requires that a measure not be applied in a manner which would constitute a means of "arbitrary or unjustifiable discrimination between countries where the same conditions prevail" or a "disguised restriction on international trade". There are three standards contained in the chapeau: first, arbitrary discrimination between countries where the same conditions prevail; second, unjustifiable discrimination between countries where the same conditions prevail; and third, a disguised restriction on international trade. In order for a measure to be applied in a manner which would constitute "arbitrary or unjustifiable discrimination between countries where the

same conditions prevail", three elements must exist. First, the application of the measure must result in *discrimination*. As we stated in *United States – Gasoline*, the nature and quality of this discrimination is different from the discrimination in the treatment of products which was already found to be inconsistent with one of the substantive obligations of the GATT 1994, such as Articles I, III or XI.[138] Second, the discrimination must be *arbitrary* or *unjustifiable* in character. We will examine this element of *arbitrariness* or *unjustifiability* in detail below. Third, this discrimination must occur *between countries where the same conditions prevail*. In *United States – Gasoline*, we accepted the assumption of the participants in that appeal that such discrimination could occur not only between different exporting Members, but also between exporting Members and the importing Member concerned.[139] Thus, the standards embodied in the language of the chapeau are not only different from the requirements of Article XX(g); they are also different from the standard used in determining that Section 609 is violative of the substantive rules of Article XI:1 of the GATT 1994.

[138] In *United States – Gasoline,* adopted 20 May 1996, WT/DS2/AB/R, p. 23, we stated: "The provisions of the chapeau cannot logically refer to the same standard(s) by which a violation of a substantive rule has been determined to have occurred."
[139] *Ibid.,* pp23–24.

151. In *United States – Gasoline*, we stated that "the purpose and object of the introductory clauses of Article XX is generally the prevention of 'abuse of the exceptions of [Article XX]'".[140] We went on to say that:

> *. . . The chapeau is animated by the principle that while the exceptions of Article XX may be invoked as a matter of legal right, they should not be so applied as to frustrate or defeat the legal obligations of the holder of the right under the substantive rules of the* General Agreement. *If those exceptions are not to be abused or misused, in other words, the measures falling within the particular exceptions must be applied reasonably, with due regard both to the legal duties of the party claiming the exception and the legal rights of the other parties concerned.*[141]

[140] *Ibid.,* p22.
[141] *Ibid.*

152. At the end of the Uruguay Round, negotiators fashioned an appropriate preamble for the new *WTO Agreement*, which strengthened the multilateral trading system by establishing an international organization, *inter alia*, to facilitate the implementation, administration and operation, and to further the objectives, of that Agreement and the other agreements resulting from that Round.[142] In recognition of the importance of continuity with the previous GATT system, negotiators used the preamble of the GATT 1947 as the template for the preamble of the new *WTO Agreement*. Those negotiators evidently believed, however, that the objective of "full use of the resources of the world" set forth in the preamble of the GATT 1947 was no longer appropriate to the world trading system of the 1990s. As a result, they decided to qualify the original objectives of the GATT 1947 with the following words:

> *... while allowing for the optimal use of the world's resources in accordance with the objective of sustainable development, seeking both to protect and preserve the environment and to enhance the means for doing so in a manner consistent with their respective needs and concerns at different levels of economic development, . . .*[143]

[142] WTO Agreement, Article III:1.
[143] Preamble of the WTO Agreement, first paragraph.

153. We note once more[144] that this language demonstrates a recognition by WTO negotiators that optimal use of the world's resources should be made in accordance with the objective of sustainable development. As this preambular language reflects the intentions of negotiators of the *WTO Agreement*, we believe it must add colour, texture and shading to our interpretation of the agreements annexed to the *WTO Agreement*, in this case, the GATT 1994. We have already observed that Article XX(g) of the GATT 1994 is appropriately read with the perspective embodied in the above preamble.[145]

[144] *Supra,* para 129.
[145] *Supra,* para 131.

154. We also note that since this preambular language was negotiated, certain other developments have occurred which help to elucidate the objectives of WTO Members with respect to the relationship between trade and the environment. The most significant, in our view, was the Decision of Ministers at Marrakesh to establish a permanent Committee on Trade and Environment (the "CTE"). In their Decision on Trade and Environment, Ministers expressed their intentions, in part, as follows:

> . . . Considering *that there should not be, nor need be, any policy contradiction between upholding and safeguarding an open, non-discriminatory and equitable multilateral trading system on the one hand, and acting for the protection of the environment, and the promotion of sustainable development on the other . . .*[146]

In this Decision, Ministers took "note" of the Rio Declaration on Environment and Development,[147] Agenda 21,[148] and "its follow-up in the GATT, as reflected in the statement of the Council of Representatives to the CONTRACTING PARTIES at their 48th Session in 1992. . ."[149] We further note that this Decision also set out the following terms of reference for the CTE:

(a) to identify the relationship between trade measures and environmental measures, in order to promote sustainable development;
(b) to make appropriate recommendations on whether any modifications of the provisions of the multilateral trading system are required, compatible with the open, equitable and non-discriminatory nature of the system, as regards, in particular:
   - the need for rules to enhance positive interaction between trade and environmental measures, for the promotion of sustainable development, with special consideration to the needs of developing countries, in particular those of the least developed among them; and
   - the avoidance of protectionist trade measures, and the adherence to effective multilateral disciplines to ensure responsiveness of the multilateral trading system to environmental objectives set forth in Agenda 21 and the Rio Declaration, in particular Principle 12; and
   - surveillance of trade measures used for environmental purposes, of trade-related aspects of environmental measures which have significant trade affects, and of effective implementation of the multilateral disciplines governing those measures.[150]

[146] Preamble of the Decision on Trade and Environment.
[147] We note that Principle 3 of the Rio Declaration on Environment and Development states: "The right to development must be fulfilled so as to equitably meet developmental and environmental needs of present and future generations." Principle 4 of the Rio Declaration on Environment and Development states that: "In order to achieve sustainable development, environmental protection shall constitute an integral part of the development process and cannot be considered in isolation from it."
[148] Agenda 21 is replete with references to the shared view that economic development and the preservation and protection should be mutually supportive. For example, paragraph 2.3(b) of Agenda 21 states: "The international economy should provide a supportive international climate for achieving environment and development goals by . . . [m]aking trade and environment mutually supportive. . ." Similarly, paragraph 2.9(d) states that an "objective" of governments should be: "To promote and support policies, domestic and international, that make economic growth

and environmental protection mutually supportive."
[149] Preamble of the Decision on Trade and Environment.
[150] Decision on Trade and Environment.

155. With these instructions, the General Council of the WTO established the CTE in 1995, and the CTE began its important work. Pending any specific recommendations by the CTE to WTO Members on the issues raised in its terms of reference, and in the absence up to now of any agreed amendments or modifications to the substantive provisions of the GATT 1994 and the *WTO Agreement* generally, we must fulfil our responsibility in this specific case, which is to interpret the existing language of the chapeau of Article XX by examining its ordinary meaning, in light of its context and object and purpose in order to determine whether the United States measure at issue qualifies for justification under Article XX. It is proper for us to take into account, as part of the context of the chapeau, the specific language of the preamble to the *WTO Agreement*, which, we have said, gives colour, texture and shading to the rights and obligations of Members under the *WTO Agreement*, generally, and under the GATT 1994, in particular.

. . .

159. The task of interpreting and applying the chapeau is, hence, essentially the delicate one of locating and marking out a line of equilibrium between the right of a Member to invoke an exception under Article XX and the rights of the other Members under varying substantive provisions (e.g., Article XI) of the GATT 1994, so that neither of the competing rights will cancel out the other and thereby distort and nullify or impair the balance of rights and obligations constructed by the Members themselves in that Agreement. The location of the line of equilibrium, as expressed in the chapeau, is not fixed and unchanging; the line moves as the kind and the shape of the measures at stake vary and as the facts making up specific cases differ.

160. With these general considerations in mind, we address now the issue of whether the *application* of the United States measure, although the measure itself falls within the terms of Article XX(g), nevertheless constitutes "a means of arbitrary or unjustifiable discrimination between countries where the same conditions prevail" or "a disguised restriction on international trade". We address, in other words, whether the application of this measure constitutes an abuse or misuse of the provisional justification made available by Article XX(g). We note, preliminarily, that the application of a measure may be characterized as amounting to an abuse or misuse of an exception of Article XX not only when the detailed operating provisions of the measure prescribe the arbitrary or unjustifiable activity, but also where a measure, otherwise fair and just on its face, is actually applied in an arbitrary or unjustifiable manner. The standards of the chapeau, in our view, project both substantive and procedural requirements.

2. *"Unjustifiable Discrimination"*

161. We scrutinize first whether Section 609 has been applied in a manner constituting "unjustifiable discrimination between countries where the same conditions prevail". Perhaps the most conspicuous flaw in this measure's application relates to its intended and actual coercive effect on the specific policy decisions made by foreign governments, Members of the WTO. Section 609, in its application, is, in effect, an economic embargo which requires *all other exporting Members*, if they wish to exercise their GATT rights, to adopt *essentially the same* policy (together with an approved enforcement program) as that applied to, and enforced on, United States domestic shrimp trawlers. As enacted by the Congress of the United States, the *statutory* provisions of Section 609(b)(2)(A) and (B) do not, in themselves, *require* that other WTO Members adopt *essentially the same* policies and enforcement practices as the United States. Viewed alone, the statute appears to permit a degree of discretion or flexibility in how the standards for determining comparability might be applied, in practice, to other countries.[158] However, any flexibility that may have been intended by Congress when it enacted the statutory provision has been effectively eliminated in the implementation of that policy through the 1996 Guidelines promulgated by the Department of State and through the practice of the administrators in making certification determinations.

[158] Pursuant to Section 609(b)(2), a harvesting nation may be certified, and thus exempted from the import ban, if:

(A) the government of the harvesting nation has provided documentary evidence of the adoption of a program governing the incidental taking of such sea turtles in the course of such harvesting that is comparable to that of the United States; and

(B) the average rate of that incidental taking by vessels of the harvesting nation is comparable to the average rate of incidental taking of sea turtles by United States vessels in the course of such harvesting . . .

162. According to the 1996 Guidelines, certification "shall be made" under Section 609(b)(2)(A) and (B) if an exporting country's program includes a requirement that all commercial shrimp trawl vessels operating in waters in which there is a likelihood of intercepting sea turtles use, at all times, TEDs comparable in effectiveness to those used in the United States.[159] Under these Guidelines, any exceptions to the requirement of the use of TEDs must be comparable to those of the United States program.[160] Furthermore, the harvesting country must have in place a "credible enforcement effort".[161] The language in the 1996 Guidelines is mandatory: certification "shall be made" if these conditions are fulfilled. However, we understand that these rules are also applied in an *exclusive* manner. That is, the 1996 Guidelines specify the *only* way that a harvesting country's regulatory program can be deemed "comparable" to the United States' program, and, therefore, they define the *only* way that a harvesting nation can be certified under Section 609(b)(2)(A) and (B). Although the 1996 Guidelines state that, in making a comparability determination, the Department of State "shall also take into account other measures the harvesting nation undertakes to protect sea turtles,"[162] in practice, the competent government officials only look to see whether there is a regulatory program requiring the use of TEDs or one that comes within one of the extremely limited exceptions available to United States shrimp trawl vessels.[163]

[159] 1996 Guidelines, p17344.

[160] As already noted, these exceptions are extremely limited and currently include only: vessels equipped exclusively with certain special types of gear; vessels whose nets are retrieved exclusively by manual rather than mechanical means; and, in exceptional circumstances, where the National Marine Fisheries Services determines that the use of TEDs would be impracticable because of special environmental conditions, vessels are permitted to restrict tow-times instead of using TEDs. See the 1996 Guidelines, p17343. In the oral hearing, the United States informed us that the exception for restricted tow-times is no longer available.

[161] 1996 Guidelines, p17344.

[162] *Ibid.*

[163] Statements by the United States at the oral hearing.

163. The actual *application* of the measure, through the implementation of the 1996 Guidelines and the regulatory practice of administrators, *requires* other WTO Members to adopt a regulatory program that is not merely *comparable*, but rather *essentially the same*, as that applied to the United States shrimp trawl vessels. Thus, the effect of the application of Section 609 is to establish a rigid and unbending standard by which United States officials determine whether or not countries will be certified, thus granting or refusing other countries the right to export shrimp to the United States. Other specific policies and measures that an exporting country may have adopted for the protection and conservation of sea turtles are not taken into account, in practice, by the administrators making the comparability determination.[164]

[164] Statement by the United States at the oral hearing.

164. We understand that the United States also applies a uniform standard throughout its territory, regardless of the particular conditions existing in certain parts of the country. The United States requires the use of approved TEDs at all times by domestic, commercial shrimp trawl vessels operating in waters where there is any likelihood that they may interact with sea turtles, regardless of the actual incidence of sea turtles in those waters, the species of those sea turtles, or other differences or disparities that may exist in different parts of the United States. It may be quite acceptable for a government, in adopting and implementing a domestic policy, to adopt a single standard applicable to all its citizens throughout that

country. However, it is not acceptable, in international trade relations, for one WTO Member to use an economic embargo to *require* other Members to adopt essentially the same comprehensive regulatory program, to achieve a certain policy goal, as that in force within that Member's territory, *without* taking into consideration different conditions which may occur in the territories of those other Members.

165. Furthermore, when this dispute was before the Panel and before us, the United States did not permit imports of shrimp harvested by commercial shrimp trawl vessels using TEDs comparable in effectiveness to those required in the United States if those shrimp originated in waters of countries not certified under Section 609. In other words, *shrimp caught using methods identical to those employed in the United States* have been excluded from the United States market solely because they have been caught in waters of *countries that have not been certified by the United States*. The resulting situation is difficult to reconcile with the declared policy objective of protecting and conserving sea turtles. This suggests to us that this measure, in its application, is more concerned with effectively influencing WTO Members to adopt essentially the same comprehensive regulatory regime as that applied by the United States to its domestic shrimp trawlers, even though many of those Members may be differently situated. We believe that discrimination results not only when countries in which the same conditions prevail are differently treated, but also when the application of the measure at issue does not allow for any inquiry into the appropriateness of the regulatory program for the conditions prevailing in those exporting countries.

166. Another aspect of the application of Section 609 that bears heavily in any appraisal of justifiable or unjustifiable discrimination is the failure of the United States to engage the appellees, as well as other Members exporting shrimp to the United States, in serious, across-the-board negotiations with the objective of concluding bilateral or multilateral agreements for the protection and conservation of sea turtles, before enforcing the import prohibition against the shrimp exports of those other Members.

. . .

167. *A propos* this failure to have prior consistent recourse to diplomacy as an instrument of environmental protection policy, which produces discriminatory impacts on countries exporting shrimp to the United States with which no international agreements are reached or even seriously attempted, a number of points must be made. First, the Congress of the United States expressly recognized the importance of securing international agreements for the protection and conservation of the sea turtle species in enacting this law. . . Apart from the negotiation of the Inter-American Convention for the Protection and Conservation of Sea Turtles[166] (the "Inter-American Convention") which concluded in 1996, the record before the Panel does not indicate any serious, substantial efforts to carry out these express directions of Congress.[167]

[166] First written submission of the United States to the Panel, Exhibit AA.
[167] Panel Report, para 7.56.

168. Second, the protection and conservation of highly migratory species of sea turtles, that is, the very policy objective of the measure, demands concerted and cooperative efforts on the part of the many countries whose waters are traversed in the course of recurrent sea turtle migrations. The need for, and the appropriateness of, such efforts have been recognized in the WTO itself as well as in a significant number of other international instruments and declarations.

. . .

169. Third, the United States did negotiate and conclude one regional international agreement for the protection and conservation of sea turtles: The Inter-American Convention.

. . .

170. The juxtaposition of (a) the *consensual* undertakings to put in place regulations providing for, *inter alia*, use of TEDs *jointly determined* to be suitable for a particular party's maritime areas, with (b) the reaffirmation of the parties' obligations under the *WTO Agreement*, including the *Agreement on Technical Barriers to Trade* and Article XI of the GATT 1994, suggests that the parties to the Inter-American Convention together marked out the equilibrium line to which we referred earlier. The Inter-American Convention demonstrates the conviction of its signatories, including the United States, that consensual and multilateral

procedures are available and feasible for the establishment of programs for the conservation of sea turtles. Moreover, the Inter-American Convention emphasizes the continuing validity and significance of Article XI of the GATT 1994, and of the obligations of the *WTO Agreement* generally, in maintaining the balance of rights and obligations under the *WTO Agreement* among the signatories of that Convention.

171. The Inter-American Convention thus provides convincing demonstration that an alternative course of action was reasonably open to the United States for securing the legitimate policy goal of its measure, a course of action other than the unilateral and non-consensual procedures of the import prohibition under Section 609. It is relevant to observe that an import prohibition is, ordinarily, the heaviest "weapon" in a Member's armoury of trade measures. The record does not, however, show that serious efforts were made by the United States to negotiate similar agreements with any other country or group of countries before (and, as far as the record shows, after) Section 609 was enforced on a world-wide basis on 1 May 1996. Finally, the record also does not show that the appellant, the United States, attempted to have recourse to such international mechanisms as exist to achieve cooperative efforts to protect and conserve sea turtles[174] before imposing the import ban.

[174] While the United States is a party to CITES, it did not make any attempt to raise the issue of sea turtle mortality due to shrimp trawling in the CITES Standing Committee as a subject requiring concerted action by states. In this context, we note that the United States, for example, has not signed the Convention on the Conservation of Migratory Species of Wild Animals or UNCLOS, and has not ratified the Convention on Biological Diversity.

172. Clearly, the United States negotiated seriously with some, but not with other Members (including the appellees), that export shrimp to the United States. The effect is plainly discriminatory and, in our view, unjustifiable. The unjustifiable nature of this discrimination emerges clearly when we consider the cumulative effects of the failure of the United States to pursue negotiations for establishing consensual means of protection and conservation of the living marine resources here involved, notwithstanding the explicit statutory direction in Section 609 itself to initiate negotiations as soon as possible for the development of bilateral and multilateral agreements.[175] The principal consequence of this failure may be seen in the resulting unilateralism evident in the application of Section 609. As we have emphasized earlier, the policies relating to the necessity for use of particular kinds of TEDs in various maritime areas, and the operating details of these policies, are all shaped by the Department of State, without the participation of the exporting Members. The system and processes of certification are established and administered by the United States agencies alone. The decision-making involved in the grant, denial or withdrawal of certification to the exporting Members, is, accordingly, also unilateral. The unilateral character of the application of Section 609 heightens the disruptive and discriminatory influence of the import prohibition and underscores its unjustifiability.

[175] Section 609(a).

173. The application of Section 609, through the implementing guidelines together with administrative practice, also resulted in other differential treatment among various countries desiring certification. Under the 1991 and 1993 Guidelines, to be certifiable, fourteen countries in the wider Caribbean/western Atlantic region had to commit themselves to require the use of TEDs on all commercial shrimp trawling vessels by 1 May 1994. These fourteen countries had a "phase-in" period of three years during which their respective shrimp trawling sectors could adjust to the requirement of the use of TEDs. With respect to all other countries exporting shrimp to the United States (including the appellees, India, Malaysia, Pakistan and Thailand), on 29 December 1995, the United States Court of International Trade directed the Department of State to apply the import ban on a world-wide basis not later than 1 May 1996.[176] On 19 April 1996, the 1996 Guidelines were issued by the Department of State bringing shrimp harvested in *all* foreign countries within the scope of Section 609, effective 1 May 1996. Thus, all countries that were not among the fourteen in the wider Caribbean/western Atlantic region had only four months to implement the requirement of compulsory use of TEDs. We acknowledge that the greatly differing periods for putting

into operation the requirement for use of TEDs resulted from decisions of the Court of International Trade. Even so, this does not relieve the United States of the legal consequences of the discriminatory impact of the decisions of that Court. The United States, like all other Members of the WTO and of the general community of states, bears responsibility for acts of all its departments of government, including its judiciary.[177]

[176] *Earth Island Institute* v. *Warren Christopher,* 913 F. Supp. 559 (CIT 1995).
[177] See *United States – Gasoline,* adopted 20 May 1996, WT/DS2/AB/R, p28. Also see, for example, Jennings and Watts (eds), *Oppenheim's International Law,* 9th ed., Vol. I (Longman's 1992), p545; and I. Brownlie, *Principles of Public International Law,* 4th ed (Clarendon Press, 1990), p450.

. . .

175. Differing treatment of different countries desiring certification is also observable in the differences in the levels of effort made by the United States in transferring the required TED technology to specific countries. Far greater efforts to transfer that technology successfully were made to certain exporting countries – basically the fourteen wider Caribbean/western Atlantic countries cited earlier – than to other exporting countries, including the appellees.[179] The level of these efforts is probably related to the length of the "phase-in" periods granted – the longer the "phase-in" period, the higher the possible level of efforts at technology transfer. Because compliance with the requirements of certification realistically assumes successful TED technology transfer, low or merely nominal efforts at achieving that transfer will, in all probability, result in fewer countries being able to satisfy the certification requirements under Section 609, within the very limited "phase-in" periods allowed them.

[179] Response by the United States to questioning by the Panel; statements by the United States at the oral hearing.

176. When the foregoing differences in the means of application of Section 609 to various shrimp exporting countries are considered in their cumulative effect, we find, and so hold, that those differences in treatment constitute "unjustifiable discrimination" between exporting countries desiring certification in order to gain access to the United States shrimp market within the meaning of the chapeau of Article XX.

3. "Arbitrary Discrimination"

177. We next consider whether Section 609 has been applied in a manner constituting "arbitrary discrimination between countries where the same conditions prevail". We have already observed that Section 609, in its application, imposes a single, rigid and unbending requirement that countries applying for certification under Section 609(b)(2)(A) and (B) adopt a comprehensive regulatory program that is essentially the same as the United States' program, without inquiring into the appropriateness of that program for the conditions prevailing in the exporting countries.[180] Furthermore, there is little or no flexibility in how officials make the determination for certification pursuant to these provisions.[181] In our view, this rigidity and inflexibility also constitute "arbitrary discrimination" within the meaning of the chapeau.

[180] *Supra,* paragraphs 161–164.
[181] In the oral hearing, the United States stated that "as a policy matter, the United States government believes that all governments should require the use of turtle excluder devices on all shrimp trawler boats that operate in areas where there is a likelihood of intercepting sea turtles" and that "when it comes to shrimp trawling, we know of only one way of effectively protecting sea turtles and that is through TEDs".

. . .

181. The certification processes followed by the United States thus appear to be singularly informal and casual, and to be conducted in a manner such that these processes could result in the negation of rights of Members. There appears to be no way that exporting Members can be certain whether the terms of Section 609, in particular, the 1996 Guidelines, are being applied in a fair and just manner by the appropriate governmental agencies of the United States. It appears to us that, effectively, exporting Members applying

for certification whose applications are rejected are denied basic fairness and due process, and are discriminated against, *vis-à-vis* those Members which are granted certification.

. . .

184. We find, accordingly, that the United States measure is applied in a manner which amounts to a means not just of "unjustifiable discrimination", but also of "arbitrary discrimination" between countries where the same conditions prevail, contrary to the requirements of the chapeau of Article XX. The measure, therefore, is not entitled to the justifying protection of Article XX of the GATT 1994. Having made this finding, it is not necessary for us to examine also whether the United States measure is applied in a manner that constitutes a "disguised restriction on international trade" under the chapeau of Article XX.

185. In reaching these conclusions, we wish to underscore what we have *not* decided in this appeal. We have *not* decided that the protection and preservation of the environment is of no significance to the Members of the WTO. Clearly, it is. We have *not* decided that the sovereign nations that are Members of the WTO cannot adopt effective measures to protect endangered species, such as sea turtles. Clearly, they can and should. And we have *not* decided that sovereign states should not act together bilaterally, plurilaterally or multilaterally, either within the WTO or in other international fora, to protect endangered species or to otherwise protect the environment. Clearly, they should and do.

186. What we *have* decided in this appeal is simply this: although the measure of the United States in dispute in this appeal serves an environmental objective that is recognized as legitimate under paragraph (g) of Article XX of the GATT 1994, this measure has been applied by the United States in a manner which constitutes arbitrary and unjustifiable discrimination between Members of the WTO, contrary to the requirements of the chapeau of Article XX. For all of the specific reasons outlined in this Report, this measure does not qualify for the exemption that Article XX of the GATT 1994 affords to measures which serve certain recognized, legitimate environmental purposes but which, at the same time, are not applied in a manner that constitutes a means of arbitrary or unjustifiable discrimination between countries where the same conditions prevail or a disguised restriction on international trade. As we emphasized in *United States – Gasoline*, WTO Members are free to adopt their own policies aimed at protecting the environment as long as, in so doing, they fulfill their obligations and respect the rights of other Members under the *WTO Agreement*.[192]

[192] Adopted 20 May 1996, WT/DS2/AB/R, p30.

United States – Import Prohibition of Certain Shrimp and Shrimp Products ('US – Shrimp/Turtle 21.5'), 2001

Short summary and commentary

As recommended by the Appellate Body in *US – Shrimp/Turtle I*, the Dispute Settlement Body (DSB) requested in 1998 that the US bring its import prohibition into conformity with its obligations under the GATT. However, at a DSB meeting in 2000, Malaysia complained that the US had not properly implemented the recommendations and rulings of the DSB, and announced that it would seek recourse under Article 21.5 of the Dispute Settlement Understanding (DSU). The DSB called upon the original panel to review the dispute.

In an effort to comply with the *Shrimp/Turtle I* recommendations, the US did not *remove* the import prohibition, but instead attempted to remedy the application of the measure in order to bring it into compliance with the chapeau of Article XX and the Appellate Body's findings. In response to the report, the US had engaged in negotiations in the Indian Ocean and Southeast Asia regarding an international agreement to conserve sea turtles, and had also imposed more flexible 'Revised Guidelines' for the implementation of the import ban. The panel declared that so long as the US showed 'ongoing serious good faith efforts to reach a multilateral agreement', the Revised Guidelines were justified under Article XX and the US was in compliance with the recommendations of *US – Shrimp/Turtle I* (Panel report, paragraph 6.1).

Malaysia appealed these findings on the basis that the US had not actually *concluded* an international agreement on the conservation of sea turtles with Malaysia, but had only pursued negotiations regarding such an agreement, asserting that the chapeau requires conclusion of an international agreement before such a measure is to be imposed. The Appellate Body, however, considered the panel's interpretation to be supported by the language of the *Shrimp/Turtle I* report, which listed the US failure to seriously *negotiate* with the complainants as an aspect of discrimination under the chapeau (AB report at paragraphs 120–122). Furthermore, the Appellate Body noted that if the *conclusion* of a multilateral agreement were a requirement for compliance under the chapeau, any country 'would have, in effect, a veto over whether the US could fulfil its WTO obligations' (*Id.* at paragraph 123). The Appellate Body found that such a requirement 'would not be reasonable', and that serious efforts to negotiate should suffice instead (*Id.*). Using the Inter-American Convention as a basis for comparison, the Appellate Body found that the US had made such 'serious, good faith efforts' (*Id.* at paragraph 133).

Malaysia also found fault with the panel's determination that the amended import ban was sufficiently *flexible* to be compliant with the chapeau. Whereas the panel had seen an important distinction between the former requirement of '*essentially the same*' policies, and the Revised Guidelines' requirement of a programme '*comparable in effectiveness*', Malaysia argued that such a requirement continued to violate the chapeau as it conditioned 'access to the US market on compliance with policies and standards "unilaterally" prescribed by the US'. The Appellate Body, however, rejected Malaysia's arguments, calling on its finding in *Shrimp/Turtle I* that 'conditioning access to a Member's domestic market on whether exporting Members comply with, or adopt, a policy or policies unilaterally prescribed . . . may, to some degree, be a common aspect of measures falling within the scope of . . . Article XX' (*Id.* at paragraphs 137–138). The Appellate Body also found that improvements in the certification process introduced a 'degree of flexibility' that would permit for the application of the measure without discrimination among Members (*Id.* at paragraph 148).

The Appellate Body therefore upheld the panel's findings that the amended application of the US import ban under the Revised Guidelines met the requirements of the Article XX chapeau, and that the measure was ultimately justified under Article XX (*Id.* at paragraph 152).

Excerpts

Report of the Appellate Body, *United States – Import Prohibition of Certain Shrimp and Shrimp Products ("Shrimp/Turtle 21.5")*, WT/DS58/AB/RW, adopted on 21 November 2001.

VI. The Chapeau of Article XX of the GATT 1994 [paras 111–152]

111. The second issue raised in this appeal is whether the Panel erred in finding that the new measure at issue is applied in a manner that no longer constitutes a means of "arbitrary or unjustifiable discrimination between countries where the same conditions prevail" and is, therefore, within the scope of measures permitted under Article XX of the GATT 1994.[53]

[53] Panel Report, para 5.137.

. . .

A. The Nature and the Extent of the Duty of the United States to Pursue International Cooperation in the Protection and Conservation of Sea Turtles [paras 115–134]

115. Before the Panel, Malaysia asserted that the United States should have negotiated and *concluded* an international agreement on the protection and conservation of sea turtles before imposing an import prohibition. Malaysia argued that "by continuing to apply a unilateral measure after the end of the reasonable period of time pending the conclusion of an international agreement, the United States failed to comply with its obligations under the GATT 1994".[61] The United States replied that it had in fact made serious, good faith efforts to negotiate and *conclude* a multilateral sea turtle conservation agreement that would include both Malaysia and the United States, and that these efforts, as detailed and documented before the Panel, should, in view of our previous ruling, be seen as sufficient to meet the requirements of the chapeau of Article XX. The Panel found as follows:

> *. . . The Panel first recalls that the Appellate Body considered "the* failure of the United States to engage the appellees, *as well as other Members exporting shrimp to the United States, in serious across-the-board negotiations* with the objective of concluding bilateral or multilateral agreements *for the protection and conservation of sea turtles,* before *enforcing the import prohibition against the shrimp exports of those other Members" bears heavily in any appraisal of justifiable or unjustifiable discrimination within the meaning of the chapeau of Article XX. From the terms used, it appears to us that the Appellate Body had in mind a negotiation, not the conclusion of an agreement. If the Appellate Body had considered that an agreement had to be concluded before any measure can be taken by the United States, it would not have used the terms "with the objective"; it would have simply stated that an agreement had to be concluded.*

. . .

We are consequently of the view that the Appellate Body could not have meant in its findings that the United States had the obligation to conclude an agreement on the protection and conservation of sea turtles in order to comply with Article XX. However, we reach the conclusion that the United States has an obligation to make serious good faith efforts to reach an agreement before resorting to the type of unilateral measure currently in place. We also consider that those efforts cannot be a "one-off" exercise. There must be a continuous process, including once a unilateral measure has been adopted pending the conclusion of an agreement. Indeed, we consider the reference of the Appellate Body to a number of international agreements promoting a multilateral solution to the conservation concerns subject to Section 609 to be evidence that a multilateral, ideally non-trade restrictive, solution is generally to be preferred when dealing with those concerns, in particular if it is established that it constitutes "an alternative course of action reasonably open".

. . .

We understand the Appellate Body findings as meaning that the United States has an obligation to make serious good faith efforts to address the question of the protection and conservation of sea turtles at the international level. We are mindful of the potentially subjective nature of the notion of serious good faith efforts and of how difficult such a test may be to apply in reality.[62] (footnotes omitted)

[61] Panel Report, para 5.1.

[62] Panel Report, paras 5.63, 5.67 and 5.76.

116. Malaysia appeals these findings of the Panel. According to Malaysia, demonstrating serious, good faith efforts to *negotiate* an international agreement for the protection and conservation of sea turtles is not sufficient to meet the requirements of the chapeau of Article XX.[63] Malaysia maintains that the chapeau

requires instead the *conclusion* of such an international agreement. As Malaysia sees it, the "pertinent observations and comments" that we made in *United States – Shrimp* that could be construed to suggest otherwise "constitute dicta" in our previous Report.[64] On this basis, Malaysia argues that the Panel used that Report improperly in attempting to justify its reasoning that serious, good faith efforts alone would be enough to meet the requirements of the chapeau.[65] Further, Malaysia submits that the Panel misread our Report with respect to the Inter-American Convention, and, consequently, did not use that Convention properly in its analysis.[66]

[63] Malaysia's appellant's submission, para 3.11.
[64] *Ibid.*, paras 3.10–3.11.
[65] *Ibid.*, para 3.11.
[66] *Ibid.*, para 3.13.

. . .

118. The chapeau of Article XX establishes three standards regarding the *application* of measures for which justification under Article XX may be sought: first, there must be no "arbitrary" discrimination between countries where the same conditions prevail; second, there must be no "unjustifiable" discrimination between countries where the same conditions prevail; and, third, there must be no "disguised restriction on international trade".[67] The Panel's findings appealed by Malaysia concern the first and second of these three standards.[68]

[67] Appellate Body Report, *United States – Shrimp, supra,* footnote 24, para 150; Appellate Body Report, *United States – Standards for Reformulated and Conventional Gasoline ("United States – Gasoline"),* WT/DS2/AB/R, adopted 20 May 1996, DSR 1996:I, 3, at 21–22.
[68] The Panel also made findings regarding disguised restriction on trade but these are not appealed (Panel Report, paras 5.138–5.144).

119. It is clear from the language of the chapeau that these two standards operate to prevent a Member from applying a measure provisionally justified under a sub-paragraph of Article XX in a manner that would result in "arbitrary or unjustifiable discrimination".[69] In *United States – Shrimp*, we stated that the measure at issue there resulted in "unjustifiable discrimination", in part because, as applied, the United States treated WTO Members differently. The United States had adopted a cooperative approach with WTO Members from the Caribbean/Western Atlantic region, with whom it had concluded a multilateral agreement on the protection and conservation of sea turtles, namely the Inter-American Convention. Yet the United States had not, we found, pursued the negotiation of such a multilateral agreement with other exporting Members, including Malaysia and the other complaining WTO Members in that case.

[69] Appellate Body Report, *United States – Shrimp, supra,* footnote 24, paras 156 and 160; Appellate Body Report, *United States – Gasoline, supra,* footnote 67 at 21–22.

120. Moreover, we observed there that Section 609, which was part of that original measure and remains part of the new measure at issue here, calls upon the United States Secretary of State to "initiate negotiations as soon as possible for the development of bilateral or multilateral agreements with other nations for the protection and conservation of . . . sea turtles" and to "initiate negotiations as soon as possible with all foreign governments which are engaged in commercial fishing operations . . . for the purpose of entering into bilateral and multilateral treaties with such countries to protect such species of sea turtles."[70] We concluded in that appeal that the United States had failed to comply with this statutory requirement in Section 609.

[70] Section 609(a). See also, Appellate Body Report, *United States – Shrimp, supra,* footnote 24, para 167.

121. As we pointed out there:

> *Apart from the negotiation of the Inter-American Convention for the Protection and Conservation of Sea Turtles . . . which concluded in 1996, the record before the Panel does not indicate any serious, substantial efforts to carry out these express directions of Congress.*[71] *(footnotes omitted)*
>
> *We also stated:*
>
> *Clearly, the United States negotiated seriously with some, but not with other Members (including the appellees), that export shrimp to the United States. The effect is plainly discriminatory and, in our view, unjustifiable.*[72]

[71] Appellate Body Report, *supra,* footnote 24, para 167.
[72] *Ibid.,* para 172.

122. We concluded in *United States – Shrimp* that, to avoid "arbitrary or unjustifiable discrimination", the United States had to provide all exporting countries "similar opportunities to negotiate" an international agreement. Given the specific mandate contained in Section 609, and given the decided preference for multilateral approaches voiced by WTO Members and others in the international community in various international agreements for the protection and conservation of endangered sea turtles that were cited in our previous Report, the United States, in our view, would be expected to make good faith efforts to reach international agreements that are comparable from one forum of negotiation to the other. The negotiations need not be identical. Indeed, no two negotiations can ever be identical, or lead to identical results. Yet the negotiations must be *comparable* in the sense that comparable efforts are made, comparable resources are invested, and comparable energies are devoted to securing an international agreement. So long as such comparable efforts are made, it is more likely that "arbitrary or unjustifiable discrimination" will be avoided between countries where an importing Member concludes an agreement with one group of countries, but fails to do so with another group of countries.

123. Under the chapeau of Article XX, an importing Member may not treat its trading partners in a manner that would constitute "arbitrary or unjustifiable discrimination". With respect to this measure, the United States could conceivably respect this obligation, and the conclusion of an international agreement might nevertheless not be possible despite the serious, good faith efforts of the United States. Requiring that a multilateral agreement be *concluded* by the United States in order to avoid "arbitrary or unjustifiable discrimination" in applying its measure would mean that any country party to the negotiations with the United States, whether a WTO Member or not, would have, in effect, a veto over whether the United States could fulfill its WTO obligations. Such a requirement would not be reasonable. For a variety of reasons, it may be possible to conclude an agreement with one group of countries but not another. The conclusion of a multilateral agreement requires the cooperation and commitment of many countries. In our view, the United States cannot be held to have engaged in "arbitrary or unjustifiable discrimination" under Article XX solely because one international negotiation resulted in an agreement while another did not.

124. As we stated in *United States – Shrimp*, "the protection and conservation of highly migratory species of sea turtles . . . demands concerted and cooperative efforts on the part of the many countries whose waters are traversed in the course of recurrent sea turtle migrations".[73] Further, the "need for, and the appropriateness of, such efforts have been recognized in the WTO itself as well as in a significant number of other international instruments and declarations".[74] For example, Principle 12 of the Rio Declaration on Environment and Development states, in part, that "[e]nvironmental measures addressing transboundary or global environmental problems should, as far as possible, be based on international consensus".[75] Clearly, and "as far as possible", a multilateral approach is strongly preferred. Yet it is one thing to *prefer* a multilateral approach in the application of a measure that is provisionally justified under one of the subparagraphs of Article XX of the GATT 1994; it is another to require the *conclusion* of a multilateral agreement as a condition of avoiding "arbitrary or unjustifiable discrimination" under the chapeau of Article XX. We see, in this case, no such requirement.

[73] Appellate Body Report, *supra,* footnote 24, para 168.
[74] *Ibid.*
[75] *Ibid.*

125. Malaysia also disagrees with certain statements made by the Panel with respect to the Inter-American Convention. The Panel found that:

> *With respect to the absence of or insufficient negotiation with some Members compared with others, the reference of the Appellate Body to the Inter-American Convention is evidence that the efforts made by the United States to negotiate with the complainants before imposing the original measure were largely insufficient. The Inter-American Convention was negotiated as a binding agreement and has entered into force on 2 May 2001. We conclude that the Inter-American Convention can reasonably be considered as a benchmark of what can be achieved through multilateral negotiations in the field of protection and conservation. While we agree that factual circumstances may influence the duration of the process or the end result, we consider that any effort alleged to be a "serious good faith effort" must be assessed against the efforts made in relation to the conclusion of the Inter-American Convention.*[76]

[76] Panel Report, para 5.71.

126. Malaysia maintains that the word "benchmark", as used by the Panel, has the connotation of a "legal standard", and asserts that nothing in the Appellate Body Report in *United States – Shrimp* suggests that the Inter-American Convention has the status of a legal standard.[77] Malaysia sees a distinction between a "benchmark", which would have the value of a "legal standard", and an "example", which would not have such a value.[78]

[77] Malaysia's appellant's submission, para 3.13.
[78] *Ibid.*

127. It should be recalled how we viewed the Inter-American Convention in *United States – Shrimp*. We stated there:

> *The Inter-American Convention thus provides convincing demonstration that an alternative course of action was reasonably open to the United States for securing the legitimate policy goal of its measure, a course of action other than the unilateral and nonconsensual procedures of the import prohibition under Section 609. It is relevant to observe that an import prohibition is, ordinarily, the heaviest "weapon" in a Member's armoury of trade measures. The record does not, however, show that serious efforts were made by the United States to negotiate similar agreements with any other country or group of countries before (and, as far as the record shows, after) Section 609 was enforced on a world-wide basis on 1 May 1996. Finally, the record also does not show that the appellant, the United States, attempted to have recourse to such international mechanisms as exist to achieve cooperative efforts to protect and conserve sea turtles before imposing the import ban.*[79]

[79] Appellate Body Report, *supra,* footnote 24, para 171.

128. Thus, in the previous case, in examining the original measure, we relied on the Inter-American Convention in two ways. First, we used the Inter-American Convention to show that "consensual and multilateral procedures are available and feasible for the establishment of programmes for the conservation of sea turtles."[80] In other words, we saw the Inter-American Convention as evidence that an alternative course of action based on cooperation and consensus was reasonably open to the United States. Second, we used the Inter-American Convention to show the existence of "unjustifiable discrimination". The Inter-

American Convention was the result of serious, good faith efforts to negotiate a regional agreement on the protection and conservation of turtles, including efforts made by the United States. In the original proceedings, we saw a clear contrast between the efforts made by the United States to conclude the Inter-American Convention and the absence of serious efforts on the part of the United States to negotiate other similar agreements with other WTO Members. We concluded there that such a disparity in efforts to negotiate an international agreement amounted to "unjustifiable discrimination".[81]

[80] *Ibid.,* para 170.
[81] *Ibid.,* para 172.

129. With this in mind, we examine what the Panel did here. In its analysis of the Inter-American Convention in the context of Malaysia's argument on "unjustifiable discrimination", the Panel relied on our original Report to state that "the Inter-American Convention is evidence that the efforts made by the United States to negotiate with the complainants before imposing the original measure were largely insufficient".[82] The Panel went on to say that "the Inter-American Convention can reasonably be considered as a benchmark of what can be achieved through multilateral negotiations in the field of protection and conservation."[83]

[82] Panel Report, para 5.71.
[83] Ibid.

130. At no time in *United States – Shrimp* did we refer to the Inter-American Convention as a "benchmark". The Panel might have chosen another and better word – perhaps, as suggested by Malaysia, "example".[84] Yet it seems to us that the Panel did all that it should have done with respect to the Inter-American Convention, and did so consistently with our approach in *United States – Shrimp*. The Panel compared the efforts of the United States to negotiate the Inter-American Convention with one group of exporting WTO Members with the efforts made by the United States to negotiate a similar agreement with another group of exporting WTO Members. The Panel rightly used the Inter-American Convention as a factual reference in this exercise of comparison. It was all the more relevant to do so given that the Inter-American Convention was the only international agreement that the Panel could have used in such a comparison. As we read the Panel Report, it is clear to us that the Panel attached a relative value to the Inter-American Convention in making this comparison, but did not view the Inter-American Convention in any way as an absolute standard. Thus, we disagree with Malaysia's submission that the Panel raised the Inter-American Convention to the rank of a "legal standard". The mere use by the Panel of the Inter-American Convention *as a basis for a comparison* did not transform the Inter-American Convention into a "legal standard". Furthermore, although the Panel could have chosen a more appropriate word than "benchmark" to express its views, Malaysia is mistaken in equating the mere use of the word "benchmark", as it was used by the Panel, with the establishment of a legal standard.

[84] *Malaysia's appellant's submission, para 3.13.*

131. The Panel noted that while "factual circumstances may influence the duration of the process or the end result, . . . any effort alleged to be a 'serious good faith effort' must be assessed against the efforts made in relation to the conclusion of the Inter-American Convention."[85] Such a comparison is a central element of the exercise to determine whether there is "unjustifiable discrimination". The Panel then analyzed the negotiation process in the Indian Ocean and South-East Asia region to determine whether the efforts made by the United States in those negotiations were serious, good faith efforts comparable to those made in relation with the Inter-American Convention.

. . .

[85] Panel Report, para 5.71.

132. On this basis and, in particular, on the basis of the "contribution of the United States to the steps that led to the Kuantan meeting and its contribution to the Kuantan meeting itself",[91] the Panel concluded that the United States had made serious, good faith efforts that met the "standard set by the Inter-American Convention".[92] In the view of the Panel, whether or not the South-East Asian MOU is a legally binding document does not affect this comparative assessment because differences in "factual circumstances have to be kept in mind".[93] Furthermore, the Panel did not consider as decisive the fact that the final agreement in the Indian Ocean and South-East Asia region, unlike the Inter-American Convention, had not been concluded at the time of the Panel proceedings. According to the Panel, "at least until the Conservation and Management Plan to be attached to the MOU is completed, the United States efforts should be judged on the basis of its active participation and its financial support to the negotiations, as well as on the basis of its previous efforts since 1998, having regard to the likelihood of a conclusion of the negotiations in the course of 2001."[94]

[91] *Ibid.,* para 5.82.
[92] *Ibid.*
[93] Panel Report. It appears that the United States was in favour of a legally binding agreement for the Indian Ocean and South-East Asia region, but a number of other parties were not, and the latter view prevailed. See, Panel Report, para 5.83.
[94] Panel Report, para 5.84.

133. We note that the Panel stated that "any effort alleged to be a 'serious good faith effort' must be assessed against the efforts made in relation to the conclusion of the Inter-American Convention."[95] In our view, in assessing the serious, good faith efforts made by the United States, the Panel did not err in using the Inter-American Convention as an *example*. In our view, also, the Panel was correct in proceeding then to an analysis broadly in line with this principle and, ultimately, was correct as well in concluding that the efforts made by the United States in the Indian Ocean and South-East Asia region constitute serious, good faith efforts comparable to those that led to the conclusion of the Inter-American Convention. We find no fault with this analysis.[96]

[95] *Ibid.,* para 5.71.
[96] We note that a multilateral conference on sea turtles was held in Manila and resulted in the adoption of the Conservation and Management Plan to be annexed to the South-East Asian MOU. We also note that the South-East Asian MOU came into effect on 1 September 2001. To our mind, these events only reinforce the finding of the Panel that the efforts made by the United States to negotiate an international agreement in the Indian Ocean and South-East Asia region constitute serious, good faith efforts comparable to those made in relation to the Inter-American Convention. The Inter-American Convention, in Article IV.2(h), provides for the use of TEDs to reduce the incidental capture and mortality of sea turtles in the course of fishing activities. Objective 1.4 of the Conservation and Management Plan attached to the South-East Asian MOU requires signatory states to "[r]educe to the greatest extent practicable the incidental capture and mortality of marine turtles in the course of fishing activities". In this respect, signatory states are directed to "[d]evelop and use gear, devices and techniques to minimise incidental capture of marine turtles in fisheries, such as devices that effectively allow the escape of marine turtles, and spatial and seasonal closures".

134. In sum, Malaysia is incorrect in its contention that avoiding "arbitrary and unjustifiable discrimination" under the chapeau of Article XX requires the *conclusion* of an international agreement on the protection and conservation of sea turtles. Therefore, we uphold the Panel's finding that, in view of the serious, good faith efforts made by the United States to negotiate an international agreement, "Section 609 is now applied in a manner that no longer constitutes a means of unjustifiable or arbitrary discrimination, as identified by the Appellate Body in its Report."[97]

[97] Panel Report, para 5.137. We do wish to note, though, that there is one observation by the Panel with which we do not agree. In assessing the good faith efforts made by the United States, the Panel stated that:

> The United States is a demandeur in this field and given its scientific, diplomatic and financial means, it is reasonable to expect rather more than less from that Member in terms of serious good faith efforts. Indeed, the capacity of persuasion of the United States is illustrated by the successful negotiation of the Inter-American Convention. (Panel Report, para 5.76)

We are not persuaded by this line of reasoning. As we stated in our previous Report, the chapeau of Article XX is "but one expression of the principle of good faith" (Appellate Body Report, *United States – Shrimp, supra,* footnote 24, para 158). This good faith notion applies to all WTO Members equally.

B. The Flexibility of the Revised Guidelines [paras 135–152]

135. We now turn to Malaysia's arguments relating to the flexibility of the Revised Guidelines. Malaysia argued before the Panel that the measure at issue results in "arbitrary or unjustifiable discrimination" because it conditions the importation of shrimp into the United States on compliance by the exporting Members with policies and standards "unilaterally" prescribed by the United States.[98] Malaysia asserted that the United States "unilaterally" imposed its domestic standards on exporters.[99] With respect to this argument, the Panel found:

> *It seems that whereas the Appellate Body found that requiring the adoption of essentially the same regime constituted arbitrary discrimination, it accepted – at least implicitly – that a requirement that the US and foreign programmes be "comparable in effectiveness" would be compatible with the obligations of the United States under the chapeau of Article XX. This is because it would "permit a degree of discretion or flexibility in how the standards for determining comparability might be applied, in practice, to other countries". We therefore conclude that if,* in practice, *the implementing measure provides for "comparable effectiveness", the finding of the Appellate Body in terms of lack of flexibility will have been addressed.*[100] *(footnote omitted)*

[98] Panel Report, para 3.131.
[99] *Ibid.,* paras 3.125 and 3.127.
[100] *Ibid.,* para 5.93.

136. Malaysia disagrees with the Panel that a measure can meet the requirements of the chapeau of Article XX if it is flexible enough, both in design and application, to permit certification of an exporting country with a sea turtle protection and conservation programme "comparable" to that of the United States. According to Malaysia, even if the measure at issue allows certification of countries having regulatory programs "comparable" to that of the United States, and even if the measure is applied in such a manner, it results in "arbitrary or unjustifiable discrimination" because it conditions access to the United States market on compliance with policies and standards "unilaterally" prescribed by the United States. Thus, Malaysia puts considerable emphasis on the "unilateral" nature of the measure, and Malaysia maintains that our previous Report does not support the conclusion of the Panel on this point.[101]

[101] Malaysia's appellant's submission, paras 3.17–3.19.

137. We recall that, in *United States – Shrimp*, we stated:

> *It appears to us . . . that* conditioning access to a Member's domestic market on whether exporting Members comply with, or adopt, a policy or policies unilaterally prescribed by the importing Member may, to some degree, be a common aspect of measures falling within the scope of one or another of the exceptions (a) to (j) of Article XX. *Paragraphs (a) to (j) comprise measures that are recognized as* exceptions to substantive obligations *established in the GATT 1994, because the domestic policies embodied in such measures have been recognized as important and legitimate in character. It is not necessary to assume that*

> *requiring from exporting countries compliance with, or adoption of, certain policies (although covered in principle by one or another of the exceptions) prescribed by the importing country, renders a measure* a priori *incapable of justification under Article XX. Such an interpretation renders most, if not all, of the specific exceptions of Article XX inutile, a result abhorrent to the principles of interpretation we are bound to apply*[102] *(emphasis added).*

[102] Appellate Body Report, *supra,* footnote 24, para 121.

138. In our view, Malaysia overlooks the significance of this statement. Contrary to what Malaysia suggests, this statement is not "*dicta*". As we said before, it appears to us "that conditioning access to a Member's domestic market on whether exporting Members comply with, or adopt, a policy or policies unilaterally prescribed by the importing Member may, to some degree, be a common aspect of measures falling within the scope of one or another of the exceptions (a) to (j) of Article XX." This statement expresses a principle that was central to our ruling in *United States – Shrimp*.

139. A separate question arises, however, when examining, under the chapeau of Article XX, a measure that provides for access to the market of one WTO Member for a product of other WTO Members *conditionally*. Both Malaysia and the United States agree that this is a common aspect of the measure at issue in the original proceedings and the new measure at issue in this dispute.

140. In *United States – Shrimp*, we concluded that the measure at issue there did not meet the requirements of the chapeau of Article XX relating to "arbitrary or unjustifiable discrimination" because, through the application of the measure, the exporting members were faced with "a single, rigid and unbending requirement"[103] to adopt *essentially the same* policies and enforcement practices as those applied to, and enforced on, domestic shrimp trawlers in the United States. In contrast, in this dispute, the Panel found that this new measure is more flexible than the original measure and has been applied more flexibly than was the original measure. In the light of the evidence brought by the United States, the Panel satisfied itself that this new measure, in design and application, does *not* condition access to the United States market on the adoption by an exporting Member of a regulatory programme aimed at the protection and the conservation of sea turtles that is *essentially the same* as that of the United States.

[103] Appellate Body Report, *supra,* footnote 24, para 177.

141. As the Panel's analysis suggests, an approach based on whether a measure requires "essentially the same" regulatory programme of an exporting Member as that adopted by the importing Member applying the measure is a useful tool in identifying measures that result in "arbitrary or unjustifiable discrimination" and, thus, do *not* meet the requirements of the chapeau of Article XX. However, this approach is not sufficient for purposes of judging whether a measure *does* meet the requirements of the chapeau of Article XX. Therefore, in construing our previous Report, the Panel inferred from our reasoning there that a measure requiring United States and foreign regulatory programmes to be "comparable in effectiveness", as opposed to being "essentially the same", would, absent some other shortcoming, comply with the chapeau of Article XX. On this, the Panel stated:

> *It seems that whereas the Appellate Body found that requiring the adoption of essentially the same regime constituted arbitrary discrimination, it accepted – at least implicitly – that a requirement that the US and foreign programmes be "comparable in effectiveness" would be compatible with the obligations of the United States under the chapeau of Article XX. This is because it would "permit a degree of discretion or flexibility in how the standards for determining comparability might be applied, in practice, to other countries". We therefore conclude that if,* in practice, *the implementing measure provides for "comparable effectiveness", the finding of the Appellate Body in terms of lack of flexibility will have been addressed.*[104] *(footnote omitted)*

[104] Panel Report, para 5.93.

142. The Panel reads our previous Report to state that a major deficiency of the original measure was its lack of flexibility, in both design and application. The Panel sees our previous Report as suggesting that the original measure was applied in a manner which constituted "unjustifiable discrimination" essentially "because the application of the measure at issue did not allow for any inquiry into the appropriateness of the regulatory program for the conditions prevailing in the exporting countries".[105] The Panel reasons that a measure that, in its design and application, allows certification of exporting Members having regulatory programmes "comparable in effectiveness" to that of the United States does take into account the specific conditions prevailing in the exporting WTO Members and is, therefore, flexible enough to meet the requirements of the chapeau of Article XX.

[105] Panel Report, para 5.92.

143. Given that the original measure in that dispute required "essentially the same" practices and procedures as those required in the United States, we found it necessary in that appeal to rule only that Article XX did not allow such inflexibility. Given the Panel's findings with respect to the flexibility of the new measure in this dispute, we find it necessary in this appeal to add to what we ruled in our original Report. The question raised by Malaysia in this appeal is whether the Panel erred in inferring from our previous Report, and thereby finding, that the chapeau of Article XX permits a measure which requires only "comparable effectiveness".

144. In our view, there is an important difference between conditioning market access on the adoption of essentially the same programme, and conditioning market access on the adoption of a programme *comparable in effectiveness*. Authorizing an importing Member to condition market access on exporting Members putting in place regulatory programmes *comparable in effectiveness* to that of the importing Member gives sufficient latitude to the exporting Member with respect to the programme it may adopt to achieve the level of effectiveness required. It allows the exporting Member to adopt a regulatory programme that is suitable to the specific conditions prevailing in its territory. As we see it, the Panel correctly reasoned and concluded that conditioning market access on the adoption of a programme *comparable in effectiveness*, allows for sufficient flexibility in the application of the measure so as to avoid "arbitrary or unjustifiable discrimination". We, therefore, agree with the conclusion of the Panel on "comparable effectiveness".

145. Malaysia also argues that the measure at issue is not flexible enough to meet the requirement of the chapeau of Article XX relating to "unjustifiable or arbitrary discrimination" because the Revised Guidelines do not provide explicitly for the specific conditions prevailing in Malaysia.[106]

[106] According to Malaysia, the specificity of its case rests on the fact that shrimp trawling is not practised in Malaysia; shrimp is a by-catch from fish trawling and therefore, the incidental catch of sea turtles is due to fish trawling, not shrimp trawling. See, Malaysia's appellant's submission, para 3.21 and Panel Report, para 3.128. In addition, Malaysia stated:

> Malaysia is a nesting ground but it is not known to be a feeding ground for sea turtles and the nesting season in Malaysia does not overlap with the shrimp season. The Loggerheads and the Kemps released rarely nested on Malaysian beaches and did not occur in Malaysian waters respectively and the high mortality of sea turtles that is reported in the shrimp trawls in the United States relate to both these sea turtles. The Green Turtle, the Hawksbill, Leatherback and Olive Ridley are the major sea turtle species in Malaysia. Green turtles were resident in sea grass beds which were found in shallow coastal waters, whilst the Hawksbills were found in coral reef. Trawling was prohibited in these areas. During the nesting season, the Green turtles remain close to the shore in areas where trawling was also prohibited. During long distance migrations between feeding and nesting grounds, turtles were actively swimming close to the surface of the water which made them more vulnerable to drift nets and long lines rather than trawl nets. In Malaysia, trawling targeted fish for the most part of the year and thus the incidental capture of sea turtles was due to fish trawls and not shrimp trawls (Malaysia's response to questioning at the oral hearing).

146. We note that the Revised Guidelines contain provisions that permit the United States authorities to take into account the specific conditions of Malaysian shrimp production, and of the Malaysian sea turtle conservation programme, should Malaysia decide to apply for certification. The Revised Guidelines explicitly state that "[if] the government of a harvesting nation demonstrates that it has implemented and is enforcing a comparably effective regulatory program to protect sea turtles in the course of shrimp trawl fishing without the use of TEDs, that nation will also be eligible for certification".[107] Likewise, the Revised Guidelines provide that the "Department of State will take fully into account any demonstrated differences between the shrimp fishing conditions in the United States and those in other nations as well as information available from other sources."[108]

[107] Revised Guidelines, Section II.B; see, Panel Report, p105.
[108] *Ibid.*

147. Further, the Revised Guidelines provide that the import prohibitions that can be imposed under Section 609 do not apply to shrimp or products of shrimp "harvested in any other manner or under any other circumstances that the Department of State may determine, following consultations with the [United States National Marine Fisheries Services], does not pose a threat of the incidental taking of sea turtles".[109] Under Section II.B(c)(iii) of the Revised Guidelines (*Additional Sea Turtle Protection Measures*), the "Department of State recognizes that sea turtles require protection throughout their life-cycle, not only when they are threatened during the course of commercial shrimp trawl harvesting."[110] Additionally, Section II.B(c)(iii) states that "[i]n making certification determinations, the Department shall also take fully into account other measures the harvesting nation undertakes to protect sea turtles, including national programmes to protect nesting beaches and other habitat, prohibitions on the direct take of sea turtles, national enforcement and compliance programmes, and participation in any international agreement for the protection and conservation of sea turtles."[111] With respect to the certification process, the Revised Guidelines specify that a country that does not appear to qualify for certification will receive a notification that "will explain the reasons for this preliminary assessment, suggest steps that the government of the harvesting nation can take in order to receive a certification, and invite the government of the harvesting nation to provide . . . any further information." Moreover, the Department of State commits itself to "actively consider any additional information that the government of the harvesting nation believes should be considered by the Department in making its determination concerning certification."[112]

[109] Revised Guidelines, Section I.B; see, Panel Report, p103.
[110] Revised Guidelines, Section II.B(c)(iii); see, Panel Report, p106.
[111] *Ibid.*
[112] Revised Guidelines, Section II.C, Panel Report, p107. See also, Revised Guidelines, Section II.D, Panel Report, p108.

148. These provisions of the Revised Guidelines, on their face, permit a degree of flexibility that, in our view, will enable the United States to consider the particular conditions prevailing in Malaysia if, and when, Malaysia applies for certification. As Malaysia has not applied for certification, any consideration of whether Malaysia would be certified would be speculation.[113]

[113] In this respect, we note that the European Communities stated that:

> . . . the complaint by Malaysia in this case is somewhat premature. As it appears Malaysia has not yet applied for certification and it is therefore not yet clear how the contested legislation would apply to imports of shrimp and shrimp products from Malaysia. (European Communities' third participant's submission, para 27).

149. We need only say here that, in our view, a measure should be designed in such a manner that there is sufficient flexibility to take into account the specific conditions prevailing in *any* exporting Member, including, of course, Malaysia.[114] Yet this is not the same as saying that there must be specific provisions

in the measure aimed at addressing specifically the particular conditions prevailing in *every individual* exporting Member. Article XX of the GATT 1994 does not require a Member to anticipate and provide explicitly for the specific conditions prevailing and evolving in *every individual* Member.

[114] Appellate Body Report, *United States – Shrimp, supra,* footnote 24, para 164.

150. We are, therefore, not persuaded by Malaysia's argument that the measure at issue is not flexible enough because the Revised Guidelines do not explicitly address the specific conditions prevailing in Malaysia.

. . .

152. For all these reasons, we uphold the finding of the Panel, in paragraph 6.1 of the Panel Report, that "Section 609 of Public Law 101–162, as implemented by the Revised Guidelines of 8 July 1999 and as applied so far by the [United States] authorities, is justified under Article XX of the GATT 1994 as long as the conditions stated in the findings of this Report, in particular the ongoing serious, good faith efforts to reach a multilateral agreement, remain satisfied".[117]

[117] Panel Report, para 6.1. The Panel stated that its findings of justification stand, *"as long as"* certain conditions it set out in its Report, in particular, the good faith efforts to reach a multilateral agreement, continue to be met. In this respect, we note that the United States negotiated and concluded a Memorandum of Understanding with certain countries in the Indian Ocean and South-East Asia region, the South-East Asian MOU. See, *supra,* footnote 96. This agreement took effect on 1 September 2001, almost two and a half months after the circulation of the Panel Report. The participants have not disputed the existence of this agreement. There was some dispute at the oral hearing as to the legally binding nature of this agreement. Basic Principle 4 of that agreement states:

> This Memorandum of Understanding, including the Conservation and Management Plan, may be amended by consensus of the signatory States. When appropriate, the signatory States will consider amending this Memorandum of Understanding to make it legally binding.

At the oral hearing, the United States stated that "[The South-East Asian MOU] is considered a political undertaking that does not have binding consequences under international law". Malaysia stated that "The [South-East Asian] MOU . . . would have the status of a treaty under the Vienna Convention of the law of treaties, because 'treaty' has been defined as an international agreement that is concluded between States in written form and governed by international law, whether embodied in a single instrument or in two or more related instruments, whatever its particular designation." We need not judge this issue, and we do not. Even so, we note that, whether legally binding or not, the Memorandum of Understanding reinforces the Panel's finding that the United States had indeed made serious good faith efforts to negotiate a multilateral agreement.

United States – Measures Affecting the Cross-Border Supply of Gambling and Betting Services ('US – Gambling'), 2005

Short summary and commentary

In *US – Gambling*, Antigua & Barbuda, one of the smallest Members of the WTO, challenged various US measures claiming that together they constituted a 'total prohibition' of the cross-border supply of gambling and betting services to the US, in violation of Article XVI of the GATS on market access and the US' commitments under its schedule of commitments.

The US acknowledged that several federal statutes resulted in a statewide prohibition of the 'remote supply' of most gambling and betting services (Panel report, paragraph 6.359). 'Remote supply' refers to any situation where the supplier (*domestic or foreign*) and the consumer of gambling and betting services are not physically together.

The Appellate Body confirmed the panel's finding that the US had indeed made commitments in gambling and betting services, although the schedule did not explicitly mention the words 'gambling and betting services'. The Appellate Body also confirmed the panel's finding that domestic regulation banning the remote supply of gambling services constituted a per se market access restriction in 'the form of numerical quotas' as referred to in Article XVI:2(a) of the GATS. As a result, the panel concluded that certain US laws that banned the 'remote supply' of gambling and betting services, effectively imposing a 'zero quota' on the provision of those 'remote supply' gambling services, violated the US market access commitment under Article XVI:2(a) and (c) of the GATS.

The Appellate Body upheld the panel's findings with respect to three federal laws (the Wire Act, the Travel Act, and the Illegal Gambling Business Act) (albeit with slightly different reasoning) but reversed the panel's finding of violation for the state laws at issue. By confirming the (controversial) panel ruling that the US domestic regulation banning the remote supply of gambling services is a prohibited market access restriction under Article XVI, the Appellate Body set an important landmark for the interpretation of central provisions of the GATS.

In order to justify its restrictions on remote gambling, the US invoked the GATS' general exceptions clause for measures necessary to protect public morals or to maintain public order (Article XIV(a)) and for measures necessary to secure compliance with other WTO-consistent US laws (Article XIV(c)). The panel found that the US laws could not be justified under either of the two sub-paragraphs of Article XIV.

In determining whether the measures found in violation of the GATS' market access restrictions fell under the scope of sub-paragraphs (a) and/or (c) of Article XIV, the Appellate Body upheld the panel's finding that 'the concerns which the Wire Act, the Travel Act and the Illegal Gambling Business Act seek to address fall within the scope of "public morals" and/or "public order"', which address problems of money-laundering, fraud, compulsory gambling and underage gambling that accompany internet gambling (AB report, paragraph 373). However, the Appellate Body reversed the panel's finding that the US measures were *not necessary* to protect public morals/maintain public order and instead found that the measures fulfilled the necessity requirement under sub-paragraphs (a) and (c) of Article XIV (*Id.* at paragraph 327). The Appellate Body's conclusions with respect to the necessity requirement are described in Chapter 3: The Necessity Requirement.

After finding that the US measures could be justified under sub-paragraph (a) of Article XIV, the Appellate Body – keeping in line with the jurisprudence under Article XX of the GATT and the approach of the panel – went on to examine whether or not the US measures met the requirements of the chapeau of Article XIV. Like the introductory clause of Article XX of the GATT, the chapeau of Article XIV requires that measures be applied in a manner that does not constitute an arbitrary or unjustifiable discrimination between countries where like conditions prevail, or a disguised restriction on trade in services.

The panel had concluded that the US failed to comply with the chapeau because it was more lax in enforcing its laws against domestic providers of *remote supply* gambling services compared to similar foreign providers, and because the US had not taken a position on internet gambling per se with regard to horse wagering services (Panel report, paragraph 6.607).

The Appellate Body reversed the panel's finding that the US failed to demonstrate a consistent enforcement of the prohibition of remote gambling services, notably with regard to certain American betting companies (AB report, paragraph 357). Specifically, concerning the alleged non-enforcement of certain laws against US remote suppliers of gambling services, the Appellate Body noted that the panel came to its conclusion on the basis of only five isolated instances of non-enforcement (*Id.* at paragraph 355). According to the Appellate Body, such isolated instances of enforcement are to be placed in the context of the overall pattern of enforcement (*Id.*).

However, the Appellate Body subsequently concluded that the US failed to demonstrate that the prohibitions contained in the Interstate Horseracing Act were applied to both foreign and domestic service suppliers of remote betting services for horse racing (*Id.* at paragraph 371). For this reason alone, the Appellate Body concluded that the US had not established that these measures satisfied the requirements of the chapeau (*Id.* at paragraph 372).

Although *US – Gambling* did not involve environmental measures, it nevertheless indicates how WTO tribunals may approach general exceptions clauses (including environmental and health exceptions), both in the GATT and the GATS. With respect to the GATS, *US – Gambling* is also important for its broad definition of Article XVI on market access. According to the Appellate Body, this article may cover measures that might not have been expected to qualify as market access restrictions. This is especially relevant given that the GATS contains no equivalent to Article XX(g) for the protection of exhaustible natural resources. A broad provision without an Article XX(g)-type of environmental exception could have particularly far-reaching implications for governmental regulatory prerogatives. It could lead to a situation where a broad range of legitimate environmental measures are considered in violation of the GATS' market access provisions that could not be justified under an exceptions clause. Also noteworthy is the *US – Gambling* approach to the public morals/public order exception in Article XIV(a), an exception that is different under GATT Article XX(a), which refers to public morals, but not public order. The public morals/public order exception may gain relevance, given the absence of an exception for the protection of exhaustible natural resources in the GATS. Finally, *US – Gambling* demonstrates that commitments in Members' schedules may cover services not explicitly mentioned in them.

The *US – Gambling* approach to the necessity test is discussed in Chapter 3: The Necessity Requirement.

Excerpts

Report of the Appellate Body, *United States – Measures Affecting the Cross-Border Supply of Gambling and Betting Services*, WT/DS285/AB/R, adopted on 20 April 2005.

VII. Article XIV of the GATS: General Exceptions [paras 266–372]

. . .

C. The Panel's substantive analysis under Article XIV [paras 291–372]

. . .

3. The chapeau of Art. XIV [paras 338–369]

338. Notwithstanding its finding that the measures at issue are *not* provisionally justified, the Panel examined whether those measures satisfy the requirements of the chapeau of Article XIV "so as to assist the parties

in resolving the underlying dispute in this case".[426] This examination is the subject of appeals by both participants. Unlike the Panel, we have found the Wire Act, the Travel Act, and the IGBA to fall within the scope of Article XIV(a). Therefore, we must now review the Panel's examination under the chapeau.

[426] Panel Report, para 6.566.

339. The chapeau of Article XIV provides:

> Subject to the requirement that such measures are not applied in a manner which would constitute a means of arbitrary or unjustifiable discrimination between countries where like conditions prevail, or a disguised restriction on trade in services, nothing in this Agreement shall be construed to prevent the adoption or enforcement by any Member of measures [of the type specified in the subsequent paragraphs of Article XIV].

The focus of the chapeau, by its express terms, is on the *application* of a measure already found by the Panel to be inconsistent with one of the obligations under the GATS but falling within one of the paragraphs of Article XIV.[427] By requiring that the measure be *applied* in a manner that does not to constitute "arbitrary" or "unjustifiable" discrimination, or a "disguised restriction on trade in services", the chapeau serves to ensure that Members' rights to avail themselves of exceptions are exercised reasonably, so as not to frustrate the rights accorded to other Members by the substantive rules of the GATS.[428]

[427] Appellate Body Report, *US – Gasoline,* p22, DSR 1996:I, 3, at 20.
[428] *Ibid.,* p22, DSR 1996:I, 3, at 20–21.

340. The Panel found that:

> *. . . the United States has not demonstrated that it does not apply its prohibition on the remote supply of wagering services for horse racing in a manner that does not constitute "arbitrary and unjustifiable discrimination between countries where like conditions prevail" and/or a "disguised restriction on trade" in accordance with the requirements of the chapeau of Article XIV.*[429]

[429] Panel Report, para 6.608.

341. In reviewing the Panel's treatment of the chapeau to Article XIV, we begin with Antigua's allegations of error, and then turn to those raised by the United States, proceeding as follows: (a) first, we examine Antigua's claim that the Panel should not have analyzed the United States' defence under the chapeau; (b) second, we analyze Antigua's allegation that the Panel erred by focusing its discussion under the chapeau on the *remote supply* of gambling services rather than on the entire gambling industry; (c) thirdly, we address the United States' argument that the Panel articulated and applied a standard under the chapeau that is inconsistent with its terms; (d) fourthly, we review the Panel's finding on the alleged non-enforcement of certain laws against United States remote suppliers of gambling services; and (e) finally, we examine whether, in its analysis under the chapeau of Article XIV, the Panel fulfilled its obligations under Article 11 of the DSU.

. . .

(b) Did the Panel Improperly "Segment" the Gambling and Betting Industry in its Analysis? [paras 346–347]

346. In examining whether discrimination exists in the United States' application of the Wire Act, the Travel Act, and the IGBA, the Panel found that "some of the concerns the United States has identified are specific only to the remote supply of gambling and betting services".[435] As a result, the Panel determined

that it would have been "inappropriate", in the context of determining whether WTO-consistent alternative measures are reasonably available, to compare the United States' treatment of concerns relating to the *remote* supply of gambling services, with its treatment of concerns relating to the *non*-remote supply of such services. Antigua characterizes this approach as an improper "segment[ation]" of the gambling industry, the result of which was to "exclude a substantial portion of gambling and betting services from any analysis at all".[436]

[435] Panel Report, para 6.498.
[436] Antigua's other appellant's submission, para 142.

347. We have already observed that the Panel found, on the basis of evidence adduced by the United States, that the *remote* supply of gambling services gives rise to particular concerns.[437] We see no error in the Panel's maintaining such a distinction for purposes of analysing any discrimination in the application of the three federal statutes. Such an approach merely reflects the view that the distinctive characteristics of the remote supply of gambling services may call for distinctive regulatory methods, and that this could render a comparison between the treatment of remote and non-remote supply of gambling services inappropriate.

[437] *Supra,* para 313.

(c) Did the Panel Fail to Take Account of the "Arbitrary" or "Unjustifiable" Nature of the Discrimination Referred to in the Chapeau? [paras 348–351]

348. We consider next whether, contrary to the United States' allegations, the Panel accurately described and applied the correct interpretation of the chapeau of Article XIV. On the basis of the arguments advanced by Antigua, the Panel examined certain instances of alleged discrimination in the application of the Wire Act, the Travel Act and the IGBA.[438] In the course of this analysis, the Panel found that the United States had not prosecuted certain domestic remote suppliers of gambling services,[439] and that a United States statute (the Interstate Horseracing Act) could be understood, on its face, to permit certain types of remote betting on horse racing within the United States.[440] On the basis of these two findings, the Panel concluded that:

> *. . . the United States has not demonstrated that it applies its prohibition on the remote supply of these services in a* consistent manner *as between those supplied domestically and those that are supplied from other Members. Accordingly, we believe that the United States has not demonstrated that it does not apply its prohibition on the remote supply of wagering services for horse racing in a manner that does not constitute "arbitrary and unjustifiable discrimination between countries where like conditions prevail" and/or a "disguised restriction on trade" in accordance with the requirements of the chapeau of Article XIV*[441] *(emphasis added).*

[438] Panel Report, para 6.584.
[439] *Ibid.,* para 6.588.
[440] Panel Report, para 6.599:

> . . . the text of the revised statute does appear, on its face, to permit interstate pari-mutuel wagering over the telephone or other modes of electronic communication, which presumably would include the Internet, as long as such wagering is legal in both states.

[441] *Ibid.,* para 6.607.

349. The United States contends that the Panel's reasoning, in particular its standard of "consistency", reveals that the Panel, in fact, assessed only whether the United States treats domestic service suppliers

differently from foreign service suppliers. Such an assessment is inadequate, the United States argues, because the chapeau also requires a determination of whether differential treatment, or discrimination, is "arbitrary" or "unjustifiable".

350. The United States based its defence under the chapeau of Article XIV on the assertion that the measures at issue prohibit the remote supply of gambling and betting services by *any supplier*, whether domestic or foreign. In other words, the United States sought to justify the Wire Act, the Travel Act and the IGBA on the basis that there is *no discrimination* in the manner in which the three federal statutes are applied to the remote supply of gambling and betting services.[442] The United States could have, but did not, put forward an additional argument that *even if* such discrimination exists, it does not rise to the level of "arbitrary" or "unjustifiable" discrimination.

[442] *Supra,* para 287.

351. In the light of the arguments before it, we do not read the Panel to have ignored the requirement of "arbitrary" or "unjustifiable" discrimination by articulating the standard under the chapeau of Article XIV as one of "consistency".[443] Rather, the Panel determined that Antigua had rebutted the United States' claim of no discrimination *at all* by showing that domestic service suppliers are permitted to provide remote gambling services in situations where foreign service suppliers are not so permitted. We see no error in the Panel's approach.

[443] See Panel Report, paras 6.578–6.581, where the Panel discusses Appellate Body decisions relating to the chapeau of Article XX of the GATT 1994. In particular, we note the Panel's quotation of the relevant portion of paragraph 150 of the Appellate Body decision in *US – Shrimp,* which states:

> [under the chapeau, first,] the application of the measure must result in *discrimination.* As we stated in *United States – Gasoline,* the nature and quality of this discrimination is different from the discrimination in the treatment of products which was already found to be inconsistent with one of the substantive obligations of the GATT 1994, such as Articles I, III or XI. Second, the discrimination must be *arbitrary* or *unjustifiable* in character (original emphasis; footnote omitted). (Panel Report, para 6.578 (quoting Appellate Body Report, *US – Shrimp,* para 150))

(d) Did the Panel Err in its Examination of the Alleged Non-Enforcement of the Measures at Issue Against Domestic Service Suppliers? [paras 352–357]

352. In the course of examining whether the Wire Act, the Travel Act and the IGBA are applied consistently with the chapeau of Article XIV, the Panel considered whether these laws are enforced in a manner that discriminates between domestic and foreign service suppliers. Antigua identified four United States firms that it claimed engage in the remote supply of gambling services but have not been prosecuted under any of the three federal statutes: Youbet.com, TVG, Capital OTB and Xpressbet.com.[444] Antigua contrasted this lack of enforcement with the case of an Antiguan service supplier that "had modelled [its] business on that of Capital OTB" but was nevertheless prosecuted and convicted under the Wire Act.[445] In support of its argument that it applies these statutes equally to domestic and foreign service suppliers, the United States submitted statistical evidence to show that most cases prosecuted under these statutes involved gambling and betting services solely within the United States.[446]

[444] *Ibid.,* para 6.585.
[445] *Ibid.*
[446] *Ibid.,* para 6.586.

353. The Panel also "note[d] indications by the United States" that prosecution proceedings were pending against one domestic remote supplier of gambling services (Youbet.com), but stated that it had no evidence as to whether any enforcement action was being taken against the other three domestic remote suppliers of gambling services identified by Antigua.[447] As to foreign service suppliers, the Panel observed

that it had evidence of the prosecution of one Antiguan operator for violations of the Wire Act.[448] The Panel found this evidence "inconclusive" and concluded that the United States had not shown that it enforces its prohibition against the remote supply of gambling services on the three domestic service suppliers in a manner consistent with the chapeau of Article XIV.[449]

[447] *Ibid.,* para 6.588.
[448] *Ibid.*
[449] *Ibid.,* para 6.589.

354. We observe, first, that none of the three federal statutes distinguishes, on its face, between domestic and foreign service suppliers.[450] We agree with the Panel that, in the context of facially neutral measures, there may nevertheless be situations where the selective prosecution of persons rises to the level of discrimination. In our view, however, the evidence before the Panel could not justify finding that, notwithstanding the neutral language of the statute, the facts are "inconclusive" to establish "non-discrimination" in the United States' enforcement of the Wire Act. The Panel's conclusion rests, not only on an inadequate evidentiary foundation, but also on an incorrect understanding of the type of conduct that can, as a matter of law, be characterized as discrimination in the enforcement of measures.

[450] *Supra,* paras 258–263.

355. In this case, the Panel came to its conclusion – that the United States failed to establish non-discrimination in the enforcement of its laws – on the basis of only five cases: one case of prosecution against a foreign service supplier; one case of "pending" prosecution against a domestic service supplier;[451] and three cases with no evidence of prosecution against domestic service suppliers. From these five cases, the Panel in effect concluded that the United States' defence had been sufficiently rebutted to warrant a finding of "inconclusiveness".

[451] Panel Report, para 6.588.

356. In our view, the proper significance to be attached to isolated instances of enforcement, or lack thereof, cannot be determined in the absence of evidence allowing such instances to be placed in their proper context. Such evidence might include evidence on the *overall* number of suppliers, and on *patterns* of enforcement, and on the reasons for particular instances of non-enforcement. Indeed, enforcement agencies may refrain from prosecution in many instances for reasons unrelated to discriminatory intent and without discriminatory effect.

357. Faced with the limited evidence the parties put before it with respect to enforcement, the Panel should rather have focused, as a matter of law, on the wording of the measures at issue. These measures, on their face, do *not* discriminate between United States and foreign suppliers of remote gambling services.[452] We therefore *reverse* the Panel's finding, in paragraph 6.589 of the Panel Report, that:

> *. . . the United States has failed to demonstrate that the manner in which it enforced its prohibition on the remote supply of gambling and betting services against TVG, Capital OTB and Xpressbet.com is consistent with the requirements of the chapeau.*

[452] *Supra,* paras 258–263.

(e) Did the Panel Fail to Comply with Article 11 of the DSU in its Analysis of Video Lottery Terminals, Nevada Bookmakers and the Interstate Horseracing Act? [paras 358–366]

. . .

361. We now turn to the United States' Article 11 claim relating to the chapeau. The Panel examined the scope of application of the Interstate Horseracing Act ("IHA").[457] Before the Panel, Antigua relied on the

text of the IHA, which provides that "[a]n interstate off-track wager *may be accepted* by an off-track betting system" where consent is obtained from certain organizations.[458] Antigua referred the Panel in particular to the definition given in the statute of "interstate off-track wager":

> *[T]he term . . . "interstate off-track wager" means a legal wager placed or accepted in one State with respect to the outcome of a horserace taking place in another State and includes pari-mutuel wagers, where lawful in each State involved,* placed or transmitted by an individual in one State via telephone or other electronic media and accepted by an off-track betting system in the same or another State, *as well as the combination of any pari-mutuel wagering pools*[459] *(emphasis added).*

Thus, according to Antigua, the IHA, on its face, authorizes *domestic* service suppliers, but not *foreign* service suppliers, to offer remote betting services in relation to certain horse races.[460] To this extent, in Antigua's view, the IHA "exempts"[461] domestic service suppliers from the prohibitions of the Wire Act, the Travel Act, and the IGBA.[462]

457 We understand the Panel to have predicated its examination of the IHA on its view that the services under the IHA include services subject to the specific commitment undertaken by the United States in subsector 10.D of its Schedule.
458 Section 3004 of Title 15 of the United States Code, Exhibit AB-82 submitted by Antigua to the Panel (emphasis added).
459 Section 3002 of Title 15 of the United States Code, Exhibit AB-82 submitted by Antigua to the Panel.
460 Antigua submitted additional evidence in support of its reading of the IHA. See, for example, Panel Report, footnote 1061 to para 6.599 and footnote 1062 to para 6.600 (citing, *inter alia,* Congressional Record, House of Representatives Proceedings and Debates of the 106th Congress, Second Session (26 October 2000) 146 Cong. Rec. H 11230, 106th Cong. 2nd Sess. (2000), Exhibit AB-124 submitted by Antigua to the Panel); and United States General Accounting Office, *Internet Gambling: An Overview of the Issues* (December 2002), Appendix II, Exhibit AB-17 submitted by Antigua to the Panel.
461 Panel Report, para 6.595 (quoting Antigua's statement at the first substantive panel meeting, para 92).
462 The Wire Act, the Travel Act, and the IGBA prohibit a broad range of gambling and betting activities when they involve foreign or interstate commerce (Panel Report, paras 6.362, 6.367 and 6.375).

362. The United States disagreed, claiming that the IHA – a civil statute – cannot "repeal"[463] the Wire Act, the Travel Act or the IGBA – which are criminal statutes – *by implication*, that is, merely by virtue of the IHA's adoption *subsequent* to that of the Wire Act, the Travel Act, and the IGBA.[464] Rather, under principles of statutory interpretation in the United States, such a repeal could be effective only if done *explicitly*, which was not the case with the IHA.[465]

463 Panel Report, para 6.597 (quoting United States' response to Question 21 posed by the Panel, Panel Report, pC-50).
464 Panel Report, para 6.595 (citing, *inter alia,* United States' first written submission to the Panel, paras 33–35); United States' second written submission to the Panel, para 63; and United States' response to Question 21 posed by the Panel, Panel Report, pC-50. See also Panel Report, para 6.597 (citing, *inter alia,* United States' response to Question 21 posed by the Panel, Panel Report, pC-50); and Presidential Statement on Signing the Departments of Commerce, Justice, State, the Judiciary and Related Agencies Appropriation Act, 21 December 2000, Exhibit US-17 submitted by the United States to the Panel, pp3155–3156.
465 United States' response to Question 21 posed by the Panel, Panel Report, pC-50; United States' second written submission to the Panel, paras 63–64.

363. Thus, the Panel had before it conflicting evidence as to the relationship between the IHA, on the one hand, and the measures at issue, on the other. We have already referred to the discretion accorded to panels, as fact-finders, in the assessment of the evidence.[466] As the Appellate Body has observed on previous occasions, "not every error in the appreciation of the evidence (although it may give rise to a question of law) may be characterized as a failure to make an objective assessment of the facts."[467]

[466] *Supra*, para 330.
[467] Appellate Body Report, *EC – Hormones,* para 133. See also Appellate Body Report, *Japan – Apples,* para 222.

364. In our view, this aspect of the United States' appeal essentially challenges the Panel's failure to accord sufficient weight to the evidence submitted by the United States with respect to the relationship under United States law between the IHA and the measures at issue. The Panel had limited evidence before it, as submitted by the parties, on which to base its conclusion. This limitation, however, could not absolve the Panel of its responsibility to arrive at a conclusion as to the relationship between the IHA and the prohibitions in the Wire Act, the Travel Act, and the IGBA. The Panel found that the evidence provided by the United States was not sufficiently persuasive to conclude that, as regards wagering on horse racing, the remote supply of such services by *domestic* firms continues to be prohibited notwithstanding the plain language of the IHA. In this light, we are not persuaded that the Panel failed to make an objective assessment of the facts.

. . .

(f) Conclusion under the Chapeau [paras 367–369]

367. In paragraph 6.607 of the Panel Report, the Panel expressed its overall conclusion under the chapeau of Article XIV as follows:

> *the United States has not demonstrated that it does not apply its prohibition on the remote supply of wagering services for horse racing in a manner that does not constitute "arbitrary and unjustifiable discrimination between countries where like conditions prevail" and/or a "disguised restriction on trade" in accordance with the requirements of the chapeau of Article XIV.*

368. This conclusion rested on the Panel's findings relating to two instances allegedly revealing that the measures at issue discriminate between domestic and foreign service suppliers, contrary to the defence asserted by the United States under the chapeau. The first instance found by the Panel was based on "inconclusive" evidence of the alleged non-enforcement of the three federal statutes.[470] We have reversed this finding.[471] The second instance found by the Panel was based on "the ambiguity relating to" the scope of application of the IHA and its relationship to the measures at issue.[472] We have upheld this finding.[473]

[470] Panel Report, paras 6.589 and 6.607.
[471] *Supra,* para 357.
[472] Panel Report, para 6.607.
[473] *Supra,* paras 364 and 366.

369. Thus, *our* conclusion – that the Panel did not err in finding that the United States has not shown that its measures satisfy the requirements of the chapeau – relates solely to the possibility that the IHA exempts only *domestic* suppliers of remote betting services for horse racing from the prohibitions in the Wire Act, the Travel Act and the IGBA. In contrast, the *Panel's* overall conclusion under the chapeau was broader in scope. As a result of our reversal of one of the two findings on which the Panel relied for its conclusion in paragraph 6.607 of the Panel Report, we must *modify* that conclusion. We *find*, rather, that the United States has not demonstrated that – in the light of the existence of the IHA – the Wire Act, the Travel Act and the IGBA are applied consistently with the requirements of the chapeau. Put another way, we uphold the Panel, but only in part.

CHAPTER 3

The Necessity Requirement

BACKGROUND

The rules of the WTO are directed at the liberalization of international trade in goods and services. They build upon basic principles, such as the prohibitions against discrimination between goods and services from different foreign countries (most-favoured nation principle) and between foreign and domestic products or services (national treatment principle), and the prohibition against quantitative export and import restrictions. The various agreements also set out the conditions under which Members are allowed to deviate from these principles, as well as conditions under which other restrictions on trade may be imposed.

One such condition consists of the requirement that a trade-restrictive measure be 'necessary' to attain a specified legitimate policy objective, such as the protection of the environment or the protection of human or animal life or health. This 'necessity requirement' can take different forms depending on the specific WTO agreement it is contained in. The General Agreement on Tariffs and Trade (GATT), the Agreement on Technical Barriers to Trade (TBT Agreement) and the Agreement on Sanitary and Phytosanitary Measures (SPS Agreement) each contain a variation of the so-called 'necessity test'. As will be shown below, the GATT incorporates its necessity tests in Article XX on general exceptions, which allows for derogations from other GATT obligations under specified conditions. The SPS and the TBT Agreements have incorporated their necessity requirements as positive rules laying out the conditions under which a Member may adopt trade-restrictive sanitary or phytosanitary measures or technical regulations, as defined under the respective agreements.

DISCUSSION OF RELEVANT WTO PROVISIONS

Articles XX(a), (b) and (d) of the GATT

The GATT includes a necessity test in certain paragraphs of its Article XX, the provision setting out an exhaustive list of 'general exceptions' that a Member can invoke as a defence to what otherwise would be a breach of GATT obligations. The relevant sections of Article XX provide that 'nothing in [the] Agreement shall be construed to prevent the adoption or enforcement . . . of measures: (a) necessary to protect public morals;

(b) necessary to protect human, animal or plant life or health; . . . [or] (d) necessary to secure compliance with laws or regulations which are not inconsistent with the provisions of this Agreement.' The other exceptions listed in Article XX are designed in a different manner and do not contain a necessity requirement.

When deciding whether or not an otherwise GATT-inconsistent measure can be saved under an Article XX(a), (b) or (d) exception, panels must determine whether or not the measure is 'necessary' to fulfil the legitimate objectives listed under the respective paragraphs. Several GATT and WTO panels have interpreted the term 'necessary' within the context of the relevant Article XX exceptions. However, the exact scope and meaning of the necessity test as interpreted by GATT and, later, by WTO tribunals remain unclear.

The pre-WTO GATT panels (i.e. those applying GATT 1947, prior to 1994) interpreted the term 'necessary' to mean that a contracting party could only justify a violation of GATT rules if there were no alternative GATT-consistent measures available that the party could reasonably be expected to employ. In cases where no other GATT-consistent measures were available, the contracting party would have to apply the reasonably available measure that was least inconsistent with other GATT provisions. This requirement to apply the 'least inconsistent' measure (often referred to as the 'least-trade-restrictive approach') was laid out by a GATT panel in 1990 in *US – Section 33*, and restated in 1991 in *Thailand – Cigarettes* (*US – Section 337* panel report, paragraph 5.26; *Thailand – Ciagrettes* panel report, paragraph 74).

These interpretations by pre-WTO GATT panels gave some guidance for the implementation of the necessity test. However, they also left many questions open, including questions about the meaning and scope of what exactly constitutes a 'reasonably available alternative measure'. The 'least-trade-restrictive approach' has been a major focus of criticism, mainly by those who claim that it fails to give adequate consideration to societal values other than trade.

In 2001, the WTO Appellate Body issued its decision in *Korea – Beef*, which reaffirmed the approach taken in *US – Section 337* and *Thailand – Cigarettes*, but added new factors to the traditional necessity test. The dispute involved a difference in treatment of domestic and imported beef, which Korea alleged was 'necessary' to protect consumers against fraudulent practices condemned by Korea's Unfair Competition Act. In interpreting the meaning of 'necessary' under Article XX(d), the Appellate Body first stated that for a measure to be necessary, the measure does not need to be 'indispensable' or 'inevitable' (*Korea – Beef* AB report, paragraph 161). Rather, the Appellate Body suggested that a 'necessary' measure was situated somewhere between an 'indispensable' measure and a measure 'making a contribution to' a goal, albeit significantly closer to the pole of 'indispensable' (*Id.*). The Appellate Body created a three factor balancing test for deciding whether or not a measure is necessary when it is not per se indispensable. The three factors to be considered are: (i) the contribution made by the (non-indispensable) measure to the legitimate objective; (ii) the importance of the common interests or values protected; and (iii) the impact of the measure on trade (*Id.* at paragraph 164). The Appellate Body indicated that these elements of the weighing and balancing process were part of the determination whether an alternative GATT-consistent or less inconsistent measure was reasonably available (*Id.* at paragraph 166).

It is important to note also that in determining whether an alternative measure was reasonably available, the Appellate Body in *Korea – Beef* confirmed the panel's approach to consider factors such as the domestic costs of an alternative measure (*Id.* at paragraph

173). In that case, the panel had noted that Korea had not demonstrated that the costs under the alternative measure would be too high (*Id.* at paragraph 174).

Only a few months after *Korea – Beef*, the Appellate Body issued its ruling in *EC – Asbestos.* In this decision, the Appellate Body examined whether a French ban on the manufacturing, sale, and import of asbestos fibres was 'necessary' to protect the health of workers and consumers, as required under Article XX(b). In accordance with pre-WTO GATT cases and *Korea – Beef*, the Appellate Body reaffirmed that a Member was free to choose its level of protection (*EC – Asbestos* AB report, paragraph 174). It also implicitly concluded that the balancing test laid out in *Korea – Beef*, with respect to Article XX(d), was also applicable under Article XX(b). In applying (parts of) the weighing and balancing test established in *Korea – Beef*, the Appellate Body confirmed the importance of the value to be protected, noting the preservation of human life and health (at issue in *EC – Asbestos*) was 'both vital and important in the highest degree', thus making it easier to meet the necessity requirements (*Id.* at paragraph 172). In that context, the Appellate Body explained that the weighing and balancing process also established the answer to the question of whether or not there was an alternative, less trade restrictive, measure that would achieve the same end as the contested measure.

It is also noteworthy that the Appellate Body in *EC – Asbestos* recognized that difficulties in the implementation of an alternative measure could be considered when determining whether an alternative measure was reasonably available (*Id.* at paragraph 169). However, it found that an alternative measure could still be considered reasonably available, even if it involved administrative or other difficulties in implementation. More recently, in *US – Gambling* (which involved the GATS), the Appellate Body found that an alternative measure that is merely theoretical in nature, may not be considered reasonably available (*US – Gambling* AB report, paragraph 308). This would include situations where the responding Member is not capable of taking an alternative measure or situations where the measure imposes an undue burden on that Member (e.g. prohibitive cost or substantial technical difficulties).

Articles 2.2 and 5.6 of the SPS Agreement [including footnote 3]

The SPS Agreement establishes binding rules and disciplines to prevent countries from using sanitary and phytosanitary measures as disguised barriers to trade. It expressly affirms that WTO Members have the right to enact and maintain SPS measures to protect the life and health of humans, animals and plants (Article 2.1). According to Article 2.2 of the SPS Agreement, however, the measures must be 'based on scientific principles' and 'not maintained without scientific evidence'. They must also be 'applied only to the extent *necessary* to protect the human, animal or plant life or health'. Thus, under the SPS Agreement, the necessity requirement is a positive obligation, and is not contained in an exception. As will be shown in more detail below, this has important consequences for the allocation of the burden of proof.

In addition to the obligations in Article 2.2, WTO Members may not arbitrarily or unjustifiably discriminate against another Member 'where identical or similar conditions prevail' in each Member's territory, nor may they use SPS measures as disguised barriers to trade (Article 2.3). The sum of these obligations constitutes a refinement of Article XX(b) of the GATT. Accordingly, the SPS Agreement explicitly provides that measures in conformity with its provisions are presumed to be in accordance with Article XX(b). It is important to note, however, that Article 2.2 of the SPS Agreement, in contrast to Article XX(b), deals only with the application of regulations, not regulations themselves.

Article 5 of the SPS Agreement builds on the basic obligations under Article 2.2 mentioned above. Paragraph 6 of Article 5 instructs WTO Members to ensure that their sanitary and phytosanitary measures be 'not more trade-restrictive than required to achieve their appropriate level of sanitary or phytosanitary protection, taking into account technical and economic feasibility'. A footnote to Article 5.6 clarifies that 'a measure is not more trade-restrictive than required unless there is another measure, reasonably available taking into account technical and economic feasibility, that achieves the appropriate level of sanitary or phytosanitary protection and is significantly less restrictive to trade'. Thus, the SPS Agreement seems to apply a slightly different set of criteria to the necessity test than that contained in paragraphs (b) and (d) of Article XX and their respective jurisprudence. Specifically, case law relating to the SPS Agreement has identified three cumulative requirements to determine whether an alternative measure is 'reasonably available':

1. the alternative measure is 'reasonably available taking into account technical and economic feasibility';
2. the alternative measure 'achieves the Member's appropriate level of sanitary protection'; and
3. the alternative measure is 'significantly less restrictive to trade' than the sanitary measure contested (*Australia – Salmon* AB report, paragraph 194).

Article 2.2 of the TBT Agreement

The TBT Agreement establishes rules for technical regulations, defined in Annex 1, paragraph 1 of the TBT Agreement as 'document[s] which lay down product characteristics or their related processes and production methods'. Like the GATT and the SPS Agreement, the TBT Agreement contains the national treatment and the most-favoured nation principles. The TBT also contains a necessity test: pursuant to Article 2.2 of the TBT Agreement, Members must 'ensure that technical regulations are not prepared, adopted or applied with a view to or the effect of creating unnecessary obstacles to international trade'. Building on the latter requirement, the same Article 2.2 adds that technical regulations are not permitted to 'be more trade-restrictive than necessary to fulfil a legitimate objective, taking account of the risks non-fulfilment would create'. The Agreement sets out a non-exhaustive list of legitimate objectives that includes, *inter alia*, national security requirements, the prevention of deceptive practices, and the protection of human health or safety, animal or plant life or health, and the environment.

Comparing the Necessity Requirement under the GATT, SPS and TBT Agreements

The necessity standard in the SPS Agreement builds on pre-WTO GATT jurisprudence relating to Article XX. As a consequence, the SPS Agreement's necessity test demands an inquiry as to whether or not an alternative measure is available. The test regarding alternative measures under the SPS Agreement shares important features with the test under the GATT and its application under recent WTO jurisprudence. For example, in order to determine whether a measure is reasonably available, the SPS Agreement explicitly takes into account technical and economic feasibility. Although these elements are not mentioned in Article XX of the GATT, recent WTO tribunals have taken into account the difficulties of implementing an alternative measure, including consideration of administrative difficulties and costs (see, most recently, *DR – Cigarettes,* AB report, paragraphs 65–70). In the same context, tribunals have clarified that it is not enough for an alternative measure be available merely in theory (*Id.*). Thus, the two standards seem to be similar in this respect.

Also, the SPS Agreement requires that a reasonably available measure achieve the *appropriate* level of sanitary protection. This seems to match jurisprudence pertaining to Article XX of the GATT, in that both the latter and the SPS Agreement require that alternative measures achieve the level of protection chosen by the WTO Member.

While these similarities seem striking, the two tests also appear to differ in some respects. For example, the SPS Agreement notes that a measure is only to be considered as reasonably available if it is *significantly* less trade-restrictive. This seems to be a rejection of the least-trade-restrictive approach adopted in pre-WTO GATT jurisprudence pertaining to Article XX of the GATT, where the degree to which an alternate measure was less restrictive did not seem to matter. Although post-GATT WTO jurisprudence does not appear to have endorsed such a strict least-trade-restrictive approach, it does not seem to go as far as to explicitly require that a potential alternative measure be *significantly* less trade-restrictive.

Another difference between the two necessity standards under the GATT and the SPS Agreement is the allocation of the burden of proof. Under the GATT, the responding party has to prove that the challenged measure is 'necessary' and thus that no alternative measure is reasonably available. In contrast, under the SPS Agreement, it is the complaining party who must prove, at least *prima facie,* that an alternative measure meeting the three elements required under the SPS Agreement is reasonably available. For example, in *Japan – Varietals,* a dispute involving the SPS Agreement, the complaining party was required to explicitly suggest specific alternative measures and establish a *prima facie* case of inconsistency with each of the elements required under Article 5.6. This approach stands in stark contrast to jurisprudence pertaining to Article XX(b) and (d) of the GATT, according to which the burden of proof lies with the responding Member. The difference in the allocation of the burden of proof under the GATT and the SPS Agreement is due to the context. The necessity test under the GATT is contained in the exceptions clause which only comes to bear once the challenging party has proved that another GATT obligation has been violated. On the other hand, under the SPS Agreement, the necessity test exists as a positive obligation. Thus, any sanitary and phytosanitary measure that restricts trade must be 'necessary', not just one which has been found to violate one of the basic GATT disciplines.

Finally, another important aspect of the SPS Agreement – relating only indirectly to the necessity test – consists of the additional requirements that sanitary and phytosanitary measures be based on scientific evidence and risk assessment, prerequisites not included under Article XX of the GATT. It is on the basis of these requirements that measures have been found to violate WTO rules; while none of the four SPS measures examined under the WTO to date were found to violate the SPS Agreement's provisions on necessity, all except one (*Australia – Salmon*, due to lack of factual evidence) were found to violate the SPS Agreement's risk assessment requirements (*EC – Hormones*, *Japan – Varietals*, and *Japan – Apples*).

The TBT Agreement's requirement that a technical regulation must not be 'more trade-restrictive than necessary to fulfil a legitimate objective' resembles – at least in part – the terminology used in the SPS Agreement that measures must not be 'more trade-restrictive than required to achieve their appropriate level of sanitary of phytosanitary protection'. However, several differences can be identified between the texts of necessity standards set out in the SPS and the TBT Agreements. First, the TBT Agreement (like GATT Article XX) does not refer to the 'appropriate level of protection', but only mentions the fulfilment of a legitimate objective. This omission arguably does not hinder WTO tribunals from allowing WTO Members to determine their level of protection, however. Moreover, the TBT Agreement, similar to the GATT and in contrast to the SPS Agreement, does not add that 'technical and economic feasibility' must be taken into account, nor does it include a footnote defining what 'not more trade-restrictive than necessary' means. But in contrast to the SPS Agreement and GATT Article XX, the TBT Agreement does require taking into account the 'risks non-fulfilment would create'. Although it is unclear what this addition actually implies, it might be comparable to GATT case law which – in determining whether a measure is necessary – takes into account the contribution made by a (non-indispensable) measure to the achievement of the legitimate objective.

Overall, the TBT Agreement appears to give significantly less guidance regarding the necessity test than the SPS Agreement. As a consequence most aspects of that test in the context of the TBT Agreement await further clarification by WTO case law. As of this writing, no case had shed any light on the necessity test under the TBT Agreement. Recently, however, *EC – Sardines* has addressed the topic of 'legitimate objectives' under the TBT Agreement, an issue closely linked to the necessity test, and described below.

Articles VI and XIV of the GATS

The General Agreement on Trade in Services (GATS) establishes a legal framework for trade in services and a goal of progressive liberalization. Necessity requirements are among its many rules.

Similar to the GATT, the GATS allows Members to derogate from their obligations on services trade liberalization under certain circumstances. These circumstances include the general and security exceptions listed in GATS Articles XIV and XIV bis, respectively. GATS Article XIV parallels certain general exceptions under GATT Article XX. It allows measures that are necessary to: (a) protect public morals and maintain public order; (b) protect human, animal or plant life or health; and (c) secure compliance with laws or regulations that are not inconsistent with the provisions of the GATS. Article XIV bis establishes a security exception, stating that nothing in the GATS shall be construed to prevent any Member from taking any action that it considers necessary for the protection of its essential security interests. Building on prior necessity jurisprudence under Article

Table 3.1: *Necessity requirements*

Agreement	*Provision*	*Text*
GATT	Article XX(b) and (d)	Subject to the requirement that such measures are not applied in a manner which would constitute a means of arbitrary or unjustifiable discrimination between countries where the same conditions prevail, or a disguised restriction on international trade, nothing in this Agreement shall be construed to prevent the adoption or enforcement by any contracting party of measures: . . . (b) necessary to protect human, animal or plant life or health; [and] . . . (d) necessary to secure compliance with laws or regulations which are not inconsistent with the provisions of this Agreement, including those relating to customs enforcement, the enforcement of monopolies operated under paragraph 4 of Article II and Article XVII, the protection of patents, trade marks and copyrights, and the prevention of deceptive practices
SPS Agreement	Article 2.2	Sanitary or phytosanitary measures which conform to international standards, guidelines or recommendations shall be deemed to be necessary to protect human, animal or plant life or health, and presumed to be consistent with the relevant provisions of this Agreement and of GATT 1994.
	Article 5.6	Without prejudice to paragraph 2 of Article 3, when establishing or maintaining sanitary or phytosanitary measures to achieve the appropriate level of sanitary or phytosanitary protection, Members shall ensure that such measures are not more trade-restrictive than required to achieve their appropriate level of sanitary or phytosanitary protection, taking into account technical and economic feasibility.[3] [3] For purposes of paragraph 6 of Article 5, a measure is not more trade-restrictive than required unless there is another measure, reasonably available taking into account technical and economic feasibility, that achieves the appropriate level of sanitary or phytosanitary protection and is significantly less restrictive to trade.
TBT Agreement	Article 2.2	Members shall ensure that technical regulations are not prepared, adopted or applied with a view to or with the effect of creating unnecessary obstacles to international trade. For this purpose, technical regulations shall not be more trade-restrictive than necessary to fulfil a legitimate objective, taking account of the risks non-fulfilment would create. Such legitimate objectives are, *inter alia:* national security requirements; the prevention of deceptive practices; protection of human health or safety, animal or plant life or health, or the environment. In assessing such risks, relevant elements of consideration are, *inter alia*: available scientific

Table 3.1: *Necessity requirements (continued)*

Agreement	*Provision*	*Text*
		and technical information, related processing technology or intended end-uses of products.
GATS	Article XIV (a),(b) and (c)	Subject to the requirement that such measures are not applied in a manner which would constitute a means of arbitrary or unjustifiable discrimination between countries where like conditions prevail, or a disguised restriction on trade in services, nothing in this Agreement shall be construed to prevent the adoption or enforcement by any Member of measures: (a) necessary to protect public morals or to maintain public order;[5] (b) necessary to protect human, animal or plant life or health; (c) necessary to secure compliance with laws or regulations which are not inconsistent with the provisions of this Agreement . . . [5] The public order exception may be invoked only where a genuine and sufficiently serious threat is posed to one of the fundamental interests of society.

XX of the GATT, the recent *US – Gambling* reports elaborate the meaning of the necessity requirement under Article XIV of the GATS in great detail. No jurisprudence exists in relation to the security exception under GATS Article XIV bis.

The GATS also includes references to necessity in rules and obligations. Specifically, these necessity requirements are included in GATS Article VI, entitled Domestic Regulation. The language of Article VI.4 does not currently contain a straightforward necessity requirement, and there is thus no clarifying GATS jurisprudence. Article VI.4 does establish a negotiating mandate related to necessity. Specifically, paragraph 4 directs negotiators to consider disciplines to the effect that 'measures relating to qualification requirements and procedures, technical standards and licensing requirements do not constitute unnecessary barriers to trade in services'. Article VI.4 further states that the future rules on domestic regulations shall aim to ensure that measures are 'not more burdensome than necessary to ensure the quality of the service'. Members are currently considering what sort of necessity requirements to include in such future disciplines. These negotiations have given rise to serious concerns among civil society groups, who fear that a necessity test in future disciplines on domestic regulation will constrain legitimate and significant domestic regulatory prerogatives.

SELECTED ISSUES RELATING TO THE NECESSITY REQUIREMENT

Legitimate objectives

The examination of the necessity test under the GATT, the SPS and the TBT Agreements makes clear that the objective that a trade-restrictive measure aims to pursue plays an important role in determining the measure's consistency with WTO rules. Each agreement specifies certain objectives that are 'legitimate'. Whereas some agreements list legitimate objectives exhaustively, others set forth legitimate objectives as part of an open list. GATT Article XX, for example, lists ten exceptions (and objectives) under which Members can derogate from their obligations under the GATT (but of which only three are relevant to the necessity test). The SPS Agreement limits the objectives of sanitary and phytosanitary measures by defining such measures according to their objectives and dividing the types of SPS measures into four categories. In contrast, the TBT Agreement gives an exemplary list of legitimate objectives, leaving room for other unspecified objectives.

In some cases, agreements refer to narrow legitimate objectives, whereas in others they refer to more open and broad objectives. For example, paragraph (d) of GATT Article XX refers to measures 'necessary to secure compliance with laws or regulations'. This paragraph thus covers a wide array of policy objectives and in some ways can be compared to an open list of objectives within the overall objective of securing compliance with laws and regulations. In contrast, paragraph (b) of GATT Article XX refers to a narrower objective, namely 'to protect human, animal or plant life or health'. But here, too, the exception under paragraph (b) in fact encompasses an entire set of legitimate objectives. The SPS Agreement, which grew out of paragraph (b) of Article XX of the GATT, has a set of similarly narrow legitimate objectives also relating to human, animal and plant life and health. However, the scope of the SPS Agreement as a whole is narrower than the scope of Article XX(b). This is due to the manner in which Annex A to the SPS Agreement defines SPS measures with respect to their objective. In defining SPS measures, the SPS Agreement specifies the *objects* that a measure may protect (human, animal and plant life or health) as well as the *types of risks* from which human, animal and plant life or health may be protected. The TBT Agreement also explicitly refers to the 'protection of human health or safety, animal or plant life or health' as one possible legitimate objective within its non-exhaustive list of legitimate objectives.

The legitimate objective that has arguably sparked the most controversy is the protection of the environment. While the necessity test under Article 2.2 of the TBT Agreement explicitly mentions the 'protection of the environment' as one possible policy objective, this goal remains notably absent from both the GATT and SPS Agreements. While it can be argued that the objective to protect animal or plant life or health also encompasses environmental protection measures, it is still noteworthy that the two agreements do not refer to the 'environment'. This omission is more understandable with respect to GATT Article XX, which was initially drafted in 1947. In this context one should recall the reference to the 'conservation of exhaustible natural resources' in GATT Article XX(g). Interestingly, however, the necessity test does not apply to measures falling under paragraph (g) because the paragraph covers measures 'relating to' (but not 'necessary for') the conservation of exhaustible natural resources. Panels and the Appellate Body have generally held that the term 'relating to' in Article XX(g) does not require a measure to be 'necessary or essential' to the conservation of the exhaustible natural resource. Thus, the test relating to the conservation of natural resources differs from the necessity test under Articles XX(b) and (d). Arguably, the conditions under Article XX(g) are easier to fulfil. Chapter 2: General Exceptions Clauses provides a more detailed analysis of paragraph (g) of GATT Article XX.

It is unclear how the structures used in the various agreements (i.e. exhaustive lists of legitimate objectives versus open lists; broad versus narrow objectives) will influence the manner in which the WTO tribunals will approach questions relevant to the legitimacy of an objective, or their precise role in the necessity test. Questions that arise in this context include whether or not objectives that are not explicitly listed in an open list can be legitimate. Do dispute settlement panels have the authority to decide whether or not an objective is legitimate, and how should the determination be made? Will the fact that objectives are explicitly listed influence the balancing required under the necessity test? Will narrowly defined objectives be treated differently from broader objectives under the necessity test?

While jurisprudence on these issues is largely non-existent, a recent case has clarified at least some of these questions. The decision in *EC – Sardines* seems to indicate that under the TBT Agreement, non-listed objectives can be considered as legitimate. At the same time, however, the Appellate Body in *EC – Sardines* agreed with the panel which stated that 'there must be an examination and a determination on the legitimacy of the objectives of the measure' (*EC – Sardines* AB report, paragraph 286). This arguably leaves some space for the WTO dispute settlement bodies to question the legitimacy of a Member's chosen (unlisted) policy objective. What these statements mean in practice remains to be seen in future WTO case law pertaining to the TBT Agreement.

The issue of legitimate objectives has sparked much discussion among trade policy makers, academics and civil society groups. Whether or not to establish exclusive lists of legitimate policy objectives is a central issue of debate, particularly in the negotiations to establish new rules for trade in services. In the context of the GATS negotiations on domestic regulation, negotiators are considering another option; specifically, suggestions have been made to simply refer to the notion of 'national policy objectives', without an explicit mention of any specific objectives. It remains to be seen whether this approach will find its way into new language in future GATS disciplines.

International standards and the presumption of necessity

Both the SPS and the TBT Agreements seek to promote international harmonization. With this as a goal, both agreements give privileged treatment to rules which 'conform to' or are 'based on' international standards, guidelines or recommendations. However, at least with respect to the SPS Agreement, WTO jurisprudence indicates no obligation on Members to abide by these international standards. As of this writing, case law has not clarified the question of whether or not international standards create an obligation for Members under the TBT Agreement.

Pursuant to Article 3.2 of the SPS Agreement, 'measures which conform to international standards, guidelines or recommendations shall be deemed to be necessary to protect human, animal or plant life or health,' as required by Article 2.2 and 5.6 of the SPS Agreement.

Similarly, Article 2.5 of the TBT Agreement provides that a technical regulation that pursues one of the legitimate objectives explicitly mentioned in the TBT Agreement and which is in accordance with relevant international standards 'shall be rebuttably presumed not to create an unnecessary obstacle to international trade'. This provision seems to imply that a technical regulation in accordance with international standards is presumed not to be 'more trade-restrictive than necessary to fulfil a legitimate objective', as required under Article 2.2 of the TBT Agreement.

Interestingly, under the TBT Agreement, the 'presumption' can be rebutted, while under the SPS Agreement, international standards are 'deemed' to be consistent with the disciplines of the SPS Agreement. Moreover, while the TBT Agreement only allows the presumption that international standards do not 'create unnecessary obstacles to trade' (while saying nothing about other provisions such as national and most-favoured nation treatment), the SPS Agreement specifically provides a similar presumption with respect to all requirements of the SPS Agreement and the GATT. As of this writing, no case law exists interpreting Article 2.5 of the TBT Agreement.

Table 3.2: *Presumption of necessity*

Provision	*Text*
SPS Agreement, Article 3.2	Sanitary or phytosanitary measures which conform to international standards, guidelines or recommendations shall be deemed to be necessary to protect human, animal or plant life or health, and presumed to be consistent with the relevant provisions of this Agreement and of GATT 1994
TBT Agreement, Article 2.5	A Member preparing, adopting or applying a technical regulation which may have a significant effect on trade of other Members shall, upon the request of another Member, explain the justification for that technical regulation in terms of the provisions of paragraphs 2 to 4. Whenever a technical regulation is prepared, adopted or applied for one of the legitimate objectives explicitly mentioned in paragraph 2, and is in accordance with relevant international standards, it shall be rebuttably presumed not to create an unnecessary obstacle to international trade

SELECTED LITERATURE

Marceau, G. and Trachtman, J. P. (forthcoming) *A Map of the World Trade Organization Law of Domestic Regulation of Goods: The Technical Barriers to Trade Agreement, the*

Sanitary and Phytosanitary Measures Agreement, and the General Agreement on Tariffs and Trade, Columbia Law School Series on WTO Law and Policy, vol 1: Trade and Health
Neumann, J. and Tuerk, E. (2003) 'Necessity revisited – proportionality in WTO law after Korea-Beef; EC-Asbestos and EC-Sardines', *Journal of World Trade*, vol 37, p199
Sykes, A. O. (2003) 'The Least Trade Restrictive Means', *University of Chicago Law Review*, vol 70, p403

SELECTED JURISPRUDENCE UNDER THE GATT, THE SPS AND TBT AGREEMENTS, AND THE GATS

The following are excerpts of GATT and WTO cases that are relevant for a discussion of the necessity requirements under the various WTO Agreements. The excerpts are preceded by a short summary and commentary of the corresponding case, aiming to put the excerpts into context. The disputes are divided into three groups bsed on whether they discuss the GATT, the SPS or the TBT Agreements. Within those sub-sections, the disputes are arranged chronologically. The summaries do not encompass all the issues raised in the cases, but focus primarily on issues relating to necessity, and are thus not comprehensive for other purposes.

Articles XX(b) and (d) of the GATT

United States – Section 337 of the Tariff Act of 1930 ('US – Section 337'), 1989

Short summary and commentary

US – Section 337 dealt with a procedure under a section of the US Tariff Act of 1930 that, among other things, offered streamlined procedures for banning allegedly patent-infringing goods from entry into the US. The European Communities challenged the law, alleging a violation of Article III:4 of the GATT (requiring national treatment). Specifically, the European Communities claimed that domestic patent infringers could only be sued in US courts under regular court procedures while foreign infringers of patents could be subject to the streamlined procedure under Section 337.

The US countered that even if Section 337 were in violation of Article III:4, such procedures were necessary for the enforcement of patent laws and were therefore permitted under the Article XX(d) exception of the GATT. Under certain circumstances, the Article XX(d) exception permits 'measures necessary to secure compliance with laws or regulations'.

The GATT panel found a violation of Article III of the GATT and rejected the US defence with respect to most aspects of the measure. However, the panel agreed that the specific Section 337 procedural remedy, under which products could be barred from entering into the US, might be justified under Article XX(d). The panel reasoned that, given the fact that foreign producers could ignore regular court remedies and that their assets might not be available in the US to satisfy judgments against them, the specific procedure under Section 337 could indeed be viewed as 'necessary to secure compliance with' US patent laws (Panel report, paragraphs 5.31–5.33). Nevertheless, the panel found that other aspects of the Section 337 procedure could not be considered necessary (*Id.* at paragraph 5.34). As a result, the panel concluded that the measure was not justifiable under Article XX(d) of the GATT.

US – Section 337 was the first dispute to interpret the meaning of the term 'necessary' under Article XX of the GATT. The panel found that an otherwise GATT-inconsistent measure can only be considered 'necessary' if no alternative measure is (1) reasonably available to the defending country, and (2) 'not inconsistent with other GATT provisions' (Panel report, paragraph 5.26). In cases where no GATT-consistent measure is reasonably available, the challenged country must apply a reasonably available measure 'which entails the least degree of inconsistency' with the other GATT provisions (*Id.*).

This version of the necessity test was developed in the context of paragraph (d) of GATT Article XX, but was subsequently applied in *Thailand – Cigarettes*, which involved paragraph (b) of Article XX. As of this writing, WTO panels addressing the necessity requirements under Articles XX(b) and (d) still refer to the *US – Section 337* criteria.

Excerpts

Report of the Panel, *United States – Section 337 of the Tariff Act of 1930*, BISD 36S/345, adopted on 7 November 1989.

(v) Article XX(d)

(a) The conditions attached to the use of Article XX(d)

. . .

(b) The 'necessary to secure compliance' condition [paragraphs 5.25–5.27]

. . .

5.26 It was clear to the Panel that a contracting party cannot justify a measure inconsistent with another GATT provision as "necessary" in terms of Article XX(d) if an alternative measure which it could reasonably be expected to employ and which is not inconsistent with other GATT provisions is available to it. By the same token, in cases where a measure consistent with other GATT provisions is not reasonably available, a contracting party is bound to use, among the measures reasonably available to it, that which entails the least degree of inconsistency with other GATT provisions. The Panel wished to make it clear that this does not mean that a contracting party could be asked to change its substantive patent law or its desired level of enforcement of that law, provided that such law and such level of enforcement are the same for imported and domestically-produced products. However, it does mean that, if a contracting party could reasonably secure that level of enforcement in a manner that is not inconsistent with other GATT provisions, it would be required to do so.

Thailand – Restrictions on Importation of and Internal Taxes on Cigarettes ('Thailand – Cigarettes'), 1990

Short summary and commentary

At issue in *Thailand – Cigarettes* was a Thai health regulation restricting the import of foreign cigarettes. This was the first case to examine the human health exception under paragraph (b) of GATT Article XX, which covers measures 'necessary to protect human, animal or plant life or health'. As in *US – Section 337*, the panel report was adopted. Although panels still build on the *US – Section 337* criteria, WTO jurisprudence has further fine-tuned the necessity test under paragraphs (b) and (d) of the GATT.

In *Thailand – Cigarettes*, the US alleged, *inter alia*, that the Thai restrictions on imports of cigarettes were inconsistent with Article XI of the GATT (which prohibits the use of quantitative restrictions on imports), and that the restrictions were not justified by the exceptions contained in Article XX(b). Thailand claimed that its import restrictions were justified on grounds of public health, noting that the restrictions were to protect the public from harmful ingredients in imported cigarettes and to reduce the consumption of cigarettes in Thailand. In its report submitted to the parties, the panel agreed with the US' allegations regarding both Articles XI and XX(b). Specifically, the panel concluded that Thailand's practice of prohibiting the importation of foreign cigarettes while allowing the sale of domestic cigarettes could not be considered as 'necessary' within the meaning of Article XX(b).

The panel noted that the import restrictions could be considered 'necessary' only if there was no alternative measure consistent with the GATT, or less inconsistent with it, which Thailand could reasonably be expected to employ to achieve its health policy objectives (Panel report, paragraph 75). The panel found that there was indeed a GATT-consistent alternative measure available, which could achieve the quality-related concerns about cigarettes, and thereby protect the public from harmful ingredients in imported cigarettes (*Id.* at paragraph 77). Specifically, the panel suggested that a non-discriminatory regulation requiring complete disclosure of ingredients, coupled with a ban on unhealthy substances, would be reasonably available (*Id.*). As a result, the panel concluded that the quantitative restriction under Article XI applied by Thailand was not 'necessary' (*Id.*).

In addressing Thailand's goal to reduce the consumption of cigarettes (i.e. quantity-related goals), the panel suggested a ban on advertising of both domestic and imported cigarettes as an alternative measure (*Id.* at paragraph 78). Even if such an advertising ban would potentially violate GATT Article III:4, the panel found that the violation would 'have to be regarded as unavoidable and therefore necessary within the meaning of Article XX(b)' (*Id.*).

As mentioned above, *Thailand – Cigarettes* builds on the interpretation of the term 'necessary' as elaborated in the *US – Section 337* report. Both cases focused primarily on the question of whether or not a GATT-consistent or less inconsistent alternative measure was reasonably available.

Excerpts

Report of the Panel, *Thailand – Restrictions on Importation of and Internal Taxes on Cigarettes*, BISD 37S/200, adopted on 7 November 1990.

(iii) Article XX(b) [paras 72–81]

. . .

74. The Panel noted that a previous panel had discussed the meaning of the term "necessary" in the context of Article XX(d), which provides an exemption for measures which are "necessary to secure compliance with laws or regulations which are not inconsistent" with the provisions of the General Agreement. The panel had stated that

> *"a contracting party cannot justify a measure inconsistent with other GATT provisions as 'necessary' in terms of Article XX(d)* if an alternative measure which it could reasonably be expected to employ and which is not inconsistent with other GATT provisions is available to it. *By the same token, in cases where a measure consistent with other GATT provisions is not reasonably available, a contracting party is bound to use, among the measures reasonably available to it, that which entails the least degree of inconsistency with other GATT provisions" (emphasis supplied).*[2]

The Panel could see no reason why under Article XX the meaning of the term "necessary" under paragraph (d) should not be the same as in paragraph (b). In both paragraphs the same term was used and the same objective intended: to allow contracting parties to impose trade restrictive measures inconsistent with the General Agreement to pursue overriding public policy goals to the extent that such inconsistencies were unavoidable. The fact that paragraph (d) applies to inconsistencies resulting from the enforcement of GATT-consistent laws and regulations while paragraph (b) applies to those resulting from health-related policies therefore did not justify a different interpretation of the term "necessary".

[2] Report of the panel on *"United States – Section 337 of the Tariff Act of 1930"* (L/6439, paragraph 5.26, adopted on 7 November 1989).

75. The Panel concluded from the above that the import restrictions imposed by Thailand could be considered to be "necessary" in terms of Article XX(b) only if there were no alternative measure consistent with the General Agreement, or less inconsistent with it, which Thailand could reasonably be expected to employ to achieve its health policy objectives. The Panel noted that contracting parties may, in accordance with Article III:4 of the General Agreement, impose laws, regulations and requirements affecting the internal sale, offering for sale, purchase, transportation, distribution or use of imported products provided they do not thereby accord treatment to imported products less favourable than that accorded to "like" products of national origin. The United States argued that Thailand could achieve its public health objectives through internal measures consistent with Article III:4 and that the inconsistency with Article XI:1 could therefore not be considered to be "necessary" within the meaning of Article XX(b). The Panel proceeded to examine this issue in detail.

. . .

77. The Panel then examined whether the Thai concerns about the *quality* of cigarettes consumed in Thailand could be met with measures consistent, or less inconsistent, with the General Agreement. It noted that other countries had introduced strict, non-discriminatory labelling and ingredient disclosure regulations which allowed governments to control, and the public to be informed of, the content of cigarettes. A non-discriminatory regulation implemented on a national treatment basis in accordance with Article III:4 requiring complete disclosure of ingredients, coupled with a ban on unhealthy substances, would be an alternative consistent with the General Agreement. The Panel considered that Thailand could reasonably be expected to take such measures to address the quality-related policy objectives it now pursues through an import ban on all cigarettes whatever their ingredients.

78. The Panel then considered whether Thai concerns about the *quantity* of cigarettes consumed in Thailand could be met by measures reasonably available to it and consistent, or less inconsistent, with the General Agreement. The Panel first examined how Thailand might reduce the *demand* for cigarettes in a manner consistent with the General Agreement. The Panel noted the view expressed by the WHO that the demand for cigarettes, in particular the initial demand for cigarettes by the young, was influenced

by cigarette advertisements and that bans on advertisement could therefore curb such demand. At the Forty-third World Health Assembly a resolution was approved stating that the WHO is:

> *"Encouraged by . . . recent information demonstrating the effectiveness of tobacco control strategies, and in particular . . . comprehensive legislative bans and other restrictive measures to effectively control the direct and the indirect advertising, promotion and sponsorship of tobacco".*[1]

[1] Forty-third World Health Assembly, Fourteenth plenary meeting, Agenda Item 10, 17 May 1990 (A43/VR/14; WHA43-16).

The resolution goes on to urge all member states of the WHO

> *"to consider including in their tobacco control strategies plans for legislation or other effective measures at the appropriate government level providing for:*
> . . .
> *(c) progressive restrictions and concerted actions to eliminate eventually all direct and indirect advertising, promotion and sponsorship concerning tobacco".*[1]

A ban on the advertisement of cigarettes of both domestic and foreign origin would normally meet the requirements of Article III:4. It might be argued that such a general ban on all cigarette advertising would create unequal competitive opportunities between the existing Thai supplier of cigarettes and new, foreign suppliers and was therefore contrary to Article III:4.[2] Even if this argument were accepted, such an inconsistency would have to be regarded as unavoidable and therefore necessary within the meaning of Article XX(b) because additional advertising rights would risk stimulating demand for cigarettes. The Panel noted that Thailand had already implemented some non-discriminatory controls on demand, including information programmes, bans on direct and indirect advertising, warnings on cigarette packs, and bans on smoking in certain public places.

[1] Forty-third World Health Assembly, Fourteenth plenary meeting, Agenda Item 10, 17 May 1990 (A43/VR/14; WHA43.16).
[2] On the requirement of equal competitive opportunities, see the Report of the panel on *"United States – Section 337 of the Tariff Act of 1930"* (L/6439, paragraph 5.26, adopted on 7 November 1989).

United States – Restrictions on Imports of Tuna ('US – Tuna/Dolphin I'), 1991 (NOT ADOPTED)

Short summary and commentary

In 1991 and 1994, two pre-WTO cases, *US – Tuna/Dolphin I* and *US – Tuna/Dolphin II*, built on the necessity test as laid out in *US – Section 337* and *Thailand – Cigarettes*.

US – Tuna/Dolphin I addressed the implementation of the 1972 US Marine Mammal Protection Act (MMPA). This act banned the import of tuna caught outside the US through methods that resulted in higher rates of dolphin mortality than those rates allowed by US laws governing domestic producers and those rates actually achieved by US industry. The panel held that the US measure violated Article III of the GATT and could not be justified under Article XX(b). The panel reached this conclusion primarily based on reasons relating to the question of extrajurisdictional protection, an issue not discussed in this chapter of the Guide, but in Chapter 5: Extraterritoriality. However, the panel also found that even if Article XX(b) were interpreted to permit extrajurisdictional protection of life and health, the measure would not meet the necessity requirement because the US had not demonstrated 'that it had exhausted all options reasonably available to pursue its dolphin protection objectives through measures consistent with the GATT' (Panel report, paragraph 5.28).

The *US – Tuna/Dolphin I* and *II* reports were never adopted by the GATT Council, making their findings less consequential for subsequent panels. Nevertheless, the panel reports constitute important steps for the evolution of the trade and environment debate, including the necessity test.

Excerpts

Report of the Panel, *United States – Restrictions on Imports of Tuna ("US – Tuna/Dolphin I")*, DS21/R – 39S/155 (3 September 1991), NOT ADOPTED.

Article XX(b) [paras 5.24–5.29]

. . .

5.28. The Panel considered that the United States' measures, even if Article XX(b) were interpreted to permit extra-jurisdictional protection of life and health, would not meet the requirement of necessity set out in that provision. The United States had not demonstrated to the Panel – as required of the party invoking an Article XX exception – that it had exhausted all options reasonably available to it to pursue its dolphin protection objectives through measures consistent with the General Agreement, in particular through the negotiation of international cooperative arrangements, which would seem to be desirable in view of the fact that dolphins roam the waters of many states and the high seas. Moreover, even assuming that an import prohibition were the only resort reasonably available to the United States, the particular measure chosen by the United States could in the Panel's view not be considered to be necessary within the meaning of Article XX(b). The United States linked the maximum incidental dolphin taking rate which Mexico had to meet during a particular period in order to be able to export tuna to the United States to the taking rate actually recorded for United States fishermen during the same period. Consequently, the Mexican authorities could not know whether, at a given point of time, their policies conformed to the United States' dolphin protection standards. The Panel considered that a limitation on trade based on such unpredictable conditions could not be regarded as necessary to protect the health or life of dolphins.

United States – Restrictions on Imports of Tuna ('US – Tuna/Dolphin II'), 1994 (NOT ADOPTED)

Short summary and commentary

Three years after *US – Tuna/Dolphin I*, a second GATT panel heard another challenge brought against the MMPA. This time the complainant was the European Economic Community (EEC), specifically targeting the secondary embargo provision of the MMPA. The secondary nation embargo provided that any nation that exported yellowfin tuna or yellowfin tuna products to the US and that also imported yellowfin tuna or yellowfin tuna products subject to the direct prohibition on import into the US, had to be certified. In addition such nation also had to provide reasonable proof that it had not imported products subject to the direct prohibition within the preceding six months.

As in *US – Tuna/Dolphin I*, the panel found the measure to violate Article XI. In addressing the necessity test under Article XX(b), the panel introduced a new development in the interpretation of Article XX(b). The US argued that its measures met the necessity requirement since 'necessary', in this sense, simply meant 'needed'. The EEC disagreed, stating that the normal meaning of the term 'necessary' meant 'indispensable' or 'unavoidable'. The panel noted instead that 'necessary' meant that 'no alternative existed' (Panel report, paragraph 5.35). In this context, the panel, citing *US – Section 337* and *Thailand – Cigarettes*, explained that 'necessary' meant that there was no alternative measure reasonably available that was not inconsistent with other GATT provisions, or – in absence of such a measure – that there was no reasonably available measure that was less inconsistent with other GATT provisions (*Id.*).

Thus, the panel confirmed that the necessity test obliges member states to find the least degree of inconsistency with other GATT provisions. However, the *US – Tuna/ Dolphin II* panel did not analyse the availability of alternative measures. Rather, it examined whether the US' measures were effective for the objectives that the US wished to achieve. The panel observed that 'the intermediary nation embargo could not, by itself, further the US' stated conservation objectives' (*Id.* at paragraph 5.36). The embargo 'would only achieve its intended effect if it were followed by changes in policies or practices, not in the country exporting tuna to the US, but in third countries from which the exporting country imported the tuna' (*Id.*).

'The panel concluded that measures taken so as to force other countries to change their polices, and that were effective only if such changes occurred, could not be considered "necessary" for the protection of animal life or health in the sense of Article XX(b)' (*Id.* at para 5.39). This approach is discussed in more detail in Chapter 5: Extraterritoriality.

Excerpts

Report of the Panel, *United States – Restrictions on Imports of Tuna ("Tuna/Dolphin II")*, DS29/R (16 June 1994), NOT ADOPTED.

D. Article XX (b)

. . .

1. To protect human, animal or plant life or health

. . .

2. "Necessary" [paras 5.34–5.39]

5.34 The Panel then examined the second of the above three questions, namely whether the primary and intermediary nation embargoes imposed by the United States on yellowfin tuna could be considered to be "necessary" for the protection of the living things within the meaning of Article XX (b). The United States argued that its measures met this requirement, since "necessary" in this sense simply meant "needed". The EEC disagreed, stating that the normal meaning of the term "necessary" was "indispensable" or "unavoidable". The EEC further argued that adopted panel reports had stated that a measure otherwise inconsistent with the General Agreement could only be justified as necessary under Article XX(b) if no other consistent measure, or more consistent measure, were reasonably available to fulfill the policy objective.

5.35 The Panel proceeded first to examine the relationship established by Article XX(b) between the trade measure and the policy of protecting living things. It noted that, in the ordinary meaning of the term, "necessary" meant that no alternative existed. A previous panel, in discussing the use of the same term in Article XX(d), stated that

> *"a contracting party cannot justify a measure inconsistent with another GATT provision as 'necessary' in terms of Article XX(d) if an alternative measure which it could reasonably be*

> *expected to employ and which is not inconsistent with other GATT provisions is available to it. By the same token, in cases where a measure consistent with other GATT provisions is not reasonably available, a contracting party is bound to use, among the measures reasonably available to it, that which entails the least degree of inconsistency with other GATT provisions."*[85]

This interpretation had also been accepted by another panel specifically examining Article XX(b).[86] The Panel agreed with the reasoning of these previous panels. The Panel then proceeded to examine whether the trade embargoes imposed by the United States could be considered to be 'necessary' in this sense to protect the life or health of dolphins.

[85] Report of the Panel on *United States – Section 337 of the Tariff Act of 1930,* adopted 7 November 1989, L/6439, 36S/345, 392, para 5.26
[86] Report of the Panel on *Thailand – Restrictions on importation of and internal taxes on cigarettes,* DS10/R, adopted 7 November 1990, 37S/200, 223

5.36 The Panel noted that measures taken under the *intermediary* nation embargo prohibited imports from a country of any tuna, whether or not the particular tuna was harvested in a manner that harmed or could harm dolphins, and whether or not the country had tuna harvesting practices and policies that harmed or could harm dolphin, as long as it was from a country that imported tuna from countries maintaining tuna harvesting practices and policies not comparable to those of the United States. The Panel observed that the prohibition on imports of tuna into the United States taken under the intermediary nation embargo could not, by itself, further the United States conservation objectives. The intermediary nation embargo would achieve its intended effect only if it were followed by changes in policies or practices, not in the country exporting tuna to the United States, but in third countries from which the exporting country imported tuna.

5.37 The Panel also recalled that measures taken under the *primary* nation embargo prohibited imports from a country of any tuna, whether or not the particular tuna was harvested in a way that harmed or could harm dolphins, as long as the country's tuna harvesting practices and policies were not comparable to those of the United States. The Panel observed that, as in the case of the intermediary nation embargo, the prohibition on imports of tuna into the United States taken under the primary nation embargo could not possibly, by itself, further the United States objective of protecting the life and health of dolphins. The primary nation embargo could achieve its desired effect only if it were followed by changes in policies and practices in the exporting countries. In view of the foregoing, the Panel observed that both the primary and intermediary nation embargoes on tuna were taken by the United States so as to force other countries to change their policies with respect to persons and things within their own jurisdiction, since the embargoes required such changes in order to have any effect on the protection of the life or health of dolphins.

5.38 The Panel then examined whether, under Article XX(b), measures necessary to protect the life or health of animals could include measures taken so as to force other countries to change their policies within their own jurisdictions, and requiring such changes in order to be effective. The Panel noted that the text of Article XX is not explicit on this question. The Panel then recalled its reasoning under its examination of Article XX(g) that Article XX, as a provision for exceptions, should be interpreted narrowly and in a way that preserves the basic objectives and principles of the General Agreement. If Article XX(b) were interpreted to permit contracting parties to deviate from the basic obligations of the General Agreement by taking trade measures to implement policies within their own jurisdiction, including policies to protect living things, the objectives of the General Agreement would be maintained. If however Article XX(b) were interpreted to permit contracting parties to impose trade embargoes so as to force other countries to change their policies within their jurisdiction, including policies to protect living things, and which required such changes to be effective, the objectives of the General Agreement would be seriously impaired.

5.39 The Panel concluded that measures taken so as to force other countries to change their policies, and that were effective only if such changes occurred, could not be considered "necessary" for the protection of animal life or health in the sense of Article XX(b). Since an essential condition of Article XX(b) had not been met, the Panel did not consider it necessary to examine the further issue of whether the United States measures had also met the other requirements of Article XX. The Panel accordingly found that the import prohibitions on tuna and tuna products maintained by the United States inconsistently with Article XI:1 were not justified by Article XX(b).

Korea – Measures Affecting Imports of Fresh, Chilled and Frozen Beef ('Korea – Beef'), 2001

Short summary and commentary

The first WTO case involving an analysis of the term 'necessary' under Article XX of the GATT is *Korea – Beef.* One of the measures at issue in this case was a 'dual retail system' for the sale of domestic and imported beef. The regulation (challenged by Australia and the US) required that small stores carry either only domestic or only imported beef. The regulation also required that large stores sell imported beef in a section of the store separate from the section where domestic beef was sold.

Korea invoked a defence under Article XX(d) of the GATT (which covers measures 'necessary to secure compliance with laws or regulations which are not inconsistent with the provisions of the GATT') alleging that the dual retail system was necessary to protect consumers from fraudulent practices condemned by Korea's Unfair Competition Act. The relevant fraudulent practices involved retailers selling foreign beef as higher quality domestic beef. Korea claimed that the dual retail system was more effective than an alternative *ex post* enforcement system, which could not lead to the desired level of anti-fraud enforcement. Also, Korea alleged that it did not have the necessary resources for the alternative *ex post* policing system.

The WTO panel rejected Korea's defence, concluding that the dual retail system could not be justified pursuant to Article XX(d) of the GATT because it was a disproportionate measure not necessary to secure compliance with the Korean law against deceptive practices and that other alternative measures were 'reasonably available'. The panel's conclusion, appealed by Korea, was subsequently upheld by the Appellate Body, which found that Korea had not discharged its burden of demonstrating, under Article XX(d), that alternative WTO-consistent measures for detecting and suppressing deceptive practices in the beef retail sector were not 'reasonably available' (AB report, paragraph 182).

In examining whether or not the measure at issue was 'necessary', as required under paragraph (d) of Article XX, the Appellate Body introduced two important clarifications with respect to pre-WTO jurisprudence relating to the necessity test (*Id.* at paragraphs 160–166). First, the Appellate Body stated that the word 'necessary' did not mean 'indispensable' or 'of absolute necessity' or 'inevitable' (*Id.* at paragraph 161). Thus, according to the Appellate Body, the scope of the paragraph (d) exception encompasses not only indispensable measures, but also some dispensable ones (*Id.*). Second, the Appellate Body developed a new weighing and balancing process for determining whether or not a dispensable measure can be considered necessary. The Appellate Body listed three factors to consider when determining whether a measure was in fact 'necessary': (1) the contribution the compliance measure makes to the enforcement of the law or regulation at issue; (2) the importance of the common interests or values that the law or regulation pursues; and (3) the trade impacts of the law or regulation (*Id.* at paragraph 164). For further clarification, the Appellate Body also noted that the weighing and balancing process was 'comprehended in the determination of whether a WTO-consistent alternative measure which the Member concerned could "reasonably be expected to employ" is available, or whether a less WTO-inconsistent measure is "reasonably available"' as required by *US – Section 337* (*Id.* at paragraph 166).

In examining whether or not alternative measures were reasonably available, the Appellate Body first found that the panel's examination of enforcement measures applicable to the same illegal behaviour relating to similar products was legitimate (*Id.* at paragraphs 167–172). The Appellate Body agreed with the panel that the alternative measures (investigations, prosecutions, fines and record-keeping) that were used in related product areas, were also 'reasonably available' to Korea to secure compliance with the Unfair Competition Act in the beef sector (*Id.* at paragraphs 173–174). In this context, the Appellate Body, again affirming the panel's conclusion, rejected Korea's claim that Korea could not achieve its desired level of enforcement by using conventional WTO-consistent enforcement measures (*Id.* at paragraph 180). Although the Appellate Body affirmed Members' right to determine their own level of enforcement of their laws and regulations, the Appellate Body remained unconvinced that the desired level of enforcement could not be achieved through conventional enforcement, if more resources were utilized (*Id.* at paragraphs 175–180). Finally, the Appellate Body pointed out that the dual system shifted most costs from the national budget to imported goods and retailers of imported goods, whereas a WTO-consistent measure of enforcement would not involve such shifting of enforcement costs (*Id.* at paragraph 181). For all of these reasons, the Appellate Body concluded that the dual retail system was not 'necessary'.

The weighing and balancing process elaborated by the Appellate Body gives additional guidance on how to apply the necessity test under Article XX of the GATT. It is interesting to note that, ironically, the Appellate Body in *Korea – Beef*, while presenting an outline of the weighing and balancing process, did not actually apply it in a clear manner. The process suggested by the Appellate Body was applied in the subsequent *EC – Asbestos*, which interpreted the term 'necessary' under Article XX(b). In that case, the Appellate Body was more explicit in applying the elements of the weighing and balancing process.

Excerpts

Report of the Appellate Body, *Korea – Measures Affecting Imports of Fresh, Chilled and Frozen Beef*, WT/DS161/AB/R, WT/DS169/AB/R, adopted on 10 January 2001.

VI. Dual Retail System

A. Article III:4 of the GATT 1994

. . .

B. Article XX(d) of the GATT 1994 [paras 152–185]

. . .

159. We turn, therefore, to the question of whether the dual retail system is "necessary" to secure compliance with the *Unfair Competition Act*. Once again, we look first to the ordinary meaning of the

word "necessary", in its context and in the light of the object and purpose of Article XX, in accordance with Article 31(1) of the *Vienna Convention*.

160. The word "necessary" normally denotes something "that cannot be dispensed with or done without, requisite, essential, needful".[102] We note, however, that a standard law dictionary cautions that:

> *"[t]his word must be considered in the connection in which it is used, as it is a word susceptible of various meanings. It may import absolute physical necessity or inevitability, or it may import that which is only convenient, useful, appropriate, suitable, proper or conducive to the end sought. It is an adjective expressing degrees, and may express mere convenience or that which is indispensable or an absolute physical necessity."*[103]

[102] *The New Shorter Oxford English Dictionary* (Clarendon Press, 1993), Vol. II, p1895.
[103] *Black's Law Dictionary* (West Publishing, 1995), p1029.

161. We believe that, as used in the context of Article XX(d), the reach of the word "necessary" is not limited to that which is "indispensable" or "of absolute necessity" or "inevitable". Measures which are indispensable or of absolute necessity or inevitable to secure compliance certainly fulfill the requirements of Article XX(d). But other measures, too, may fall within the ambit of this exception. As used in Article XX(d), the term "necessary" refers, in our view, to a range of degrees of necessity. At one end of this continuum lies "necessary" understood as "indispensable"; at the other end, is "necessary" taken to mean as "making a contribution to". We consider that a "necessary" measure is, in this continuum, located significantly closer to the pole of "indispensable" than to the opposite pole of simply "making a contribution to".[104]

[104] We recall that we have twice interpreted Article XX(g), which requires a measure *"relating* to the conservation of exhaustible natural resources" (emphasis added). This requirement is more flexible textually than the "necessity" requirement found in Article XX(d). We note that, under the more flexible *"relating to"* standard of Article XX(g), we accepted in *United States – Gasoline* a measure because it presented a *"substantial* relationship" (emphasis added), i.e., *a close and genuine* relationship of ends and means, with the conservation of clean air *(Supra,* footnote 98, p19). In *United States – Shrimp* we accepted a measure because it was *"reasonably related"* to the protection and conservation of sea turtles *(Supra,* footnote 98, at para 141).

162. In appraising the "necessity" of a measure in these terms, it is useful to bear in mind the context in which "necessary" is found in Article XX(d). The measure at stake has to be "necessary to ensure compliance with laws and regulations . . . , *including* those relating to customs enforcement, the enforcement of [lawful] monopolies . . . , the protection of patents, trade marks and copyrights, and the prevention of deceptive practices" (emphasis added). Clearly, Article XX(d) is susceptible of application in respect of a wide variety of "laws and regulations" to be enforced. It seems to us that a treaty interpreter assessing a measure claimed to be necessary to secure compliance of a WTO-consistent law or regulation may, in appropriate cases, take into account the relative importance of the common interests or values that the law or regulation to be enforced is intended to protect. The more vital or important those common interests or values are, the easier it would be to accept as "necessary" a measure designed as an enforcement instrument.

163. There are other aspects of the enforcement measure to be considered in evaluating that measure as "necessary". One is the extent to which the measure contributes to the realization of the end pursued, the securing of compliance with the law or regulation at issue. The greater the contribution, the more easily a measure might be considered to be "necessary". Another aspect is the extent to which the compliance measure produces restrictive effects on international commerce,[105] that is, in respect of a measure inconsistent with Article III:4, restrictive effects *on imported goods*. A measure with a relatively slight impact upon imported products might more easily be considered as "necessary" than a measure with intense or broader restrictive effects.

[105] We recall that the last paragraph of the Preamble of the GATT of 1994 reads as follows: "Being desirous of contributing to these objectives by entering into reciprocal and mutually advantageous arrangements directed to the substantial reduction of tariffs and other barriers to trade *and to the elimination of discriminatory treatment in international commerce*" (emphasis added).

164. In sum, determination of whether a measure, which is not "indispensable", may nevertheless be "necessary" within the contemplation of Article XX(d), involves in every case a process of weighing and balancing a series of factors which prominently include the contribution made by the compliance measure to the enforcement of the law or regulation at issue, the importance of the common interests or values protected by that law or regulation, and the accompanying impact of the law or regulation on imports or exports.

165. The panel in *United States – Section 337* described the applicable standard for evaluating whether a measure is "necessary" under Article XX(d) in the following terms:

> *It was clear to the Panel that a contracting party cannot justify a measure inconsistent with another GATT provision as "necessary" in terms of Article XX(d) if an alternative measure which it could reasonably be expected to employ and which is not inconsistent with other GATT provisions is available to it. By the same token, in cases where a measure consistent with other GATT provisions is not reasonably available, a contracting party is bound to use, among the measures reasonably available to it, that which entails the least degree of inconsistency with other GATT provisions.*[106]

[106] Panel report, *United States – Section 337, supra,* footnote 69, para 5.26.

166. The standard described by the panel in *United States – Section 337* encapsulates the general considerations we have adverted to above. In our view, the weighing and balancing process we have outlined is comprehended in the determination of whether a WTO-consistent alternative measure which the Member concerned could "reasonably be expected to employ" is available, or whether a less WTO-inconsistent measure is "reasonably available".

167. The Panel followed the standard identified by the panel in *United States – Section 337*. It started scrutinizing whether the dual retail system is "necessary" under paragraph (d) of Article XX by stating:

> *Korea has to convince the Panel that, contrary to what was alleged by Australia and the United States, no alternative measure consistent with the WTO Agreement is reasonably available at present in order to deal with misrepresentation in the retail market as to the origin of beef.*[107]

[107] Panel Report, para 659.

168. The Panel first considered a range of possible alternative measures, by examining measures taken by Korea with respect to situations involving, or which could involve, deceptive practices similar to those which in 1989–1990 had affected the retail sale of foreign beef. The Panel found that Korea does not require a dual retail system in *related product areas*, but relies instead on traditional enforcement procedures. There is no requirement, for example, for a dual retail system separating domestic Hanwoo beef from domestic dairy cattle beef.[108] Nor is there a requirement for a dual retail system for any other meat or food product, such as pork or seafood.[109] Finally, there is no requirement for a system of separate restaurants, depending on whether they serve domestic or imported beef, even though approximately 45 per cent of the beef imported into Korea is sold in restaurants.[110] Yet, in all of these cases, the Panel found that there were numerous cases of fraudulent misrepresentation.[111] For the Panel, these examples indicated that misrepresentation of origin could, in principle, be dealt with "on the basis of basic methods . . . such as normal policing under the Korean *Unfair Competition Act*."[112]

[108] In 1998, domestic dairy cattle beef amounted to 12 percent of total beef consumption in Korea. Panel Report, para 661.
[109] *Ibid.,* para 662.
[110] *Ibid.,* para 663.
[111] *Ibid.,* paras 661–663, including footnote 366, in which the Panel noted "that the *Livestock Times* reported that the deceptive beef marketing practice was widespread in restaurants (where price differential was 58 per cent)".
[112] *Ibid.,* para 664.

169. Korea argues, on appeal, that the Panel, by drawing conclusions from the absence of any requirement for a dual retail system in related product areas, introduces an illegitimate "consistency test" into Article XX(d). For Korea, the proper test for "necessary" under Article XX(d):

> *. . . is to see whether another means exists which is less restrictive than the one used and which can reach the objective sought. Whether such means will be applied* consistently *to other products or not is not a matter of concern for the necessity requirement under Article XX(d).*[113]

[113] Korea's appellant's submission, para 167.

170. Examining enforcement measures applicable to the same illegal behaviour relating to like, or at least similar, products does not necessarily imply the introduction of a "consistency" requirement into the "necessary" concept of Article XX(d). Examining such enforcement measures may provide useful input in the course of determining whether an alternative measure which could "reasonably be expected" to be utilized, is available or not.

171. The enforcement measures that the Panel examined were measures taken to enforce the same law, the *Unfair Competition Act*.[114] This law provides for penal and other sanctions[115] against any "unfair competitive act", which includes any:

> Act misleading the public to understand the place of origin of any goods *either by falsely marking that place on any commercial document or communication, in said goods or any advertisement thereof* or in any manner of misleading the general public, *or by selling, distributing, importing or exporting goods bearing such mark*[116] *(emphasis added).*

The language used in this law to define an "unfair competitive act" – "any manner of misleading the general public" – is broad. It applies to all the examples raised by the Panel – domestic dairy beef sold as Hanwoo beef, foreign pork or seafood sold as domestic product, as well as to imported beef served as domestic beef in restaurants.

[114] In GATT case law, comparisons have been made between enforcement measures taken in different *jurisdictions.* In the *US – Measures Affecting Alcoholic and Malt Beverages case,* the panel said that "[t]he fact that not all fifty states maintain discriminatory distribution systems indicates to the Panel that alternative measure for enforcement of state excise tax laws do indeed exist". Adopted 19 June 1992, BISD 39S/206, para 5.43. In the *United States – Section 337* case, the panel "did not consider that a different scheme for imports alleged to infringe process patents is necessary, since many countries grant to their civil courts jurisdiction over imports of products manufactured abroad under processes protected by patents of the importing country" *(Supra,* footnote 69, para 5.28).
[115] *Unfair Competition Prevention and Business Secret Protection Act,* Article 2(1)(c), Article 8.
[116] *Unfair Competition Prevention and Business Secret Protection Act,* Article 2(1)(c) (from translation provided by Korea as Exhibit 28 of its second submission to the Panel).

172. The application by a Member of WTO-*compatible* enforcement measures to the same kind of illegal behaviour – the passing off of one product for another – for like or at least similar products, provides a suggestive indication that an alternative measure which could "reasonably be expected" to be employed may well be available. The application of such measures for the control of the same illegal behaviour for

like, or at least similar, products raises doubts with respect to the objective *necessity* of a different, much stricter, and WTO-inconsistent enforcement measure. The Panel was, in our opinion, entitled to consider that the "examples taken from outside as well as within the beef sector indicate that misrepresentation of origin can indeed be dealt with on the basis of basic methods, consistent with the *WTO Agreement*, and thus less trade restrictive and less market intrusive, such as normal policing under the Korean *Unfair Competition Act*."[117]

[117] Panel Report, para 664.

173. Having found that possible alternative enforcement measures, consistent with the *WTO Agreement*, existed in other related product areas, the Panel went on to state that:

> *. . . it is for Korea to demonstrate that such an alternative measure is not reasonably available or is unreasonably burdensome, financially or technically, taking into account a variety of factors including the domestic costs of such alternative measure, to ensure that consumers are not misled as to the origin of beef.*[118]

[118] Panel Report, para 665.

174. The Panel proceeded to examine whether the alternative measures or "basic methods" – investigations, prosecutions, fines, and record-keeping – which were used in related product areas, were "reasonably available" to Korea to secure compliance with the *Unfair Competition Act*. The Panel concluded "that Korea has not demonstrated to the satisfaction of the Panel that alternative measures consistent with the WTO Agreement were not reasonably available".[119] Thus, as noted at the outset, the Panel found that the dual retail system was "a disproportionate measure not necessary to secure compliance with the Korean law against deceptive practices".[120] The dual retail system was, therefore, not justified under Article XX(d).[121]

[119] *Ibid.*, para 674.
[120] *Ibid.*, para 675.
[121] *Ibid.*

175. Korea also argues on appeal that the Panel erred in applying Article XX(d) because it did not "pay due attention to the level of enforcement sought".[122] For Korea, under Article XX(d), a panel must:

> *. . . examine whether a means reasonably available to the WTO Member could have been used in order to reach the objective sought without putting into question the level of enforcement sought.*[123]

For Korea, alternative measures must not only be reasonably available, but must also *guarantee* the level of enforcement sought which, in the case of the dual retail system, is the *elimination* of fraud in the beef retail market.[124] With respect to investigations, Korea argues that this tool can only reveal fraud *ex post*, whereas the dual retail system can combat fraudulent practices *ex ante*.[125] Korea contends that *ex post* investigations do not *guarantee* the level of enforcement that Korea has chosen, and therefore should not be considered. With respect to policing, Korea believes that this option is not "reasonably available", because Korea lacks the resources to police thousands of shops on a round-the-clock basis.

[122] Korea's appellant's submission, para 182.
[123] *Ibid.*, para 181.
[124] *Ibid.*, paras 181, 185.
[125] *Ibid.*, para 192.

176. It is not open to doubt that Members of the WTO have the right to determine for themselves the level of enforcement of their WTO-consistent laws and regulations. We note that this has also been recognized by the panel in *United States – Section 337*, where it said: "The Panel wished to make it clear that this [the obligation to choose a reasonably available GATT-consistent or less inconsistent measure] does not mean that a contracting party could be asked to change its substantive patent law or its desired *level of enforcement* of that law. . ." (emphasis added). The panel added, however, the caveat that "provided that such law and such *level of enforcement* are the same for imported and domestically-produced products".[126]

[126] Panel report, *United States – Section 337, supra,* footnote 69, para 5.26.

177. We recognize that, in establishing the dual retail system, Korea could well have intended to secure a higher level of enforcement of the prohibition, provided by the *Unfair Competition Act*, of acts misleading the public *about the origin of beef* (domestic or imported) *sold by retailers*, than the level of enforcement of the same prohibition of the *Unfair Competition Act* with respect to *beef served in restaurants*, or the sale by *retailers* of *other meat or food products*, such as *pork or seafood*.

178. We think it unlikely that Korea intended to establish a level of protection that *totally eliminates* fraud with respect to the origin of beef (domestic or foreign) sold by retailers. The total elimination of fraud would probably require a total ban of imports. Consequently, we assume that in effect Korea intended to *reduce considerably* the number of cases of fraud occurring with respect to the origin of beef sold by retailers. The Panel did find that the dual retail system "does appear to reduce the opportunities and thus the temptations for butchers to misrepresent foreign beef for domestic beef".[127] And we accept Korea's argument that the dual retail system *facilitates* control and permits combatting fraudulent practices *ex ante*. Nevertheless, it must be noted that the dual retail system is only an *instrument* to achieve a significant reduction of violations of the *Unfair Competition Act*. Therefore, the question remains whether other, conventional and WTO-consistent instruments can not reasonably be expected to be employed to achieve the same result.

[127] Panel Report, para 658.

179. Turning to investigations, the Panel found that Korea, in the past, had been able to distinguish imported beef from domestic beef, and had, in fact, published figures on the amount of imported beef fraudulently sold as domestic beef. This meant that Korea was able, in fact, to detect fraud.[128] On fines, the Panel found that these could be an effective deterrent, as long as they outweighed the potential profits from fraud.[129] On record-keeping, the Panel felt that if beef traders at all levels were required to keep records of their transactions, then effective investigations could be carried out.[130] Finally, on policing, the Panel noted that Korea had not demonstrated that the costs would be too high.[131] For all these reasons, the Panel considered "that Korea has not demonstrated to the satisfaction of the Panel that alternative measures consistent with the WTO Agreement were not reasonably available".[132] Thus, as already noted, the Panel found that the dual retail system was "a disproportionate measure not necessary to secure compliance with the Korean law against deceptive practices".[133]

[128] *Ibid.*, para 668.
[129] *Ibid.*, para 669.
[130] *Ibid.*, para 672.
[131] *Ibid.*, para 673.
[132] *Ibid.*, para 674.
[133] *Ibid.*, para 675.

180. We share the Panel's conclusion. We are not persuaded that Korea could not achieve its desired level of enforcement of the *Unfair Competition Act* with respect to the origin of beef sold by retailers by using conventional WTO-consistent enforcement measures, if Korea would devote more resources to its

enforcement efforts on the beef sector. It might also be added that Korea's argument about the lack of resources to police thousands of shops on a round-the-clock basis is, in the end, not sufficiently persuasive. Violations of laws and regulations like the Korean *Unfair Competition Act* can be expected to be routinely investigated and detected through selective, but well-targeted, controls of potential wrongdoers. The control of records will assist in selecting the shops to which the police could pay particular attention.

181. There is still another aspect that should be noted relating to both the method actually chosen by Korea – its dual retail system for beef – and alternative traditional enforcement measures. Securing through conventional, WTO-consistent measures a higher level of enforcement of the *Unfair Competition Act* with respect to the retail sale of beef, could well entail higher enforcement costs for the national budget. It is pertinent to observe that, through its dual retail system, Korea has in effect shifted all, or the great bulk, of these potential costs of enforcement (translated into a drastic reduction of competitive access to consumers) to imported goods and retailers of imported goods, instead of evenly distributing such costs between the domestic and imported products. In contrast, the more conventional, WTO-consistent measures of enforcement do not involve such onerous shifting of enforcement costs which ordinarily are borne by the Member's public purse.

182. For these reasons, we uphold the conclusion of the Panel that Korea has not discharged its burden of demonstrating under Article XX(d) that alternative WTO-consistent measures were not "reasonably available" in order to detect and suppress deceptive practices in the beef retail sector,[134] and that the dual retail system is therefore not justified by Article XX(d).[135]

[134] Panel Report, para 674.
[135] *Ibid.,* para 675.

European Communities – Measures Affecting Asbestos and Products Containing Asbestos ('EC – Asbestos'), 2001

Short summary and commentary

EC – Asbestos involved a claim by Canada that a French ban on the manufacturing, sale, and import of asbestos fibres violated, *inter alia*, GATT Article III:4 on national treatment. The stated purpose of the ban was to protect the health of workers and consumers from the carcinogenicity of asbestos fibres. Although the Appellate Body concluded that the French measure was not in violation of Article III of the GATT, it went on to examine the panel's finding that the measure was justified under Article XX(b). The Appellate Body confirmed the panel's conclusion that the measure fell within the category of measures embraced by Article XX(b) of the GATT, and reiterated that it was undisputed that WTO Members had the right to determine their own levels of health protection (AB report, paragraph 168).

The Appellate Body then addressed Canada's argument that the panel had erred in finding that 'controlled use' was not a reasonably available alternative to the outright ban. Referring to *Thailand – Cigarettes* and *Korea – Beef*, the Appellate Body recalled that Article XX(b) of the GATT requires the examination of whether or not there is an alternative measure consistent or less inconsistent with the GATT, which a Member could reasonably be expected to employ to achieve its objectives (*Id.* at paragraph 170). Confirming the 'weighing and balancing process' laid down in *Korea – Beef*, the Appellate Body reiterated two aspects of that process. First, it referred to the extent to which the alternative measure 'contributes to the realization of the end pursued' and second, it reiterated the concept that the more 'vital or important' the common interests being pursued, the easier it would be for a measure to satisfy the necessity requirement (*Id.* at paragraph 172). With respect to the first of the two elements, the Appellate Body noted that in the specific case, 'controlled use' would not allow France to achieve its chosen level of health protection by halting the spread of asbestos-related health risks (*Id.* at paragraph 174). In addition, in applying the second aspect of the weighing and balancing process, the Appellate Body emphasized that the objective pursued by the French measure – the preservation of human life and health – was indeed 'both vital and important in the highest degree' (*Id.* at paragraph 172). Consequently, the Appellate Body concluded that 'controlled use' had not been shown to be a reasonably available, less trade-restrictive, alternative measure able to achieve the same result as the measure at issue (*Id.*).

EC – Asbestos was the first to accept a Member's defence under Article XX(b).

Excerpts

Report of the Appellate Body, *European Communities – Measures Affecting Asbestos and Products Containing Asbestos*, WT/DS135/AB/R, adopted on 5 April 2001.

VII. Article XX(b) of the GATT 1994 and Article 11 of the DSU

. . .

A. "To Protect Human Life or Health"

. . .

B. "Necessary" [paras 164–175]

. . .

169. In its fourth argument, Canada asserts that the Panel erred in finding that "controlled use" is not a reasonably available alternative to the Decree. This last argument is based on Canada's assertion that, in *United States – Gasoline*, both we and the panel held that an alternative measure "can only be ruled out if it is shown to be impossible to implement".[161] We understand Canada to mean by this that an alternative measure is only excluded as a "reasonably available" alternative if implementation of that measure is "impossible". We certainly agree with Canada that an alternative measure which is impossible to implement is not "reasonably available". But we do not agree with Canada's reading of either the panel report or our report in *United States – Gasoline*. In *United States – Gasoline*, the panel held, in essence, that an alternative measure did not *cease* to be "reasonably" available simply because the alternative measure involved *administrative difficulties* for a Member.[162] The panel's findings on this point were not appealed, and, thus, we did not address this issue in that case.

[161] Canada's appellant's submission, para 202, referring to, *inter alia,* para 130 of that submission.
[162] See Panel Report, *United States – Gasoline, supra,* footnote 15, paras 6.26 and 6.28.

170. Looking at this issue now, we believe that, in determining whether a suggested alternative measure is "reasonably available", several factors must be taken into account, besides the difficulty of implementation. In *Thailand – Restrictions on Importation of and Internal Taxes on Cigarettes*, the panel made the following observations on the applicable standard for evaluating whether a measure is "necessary" under Article XX(b):

> *The import restrictions imposed by Thailand could be considered to be "necessary" in terms of Article XX(b) only if there were no alternative measure consistent with the General Agreement, or less inconsistent with it, which Thailand could* reasonably be expected to employ to achieve its health policy objectives[163] *(emphasis added).*

[163] Adopted 20 February 1990, BISD 37S/200, para 75.

171. In our Report in *Korea – Beef*, we addressed the issue of "necessity" under Article XX(d) of the GATT 1994.[164] In that appeal, we found that the panel was correct in following the standard set forth by the panel in *United States – Section 337 of the Tariff Act of 1930*:

> *It was clear to the Panel that a contracting party cannot justify a measure inconsistent with another GATT provision as "necessary" in terms of Article XX(d) if an alternative measure which it could reasonably be expected to employ and which is not inconsistent with other GATT provisions is available to it. By the same token, in cases where a measure consistent with other GATT provisions is not reasonably available, a contracting party is bound to use, among the measures reasonably available to it, that which entails the least degree of inconsistency with other GATT provisions.*[165]

[164] *Supra,* footnote 49, paras 159 ff.

[165] Adopted 7 November 1989, BISD 36S/345, para 5.26; we expressly affirmed this standard in our Report in *Korea – Beef, supra,* footnote 49, para 166.

172. We indicated in *Korea – Beef* that one aspect of the "weighing and balancing process . . . comprehended in the determination of whether a WTO-consistent alternative measure" is reasonably available is the extent to which the alternative measure "contributes to the realization of the end pursued".[166] In addition, we observed, in that case, that "[t]he more vital or important [the] common interests or values" pursued, the easier it would be to accept as "necessary" measures designed to achieve those ends.[167] In this case, the objective pursued by the measure is the preservation of human life and health through the elimination, or reduction, of the well-known, and life-threatening, health risks posed by asbestos fibres. The value pursued is both vital and important in the highest degree. The remaining question, then, is whether there is an alternative measure that would achieve the same end and that is less restrictive of trade than a prohibition.

[166] Appellate Body Report, *Korea – Beef, supra,* footnote 49, paras 166 and 163.

[167] *Ibid.,* para 162.

173. Canada asserts that "controlled use" represents a "reasonably available" measure that would serve the same end. The issue is, thus, whether France could reasonably be expected to employ "controlled use" practices to achieve its chosen level of health protection – a halt in the spread of asbestos-related health risks.

174. In our view, France could not reasonably be expected to employ *any* alternative measure if that measure would involve a continuation of the very risk that the Decree seeks to "halt". Such an alternative measure would, in effect, prevent France from achieving its chosen level of health protection. On the basis of the scientific evidence before it, the Panel found that, in general, the efficacy of "controlled use" remains to be demonstrated.[168] Moreover, even in cases where "controlled use" practices are applied "with greater certainty", the scientific evidence suggests that the level of exposure can, in some circumstances, still be high enough for there to be a "significant residual risk of developing asbestos-related diseases".[169] The Panel found too that the efficacy of "controlled use" is particularly doubtful for the building industry and for DIY enthusiasts, which are the most important users of cement-based products containing chrysotile asbestos.[170] Given these factual findings by the Panel, we believe that "controlled use" would not allow France to achieve its chosen level of health protection by halting the spread of asbestos-related health risks. "Controlled use" would, thus, not be an alternative measure that would achieve the end sought by France.

[168] Panel Report, para 8.209.

[169] *Ibid.,* paras 8.209 and 8.211.

[170] *Ibid.,* paras 8.213 and 8.214.

Dominican Republic – Measures Affecting the Importation and Internal Sale of Cigarettes ('DR – Cigarettes'), 2005

Short summary and commentary

In this case, Honduras complained against certain measures imposed by the Dominican Republic (DR), in connection with the import and sales of cigarettes. The measures at issue included transitional surcharges imposed on all imports, a foreign exchange fee on all imports, a requirement that tax stamps be attached to packets of cigarettes, certain rules and practices for determining the tax base, and the requirement that cigarette importers post a bond to ensure payment of taxes.

Honduras claimed that certain of these measures violated the GATT obligations on MFN (most-favoured nation) treatment (Article II:1(b)), national treatment (Articles III:4 and III:2), quantitative restrictions (Article XI:1) and certain obligations regarding the publication and administration of trade regulations (Article X:1). The panel found that the transitional surcharge violated Article II, and that the tax stamp requirement violated Article III:4. The Dominican tax stamp regulation laid down that the stamps needed to be affixed in the territory of the DR and under the supervision of its tax authorities. The panel found that this violated national treatment because this resulted in 'additional costs and processes for imported products', although this measure applied indistinctly to imported and domestic cigarettes (this finding was not appealed) (AB report, paragraph 57, referring to panel report). The panel also found that the Dominican Republic failed to show that the tax stamp requirement was necessary according to GATT Article XX(d). The panel exercised judicial economy on Honduras' claim that the requirement amounted to arbitrary or unjustified discrimination or to a disguised restriction on trade (the chapeau of Article XX).

On appeal, the Appellate Body upheld the panel's finding that the tax stamp requirement was not 'necessary' within the meaning of GATT Article XX(d) (*Id.* at paragraph 73). In its analysis, the Appellate Body focused on the question of whether or not the DR's specific requirement was necessary in order to seek compliance with its tax laws. The Appellate Body, as did the panel, based its analysis on its previous approaches to the concept of 'necessity' as laid out in *Korea – Beef, EC – Asbestos* and in *US – Gambling*.

Along these lines, the Appellate Body stated that an assessment of the 'necessity' of a measure involves an inquiry as to whether or not reasonably available, WTO-consistent (or less-WTO inconsistent) alternative measures exist (AB report, paragraphs 66–68). This inquiry must be assessed in light of the weighing and balancing of factors, which will usually include: (1) the importance of interests and values protected, (2) the contribution of the measure to the objective pursued, and (3) the restrictive impact on trade (*Id.* at paragraphs 68–69).

The Appellate Body also recalled its previous statements that such an analysis should involve a 'comparison between the challenged measure and possible alternatives'; that for a measure to be reasonably available, it must not be only theoretically available (e.g. it must not impose undue burdens on the Member such as prohibitive costs or substantial technical difficulties); and that a reasonable available alternative must preserve the Member's right to achieve its desired level of protection with respect to the objective pursued (*Id.* at paragraphs 65–70). Based on these interpretations, the Appellate Body concluded that the panel had conducted an 'appropriate analysis' of the issue (*Id.* at paragraphs 71–72).

Examining the panel's analysis, as confirmed by the Appellate Body, a series of aspects may warrant attention and give guidance for the future application of this interpretation of necessity. One aspect relates to the interests and values protected. The panel found that the interests protected (namely the avoidance of tax evasion) constitute 'most important interests' for states, particularly for developing countries (Panel report, paragraph 7.215). In that context, the panel did not question the Dominican Republic's position that the Dominican Republic was in fact pursuing a zero tolerance policy towards tax evasion and tobacco smuggling (*Id.* at paragraph 7.228). The panel did, however, find that *the measures as they stood, did not secure this zero tolerance level of enforcement* (*Id.* at paragraph 7.229).

Having considered the measure's impact on trade (the panel found that the tax stamp requirement had no 'intensive restrictive effects on trade' in light of the fact that Honduras' cigarette imports had increased in recent years), the panel then turned to assessing the measure's contribution to the objective pursued (*Id.* at paragraph 7.215). This aspect was key to the panel's conclusion. First, the panel recognized that tax stamps in general may be a useful tool for enforcement. However, it found that the tax stamp requirement only provided 'limited effectiveness' in preventing smuggling and tax evasion of cigarettes. In fact, the panel found that there is '*no causal link between allowing tax stamps to be affixed abroad and the forgery of tax stamps*' (*Id.* at paragraph 7.226). The DR's rigid requirements for the affixation of tax stamps would only address those tobacco products that enter legally into the country, while not preventing smuggling of cigarettes with forged tax stamps (*Id.*). Next, the panel found that 'other factors, . . . *may play a more important role in the forgery of tax stamps, the tax evasion and the smuggling of tobacco products*', such as incorporating more security features in the tax stamps (to make forgery more costly), and utilizing police controls at roads and at different commercial levels (*Id.*).

In this vein, the panel identified (on the basis of Honduras' arguments) 'reasonably available, less GATT-inconsistent alternative measures', such as providing secure stamps to foreign exporters, so that they can place the stamps themselves, prior to importation, and if necessary, accompanying the stamps with pre-shipment inspection and certification (*Id.* at paragraph 7.227). The panel concluded that the Dominican Republic had not shown that the alternatives were not reasonably available because it had not proven that the alternatives were 'not able to achieve that same level of enforcement' that the Dominican Republic had chosen to attain (*Id.* at paragraph 7.226). The panel concluded that the Dominican Republic had not proven that the measures are necessary under Article XX(d) (*Id.* at paragraph 7.330). It then exercised judicial economy on the chapeau of Article XX(d) (*Id.* at paragraph 7.331).

The Appellate Body, for its part, agreed fully with the legal analysis of the panel. It noted that the panel gave substantial weight to its finding that the incumbent tax stamp requirement was of limited effectiveness in achieving the DR's goals and called this 'appropriate' and in line with its earlier jurisprudence (AB report, paragraph 71). The Appellate Body also considered the panel's analysis of the alternative measures and the 'equivalence' with regard to the level of enforcement of the tax laws as 'appropriate', noting the weight the panel granted to the limited contribution of the tax stamp requirement to the DR's goals (*Id.* at paragraph 72).

Excerpts

Report of the Appellate Body, Dominican Republic – Measures Affecting the Importation and Internal Sale of Cigarettes, *WT/DS302/AB/R, adopted on 19 May 2005.*

IV. The Necessity Analysis under Article XX(d) of the GATT 1994 in relation to the Tax Stamp Requirement [paras 57–74]

. . .

57. The Dominican Republic requires that tax stamps be affixed to cigarette packets in the territory of the Dominican Republic under the supervision of the Dominican Republic's tax authorities (the "tax stamp requirement"). The Panel found that the tax stamp requirement is inconsistent with the national treatment obligation set out in Article III:4 of the GATT 1994.[41] According to the Panel, although the tax stamp requirement is applied in a formally equal manner to domestic and imported cigarettes, it modifies the conditions of competition in the market place to the detriment of imports. The Panel found that the tax stamp requirement results in additional processes and costs for imported products, and leads to imported cigarettes being presented to final consumers in a less appealing manner. Having found that the tax stamp requirement was inconsistent with Article III:4 of the GATT 1994, the Panel then examined the Dominican Republic's argument, under Article XX(d) of the GATT 1994, that the tax stamp requirement is necessary to secure compliance with the Dominican Republic tax laws and regulations, to fight tax evasion, and to prevent smuggling of cigarettes. The Panel concluded that the Dominican Republic had failed to establish that the tax stamp requirement is justified under Article XX(d) of the GATT 1994.[42]

[41] Panel Report, paras 7.198 and 8.1(e).
[42] *Ibid.,* paras 7.232, 7.233 and 8.1(e).

58. On appeal, the Dominican Republic limits its challenge to the Panel's finding that the tax stamp requirement is not justified under Article XX(d) of the GATT 1994. The Dominican Republic does not appeal the Panel's finding that the tax stamp requirement is inconsistent with the national treatment obligation set out in Article III:4 of the GATT 1994. Therefore, we need not express any view on the finding under Article III:4.

59. In considering the Dominican Republic's argument under Article XX(d), the Panel began its analysis by assuming that the tax laws and regulations to be enforced through the tax stamp requirement are not inconsistent with the provisions of the GATT 1994. The Panel then examined whether the tax stamp requirement is "necessary" to secure compliance with those laws and regulations. The Panel acknowledged that "the collection of tax revenue (and, conversely, the prevention of tax evasion) is a most important interest" for the Dominican Republic.[43] The Panel also said that "the measure has not had any intense restrictive effects on trade".[44] The Panel found, however, no supporting evidence "that there is a causal link between allowing stamps to be affixed abroad and the forgery of tax stamps."[45] According to the Panel, the requirement of affixing tax stamps in the Dominican Republic and under the supervision of the Dominican Republic authorities "would only serve to guarantee that those tobacco products that enter legally into the country and go through the proper customs procedures will carry authentic tax stamps as a proof that the appropriate tax has been paid."[46] The Panel added that the tax stamp requirement, "in and of itself, would not prevent the forgery of tax stamps, nor smuggling and tax evasion."[47] In the opinion of the Panel, the Dominican Republic did not discharge its duty to prove why other reasonably available GATT-consistent or less GATT-inconsistent measures would not be able to achieve the level of enforcement with regard to tax collection and cigarette smuggling that the Dominican Republic sought to attain with the tax stamp requirement.[48] For the Panel, a reasonably available alternative to the tax stamp requirement would be to provide secure tax stamps to foreign exporters.[49] In this light, the Panel concluded that the tax stamp requirement is not "necessary" to secure compliance with the Dominican Republic's tax laws and regulations. Accordingly, the Panel found that the tax stamp requirement is not justified under Article XX(d) of the GATT 1994.[50]

[43] *Ibid.*, para 7.215.
[44] *Ibid.*, para 7.215.
[45] *Ibid.*, para 7.226.
[46] *Ibid.*
[47] *Ibid.*
[48] *Ibid.*
[49] Thus, tax stamps would be affixed on cigarette packets in the course of the foreign manufacturer's production process and prior to importation into the Dominican Republic.
[50] Given its conclusion that the tax stamp requirement is not "necessary" under Article XX(d), the Panel considered that it did not need to analyze consistency of the measure with the chapeau of Article XX.

60. The Dominican Republic claims that the Panel erred in interpreting and applying the term "necessary" in Article XX(d) of the GATT 1994. The Dominican Republic relies mainly on the Appellate Body Report in *Korea – Various Measures on Beef*, contending that, determining whether a measure is "necessary" under Article XX(d), involves in every case a process of weighing and balancing a series of factors.[51] According to the Dominican Republic, a panel must weigh and balance the following four factors as part of the necessity analysis: (1) the trade impact of the measure; (2) the importance of the interests protected by the measure; (3) the contribution of the measure to the end pursued; and (4) the existence of alternative measures that a Member could reasonably be expected to employ.[52] Thus, "the Panel improperly interpreted and applied the term 'necessary' because it failed to examine fully all the factors relevant to determining whether a measure is 'necessary' under Article XX(d), including weighing and balancing them, as required by Article XX(d)."[53] The Dominican Republic adds that a proper weighing and balancing of the relevant factors leads to the conclusion that the tax stamp requirement is "necessary" within the meaning of Article XX(d) of the GATT 1994. In particular, the Dominican Republic contends that affixation of tax stamps in the presence of a tax inspector contributes more to the prevention of tax evasion than affixation abroad, without the presence of a tax inspector. The Dominican Republic underlines that affixing the stamp abroad would make it possible for cigarettes smuggled into the Dominican Republic to be sold as stamped, while evading import taxes. This would be prevented by the requirement to affix stamps in the Dominican Republic in the presence of a tax inspector, unless the stamp is forged. Thus, for the Dominican Republic, the tax stamp requirement not only seeks to ensure the authenticity of tax stamps, but also "contributes importantly to reducing the volume of smuggled cigarettes and increasing the volume of cigarettes bearing 'authentic tax stamps,".[54]

[51] Dominican Republic's appellant's submission, para 30 (referring to Appellate Body Report, *Korea – Various Measures on Beef,* para 164).
[52] *Ibid.*, para 31.
[53] Dominican Republic's appellant's submission, para 30.
[54] *Ibid.*, para 45.

61. Regarding the question of the existence of alternative measures that a Member could reasonably be expected to employ in place of the GATT-inconsistent measure, the Dominican Republic submits that the Panel erred in concluding that an alternative measure is reasonably available. According to the Dominican Republic, the alternative identified by the Panel – providing secure tax stamps to foreign exporters – is not a reasonably available alternative because it would increase the risk of smuggling and tax evasion, as compared with the tax stamp requirement, and, therefore, would be less likely to secure the goals pursued by the tax stamp requirement.

62. For Honduras, the Dominican Republic's contention that the Panel did not properly weigh and balance the relevant factors in its analysis under Article XX(d) should be rejected. Honduras maintains that "the Panel properly set out and applied the appropriate factors in its assessment of the measure under Article XX(d)."[55] Honduras adds that "the Panel did examine the relevant factors in its assessment of whether there were less trade restrictive alternative measures that the Dominican Republic could have employed."[56]

[55] Honduras' appellee's submission, para 37.
[56] *Ibid.*, para 65.

63. At the oral hearing, Honduras drew attention to the fact that, on 25 October 2004, the Dominican Republic enacted a new decree modifying the tax stamp requirement to allow tax stamps to be affixed abroad at the time of production.[57] The Dominican Republic confirmed that it had enacted the new decree. Honduras stated that, pursuant to this new measure, it had recently exported to the Dominican Republic a shipment of cigarettes with stamps attached at the factory. Honduras expressed surprise that, in these circumstances, the Dominican Republic continues to maintain that the only measure reasonably available to it is affixation of tax stamps within the Dominican Republic, under the supervision of the tax authorities. Both participants nevertheless requested the Appellate Body to rule on whether the original measure is justified under Article XX(d) of the GATT 1994.

[57] The new decree was enacted after the issuance of the Panel Report to the parties on 20 October 2004. We also referred to the enactment of the new decree in paragraph 14 of this Report.

64. We begin our consideration of Article XX(d) by noting that the analysis of a measure under Article XX is two-tiered:

> *In order that the justifying protection of Article XX may be extended to it, the measure at issue must not only come under one or another of the particular exceptions – paragraphs (a) to (j) – listed under Article XX; it must also satisfy the requirements imposed by the opening clauses of Article XX. The analysis is, in other words, two-tiered: first, provisional justification by reason of characterization of the measure under XX(g); second, further appraisal of the same measure under the introductory clauses of Article XX.*[58]

[58] Appellate Body Report, *US – Gasoline,* p22, DSR 1996:I, 3, at p20.

65. In *Korea – Various Measures on Beef*, the Appellate Body explained the analysis to be undertaken in considering the justification of a measure under paragraph (d) of Article XX:

> *For a measure . . . to be justified provisionally under paragraph (d) of Article XX, two elements must be shown. First, the measure must be one designed to "secure compliance" with laws or regulations that are not themselves inconsistent with some provision of the GATT 1994. Second, the measure must be "necessary" to secure such compliance.*[59]

[59] Appellate Body Report, *Korea – Various Measures on Beef,* para 157.

66. The Appellate Body also explained that determining whether a measure is "necessary" within the meaning of Article XX(d):

> *. . . involves in every case a process of weighing and balancing a series of factors which prominently include the contribution made by the compliance measure to the enforcement of the law or regulation at issue, the importance of the common interests or values protected by that law or regulation, and the accompanying impact of the law or regulation on imports or exports.*[60]

[60] Appellate Body Report, *Korea – Various Measures on Beef,* para 164.

67. The Appellate Body also referred to the GATT panel report in *US – Section 337*, in particular to the statement that a Member's inconsistent measure cannot be deemed to be necessary "if an alternative

measure which it could reasonably be expected to employ and which is not inconsistent with other GATT provisions is available to it."[61]

[61] *Ibid.*, para 165 (quoting GATT Panel Report, *US – Section 337*, para 5.26).

68. In *EC – Asbestos*, the Appellate Body considered whether the measure challenged in those proceedings was "necessary" to protect public health within the meaning of Article XX(b) of the GATT 1994. The Appellate Body stated that "in determining whether a suggested alternative measure is 'reasonably available', several factors must be taken into account, besides the difficulty of implementation."[62] Relying on its Report in *Korea – Various Measures on Beef*, the Appellate Body reiterated, in the context of Article XX(b), that "one aspect of the 'weighing and balancing process . . . comprehended in the determination of whether a WTO-consistent alternative measure' is reasonably available is the extent to which the alternative measure 'contributes to the realization of the end pursued'."[63] Another factor to be taken into account in determining whether an alternative measure is reasonably available is the importance of the interests or values pursued: "[t]he more vital or important [the] common interests or 'values' pursued, the easier it would be to accept as 'necessary' measures designed to achieve those ends."[64]

[62] Appellate Body Report, *EC – Asbestos*, para 170.
[63] *Ibid.*, para 172 (quoting Appellate Body Report, *Korea – Various Measures on Beef*, paras 166 and 163).
[64] *Ibid.*, para 172 (quoting Appellate Body Report, *Korea – Various Measures on Beef*, para 162).

69. In *US – Gambling*, the Appellate Body considered the "necessity" test in the context of Article XIV of the *General Agreement on Trade in Services.* The Appellate Body confirmed that an assessment of the "necessity" of a measure involves a weighing and balancing of "the 'relative importance' of the interests or values furthered by the challenged measure", along with other factors, which will usually include "the contribution of the measure to the realization of the ends pursued by it [and] the restrictive impact of the measure on international commerce."[65] The Appellate Body went on to explain that:

> *A comparison between the challenged measure and possible alternatives should then be undertaken, and the results of such comparison should be considered in the light of the importance of the interests at issue. It is on the basis of this "weighing and balancing" and comparison of measures, taking into account the interests or values at stake, that a panel determines whether a measure is "necessary" or, alternatively, whether another, WTO-consistent measure is "reasonably available".*[66]

[65] Appellate Body Report, *US – Gambling*, para 306.
[66] *Ibid.*, para 307.

70. The Appellate Body Reports in *Korea – Various Measures on Beef*, *EC – Asbestos* and *US – Gambling* indicate that, in the assessment of whether a proposed alternative to the impugned measure is reasonably available, factors such as the trade impact of the measure, the importance of the interests protected by the measure, or the contribution of the measure to the realization of the end pursued, should be taken into account in the analysis. The weighing and balancing process of these three factors also informs the determination whether a WTO-consistent alternative measure which the Member concerned could reasonably be expected to employ is available, or whether a less WTO-inconsistent measure is reasonably available. Furthermore, in *US – Gambling*, the Appellate Body indicated:

> *An alternative measure may be found not to be "reasonably available", however, where it is merely theoretical in nature, for instance, where the responding Member is not capable of taking it, or where the measure imposes an undue burden on that Member, such as prohibitive costs or substantial technical difficulties. Moreover, a "reasonably available" alternative*

measure must be a measure that would preserve for the responding Member its right to achieve its desired level of protection with respect to the objective pursued . . . .[67]

[67] *Ibid.*, para 308.

71. In assessing whether a WTO-consistent measure was reasonably available, the Panel in the present case discussed the factors identified by the Appellate Body in previous appeals, namely, the importance of the interests protected by the tax stamp requirement, its trade impact and its contribution to the realization of the end pursued. As regards the first factor, "the Panel [did] not disagree with the Dominican Republic's argument that tax stamps may be a useful instrument to monitor tax collection on cigarettes and, conversely, to avoid tax evasion".[68] The Panel also recognized that "the collection of tax revenue (and, conversely, the prevention of tax evasion) is a most important interest for any country and particularly for a developing country such as the Dominican Republic".[69] With respect to the trade impact of the measure, the Panel noted that the tax stamp requirement did not prevent Honduras from exporting cigarettes to the Dominican Republic and that its exports had increased significantly over recent years.[70] Accordingly, the Panel assumed "that the measure has not had any intense restrictive effects on trade".[71] As far as the third factor is concerned, the Panel noted the Dominican Republic's claim that "the tax stamp requirement secures compliance with its tax laws and regulations generally, and more specifically with the provisions governing the Selective Consumption Tax".[72] The Panel, however, was of the view that the tax stamp requirement was of limited effectiveness in preventing tax evasion and cigarette smuggling. According to the Panel, requiring that tax stamps be affixed in the Dominican Republic under the supervision of the tax authorities "in and of itself, would not prevent the forgery of tax stamps, nor smuggling and tax evasion".[73] In this respect, the Panel indicated that other factors, such as security features incorporated into the tax stamps, or police controls on roads and at different commercial levels, would play a more important role in preventing forgery of tax stamps, tax evasion and smuggling of tobacco products.[74] Having considered the importance of the interests protected by the tax stamp requirement, its trade impact, and its contribution to the realization of the end pursued, we are of the view that the Panel conducted an appropriate analysis, following the approach set out in the Appellate Body Reports in *Korea – Various Measures on Beef* and in *EC – Asbestos*, and affirmed in *US – Gambling*. We see no error in the approach taken by the Panel or in the results of its analysis. We note that, in this particular case, the Panel's conclusion concerning the contribution of the measure to the realization of the end pursued is based on findings of fact (limited effectiveness of the tax stamp requirement in preventing forgery, smuggling and tax evasion; greater effectiveness and efficiency of measures such as security features incorporated into the tax stamps or police controls) that have not been challenged under Article 11 of the DSU and, therefore, fall outside the scope of appellate review.

[68] Panel Report, para 7.217.
[69] Panel Report, para 7.215.
[70] *Ibid.*
[71] *Ibid.*
[72] *Ibid.*, para 7.210.
[73] *Ibid.*, para 7.226.
[74] *Ibid.*

72. Having assessed the importance of the interests protected by the tax stamp requirement, its trade impact, and its contribution to the realization of the end pursued, the Panel also considered whether a WTO-consistent alternative measure is reasonably available to secure compliance with the Dominican Republic's tax laws and regulations appropriate to the level of enforcement pursued by the Dominican Republic. In the light of its analysis of the relevant factors, especially the measure's contribution to the realization of the end pursued, the Panel opined that the alternative of providing secure tax stamps to foreign exporters, so that those tax stamps could be affixed on cigarette packets in the course of their own production process, prior to importation, would be equivalent to the tax stamp requirement in terms

of allowing the Dominican Republic to secure the high level of enforcement it pursues with regard to tax collection and the prevention of cigarette smuggling.[75] The Panel gave substantial weight to its finding that the tax stamp requirement is of limited effectiveness in preventing tax evasion and cigarette smuggling; in particular, it found "no evidence to conclude that the tax stamp requirement secures a zero tolerance level of enforcement with regard to tax collection and the prevention of cigarette smuggling."[76] We consider that the Panel conducted an appropriate analysis, following the approach set out in *Korea – Various Measures on Beef* and in *EC – Asbestos*, and affirmed in *US – Gambling*. We see no reason to disturb the Panel's conclusions in respect of the existence of a reasonably available alternative measure to the tax stamp requirement.

[75] Panel Report, para 7.228.
[76] *Ibid.,* para 7.229.

73. In the light of these considerations, we *uphold* the Panel's finding, in paragraphs 7.232, 7.233 and 8.1(e) of the Panel Report, that the tax stamp requirement is not "necessary" within the meaning of Article XX(d) of the GATT 1994 and, therefore, is not justified under Article XX(d) of the GATT 1994.

74. The Dominican Republic requests us to complete the legal analysis under Article XX of the GATT 1994 should we find that the Panel misinterpreted or misapplied the term "necessary" in Article XX(d) of the GATT 1994. As we agree with the Panel's interpretation of the term "necessary" and we uphold the Panel's finding that the tax stamp requirement is not "necessary" within the meaning of Article XX(d) of the GATT 1994, the contingency on which the Dominican Republic's request is based does not arise and, therefore, there is no need for us to complete the legal analysis under Article XX of the GATT 1994.

SPS Agreement

Australia – Measures Affecting Importation of Salmon from Canada ('Australia – Salmon'), 1998

Short summary and commentary

Australia – Salmon was the first SPS case that expressly addressed the requirement under Article 5.6 that measures not be 'more trade-restrictive than required to achieve their appropriate level of sanitary or phytosanitary protection, taking into account technical and economic feasibility.' The case involved a Canadian challenge to Australia's import prohibition of certain fresh, chilled and frozen salmon. Australia based its measure on studies of several fish disease agents that were found in uncooked salmon of Canadian and US origin, and that were considered a risk to Australian salmon populations. Canada claimed, among other things, that Australia's policy was more trade-restrictive than required to achieve Australia's appropriate level of protection, and therefore in violation of Article 5.6 of the SPS Agreement.

Based on a lack of factual findings by the panel, the Appellate Body reversed the panel's finding that Australia had acted inconsistently with Article 5.6 and did not come to a conclusion itself on whether the import ban did, in fact, violate Article 5.6. Nevertheless, the Appellate Body completed the panel's legal analysis; specifically, it agreed with the three-pronged test the panel developed for Article 5.6., including the footnote to this provision, and found a violation of Article 5.6 (AB report, paragraph 194). Pursuant to this a measure is to be considered 'more trade-restrictive than required' only if there is another sanitary measure that meets the following three cumulative requirements:

1. That the measure is 'reasonably available taking into account technical and economic feasibility';
2. That the measure 'achieves [Australia's] appropriate level of sanitary . . . protection'; and
3. That the measure is 'significantly less restrictive to trade' than the sanitary measure contested (*Id.*).

Applying this three-pronged test to alternative measures, the panel found that each of the test's elements was met, and thus that Australia had acted inconsistently with Article 5.6.

Based on the panel's factual finding, the Appellate Body also considered the first element of the test met (*Id.* at paragraph 195). However, with respect to the second element, which requires that alternative measures meet the appropriate level of protection, the Appellate Body was unable to come to a conclusion, due to the insufficiency of the factual findings of the panel. However, it examined the panel's legal analysis in great detail and disagreed with the reasoning of the panel that the level of protection reflected in a sanitary measure could be presumed to be at least as high as the level of protection considered to be appropriate by the Member imposing the measure (*Id.* at paragraph 196). Rejecting this argument, the Appellate Body found that the 'determination of the appropriate level of protection, . . . is a *prerogative* of the Member concerned and not of a panel or of the Appellate Body' (*Id.* at paragraph 199). Moreover, the Appellate Body explained that the SPS Agreement – although not explicitly obliging Members to determine the appropriate level of protection – contained such an implicit obligation (*Id.* at paragraph 205). It clarified that the determination did not have to be quantitative but, at the same time, could not be determined 'with such vagueness or equivocation that the application of the relevant provisions of the *SPS Agreement*, such as Article 5.6, becomes impossible' (*Id.* at paragraph 206). It stressed that the 'appropriate level of protection' and the SPS measure had to be clearly distinguished, the first being the objective and the second the instrument (*Id.* at paragraph 200). Only in cases where a Member did not determine its appropriate level of protection, could such a level be 'established by panels on the basis of the level of protection reflected in the SPS measure actually applied' (*Id.* at paragraph 207).

Australia – Salmon is important for at least two reasons. First, it clearly sets out the elements to be considered under Article 5.6 of the SPS Agreement, which incorporates a form of the 'necessity test'. Second, it illustrates an application of the second element under Article 5.6, namely whether or not the alternative measure achieves the Member's appropriate level of protection. In this context, the Appellate Body's findings that each Member has the prerogative to set its own level of protection, and that there is an (implicit) obligation of the Member under the SPS Agreement to determine its appropriate level of protection, are of particular relevance.

Excerpts

Report of the Appellate Body, *Australia – Measures Affecting Importation of Salmon*, WT/DS18/AB/R, adopted on 6 November 1998.

V. The *SPS Agreement*

. . .

D. Article 5.6 of the SPS Agreement [paras 179–213]

. . .

194. We agree with the Panel that Article 5.6 and, in particular, the footnote to this provision, clearly provides a three-pronged test to establish a violation of Article 5.6. As already noted, the three elements of this test under Article 5.6 are that there is an SPS measure which:

(1) is reasonably available taking into account technical and economic feasibility;
(2) achieves the Member's appropriate level of sanitary or phytosanitary protection; and
(3) is significantly less restrictive to trade than the SPS measure contested.

These three elements are cumulative in the sense that, to establish inconsistency with Article 5.6, all of them have to be met. If any of these elements is not fulfilled, the measure in dispute would be consistent with Article 5.6. Thus, if there is no alternative measure available, taking into account technical and economic feasibility, *or* if the alternative measure does not achieve the Member's appropriate level of sanitary or phytosanitary protection, *or* if it is not significantly less trade-restrictive, the measure in dispute would be consistent with Article 5.6.

195. With regard to the first element of this test, we note the Panel's factual finding that there are alternative SPS measures that are reasonably available, taking into account technical and economic feasibility. We, therefore, consider that the first element of the test under Article 5.6 is met.

196. With regard to the second element of the test under Article 5.6, i.e. whether the available alternative SPS measures meet the appropriate level of protection, we note that the Panel stated in paragraph 8.173 of its Report, that "[t]o determine whether any of the alternative measures meet Australia's appropriate level of protection, we should [. . .] examine whether these alternatives meet the level of protection currently achieved by the measure at issue". As already noted, this statement is based on the Panel's premise that "the *level of* protection implied or reflected in a sanitary *measure* or regime imposed by a WTO Member can be presumed to be at least as high as the level of protection considered to be *appropriate* by that Member." We disagree with the Panel.

. . .

200. The "appropriate level of protection" established by a Member and the "SPS measure" have to be clearly distinguished.[160] They are not one and the same thing. The first is an *objective*, the second is an *instrument* chosen to attain or implement that objective.

[160] That the level of protection and the SPS measure applied have to be clearly distinguished results already from our Report in *European Communities – Hormones,* WT/DS26/AB/R, WT/DS48/AB/R, adopted 13 February 1998, para 214.

201. It can be deduced from the provisions of the *SPS Agreement* that the determination by a Member of the "appropriate level of protection" logically precedes the establishment or decision on maintenance of an "SPS measure". The provisions of the *SPS Agreement* also clarify the correlation between the "appropriate level of protection" and the "SPS measure".

. . .

204. We, therefore, conclude that the Panel's statement that "to determine whether any of the alternative measures meet Australia's appropriate level of protection, we should [. . .] examine whether these alternatives meet the level of protection currently achieved by the measure at issue" is wrong. What is required under Article 5.6 is an examination of whether possible alternative SPS measures meet the appropriate level of protection *as determined by the Member concerned*.

205. We recognize that the *SPS Agreement* does not contain an *explicit* provision which obliges WTO Members to determine the appropriate level of protection. Such an obligation is, however, implicit

in several provisions of the *SPS Agreement*, in particular, in paragraph 3 of Annex B, Article 4.1,[161] Article 5.4 and Article 5.6 of the *SPS Agreement*.[162] With regard to Article 5.6, for example, we note that it would clearly be impossible to examine whether alternative SPS measures achieve the appropriate level of protection if the importing Member were not required to determine its appropriate level of protection.

[161] Reasonable questions from interested Members within the meaning of paragraph 3 of Annex B can arise, in particular, with respect to the application of Article 4 of the *SPS Agreement.* Articles 4.1 and 4.2 imply, in our view, a clear obligation of the importing Member to determine its appropriate level of protection.

[162] Furthermore, it could be argued that an implicit obligation for a Member to determine the appropriate level of protection results also from Article 5.8 and Article 12.4 of the *SPS Agreement.*

206. We thus believe that the *SPS Agreement* contains an implicit obligation to determine the appropriate level of protection. We do not believe that there is an obligation to determine the appropriate level of protection in quantitative terms. This does not mean, however, that an importing Member is free to determine its level of protection with such vagueness or equivocation that the application of the relevant provisions of the *SPS Agreement*, such as Article 5.6, becomes impossible. It would obviously be wrong to interpret the *SPS Agreement* in a way that would render nugatory entire articles or paragraphs of articles of this Agreement and allow Members to escape from their obligations under this Agreement.

207. While in this case Australia determined its appropriate level of protection, and did so with sufficient precision to apply Article 5.6, we believe that in cases where a Member does not determine its appropriate level of protection, or does so with insufficient precision, the appropriate level of protection may be established by panels on the basis of the level of protection reflected in the SPS measure actually applied. Otherwise, a Member's failure to comply with the implicit obligation to determine its appropriate level of protection – with sufficient precision – would allow it to escape from its obligations under this Agreement and, in particular, its obligations under Articles 5.5 and 5.6.

Japan – Measures Affecting Agricultural Products ('Japan – Varietals'), 1999

Short summary and commentary

In *Japan – Varietals*, the US challenged a Japanese prohibition on importing individual varieties of some agricultural products until each variety had been tested with the required quarantine treatment (varietal testing requirement). Japan established the prohibition on the ground that the imports could carry pests that could damage Japanese fruit. The US alleged, *inter alia*, that the measure was more restrictive than required to achieve Japan's appropriate level of protection, thus violating Article 5.6 of the SPS Agreement. The US argued that there was another alternative measure available which fulfilled the three cumulative requirements under Article 5.6 (as established in *Australia – Salmon*), namely the 'testing-by-product' alternative. The panel agreed with the US that this alternative fulfilled two of the three required elements. It found that: (1) the alternative was a measure that was reasonably available, taking into account technical and economic feasibility, and (2) the alternative measure was significantly less restrictive to trade than the varietal testing requirement (AB report, paragraph 96). However, it found that there was insufficient evidence to prove that the testing-by-product alternative would achieve Japan's appropriate level of protection, and as a consequence did not find a violation of Article 5.6 with regard to the testing-by-product alternative (*Id.*). The Appellate Body rejected the US' appeal from the panel's finding under Article 5.6 with regard to the testing-by-product alternative.

While rejecting the US' claim that testing-by-product was an alternative measure meeting all of the elements under Article 5.6, the panel found that another alternative, namely the 'determination of sorption levels', met all of the elements under Article 5.6 (*Id.* at paragraph 125). The Appellate Body, however, rejected this conclusion, stating that it was reached in a manner inconsistent with the rules of burden of proof (*Id.* at paragraph 131). Specifically, the Appellate Body did not accept the fact that the 'determination of sorption levels' alternative was suggested by the experts advising the panel, rather than the US (*Id.* at paragraphs 126, 130). The Appellate Body pointed out that pursuant to the rules on the burden of proof, the US would have had to establish a *prima facie* case that there was an alternative measure that met all three elements under Article 5.6, something the US had not specifically argued with respect to the determination of sorption levels (*Id.* at paragraph 126).

This case is interesting insofar as it clearly shows that the complaining party must explicitly suggest specific alternative measures and establish a *prima facie* case of inconsistency with each of the elements required under Article 5.6. In contrast, under Articles XX(b) and (d) of the GATT, the burden of proof lies with the responding Member. Moreover, while the Appellate Body in *Japan – Varietals* did not accept the fact that the panel found a reasonable alternative based on suggestions of experts rather than the complaining party, the panels in some of the cases involving Articles XX(b) and (d) appeared to have fairly extensive freedom in suggesting and assessing alternative measures (see *Thailand – Cigarettes* and *Korea – Beef*, in particular).

Excerpts

Report of the Appellate Body, *Japan – Measures Affecting Agricultural Products*, WT/DS76/AB/R, adopted on 19 March 1999.

VI. General Issues

A. Burden of Proof [paras 118–131]

. . .

124. As noted above, the United States argued that "testing by product" is an alternative measure which meets the three cumulative elements under Article 5.6. The Panel was not, however, convinced that there was sufficient evidence to find that "testing by product" would achieve Japan's appropriate level of protection.[76]

[76] The United States appeals from this finding, but we have upheld it *(supra,* para 100*)*.

125. The Panel then turned its attention to an alternative measure which had been *suggested* by the experts advising the Panel, i.e., the "determination of sorption levels".[77] The Panel explained that it *deduced* this alternative measure from the written answers of the experts to the Panel's questions and from their statements at the Panel's meeting with the experts.[78] We note that the Panel explicitly stated that the United States, as complaining party, did *not specifically argue* that the "determination of sorption levels" met any of the three elements under Article 5.6.[79] On the basis of the evidence before it, including its deductions from the views expressed by the experts,[80] the Panel came to the conclusion that it could be presumed that the "determination of sorption levels was an alternative measure which would meet all of the elements under Article 5.6".[81] The Panel pointed out that the United States had "given views which were consistent with" the argument that this alternative measure met the first and third elements under

Article 5.6 and had "suggest[ed]" that it would meet the second element.[82]

[77] Panel Report, para 8.74.
[78] *Ibid.*
[79] Panel Report, footnotes 328, 332 and 333. See *supra,* para 119. We note that the United States stated in its Appellee's Submission, para 79, that it "emphasized [testing by product] in its Article 5.6 arguments because this alternative meets the requirements of Article 5.6, and because *there is no scientific evidence to support even limited sorption testing"* (emphasis added). We also note that the United States declared before the Panel in its Comments on the Experts' Reponses (p3), that "it is not necessary in the context of this dispute for the United States to address the merits of [the 'determination of sorption levels'], nor is it within the scope of the Panel's terms of reference to make findings with respect to the comparative efficacy of alternative treatments proposed by technical experts."
[80] See Panel Report, paras 8.92 and 8.93 (on the first element) and para. 8.100 (on the second element).
[81] See Panel Report, para 8.94 (on the first element), para 8.97 (on the third element), para 8.101 (on the second element) and para 8.103 (on all three elements).
[82] Panel Report, paras 8.91, 8.95 and 8.98.

126. Pursuant to the rules on burden of proof set out above, we consider that it was for the United States to establish a *prima facie* case that there is an alternative measure that meets all three elements under Article 5.6 in order to establish a *prima facie* case of inconsistency with Article 5.6. Since the United States did not even claim before the Panel that the "determination of sorption levels" is an alternative measure which meets the three elements under Article 5.6, we are of the opinion that the United States did not establish a *prima facie* case that the "determination of sorption levels" is an alternative measure within the meaning of Article 5.6.

. . .

130. In the present case, the Panel was correct to seek information and advice from experts to help it to understand and evaluate the evidence submitted and the arguments made by the United States and Japan with regard to the alleged violation of Article 5.6. The Panel erred, however, when it used that expert information and advice as the basis for a finding of inconsistency with Article 5.6, since the United States did not establish a *prima facie* case of inconsistency with Article 5.6 based on claims relating to the "determination of sorption levels". The United States did not even *argue* that the "determination of sorption levels" is an alternative measure which meets the three elements under Article 5.6.

131. We, therefore, reverse the Panel's finding that it can be presumed that the "determination of sorption levels" is an alternative SPS measure which meets the three elements under Article 5.6, because this finding was reached in a manner inconsistent with the rules on burden of proof.

TBT Agreement

European Communities – Trade Description of Sardines ('EC – Sardines'), 2002

Short summary and commentary

In *EC – Sardines,* Peru challenged an EC measure regulating the marketing of certain species of fish sold in the European Communities. Specifically, the dispute concerned a regulation, which provided in part that only products prepared from *Sardina pilchardus* (a specific species of sardines that can be found in the North Atlantic, the Black Sea and the Mediterranean) could be marketed as preserved sardines. Thus, given that the species of sardines found in the Pacific near the Peruvian coast did not belong to the particular species identified in the EC regulation, Peruvian 'sardines' could not be marketed with the words 'sardines' on their packaging.

Peru alleged, *inter alia*, that the measure violated Articles 2.1 (national and most-favoured nation treatment requirements), 2.2 (necessity requirements) and 2.4 (international standards) of the TBT Agreement. The panel agreed with Peru's claim that the measure was inconsistent with Article 2.4 of the TBT Agreement. It relied on the principle of judicial economy to refrain from examining the consistency of the measure with Articles 2.1 and 2.2 of the TBT Agreement, as well as with Article III.4 of the GATT. On appeal, the Appellate Body upheld the panel's finding that the EC regulation was inconsistent with Article 2.4 of the TBT Agreement. Article 2.4 provides that '[w]here technical regulations are required and relevant international standards exist or their completion is imminent, Members shall use them, or the relevant parts of them, as a basis for their technical regulations except when such international standards or relevant parts would be an ineffective or inappropriate means for the fulfilment of the legitimate objectives pursued. . . .'

Although *EC – Sardines* did not address the necessity concept for reasons of judicial economy, the case remains relevant for the discussion of necessity under the TBT Agreement.

Most importantly, the case addressed issues relating to 'legitimate objectives'. In that context, it first addressed the question of how the notion of legitimate objectives in Article 2.4 of the TBT Agreement relates to the concept of legitimate objectives under Article 2.2. Article 2.4 requires Members to use international standards as a basis for their technical regulation except where such standards would be an 'ineffective or inappropriate means for the fulfilment of the legitimate objectives pursued'. Article 2.2 provides that measures must 'not be more trade restrictive than necessary to fulfil a legitimate objective' and sets forth an open list of such legitimate objectives. Regarding the relationship between Articles 2.4 and 2.2 of the TBT Agreement, the Appellate Body specifically stated that 'legitimate objectives' as referred to in Article 2.4 had to be interpreted in the context of Article 2.2 (AB report, paragraph 286). Against that background, it specified that the scope of legitimate objectives in Article 2.4 must include and go beyond those objectives explicitly mentioned in Article 2.2 of the TBT Agreement (*Id.*).

Second, *EC – Sardines* raised the issue of whether or not panels and/or the Appellate Body are allowed to question the legitimacy of policy objectives referred to in Article 2.4 of the TBT Agreement. The Appellate Body declared that it indeed had the authority, at least in the context of Article 2.4 of the TBT Agreement, to question the legitimacy of certain policy objectives (*Id.*). Specifically, it agreed with the panel that the second sentence of Article 2.4 implies that WTO tribunals must examine and determine the legitimacy of measures' objectives (*Id.*). In the end, however, neither the panel, nor the Appellate Body questioned the legitimacy of the objectives in question (i.e. market transparency, consumer protection and fair competition). This was the case even though none of these three policy objectives are explicitly mentioned in the indicative list of Article 2.2 of the TBT Agreement. The panel clarified that it had refrained from analysing the legitimacy of these objectives mainly because the disputing parties essentially agreed upon the legitimacy of the objectives, and because it saw no reason to disagree with the parties' assessment in this respect (*Id.* at paragraph 263).

In addition to the issue of legitimate objectives, *EC – Sardines* addressed international standards. Specifically, it raised the question of whether or not the EC based its measure on the relevant international standards. This question matters for the necessity test under the TBT Agreement because Article 2.5 of the TBT establishes a rebuttable presumption that measures that are in accordance with international standards do not create *unnecessary* obstacles to international trade (emphasis added). In these cases, it is presumed that the measure applied is necessary. However, in *EC – Sardines*, the Appellate Body found that the European Communities had not based its measure on international standards (*Id.* at paragraphs 257–258). The Appellate Body did not proceed to examine whether the measure was more trade-restrictive than necessary (TBT Article 2.2) for reasons of judicial economy. Because the Appellate Body did not specifically address the necessity requirement, the discussion of whether the EC measure was based on international standards is not reflected in the excerpts below.

Finally, it is worth noting that the Appellate Body analysed the issue of whether or not the European Communities' failure to base its measure on international standards was consistent with the TBT Agreement. Again, the Appellate Body referred to Article 2.4 of the TBT Agreement, second sentence, which states that WTO Members need not use international standards as a basis for their technical regulations 'when such international standards or relevant parts would be an ineffective or inappropriate means of the fulfilment of the legitimate objective pursued'. The Appellate Body upheld the panel's finding that Peru had fulfilled its burden of proof to demonstrate that the Codex standard at issue was not 'ineffective or inappropriate' to fulfil the legitimate objectives of the EC measure and thus confirmed the panel's finding of a violation of Article 2.4 of the TBT Agreement (*Id.* at paragraphs 290–291). In that context, the Appellate Body's ruling in *EC – Sardines* provides some guidance as to the concept of a 'relevant international standard' as referred to in Article 2.4 (*Id.* at paragraphs 217–227). It also gives directions as to when such a standard would be an 'ineffective or inappropriate' means for the fulfilment of certain legitimate objectives (*Id.* at paragraphs 284–291). Due to space constraints these aspects are not reproduced in the excerpts below.

Thus, *EC – Sardines*, while not directly relating to the necessity test, is relevant primarily because it brings clarification to related issues, including the question of legitimate objectives and international standards.

Excerpts

Report of the Appellate Body, *European Communities – Trade Description of Sardines*, WT/DS231/AB/R, adopted on 23 October 2002.

IX. The Question of the "Ineffectiveness or Inappropriateness" of Codex Stan 94

. . .

B. Whether Codex Stan 94 is an Effective and Appropriate Means to Fulfil the "Legitimate Objectives" Pursued by the European Communities Through the EC Regulation

. . .

1. The Interpretation of the Second Part of Article 2.4 [paras 285–286]

. . .

286. As to the second question, we are of the view that the Panel was also correct in concluding that "the 'legitimate objectives' referred to in Article 2.4 must be interpreted in the context of Article 2.2", which

refers also to "legitimate objectives", and includes a description of what the nature of some such objectives can be.[208] Two implications flow from the Panel's interpretation. First, the term "legitimate objectives" in Article 2.4, as the Panel concluded, must cover the objectives explicitly mentioned in Article 2.2, namely: "national security requirements; the prevention of deceptive practices; protection of human health or safety, animal or plant life or health, or the environment". Second, given the use of the term "*inter alia*" in Article 2.2, the objectives covered by the term "legitimate objectives" in Article 2.4 extend beyond the list of the objectives specifically mentioned in Article 2.2. Furthermore, we share the view of the Panel that the second part of Article 2.4 implies that there must be an examination and a determination on the legitimacy of the objectives of the measure.[209]

[208] Panel Report, para 7.118.
[209] *Ibid.*, para 7.122.

Article XIV of the GATS

United States – Measures Affecting the Cross-Border Supply of Gambling and Betting Services ('US – Gambling'), 2005

Short summary and commentary

US – Gambling is one of the first WTO cases entirely based on the General Agreement on Trade in Services (GATS). The case is described in more detail in Chapter 2: General Exceptions Clauses. It involved a complaint by Antigua & Barbuda challenging various US measures (including federal and state laws, as well as court decisions, policy statements, government actions, websites and agreements between US enforcement agencies and credit card companies), which, according to Antigua, constituted a 'total prohibition' of the cross-border supply of gambling and betting services to the US.

Both the panel and the Appellate Body found that three US federal laws violated the US market access commitment under Article XVI(a) and (c) of the GATS (the Wire Act, the Travel Act and the Illegal Gambling Business Act) because they banned the 'remote supply' of gambling and betting services, thereby, effectively imposing a 'zero quota' on the provision of those 'remote supply' gambling services.

In its defence, the US stated that its measures were justified on the basis of the GATS' general exceptions for measures necessary to protect public morals and/or to maintain public order (Article XIV(a)) and for measures necessary to secure compliance with other WTO-consistent US laws (Article XIV(c)). Concluding that the measures were not 'necessary' to achieve the policy goals under sub-paragraphs (a) and (c) of Article XIV, the panel found that the US restrictions could not be justified under either Article XIV(a) or Article XIV(c) (Panel report, paragraphs 6.533–6.535). Although the Appellate Body reversed the panel's finding that the US measures were not *necessary* to protect public morals/maintain public order, the Appellate Body also found that the US had not demonstrated that its measures were consistent with the requirements of the chapeau of GATS Article XIV (AB report, paragraphs 318–321 and 370).

US – Gambling represented the first case in which a Member invoked the general exception for public morals/public order. Both the panel and the Appellate Body found similarity in the language between the general exceptions provisions of the GATT and the GATS, and accordingly applied the two-tier test developed in Article XX jurisprudence. The first step thus included an analysis of whether or not the measure was 'necessary' to achieve the specific legitimate policy objective. The two-tier analysis is described in detail in Chapter 2: General Exceptions Clauses.

In its analysis of GATS Article XIV, the panel included the 'weighing and balancing' of different factors as laid out by the Appellate Body in its decision on *Korea – Beef* (AB report, paragraphs 300–301). The panel first looked at three factors: (1) the importance of the interest/values protected (stating that the measure served societal interests that are *vital and important in the highest degree*); (2) the contribution of the measure to the ends pursued (stating that the US measures *must* contribute to the ends pursued, at least to *some* extent); and (3) the trade impact of the measure (stating that there is a *significant restrictive* impact on trade) (*Id.* at paragraph 301). The panel then turned to a prior Appellate Body statement, which set forth that a Member must first explore and exhaust all GATT/WTO-compatible alternatives before resorting to WTO-inconsistent alternatives. In that context, the panel found that by rejecting Antigua's invitation to engage in negotiations, the US had failed to explore – in good faith – the possibility of finding a reasonably available WTO-consistent alternative (*Id.*). Thus, the panel concluded that the US measure could not be justified under sub-paragraph (a) of GATS Article XIV.

On appeal, the Appellate Body reversed the panel's finding and further clarified the necessity test with a number of statements. The Appellate Body noted that the factors involved in the weighing and balancing process were not exhaustive (*Id.* at paragraph 306). It also stated that, when comparing the challenged measure to possible alternatives, the importance of the interest at issue plays a key role in determining the ultimate necessity of the measure (*Id.*).

With respect to the reasonable availability of an alternative measure, the Appellate Body found that an alternative that is merely theoretical may not be considered a reasonably available alternative (*Id.* at paragraph 308). It referred to examples such as situations in which the responding Member is not capable of taking an alternative measure and situations in which the alternative measure would impose an undue burden on that Member (e.g. prohibitive cost or substantial technical difficulties) (*Id.*). In that context, the Appellate Body also noted that a reasonably available alternative measure must preserve the Member's right to achieve its desired level of protection with respect to the objective pursued (*Id.*).

The Appellate Body also made important statements with respect to the burden of proof. It clarified that the responding party did not, in the first instance, need to explore the universe of reasonably available measures (*Id.* at paragraph 309). Rather, the responding parts merely had to make a *prima facie* case that its measure was necessary (*Id.* at paragraph 310). The Appellate Body clarified that once the complaining party raised a WTO consistent-alternative, the responding party then needed to demonstrate that the suggested alternative was not reasonably available (*Id.* at paragraph 311).

Based on these considerations, the Appellate Body ultimately reversed the panel's finding that negotiating with Antigua would have been an appropriate alternative for the US (*Id.* at paragraph 321). According to the Appellate Body, such negotiations were not appropriate, as 'consultations are by definition a process, the results of which are uncertain and therefore not capable of comparison with the measures at issue' (*Id.* at paragraphs 317–318). Thus, the Appellate Body found that the three US federal laws were necessary to protect public morals or to maintain public order within the meaning of GATS Article XIV(a) (*Id.*). Similarly, the Appellate Body also reversed the finding regarding the necessity test under GATS Article XIV(c).

Subsequently, the panel and the Appellate Body analysed whether or not the US measure complied with the requirements of the chapeau of Article XIV, and both – albeit based on different reasoning – found that the US failed to demonstrate that the application of its laws did not result in an unjustifiable or arbitrary discrimination or in a disguised restriction on international trade. This aspect of the dispute is addressed in more detail in Chapter 2: General Exceptions Clauses.

Excerpts

Report of the Appellate Body, *United States – Measures Affecting the Cross-Border Supply of Gambling and Betting Services*, WT/DS285/AB/R, adopted on 20 April 2005.

VII. Article XIV of the GATS: General Exceptions [paras 266–372]

. . .

C. The Panel's substantive analysis under Article XIV [paras 291–372]

. . .

1. Justification of the Measures Under Paragraph (a) of Article XIV [paras 293–334]

. . .

(b) The Requirement that a Measure be "Necessary" Under Art. XIV(a) [paras 300–327]

. . .

300. In the second part of its analysis under Article XIV(a), the Panel considered whether the Wire Act, the Travel Act and the IGBA are "necessary" within the meaning of that provision. The Panel found that the US had not demonstrated the "necessity" of those measures.[366]

[366] *Ibid.*

301. This finding rested on the Panel's determinations that: (i) "the interests and values protected by [the Wire Act, the Travel Act, and the IGBA] serve very important societal interests that can be characterized as 'vital and important in the highest degree'";[367] (ii) the Wire Act, the Travel Act, and the IGBA "must contribute, at least to some extent", to addressing the United States' concerns "pertaining to money laundering, organized crime, fraud, underage gambling and pathological gambling";[368] (iii) the measures in question "have a significant restrictive trade impact";[369] and (iv) "[i]n rejecting Antigua's invitation to engage in bilateral or multilateral consultations and/or negotiations, the United States failed to pursue in good faith a course of action that could have been used by it to explore the possibility of finding a reasonably available WTO-consistent alternative".[370]

[367] *Ibid.*, para 6.492:

> On the basis of the foregoing, it is clear to us that the interests and values protected by the Wire Act, the Travel Act (when read together with the relevant state laws) and the Illegal Gambling Business Act (when read together with the relevant state laws) serve very important societal interests that can be characterized as "vital and important in the highest degree" in a similar way to the characterization of the protection of human life and health against a life-threatening health risk by the Appellate Body in *EC – Asbestos* (quoting Appellate Body Report, *EC – Asbestos,* para 172).

[368] *Ibid.*, para 6.494.

[369] *Ibid.*, para 6.495.
[370] *Ibid.*, para 6.531.

302. Each of the participants appeals different aspects of the analysis undertaken by the Panel in determining whether the "necessity" requirement in Article XIV(a) was satisfied. According to Antigua, the Panel failed to establish a sufficient "nexus" between gambling and the concerns raised by the United States.[371] In addition, Antigua claims that the Panel erroneously limited its discussion of "reasonably available alternatives". In its appeal, the United States argues that the Panel departed from the way in which "reasonably available alternative" measures have been examined in previous disputes and erroneously imposed "a procedural requirement on the United States to consult or negotiate with Antigua before the United States may take measures to protect public morals [or] protect public order".[372]

[371] Antigua's other appellant's submission, para 97.
[372] United States' appellant's submission, para 139.

303. We begin our analysis of this issue by examining the legal standard of "necessity" in Article XIV(a) of the GATS. We then turn to the participants' appeals regarding the Panel's interpretation and application of this requirement.

(i) Determining "necessity" under Article XIV(a)

304. We note, at the outset, that the standard of "necessity" provided for in the general exceptions provision is an objective standard. To be sure, a Member's characterization of a measure's objectives and of the effectiveness of its regulatory approach – as evidenced, for example, by texts of statutes, legislative history and pronouncements of government agencies or officials – will be relevant in determining whether the measure is, objectively, "necessary". A panel is not bound by these characterizations,[373] however, and may also find guidance in the structure and operation of the measure and in contrary evidence proffered by the complaining party. In any event, a panel must, on the basis of the evidence in the record, independently and objectively assess the "necessity" of the measure before it.

[373] Appellate Body Report, *India – Patents (US)*, para 66.

305. In *Korea – Various Measures on Beef,* the Appellate Body stated, in the context of Article XX(d) of the GATT 1994, that whether a measure is "necessary" should be determined through "a process of weighing and balancing a series of factors".[374] The Appellate Body characterized this process as one:

> *. . . comprehended in the determination of whether a WTO-consistent alternative measure which the Member concerned could "reasonably be expected to employ" is available, or whether a less WTO-inconsistent measure is "reasonably available".*[375]

[374] Appellate Body Report, *Korea – Various Measures on Beef,* para 164.
[375] Appellate Body Report, *Korea – Various Measures on Beef,* para 166.

306. The process begins with an assessment of the "relative importance" of the interests or values furthered by the challenged measure.[376] Having ascertained the importance of the particular interests at stake, a panel should then turn to the other factors that are to be "weighed and balanced". The Appellate Body has pointed to two factors that, in most cases, will be relevant to a panel's determination of the "necessity" of a measure, although not necessarily exhaustive of factors that might be considered.[377] One factor is the contribution of the measure to the realization of the ends pursued by it; the other factor is the restrictive impact of the measure on international commerce.

[376] *Ibid.*, para 162. See also Appellate Body Report, *EC – Asbestos,* para 172.

[377] Appellate Body Report, *Korea – Various Measures on Beef,* para 164.

307. A comparison between the challenged measure and possible alternatives should then be undertaken, and the results of such comparison should be considered in the light of the importance of the interests at issue. It is on the basis of this "weighing and balancing" and comparison of measures, taking into account the interests or values at stake, that a panel determines whether a measure is "necessary" or, alternatively, whether another, WTO-consistent measure is "reasonably available".[378]

[378] *Ibid.,* para 166.

308. The requirement, under Article XIV(a), that a measure be "necessary" – that is, that there be no "reasonably available", WTO-consistent alternative – reflects the shared understanding of Members that substantive GATS obligations should not be deviated from lightly. An alternative measure may be found not to be "reasonably available", however, where it is merely theoretical in nature, for instance, where the responding Member is not capable of taking it, or where the measure imposes an undue burden on that Member, such as prohibitive costs or substantial technical difficulties. Moreover, a "reasonably available" alternative measure must be a measure that would preserve for the responding Member its right to achieve its desired level of protection with respect to the objective pursued under paragraph (a) of Article XIV.[379]

[379] Appellate Body Report, *EC – Asbestos,* paras 172–174. See also Appellate Body Report, *Korea – Various Measures on Beef,* para 180.

309. It is well-established that a responding party invoking an affirmative defence bears the burden of demonstrating that its measure, found to be WTO-inconsistent, satisfies the requirements of the invoked defence.[380] In the context of Article XIV(a), this means that the responding party must show that its measure is "necessary" to achieve objectives relating to public morals or public order. In our view, however, it is not the responding party's burden to show, in the first instance, that there are *no* reasonably available alternatives to achieve its objectives. In particular, a responding party need not identify the universe of less trade-restrictive alternative measures and then show that none of those measures achieves the desired objective. The WTO agreements do not contemplate such an impracticable and, indeed, often impossible burden.

[380] Appellate Body Report, *US – Gasoline,* pp22–23, DSR 1996:I, 3, at p21; Appellate Body Report, *US – Wool Shirts and Blouses,* pp15–16, DSR 1997:I, 323, at 337; Appellate Body Report, *US – FSC (Article 21.5 – EC),* para 133.

310. Rather, it is for a responding party to make a *prima facie* case that its measure is "necessary" by putting forward evidence and arguments that enable a panel to assess the challenged measure in the light of the relevant factors to be "weighed and balanced" in a given case. The responding party may, in so doing, point out why alternative measures would not achieve the same objectives as the challenged measure, but it is under no obligation to do so in order to establish, in the first instance, that its measure is "necessary". If the panel concludes that the respondent has made a *prima facie* case that the challenged measure is "necessary" – that is, "significantly closer to the pole of 'indispensable' than to the opposite pole of simply 'making a contribution to'"[381] – then a panel should find that challenged measure "necessary" within the terms of Article XIV(a) of the GATS.

[381] Appellate Body Report, *Korea – Various Measures on Beef,* para 161.

311. If, however, the complaining party raises a WTO-consistent alternative measure that, in its view, the responding party should have taken, the responding party will be required to demonstrate why its challenged measure nevertheless remains "necessary" in the light of that alternative or, in other words,

why the proposed alternative is not, in fact, "reasonably available". If a responding party demonstrates that the alternative is not "reasonably available", in the light of the interests or values being pursued and the party's desired level of protection, it follows that the challenged measure must be "necessary" within the terms of Article XIV(a) of the GATS.

(ii) Did the Panel err in its analysis of the "necessity" of the measures at issue?

312. In considering whether the United States' measures are "necessary" under Article XIV(a) of the GATS, the Panel began by considering the factors set out by the Appellate Body in *Korea – Various Measures on Beef* as they apply to the Wire Act, the Travel Act, and the IGBA. Antigua claims that the Panel erred in concluding, in the course of its analysis of these factors, that the three federal statutes contribute to protecting the interests raised by the United States.

313. The Panel set out, in some detail, how the United States' evidence established a specific connection between the remote supply of gambling services and each of the interests identified by the United States,[382] except for organized crime.[383] In particular, the Panel found such a link in relation to money laundering,[384] fraud,[385] compulsive gambling[386] and underage gambling.[387] Considering that the three federal statutes embody an outright prohibition on the remote supply of gambling services,[388] we see no error in the Panel's approach, nor in its finding, in paragraph 6.494 of the Panel Report, that the Wire Act, the Travel Act and the IGBA 'must contribute' to addressing those concerns.[389]

[382] Panel Report, paras 6.498–6.520.
[383] The Panel found that the United States had not submitted "concrete evidence" showing the *particular* vulnerability of the remote supply of gambling services to involvement by organized crime. Therefore, the Panel concluded, the United States had not demonstrated why the means used to regulate non-remote supply of gambling services could not sufficiently guard against the risk of organized crime (Panel Report, para 6.520).
[384] Panel Report, paras 6.500–6.504.
[385] *Ibid.,* paras 6.507 and 6.508.
[386] *Ibid.,* paras 6.511–6.513.
[387] *Ibid.,* paras 6.516–6.518.
[388] *Supra,* paras 258–263.
[389] The Appellate Body employed similar reasoning with respect to a prohibition on the import of products containing asbestos. See Appellate Body Report, *EC – Asbestos,* para 168:

> By prohibiting all forms of amphibole asbestos, and by severely restricting the use of chrysotile asbestos, the measure at issue is clearly designed and apt to achieve that level of health protection.

314. In addition, the United States and Antigua each appeals different aspects of the Panel's selection of alternative measures to compare with the Wire Act, the Travel Act, and the IGBA. The United States argues that the Panel erred in examining the one alternative measure that it did consider, and Antigua contends that the Panel erred in failing to consider additional alternative measures.

315. In its "necessity" analysis under Article XIV(a), the Panel appeared to understand that, in order for a measure to be accepted as "necessary" under Article XIV(a), the responding Member must have first "*explored and exhausted*" all reasonably available WTO-compatible alternatives before adopting its WTO-inconsistent measure.[390] This understanding led the Panel to conclude that, in this case, the United States had "an obligation to consult with Antigua before and while imposing its prohibition on the cross-border supply of gambling and betting services".[391] Because the Panel found that the United States had not engaged in such consultations with Antigua, the Panel also found that the United States had not established that its measures are "necessary" and, therefore, provisionally justified under Article XIV(a).[392]

[390] Panel Report, para 6.528 (emphasis added). See also paras 6.496, 6.522 and 6.534.
[391] *Ibid.*, para 6.531. See also para 6.534.
[392] *Ibid.*, paras 6.533–6.535.

316. In its appeal of this finding, the United States argues that "[t]he Panel relied on the 'necessity' test in Article XIV as the basis for imposing a procedural requirement on the United States to consult or negotiate with Antigua before the United States may take measures to protect public morals [or] protect public order".[393] The United States submits that the requirement in Article XIV(a) that a measure be "necessary" indicates that "necessity is a property of the measure itself" and, as such, "necessity" cannot be determined by reference to the efforts undertaken by a Member to negotiate an alternative measure.[394] The United States further argues that in previous disputes, the availability of alternative measures that were "merely theoretical" did not preclude the challenged measures from being deemed to be "necessary".[395] Similarly, the United States argues, the fact that measures might theoretically be available after engaging in consultations with Antigua does not preclude the "necessity" of the three federal statutes.

[393] United States' appellant's submission, para 139.
[394] *Ibid.,* para 142.
[395] *Ibid.,* para 152.

317. In our view, the Panel's "necessity" analysis was flawed because it did not focus on an alternative measure that was reasonably available to the United States to achieve the stated objectives regarding the protection of public morals or the maintenance of public order. Engaging in consultations with Antigua, with a view to arriving at a negotiated settlement that achieves the same objectives as the challenged United States' measures, was not an appropriate alternative for the Panel to consider because consultations are by definition a process, the results of which are uncertain and therefore not capable of comparison with the measures at issue in this case.

318. We note, in addition, that the Panel based its requirement of consultations, in part, on "the existence of [a] specific market access commitment [in the United States' GATS Schedule] with respect to cross-border trade of gambling and betting services".[396] We do not see how the existence of a specific commitment in a Member's Schedule affects the "necessity" of a measure in terms of the protection of public morals or the maintenance of public order. For this reason as well, the Panel erred in relying on consultations as an alternative measure reasonably available to the United States.

[396] Panel Report, para 6.531.

319. We turn now to Antigua's allegation that the Panel improperly limited its examination of possible alternative measures against which to compare the Wire Act, the Travel Act, and the IGBA. Antigua claims that the Panel "erred in limiting" its search for alternatives to the universe of *existing* United States regulatory measures.[397] Antigua also alleges that the Panel erred by examining only those measures that had been explicitly identified by Antigua even though "Antigua was never given the opportunity to properly rebut the Article XIV defence".[398]

[397] Antigua's other appellant's submission, para 103.
[398] *Ibid.,* para 104.

320. We observe, first, that the Panel did not state that it was limiting its search for alternatives in the manner alleged by Antigua. Secondly, although the Panel *began* its analysis of alternative measures by considering whether the United States already employs measures less restrictive than a prohibition to achieve the same objectives as the three federal statutes,[399] its inquiry did not end there. The Panel obviously did consider alternatives not currently in place in the United States, as evidenced by its (ultimately erroneous) emphasis on the United States' alleged failure to pursue consultations with Antigua.[400] Finally, we do not see why the Panel should have been expected to continue its analysis into additional alternative measures, which Antigua itself failed to identify. As we said above,[401] it is not for the responding party to identify the universe of alternative measures against which its own measure should be compared. It is only if such an alternative is raised that this comparison is required.[402] We therefore dismiss this aspect of Antigua's appeal.

[399] See Panel Report, paras 6.497–6.498. This type of approach was expressly encouraged by the Appellate Body in *Korea – Various Measures on Beef,* para 172:

> The application by a Member of WTO-*compatible* enforcement measures to the same kind of illegal behaviour – the passing off of one product for another – for like or at least similar products, provides a suggestive indication that an alternative measure which could "reasonably be expected" to be employed may well be available. The application of such measures for the control of the same illegal behaviour for like, or at least similar, products raises doubts with respect to the objective *necessity* of a different, much stricter, and WTO-inconsistent enforcement measure (original emphasis).

[400] *Supra,* paras 315–318.
[401] *Supra,* para 309.
[402] *Supra,* paras 310–311.

321. In our analysis above, we found that the Panel erred in assessing the necessity of the three United States statutes against the possibility of consultations with Antigua because such consultations, in our view, cannot qualify as a reasonably available alternative measure with which a challenged measure should be compared.[403] For this reason, we *reverse* the Panel's finding, in paragraph 6.535 of the Panel Report, that, because the United States did not enter into consultations with Antigua:

> *. . . the United States has not been able to provisionally justify, under Article XIV(a) of the GATS, that the Wire Act, the Travel Act (when read together with the relevant state laws) and the Illegal Gambling Business Act (when read together with the relevant state laws) are necessary to protect public morals and/or public order within the meaning of Article XIV(a).*

[403] *Supra,* para 317.

322. Having reversed this finding, we must consider whether, as the United States contends,[404] the Wire Act, the Travel Act and the IGBA are properly characterized as "necessary" to achieve the objectives identified by the United States and accepted by the Panel. The Panel's analysis, as well as the factual findings contained therein, are useful for our assessment of whether these measures satisfy the requirements of paragraph (a) of Article XIV.

[404] United States' appellant's submission, para 176.

323. As we stated above, a responding party must make a *prima facie* case that its challenged measure is "necessary". A Panel determines whether this case is made through the identification, and weighing and balancing, of relevant factors, such as those in *Korea – Various Measures on Beef*, with respect to the measure challenged. In this regard, we note that the Panel: (i) found that the three federal statutes protect "very important societal interests";[405] (ii) observed that "strict controls may be needed to protect [such] interests";[406] and (iii) found that the three federal statutes contribute to the realization of the ends that they pursue.[407] Although the Panel recognized the "significant restrictive trade impact"[408] of the three federal statutes, it expressly tempered this recognition with a detailed explanation of certain characteristics of, and concerns specific to, the remote supply of gambling and betting services. These included: (i) "the volume, speed and international reach of remote gambling transactions";[409] (ii) the "virtual anonymity of such transactions";[410] (iii) "low barriers to entry in the context of the remote supply of gambling and betting services";[411] and the (iv) "isolated and anonymous environment in which such gambling takes place".[412] Thus, this analysis reveals that the Panel did not place much weight, in the circumstances of this case, on the restrictive trade impact of the three federal statutes. On the contrary, the Panel appears to have accepted virtually all of the elements upon which the United States based its assertion that the three federal statutes are "indispensable".[413]

[405] Panel Report, paras 6.492 and 6.533.

[406] *Ibid.*, para 6.493.
[407] *Ibid.*, para 6.494.
[408] *Ibid.*, para 6.495.
[409] *Ibid.*, para 6.505.
[410] *Ibid.*
[411] *Ibid.*, para 6.507.
[412] *Ibid.*, para 6.514.
[413] Ibid., para 6.534.

324. The Panel further, and in our view, tellingly, stated that:

> . . . *the United States has legitimate specific concerns with respect to money laundering, fraud, health and underage gambling that are specific to the remote supply of gambling and betting services,* which suggests that the measures in question are "necessary" within the meaning of Article XIV(a)[414] *(emphasis added).*

[414] Panel Report, para 6.534.

325. From all of the above, and in particular from the summary of its analysis made in paragraphs 6.533 and 6.534 of the Panel Report, we understand the Panel to have acknowledged that, *but for* the United States' alleged refusal to accept Antigua's invitation to negotiate, the Panel would have found that the United States had made its *prima facie* case that the Wire Act, the Travel Act and the IGBA are "necessary", within the meaning of Article XIV(a). We thus agree with the United States that the "sole basis" for the Panel's conclusion to the contrary was its finding relating to the requirement of consultations with Antigua.[415]

[415] United States' appellant's submission, para 137.

326. Turning to the Panel's analysis of alternative measures, we observe that the Panel dismissed, as irrelevant to its analysis, measures that did not take account of the specific concerns associated with *remote* gambling.[416] We found above that the Panel erred in finding that consultations with Antigua constitutes a measure reasonably available to the United States.[417] Antigua raised no other measure that, in the view of the Panel, could be considered an alternative to the prohibitions on remote gambling contained in the Wire Act, the Travel Act, and the IGBA. In our opinion, therefore, the record before us reveals no reasonably available alternative measure proposed by Antigua or examined by the Panel that would establish that the three federal statutes are not "necessary" within the meaning of Article XIV(a). Because the United States made its *prima facie* case of "necessity", and Antigua failed to identify a reasonably available alternative measure, we conclude that the United States demonstrated that its statutes are "necessary", and therefore justified, under paragraph (a) of Article XIV.

[416] Panel Report, paras 6.497–6.498.
[417] *Supra*, para 317

327. For all these reasons, we *find* that the Wire Act, the Travel Act and the IGBA are "measures . . . necessary to protect public morals or to maintain public order", within the meaning of paragraph (a) of Article XIV of the GATS.[418]

[418] We address in the next sub-section of this Report the appeals raised by Antigua and the United States under Article 11 of the DSU, with respect to the Panel's analysis under Article XIV(a) of the GATS, and find them to be either without merit or not necessary to rule on in order to resolve this dispute.

. . .

2. Justification of the Measures Under Paragraph (c) of Article XIV [paras 335–337]

335. The Panel found, in paragraph 6.565 of the Panel Report, that:

> *. . . the United States has not been able to provisionally justify that the Wire Act, the Travel Act (when read together with the relevant state laws) and the Illegal Gambling Business Act (when read together with the relevant state laws) are necessary within the meaning of Article XIV(c) of GATS to secure compliance with the RICO statute . . . . (footnotes omitted)*

336. The United States appeals this finding on the same grounds that it appeals the Panel's finding that the United States had not established that the Wire Act, the Travel Act and the IGBA are within the scope of Article XIV(a). The Panel's finding under Article XIV(c) rests on the same basis as its finding under Article XIV(a), namely that the measures are not "necessary" because, in failing to engage in consultations with Antigua, the United States failed to explore and exhaust all reasonably available alternative measures. Given that we have reversed this finding under Article XIV(a), we also *reverse* the Panel's finding in paragraph 6.565 of the Panel Report on the same ground.

337. The United States requests us to complete the analysis and find that the Wire Act, the Travel Act, and the IGBA are "necessary", within the meaning of Article XIV(c), to secure compliance with the RICO statute. We found in the previous section of this Report that the Wire Act, the Travel Act, and the IGBA fall under paragraph (a) of Article XIV. As a result, it is *not necessary for us to determine* whether these measures are also justified under paragraph (c) of Article XIV.

. . .

3. The chapeau of Article XIV [paras 338–369]

338. Notwithstanding its finding that the measures at issue are *not* provisionally justified, the Panel examined whether those measures satisfy the requirements of the chapeau of Article XIV "so as to assist the parties in resolving the underlying dispute in this case".[426] This examination is the subject of appeals by both participants. Unlike the Panel, we have found the Wire Act, the Travel Act, and the IGBA to fall within the scope of Article XIV(a). Therefore, we must now review the Panel's examination under the chapeau.

[426] Panel Report, para 6.566.

339. The chapeau of Article XIV provides:

> *Subject to the requirement that such measures are not applied in a manner which would constitute a means of arbitrary or unjustifiable discrimination between countries where like conditions prevail, or a disguised restriction on trade in services, nothing in this Agreement shall be construed to prevent the adoption or enforcement by any Member of measures [of the type specified in the subsequent paragraphs of Article XIV].*

The focus of the chapeau, by its express terms, is on the *application* of a measure already found by the Panel to be inconsistent with one of the obligations under the GATS but falling within one of the paragraphs of Article XIV.[427] By requiring that the measure be *applied* in a manner that does not to constitute "arbitrary" or "unjustifiable" discrimination, or a "disguised restriction on trade in services", the chapeau serves to ensure that Members' rights to avail themselves of exceptions are exercised reasonably, so as not to frustrate the rights accorded to other Members by the substantive rules of the GATS.[428]

[427] Appellate Body Report, *US – Gasoline,* p22, DSR 1996:I, 3, at 20.
[428] *Ibid.,* p22, DSR 1996:I, 3, at 20–21.

340. The Panel found that:

> *. . . the United States has not demonstrated that it does not apply its prohibition on the remote supply of wagering services for horse racing in a manner that does not constitute "arbitrary and unjustifiable discrimination between countries where like conditions prevail" and/or a "disguised restriction on trade" in accordance with the requirements of the chapeau of Article XIV.*[429]

[429] Panel Report, para 6.608.

341. In reviewing the Panel's treatment of the chapeau to Article XIV, we begin with Antigua's allegations of error, and then turn to those raised by the United States, proceeding as follows: (a) first, we examine United States' Antigua's claim that the Panel should not have analyzed the defence under the chapeau; (b) secondly, we analyze Antigua's allegation that the Panel erred by focusing its discussion under the chapeau on the *remote supply* of gambling services rather than on the entire gambling industry; (c) thirdly, we address the United States' argument that the Panel articulated and applied a standard under the chapeau that is inconsistent with its terms; (d) fourthly, we review the Panel's finding on the alleged non-enforcement of certain laws against United States remote suppliers of gambling services; and (e) finally, we examine whether, in its analysis under the chapeau of Article XIV, the Panel fulfilled its obligations under Article 11 of the DSU.

. . .

4. Overall Conclusion on Article XIV [paras 370–372]

370. Our findings under Article XIV lead us to modify the overall conclusions of the Panel in paragraph 7.2(d) of the Panel Report.[474] The Panel found that the United States failed to justify its measures as "necessary" under paragraph (a) of Article XIV, and that it also failed to establish that those measures satisfy the requirements of the chapeau.

[474] See also Panel Report, para 6.608.

371. We have found instead that those measures satisfy the "necessity" requirement. We have also upheld, but only in part, the Panel's finding under the chapeau. We explained that the only inconsistency that the Panel could have found with the requirements of the chapeau stems from the fact that the United States did not demonstrate that the prohibition embodied in the measures at issue applies to both foreign *and* domestic suppliers of remote gambling services, notwithstanding the IHA – which, according to the Panel, "does appear, on its face, to permit"[475] *domestic* service suppliers to supply remote betting services for horse racing. In other words, the United States did not establish that the IHA does not alter the scope of application of the challenged measures, particularly vis-à-vis domestic suppliers of a specific type of remote gambling services. In this respect, we wish to clarify that the Panel did not, and we do not, make a finding as to whether the IHA does, in fact, permit domestic suppliers to provide certain remote betting services that would otherwise be prohibited by the Wire Act, the Travel Act and/or the IGBA.

[475] *Ibid.*, para 6.599.

372. Therefore, we *modify* the Panel's conclusion in paragraph 7.2(d) of the Panel Report. We *find*, instead, that the United States has demonstrated that the Wire Act, the Travel Act and the IGBA fall within the scope of paragraph (a) of Article XIV, but that it has not shown, in the light of the IHA, that the prohibitions embodied in these measures are applied to both foreign and domestic service suppliers of remote betting services for horse racing. For this reason alone, we *find* that the United States has not established that these measures satisfy the requirements of the chapeau. Here, too, we uphold the Panel, but only in part.

CHAPTER 4

Processes and Production Methods

BACKGROUND

Introduction

Processes and production methods (PPMs) relate to the manner in which products are made and natural resources are extracted, grown or harvested. Many PPMs can negatively affect the environment and human health. For example, production methods can pollute the air or water, and certain methods of harvesting can lead to resource depletion or harm to endangered species. Most countries have adopted policies and rules aimed at avoiding or mitigating the harmful effects caused by PPMs. These policies, referred to as 'PPM-based measures', can affect international trade. Trade-affecting PPM-based measures include, among other things, import and export restrictions on products produced in a certain way, labelling requirements regarding the production method used to produce a product, tax schemes based on production methods, and border tax adjustments levied on imported products to counterbalance PPM-based domestic taxation.

Some PPM-based measures have been challenged under the dispute settlement mechanisms of the 1947 General Agreement on Tariffs and Trade (GATT 1947) and, later, of the World Trade Organization (WTO). All but one of the PPM-based measures brought to GATT/WTO panels, have been found to violate GATT/WTO rules. In the past, both free trade sceptics and free trade proponents have claimed that the WTO rules prohibit PPM-based restrictions – perhaps because until *US – Shrimp/Turtle 21.5* in 2001, all challenged PPM-based measures were decided in favour of the complaining state. Recently, however, it has become clear that PPM-based measures affecting trade are not prohibited by WTO rules per se. Yet the extent to which PPM-based measures are permitted under the various agreements and provisions remains vague. The evolution of GATT and WTO case law relating to PPM-based measures gives at least some insight as to the direction in which WTO jurisprudence might be heading.

The PPM debate reflects the WTO Members' unwillingness to deal with contentious issues within the negotiating process. The two *US – Tuna/Dolphin* disputes in the early 1990s clearly made the PPM question a central issue in the trade and environment discussions. However, Members did not address the issue during the Uruguay Round of negotiations leading to the creation of the WTO. Instead, they left the PPM-related ambiguities for the WTO tribunals to resolve.

Why are PPM-based measures so controversial?

Several factors explain why the use of trade-related environmental PPM-based measures is controversial. First, by limiting imports to products produced in a specific manner, a WTO Member may make it more difficult and expensive for exporters from other countries to sell in its market, as they will have to adapt their PPMs to the requirements of the importing country. Financial burdens and technical difficulties created by PPM-based measures can be especially hard on smaller producers and on producers in developing countries. Critics of trade-related PPM-based measures also claim that PPM-based import restrictions impinge upon the sovereignty of the exporting state because they aim to influence PPMs abroad. The claim regarding national sovereignty is linked to the idea that the importing state is imposing its values or ethical and cultural preferences on the exporting state. This criticism is generally countered with the argument that the importing state is not demanding the use of a particular PPM in the exporting country, but is only regulating what enters its own territory. This argument is based on the idea that countries are encouraged by international instruments such as the 1992 Rio Principles on Sustainable Development to adopt sustainable consumption and production patterns, and the use of appropriate PPM-based measures is one way of achieving that goal. Finally, an important critique concerns questions of equity: while PPM-based measures are most frequently used by rich, importing countries, the products that are denied entrance into these important markets are frequently those of developing countries. Since much trade is North–North or South–South, this critique may not be entirely adequate, but the point remains that such measures pose a particular burden on southern exporters.

Distinction between product-related and non-product-related PPM-based measures

In the trade context PPM-based measures are usually divided into two categories: product-related PPM-based measures and non-product-related PPM-based measures. Product-related PPM-based measures are applied to guarantee the quality, safety and functionality of the product. The measures aim to protect the environment or the user/consumer from potential damage caused by the product itself or by a substance incorporated in the product. Usually, a product-related PPM is directly detectable in the end product. For example, pesticide residues can be detected in fruit cultivated with a specific pesticide. Sometimes, however, the production process cannot be directly detected in the product. In these cases, the production method still relates to the product because the specific process required by the PPM-based measure aims at influencing the end product. For example, food safety measures incorporate precise and strict sanitary standards for pasteurization of milk, packing of meat, etc., with the objective of assuring the healthful quality of the resulting products. However, the sanitary standard applied cannot necessarily be detected in the end product.

The ongoing debate on PPM-based measures, however, focuses more heavily on the second category: the non-product-related measures. Non-product-related PPM-based measures aim to avoid or minimize harm caused by the way in which a product is manufactured or harvested, not by the product itself. These PPMs are not detectable in the end product and do not directly affect the user/consumer. For example, a measure may attempt to regulate manufacturing processes in order to protect: a transboundary water course from upstream pollution; children or other workers from hazardous working conditions; endangered species from extinction through incidental killing; or the ozone layer from the use of ozone depleting substances, and so on.

Some measures, rather than relating to the *manner* in which a product is produced, relate to the *producer* if the product. These measures are sometimes referred to as 'producer characteristics standards'. Jurisprudence relating producer characteristics is often linked to or relevant for PPM-related issues. Examples include: the unadopted pre-WTO GATT report *US – Taxes on Automobiles*, and the more recent WTO reports in *US – Reformulated Gasoline, Indonesia – Automobile and Canada – Automobile Industry*.

Distinction between country-based and origin-neutral PPM-based measures

Besides distinguishing between product-related and non-product-related PPM-based measures, GATT and WTO tribunals, as well as commentators, have distinguished between country-based and origin-neutral PPM-based measures. For example, an importing country that bans the import of a product from countries that do not regulate production in a specific way is applying a country-based PPM-based measure (or what might also be referred to as a 'government policy standard'). This type of measure stands in contrast to a measure which focuses solely on the manner in which the product is produced. Because the latter relates to the production method actually used for producing a product, and not to the regulation in force in the country of production, this type of measure qualifies as origin-neutral. Several commentators stress the importance of the distinction between these two types of PPM-based measures, noting that origin-neutral PPM-based measures are more likely to be found consistent with certain provisions of the GATT (*See*, e.g. Charnovitz 2002; Howse and Regan 2000). A recent WTO report (*Canada – Automotive Industry*) also seemed to focus more heavily on the question of whether the PPM-based measure at issue was country-based or origin-neutral, rather than whether or not the measure was product-related.

In this context it is important to note, however, that origin-neutral measures that focus on the PPM actually used are generally much more difficult to implement than country-based measures because they may require complicated certification or other verification systems.

Extraterritorial characteristics of PPM-based measures

Trade-affecting PPM-based measures that are not related to the product often aim to protect natural resources, the environment, humans, animals, plants, etc. that are located (at least in part) outside the territorial boundaries of the country taking the measure. This is due to the fact that these types of measures focus on the effects of the manner in which products are produced or harvested, rather than on the effect of the product per se. Aspects relating to extraterritoriality are addressed in Chapter 5.

ECO-LABELLING

Eco-labels provide consumers, retailers, government officials and other interested parties with information about the environmental characteristics and impacts of labelled products and services. (The term eco-label has not been officially defined; here, the term is used broadly to include mandatory and voluntary labelling schemes that relate directly to the product or are 'non-product-related'.) Eco-labels allow purchasers to make more informed choices about the goods and services they buy and signal their preferences to manufacturers and service providers. Often, eco-labels provide information on how products were produced; thus, they are closely linked to the debate on PPM-based measures, and non-product-related PPM-based measures in particular. Some perceive eco-labelling schemes as trade restrictions, reducing access to the markets of countries applying the schemes and increasing costs for producers and exporters.

With respect to eco-labelling, a host of legal questions arise in the context of WTO rules: (i) which WTO rules and agreements apply to labelling schemes; (ii) do these rules also apply to voluntary labelling schemes; (iii) do these rules apply to labelling schemes that are based on the production method, including those schemes that apply criteria that are not directly related to the end-product; and (iv) if so, do those rules allow the use of non-product-related PPMs?

The WTO Agreements that potentially apply to eco-labelling schemes include the GATT, the Agreement on Technical Barriers to Trade (TBT), and the Agreement on Sanitary and Phytosanitary Measures (SPS). Each agreement contains its own set of rules, some of which overlap with the scope and rules contained in other agreements. The GATT contains several obligations that could apply to mandatory labels, notably its prohibitions of discrimination and quantitative restrictions, and its exceptions for environmental measures (Articles III, XI and XX). However, although the question has not been fully tested, labelling schemes for products are most likely to fall under the TBT Agreement rather than the GATT. According to the TBT Agreement both technical regulations (mandatory measures) and standards (voluntary measures) are documents that may 'include or deal exclusively with ... *labelling requirements* as they apply to a product, process or production method' (Annex 1, paragraphs 1 and 2 of the TBT Agreement). At the same time, the SPS Agreement is also relevant for labels. The SPS Agreement applies to all sanitary and phytosanitary measures taken by Members, including packaging and *labelling requirements,* as long as they are aimed at protecting humans, animals and plants within the territory of the Member applying the measure from risks arising from the spread of pests, diseases and disease-causing organisms, as well as from additives, contaminants and toxins or disease-causing organisms in foods, beverages and feedstuffs. For example, concerns have been raised in the SPS Committee rather than the TBT Committee with respect to the EU's regulation on the labelling and traceability of genetically modified organisms (Note of the Secretariat to the SPS Committee, Specific Trade Concerns, items 54 and 55, G/SPS/GEN/204/Rev. 4, 2 March 2004). To date, however, only one WTO dispute, *EC – Sardines*, has specifically addressed a labelling scheme. In that case, the mandatory labelling scheme at issue was examined under the TBT Agreement. No case has yet addressed an *eco*-labelling scheme.

The only agreement that would appear to apply to *voluntary* labelling schemes is the TBT Agreement. It is the only agreement to explicitly cover documents '*with which compliance is not mandatory*', also referred to as 'standards' (TBT Agreement, Annex 1, paragraph. 2). Provisions for voluntary labels, including privately administered labels, are contained in the TBT Agreement's Code of Good Practice for the Preparation, Adoption and Application of Standards in Annex 3 of the TBT Agreement. The Code of Good Practice incorporates many of the same elements that are applicable to mandatory labels, but in a form that can be characterized as guidance. Standardizing bodies may, on their own initiative, notify the WTO that they have chosen to accept and comply with the Code of Good Practice. While WTO Members are called to ensure that their central government's standardizing bodies accept and comply with the Code of Good Practice, they are only called to 'take such reasonable measures as may be available to them' to ensure that local governmental bodies and non-governmental organizations within their territories comply with the relevant provisions for standards (TBT Agreement, Article 4). It is currently unclear what types of actions Members must take to satisfy the 'reasonable measures' requirement. No jurisprudence has addressed issues relating to voluntary standards.

DISCUSSION OF RELEVANT WTO PROVISIONS

The GATT (Articles I, III, XI and XX)

The four relevant GATT provisions in the context of PPM-based measures are: Article I on most-favoured nation treatment, Article III on national treatment, Article XI on the elimination of quantitative restrictions, and the general exceptions clause under Article XX. PPM-based measures could potentially violate any of the first three provisions referred to above. If a violation is found, the PPM-based measure can still be permissible if it qualifies as an exception under Article XX.

Article I

GATT Article I provides that with respect to customs duties, taxes and internal regulations, any advantage, favour, privilege or immunity granted by a party to any product must be accorded immediately and unconditionally to the like product of all other parties. Although environment-related disputes have primarily involved Articles III and XI of the GATT (both of which are discussed in the following paragraphs) the interpretation of Article I remains relevant for the PPM-debate.

Two recent WTO disputes, *Indonesia – Automobile* and *Canada – Automotive Industry*, examined the consistency of a non-product-related PPM with Article I of the GATT. In *Indonesia – Automobile*, the panel pointed out that under Article I of the GATT, the tax and customs duty benefits at issue could not 'be made conditional on any criteria that is not related to the imported product itself'. This seemed to be a categorical rejection of non-product-related PPM-based measures under Article I. However, two years later in 2000, the Appellate Body in *Canada – Automotive Industry* clarified that the focus should not be on the fact that the advantage granted is made conditional on non-product-related criteria, but rather on 'whether or not such conditions discriminate with respect to the origin of products'. Thus, this decision abandoned the product-related/non-product-related distinction for the country-based/origin-neutral distinction.

Article III

Article III incorporates the central national treatment obligation of the GATT. It imposes the principle of non-discrimination between domestically produced goods and 'like' imported goods. Paragraph 1 establishes the basic principle that internal taxes and regulations 'should not be applied to imported or domestic products so as to afford protection to domestic production'. This principle is specifically incorporated into the obligations established in other provisions of Article III. Paragraph 2 requires national treatment with respect to internal taxation (including value added taxes, sales taxes or excise taxes). Paragraph 4 requires the same for regulations affecting the sale and use of goods in general. GATT/WTO disputes involving PPM-based measures have often entailed an examination of two main issues surrounding Article III. First, what is the scope of Article III with respect to PPM-based measures, and second, how are 'like products' treated under Article III?

Scope of Article III

The first issue asks whether the scope of Article III extends to PPM-based measures. If Article III does not apply – as decided by *US – Tuna/Dolphin I* and *II* GATT panels – the PPM-based measures cannot be a violation of Article III. However, these measures could still violate the Article XI prohibition on quantitative restrictions. This is precisely the result in (unadopted) *US – Tuna/Dolphin I* and *II*. In these two disputes, the panels decided that the US law prohibiting the import of yellow-fin tuna caught with purse-seine nets unless the government of the harvesting country proved that its programme regulating dolphin kill rates was comparable to that of the US, violated Article XI of the GATT. The more recent *US – Shrimp/Turtle* disputes also involved PPM-based measures similar to those under the *US – Tuna/Dolphin* disputes. At issue in the *US – Shrimp/Turtle* decisions was a measure banning the importation of shrimp harvested in a way which might harm sea turtles, unless certified by the US. As in the *US – Tuna/Dolphin* disputes, the measure at issue was examined under Article XI rather than under Article III of the GATT. In the *US – Shrimp/Turtle* disputes, however, the panels did not examine the relationship between Articles III and XI of the GATT, nor did they discuss the scope of Article III, probably because neither of the parties questioned the application of Article XI.

Commentators have pointed out that if the approach of the *US – Tuna/Dolphin* panels (that PPM-based measures fall outside the scope of Article III of the GATT) were to be followed, those *PPM-based* internal measures that do not qualify as a quantitative restriction under Article XI might not be subject to GATT rules at all because they would fall outside of its scope. At the same time, internal *product-based* measures would have to comply with the conditions under Article III of the GATT (*See*, e.g. Howse and Regan 2000).

The question of whether Article III or XI is applicable for PPM-based measures is also important for another reason: arguably, a measure can more easily be found to violate the straightforward prohibition of Article XI, rather than to violate the much more complicated non-discrimination principle under Article III. However, to date, the relationship between Article III, dealing with so-called 'internal measures', and Article XI, dealing with so-called 'border measures' remains unclear. Note Ad Article III gives some guidance. It provides that 'internal measures' that are applied to imported products at the time of importation, are to be regarded as internal measures pursuant to Article III. The note does not, however, clearly address the question of whether such coverage of internal measures would be exclusive and thus does not preclude the possibility that a measure examined under Article III be additionally examined under Article XI.

Addressing the scope of Article III and its relationship to Article XI, the *EC – Asbestos* panel in September 2000 found that a French ban on the manufacture, import and export, and domestic sales and transfer of certain asbestos and asbestos-containing products fell under the scope of Article III and Note Ad Article III. The claimant (Canada) had proposed that, even if the French measure were an internal measure falling within the scope of Article III, this did not prevent the French measure from also falling under the scope of Article XI and that, if the panel found that the measure could not be examined in light of the two different articles, the measure had to be examined under Article XI. After having concluded that Article III:4 of the GATT 1994 applied to the ban on importing asbestos and asbestos-containing products, the panel found it unnecessary to examine the claimant's arguments on the exclusive application of Article XI:1 to the part of an internal measure dealing with the treatment of imported products. While it did not endorse the simultaneous application of Articles III and XI to different aspects of the same measure, the panel did not explicitly exclude such a possibility (*EC – Asbestos* panel report, paragraphs 8.83–8.100). The panel's findings on this issue were not appealed and thus were not subsequently discussed in the Appellate Body report.

Similarly, in July 2000 the panel in *Korea – Beef* found one of the measures at issue inconsistent with GATT Article III:4 but exercised judicial economy with respect to the claim that the same measure also violated Article XI (*Korea – Beef* panel report, paragraph 705).

The approach of the panels in *Korea – Beef* and *EC – Asbestos* (although not involving non-product-related PPM-based measures) seems to suggest that even if a measure does fall under the scope of Article III, it does not necessarily preclude an additional examination under Article XI. For reasons of judicial economy, a panel would likely not examine a measure under Article XI after finding a measure *inconsistent* with Article III, but might proceed to examine Article XI legality if it found that a measure was *consistent* with Article III.

Like products

The second legal question regarding Article III is whether products can be distinguished based on factors not directly relating to the product as such. This relates to the jurisprudence on 'likeness' or 'like products'. The question of like products is important because Article III requires that an imported product be treated no less favourably than 'like' products of national origin. This issue is discussed in detail in Chapter 1: Like Products, including an analysis of the various criteria used by WTO panels to determine whether or not two products are 'like'. The present chapter limits itself to the specific question of whether products can be distinguished pursuant to one specific criterion: the method of production.

Four pre-WTO GATT panel reports interpreted Article III and addressed the question of likeness in the context of PPMs: *US – Tuna/Dolphin I* and *II*, *US – Malt Beverages*, and *US – Taxes on Automobiles* (only *US – Malt Beverages* was adopted). In addition, two WTO disputes have addressed the same issue: *US – Reformulated Gasoline* and *Indonesia – Automobile.* All of the reports rejected distinctions between products based on the PPMs at issue. The two WTO reports and the one adopted GATT report all involved producer characteristics standards. Thus, it is not entirely clear what this jurisprudence means for other types of non-product-related PPMs.

In addition to the question of whether products can be distinguished according to the PPM used, GATT/WTO jurisprudence has addressed the question whether products can be distinguished based on whether the measure at issue was or was not 'applied ... so as to afford protection to domestic production' as provided in Article III:1. This inquiry is frequently referred to as the 'aims and effects test'. The aims and effects test is relevant in the context of PPMs insofar as it could justify a measure adopted for environmental or other non-protectionist purposes. Under the aims and effects test, the question of whether a regulation has a protective aim or effect is part of the 'likeness' analysis: if the conclusion is that the aim and effect of a measure is not protective, products could be considered 'unlike'. To date, the aims and effects test has not been applied or analysed in a specific PPM-based measure context. While the concept of the aims and effects test is interesting for the PPM discussion, it must be noted that WTO jurisprudence is generally understood to reject the aims and effects test (*see* e.g. *Japan – Alcoholic Beverages,* which examined the legality of a non-PPM-based tax measure under paragraphs 1 and 2 of GATT Article III). However, commentators continue to write on the subject, suggesting that certain issues relating to the aims and effects test are not yet completely resolved. More details on the aims and effects test can be found in Chapter 1: Like Products.

Article XI

Article XI of the GATT prohibits the use of quantitative restrictions but, in reality, its scope is broader. Pursuant to its first paragraph, Article XI disallows 'prohibitions or restrictions other than duties, taxes or other charges' on the importation and exportation of products from or into other Member countries.

Thus, Article XI bans a whole range of import restraints other than 'duties, taxes or other charges'. While it is obvious that the Article covers quotas on imports, the language does not offer a clear understanding of the scope beyond quotas. Since the language refers to restrictions 'on the importation of products', Article XI arguably does not cover restrictions placed on imports after entry. These internal measures are instead dealt with under Article III. However, as seen above in the paragraphs on Article III, the scope of Articles III and XI and their potential overlap or mutual exclusion are not as clear as it might seem.

The panel in *US – Shrimp/Turtle I* found that the measure at issue (imposing an import ban on shrimp and shrimp products harvested by vessels of foreign nations that were not previously certified by the US) fell under the scope of Article XI. This finding was not challenged and the question of whether Article III could apply simultaneously was not addressed. In another case (*Korea – Beef*), the panel found one of the measures at issue inconsistent with GATT Article XI and held that for reasons of judicial economy, it was not necessary to address the question of whether the measure also violated Article III of the GATT.

In sum, the measures of some of the most prominent trade and environment disputes (*US – Tuna/Dolphin I* and *II* and *US – Shrimp/Turtle I* and *21.5)* were examined under Article XI rather than Article III. However, *US – Shrimp/Turtle I* and *Korea – Beef* seem to indicate that an examination under Article XI does not necessarily preclude an examination under Article III, and vice versa. This conclusion, however, will remain speculative as long as WTO tribunals do not explicitly clarify the relationship between Articles III and XI.

Article XX

If a PPM-based measure is found to violate one of the GATT obligations, including Articles I, III or XI described above, the defending Member may still be able to justify the challenged measure under Article XX. Article XX lists ten exceptions to the obligations of the GATT. Two of the ten exceptions are particularly relevant in the context of protecting the environment and human health: paragraph (b) covers measures 'necessary to protect human, animal or plant life or health' and paragraph (g) applies to measures 'relating to the conservation of exhaustible natural resources if such measures are made effective in conjunction with restriction on domestic production and consumption'.

WTO jurisprudence (*US – Reformulated Gasoline* and *US – Shrimp/Turtle I* and *21.5)* indicates that non-product-related PPM-based measures are not per se excluded from the scope of the exceptions listed in Article XX. *US – Shrimp/Turtle 21.5* (for the first time in GATT/WTO history) found that the non-product-related PPM-based measure at issue was justified under Article XX and was therefore permissible under the GATT. While in *US – Reformulated Gasoline* and *US – Shrimp/Turtle I* the non-product-related PPM-based measures examined also qualified under paragraph (g) as 'measures relating to the conservation of exhaustible natural resources', the Appellate Body, did not reach the same conclusion as *US – Shrimp/Turtle 21.5.* In these cases, the Appellate Body found that the measures did not fulfil the requirements set out in the chapeau of Article XX, which requires that a measure not 'constitute a means of arbitrary or unjustifiable discrimination between countries where the same conditions prevail, or a disguised restriction on international trade'. Thus, to date, the only non-product-related PPM-based measure found to fulfil those requirements was the measure at issue in *US – Shrimp/Turtle 21.5.* It is worth noting, however, that neither the *US – Reformulated Gasoline* nor the *US – Shrimp/Turtle I* decisions found the measures at issue in those cases inconsistent with the requirements of the chapeau because of the fact that they were PPM-based. They focused instead on other issues, including: (1) the requirement to take into account the particular circumstances in the exporting country in making administrative determinations more flexible; (2)

the requirement of due process and transparency in administrative proceedings; and (3) the need to conduct serious efforts to negotiate a treaty with affected countries before adopting trade measures.

Thus, it is reasonable to conclude that non-product related PPM-based measures, even if found inconsistent with Articles I, III or XI, can be GATT-consistent. The *US – Shrimp/Turtle 21.5* decision erases any remaining doubt in this respect. However, the approach to finding PPM-based measures as GATT-illegal a priori, and justified only under the GATT's exceptions, continues to be subject to criticism. There is a concern among civil society and some commentators that Article XX might not offer sufficient protection for many PPM-based measures under the current legal status quo. *Inter alia,* Article XX's ability to cover PPM-based measures is diluted by the fact that Article XX is limited to an exclusive set of national policies. Moreover, Article XX shifts the burden of proof from the complainant to the defendant. This can have a determinative effect on the outcome of the dispute.

There is a debate as to the appropriate legal provision under which non-product-related PPMs should be addressed – under Article III or Article XX. Some commentators claim that in case of an allegation of an Article III violation, non-product-related PPM analysis should first be made under Article III. They believe that PPM-based measures (including non-product-related measures) should not be per se prohibited under Article III, nor should they be excluded from the scope of Article III altogether. Instead, these commentators are of the view that only protectionist PPM-based measures should be found in violation of Article III (*See,* e.g. Howse and Regan 2000). Other commentators argue that measures using non-product-related PPMs to distinguish between physically indistinguishable products violate Article III, and that the permissibility of these measures should be analysed under Article XX exceptions. (*See,* e.g. Gaines 2002.)

In sum, it remains unclear whether or not Article III allows distinctions based on the processes or productions methods used for otherwise 'like' products. However, tribunals have given refuge to non-product-related PPM-based measures under Article XX. Whether the sole protection under Article XX is sufficient continues to be questioned due to the reasons mentioned above regarding the burden of proof and the limitation of Article XX to exclusive policies.

Annex A of the SPS Agreement

In the past, the PPM debate has focused largely on the interpretation of the GATT. However, since the creation of the WTO in 1994, two additional agreements, the SPS Agreement and the TBT Agreement, have gained significance in the PPM context (PPM-based measures in the context of the TBT Agreement are discussed below). To date, WTO tribunals have examined a few product-related PPM-based measures under the SPS Agreement, namely in the well-known *EC – Hormones* dispute and the more recent *Japan – Apples* dispute, but no non-product-related PPM-based measures have been examined. PPM-based measures, both product- and non-product-related, have yet to be tested under the TBT Agreement in the context of WTO dispute settlement. Because many PPM-based measures are sanitary or phytosanitary measures, or technical regulations or standards, it is important to keep these agreements in mind when analysing the PPM issue.

A preliminary question to ask when examining PPM-based measures under the SPS Agreement is whether the Agreement covers such measures in the first place. The answer to that question lies in the definition of SPS measures in Annex A of the SPS Agreement, which specifies that SPS measures 'include all relevant laws, decrees, regulations, requirements and procedures including, *inter alia*, ... processes and production methods . . .'. The definition does not specify, however, *which* processes and production methods are covered by the Agreement. Thus, it is unclear whether the reference to 'processes and production methods' covers only product-related PPM-measures, or also non-product-related PPM-based measures. Very little literature is available to shed light on this question.

Nevertheless, the definition under Annex A does give some indication as to what types of PPM-based measures may or may not be covered. It distinguishes between four categories of SPS measures: (1) measures that are adopted 'to protect animal or plant life or health within the territory of the Member from risks arising from the entry, establishment or spread of pests, diseases, disease-carrying organisms or disease-causing organisms' (internal footnotes omitted); (2) measures taken 'to protect human or animal life or health within the territory of the Member from risks arising from additives, contaminants, toxins or disease-causing organisms in foods, beverages or feedstuffs'; (3) measures applied 'to protect human life or health within the territory of the Member from risks arising from diseases carried by animals, plants or products thereof, or from the entry, establishment or spread of pests'; and finally, (4) measures established 'to prevent or limit other damage within the territory of the Member from the entry, establishment or spread of pests'.

At least the second of the four categories above covers only product-related PPM-based measures by referring to risks relating to 'food, beverages or feedstuffs'. The coverage of the other categories is less clear; however, the SPS Agreement confines the scope of all four categories to measures aimed at preventing harm only *within the country of import*. Because many trade-related PPM-based measures have extraterritorial effect, this territorial limitation thereby seems to exclude several non-product-specific PPM-based measures from the scope of the SPS Agreement. For a more detailed overview of the extraterritorial effects of PPM-based measures, see Chapter 5: Extraterritoriality. Despite this limitation, PPM-based measures aimed at preventing transboundary harm or harm to migratory animal species might be considered to aim at preventing harm 'within the country'. It is unclear how this territorial restriction would relate to the protection of the global commons, but in this context it is important to recall that the SPS definition focuses on harms caused by diseases and pests. This implies that the protection of certain global commons such as the climate or the ozone layer through the use of PPM-based measures is unlikely to be covered by the SPS Agreement.

PPM-based measures that are within the scope of the SPS Agreement are permitted provided that they are consistent with its obligations regarding necessity, scientific evidence, risk assessment and non-discrimination. These requirements are discussed in detail in Chapter 3: The Necessity Requirement and Chapter 6: The Role of Science and the Precautionary Principle, respectively. As seen above, the non-discrimination obligations in Articles I and III of the GATT have been at the centre of jurisprudence involving PPM-based measures, including an interpretation of the term 'like products'. In contrast to Articles I and III of the GATT, the SPS Agreement's obligation on non-discrimination does not refer to the concept of likeness. Instead, it includes non-discrimination language that is almost identical to the chapeau of Article XX of the GATT. Thus it does not hinge upon the question of 'like products', but rather instructs Members to 'ensure that their sanitary and phytosanitary measures do not arbitrarily or unjustifiably discriminate between Members where identical or similar conditions prevail'. As a result, disputes arising under the SPS Agreement involving PPM-based measures are likely to raise a host of completely different questions from those raised under GATT Articles I and III.

PPM-based measures that are not within the SPS Agreement's scope of application will (most likely) fall instead under the scope of the TBT Agreement or the GATT.

Annex 1 and Article 2 of the TBT Agreement

The TBT Agreement provides specific disciplines for two categories of domestic regulatory measures: technical regulations and standards. As set forth in Annex 1 to the TBT Agreement, *technical regulations* are mandatory rules that regulate 'product characteristics or their related processes and production methods'. *Standards* are non-mandatory rules, guidelines or characteristics 'for products or related processes and production methods'. At first glance, both definitions seem to imply that only product-related PPM-based measures are covered. However, the slight variations used in the language for the two types of TBT measures have raised some questions in this respect. To date, these questions remain unanswered.

It is noteworthy that the last sentence of both definitions states that the technical regulation or the standard 'may also include or deal exclusively with terminology, symbols, packaging, marking or labelling requirements as they apply to a product, process or production method'. While the first sentence in the relevant definition (quoted above in the text) refers to 'related processes and production methods', suggesting to cover only *product-related* PPMs, the last sentence lacks such a reference. This last sentence could therefore be seen to include non-product-related PPMs as well. One could also argue, however, that the last sentence has to be seen in the context of the first sentence, and therefore is also implicitly informed by the word 'related'.

PPM-based measures that are mandatory and found to fall within the TBT Agreement's scope are subject to a series of restrictions. First, Article 2.1 of the TBT Agreement contains the national treatment and the most-favoured nation principles according to which WTO Members must accord to imported products 'treatment no less favourable than that accorded to like products of national origin and to like products originating in any other country'. Second, according to Article 2.2 of the TBT Agreement, Members must 'ensure that technical regulations are not prepared, adopted or applied with a view to or the effect of creating unnecessary obstacles to international trade' and, for that purpose, that technical regulations are not permitted to 'be more trade-restrictive than necessary to fulfil a legitimate objective, taking account of the risks non-fulfilment would create'. Third, the TBT Agreement requires WTO Members to use relevant international standards (where they exist or where they are about to be completed) as a basis for their technical regulations, unless the international standards would be an ineffective or inappropriate means for achieving the legitimate objective in question. The second and third requirements mentioned are discussed in detail in Chapter 3: The Necessity Requirement.

Unlike the non-discrimination obligation in the SPS Agreement, which is similar to the one used in the chapeau to Article XX of the GATT, the non-discrimination provisions under the TBT Agreement are closer to the non-discrimination clauses of Articles I and III of the GATT (national treatment and most-favoured nation treatment). Thus, like Article III of the GATT, and in contrast to the SPS Agreement, an analysis of the consistency of a PPM-based measure with the TBT Agreement is likely to hinge upon a 'like product' test. However, in contrast to the GATT, the TBT Agreement offers no exceptions to the national and most-favoured treatment obligations in its body text. It only contains language similar to the chapeau of the Article XX exceptions clause. Thus, the TBT Agreement could be perceived to be stricter than the GATT. Arguably, though, the preamble should at least serve as a guide to interpret the rest of the Agreement.

While it remains unclear how the 'like product' test under the TBT Agreement compares to the corresponding analysis under Article III of the GATT, it could be argued that the TBT 'like product' test should allow more leeway to consider products to be 'unlike'. Otherwise some technical regulations could be found inconsistent with Article 2.1 while they would be justified under Article XX of the GATT (*see,* e.g. Marceau and Trachtman, forthcoming).

In cases where PPM-based measures are found to fall outside the scope of the TBT Agreement, the GATT's Article I, III or XI (as well as Article XX) will likely apply.

SELECTED LITERATURE

Charnovitz, S. (2002) 'The Law of Environmental "PPMs" in the WTO: Debunking the Myth of Illegality', *Yale Journal of International Law*, vol 27, p59

Gaines, S. (2002) 'Processes and Production Methods: How to produce sound policy for environmental PPM-based trade measures?', *Columbia Journal of Environmental Law*, vol 27, p383

Howse, R. and Regan, D. (2000) 'The product/process distinction – An illusory basis for disciplining "unilateralism" in trade policy', *European Journal of International Law*, vol 11, p249

Marceau, G. and Trachtman, J. P. (forthcoming) *A Map of the World Trade Organization Law of Domestic Regulation of Goods: The Technical Barriers to Trade Agreement, the Sanitary and Phytosanitary Measures Agreement, and the General Agreement on Tariffs and Trade,* Columbia Law School Series on WTO Law and Policy, vol 1: Trade and Health

Organisation for Economic Co-operation and Development (11 August, 1997) *Processes and Production Methods (PPMs): Conceptual Framework and Considerations on Use of PPM-based Trade Measures,* OECD/GD(97)137 at www.oecd.org

SELECTED JURISPRUDENCE UNDER ARTICLES I, III AND XX OF THE GATT

The following are excerpts of GATT and WTO cases that are relevant for a discussion of PPM-based measures. The excerpts are preceded by a short summary and commentary of the corresponding case, aiming to put the excerpts into context. The disputes are divided into three groups depending on whether they discuss GATT Article I, GATT Article III (and XX), or GATT Article XX. Within those sub-sections, the disputes are arranged chronologically. The summaries do not encompass all the issues raised in the cases, but focus primarily on issues regarding PPMs, and are thus not comprehensive for other purposes. A number of the cases discussed here are also discussed in Chapter 1: Like Products and Chapter 5: Extraterritoriality, both covering issues inherently linked to the PPMs question.

Because no non-product-related PPM issues have been raised under disputes involving the TBT or the SPS Agreements, the PPM-related disputes below all relate to the GATT. Specifically, they involve violations of Articles I, III or XI of the GATT, and in part they also address discussions of Article XX on general exceptions. As violations of GATT Articles I, III or XI can be justified under the GATT's general exceptions set forth in Article XX, a violation of one of those articles does not necessarily imply a general PPM prohibition under GATT. The typical 'trade and environment' disputes involving non-product-related PPM-based measures under the GATT (*US – Tuna/Dolphin I* and *II*, *US – Taxes on Automobiles*, *US – Reformulated Gasoline*, and *US – Shrimp/Turtle I* and *21.5*) all involved Article XX defences. Of these, only the *US – Shrimp/Turtle 21.5* decision found that the measure at issue qualified as an exception under Article XX. However, some of the other cases also indicate that the scope of Article XX does not exclude non-product-related PPM-based measures.

Additional disputes relevant for the PPM issue are addressed in Chapter 1: Like Products. Most importantly, these include *Japan – Alcoholic Beverages* and *EC – Asbestos.*

Article I of the GATT

Belgian Family Allowances, 1952

Short summary and commentary

Belgian Family Allowances addressed the PPM issue in the context of Article I of the GATT. *Belgian Family Allowances* is generally considered to be the first PPM-related GATT dispute. In this dispute, Norway and Denmark alleged a violation of Article I of the GATT on most-favoured nation treatment. At issue was the application of a Belgian law which charged an import tax on foreign goods purchased by Belgian government bodies. However, some countries were exempted from this tax if they applied a system of family allowances similar to that which was applied in Belgium. The complainants argued that a tax exemption was given to Sweden but not to them, although they had similar family allowance programmes. The panel found a violation irrespective of the nature of the various family allowance systems. The mere fact that the Belgian law treated products differently based on whether the country of origin had in place a specific government policy sufficed for the tribunal to find discrimination in violation of Article I of the GATT (Panel report, paragraph 3.) The dispute did not involve any exceptions under Article XX of the GATT.

This early GATT report left many questions open. While it appears to indicate that GATT Article I does not permit discrimination based on the regulations of a country, it does not make clear whether or not origin-neutral PPM-based measures might be permitted. The panel also did not explicitly address the fact that the measure in question was not product-related. Two recent WTO disputes interpreted and clarified the *Belgian Family Allowances* report to some extent. The *Indonesia – Automobile* decision referred to *Belgian Family Allowances* to support its finding that an advantage under Article I could not 'be made conditional on any criteria that is not related to the imported product itself' (*Indonesia – Automobile* Panel report, paragraph 14.143). Subsequently, the Appellate Body in *Canada – Automotive Industry* also referred to *Belgian Family Allowances*, to explain its finding regarding non-product-related conditions, noting that *Belgian Family Allowances* dealt with a measure that distinguished between countries of origin based on the system of family allowances in force in their territories (for details please see respective summaries and excerpts below) (*Canada – Automotive Industry* Panel report, paragraph 10.28).

Thus, with these clarifications, one might read the *Belgian Family Allowances* report as follows: *origin-based* non-product-related PPM-based measures are prohibited under Article I of the GATT, but *origin-neutral* non-product-related PPM-based measures might be permitted.

Excerpts

Report of the Panel, *Belgian Family Allowances*, G/32 – 1S/59, adopted on 7 November 1952.

I. Examination of the Legal Issues Involved [paras 1–7]

. . .

3. According to the provisions of paragraph 1 of Article I of the General Agreement, any advantage, favour, privilege or immunity granted by Belgium to any product originating in the territory of any country with respect to all matters referred to in paragraph 2 of Article III shall be granted immediately and unconditionally to the like product originating in the territories of all contracting parties. Belgium has granted exemption from the levy under consideration to products purchased by public bodies when they originate in Luxemburg and the Netherlands, as well as in France, Italy, Sweden and the United Kingdom. If the General Agreement were definitively in force in accordance with Article XXVI, it is clear that that exemption would have to be granted unconditionally to all other contracting parties (including Denmark and Norway). The consistency or otherwise of the system of family allowances in force in the territory of a given contracting party with the requirements of the Belgian law would be irrelevant in this respect, and the Belgian legislation would have to be amended insofar as it introduced a discrimination between countries having a given system of family allowances and those which had a different system or no system at all, and made the granting of the exemption dependent on certain conditions.

Canada – Certain Measures Affecting the Automotive Industry ('Canada – Automotive Industry'), 2000

Short summary and commentary

In *Canada – Automotive Industry*, Japan and the European Communities alleged, among other things, a violation of GATT Article I requiring most-favoured nation treatment. The case involved a measure that exempted certain manufacturers from import duties based on their manufacturing presence and the level of value added in Canada. Thus, the challenged measures accorded import duty exemptions based on the characteristics of the manufacturers, not on the characteristics of the products as such. The panel found that these exemptions violated Article I, a finding upheld by the Appellate Body without explicitly addressing the panel's reasoning as far as concerns the issues discussed here.

The panel's finding that the exemptions violated the GATT was not based on the fact that the exemptions did not relate to the products as such. Rather, the panel seemed to indicate that, contrary to the arguments advanced by Japan, non-product-related measures are not per se inconsistent with Article I of the GATT (Panel report, paragraph 10.29). In analysing Article I, the panel explained that the finding of a violation will depend 'upon whether or not such conditions discriminate with respect to the origin of products' rather than on the simple fact that the advantage 'is granted on conditions that are not related to the imported products themselves' (*Id.*).

Excerpts

Report of the Panel, *Canada – Certain Measures Affecting the Automotive Industry*, WT/DS/139/R (11 February 2000), adopted as modified by the Appellate Body Report on 19 June 2000.

(b) Whether the import duty exemption is awarded "immediately and unconditionally" [paras 10.18–10.30].

. . .

10.28 With respect to the Panel Report on *Indonesia – Autos*, we note that the panel determined that certain customs duty and tax benefits provided by Indonesia to imports of "National Cars" and parts and components thereof from Korea were advantages within the meaning of Article I, and that these "National Cars" and their parts and components imported from Korea were like other similar motor vehicles and parts and components from other Members. The panel then proceeded to

> *"... examine whether the advantages accorded to national cars and parts and components thereof from Korea are unconditionally accorded to the products of other Members, as required by Article I. The GATT case law is clear to the effect that any such advantage (here tax and customs duty benefits) cannot be made conditional on any criteria that is not related to the imported product itself."*[815]

Significantly, in support of the statement that "the GATT case law is clear to the effect that any such advantage (...) cannot be made conditional on any criteria that is not related to the imported product itself", the panel referred to the Panel Report on *Belgian Family Allowances*.[816] As discussed above, that Panel Report dealt with a measure which distinguished between countries of origin depending upon the

[815] Panel Report on *Indonesia – Autos, supra* note 270, para 14.143.

system of family allowances in force in their territories. We further note that, following this statement, the panel on *Indonesia – Autos* identified certain conditions which entailed discrimination between imports of the subject products from Korea and like products from other Members, and found that these measures were thus inconsistent with Article I of the GATT.[817] The statement in the Panel Report that an advantage within the meaning of Article I "cannot be made conditional on any criteria that is not related to the imported product itself" must therefore in our view be seen in relation to conditions which entailed different treatment of like products depending upon their origin.

[816] *Ibid.,* para 14.144.
[817] *Ibid.,* paras 14.145–148.

10.29 In sum, we believe that the panel decisions and other sources referred to by Japan do not support the interpretation of Article I:1 advocated by Japan in the present case according to which the word "unconditionally" in Article I:1 must be interpreted to mean that subjecting an advantage granted in connection with the importation of a product to conditions not related to the imported product itself is *per se* inconsistent with Article I:1, regardless of whether such conditions are discriminatory with respect to the origin of products. Rather, they accord with the conclusion from our analysis of the text of Article I:1 that whether conditions attached to an advantage granted in connection with the importation of a product offend Article I:1 depends upon whether or not such conditions discriminate with respect to the origin of products.

10.30 In light of the foregoing considerations, we reject Japan's argument that, by making the import duty exemption on motor vehicles conditional on criteria that are not related to the imported products themselves, Canada fails to accord the exemption immediately and unconditionally to the like product originating in the territories of all WTO Members. In our view, Canada's import duty exemption cannot be held to be inconsistent with Article I:1 simply on the grounds that it is granted on conditions that are not related to the imported products themselves. Rather, we must determine whether these conditions amount to discrimination between like products of different origins.

Article III (and XX) of the GATT

United States – Restrictions on Imports of Tuna ('US– Tuna/Dolphin I'), 1991 (NOT ADOPTED) and United States – Restrictions on Imports of Tuna ('US – Tuna/Dolphin II'), 1994 (NOT ADOPTED)

Short summary and commentary

U.S. – Tuna/Dolphin I was the first dispute to involve an environmental non-product-related PPM-based measure. It addressed the PPM-issue primarily in its interpretation of Article III (on national treatment), and to some extent, in the context of Article XI (on the prohibition of quantitative restrictions). However, in contrast to *Belgian Family Allowances,* it also involved interpretations of Articles XX(b) and (g). At issue was a US regulation imposing an embargo on yellow-fin tuna (and products thereof) caught in a specific way that incidentally killed or injured dolphins. If the harvesting and exporting country proved that its incidental dolphin kill rates did not exceed, by a certain margin, the rate of the US fleet, however, that country was certified and not subject to the embargo. The regulations also banned yellow-fin tuna and products from 'intermediary nations' (secondary nation embargo) unless these countries proved that they also banned tuna and products produced in countries subject to the primary ban.

Mexico complained that this regulatory scheme violated Article XI of the GATT prohibiting quantitative restrictions on importation. The US, in turn, responded that the measures instead fell within the scope of Article III:4 (which permits the application of internal regulations on a non-discriminatory basis) and Note Ad Article III (which permits enforcement of such internal regulations at the time or point of importation). The panel ruled that Article III and Note Ad Article III only covered measures applying to products as such. (*US – Tuna/Dolphin I* Panel report, paragraph 5.11). Thus, because the panel found that the US regulation did not affect tuna as a product, it concluded that the regulation did not fall under the scope of Article III, but instead qualified as a quantitative restriction under Article XI.

The US argued that even if a violation of Article XI or III of the GATT were found, both the primary and the secondary embargo could be justified under Articles XX(b) and (g) of the GATT, which provide general exceptions to measures 'necessary to protect human, animal or plant life or health' and measures 'relating to the conservation of exhaustible natural resources'. The US also argued that the secondary embargo was justified under Article XX(d), which covers measures necessary to enforce laws or regulations that are not themselves GATT inconsistent.

The panel concluded that the measure was not justified under Article XX(b) because that article should not be used to protect extraterritorial life or health. The panel found that if it were to justify the US measure under Article XX(b) of the GATT, it would allow a party to unilaterally determine life or health protection policies from which other parties could not deviate, without jeopardizing trading rights guaranteed by the GATT. For largely the same reason, the panel rejected justification under Article XX(g) as well. Since the primary embargo was inconsistent, the panel also found that the secondary embargo was not justified under Article XX(d). Discussions and excerpts regarding the panel's interpretation of Article XX can be found in Chapter 2: General Exceptions Clauses and Chapter 5: Extraterritoriality.

Due to strong opposition by environmental groups and the US public, and the fear of jeopardizing the ongoing negotiations of the North American Free Trade Agreement (NAFTA), the Report was never presented for approval by the GATT Council and thus was never adopted. As a result, the European Economic Community (EEC) and the Netherlands initiated a subsequent challenge of the same US measures, which led the *US – Tuna/Dolphin II* ruling in 1994. In *US – Tuna/Dolphin II*, the PPM-issue was also addressed under Articles III, XI and XX of the GATT. The panel report confirmed that Article III did not apply to laws not affecting the product as such (*US – Tuna/Dolphin II* Panel report, paragraph 5.8). Furthermore, the ruling specified that the US bans distinguished between tuna products according to the harvesting practices of primary nations and the import policies of 'intermediary' nations, and that these practices and policies could not have any impact on the inherent character of tuna as a product, thus making Article III inapplicable (*Id.* at paragraph 5.9). Instead, the panel found a violation of Article XI of the GATT prohibiting quantitative restrictions.

In contrast to the previous panel in *US – Tuna/Dolphin I*, this panel found that Article XX(g) of the GATT applied to policies related to the conservation of exhaustible natural resources located *within* the territory of the party invoking the provision *and* to policies aimed at conserving dolphins *outside* its territory, but only by exercising its jurisdiction on its nationals and vessels (*Id.* at paragraphs 5.15–5.17). However, just as in *US – Tuna/Dolphin I*, the panel rejected justification for the embargo under Article

XX by concluding that measures taken to force other countries to change their policies, and that are effective only if such changes occur, could not be justified under Article XX(g) (*Id.* at paragraph 5.27).

Similarly, the panel found that a policy to protect the life and health of dolphins outside its territory was covered by paragraph (b), but rejected justification of the US measures for the same reasons as it rejected justification under paragraph (g).

US – Tuna/Dolphin II was not adopted by the GATT Council.

With respect to the PPM issue, the two *US – Tuna/Dolphin* disputes each looked at the scope of coverage of Article III and concluded that non-product-related PPMs did not fall under the scope of Article III (*US – Tuna/Dolphin I* Panel report, paragraph 5.11 and *US – Tuna/Dolphin II* Panel report, paragraph 5.8). The first of the two reports additionally noted that even if Article III were to apply, the US ban would not meet the requirements under Article III because Article III:4 required that the US accord Mexican tuna *as a product* treatment no less favourable to that accorded US tuna *as a product*, independent of the incidental dolphin kill rates (*US Tuna/Dolphin I* Panel report, paragraph 5.15). *US – Tuna/Dolphin II*, concluding that Article III did not apply, did not address the issue of 'like products' or the question of whether products can be distinguished based on factors not directly relating to the product as such.

Both reports concluded that the US measures fell under the scope of Article XI on quantitative restrictions. Commentators have noted that if Article III is viewed as not covering non-product-related PPM-based measures, it is possible that such measures, which do not fall under the scope of Article XI, would not be subject to GATT disciplines. This would result in a situation in which certain non-product-related PPMs – in contrast to product-related measures – would escape GATT strictures.

As of June 2005 there has been no subsequent decision explicitly addressing the issue of Article III's scope and applicability to questions of PPM measures. In *US – Shrimp/Turtle I*, which challenged a measure similar to the measure at issue in the *US – Tuna/Dolphin* disputes, the WTO Appellate Body reviewed the challenged US measure again under Article XI, not Article III. However it is worth noting that the Appellate Body probably did not take a position on the scope of Article III because the treatment under Article XI had not been contested.

In concluding that the US measure failed to comply with the conditions set out in the Article XX exceptions, the *US – Tuna/Dolphin I* and *II* decisions led many to believe that the GATT system as a whole generally prohibited the use of non-product-related PPM-based measures. However, the reports did not explicitly take a position on the product-related/non-product-related distinction in the context of Article XX. Rather, as discussed above, the panels focused instead on extraterritoriality. Nonetheless, because the effects of many (or most) non-product-related PPM-based measures are extraterritorial, the prohibition of measures with extraterritorial effects under Article XX has a direct impact on the general treatment of non-product-related PPM-based measures under the same article.

The *US – Shrimp/Turtle* decisions that followed half a decade later under the newly established WTO (described below) took a more flexible approach to the interpretation of the Article XX exceptions, and, in *US – Shrimp/Turtle 21.5*, led to the first non-product-related PPM-based measure to be allowed under GATT rules.

Issues relating to extraterritoriality and Article XX are addressed separately in Chapter 5: Extraterritoriality and Chapter 2: General Exceptions Clauses. Although *US*

– *Tuna/Dolphin I* and *II*'s discussion of Article XX are (indirectly) relevant for the PPM-issue, the respective excerpts are not included here, but instead in Chapter 5: Extraterritoriality. Thus, the excerpts printed below only relate to Articles III and XI of the GATT, not to Article XX.

Excerpts

Report of the Panel, *United States – Restrictions on Imports of Tuna ("Tuna/Dolphin I")*, DS21/R – 39S/155 (3 September 1991), NOT ADOPTED.

Categorization as internal regulations (Article III) or quantitative restrictions (Article XI) [paras 5.8–5.16]

. . .

5.11 The text of Article III:1 refers to the application to imported or domestic *products* of "laws, regulations and requirements affecting the internal sale ... of *products*" and "internal quantitative regulations requiring the mixture, processing or use of *products*"; it sets forth the principle that such regulations on *products* not be applied so as to afford protection to domestic production. Article III:4 refers solely to laws, regulations and requirements affecting the internal sale, etc. of *products*. This suggests that Article III covers only measures affecting products as such. Furthermore, the text of the Note Ad Article III refers to a measure "which applies to an imported *product* and the like domestic *product* and is collected or enforced in the case of the imported *product* at the time or point of importation". This suggests that this Note covers only measures applied to imported products that are of the same nature as those applied to the domestic products, such as a prohibition on importation of a product which enforces at the border an internal sales prohibition applied to both imported and like domestic products.

5.12 A previous panel had found that Article III:2, first sentence, "obliges contracting parties to establish certain competitive conditions for imported *products* in relation to domestic *products*".[35] Another panel had found that the words "treatment no less favourable" in Article III:4 call for effective equality of opportunities for imported *products* in respect of the application of laws, regulations or requirements affecting the sale, offering for sale, purchase, transportation, distribution or use of *products*, and that this standard has to be understood as applicable to each individual case of imported *products*.[36] It was apparent to the Panel that the comparison implied was necessarily one between the measures applied to imported products and the measures applied to like domestic products.

[35] Panel report on *"United States – Taxes on Petroleum and Certain Imported Substances"*, adopted 17 June 1987, BISD 34S/136, 158, para 5.1.9.
[36] Panel report on *"United States – Section 337 of the Tariff Act of 1930"*, adopted 7 November 1989, BISD 36S/345, 386–7, paras 5.11, 5.14.

5.13 The Panel considered that, as Article III applied the national treatment principle to both regulations and internal taxes, the provisions of Article III:4 applicable to regulations should be interpreted taking into account interpretations by the CONTRACTING PARTIES of the provisions of Article III:2 applicable to taxes. The Panel noted in this context that the Working Party Report on Border Tax Adjustments, adopted by the CONTRACTING PARTIES in 1970, had concluded that:

> *"... there was convergence of views to the effect that* taxes directly levied on products were eligible for tax adjustment... *Furthermore, the Working Party concluded that there was convergence of views to the effect that certain taxes that were not directly levied on products were not eligible for adjustment, [such as] social security charges whether on employers or employees and payroll taxes."*[37]

Thus, under the national treatment principle of Article III, contracting parties may apply border tax adjustments with regard to those taxes that are borne by products, but not for domestic taxes not directly levied on products (such as corporate income taxes). Consequently, the Note Ad Article III covers only internal taxes that are borne by products. The Panel considered that it would be inconsistent to limit the application of this Note to taxes that are borne by products while permitting its application to regulations not applied to the product as such.

[37] BISD 18S/97, 100–101, para 14.

5.14 The Panel concluded from the above considerations that the Note Ad Article III covers only those measures that are applied to the product as such. The Panel noted that the MMPA regulates the domestic harvesting of yellowfin tuna to reduce the incidental taking of dolphin, but that these regulations could not be regarded as being applied to tuna products as such because they would not directly regulate the sale of tuna and could not possibly affect tuna as a product. Therefore, the Panel found that the import prohibition on certain yellowfin tuna and certain yellowfin tuna products of Mexico and the provisions of the MMPA under which it is imposed did not constitute internal regulations covered by the Note Ad Article III.

5.15 The Panel further concluded that, even if the provisions of the MMPA enforcing the tuna harvesting regulations (in particular those providing for the seizure of cargo as a penalty for violation of the Act) were regarded as regulating the sale of tuna as a product, the United States import prohibition would not meet the requirements of Article III. As pointed out in paragraph 5.12 above, Article III:4 calls for a comparison of the treatment of imported tuna as a product with that of domestic tuna *as a product*. Regulations governing the taking of dolphins incidental to the taking of tuna could not possibly affect tuna as a product. Article III:4 therefore obliges the United States to accord treatment to Mexican tuna no less favourable than that accorded to United States tuna, whether or not the incidental taking of dolphins by Mexican vessels corresponds to that of United States vessels.

Report of the Panel, *United States – Restrictions on Imports of Tuna ("US – Tuna/Dolphin II")*, DS29/R (16 June 1994), NOT ADOPTED.

B. Articles III and XI [paras 5.6–5.10]

. . .

5.8 The Panel proceeded first to examine whether the United States measures, although applied at the border, should nonetheless be examined under the national treatment provisions of Article III. The Panel observed that a Note to Article III extends the scope of Article III to domestic measures enforced at the time or point of importation as follows:

> *"any law, regulation or requirement … which applies to an imported product and to the like domestic product and is … enforced in the case of the imported product at the time or point of importation, is nevertheless to be regarded as … a law, regulation or requirement … subject to the provisions of Article III."*

The Panel observed however that this provision can only be invoked in respect of a measure which "applies to an imported product and to the like domestic product". The Panel also noted that the national treatment standard, as it relates to laws, regulations and requirements, is specified in Article III:4:, which states:

> *"The* products *of the territory of any contracting party imported into the territory of any other contracting party shall be accorded treatment no less favourable than that accorded to like* products *of national origin in respect of all laws, regulations and requirements affecting their internal sale, offering for sale, transportation, distribution or use. . ." (emphasis added).*

The Panel noted that Article III calls for a comparison between the treatment accorded to domestic and imported like *products*, not for a comparison of the policies or practices of the country of origin with those of the country of importation. The Panel found therefore that the Note ad Article III could only permit the enforcement, at the time or point of importation, of those laws, regulations and requirements that affected or were applied to the imported and domestic products considered *as products*. The Note therefore could not apply to the enforcement at the time or point of importation of laws, regulations or requirements that related to policies or practices that could not affect the product as such, and that accorded less favourable treatment to like products not produced in conformity with the domestic policies of the importing country.

5.9 The Panel then examined in this light the measures taken by the United States. It noted that the import embargoes distinguished between tuna products according to harvesting practices and tuna import policies of the exporting countries; that the measures imposed by the United States in respect of domestic tuna similarly distinguished between tuna and tuna products according to tuna harvesting methods; and that none of these practices, policies and methods could have any impact on the inherent character of tuna as a product. The Panel therefore concluded that the Note ad Article III was not applicable.

United States – Measures Affecting Alcoholic and Malt Beverages ('US – Malt Beverages'), 1992

Short summary and commentary

This dispute involved the interpretation of Article III:2 (relating to national treatment on internal taxation) in light of a non-product-related PPM-based measure. Canada brought a complaint against the US arguing, among other things, that an excise tax credit for small beer breweries, both domestic and foreign, violated GATT Article III on national treatment because the tax measure discriminated against Canada's large breweries. The panel held that beer from small beer breweries was 'like' beer from large breweries, and concluded that the tax thus violated Article III:2 because it impermissibly discriminated between like products (Panel report, paragraph 5.19).

While this panel report was adopted and thus has legal weight for WTO jurisprudence, its result probably should not be interpreted as a blanket prohibition on distinguishing between products based on non-product-related PPMs. This is because the challenged measure did not focus on the *manner* of production, but rather on the characteristics of the producer/manufacturer. However, it is significant in that it is the only adopted decision involving an origin-neutral non-product-related PPM-based measure found in violation of GATT Article III.

A further important aspect of the case is its application of the so-called aims and effects test. This issue is addressed in Chapter 1: Like Products.

Excerpts

Report of the Panel, *United States – Measures Affecting Alcoholic and Malt Beverages*, DS23/R – 39S/206, adopted on 19 June 1992.

State Excise Tax Credits Based on Annual Production [paras 5.18–5.19]

. . .

5.19 The Panel further noted that the parties disagreed as to whether or not the tax credits in **Minnesota** were available in the case of imported beer from small foreign breweries. The Panel considered that beer produced by large breweries is not unlike beer produced by small breweries. Indeed, the United States did not assert that the size of the breweries affected the nature of the beer produced or otherwise affected beer as a product. Therefore, in the view of the Panel, even if Minnesota were to grant the tax credits on a non-discriminatory basis to small breweries inside and outside the United States, imported beer from large breweries would be "subject ... to internal taxes ... in excess of those applied ... to like domestic products" from small breweries and there would still be an inconsistency with Article III:2, first sentence. Accordingly, the Panel found that the state excise tax credits provided by **Kentucky**, **Minnesota**, **Ohio** and **Wisconsin** to domestic breweries based on annual beer production, but not to imported beer, are inconsistent with Article III:2, first sentence.

United States – Taxes on Automobiles ('US – Taxes on Automobiles'), 1994 (NOT ADOPTED)

Short summary and commentary

US – Taxes on Automobiles addressed the PPM issue in the context of Article III:4 (relating to national treatment on internal regulation). The European Community challenged, among other things, the US Corporate Average Fuel Economy (CAFE) regulations as they applied to cars. The CAFE standards required that average fuel economy for passenger automobiles (manufactured by any manufacturer) not fall below a certain set level. A manufacturer was deemed to be any person engaged in the business of producing or assembling automobiles in the US, or importing them. A manufacturer had to meet average fuel economy standards for both its imported and domestic fleets, calculated separately. An automobile was counted in the domestic fleet if less than 25 per cent of its value was imported. The EC argued that the regulations, which were based on a fleet averaging method that treated domestic and foreign cars separately, violated the national treatment clause of Article III:4 of the GATT.

The panel found that the CAFE regulations were inconsistent with GATT Article III:4 because the regulations differentiated between domestic and imported products based on non-product-related factors (Panel report, paragraphs 5.54, 5.55). Because the CAFE fleet averaging method was based on the ownership or control relationship of the car manufacturer, the measure did not relate to the cars as products, and therefore could result in imported products being treated less favourably than 'like' domestic products – a violation of Article III's national treatment obligation (*Id.*).

The US also asserted that, because the CAFE scheme was intended to conserve exhaustible natural resources by encouraging the sale of fuel efficient cars, even if the panel were to find the CAFE regulations inconsistent with Article III:4, those regulations should nevertheless be upheld under the exception set forth in Article XX(g) of the GATT. Although the panel agreed that it was clear that the goal of the CAFE scheme was to enhance the fuel efficiency of cars in the US, it did not find that Article XX(g) of the GATT protected the regulations. The panel concluded that Article XX(g) did not protect the measure because the separate fleet accounting method was not 'primarily aimed at' the conservation of exhaustible natural resources.

If, however, the fleet averaging system applied to foreign cars in the same manner as it applied to domestic cars, the panel suggested that such a system could fall within the exception set forth in Article XX(g). Thus, there are two important aspects to the panel's findings on the GATT-consistency of the CAFE regulations. First, the panel found that the fleet averaging system violated the GATT's national treatment discipline because the US regulations were dependent on factors not directly related to the products as such (*Id.* at paragraph 5.55). Second, the panel noted that the fleet averaging method could, in some cases, meet the requirements in paragraph (g) of Article XX. In essence, therefore, the panel implicitly and indirectly ruled that Article XX could potentially permit a non-product-related PPM-based measure that relied on the characteristics of the producers.

The GATT Council never adopted this decision.

The excerpts below relate only to Article III:4, not Article XX of the GATT because the panel's discussion of Article XX does not touch upon the product-related/non-product-related issue. More information on the evolution of Article XX(g) on the conservation of exhaustible natural resources can be found in Chapter 2: General Exceptions Clauses.

Excerpts

Report of the Panel, *United States – Taxes on Automobiles*, DS31/R (11 October 1994), NOT ADOPTED.

(ii) Article III:4 [paras. 5.44–5.46]

. . .

5.45 The Panel considered first whether in terms of Article III:4 the CAFE measure was a requirement "affecting" the internal sale, offering for sale, purchase, transportation, distribution or use of a product. The Panel noted that for a measure to be subject to Article III, it does not have to regulate a product directly. It only has to affect the conditions of competition between domestic and imported products. A previous panel had explained this principle:

> *"In addition, the text of paragraph 4 referred both in English and French to laws and regulations and requirements* affecting *internal sale, purchase, etc., and not to laws, regulations and requirements governing the conditions of sale or purchase. The selection of the word 'affecting' would imply, in the opinion of the Panel, that the drafters of the Article intended to cover in paragraph 4 not only the laws and regulations which directly governed the conditions of sale or purchase but also any laws or regulations which might adversely modify the conditions of competition between the domestic and imported products on the internal market."*[148]

The Panel observed that the CAFE measure was not applied to cars as such, but that it regulated the conduct of manufacturers and importers. The Panel therefore examined whether regulations applied to manufacturers of cars, and not directly to cars, could "affect" the product in terms of Article III:4. As previously noted by the Panel, the purpose of Article III is to ensure that imported products benefit from conditions of competition no less favourable than like domestic products. Since conditions of competition could easily be modified by regulations applied directly to producers or importers and not to a product, the Panel considered that the direct application of a regulation to a producer did not mean that the regulation could not "affect" the conditions of competition of the product. A previous panel had applied this principle and stated:

> *"Nor could the applicability of Article III:4 be denied on the ground that most of the procedures in the case before the Panel are applied to persons rather than products, since the factor determining whether persons might be susceptible to Section 337 proceedings or federal district court procedures is the source of the challenged products, that is whether they are of United States origin or imported."*[149]

[148] Report of the Panel on *Italian Discrimination against imported agricultural machinery,* adopted 23 October 1958, BISD 7S/60, 64 at para 12.
[149] Report of the Panel on *United States – Section 337 of the Tariff Act of 1930,* adopted 7 November 1989, BISD 36S/345, para 5.10.

. . .

(b) Fleet Averaging [paras 5.50–5.55]

. . .

5.51 The Panel proceeded to examine the argument of the United States that the CAFE regulation provided all manufacturers or importers with the same flexibility in meeting its requirements, and that imported cars were consequently accorded treatment no less favourable than domestic cars. This raised in the view of the Panel the question of whether Article III permitted the application to imported products of measures applied to domestic products that differentiated between them on the basis of the ownership or control of the manufacturers or importers, since this was the element that defined the scope of the products to be averaged under fleet averaging requirement.

5.52 The Panel examined this issue in the light of the text of Article III. It observed that Article III prescribes in general the treatment to be accorded to imported *products* in relation to domestic products. In particular, Article III:1, which sets out the principle underlying Article III, refers to treatment resulting from measures applied to products. Article III:4 refers only to laws, regulations and requirements affecting the internal sale, offering for sale, purchase, transportation, distribution or use of products. The Panel noted that these activities relate to the product *as a product*, from its introduction into the market to its final consumption. They do not relate directly to the producer. The Panel further noted that a similar principle underlies the treatment of taxes under Art. III:2. A Working Party report had interpreted this provision as permitting domestic taxes to be applied to foreign products (i.e. border adjusted) only when the taxes were "directly levied on products":

> *"[T]here was a convergence of views to the effect that taxes directly levied on products were eligible for tax adjustment. Examples of such taxes comprised specific excise duties, sales taxes and cascade taxes and the tax on value added... Furthermore, the Working Party concluded that there was convergence of views to the effect that certain taxes that were not directly levied on products were not eligible for adjustment. Examples of such taxes were social security charges whether on employers or employees and payroll taxes."*[150]

The Panel noted that the domestic taxes mentioned in the Working Party report that could be applied also to foreign products (i.e. border adjusted) were based on factors directly related to the product, for example its sale within the importing country. Those that could not be so applied were not directly related to the product, but to other factors such as the income of the producer.

[150] Report of the Working Party on *Border Tax Adjustments,* adopted on 2 December 1970, BISD 18S/97.

5.53 The Panel considered that this limitation on the range of domestic policy measures that may be applied also to imported products reflected one of the central purposes of Article III: to ensure the security of tariff bindings. Contracting parties could not be expected to negotiate tariff commitments if these could be frustrated through the application of measures affecting imported products subject to tariff commitments and triggered by factors unrelated to the products as such. If it were permissible to justify under Article III less favourable treatment to an imported product on the basis of factors not related to the product as such, Article III would not serve its intended purpose. Equally important, the right to unconditional most-favoured nation treatment in the application of Article III:4, which is specifically mentioned in Article I:1, would not be assured.

5.54 These considerations confirmed in the view of the Panel that Article III:4 does not permit treatment of an imported product less favourable than that accorded to a like domestic product, based on factors not directly relating to the product as such. The Panel found therefore that, to the extent that treatment under the CAFE measure was based on factors relating to the control or ownership of producers/importers, it could not in accordance with Article III:4 be applied in a manner that also accorded less favourable treatment to products of foreign origin. It was therefore not necessary to examine whether treatment based on these factors was also applied so as to afford protection to domestic production.

5.55 The Panel concluded that the fleet averaging requirement based on the ownership or control relationship of the car manufacturer did not relate to cars as products. This requirement could thus result in treatment less favourable than that accorded to like domestic products. Therefore it could not be imposed consistently with Article III:4 so as to affect also cars of foreign origin.

United States – Standards for Reformulated and Conventional Gasoline ('US – Reformulated Gasoline'), 1996

Short summary and commentary

In *US – Reformulated Gasoline*, the panel interpreted a non-product-related PPM-based measure in the context of Article III:4 (relating to national treatment on internal regulation). In the dispute, Brazil and Venezuela challenged the implementation of the US Clean Air Act (CAA). The dispute had begun in 1990 when the US Congress amended the CAA to instruct the US Environmental Protection Agency (EPA) to issue regulations reducing vehicle emissions caused by gasoline in order to improve air quality in the most polluted areas of the US. The amended CAA called for a 20–25 per cent reduction in emissions of toxic air pollutants and ozone-forming volatile organic compounds from 'reformulated gasoline' (which was sold in highly polluted areas). It also required that conventional gasoline (which was sold in the rest of the country) remain as clean as it was in 1990. This led to the adoption of regulations in 1993, which required that the chemical characteristics of the gasoline comply with defined levels. While the levels were fixed for certain chemicals, others were expressed as non-degradation requirements by reference to baselines representing gasoline quality in 1990. The regulations laid out how to determine the baselines for the reduction in air pollutants for reformulated gasoline. Domestic refineries in existence prior to 1990 could use one of several methods to determine their 'individual baseline' derived from refinery-specific data. In contrast, US refineries built after 1990 and all foreign refineries were required to use a statutory baseline representing average US 1990 gasoline quality. The statutory baseline in some circumstances was less advantageous than the baselines that could be individually established by domestic refineries. The EPA justified this differential treatment of foreign refineries by arguing that there might be insufficient reliable information regarding the quality of gasoline produced in 1990 to determine the baseline for individual foreign refineries.

The WTO panel upheld Venezuela's allegation that the EPA regulation violated Article III:4 on national treatment, holding that Article III:4 does not allow foreign products to be treated less favourably than like, domestic products based 'on the characteristics of the producer and the nature of data held by it' (Panel report, paragraph 6.11). The panel found that imported and domestic gasoline were 'like' products and noted that the US had not denied that these were 'like' per se (*Id.* at paragraph 6.9). It noted that instead, the US claimed that the situation of the producers should be taken into account when examining the treatment of the imported and domestic products (*Id.*). The US argued that its regulations met the requirements of Article III:4 because they treated imported gasoline similarly to gasoline from similarly situated domestic parties. However, the panel noted that Article III:4 deals with the treatment to be accorded to 'like' products, which does not allow less favourable treatment based on 'extraneous factors' such as the characteristics of the producer and the data held by it (*Id.* at paragraphs 6.11–6.12). It thus concluded that chemically identical imported and domestic gasoline were 'like' products, and that by failing to give foreign refineries the chance to use an individual baseline, the EPA regulation accorded importers treatment less favourable than domestic producers, and hence violated Article III:4 of the GATT. This holding was not appealed and therefore was not addressed in the decision of the Appellate Body.

The panel also rejected the US' defences based on the Article XX(b) and (g) exceptions. The Appellate Body agreed, but came to the conclusion based on different reasoning. It reversed the panel's finding that the US measure did not fall within the scope of Article XX(g). It concluded that the measure qualified for provisional justification under Article XX(g), but failed to meet the requirements of the chapeau of Article XX. That clause specifies that measures may not be applied in a manner which constitutes a disguised barrier to trade, or a means of arbitrary or unjustifiable discrimination between countries where the same conditions prevail. The Appellate Body explained that the chapeau was not so much about the measure as such, but rather the manner in which the measure applied (AB report, section IV). In the case at issue, the Appellate Body found that the US could have either applied statutory baselines to all refiners, or made individual baselines available to all refiners (*Id.*). It rejected the US' explanations that the differential treatment was necessary for practical reasons of verification and enforcement (*Id.*).

Although the Appellate Body did not explicitly address the product-related/non-product-related distinction, its conclusion that the measures at issue fell under the scope of Article XX(g) gives a fairly clear indication that non-product-related measures are not per se excluded from paragraph (g) of Article XX. Also, the Appellate Body did not indicate that the chapeau categorically prohibits the use of non-product-related PPM-based measures. This was confirmed in the subsequent *US – Shrimp/Turtle 21.5* ruling (described below). In *US – Shrimp/Turtle 21.5*, the Appellate Body, although not addressing the non-product-related PPM-based characteristics of the measure at issue, found that the PPM-based measure fulfilled all requirements under paragraph (g) of Article XX and its chapeau.

In sum, *US – Reformulated Gasoline* shows that non-product-related PPM-based measures that involve (at least certain types of) producer characteristics standards are likely to be found inconsistent with Article III:4 of the GATT based on the holding that such 'extraneous factors' may not be used as a basis for according less favourable treatment to 'like' products (Panel report, paragraph 6.12). What this interpretation of Article III:4 means for other types of non-product-related measures remains unclear. However, it is important to keep in mind that non-product-related measures were not found to be per se excluded from justification under Article XX. Thus, certain non-product-related PPM-based measures found in violation of Article III can still be found to be GATT-consistent.

The excerpts below relate only to Article III:4, not Article XX, of the GATT because neither the panel's nor the Appellate Body's discussion of Article XX addressed the product-related/non-product-related distinction. Also, as mentioned above, the panel's findings regarding Article III:4 were not appealed; therefore, only excerpts of the panel report, not the Appellate Body Report, are printed below.

Excerpts

Report of the Panel, *United States – Standards for Reformulated and Conventional Gasoline*, WT/DS2/R (29 January 1996), adopted as modified by the Appellate Body Report on 20 May 1996.

1. Article III:4 [paras 6.5–6.16]

. . .

6.9 In light of the foregoing, the Panel proceeded to examine whether imported and domestic gasoline were like products under Article III:4. The Panel observed first that the United States did not argue that imported gasoline and domestic gasoline were not like *per se*. It had argued rather that with respect to the treatment of the imported and domestic products, the situation of the parties dealing in the gasoline must be taken into consideration. The Panel, recalling its previous discussion of the factors to be taken into account in the determination of like product, noted that chemically-identical imported and domestic gasoline by definition have exactly the same physical characteristics, end-uses, tariff classification, and are perfectly substitutable. The Panel found therefore that chemically-identical imported and domestic gasoline are like products under Article III:4.

6.10 The Panel next examined whether the treatment accorded under the Gasoline Rule to imported gasoline was less favourable than that accorded to like gasoline of national origin.

6.11 The Panel then examined the US argument that the requirements of Article III:4 are met because imported gasoline is treated similarly to gasoline from *similarly situated* domestic parties – domestic refiners with limited 1990 operations and blenders. According to the United States, the difference in treatment between imported and domestic gasoline was justified because importers, like domestic refiners with limited 1990 operations and blenders, could not reliably establish their 1990 gasoline quality, lacked consistent sources and quality of gasoline, or had the flexibility to meet a statutory baseline since they were not constrained by refinery equipment and crude supplies. The Panel observed that the distinction in the Gasoline Rule between refiners on the one hand, and importers and blenders on the other, which affected the treatment of imported gasoline with respect to domestic gasoline, was related to certain differences in the characteristics of refiners, blenders and importers, and the nature of the data held by them. However, Article III:4 of the General Agreement deals with the treatment to be accorded to like products; its wording does not allow less favourable treatment dependent on the characteristics of the producer and the nature of the data held by it. The Panel noted that in the *Malt Beverages* case, a tax regulation according less favourable treatment to beer on the basis of the size of the producer was rejected.[29] Although this finding was made under Article III:2 concerning fiscal measures, the Panel considered that the same principle applied to regulations under Article III:4. Accordingly, the Panel rejected the US argument that the requirements of Article III:4 are met because imported gasoline is treated similarly to gasoline from similarly situated domestic parties.

[29] *"United States – Measures Affecting Alcoholic and Malt Beverages"*, BISD 39S/206, para 5.19 (adopted on 19 June 1992).

6.12 Apart from being contrary to the ordinary meaning of the terms of Article III:4, any interpretation of Article III:4 in this manner would mean that the treatment of imported and domestic goods concerned could no longer be assured on the objective basis of their likeness as products. Rather, imported goods would be exposed to a highly subjective and variable treatment according to extraneous factors. This would thereby create great instability and uncertainty in the conditions of competition as between domestic and imported goods in a manner fundamentally inconsistent with the object and purpose of Article III.

Indonesia – Certain Measures Affecting the Automotive Industry ('Indonesia – Automobile'), 1998 (This decision was not appealed.)

Short summary and commentary

Indonesia – Automobile questioned the consistency of Indonesia's tax regime under the GATT. Indonesia imposed higher duties and sales taxes on imported products of manufacturers that did not use a certain amount of Indonesian auto parts or Indonesian labour. In addressing a complaint brought by Japan, the European Communities, and the US, the WTO panel noted that the measure at issue created a situation in which an imported car, alike in all functional aspects, would be taxed at a higher rate simply because of its origin or lack of sufficient local content. The panel found that this 'distinction between the products, which results in different levels of taxation, is not based on the products per se, but rather on such factors as the nationality of the producer or the origin of the parts and components contained in the product' (Panel report, paragraph 14.112). Consequently, the panel found that 'such an origin-based distinction in respect of internal taxes' violated Article III:2 of the GATT, which prohibits tax discrimination of like products (*Id.* at paragraph 14.113).

The language used by the panel seems to prohibit any distinction between products based on non-product-related measures under GATT Article III:2. However, the fact that the dispute involved an origin-based measure suggests that origin-neutral measures might be treated differently. The reasoning in the subsequent *Canada – Automotive Industry* dispute (see below) offers a more complete explanation in this respect. Most importantly, the panel in *Canada – Automotive Industry* specifically referred to the statement by the *Indonesia – Automobile* panel that an advantage within the meaning of Article I 'cannot be made conditional on any criteria that is not related to the imported product itself' and explained that such a statement must 'be seen in relation to conditions which entailed different treatment of like products depending upon their origin' (*Canada – Automotive Industry* panel report, paragraph 10.28). Thus, *Indonesia – Automobile* should probably be understood to focus more on the origin-based/origin-neutral distinction, rather than on the question of whether or not a measure is or is not product-related.

Excerpts

Report of the Panel, *Indonesia – Certain Measures Affecting the Automotive Industry*, WT/DS54/R, WT/DS55/R, WT/DS59/R, WT/DS64/R, adopted on 23 July 1998. (This decision was not appealed.)

2. Article III:2 of GATT [paras 14.102–14.117]

. . .

(a) Article III:2, first sentence [paras 14.104–14.114]

. . .

14.112 More importantly, we note that because of the structure of the tax regime under examination, any imported like products would necessarily be taxed in excess of domestic like products. In considering the broader arguments put forward by the complainants that the tax measures in dispute violate Article III:2 because they discriminate not on the basis of factors affecting the properties, nature, qualities or end use of the products, but on origin-related criteria, we recall that the Appellate Body decisions in *Alcoholic Beverages (1996)* and *Periodicals* suggest that the term "like products" as used in Article III:2 should be interpreted narrowly.[705] We note, however, that in this case the "like products" issue is not the same as the "like products" issue in the *Alcoholic Beverages (1996)* case. There, the internal tax imposed on domestic shochu was the same as that imposed on imported shochu; the higher tax imposed on imported vodka was also imposed on domestic vodka. Identical products (not considering brand differences) were taxed identically. The issue was whether the differences between the two products shochu and vodka, as defined for tax purposes, were so minor that shochu and vodka should be considered to be like products and therefore subject to the requirement of Article III:2, first sentence, that one should not be taxed in excess of the other. Here, the situation is quite different. The distinction between the products, which results in different levels of taxation, is not based on the products *per se*, but rather on such factors as the nationality of the producer or the origin of the parts and components contained in the product. As such, an imported product identical in all respects to a domestic product, except for its origin or the origin of its parts and components or other factors not related to the product itself, would be subject to a different level of taxation.

[705] *Alcoholic Beverages (1996),* op. cit., Appellate Body Report, pp19–20*; Periodicals,* op. cit.,Appellate Body Report, p22.

14.113 In *Periodicals*, the Appellate Body recognized the possibility of using hypothetical imports to determine whether a measure violates Article III:2, although in that case the Appellate Body rejected the hypothetical example used by the Panel.[706] But this case is different. Under the Indonesian car programmes, the distinction between the products for tax purposes is based on such factors as the nationality of the producer or the origin of the parts and components contained in the product. Appropriate hypotheticals are therefore easily constructed. An imported motor vehicle alike in all aspects relevant to a likeness determination would be taxed at a higher rate simply because of its origin or lack of sufficient local content.[707] Such vehicles certainly can exist (and, as demonstrated above, do in fact exist). In our view, such an origin-based distinction in respect of internal taxes suffices in itself to violate Article III:2, without the need to demonstrate the existence of actually traded like products.[708] This is directly in accord with the broad purposes of Article III:2, as outlined by the Appellate Body in paragraph 14.108, *infra*.

[706] *Periodicals,* op.cit., Appellate Body Report, pp20–21.

[707] Thus, although there is no evidence in the record of such actual imports, it can be found that any imported motorcycles of 250 cc or less, which are like Indonesian made motorcycles of 250 cc or less, would be taxed in excess of the latter; any imported combines, minibuses, vans and pick-ups, which are like Indonesian made combines, minibuses, vans and pick-ups, including those with a local content of 60 % or more, would be taxed in excess of the latter; any imported buses, which are like Indonesian made buses, would be taxed in excess of the latter; any imported sedans and stations wagons of less than 1,600 cc, which are like Indonesian made sedans and station wagons of less than 1,600 cc, including those with a local content of 60 % or more, would be taxed in excess of the latter.

[708] This finding is in accord with a number of previous panel reports concluding that differences in producers' characteristics, which do not affect the products' characteristics, cannot justify a different tax treatment of the products involved. See, e.g*., Malt Beverages,* at para 5.19 ("beer produced by large breweries is not unlike beer produced by small breweries"); Gasoline, at para 6.11 ("Article III:4 of the General Agreement deals with the treatment to be accorded to like products; its wording does not allow less favourable treatment dependent on the characteristics of the producer."); Panel Report on *United States – Measures Affecting the Importation, Internal Sale and Use of Tobacco,* adopted 4 October 1994, DS44/R, para 97 ("The Panel thus considered that the system for calculation of the BDA on imported tobacco itself, not just the manner in which it was currently applied, was inconsistent with Article III:2 because it carried with it the risk of discriminatory treatment of imports in respect of internal taxes.").

Article XX of the GATT

United States – Import Prohibition of Certain Shrimp and Shrimp Products ('US – Shrimp/Turtle I'), 1998 and United States – Import Prohibition of Certain Shrimp and Shrimp Products ('US – Shrimp/Turtle 21.5'), 2001

Short summary and commentary

US – Shrimp/Turtle I and *21.5* involved a non-product-related PPM-based measure similar to the measure at issue in (unadopted) *US – Tuna/Dolphin I* and *II*. However, in contrast to the *US – Tuna/Dolphin* reports, the *US – Shrimp/Turtle* reports did not explicitly address the PPM characteristic of the measure. In spite of this, the case is crucial for PPM-based measures because *US – Shrimp/Turtle 21.5* was the first dispute to find a non-product-related PPM-based measure GATT-consistent based on the Article XX exceptions clause of the GATT. The measure at issue in *US – Shrimp/Turtle I* was a 1989 amendment to the US Endangered Species Act (ESA). This amendment, referred to as Section 609, prohibited the importation of shrimp harvested in a way that might harm sea turtles. However, if the exporting country was certified by the US administration as having a regulatory programme to prevent incidental turtle mortality, comparable to that of the US, or if it were certified as having a fishing environment that did not pose risks to sea turtles from shrimping, the importation of shrimp was permitted.

India, Malaysia, Pakistan and Thailand alleged that the shrimp embargo violated GATT Article XI, which prohibits the use of quantitative restrictions. The US did not dispute the violation of Article XI. Rather, it invoked paragraphs (b) and (g) of Article XX as a defence. These provisions permit Members to maintain measures necessary for the protection of animal life, and measures related to the conservation of exhaustible natural resources, even if those measures are inconsistent with another GATT provision. The WTO panel found a violation of GATT Article XI, and rejected the US' defences. The panel explained that Article XX did not allow measures aimed at compelling another party to change its policies to be consistent with the policies of the party enacting the measures (*US – Shrimp/Turtle I* AB report, paragraph116). To allow such measures would constitute a threat to the multilateral trading system as a whole, and would be contrary to the object and purpose of the WTO Agreements (*Id.*). Thus, the panel concluded that the measures fell outside the scope of Article XX (*Id.*). Like the *US – Tuna/Dolphin II* ruling, the WTO panel report had the effect of excluding from the scope of Article XX most types of measures with extraterritorial effects, thereby also excluding most types of non-product-related PPM-based measures.

The Appellate Body upheld the panel's final conclusion that the ban was not justified under Article XX, but based its holding on different reasons. The Appellate Body explicitly and forcefully rejected the reasoning of the panel that Article XX could not justify measures that condition access to domestic markets on whether the exporting state complies with or adopts a policy or policies unilaterally prescribed by the importing state (*Id.* at paragraph 121). Therefore, the Appellate Body implicitly allowed measures impacting processes and production methods used in jurisdictions outside the country enacting the measures.

The Appellate Body found that the import ban at issue was provisionally justified under Article XX(g), but that the measure failed to meet the requirements of the chapeau of Article XX (*Id.* at paragraphs 125–145, 184). The latter prohibits measures that are applied in a manner that constitutes a means of arbitrary or unjustifiable discrimination between countries where the same conditions prevail, or in a manner which constitutes a disguised barrier to trade. The Appellate Body prescribed a series of requirements necessary for measures to fulfil the chapeau's obligations, including an obligation to take into account the particular circumstances in the exporting country and make administrative determinations more flexible, to allow for due process and transparency in the administrative proceedings, and to conduct serious efforts to negotiate a treaty with affected countries before adopting trade measures. The Appellate Body did not require that a measure be product-related in order to fulfil the requirements under Article XX. Nor did it require that a measure be origin-neutral or jurisdictionally limited.

In 2001 Malaysia brought a second challenge to the WTO, alleging that the US had not taken the necessary steps to comply with the recommendations and rulings contained in the *US – Shrimp/Turtle I* reports. The panel found that the US measure was now applied in a manner that met the requirements of Article XX of the GATT (*US – Shrimp/ Turtle 21.5* panel report, paragraph 5.137). Upon appeal in the implementation dispute, the Appellate Body upheld panel findings that the US had met its obligation to exercise ongoing good faith efforts in pursuit of international sea turtle protections, and that the US had achieved sufficient flexibility in its regulatory regime to eliminate the unjustified and arbitrary discrimination prohibited by the Article XX chapeau (*US – Shrimp/Turtle 21.5* AB report, paragraphs 134, 144). The new guidelines allowed certification of importer programmes that protected sea turtles using means other than the method prescribed by the US, as long as they were comparably effective in preventing turtle mortality. They also allowed imports from shrimp trawlers operating in uncertified countries as long as they were using a turtle-friendly method (shipment-by-shipment approach as opposed to country-based approach). The panel in *US – Shrimp/Turtle 21.5* found that it was not enough to certify countries with programmes comparably effective but that it was also essential that the US was allowing certified turtle-friendly shipments from non-certified countries (*Id.* at paragraph 123). The US did not appeal this holding and the Appellate Body did not take a position on this. Thus, *US – Shrimp/Turtle 21.5* does not answer the question whether the shipment-by-shipment (origin-neutral) approach was a necessary requirement. It is noteworthy, however, that the Appellate Body did not mention this as a requirement in its first decision. Also, the willingness of the Appellate Body to permit measures that condition access to domestic markets on whether the exporting state complies with or adopts a 'policy' or 'policies' prescribed by the importing state, might be an indication that Article XX also permits country-based trade measures as long as they are sufficiently flexible and fulfil the other conditions under the chapeau of Article XX.

The *US – Shrimp/Turtle* decisions indicate that non-product-related PPM-based measures can be GATT-compliant. In that context, it should first be noted that the Appellate Body, when laying down the tests under the chapeau of Article XX, did not categorically rule as impermissible country-based non-product-related PPM-based measures. However, the version of the US measure held GATT-consistent in *US – Shrimp/ Turtle 21.5* was not country-based but origin-neutral in that it allowed the entry of shrimp where the manufacturer (as opposed to the country of export) was certified. Second, it is noteworthy that the Appellate Body assumed that the sea turtles the US meant to protect traversed US waters. In doing so, the Appellate Body appears to have limited its sanctification of non-product-related PPM-based measures to measures with a 'sufficient nexus' between the natural resource to be protected and the country enacting the environmental measure. As a consequence, it remains unclear what *US – Shrimp/Turtle I* and *21.5* mean for PPM-based measures aimed at protecting natural resources existing solely outside the territory of the party enacting a challenged measure.

As mentioned above, *US – Shrimp/Turtle I* did not examine Article III. Instead the discussion focused on the interpretation of Article XX. However, the analysis of Article XX in *US – Shrimp/Turtle I* did not address the product/process distinction. Instead, *US – Shrimp/Turtle I* examined other aspects of Article XX including issues relating to the extraterritorial effects of measures. These are discussed in more detail in Chapter 5: Extraterritoriality. *US – Shrimp/Turtle I* only implicitly found that non-product-related PPM-based measures could fall within the scope of Article XX(g) and fulfil the requirements of the chapeau of Article XX. In addition, Chapter 2: General Exceptions Clauses, extensively discusses this issue. As a result, the relevant excerpts are reproduced, instead, in Chapter 5: Extraterritoriality and Chapter 2: General Exceptions Clauses.

CHAPTER 5

Extraterritoriality

BACKGROUND

Introduction

Trade and environment disputes sometimes involve assertions that the challenged measure is 'extraterritorial' or 'extrajurisdictional', and therefore violates World Trade Organization (WTO) rules. These terms have not always been used with sufficient legal precision, however, and the claim that extraterritoriality automatically leads to WTO-inconsistency conflates different legal inquiries.

To conduct an adequate legal analysis in this area, one must distinguish between the concept of extraterritoriality in the context of customary international law on jurisdiction and the concept of extraterritoriality in the context of WTO law. For instance, an extraterritorial measure might be considered permissible under customary international law, but in violation of WTO rules or vice versa.

The exercise of 'jurisdiction' is considered by customary international law to involve any (or all) of three types of governmental authority:

(i) the authority to prescribe or apply laws to persons and activities;
(ii) the authority to enforce those laws through the application of sanctions; and/or
(iii) the authority to exercise judicial power over a particular person or object.

States have the right to exercise these powers based on different grounds. Customary international law recognizes five basic principles for exercising jurisdiction: (i) the territorial principle; (ii) the effects principle; (iii) the nationality principle; (iv) the universality principle; and (v) the protective principle.

The *territorial principle* holds that a state has the right to exercise jurisdiction to prescribe and enforce laws, and adjudicate over all persons and objects within its territory. Territorial jurisdiction applies to the land within the state's boundaries, the territorial sea as specified in international law of the sea, and the airspace above the land and territorial waters. Under this principle, a state has the right, for example, to prohibit a person in its territory from killing a human being or a member of an endangered species located in its territory, or from emitting pollution in its territory. Territorial jurisdiction is an essential element of the sovereign state. Several states have extended the territorial principle to include jurisdiction to prosecute and punish crimes commenced within their territory, but completed or consummated in the territory of another state. Similarly, some states apply their territorial jurisdiction to actions commenced in another state but completed or consummated within their territory. The territorial principle is generally viewed as the most important basis for jurisdiction.

According to the *effects principle*, which derives from the territorial principle, a state has the right to exercise prescriptive jurisdiction over actions that have substantial effects within its territory. Here, jurisdiction is exercised extraterritorially on the basis of the effects or consequences in the territory of the state exercising jurisdiction. Under the effects principle, a state has the right, for instance, to prohibit a person from shooting across a border to kill a human being or a member of an endangered species located in its territory, or from emitting pollution in another state that has harmful effects in its territory. The effects principle is controversial when the only effect is economic, such as the US' exercise of jurisdiction in anti-trust proceedings.

Like the territorial principle, the *nationality principle* is widely accepted and non-controversial. Under this principle, a state has the right to exercise its jurisdiction over its nationals wherever they are located. Nationality as a basis for jurisdiction includes the nationality of individuals, corporations, vessels, aircraft and spacecraft. Under this principle, a state has the right, for example, to prohibit its nationals from killing human beings or members of an endangered species, or from polluting – regardless of where the nationals and the endangered species are located.

It is generally accepted that states also have jurisdiction to prescribe laws with respect to certain types of conduct outside its territory by persons that are not its nationals. In this context, the two grounds for jurisdiction are the universality and the protective principles. According to the *universality principle*, a state has the right to exercise jurisdiction over universally condemned activities, such as slavery, torture and genocide. Pursuant to the *protective principle*, a state has the right to exercise jurisdiction in order to protect vital national interests, such as the integrity of its currency. Under this principle, a state has the right to prohibit counterfeiting of its currency anywhere in the world.

The relationship between extraterritoriality, customary international law, and the WTO

To understand how the concepts of extraterritorial jurisdiction and WTO consistency/inconsistency interrelate, consider the US' import ban on shrimp caught without turtle excluder devices (TEDs), devices used to reduce the harms caused by shrimping to sea turtles. Some critics have claimed that the ban is 'extraterritorial' because the effects of the ban are felt outside the territory of the US (the country enacting the measure), and that the ban therefore violates the WTO agreement. What critics mean by 'extraterritorial' is unclear. According to the latest edition of Black's Law Dictionary, the adjective 'extraterritorial' means 'beyond the geographic limits of a particular jurisdiction' (Black's Dictionary, 8th ed., 2004). Based on this definition, one can argue that the US did not in fact apply its laws in an extraterritorial manner. That is, the US did not apply its laws 'beyond the geographic limits of [its] jurisdiction', as it did not directly prohibit anyone outside its territory from fishing without TEDs. The decisions to impose and how to administer the ban were made in the US, and the actual refusal of import occurs at US ports, which are located within the territorial jurisdiction of the US.

On the other hand, one might argue that the US measures restricted fishermen abroad from exporting their product into the US and is therefore extraterritorial. Thus, while the *application* of the US law was not extraterritorial, the *effects* of the measure nevertheless were extraterritorial.

If the effects of a measure are 'extraterritorial', it does not necessarily mean that the measure is 'impermissible' under customary international law or 'WTO-inconsistent'.

For example, several aspects of the US measure on TEDs indicate that the territoriality principle justifies this type of measure. First, the import prohibition imposed by the US on its domestic importers is clearly an application of laws over persons *within* US territory, and thus an application of the territoriality principle. In addition, the US measure attempted to prevent its society and the market within its territory from engaging in unsustainable consumption patterns, that is purchasing and consuming shrimp harvested in a way that threatened endangered species of turtles. Additionally, the territoriality principle would also apply if the turtles were sometimes located within the territory of the U S (i.e. while migrating). Finally, even if the turtles were never located in the US, the effects principle would provide a basis for jurisdiction if the species' extinction had effects in the US. In sum, the US measure discussed here arguably falls within the ambit of measures covered by the territoriality principle, the effects principle, or both, which would provide a valid basis for exercising jurisdiction under customary international law.

However, because countries may agree to limit such customary international law rights in treaties such as trade agreements, the question remains whether or not measures, such as the US measure at issue, are forbidden under GATT/WTO law. In this context, it should also be noted that, even if a measure were found illegal under customary international law, this would not automatically constitute a violation of WTO rules. There is no language in the WTO agreements that would lead to such a wide-ranging result. Another conclusion would transform a violation of international law into a WTO violation, subject to WTO dispute settlement.

The link between extraterritoriality and PPM-based measures

As of this writing, the GATT and WTO disputes that raised questions relating to extraterritoriality generally involved measures based on processes and production methods (PPMs) that were not related to the product (referred to as non-product-related PPM-based measures). These measures are described in detail in Chapter 4: Processes and Production Methods. In short, these measures are rules that are defined in terms of PPMs that do not affect the end-product; often they are aimed at avoiding or mitigating harmful effects caused by methods of production. Some PPM-based measures can affect international trade, including, for example, import restrictions or labelling requirements on goods produced in a certain way. Typically, trade-related PPM-based measures (that are not product-related) aim at protecting something located (at least in part) outside the territorial boundaries of the country enacting the measure. The country enacting the measure may, for example, be trying to protect natural resources, humans, animals, plants, ecosystems or the environmental quality in the producing state or in ecosystems beyond any state's jurisdiction.

Critics associate PPM-based trade restrictions with extraterritoriality and sometimes illegality because, in their view, the country enacting the PPM-based measure is telling producers in exporting countries *how* to produce or harvest their goods, by conditioning market access on the PPM used. It is undisputable that non-product-related PPM-based import restrictions can have extraterritorial effects. It is also the case, however, that all *product-related* import restrictions (PPM-based or not), have similar extraterritorial effects. For example, by closing the borders to a hazardous product, an importing state can affect *what* producers in exporting states produce.

The question of whether or not non-product-related PPM-based measures are consistent with the WTO rules is discussed in detail in Chapter 4: Processes and Production Methods. Interestingly, jurisprudence relating to the GATT deals with this question primarily in the context of the like products discussion under Articles I and III of the GATT on most-favoured nation and national treatment (see Chapter 1: Like Products). Whereas extraterritoriality has been examined under Article XX, nowhere have WTO tribunals explicitly addressed the PPMs issue in interpreting Article XX.

DISCUSSION OF RELEVANT WTO PROVISIONS

Article XX of the GATT

The General Agreement on Tariffs and Trade (GATT) does not explicitly address the subjects of jurisdiction or extraterritoriality. Article XX(b) allows Members to take measures to protect life and health. It does not expressly limit the application of that provision territorially, nor does it set forth nationality requirements. Similarly, Article XX(g) allows Members to adopt policies relating to the protection of exhaustible natural resources, without limiting that protection in terms of the location of the natural resource. These comments pertain to both the 1947 and 1994 versions of the GATT.

The (unadopted) *US – Tuna/Dolphin* reports extensively interpreted Articles XX(b) and (g) in this context. The disputes involved a US law that prohibited the import of yellowfin tuna (or products of such fish) caught with purse-seine nets, unless the government of the harvesting country proved that its programme regulating dolphin kill rates was comparable to that of the US. After finding a violation of Article XI of the GATT (which prohibits quantitative restrictions), the panel in *US – Tuna Dolphin I* rejected the US defence under the Article XX exceptions clause. It excluded from the scope of Articles XX(b) and (g) all measures protecting human, animal or plant life, or relating to the conservation of exhaustible natural resources *outside* the jurisdiction of the party taking the measure. The panel stated that if Article XX(b) or (g) permitted a country to protect life or health or the conservation of natural resources outside that country's territory, each GATT party could unilaterally determine the life, health and conservation policies of other parties, as those other parties could not deviate from such policies without jeopardizing trading rights guaranteed by the GATT (*US – Tuna/Dolphin I* panel report, paragraphs 5.27, 5.32).

The (unadopted) *US – Tuna/Dolphin II* panel report included a slightly broader reading of Article XX(b) and (g). In addition to the measures aiming to protect and conserve dolphins *within* the territory of the enacting state, the panel found admissible measures involving states' exercise of *jurisdiction over their own nationals and vessels* (*US – Tuna/Dolphin II* panel report, paragraphs 5.15–5.17, 5.20, 5.31–5.33). Nevertheless, the panel rejected justification of the US measure under Articles XX(b) and (g). It found that the US had taken the measures so as to force other countries to change their policies with respect to persons and things within the jurisdiction of those countries. Thus, the panel concluded that the measure could not be considered as fulfilling the requirements under paragraph (g) of Article XX, nor could the measure be considered as 'necessary' as required under paragraph (b) of Article XX (*Id.* at paragraphs 5.23–5.26 and 5.36–5.39).

US – Shrimp/Turtle I was the first and, as of this writing, the only WTO dispute to address questions of extraterritoriality. It involved a measure banning the import of shrimp and shrimp products unless they were taken from the waters of a country certified as complying with US standards for the protection of sea turtles. After finding a violation of Article XI on quantitative restrictions, the panel rejected justification under Article XX(g) holding, *inter alia*, that a measure cannot be considered as falling within the scope of Article XX if it operates so as to affect other governments' policies in a way that threatens the multilateral trading system (*US – Shrimp/Turtle I* panel report, paragraph 7.51).

The Appellate Body explicitly rejected the panel's approach, finding that most measures justified by Article XX would have the characteristic of affecting other governments' policies by conditioning access into the importing country's market (*US – Shrimp/Turtle I* AB report, paragraph 121). With respect to the location of the natural resource to be protected (here sea turtles), the Appellate Body in *US – Shrimp/Turtle I* found it unnecessary to consider whether or not there is an implied territorial limitation in Article XX. It found that migratory species occurring within US waters provided sufficient nexus for a measure to be justified under Article XX(g) (*Id.* at paragraph 133).

From the disputes described above, two key questions can be distilled. First, do Articles XX(b) and (g) a priori exclude measures to protect human, animal and plant life or health and exhaustible natural resources located *outside* the jurisdiction of the Member adopting the measure? Second, can measures fall under the scope of Articles XX(b) or (g) if they make access to a country's market conditional upon the exporting state's adoption of a specific policy?

The first question regarding the location of the object to be protected remains largely unanswered. The relevant dispute today is *US – Shrimp/Turtle I.* In this case, the Appellate Body clearly distanced itself from the narrow rulings of the *US – Tuna/Dolphin* disputes. However, *US – Shrimp/Turtle I* does not answer the question as to the location of the object to be protected or conserved. Instead, the Appellate Body avoided the issue by clearly stating that it considered that the protected migratory species at issue occurred in US waters and that this created a 'sufficient nexus' for the purposes of Article XX(g) (*Id.*).

With respect to the second question, that is whether or not a measure may make access to a country's market conditional upon the exporting state adopting a specific policy, it should be noted that the types of measures at issue in the *US – Tuna/Dolphin* and the *US – Shrimp/Turtle* disputes, although with *effect* beyond the jurisdiction of the US, were not exercised extrajurisdictionally. The US was not prescribing or enforcing its measure outside its jurisdictional authority as provided by customary international law. The fishermen outside US jurisdiction were allowed to continue to exercise their activities under the rules of their countries, but the US simply did not allow their products into its territory. Thus, this question is not about a measure taken extrajurisdictionally, but about a measure taken within the importing state's jurisdictional authority but with some possible effects on other countries. In *US – Shrimp/Turtle I* the Appellate Body clearly concluded that these types of measures are not per se excluded from the scope of exceptions listed under Article XX of the GATT (*Id.* at paragraph 121). It explicitly pointed out that most measures falling under the scope of Article XX would have the characteristic of affecting other governments' policies by conditioning access into the importing country's market (*Id.*).

Annex A of the SPS Agreement

The Agreement on Sanitary and Phytosanitary Measures (SPS Agreement), in contrast to the GATT, includes explicit references to territorial restrictions of measures. SPS measures are defined in Annex A to the Agreement. The definition distinguishes between four categories of SPS measures: Those applied:

(a) to protect animal or plant life or health *within the territory of the Member* from risks arising from the entry, establishment or spread of pests, diseases, disease-carrying organisms or disease-causing organisms;
(b) to protect human or animal life or health *within the territory of the Member* from risks arising from additives, contaminants, toxins or disease-causing organisms in foods, beverages or feedstuffs;
(c) to protect human life or health *within the territory of the Member* from risks arising from diseases carried by animals, plants or products thereof, or from the entry, establishment or spread of pests; or
(d) to prevent or limit other damage *within the territory of the Member* from the entry, establishment or spread of pests (emphasis added).

All four categories refer to measures aimed at preventing harm only 'within the country of import'. It is also notable that the SPS Agreement only covers measures that relate to specific types of risks, such as those relating to pests or those that are food-related.

While the SPS Agreement presumably does not apply to measures aimed at protecting human, animal or plant life or health wholly outside of the territory of the enacting state, the Agreement does not prohibit the use of such measures. In cases where the SPS Agreement does not apply, measures might fall under the scope of the GATT or the TBT Agreement. For a more detailed discussion of the scope of the SPS Agreement, see Chapter 4: Processes and Production Methods.

The TBT Agreement

In contrast to the SPS Agreement, the Agreement on Technical Barriers to Trade (TBT Agreement) does not contain any references to jurisdictional or territorial limitations.

Although not entirely clear, it is possible to interpret the TBT Agreement to cover only measures that are product-related. Arguably, this interpretation would indirectly exclude from the scope of the TBT Agreement measures that aim to protect health and life or the environment *outside* the jurisdiction of the state enacting the PPM-based measure. On the other hand, it is possible to argue the opposite. Article 2.2 of the TBT Agreement, for example, provides an open list of legitimate policy objectives that includes, *inter alia*, the protection of human health or safety, animal or plant life or health, or the environment without specifying whether this protection is limited to humans, animals, plants or the environment within the territory of the enacting Member. Chapter 4: Processes and Production Methods illustrates the scope of the TBT Agreement more extensively.

SELECTED LITERATURE

Charnovitz, S. (2002) 'The law of environmental "PPMs" in the WTO: Debunking the myth of illegality', *Yale Journal of International Law*, vol 27, p59

Howse, R. and Regan, D. (2000) 'The product/process distinction – An illusory basis for disciplining "unilateralism" in trade policy', *European Journal of International Law*, vol 11, p249

SELECTED JURISPRUDENCE UNDER ARTICLES XX(B) AND (G) OF THE GATT

The following are excerpts of GATT and WTO cases that are relevant for a discussion of the principle of extraterritoriality. The excerpts are preceded by a short summary and commentary of the corresponding case, aiming to put the excerpts into context. The cases, listed in chronological order, involve the interpretation of the exceptions listed in GATT Articles XX(b) and XX(g). The interpretation of the Article XX general exceptions clause more generally is also addressed in Chapter 2: General Exceptions Clauses.

United States – Restrictions on Imports of Tuna ('US – Tuna/Dolphin I'), 1991 (NOT ADOPTED)

Short summary and commentary

In *US – Tuna/Dolphin I*, the panel interpreted the GATT as imposing jurisdictional and territorial limitations on the importing state's ability to invoke Article XX(b) and (g) to protect human, animal and plant life and health, and conserve natural resources. In the dispute, Mexico challenged a US law that prohibited the import of yellowfin tuna (or products of such fish) caught with purse-seine nets, unless the government of the harvesting country proved that its programme regulating dolphin kill rates was comparable to that of the US.

The panel found that the US measure violated Article XI of the GATT (prohibiting quantitative restrictions) and was not justified under Article XX(b), which allows parties to set their human, animal or plant life and health standards (Panel report, paragraph 5.29). It noted that Article XX(b) should not be used to protect life or health *outside* the jurisdiction of the state adopting the measure. The panel first stated that the GATT was silent with respect to jurisdictional limitations of measures and thus decided to look into the drafting history of GATT Article XX. From that history, it concluded that the drafters wanted to limit the application of Article XX(b) to the protection of life and health *within* the jurisdiction of the importing state (*Id.* at paragraph 5.26). The panel also found that Article XX should not be interpreted broadly and that to justify the US measure under Article XX(b) of the GATT would allow a party to unilaterally determine life or health protection policies from which other parties could not deviate without jeopardizing their trading rights guaranteed by the GATT (*Id.* at paragraph 5.27). For largely the same reason, the panel rejected justification under Article XX(g) as well (*Id.* at paragraphs 5.30–5.34). With respect to paragraph (g), the panel also added that this paragraph was intended to permit GATT parties to take measures primarily aimed at rendering effective restrictions on production and consumption (as stipulated in paragraph (g)) *within* their jurisdiction because a country could only effectively control production and consumption of an exhaustible natural resource to the extent that production and consumption was under its jurisdiction (*Id.* at paragraph 5.31).

It is important to note that while the panel speaks of the 'extrajurisdictional application' (*see*, e.g., *Id.* at paragraph 5.32) of Articles XX(b) and (g), this does not mean that the importing state is enacting or enforcing laws outside of its jurisdiction. Rather, the panel uses the term 'extrajurisdictional' to refer to a measure that, although enacted and enforced within the importing state's territory, is intended to *protect something outside* the territory of the importing state.

The *US – Tuna/Dolphin I* report was never presented for approval by the GATT Council and thus was never adopted.

Excerpts

Report of the Panel, *United States – Restrictions on Imports of Tuna* (hereinafter *US – Tuna/Dolphin I*), DS21/R – 39S/155 (3 September 1991), NOT ADOPTED

Article XX(b) [paras 5.24–5.29]

5.24. The Panel noted that the United States considered the prohibition of imports of certain yellowfin tuna and certain yellowfin tuna products from Mexico, and the provisions of the MMPA on which this prohibition is based, to be justified by Article XX(b) because they served solely the purpose of protecting dolphin life and health and were "necessary" within the meaning of that provision because, in respect of the protection of dolphin life and health outside its jurisdiction, there was no alternative measure reasonably available to the United States to achieve this objective. Mexico considered that Article XX(b) was not applicable to a measure imposed to protect the life or health of animals outside the jurisdiction of the contracting party taking it and that the import prohibition imposed by the United States was not necessary because alternative means consistent with the General Agreement were available to it to protect dolphin lives or health, namely international co-operation between the countries concerned.

5.25. The Panel noted that the basic question raised by these arguments, namely whether Article XX(b) covers measures necessary to protect human, animal or plant life or health outside the jurisdiction of the contracting party taking the measure, is not clearly answered by the test of that provision. It refers to life and health protection generally without expressly limiting that protection to the jurisdiction of the contracting party concerned. The Panel therefore decided to analyze this issue in the light of the drafting history of Article XX(b), the purpose of this provision, and the consequences that the interpretations proposed by the parties would have for the operation of the General Agreement as a whole.

5.26. The Panel noted that the proposal for Article XX(b) dated from the Draft Charter of the International Trade Organization (ITO) proposed by the United States, which stated in Article 32, "Nothing in Chapter IV [on commercial policy] of this Charter shall be construed to prevent the adoption or enforcement by any Member of measures: ... (b) necessary to protect human, animal or plant life or health". In the New York Draft of the ITO Charter, the preamble had been revised to read as it does at present, and exception (b) read: "For the purpose of protecting human, animal or plant life or health, if corresponding domestic safeguards under similar conditions exist in the importing country". This added proviso reflected concerns regarding the abuse of sanitary regulations by importing countries. Later, Commission A of the Second Session of the Preparatory Committee in Geneva agreed to drop this proviso as unnecessary.[42] Thus, the record indicates that the concerns of the drafters of Article XX(b) focused on the use of sanitary measures to safeguard life or health of humans, animals or plants within the jurisdiction of the importing country.

[42] EPCT/A/PV/30/7–15

5.27. The Panel further noted that Article XX(b) allows each contracting party to set its human, animal or plant life or health standards. The conditions set out in Article XX(b) which limit resort to this exception, namely that the measure taken must be "necessary" and not "constitute a means of arbitrary or unjustifiable discrimination or a disguised restriction on international trade", refer to the trade measure requiring justification under Article XX(b), not however to the life or health standard chosen by the contracting party. The Panel recalled the finding of a previous panel that this paragraph of Article XX was intended to allow contracting parties to impose trade restrictive measures inconsistent with the General Agreement to pursue overriding public policy goals to the extent that such inconsistencies were unavoidable.[43] The Panel considered that if the broad interpretation of Article XX(b) suggested by the United States were accepted, each contracting party could unilaterally determine the life or health protection policies from which other contracting parties could not deviate without jeopardizing their rights under the General Agreement; the General Agreement would then no longer constitute a multilateral framework for trade among all contracting parties but would provide legal security only in respect of trade between a limited number of contracting parties with identical internal regulations.

[43] Panel report on "Thailand – Restrictions on Importation of and Internal Taxes on Cigarettes", adopted 7 November 1990, BISD 37S/200, 222–223, DS10/R, paras 73–74.

. . .

5.29. On the basis of the above considerations, the Panel found that the United States' direct import prohibition imposed on certain yellowfin tuna and certain yellowfin tuna products of Mexico and the provisions of the MMPA under which it is imposed could not be justified under the exception in Article XX(b).

Article XX(g) [paras 5.30–5.34]

5.30. The Panel proceeded to examine whether the prohibition on imports of certain yellowfin tuna and certain yellowfin tuna products from Mexico and the MMPA provisions under which it was imposed could be justified under the exception in Article XX(g). The Panel noted that the United States, in invoking Article XX(g) with respect to its direct import prohibition under the MMPA, had argued that the measures taken under the MMPA are measures primarily aimed at the conservation of dolphin, and that the import restrictions on certain tuna and tuna products under the MMPA are "primarily aimed at rendering effective restrictions on domestic production or consumption" of dolphin. The Panel also noted that Mexico had argued that the United States measures were not justified under the exception in Article XX(g) because, *inter alia*, this provision could not be applied extrajurisdictionally.

5.31. The Panel noted that Article XX(g) required that the measures relating to the conservation of exhaustible natural resources be taken "in conjunction with restrictions on domestic production or consumption". A previous panel had found that a measure could only be considered to have been taken "in conjunction with" production restrictions "if it was primarily aimed at rendering effective these restrictions".[44] A country can effectively control the protection or consumption of an exhaustible natural resource only to the extent that the production or consumption is under its jurisdiction. This suggests that Article XX(g) was intended to permit contracting parties to take trade measures primarily aimed at rendering effective restrictions on production or consumption within their jurisdiction.

[44] Panel report on *"Canada – Measures Affecting Exports of Unprocessed Herring and Salmon"*, adopted 22 March 1988, BISD 35S/98, 114, para 4.6.

5.32. The Panel further noted that Article XX(g) allows each contracting party to adopt its own conservation policies. The conditions set out in Article XX(g) which limit resort to this exception, namely that the measures taken must be related to the conservation of exhaustible natural resources, and that they not "constitute a means of arbitrary or unjustifiable discrimination ... or a disguised restriction on international trade" refer to the trade measure requiring justification under Article XX(g), not however to the conservation policies adopted by the contracting party. The Panel considered that if the extrajurisdictional interpretation of Article XX(g) suggested by the United States were accepted, each contracting party could unilaterally determine the conservation policies from which other contracting parties could not deviate without jeopardizing their rights under the General Agreement. The considerations that led the Panel to reject an extrajurisdictional application of Article XX(b) therefore apply also to Article XX(g).

. . .

5.34. On the basis of the above considerations, the Panel found that the United States direct import prohibition on certain yellowfin tuna and certain yellowfin tuna products of Mexico directly imported from Mexico, and the provisions of the MMPA under which it is imposed, could not be justified under Article XX(g).

United States – Restrictions on Imports of Tuna ('US – Tuna/Dolphin II'), 1994 (NOT ADOPTED)

Short summary and commentary

The second *US – Tuna/Dolphin* panel report (*US – Tuna/Dolphin II*) involved the same US measures as *US – Tuna/Dolphin I,* but different plaintiffs (the European Economic Community and the Netherlands). As in the first case, the second panel also found a violation of Article XI of the GATT and rejected justification of the measure under Articles XX(b) or (g) (Panel report, paragraphs 5.27, 5.39).

In contrast to the previous report, however, *US – Tuna/Dolphin II* found that there was no valid reason to support the conclusion that Article XX(g) of the GATT applied only to policies related to the conservation of exhaustible natural resources located *within* the territory of the party invoking the provision (*Id.* at paragraph 5.20). The panel cited previous GATT cases, the concept of national jurisdiction, and Article XX(e)'s provision relating to the products of prison labour as examples of ways in which countries are allowed to enact measures relating to things located or actions taken outside of its territorial jurisdiction (*Id.* at paragraphs 5.15–5.17). Based on these considerations, the panel found that the US policy at issue, although it aimed at conserving dolphins outside its territory, fell within the range of policies covered by paragraph (g) of Article XX (*Id.* at paragraph 5.20). However, it restricted this finding exclusively to conservation based on the US' exercise of jurisdiction over its own nationals and vessels (*Id.* at paragraph 5.17). Thus, although *US – Tuna/Dolphin II* extended the scope of measures falling within the scope of Article XX(g), it did so to a very limited extent.

In the end, as in *US – Tuna/Dolphin I,* the panel rejected the argument that the embargo was justified under Article XX(g) (*Id.* at paragraph 5.27). It found that the measure had not fulfilled the conditions of Article XX(g), in that the measure was not 'primarily aimed either at the conservation of an exhaustible natural resource, or at rendering effective restrictions on domestic production or consumption' (*Id.*). The panel based it conclusion on the finding that that the US measures were taken 'so as to force other countries to change their policies with respect to persons and things within their own jurisdiction' and that they could only be effective for dolphin conservation if such changes occurred (*Id.* at paragraph 5.24).

Additionally, the panel found that policies to protect the life and health of dolphins outside its territory were covered by Article XX(b) (*Id.* at paragraph 5.33), insofar as the United States pursued the policies within its jurisdiction over its nationals and vessels. However, the panel concluded that the US measures were not 'necessary' for the protection of dolphins, and thus not justified under Article XX(b) for the same reasons that the measures were not justified under paragraph (g) (*Id.* at paragraph 5.39).

US – Tuna/Dolphin II was not adopted by the GATT Council.

Excerpts

Report of the Panel, *United States – Restrictions on Imports of Tuna* (hereinafter "*US – Tuna/Dolphin II*"), DS29/R (16 June 1994), NOT ADOPTED

C. Article XX(g) [paras 5.11–5.27]

. . .

1. Conservation of an exhaustible natural resource [paras 5.13–5.20]

. . .

5.15 The Panel observed, first, that the text of Article XX(g) does not spell out any limitation on the location of the exhaustible natural resources to be conserved. It noted that the conditions set out in the text of Article XX(g) and the preamble qualify only the trade measure requiring justification ("related to") or the manner in which the trade measure is applied ("in conjunction with", "arbitrary or unjustifiable discrimination", "disguised restriction on international trade"). The nature and precise scope of the policy area named in the Article, the conservation of exhaustible natural resources, is not spelled out or specifically conditioned by the text of the Article, in particular with respect to the location of the exhaustible natural resource to be conserved. The Panel noted that two previous panels have considered Article XX(g) to be applicable to policies related to migratory species of fish, and had made no distinction between fish caught within or outside the territorial jurisdiction of the contracting party that had invoked this provision.[81]

[81] Reports of the Panels in *Canada – Measures affecting the exports of unprocessed herring and salmon,* adopted 22 March 1988, 35S/98; *United States – Prohibition of imports of tuna and tuna products from Canada,* adopted 22 February 1982, 29S/91.

5.16 The Panel then observed that measures providing different treatment to products of different origins could in principle be taken under other paragraphs of Article XX and other Articles of the General Agreement with respect to things located, or actions occurring, outside the territorial jurisdiction of the party taking the measure. An example was the provision in Article XX(e) relating to products of prison labour. It could not therefore be said that the General Agreement proscribed in an absolute manner measures that related to things or actions outside the territorial jurisdiction of the party taking the measure.

5.17 The Panel further observed that, under general international law, states are not in principle barred from regulating the conduct of their nationals with respect to persons, animals, plants and natural resources outside of their territory. Nor are states barred, in principle, from regulating the conduct of vessels having their nationality, or any persons on these vessels, with respect to persons, animals, plants and natural resources outside their territory. A state may in particular regulate the conduct of its fishermen, or of vessels having its nationality or any fishermen on these vessels, with respect to fish located in the high seas.

. . .

5.20 The Panel then examined whether the treaties referred to might be relevant as a supplementary means of interpretation of the General Agreement under the Vienna Convention. The Panel noted that the supplementary means permitted by Article 32 of the Vienna Convention include "the preparatory work of the treaty and the circumstances of its conclusion". However, the terms of this provision make clear that its applicability is limited. Preparatory work and other supplementary means of interpretation may only be used "to confirm" an interpretation reached under the general rule of interpretation, or when application of the general rule "leaves the meaning ambiguous or obscure", or "leads to a result which is manifestly absurd or unreasonable". Even if interpretation according to the general rule had led to this result, the Panel considered that those cited treaties that were concluded prior to the conclusion of the General Agreement were of little assistance in interpreting the text of Article XX(g), since it appeared to the Panel on the basis of the material presented to it that no direct references were made to these treaties in the text of the General Agreement, the Havana Charter, or in the preparatory work to these instruments. The Panel also found that the statements and drafting changes made during the negotiation of the Havana Charter and the General Agreement cited by the parties did not provide clear support for any particular contention of the parties on the question of the location of the exhaustible natural resource in Article XX(g). In view of the above, the Panel could see no valid reason supporting the conclusion that the provisions of Article XX(g) apply only to policies related to the conservation of exhaustible natural resources located within the territory of the contracting party invoking the provision. The Panel consequently found that the policy to conserve dolphins in the eastern tropical Pacific Ocean, which the United States pursued within its jurisdiction over its nationals and vessels, fell within the range of policies covered by Article XX(g).

2. "Related to" the conservation of an exhaustible natural resource made effective "in conjunction" with restrictions on domestic production and consumption [paras 5.21–5.27]

. . .

5.23 The Panel then proceeded to examine whether the embargoes imposed by the United States could be considered to be primarily aimed at the conservation of an exhaustible natural resource, and primarily aimed at rendering effective restrictions on domestic production or consumption. In particular, the Panel examined the relationship of the United States measures with the expressed goal of dolphin conservation. The Panel noted that measures taken under the intermediary nation embargo prohibited imports from a country of any tuna, whether or not the particular tuna was harvested in a manner that harmed or could harm dolphins, and whether or not the country had tuna harvesting practices and policies that harmed or could harm dolphins, as long as it was from a country that imported tuna from countries maintaining tuna harvesting practices and policies not comparable to those of the United States. The Panel then observed that the prohibition on imports of tuna into the United States taken under the intermediary nation embargo could not, by itself, further the United States conservation objectives. The intermediary nation embargo could achieve its intended effect only if it were followed by changes in policies or practices, not in the country exporting tuna to the United States, but in third countries from which the exporting country imported tuna.

5.24 The Panel noted also that measures taken under the primary nation embargo prohibited imports from a country of any tuna, whether or not the particular tuna was harvested in a way that harmed or could harm dolphins, as long as the country's tuna harvesting practices and policies were not comparable to those of the United States. The Panel observed that, as in the case of the intermediary nation embargo, the prohibition on imports of tuna into the United States taken under the primary nation embargo could not possibly, by itself, further the United States' conservation objectives. The primary nation embargo could achieve its desired effect only if it were followed by changes in policies and practices in the exporting countries. In view of the foregoing, the Panel observed that both the primary and intermediary nation embargoes on tuna implemented by the United States were taken so as to force other countries to change their policies with respect to persons and things within their own jurisdiction, since the embargoes required such changes in order to have any effect on the conservation of dolphins.

. . .

5.26 The Panel observed that Article XX provides for an exception to obligations under the General Agreement. The long-standing practice of panels has accordingly been to interpret this provision narrowly, in a manner that preserves the basic objectives and principles of the General Agreement.[84] If Article XX were interpreted to permit contracting parties to deviate from the obligations of the General Agreement by taking trade measures to implement policies, including conservation policies, within their own jurisdiction, the basic objectives of the General Agreement would be maintained. If however Article XX were interpreted to permit contracting parties to take trade measures so as to force other contracting parties to change their policies within their jurisdiction, including their conservation policies, the balance of rights and obligations among contracting parties, in particular the right of access to markets, would be seriously impaired. Under such an interpretation, the General Agreement could no longer serve as a multilateral framework for trade among contracting parties.

[84] Reports of the Panels in *Canada – Administration of the Foreign Investment Review Act,* adopted 7 February 1984, 30S/140, 64, para5.20; *United States – Section 337 of the Tariff Act of 1930,* adopted 7 November 1989, 36S/345, 393, para 5.27.

5.27 The Panel concluded that measures taken so as to force other countries to change their policies, and that were effective only if such changes occurred, could not be primarily aimed either at the conservation of an exhaustible natural resource, or at rendering effective restrictions on domestic production or consumption, in the meaning of Article XX(g). Since an essential condition of Article XX(g) had not been met, the Panel did not consider it necessary to examine whether the United States measures had also met the other requirements of Article XX. The Panel accordingly found that the import prohibitions on tuna and tuna products maintained by the United States inconsistently with Article XI:1 were not justified by Article XX(g).

D. Article XX(b) [paras 5.28–5.39]

5.28 The Panel noted the United States argument that both the primary and intermediary nation embargoes, even if inconsistent with Articles III or XI, were justified by Article XX(b) as measures necessary to protect the life and health of dolphins. The United States argued that there was no requirement in Article XX(b) that the animals whose life or health was to be protected had to be within the jurisdiction of the country taking the measure. The United States further argued that the measures were necessary to fulfil the policy goal of protecting the life and health of dolphins. Finally, it argued that the measures met the requirement of the preamble to Article XX. The EEC and the Netherlands disagreed, stating that the animals whose life or health was to be protected had to be within the jurisdiction of the country taking the measure. The EEC and the Netherlands were further of the view that the United States measures were not necessary within the meaning of Article XX(b).

5.29 The Panel proceeded first to examine the text of Article XX(b), which, together with its preamble, states:

> *"Subject to the requirement that such measures are not applied in a manner which would constitute a means of arbitrary or unjustifiable discrimination between countries where the same conditions prevail, or a disguised restriction on international trade, nothing in this Agreement shall be construed to prevent the adoption or enforcement by any contracting party of measures:*
>
> . . .
>
> *(b) necessary to protect the human, animal or plant life or health."*

The Panel observed that the text of Article XX(b) suggested a three-step analysis:

- First, it had to be determined whether the *policy* in respect of which these provisions were invoked fell within the range of policies referred to in these provisions, that is policies to protect human, animal or plant life or health;
- Second, it had to be determined whether the *measure* for which the exception was being invoked – that is the particular trade measure inconsistent with the obligations under the General Agreement - was "necessary" to protect human, animal or plant life or health;
- Third, it had to be determined whether the measure was applied in a manner consistent with the requirement set out in the preamble to Article XX, namely that the measure not be applied in a manner which would constitute a means of arbitrary or unjustifiable discrimination between countries where the same conditions prevail or in a manner which would constitute a disguised restriction on international trade.

1. To protect human, animal or plant life and health [paragraphs 5.30–5.33]

5.30 Turning to the first of the above three questions, the Panel noted that the parties did not disagree that the protection of dolphin life or health was a policy that could come within Article XX(b). The EEC argued, however, that Article XX(b) could not justify measures taken to protect living things located outside the territorial jurisdiction of the party taking the measure. The United States disagreed. The arguments on this issue advanced by the parties were similar to those made under Article XX(g).

5.31 The Panel recalled its reasoning under Article XX(g). It observed that the text of Article XX(b) does not spell out any limitation on the location of the living things to be protected. It noted that the conditions set out in the text of Article XX(b) and the preamble qualify only the trade measure requiring justification ("necessary to") or the manner in which the trade measure is applied ("arbitrary or unjustifiable discrimination", "disguised restriction on international trade"). The nature and precise scope of the *policy area* named in the Article, the protection of living things, is not specified in the text of the Article, in particular with respect to the location of the living things to be protected.

5.32 The Panel further recalled its observation that elsewhere in the General Agreement measures according different treatment to products of different origins could in principle be taken with respect to things located, or actions occurring, outside the territorial jurisdiction of the party taking the measure. It could not therefore be said that the General Agreement proscribed in an absolute manner such measures. The Panel further recalled its observation that, under general international law, states are not in principle barred from regulating the conduct of their nationals with respect to persons, animals, plants and natural resources outside of their territory (see paragraph 5.17 above).

5.33 The Panel noted that the United States and the EEC, as under Article XX(g), based many of their arguments regarding the location of the living things to [be] protected under Article XX(b) on environmental and trade treaties other than the General Agreement. However, for the reasons advanced under its discussion of Article XX(g), the Panel did not consider that the treaties were relevant for the interpretation of the text of the General Agreement (see paragraphs 5.19–5.20). The Panel also noted that the statements and drafting changes made during the negotiation of the Havana Charter and the General Agreement did not clearly support any particular contention of the parties with respect to the location of the living thing to be protected under Article XX(b). The Panel did not see the need to settle the issue argued by the parties as to whether the intent of the drafters was to restrict measures justifiable under Article XX to sanitary measures. The Panel therefore found that the policy to protect the life and health of dolphins in the eastern tropical Pacific Ocean, which the United States pursued within its jurisdiction over its nationals and vessels, fell within the range of policies covered by Article XX(b).

2. *Necessary [paras 5.34–5.39]*

. . .

5.36 The Panel noted that measures taken under the intermediary nation embargo prohibited imports from a country of any tuna, whether or not the particular tuna was harvested in a manner that harmed or could harm dolphins, and whether or not the country had tuna harvesting practices and policies that harmed or could harm dolphin, as long as it was from a country that imported tuna from countries maintaining tuna harvesting practices and policies not comparable to those of the United States. The Panel observed that the prohibition on imports of tuna into the United States taken under the intermediary nation embargo could not, by itself, further the United States conservation objectives. The intermediary nation embargo would achieve its intended effect only if it were followed by changes in policies or practices, not in the country exporting tuna to the United States, but in third countries from which the exporting country imported tuna.

5.37 The Panel also recalled that measures taken under the primary nation embargo prohibited imports from a country of any tuna, whether or not the particular tuna was harvested in a way that harmed or could harm dolphins, as long as the country's tuna harvesting practices and policies were not comparable to those of the United States. The Panel observed that, as in the case of the intermediary nation embargo, the prohibition on imports of tuna into the United States taken under the primary nation embargo could not possibly, by itself, further the United States objective of protecting the life and health of dolphins. The primary nation embargo could achieve its desired effect only if it were followed by changes in policies and practices in the exporting countries. In view of the foregoing, the Panel observed that both the primary and intermediary nation embargoes on tuna were taken by the United States so as to force other countries to change their policies with respect to persons and things within their own jurisdiction, since the embargoes required such changes in order to have any effect on the protection of the life or health of dolphins.

5.38 The Panel then examined whether, under Article XX(b), measures necessary to protect the life or health of animals could include measures taken so as to force other countries to change their policies within their own jurisdictions, and requiring such changes in order to be effective. The Panel noted that the text of Article XX is not explicit on this question. The Panel then recalled its reasoning under its examination of Article XX(g) that Article XX, as a provision for exceptions, should be interpreted narrowly and in a way that preserves the basic objectives and principles of the General Agreement. If Article XX(b) were interpreted to permit contracting parties to deviate from the basic obligations of the General Agreement by taking trade measures to implement policies within their own jurisdiction, including policies to protect living things, the objectives of the General Agreement would be maintained. If however Article XX(b) were interpreted to permit contracting parties to impose trade embargoes so as to force other countries to change their policies within their jurisdiction, including policies to protect living things, and which required such changes to be effective, the objectives of the General Agreement would be seriously impaired.

5.39 The Panel concluded that measures taken so as to force other countries to change their policies, and that were effective only if such changes occurred, could not be considered "necessary" for the protection of animal life or health in the sense of Article XX(b). Since an essential condition of Article XX(b) had not been met, the Panel did not consider it necessary to examine the further issue of whether the United States measures had also met the other requirements of Article XX. The Panel accordingly found that the import prohibitions on tuna and tuna products maintained by the United States inconsistently with Article XI:1 were not justified by Article XX(b).

United States – Import Prohibition of Certain Shrimp and Shrimp Products ('US – Shrimp/Turtle I'), 1998

Short summary and commentary

US – Shrimp-Turtle I is the only WTO dispute to date that addresses questions relating to extraterritoriality. In addressing this issue, the Appellate Body clearly distanced itself from the restrictive approach taken by the panels in the *US – Tuna/Dolphin* disputes.

In *US – Shrimp/Turtle I* India, Malaysia, Pakistan and Thailand challenged a US measure banning the import of shrimp and shrimp products, except for those taken from waters of a country certified as complying with US standards for the protection of sea turtles. After finding a violation of Article XI on quantitative restrictions, the first level panel found that conditioning access to a Member's domestic market on whether or not exporting Members comply with or adopt a certain policy, unilaterally prescribed by the importing Member, could not be justified under Article XX – to do so would threaten the multilateral trading system (AB Report, paragraph 112, referring the panel report). Thus, the panel denied justification under Article XX(g) allowing Members to take measures to protect exhaustible natural resources (*Id.*).

On appeal, the Appellate Body explicitly rejected the panel's argument. (AB report, paragraph 122). It found that 'conditioning access to a Member's domestic market on whether exporting Members comply with, or adopt, a policy or policies unilaterally prescribed by the importing Member may, to some degree, be a common aspect of measures falling within the scope of one or another of the exceptions (a) to (j) of Article XX' (*Id.* at paragraph 121). Thus, the Appellate Body found that such unilateral acts could not be a priori excluded from the scope of the types of measures covered by Article XX(g).

With respect to the location of the natural resource, the Appellate Body explicitly refused to address the question of whether or not there is an implied jurisdictional limitation in Article XX (*Id.* at paragraph 133). It found that migratory species occurring within US waters provided sufficient nexus for a measure to be justified under Article XX(g) (*Id.*).

Despite these findings, the Appellate Body concluded that the US measures were not justified under Article XX(g) because the way in which the measures were applied amounted to unjustifiable and arbitrary discrimination, thus failing to comply with the conditions set out in the chapeau of Article XX. The Appellate Body's main reasons for denying justification under Article XX were: (i) the rigidity of the measure, (i.e. that the measure as applied required that other Members adopt *essentially the same* regulatory programme as the one used and elaborated by the US) (*Id.* at paragraph 164); (ii) the fact that shrimp caught using methods identical to those used in the US were still banned if they emanated from a non-certified country (*Id.* at paragraph 165); and (iii) the failure of the US to engage in serious across-the-board negotiations (*Id.* at paragraphs 166–172). The Appellate Body's reasoning with respect to the chapeau of Article XX is described in more detail in Chapter 2: General Exceptions Clauses.

Based on the Appellate Body's decision, migratory species occurring *within* the territory of the Member enacting the measures may be protected independent of any jurisdictional powers the Member has over nationals and vessels. However, the extent to which Members can protect resources located *solely outside* their jurisdictional boundaries remains uncertain.

In 2001, Malaysia brought a second challenge to the WTO, alleging that the US had not taken the necessary steps to comply with the recommendations and rulings contained in the *US – Shrimp/Turtle I* reports. For a summary and analysis of *US – Shrimp/Turtle 21.5*, see Chapter 2: General Exceptions Clauses and Chapter 4: Processes and Production Methods.

Excerpts

Report of the Appellate Body, *United States – Import Prohibition of Certain Shrimp and Shrimp Products* (hereinafter *US – Shrimp/Turtle I*), WT/DS58/AB/R adopted on 6 November 1998

VI. Appraising Section 609 Under Article XX of the GATT 1994 [paras 111–186]

. . .

A. The Panel's Findings and Interpretive Analysis [paras 112–124]

112. The Panel's findings, from which the United States appeals, and the gist of its supporting reasoning, are set forth below *in extenso*:

> . . . *[W]e are of the opinion that the* chapeau *[of]* Article XX, *interpreted within its context and in the light of the object and purpose of GATT and of the WTO Agreement,* only allows Members to derogate from GATT provisions so long as, in doing so, they do not undermine the WTO multilateral trading system, *thus also abusing the exceptions contained in Article XX. Such undermining and abuse would occur when a Member jeopardizes the operation of the WTO Agreement in such a way that guaranteed market access and nondiscriminatory treatment within a multilateral framework would no longer be possible. We are of the view that a* type of measure adopted by a Member *which, on its own, may appear to have a relatively minor impact on the multilateral trading system,* may *nonetheless* raise a serious threat to that system if similar measures are adopted by the same or other Members. *Thus, by allowing such type of measures even though their individual impact may not appear to be such as to threaten the multilateral trading system, one would affect the security and predictability of the multilateral trading system. We consequently find that when considering a measure under Article XX, we must determine not only whether the measure* on its own *undermines the WTO multilateral trading system, but also whether* such type of measure, *if it were to be adopted by other Members, would threaten the security and predictability of the multilateral trading system.*[77]
>
> *In our view, if an interpretation of the chapeau of Article XX were to be followed which would allow a Member* to adopt measures conditioning access to its market for a given product upon the adoption by the exporting Members of certain policies, including conservation policies, *GATT 1994 and the WTO Agreement could no longer serve as a multilateral framework for trade among Members as security and predictability of trade relations under those agreements would be threatened. This follows because, if one WTO Member were allowed to adopt such measures, then other Members would also have the right to adopt similar measures on the same subject but with differing, or even conflicting, requirements. Market access for goods could become subject to an increasing number of conflicting policy requirements for the same product and this would rapidly lead to the end of the WTO multilateral trading system.*[78]
>
> ... Section 609, as applied, is a measure conditioning access to the US market for a given product on the adoption by exporting Members of conservation policies that the

> *United States considers to be comparable to its own in terms of regulatory programmes and incidental taking.*[79]
>
> *... it appears to us that, in light of the context of the term "unjustifiable" and the object and purpose of the WTO Agreement,* the US measure at issue constitutes unjustifiable discrimination *between countries where the same conditions prevail and thus is not within the scope of measures permitted under Article XX.*[80]
>
> ...
>
> *We therefore find that* the US measure *at issue is* not within the scope of measures permitted under the chapeau of Article XX.[81] *(emphasis added)*

[77] Panel Report, para 7.44.
[78] Panel Report, para 7.45.
[79] Panel Report, para 7.48.
[80] Panel Report, para 7.49.
[81] Panel Report, para 7.62.

...

116. The general design of a measure, as distinguished from its application, is, however, to be examined in the course of determining whether that measure falls within one or another of the paragraphs of Article XX following the chapeau. The Panel failed to scrutinize the *immediate* context of the chapeau: i.e. paragraphs (a) to (j) of Article XX. Moreover, the Panel did not look into the object and purpose of the *chapeau of Article XX*. Rather, the Panel looked into the object and purpose of the *whole of the GATT 1994 and the WTO Agreement*, which object and purpose it described in an overly broad manner. Thus, the Panel arrived at the very broad formulation that measures which "undermine the WTO multilateral trading system" must be regarded as "not within the scope of measures permitted under the chapeau of Article XX". Maintaining, rather than undermining, the multilateral trading system is necessarily a fundamental and pervasive premise underlying the *WTO Agreement*; but it is not a right or an obligation, nor is it an interpretative rule which can be employed in the appraisal of a given measure under the chapeau of Article XX. In *United States – Gasoline*, we stated that it is "important to underscore that the purpose and object of the introductory clauses of Article XX is generally the prevention of '*abuse of the exceptions of [Article XX]*'"[88] (emphasis added). The Panel did not attempt to inquire into how the measure at stake was being *applied in such a manner* as to constitute *abuse or misuse of a given kind of exception*.

[88] Adopted 20 May 1996, WT/DS2/AB/R, p22.

...

121. The consequences of the interpretative approach adopted by the Panel are apparent in its findings. The Panel formulated a broad standard and a test for appraising measures sought to be justified under the chapeau; it is a standard or a test that finds no basis either in the text of the chapeau or in that of either of the two specific exceptions claimed by the United States. The Panel, in effect, constructed an *a priori* test that purports to define a category of measures which, *ratione materiae*, fall outside the justifying protection of Article XX's chapeau.[94] In the present case, the Panel found that the United States measure at stake fell within that class of excluded measures because Section 609 conditions access to the domestic shrimp market of the United States on the adoption by exporting countries of certain conservation policies prescribed by the United States. It appears to us, however, that conditioning access to a Member's domestic market on whether exporting Members comply with, or adopt, a policy or policies unilaterally prescribed by the importing Member may, to some degree, be a common aspect of measures falling within the scope of one or another of the exceptions (a) to (j) of Article XX. Paragraphs (a) to (j) comprise measures that are recognized as exceptions to substantive obligations established in the GATT 1994, because the domestic policies embodied in such measures have been recognized as important and legitimate in character. It is not necessary to assume that requiring from exporting countries compliance with, or adoption of, certain policies (although covered in principle by one or another of the exceptions)

prescribed by the importing country, renders a measure *a priori* incapable of justification under Article XX. Such an interpretation renders most, if not all, of the specific exceptions of Article XX inutile, a result abhorrent to the principles of interpretation we are bound to apply.

[94] See, for example, Panel Report, para 7.50.

122. We hold that the findings of the Panel quoted in paragraph 112 above, and the interpretative analysis embodied therein, constitute error in legal interpretation and accordingly reverse them.

B. Article XX(g): Provisional Justification of Section 609 [paras 125–145]

. . .

1. Exhaustible Natural Resources [paras 127–134]

. . .

133. Finally, we observe that sea turtles are highly migratory animals, passing in and out of waters subject to the rights of jurisdiction of various coastal states and the high seas. In the Panel Report, the Panel said:

> . . . *Information brought to the attention of the Panel, including documented statements from the experts, tends to* confirm the fact that sea turtles, in certain circumstances of their lives, migrate through the waters of several countries and the high sea . . .[118] *(emphasis added).*

The sea turtle species here at stake, i.e., covered by Section 609, are all known to occur in waters over which the United States exercises jurisdiction.[119] Of course, it is not claimed that *all* populations of these species migrate to, or traverse, at one time or another, waters subject to United States jurisdiction. Neither the appellant nor any of the appellees claims any rights of exclusive ownership over the sea turtles, at least not while they are swimming freely in their natural habitat – the oceans. We do not pass upon the question of whether there is an implied jurisdictional limitation in Article XX(g), and if so, the nature or extent of that limitation. We note only that in the specific circumstances of the case before us, there is a sufficient nexus between the migratory and endangered marine populations involved and the United States for purposes of Article XX(g).

[118] Panel Report, para 7.53.
[119] See Panel Report, para 2.6. The 1987 Regulations, 52 Fed. Reg. 24244, 29 June 1987, identified five species of sea turtles as occurring within the areas concerned and thus falling under the regulations: loggerhead (*Caretta caretta*), Kemp's ridley (*Lepidochelys kempi*), green (*Chelonia mydas*), leatherback (*Dermochelys coriacea*) and hawksbill (*Eretmochelys imbricata*). Section 609 refers to "those species of sea turtles the conservation of which is the subject of regulations promulgated by the Secretary of Commerce on 29 June, 1987".

CHAPTER 6

The Role of Science and the Precautionary Principle

BACKGROUND

Full scientific certainty almost never exists with respect to environmental and health risks, and as a result, environmental and health decision makers almost never have all of the scientific information they would like to have in order to make regulatory decisions. To address this problem, decision makers can decide to take a precautionary stance when faced with incomplete knowledge and the prospect of harm to the environment or human health. Such a precautionary approach is particularly important because numerous environmental and health risks are both complex and multifaceted. Additionally, by the time the impacts of some of these risks are fully scientifically established, it is too late to formulate an effective response – the damage has already been done and reversing the damage becomes impossible or extremely difficult. Precaution is an essential element of virtually every domestic regulatory system in the world for protecting human health and the environment. It is also an essential element of international efforts to protect human health and the environment.

Many international instruments, both binding and non-binding, specifically include or refer to the precautionary principle (or sometimes the 'precautionary approach'). The most quoted formulation of the precautionary principle is Principle 15 of the Rio Declaration, adopted at the 1992 United Nations Conference on Environment and Development (UNCED):

> *Where there are threats of serious or irreversible damage, lack of full scientific certainty shall not be used as a reason for postponing cost-effective measures to prevent environmental degradation.*

Questions have arisen as to how the precautionary principle plays out in the trade context. Is precaution recognized in trade rules? If so, what are the parameters for its application? Some commentators fear that trade rules put unwarranted limits on the application of the precautionary principle, which will result in negative impacts on the environment and human health. Others are concerned that relying on the precautionary principle at the domestic and the international levels might weaken the international trading system. Commentators from this second group argue that governments could exploit scientific uncertainty to justify measures that limit market access in situations where the actual motivation is trade protectionism.

Several recent World Trade Organization (WTO) disputes have raised the question of whether or not WTO rules allow governments to take trade-related measures based on precaution, and if so, to what extent. WTO panels and the Appellate Body have approached the question of the legitimacy of precautionary measures by examining the degree to which the precautionary principle is reflected in the Agreement on Sanitary and Phytosanitary Measures (SPS Agreement). This agreement, while not specifically mentioning the precautionary principle, places emphasis on the role of science. No dispute has explicitly addressed the precautionary principle under the General Agreement on Tariffs and Trade (GATT) or the Agreement on Technical Barriers to Trade (TBT), both of which do not explicitly refer to science or precaution in their texts.

WTO panels and the Appellate Body have also addressed the status of the precautionary principle in public international law. In *EC – Hormones*, the first dispute to involve the Agreement on Sanitary and Phytosanitary Measures (SPS), the European Communities (EC) argued that the precautionary principle had developed into a fully fledged principle of customary international law, therefore constituting a relevant 'rule of international law applicable in the relations between the parties' under Article 31(3)(c) of the Vienna Convention on the Law of Treaties (Vienna Convention). The US countered that the precautionary principle was not a principle of customary international law, and was thus irrelevant to the interpretation of WTO provisions. Canada argued with the US, but conceded that the principle was an emerging principle of law.

The Appellate Body avoided taking a position as to the question of whether or not the precautionary principle was a norm of customary international law. Instead, it held that the precautionary principle 'finds reflection' in certain existing SPS Agreement provisions, but cannot 'override' specific SPS provisions (*EC – Hormones* AB report, paragraphs 121–124).

The analysis below focuses on the relationship between the precautionary principle and WTO rules. It does not examine whether the precautionary principle is a norm of customary international law.

DISCUSSION OF RELEVANT WTO PROVISIONS

Introduction

Neither the GATT nor the SPS and TBT Agreements explicitly prohibit trade-related measures that are based on precaution. However, the SPS Agreement, in contrast to the GATT and the TBT Agreement, sets forth explicit requirements relating to science and scientific evidence, which may affect a Member's ability to take a precautionary approach. The following sections will discuss the role of science and the precautionary principle in relation to these agreements.

Article XX of the GATT

The language of the GATT (which was drafted in 1947) neither includes explicit requirements relating to science, nor specifically addresses the issue of precaution. The general exceptions clause provides that:

> *Subject to the requirement that such measures are not applied in a manner which would constitute a means of arbitrary or unjustifiable discrimination between countries where the same conditions prevail, or a disguised restriction on international trade, nothing in this Agreement shall be construed to prevent the adoption or enforcement by any contracting party of measures:*
>
> ...
>
> *(b) necessary to protect human, animal or plant life or health;*
>
> ...
>
> *(g) relating to the conservation of exhaustible natural resources if such measures are made effective in conjunction with restrictions on domestic production or consumption;*

The language of Article XX (described in detail in Chapter 2: General Exceptions Clauses) seems to leave sufficient space for Members to adopt precautionary policies to protect exhaustible natural resources and human, animal and plant life or health. However, it is still unclear whether or not the Appellate Body and panels will interpret the language in this sense. The approach will depend in large part on the tribunals' stance regarding science in the context of Article XX. To date, they have addressed some elements relating to the role of science in the context of Article XX(b). Notably, the Appellate Body in *EC – Asbestos*, explained that some important principles, developed in cases under the SPS Agreement (discussed below), were equally applicable under Article XX. These principles include the following:

- Members retain the right to determine their appropriate level of protection (*EC – Asbestos* AB report paragraph 168);
- while risks to human, animal or plant life or health must be assessed, this assessment can be either quantitative or qualitative (*Id.* at paragraph 167); and
- Members are not obliged to rely on majority scientific opinions, but may base measures that protect human, animal or plant life or health on respected sources of divergent scientific opinion (*Id.* at paragraph 178). This takes into account past experience, which has shown that majority opinions can sometimes turn out to be erroneous.

Preamble of the TBT Agreement

In the preamble of the TBT Agreement Members recognize:

> *that no country should be prevented from taking measures necessary to ensure the quality of its exports, or for the protection of human, animal or plant life or health, of the environment, or for the prevention of deceptive practices, at the levels it considers*

> *appropriate, subject to the requirement that they are not applied in a manner which would constitute a means of arbitrary or unjustifiable discrimination between countries where the same conditions prevail or a disguised restriction on international trade, and are otherwise in accordance with the provisions of this Agreement.*

Like the GATT, the TBT Agreement does not explicitly refer to science or precaution. Its preamble uses language similar to that in Article XX of the GATT, arguably allowing a Member to adopt precautionary measures for the protection of human, animal or plant life or health, or for the protection of the environment. In fact, one could argue that use of the phrase 'at the levels it considers appropriate', in conjunction with the option of a Member to take 'measures necessary . . . for the protection of human, animal or plant life or health, [or] of the environment', shows an implicit recognition or reflection of the precautionary principle. Given that the Appellate Body, in another context, has affirmed that the preamble to the Marrakesh Agreement Establishing the World Trade Organization (WTO Agreement) affected the Appellate Body's interpretation of the rights and obligations of WTO Members (*US – Shrimp/Turtle I* AB report, paragraph 155), it is reasonable to assume that the preambular language of the TBT Agreement would also inform the interpretation of rights and obligations under the TBT Agreement. However, jurisprudence has yet to clarify the role of the precautionary principle in this context.

The SPS Agreement (Articles 2.2, 5.1 and 5.7)

The role of science

The SPS Agreement explicitly recognizes the right of Members to take measures to protect human, animal or plant life or health. However, in addition to the non-discrimination and necessity requirements incorporated in the GATT and the TBT Agreements, the SPS Agreement includes a series of science-related requirements. In particular, the SPS Agreement requires that:

- SPS measures are based on scientific principles not maintained without sufficient scientific evidence (Article 2.2); and
- SPS measures are based on a risk assessment (Article 5.1).

If 'scientific evidence is insufficient', a Member may still adopt an SPS measure, provided that the measure is:

- based on available pertinent information;
- taken on a provisional basis; and
- reviewed 'within a reasonable period of time' (Article 5.7).

As of this writing, four WTO cases have addressed the question of whether and how Article 5.7, and the SPS Agreement in general, reflect the precautionary principle. All of those are described in detail below. A fifth case brought by the US, Canada and Argentina against the EC in relation to alleged measures prohibiting the entry of genetically modified organisms (GMOs) into the EC is currently pending. Finally, the EC is challenging retaliatory measures imposed by Canada and the US regarding the EC ban on beef emanating from cattle treated with certain hormones. Both of these pending cases are likely to involve a discussion of the precautionary principle under the SPS Agreement (and possibly other agreements).

The Precautionary Principle as reflected in the SPS Agreement

The Appellate Body has held that while the precautionary principle 'has not been written into the SPS Agreement as a ground for justifying SPS measures that are otherwise inconsistent with the obligations of Members', it does 'find reflection' in certain existing SPS Agreement provisions (*EC – Hormones* AB report, paragraph 124). According to the Appellate Body, this includes Article 5.7, which allows for the adoption of provisional measures, and Article 3.3, which relates to the right to adopt SPS standards that may be higher than international standards under certain conditions, and finally, the sixth paragraph of the preamble, which reflects the desire of Members to harmonize SPS measures (*Id.*). These provisions will be discussed in detail below. The Appellate Body has further held that panels charged with determining the SPS consistency of a measure should 'bear in mind that responsible, representative governments commonly act from perspectives of prudence and precaution where risks of irreversible, e.g. life-terminating, damage to human health are concerned' (*Id.*). It is also implicit from another passage in *EC – Hormones* that the right of governments to act from perspectives of prudence and precaution is not limited to situations of *irreversible* or *life threatening* damage, but that the right may extend to other risks (*Id.* at paragraph 194).

Both Article 3.3 and the sixth paragraph of the preamble explicitly recognize that WTO Members have the right to 'establish their own appropriate level of sanitary protection, *which may be higher (i.e. more cautious)* than international standards, guidelines and recommendations' (*Id.* at paragraph 124, emphasis added). A Member's right to choose its own appropriate level of protection is an important factor in recognizing the sovereign right of Members to adopt precautionary SPS measures, particularly in light of Article 2.2, which requires that SPS measures are based on 'scientific principles' and prohibits the maintenance of SPS measures 'without sufficient scientific evidence', and Article 5.1, which requires that SPS measures are based on a risk assessment.

Article 2.2: SPS measures must be based on 'Sufficient Scientific Evidence'

Article 2.2 of the SPS Agreement provides that:

> *Members shall ensure that any sanitary or phytosanitary measure is applied only to the extent necessary to protect human, animal or plant life or health, is based on scientific principles and is not maintained without sufficient scientific evidence, except as provided for in paragraph 7 of Article 5.*

According to Article 2.2, SPS measures must be based on 'scientific principles' and may not be maintained 'without sufficient scientific evidence'. As noted above, the SPS Agreement provides for an exception to this rule under Article 5.7 by allowing Members to adopt 'provisional measures' where 'relevant scientific evidence is insufficient'. In large part, WTO case law has approached Article 2.2 in the context of other, more specific, SPS provisions.

In *Australia – Salmon*, the Appellate Body considered the relationship between Article 2.2 and Articles 5.1 and 5.2. It held that where a violation of Articles 5.1 or 5.2 is found, one can presume that the more general provisions of Article 2.2 have also been violated. (*Australia – Salmon* AB report, paragraphs 137–138). The Appellate Body also emphasized, however, that a violation of Article 2.2 is not limited to situations where Articles 5.1 and/or 5.2 have been breached (*Id.*). It found that Article 2.2 establishes a separate and broader obligation than do Articles 5.1 and 5.2 (*Id.*; *see also EC – Hormones* AB report, paragraph 180 and *Japan – Varietals* AB report, paragraph 82). Despite this clear ruling, however, there has not yet been a case in which a Member has been found to have violated Article 2.2, without having been found to have violated Article 5.1 as well. Drawing on its Article 5.1 jurisprudence, the Appellate Body clarified that 'sufficient scientific evidence' under Article 2.2 could include qualified and respected divergent scientific opinion as well as mainstream scientific evidence (*Japan – Varietals* AB report, paragraph 77).

In *Japan – Varietals*, the Appellate Body affirmed that Article 2.2 must be interpreted in the context of Articles 3.3, 5.1 and 5.7 of the SPS Agreement (*Id.* at paragraph 74). The Appellate Body pointed out that Article 2.2 explicitly refers to Article 5.7, which 'operates as a qualified exemption from the obligation under Article 2.2 not to maintain SPS measures without sufficient scientific evidence', (*Id.* at paragraph 80). It deduced from this that 'an overly broad and flexible interpretation of Article 2.2 would render Article 5.7 meaningless' (*Id.*).

The Appellate Body in *Japan – Varietals* concluded that the meaning of 'sufficient' (in 'sufficient scientific evidence') was a relational concept that requires a rational or objective relationship between the SPS measure and the scientific evidence (*Id.* at paragraph 84). It further noted that the determination of whether such a relationship exists must be made 'on a case-by-case basis and will depend on the particular circumstances of the case, including the characteristics of the measure at issue and the quality and quantity of scientific evidence' (*Id.*).

In *Japan – Apples*, the panel applied the 'rational or objective relationship test' developed in *Japan – Varietals*. The panel held that the measure at issue in that case was 'on the face of it disproportionate' to the negligible risk identified by the available scientific evidence, and therefore maintained without 'sufficient scientific evidence' . (*Japan – Apples* panel report, paragraphs 8.180–8.181, 8.198–8.199). This finding was upheld by the Appellate Body, which re-emphasized the case-by-case nature of the analysis (*Japan – Apples* AB report, paragraphs 163–164).

At the meeting in which the Dispute Settlement Body adopted the panel and Appellate Body reports, the US questioned the panel and the Appellate Body's use of the term 'disproportionate'. It said 'this approach risk[s] changing the nature of the obligation under Article 2.2 from one in which Members were required to meet a threshold of evidence "sufficient" to maintain a measure to one in which evidence was weighed, in a relative sense, against the measure' (Dispute Settlement Body, Minutes of Meeting, WT/DSB/M/160 of 27 January 2004 at paragraph 8).

If this was the intention of the panel and the Appellate Body, the *Japan – Apples* decision arguably would contradict a number of rulings in the context of Article 5.1, which emphasize the right of Members to choose their own appropriate level of protection, and which need not hold that a risk assessment or sufficient scientific evidence establish any minimum magnitude of risk to justify an SPS measure. However, when the panel report is read as a whole, the apparent introduction of a type of 'proportionality' test may simply be the result of the lax use of language, rather than an intent to modify existing jurisprudence. The panel's explicit recognition that governments may legitimately act from a position of precaution reinforces this position (*Japan – Apples,* panel report, paragraph 8.105). Moreover, the Appellate Body explicitly acknowledged that while the approach adopted by the panel to assess the adequacy of the relationship between the SPS measure and the scientific evidence was appropriate in this case, such an approach may not be appropriate in all cases (*Japan – Apples* AB report, paragraph 164).

The Appellate Body's emphasis on the case-by-case nature of assessing the adequacy of the relationship between an SPS measure and scientific evidence in the context of Article 2.2 makes it difficult to derive any general rules from the jurisprudence in this area. Nonetheless, it will be interesting to see what type of methodology the panel, and perhaps the Appellate Body, will adopt in assessing the claims of a violation of Article 2.2 in the *EC – Biotech* case, discussed below.

Article 5.1: SPS measures must be based on risk assessment

Article 5.1 of the SPS Agreement provides that:

> *Members shall ensure that their sanitary or phytosanitary measures are based on an assessment, as appropriate to the circumstances, of the risks to human, animal or plant life or health, taking into account risk assessment techniques developed by the relevant international organizations.*

The requirement under Article 5.1 of the SPS Agreement to base SPS measures on a risk assessment appropriate to the circumstances has been considered in all the disputes brought under the SPS Agreement to date. In each of the SPS Agreement-related cases to date, WTO tribunals found that requirements under Article 5.1 were not fulfilled, either because the challenged Member had failed to conduct or have a risk assessment, or that it had failed to base its SPS measure on a risk assessment.

Risk assessment is defined in paragraph 4 of Annex A to the SPS Agreement. The definition distinguishes between two categories: assessments of food-borne risks to human or animal health, and assessments of disease or pest risks. With respect to the latter, risk assessment is defined as '[t]he evaluation of the *likelihood of entry, establishment or spread* of a pest or disease within a territory of an importing Member according to the sanitary or phytosanitary measures which might be applied, and of the associated *potential* biological and economic consequences' (emphasis added). With respect to food-borne risks, risk assessment is defined as 'the evaluation of the *potential for adverse effects* on human or animal health arising from the presence of additives, contaminants, toxins or disease-causing organisms in food, beverages or feedstuffs' (emphasis added).

The Appellate Body has addressed a number of questions raised with respect to Article 5.1. As a general rule, the Appellate Body has held that Article 5.1 could be viewed as a specific application of the basic obligations contained in Article 2.2 of the SPS Agreement (which requires that SPS measures be based on scientific principles and is not maintained without sufficient scientific evidence) (*EC – Hormones* AB report, paragraph 180).

The Appellate Body specifically addressed the requirement that SPS measures be 'based on' risk assessment. It explained that the term 'based on' required a *rational relationship* between the measure and the risk assessment, and that the results of the risk assessment had to sufficiently warrant the SPS measure (*Id.* at paragraph 193). At the same time, however, the Appellate Body clarified that the provision requiring that the risk assessment is *appropriate to the circumstances* gives Members a certain degree of flexibility in meeting the requirements of Article 5.1 (*Id.* at paragraph 129; *see also Japan – Apples* Panel report, paragraph 8.239).

Furthermore, while Article 5.1 requires Members to 'base' their SPS measures on a risk assessment, the Appellate Body has made clear that a Member is not obliged to *undertake* the risk assessment itself. The Member may instead rely on a risk assessment carried out by another Member or an international organization (*EC – Hormones* AB report, paragraph 190). In this context, the question arises as to who bears the cost of undertaking a risk assessment in cases where no relevant risk assessment exists. This is an important question in terms of the ability of developing countries to comply with SPS requirements, as they may not always have the resources to undertake an Article 5.1-compliant risk assessment. As of this writing, the Appellate Body has not addressed this issue. However, common sense and practice indicate that the party seeking regulatory approval may be required to conduct the necessary studies.

With regard to the types of risk taken into account in a risk assessment pursuant to Article 5.1, the Appellate Body has held that theoretical risk (that is, uncertainty inherent to scientific endeavour) is not the kind of risk to which an Article 5.1 risk assessment is directed (*Id.* at paragraph 186). At the same time, it also clarified that the risks to be taken into account in a risk assessment include not only those risks ascertainable in a science laboratory, but also 'risk in human societies as they actually exist, in other words, the actual potential for adverse effects on human health in the real world where people live and work and die' (*Id.* at paragraphs 186–187; *see also Australia – Salmon* AB report, paragraph 125). Thus, a proper risk assessment can assess the risks associated with failure to comply with good veterinary practice in the administration of hormones for growth promotion purposes, as well as the risks associated with failure of control and inspection procedures (*EC – Hormones* AB report, paragraph 205; *see also Japan – Apples* AB report, paragraphs 137–142). Despite these clarifications, it remains unclear how far the Appellate Body has opened the door for the consideration of risks that are not purely scientific, including socio-economic risks.

The Appellate Body has also clarified that a risk assessment need not establish a certain magnitude or threshold level or degree of risk (*EC – Hormones* AB report, paragraph 186; *Australia – Salmon* AB report, paragraph 124). Indeed, a Member can determine that its own appropriate level of protection is 'zero risk' (*Australia – Salmon* AB report, paragraph 125).

Additionally, the Appellate Body has recognized that while Members will generally base their SPS measures on 'mainstream' scientific opinions, it is equally legitimate for a Member to base its SPS measure on divergent scientific opinions, as long as those opinions come from qualified and respected sources (*EC – Hormones* AB report, paragraph 194).

In addressing the risk of pests or disease specifically, the Appellate Body has held that a risk assessment that 'conclude[s] that there is a *possibility*' of a risk is insufficient. Rather, a risk assessment under Article 5.1 must 'evaluate the likelihood, i.e. the "probability"', of the risk (*Australia – Salmon* AB report, paragraph 123). Additionally, where only '*some* evaluation of the likelihood' is undertaken, the risk assessment will not satisfy Article 5.1 (*Id.* at paragraph 124). However, the Appellate Body further held that the evaluation of the likelihood of a risk in a risk assessment may be expressed either quantitatively or qualitatively (*Id.*).

Finally, while Article 5.1 requires Members to 'take into account risk assessment techniques developed by the relevant international organizations', the panel in *Japan – Apples* clarified that this provision did not establish a requirement that a risk assessment had to be 'based on' or 'in conformity with' international risk assessment techniques (*Japan – Apples* panel report, paragraph 8.241).

Article 5.7: Provisional SPS measures

Article 5.7 of the SPS Agreement provides that:

> *[i]n cases where relevant scientific evidence is insufficient, a Member may provisionally adopt sanitary or phytosanitary measures on the basis of available pertinent information. . . In such circumstances, Members shall seek to obtain the additional information necessary for a more objective assessment of risk and review the sanitary or phytosanitary measure accordingly within a reasonable period of time.*

The Appellate Body first considered Article 5.7 in *Japan – Varietals*, and set forth four requirements for Members seeking to adopt and maintain a provisional measure pursuant to Article 5.7:

1 the provisional SPS measure may be imposed only where 'relevant scientific information [sic] is insufficient';
2 the measure must be adopted 'on the basis of available pertinent information';
3 the Member must 'seek to obtain the additional information necessary for a more objective assessment of risk'; and
4 the Member must 'review the measure accordingly within a reasonable period of time' (*Japan – Varietals* AB report, paragraph 89).

This four-step test has been confirmed in *Japan – Apples* (*Japan – Apples* AB report, paragraph 176). To date, panels and the Appellate Body have discussed the first, third and fourth requirements, but have not attempted to define more precisely the meaning of term 'available pertinent information' found in the second requirement.

The *Japan – Apples* panel analysed the first requirement of 'insufficient scientific information', and concluded that Article 5.7 was intended to address a situation where little, *or no reliable*, scientific evidence was available (*Japan – Apples* panel report, paragraph 8.219). The Appellate Body upheld the panel's reasoning (*Japan – Apples* AB report, paragraph 185), but added that '"relevant scientific evidence" will be "insufficient" within the meaning of Article 5.7 if the body of available scientific evidence does not allow, in quantitative or qualitative terms, the performance of an adequate assessment of risks as required under Article 5.1 and as defined in Annex A to the SPS Agreement' (*Id.* at paragraph 179). Thus, this approach links the sufficiency of relevant scientific evidence to the ability to conduct an adequate risk assessment.

In *EC – Hormones,* the Appellate Body held that the precautionary principle 'has been incorporated and given a specific meaning in Article 5.7 of the SPS Agreement' (*EC – Hormones,* AB report, paragraphs 120, 124). Thus, although the Appellate Body has acknowledged that the precautionary principle is also reflected in other provisions of the SPS Agreement, its view has been that Article 5.7 is the provision that most directly reflects the precautionary principle. However, in *Japan – Apples,* the Appellate Body explicitly held that Article 5.7 would not be 'triggered' by 'scientific uncertainty', but only by 'insufficiency of scientific evidence', and stressed that these 'two concepts are not interchangeable' (*Japan – Apples,* panel report, paragraph 184). The implications of this distinction remain unclear, given the strong interrelationship between the two concepts.

The third and fourth requirements of Article 5.7, 'to obtain the additional information necessary for a more objective assessment of risk' and to 'review the measure accordingly within a reasonable period of time', both received consideration in *Japan – Varietals.* With respect to the third requirement, the Appellate Body noted that the SPS Agreement did not specify the additional information a Member must collect and in what manner; Article 5.7 does not 'specify what actual results must be achieved' (*Japan – Varietals* AB report, paragraph 92). However, the Appellate Body stressed that 'the information sought must be germane to conducting . . . [a more objective] risk assessment, i.e. the evaluation of the likelihood of entry, establishment or spread of, *in casu,* a pest, according to the SPS measures which might be applied' (*Id.*).

As to the meaning of 'a reasonable period of time', the Appellate Body determined that such a period had 'to be established on a case-by-case basis and depends on the specific circumstances of each case, including the difficulty of obtaining the additional information and the characteristics of the provisional SPS measure' (*Id.* at paragraph 93).

Article 5.7 will probably be considered again in *EC – Biotech,* a case in which the European Communities is arguing that its challenged marketing and import bans on genetically modified organisms should be assessed under Article 5.7, to the extent that they are SPS measures.

SELECTED ISSUES RELATING TO THE ROLE OF SCIENCE AND THE PRECAUTIONARY PRINCIPLE

International standards

The TBT and the SPS Agreements seek to harmonize SPS measures and technical regulations, and therefore encourage the use of international standards, guidelines and recommendations.

In the TBT Agreement, this aim is reflected in:

- Paragraphs 2, 3 and 8 of the Preamble, which emphasize the efficiency, trade liberalization and technology transfer benefits of harmonization;
- Articles 2.4 and 5.4, which require Members to base technical regulations and conformity assessment procedures on international standards, except where such standards are ineffective or inappropriate to the Member's circumstances;
- Article 2.5, which creates a presumption that a technical regulation that conforms to an international standard does not create an unnecessary obstacle to trade;
- Articles 2.6 and 5.5, which require Members to participate in the development of international technical regulations and conformity assessment standards; and
- Article 9.1, which requires Members to participate in the development of international systems for conformity assessment.

The only case interpreting some of these provisions of the TBT Agreement (*EC – Sardines*) dealt primarily with the question of whether or not the measure at issue was based on the relevant international standards. As a result, many issues regarding the scope of the obligations relating to harmonization with international technical standards remain open.

In the SPS Agreement, the harmonization goal is principally reflected in:

- Paragraphs 4, 5 and 6 of the Preamble, which emphasize the trade benefits of harmonization, while recognizing each Member's right to maintain its own appropriate level of protection;
- Article 3.1, which requires SPS measures to be based on international standards where they exist, except as otherwise provided for in the SPS Agreement;
- Article 3.2, which establishes a presumption that SPS measures conforming to international standards are consistent with the SPS Agreement and GATT;
- Article 3.3, which gives Members the right to adopt SPS measures that result in a higher level of protection than international standard if there is a scientific justification, or as a consequence of that Member's higher appropriate level of protection in accordance with Article 5 (which includes, *inter alia*, the requirement that measures be based on risk assessment); and
- Article 3.4, which requires Members to participate in international standard setting bodies within the limits of their resources.

In *EC – Hormones*, the Appellate Body discussed the relationship between Articles 3.1 and 3.3 (*EC – Hormones* AB report, paragraphs 157–177). It held that Members are not obliged by Article 3.1 to 'conform' their domestic regulations to standards enacted by international standard setting bodies, but rather must 'base' their SPS measures on such standards (*Id.* at paragraphs 160–168). The Appellate Body found that although the SPS Agreement seeks to *promote* international harmonization, it does not create an *obligation* for Members to abide by such international standards (*Id.* at paragraph 165). The distinction that it has made between the terms 'based on' and 'conform to' leaves Members some flexibility in designing their SPS measures.

Additionally, under Article 3.3, Members may establish an SPS measure that is unrelated to any existing international standards, if other or additional scientific evidence exists, or if the Member has chosen a different (higher) appropriate level of protection.

In sum, the Appellate Body has distinguished between three situations permissible under the SPS Agreement:

1 a Member promulgates an SPS measure that conforms to an international standard, and is therefore presumed to be SPS consistent under Article 3.2 (*Id.* at paragraph 170);
2 a Member promulgates an SPS measure that is based on an international standard as required in 3.1, but differs in some respects from (*Id.* at paragraph 171); or
3 a Member promulgates an SPS measure that is different from an international standard, but is based on scientific evidence, or the Member's chosen appropriate level of protection under Article 3.3, and therefore must be consistent with other provisions of the SPS Agreement, particularly Article 5.1 on risk assessment (case law indicates that to challenge a measure adopted under Article 3.3, the complaining Member will need to establish a *prima facie* case of a violation of Article 5.1) (*Id.* at paragraphs 173–177).

It is interesting to note that the Appellate Body in *EC – Hormones* held that the relationship between Articles 3.1, 3.2 and 3.3 was qualitatively different from the relationship between Articles I or III and Article XX of the GATT. It held that Article 3.1 of the SPS Agreement excludes from its scope of application the kinds of situations covered by Article 3.3, and that Article 3.3 recognizes the autonomous right of a Member to establish a higher level of protection, provided that that Member complies with certain requirements in promulgating the SPS measures. In light of this reasoning, the Appellate Body held that Article 3.3, a provision that appears to be an exception (i.e. an affirmative defence), is in fact an autonomous right of Members. Therefore, instead of the defending party bearing the burden of proof of showing that it has complied with Article 3.3, the complaining party bears the burden of proof of showing that the defending party has violated Article 3.3 (*EC – Hormones*, AB report, paragraph 104).

The Precautionary Principle in the context of multilateral environmental agreements (MEAs)

Many multilateral environmental agreements (MEAs) refer to the precautionary principle, either in their preambles, or in the operative text of the treaties. Examples include the 1992 Convention on Biodiversity (CBD), the 1992 Framework Convention on Climate Change, the 1989 Basel Convention on the Control of Transboundary Movements of Hazardous Wastes and Hazardous Substances, and the 1996 Protocol to the Convention on the Prevention of Marine Pollution by Dumping of Wastes and other Matter. Of particular relevance is the Cartagena Protocol on Biosafety, which entered into force on 11 September 2003. This Protocol to the CBD regulates the transboundary movement of certain 'living modified organisms' and incorporates the precautionary principle in its substantive provisions.

The discussion of the precautionary principle and trade is intrinsically linked to the debate on the relationship between MEAs and WTO rules. Is there a conflict between the two sets of rules? If so, how should they be reconciled? As of this writing, WTO tribunals have not been asked to address these questions.

While pre-WTO GATT panels were hesitant to refer to international law outside the GATT, the Appellate Body has been more willing to rely on international law outside the WTO in order to interpret WTO provisions. In interpreting Article XX(g) of the GATT, the Appellate Body in *US – Reformulated Gasoline* held that the panel had failed to apply the basic principles of interpretation contained in Article 31(1) of the Vienna Convention. The Appellate Body found that Article 31(1) is a rule of customary international law and, pursuant to DSU Article 3.2, should be applied. It noted that the GATT could not be 'read in clinical isolation from public international law' (*US – Reformulated Gasoline* AB report, section IV.B). In an entire series of subsequent decisions, the Appellate Body confirmed the approach taken in *US – Reformulated Gasoline* and emphasized that the customary rules of interpretation of public international law must be applied when interpreting WTO provisions.

In *US – Shrimp/Turtle I*, the Appellate Body looked beyond the Vienna Convention to environmental treaties in interpreting specific terms used in Article XX of the GATT. The Appellate Body acknowledged the importance of environmental issues under the 'new' WTO and stressed its preference for a multilateral approach to environmental issues. In analysing Article XX(g) of the GATT, the Appellate Body had to determine whether the term 'exhaustible natural resources' included living and as well as non-living resources. Besides referring to the preamble of the WTO Agreement (which explicitly refers to sustainable development and environmental protection and preservation), the Appellate Body took into account a significant number of international conventions and declarations to interpret the term 'exhaustible natural resources' to include living resources. In doing so, the Appellate Body referred to treaties to which not all participants in the dispute were party (*US – Shrimp/Turtle I* AB report, footnotes 71–74).

Additionally, the Appellate Body relied on the Convention on International Trade in Endangered Species of Wild Fauna and Flora (CITES) in determining that sea turtles are an 'exhaustible' natural resource. Interestingly, the Appellate Body specified in a footnote that all of the participants in the appeal were Parties to CITES and that CITES at the time had 144 parties (*Id.* at footnotes 81–82).

US – Shrimp/Turtle I indicates that a future WTO tribunal, in a dispute involving an MEA incorporating the precautionary principle, might interpret WTO provisions in light of that MEA.

SELECTED LITERATURE

Briese, R. (2002) 'Precaution and cooperation in the World Trade Organization: An environmental perspective', *Australian Yearbook of International Law*, vol 22, p113

Howse, R. (2000) 'Democracy, science, and free trade: Risk regulation on trial at the World Trade Organization', *Michigan Law Review*, vol 98, p2329

Mbengue, M. M. and Thomas, U. (2005) 'The precautionary principle: Torn between biodiversity, environment-related food safety and the WTO', *International Journal of Global Environmental Issues*, vol 5, no 1/2, p36

Pauwelyn, J. (1999) 'The WTO Agreement on SPS Measures as applied in the first three SPS disputes, *EC – Hormones, Australia – Salmon, Japan – Varietals*', *Journal of International Ecomonic Law*, vol 2, p641

Walker, V. R. (1998) 'Keeping the WTO from becoming the World Trans-Science Organization: Scientific uncertainty, science policy, and factfinding in the growth hormones dispute', *Cornell International Law Journal*, vol 31, p251

World Trade Organization (2005) *World Trade Report 2005, Exploring the Links Between Trade, Standards, and the WTO* (Chapter II: Trade, Standards and the WTO), World Trade Organization, Geneva

SELECTED JURISPRUDENCE RELATING TO SCIENCE AND THE PRECAUTIONARY PRINCIPLE

The following are excerpts of WTO cases that are relevant for a discussion of the precautionary principle and the role of science in WTO law. The excerpts are preceded by a short summary and commentary of the corresponding case, aiming to put the excerpts into context. The cases are listed in chronological order. The case summaries in this chapter do not encompass all the issues raised in the cases, but focus primarily on issues relating to the precautionary principle and the role of science, and thus are not comprehensive for other purposes.

European Communities – Measures Concerning Meat and Meat Products ('EC – Hormones'), 1998

Short summary and commentary

The first case to consider the SPS Agreement, *EC – Hormones*, involved Canadian and US challenges to the EC's ban on the import of meat from cattle to which bovine growth hormones ('BGH') had been administered for the purpose of promoting growth. The import ban was an integral part of an EC directive that also prohibited the use of hormones domestically and the domestic sale of any meat products from animals so treated.

The panel found the EC measure inconsistent with a number of provisions of the SPS Agreement. On appeal, the Appellate Body also found the EC measure inconsistent with the SPS Agreement. However, in reaching this conclusion, the Appellate Body overturned or qualified the panel's reasoning in a number of respects.

Prior to considering the substantive provisions of the SPS Agreement, the Appellate Body discussed the relationship between the SPS Agreement and precautionary principle (on which the EC relied). Although the EC had not explicitly relied on Article 5.7 (which allows Members to adopt a provisional SPS measure where scientific evidence is insufficient), the Appellate Body noted that Article 5.7 was the most direct reflection of the precautionary principle in the SPS Agreement. It also pointed out that the principle was reflected in other parts of the SPS Agreement, including Article 3.3 and the sixth paragraph of the Preamble. Nonetheless, the Appellate Body held that the precautionary principle could not override the explicit provisions of the SPS Agreement, in particular Article 5.1's requirements that a Member's SPS measures be based on a risk assessment.

The Appellate Body found that the EC measure was inconsistent with Article 5.1 of the SPS Agreement as it was not sufficiently 'based on' a risk assessment. The Appellate

Body considered the nature of the risk assessment requirement in detail. It stressed the obligation of Members to base their SPS measures on a risk assessment, and interpreted Articles 5.1 and 2.2 to mean that Members must demonstrate a 'rational relationship' between a (scientific) risk assessment and an SPS measure (AB report, paragraph 193). The Appellate Body described this requirement as a 'countervailing factor' to a Member's freedom to establish its appropriate level of protection under Article 3.3 (*Id.* at paragraph 177). The Appellate Body also made a number of rulings about the substantive requirements of a risk assessment, including that: (i) a risk assessment does not need to establish a particular magnitude of risk before a Member is entitled to implement an SPS measure; (ii) if scientific opinion or risk assessments diverge, Members have the discretion to decide which scientific evidence to base their SPS measures upon; and (iii) a risk assessment may take into account not only 'risk ascertainable in a science laboratory . . . but also risk in human societies as they actually exist, in other words, the actual potential for adverse effects on human health in the real world where people live and work and die' (*Id.* at paragraph 187).

In analysing Article 3, the Appellate Body devoted a number of pages to correcting the panel's interpretation of the relationship among the sub-articles of Article 3, in particular, the fact that the panel equated 'based on' with 'conform to'. In contrast to the panel, the Appellate Body held that Article 3.1's obligation to 'base' an SPS measure on international standards was not the same thing as the requirement to 'conform' to international standards (*Id.* at paragraphs 162–166). Thus, a measure may be considered identical.

The Appellate Body further held that Article 3.3 allows Members that do not 'base' their measures on international standards to depart from the levels of protection established by international standards and to establish their own (higher) levels of protection, in accordance with their societal preferences. This right, however, is subject to compliance with Article 5. As a result of the Appellate Body's finding that the EC measure was inconsistent with Article 5.1 of the SPS Agreement, the Appellate Body also held that the EC measure was inconsistent with Article 3.3.

The Appellate Body confirmed that the burden of proof under both Articles 3.1 and 3.3 is on the Member challenging the SPS measure. Thus, even if a Member establishes a level of (health or environmental) protection that is higher than that contained in an international standard, another Member challenging this measure must make a *prima facie* case of inconsistency with the SPS Agreement.

The Appellate Body also overturned the panel's finding that the EC measure was inconsistent with Article 5.5 of the SPS Agreement. Article 5.5 requires Members to avoid arbitrary or unjustifiable distinctions in the level of protection it considers appropriate in different situations, if such distinctions result in discrimination or a disguised restriction on international trade. In interpreting this provision, the Appellate Body held that three cumulative requirements must be satisfied to establish an inconsistency with Article 5.5:

1 a Member must have adopted its own appropriate level of protection in several different, but comparable situations;
2 these levels of protection must exhibit arbitrary or unjustifiable differences; and
3 the arbitrary or unjustifiable differences must result in discrimination or is a disguised restriction on trade (*Id.* at paragraphs 214–215).

Applying this three-pronged test to the EC measure, the Appellate Body found that, while the first two requirements were established, the background to the development of the measure suggested that the primary motive was to protect public health, and did not provide any evidence of a discriminatory or protectionist motive. According to the Appellate Body, in such circumstances, the third requirement, that the measure results in discrimination or a disguised restriction on trade, is not satisfied.

All of these legal issues might be examined again in a currently pending case, in which the EC is challenging US and Canadian trade sanctions against the EC ban on growth-hormone treated beef. The EC claims that neither country had removed extra duties on EC products, although the Communities had modified its rules on beef imports to comply with the 1998 WTO ruling.

Excerpts

Report of the Appellate Body, *European Communities – Measures Concerning Meat and Meat Products (Hormones)*, WT/DS26/AB/R, WT/DS48/AB/R, adopted on 13 February 1998.

IV. Allocating the Burden of Proof in Proceedings Under the SPS Agreement [paras 97–109]

. . .

102. We find the general interpretative ruling of the Panel to be bereft of basis in the *SPS Agreement* and must, accordingly, reverse that ruling. It does not appear to us that there is any necessary (i.e. logical) or other connection between the undertaking of Members to ensure, for example, that SPS measures are "applied only to the extent necessary to protect human, animal or plant life or health . . .", and the allocation of burden of proof in a dispute settlement proceeding. Article 5.8 of the *SPS Agreement* does not purport to address burden of proof problems; it does not deal with a dispute settlement situation. To the contrary, a Member seeking to exercise its right to receive information under Article 5.8 would, most likely, be in a pre-dispute situation, and the information or explanation it receives may well make it possible for that Member to proceed to dispute settlement proceedings and to carry the burden of proving on a *prima facie* basis that the measure involved is not consistent with the *SPS Agreement*. The Panel's last reason involves, quite simply, a *non-sequitur*. The converse or a contrario presumption created by the Panel does not arise. The presumption of consistency with relevant provisions of the *SPS Agreement* that arises under Article 3.2 in respect of measures that conform to international standards may well be an incentive for Members so to conform their SPS measures with such standards. It is clear, however, that a decision of a Member not to conform a particular measure with an international standard does not authorize imposition of a special or generalized burden of proof upon that Member, which may, more often than not, amount to a *penalty*.

. . .

104. The Panel relies on two interpretative points in reaching its above finding. First, the Panel posits the existence of a "general rule – exception" relationship between Article 3.1 (the general obligation) and Article 3.3 (an exception)[61] and applies to the SPS Agreement what it calls "established practice under GATT 1947 and GATT 1994" to the effect that the burden of justifying a measure under Article XX of the GATT 1994 rests on the defending party.[62] It appears to us that the Panel has misconceived the relationship between Articles 3.1, 3.2 and 3.3, a relationship discussed below,[63] which is qualitatively different from the relationship between, for instance, Articles I or III and Article XX of the GATT 1994. Article 3.1 of the *SPS Agreement* simply excludes from its scope of application the kinds of situations covered by Article 3.3 of that Agreement, that is, where a Member has projected for itself a higher level of sanitary protection than would be achieved by a measure based on an international standard. Article 3.3 recognizes the autonomous right of a Member to establish such higher level of protection, provided that that Member complies with certain requirements in promulgating SPS measures to achieve that level. The general rule

in a dispute settlement proceeding requiring a complaining party to establish a *prima facie* case of inconsistency with a provision of the *SPS Agreement* before the burden of showing consistency with that provision is taken on by the defending party, is *not* avoided by simply describing that same provision as an "exception". In much the same way, merely characterizing a treaty provision as an "exception" does not by itself justify a "stricter" or "narrower" interpretation of that provision than would be warranted by examination of the ordinary meaning of the actual treaty words, viewed in context and in the light of the treaty's object and purpose, or, in other words, by applying the normal rules of treaty interpretation. It is also well to remember that a *prima facie* case is one which, in the absence of effective refutation by the defending party, requires a panel, as a matter of law, to rule in favour of the complaining party presenting the *prima facie* case.

[61] US Panel Report, para 8.86; Canada Panel Report, para 8.89.
[62] US Panel Report, footnote 288; Canada Panel Report, footnote 393.
[63] Paras 169–172 of this Report.

105. Secondly, the Panel relies upon the reverse presumption or implication it discovered in Article 3.2 of the SPS Agreement. As already noted, we have been unable to find any basis for that implication or presumption.

. . .

108. To the extent that the Panel[69] purports to absolve the United States and Canada from the necessity of establishing a *prima facie* case showing the absence of the risk assessment required by Article 5.1, and the failure of the European Communities to comply with the requirements of Article 3.3, and to impose upon the European Communities the burden of proving the existence of such risk assessment and the consistency of its measures with Articles 5.4, 5.5 and 5.6 *without regard to whether or not the complaining parties had already established their prima facie case*, we consider and so hold that the Panel once more erred in law.

[69] US Panel Report, paras 8.151 and 8.165; Canada Panel Report, paras 8.154 and 8.168.

. . .

VI. The Relevance of the Precautionary Principle in the Interpretation of the SPS Agreement [paras 120–125]

120. We are asked by the European Communities to reverse the finding of the Panel relating to the precautionary principle. The Panel's finding and its supporting statements are set out in the Panel Reports in the following terms:

> *The European Communities also invokes the precautionary principle in support of its claim that its measures in dispute are based on a risk assessment. To the extent that this principle could be considered as part of customary international law* and *be used to interpret Articles 5.1 and 5.2 on the assessment of risks as a customary rule of interpretation of public international law (as that phrase is used in Article 3.2 of the DSU), we consider that* this principle would not override the explicit wording of Articles 5.1 and 5.2 outlined above*, in particular since the precautionary principle has been incorporated and given a specific meaning in Article 5.7 of the SPS Agreement. We note, however, that the European Communities has explicitly stated in this case that it is not invoking Article 5.7.*

We thus find that *the precautionary principle cannot override our findings made above*, namely that the EC import ban of meat and meat products from animals treated with any of the five hormones at issue for growth promotion purposes, in so far as it also applies to meat and meat products from animals treated with any of these hormones in accordance with good practice, is, from a substantive point of view, not based on a risk assessment[85] (emphasis added).

[85] *US Panel Report, paras 8.157 and 8.158; Canada Panel Report, paras 8.160 and 8.161.*

121. The basic submission of the European Communities is that the precautionary principle is, or has become, "a general customary rule of international law" or at least "a general principle of law".[86] Referring more specifically to Articles 5.1 and 5.2 of the *SPS Agreement*, applying the precautionary principle means, in the view of the European Communities, that it is not necessary for *all* scientists around the world to agree on the "possibility and magnitude" of the risk, nor for *all* or most of the WTO Members to perceive and evaluate the risk in the same way.[87] It is also stressed that Articles 5.1 and 5.2 do not prescribe a particular type of risk assessment and do not prevent Members from being cautious in their risk assessment exercise.[88] The European Communities goes on to state that its measures here at stake were precautionary in nature and satisfied the requirements of Articles 2.2 and 2.3, as well as of Articles 5.1, 5.2, 5.4, 5.5 and 5.6 of the *SPS Agreement*.[89]

[86] EC's appellant's submission, para 91.
[87] EC's appellant's submission, para 88.
[88] EC's appellant's submission, para 94.
[89] EC's appellant's submission, para 98.

122. The United States does not consider that the "precautionary principle" represents customary international law and suggests it is more an "approach" than a "principle".[90] Canada, too, takes the view that the precautionary principle has not yet been incorporated into the corpus of public international law; however, it concedes that the "precautionary approach" or "concept" is "an *emerging* principle of law" which may in the future crystallize into one of the "general principles of law recognized by civilized nations" within the meaning of Article 38(1)(c) of the *Statute of the International Court of Justice*.[91]

[90] United States' appellee's submission, para 92.
[91] Canada's appellee's submission, para 34.

123.The status of the precautionary principle in international law continues to be the subject of debate among academics, law practitioners, regulators and judges. The precautionary principle is regarded by some as having crystallized into a general principle of customary international *environmental* law. Whether it has been widely accepted by Members as a principle of *general* or *customary international law* appears less than clear.[92] We consider, however, that it is unnecessary, and probably imprudent, for the Appellate Body in this appeal to take a position on this important, but abstract, question. We note that the Panel itself did not make any definitive finding with regard to the status of the precautionary principle in international law and that the precautionary principle, at least outside the field of international environmental law, still awaits authoritative formulation.[93]

[92] Authors like P. Sands, J. Cameron and J. Abouchar, while recognizing that the principle is still evolving, submit nevertheless that there is currently sufficient state practice to support the view that the precautionary principle is a principle of customary international law. See, for example, P. Sands, *Principles of International Environmental Law,* vol I (Manchester University Press, 1995) p212; J. Cameron, 'The status of the Precautionary Principle in International Law', in J. Cameron and T. O'Riordan (eds.), *Interpreting the Precautionary Principle* (Cameron May, 1994) 262, p283; J.Cameron and J. Abouchar, 'The status of the Precautionary Principle in International Law', in D. Freestone and E. Hey (eds.), *The Precautionary Principle in International Law* (Kluwer, 1996) 29, p52. Other authors argue that the precautionary principle has not yet reached the status of a principle of international law, or at least, consider such status doubtful, among other reasons, due to the fact that the principle is still subject to a great variety of interpretations. See, for example, P. Birnie and A. Boyle, *International Law and the Environment* (Clarendon Press, 1992), p98; L. Gündling, 'The status in International Law of the Precautionary Principle' (1990), 5:1,2,3 *International Journal of*

Estuarine and Coastal Law 25, p. 30; A. deMestral (et al), *International Law Chiefly as Interpreted and Applied in Canada,* 5th ed. (Emond Montgomery, 1993), p765; D. Bodansky, in *Proceedings of the 85th Annual Meeting of the American Society of International Law* (ASIL, 1991), p415.

[93] In *Case Concerning the Gabcíkovo-Nagymaros Project (Hungary/Slovakia)*, the International Court of Justice recognized that in the field of environmental protection ". . . new norms and standards have been developed, set forth in a great number of instruments during the last two decades. Such new norms have to be taken into consideration, and such new standards given proper weight". However, we note that the Court did not identify the precautionary principle as one of those recently developed norms. It also declined to declare that such principle could override the obligations of the Treaty between Czechoslovakia and Hungary of 16 September 1977 concerning the construction and operation of the Gabcíkovo/Nagymaros System of Locks. See, *Case Concerning the Gabcíkovo-Nagymaros Project (Hungary/Slovakia),* I.C.J. Judgement, 25 September 1997, paras 140, 111–114. Not yet reported in the I.C.J. Reports but available on internet at http://www.icj-cij.org/idecis.htm.

124. It appears to us important, nevertheless, to note some aspects of the relationship of the precautionary principle to the *SPS Agreement*. First, the principle has not been written into the *SPS Agreement* as a ground for justifying SPS measures that are otherwise inconsistent with the obligations of Members set out in particular provisions of that Agreement. Secondly, the precautionary principle indeed finds reflection in Article 5.7 of the *SPS Agreement*. We agree, at the same time, with the European Communities, that there is no need to assume that Article 5.7 exhausts the relevance of a precautionary principle. It is reflected also in the sixth paragraph of the preamble and in Article 3.3. These explicitly recognize the right of Members to establish their own appropriate level of sanitary protection, which level may be higher (i.e. more cautious) than that implied in existing international standards, guidelines and recommendations. Thirdly, a panel charged with determining, for instance, whether "sufficient scientific evidence" exists to warrant the maintenance by a Member of a particular SPS measure may, of course, and should, bear in mind that responsible, representative governments commonly act from perspectives of prudence and precaution where risks of irreversible, e.g. life-terminating, damage to human health are concerned. Lastly, however, the precautionary principle does not, by itself, and without a clear textual directive to that effect, relieve a panel from the duty of applying the normal (i.e. customary international law) principles of treaty interpretation in reading the provisions of the *SPS Agreement*.

125. We accordingly agree with the finding of the Panel that the precautionary principle does not override the provisions of Articles 5.1 and 5.2 of the SPS Agreement.

VII. Application of the SPS Agreement to Measures Enacted Before 1 January [paras 126–130]

. . .

129. We are aware that the applicability, as from 1 January 1995, of the requirement that an SPS measure be based on a risk assessment to the many SPS measures already in existence on that date, may impose burdens on Members. It is pertinent here to note that Article 5.1 stipulates that SPS measures must be based on a risk assessment, *as appropriate to the circumstances*, and this makes clear that the Members have a certain degree of flexibility in meeting the requirements of Article 5.1.

. . .

X. The Interpretation of Articles 3.1 and 3.3 of the SPS Agreement [paras 157–177]

. . .

162. We read the Panel's interpretation that Article 3.2 "equates" measures "based on" international standards with measures which "conform to" such standards, as signifying that "based on" and "conform to" are identical in meaning. The Panel is thus saying that, henceforth, SPS measures of Members *must* "conform to" Codex standards, guidelines and recommendations.

163. We are unable to accept this interpretation of the Panel. In the first place, the ordinary meaning of "based on" is quite different from the plain or natural import of "conform to". A thing is commonly said to be "based on" another thing when the former "stands" or is "founded" or "built" upon or "is supported

by" the latter.[150] In contrast, much more is required before one thing may be regarded as "conform[ing] to" another: the former must "comply with", "yield or show compliance" with the latter. The reference of "conform to" is to "correspondence in form or manner", to "compliance with" or "acquiescence", to "follow[ing] in form or nature".[151] A measure that "conforms to" and incorporates a Codex standard is, of course, "based on" that standard. A measure, however, based on the same standard might not conform to that standard, as where only some, not all, of the elements of the standard are incorporated into the measure.

[150] L. Brown (ed.), *The New Shorter Oxford English Dictionary on Historical Principles* (Clarendon Press), Vol. I, p187.
[151] L. Brown (ed.), *The New Shorter Oxford English Dictionary on Historical Principles* (Clarendon Press), Vol. I, p477.

164. In the second place, "based on" and "conform to" are used in different articles, as well as in differing paragraphs of the same article. Thus, Article 2.2 uses "based on", while Article 2.4 employs "conform to". Article 3.1 requires the Members to "base" their SPS measures on international standards; however, Article 3.2 speaks of measures which "conform to" international standards. Article 3.3 once again refers to measures "based on" international standards. The implication arises that the choice and use of different words in different places in the *SPS Agreement* are deliberate, and that the different words are designed to convey different meanings. A treaty interpreter is not entitled to assume that such usage was merely inadvertent on the part of the Members who negotiated and wrote that Agreement.[152] Canada has suggested the use of different terms was "accidental" in this case, but has offered no convincing argument to support its suggestion. We do not believe this suggestion has overturned the inference of deliberate choice.

[152] Appellate Body Report, *United States – Underwear,* adopted 25 February 1997, WT/DS24/AB/R, p17.

165. In the third place, the object and purpose of Article 3 run counter to the Panel's interpretation. That purpose, Article 3.1 states, is '[t]o harmonize [SPS] measures on as wide a basis as possible. . .'. The preamble of the *SPS Agreement* also records that the Members "[d]esir[e] to *further the use of harmonized [SPS] measures between Members* on the basis of international standards, guidelines and recommendations developed by the relevant international organizations . . ." (emphasis added). Article 12.1 created a Committee on Sanitary and Phytosanitary Measures and gave it the task, *inter alia*, of "furtherance of its objectives, in particular with respect to harmonization" and (in Article 12.2) to "encourage the use of international standards, guidelines and recommendations by all Members". It is clear to us that harmonization of SPS measures of Members on the basis of international standards is projected in the Agreement, as a *goal*, yet to be realized *in the future*. To read Article 3.1 as requiring Members to harmonize their SPS measures *by conforming those measures with international standards*, guidelines and recommendations, *in the here and now*, is, in effect, to vest such international standards, guidelines and recommendations (which are by the terms of the Codex *recommendatory* in form and nature[153]) with *obligatory* force and effect. The Panel's interpretation of Article 3.1 would, in other words, transform those standards, guidelines and recommendations into binding *norms*. But, as already noted, the *SPS Agreement* itself sets out no indication of any intent on the part of the Members to do so. We cannot lightly assume that sovereign states intended to impose upon themselves the more onerous, rather than the less burdensome, obligation by mandating *conformity* or *compliance with* such standards, guidelines and recommendations.[154] To sustain such an assumption and to warrant such a far-reaching interpretation, treaty language far more specific and compelling than that found in Article 3 of the *SPS Agreement* would be necessary.

[153] US Panel Report, para 8.59; Canada Panel Report, para 8.62.
[154] The interpretative principle of *in dubio mitius,* widely recognized in international law as a "supplementary means of interpretation", has been expressed in the following terms:

"The principle of *in dubio mitius* applies in interpreting treaties, in deference to the sovereignty of states. If the meaning of a term is ambiguous, that meaning is to be preferred which is less onerous to the party assuming an obligation, or which interferes less with the territorial and personal supremacy of a party, or involves less general restrictions upon the parties."

R. Jennings and A. Watts (eds.), *Oppenheim's International Law,* 9th ed., Vol. I (Longman, 1992), p1278. The relevant case law includes: *Nuclear Tests Case (Australia v. France),* (1974), I.C.J. Reports, p267 (International Court of Justice); *Access of Polish War Vessels to the Port of Danzig* (1931) PCIJ Rep., Series A/B, No 43, p142 (Permanent Court of International Justice); *USA–France Air Transport Services Arbitration* (1963), 38 *International Law Reports* 243 (Arbitral Tribunal); *De Pascale Claim* (1961), 40 *International Law Reports* 250 (Italian – United States Conciliation Commission). See also: I. Brownlie, *Principles of Public International Law,* 4th ed. (Clarendon Press, 1990), p631; C. Rousseau, *Droit International Public,* Vol. I (1990), p273; D. Carreau, *Droit International,* 4th ed. (Editions A. Pedone, 1994), p142; M. Díez de Velasco, *Instituciones de Derecho Internacional Público,* 9th ed., Vol. I (Editorial Tecnos, 1991), pp163–164; and B. Conforti, *Diritto Internazionale,* 3rd ed. (Editoriale Scientifica, 1987), pp99–100.

166. Accordingly, we disagree with the Panel's interpretation that "based on" means the same thing as "conform to".

. . .

169. We turn to the relationship between Articles 3.1, 3.2 and 3.3 of the *SPS Agreement*. As observed earlier, the Panel assimilated Articles 3.1 and 3.2 to one another, designating the product as the "general rule", and contraposed that product to Article 3.3 which denoted the "exception". This view appears to us an erroneous representation of the differing situations that may arise under Article 3, that is, where a relevant international standard, guideline or recommendation exists.

170. Under Article 3.2 of the *SPS Agreement*, a Member may decide to promulgate an SPS measure that conforms to an international standard. Such a measure would embody the international standard completely and, for practical purposes, converts it into a municipal standard. Such a measure enjoys the benefit of a presumption (albeit a rebuttable one) that it is consistent with the relevant provisions of the *SPS Agreement* and of the GATT 1994.

171. Under Article 3.1 of the *SPS Agreement*, a Member may choose to establish an SPS measure that is based on the existing relevant international standard, guideline or recommendation. Such a measure may adopt some, not necessarily all, of the elements of the international standard. The Member imposing this measure does not benefit from the presumption of consistency set up in Article 3.2; but, as earlier observed, the Member is not penalized by exemption of a complaining Member from the normal burden of showing a *prima facie* case of inconsistency with Article 3.1 or any other relevant article of the *SPS Agreement* or of the GATT 1994.

172. Under Article 3.3 of the *SPS Agreement*, a Member may decide to set for itself a level of protection different from that implicit in the international standard, and to implement or embody that level of protection in a measure not "based on" the international standard. The Member's appropriate level of protection may be higher than that implied in the international standard. The right of a Member to determine its own appropriate level of sanitary protection is an important right. . . As noted earlier, this right of a Member to establish its own level of sanitary protection under Article 3.3 of the *SPS Agreement* is an autonomous right and *not* an "exception" from a "general obligation" under Article 3.1.

. . .

177. Consideration of the object and purpose of Article 3 and of the *SPS Agreement* as a whole reinforces our belief that compliance with Article 5.1 was intended as a countervailing factor in respect of the right of Members to set their appropriate level of protection. In generalized terms, the object and purpose of Article 3 is to promote the harmonization of the SPS measures of Members on as wide a basis as possible, while recognizing and safeguarding, at the same time, the right and duty of Members to protect the life and health of their people. The ultimate goal of the harmonization of SPS measures is to prevent the use of such measures for arbitrary or unjustifiable discrimination between Members or as a disguised restriction on international trade, without preventing Members from adopting or enforcing measures which are both "necessary to protect" human life or health and "based on scientific principles", and without requiring them to change their appropriate level of protection. The requirements of a risk

assessment under Article 5.1, as well as of "sufficient scientific evidence" under Article 2.2, are essential for the maintenance of the delicate and carefully negotiated balance in the SPS Agreement between the shared, but sometimes competing, interests of promoting international trade and of protecting the life and health of human beings. We conclude that the Panel's finding that the European Communities is required by Article 3.3 to comply with the requirements of Article 5.1 is correct and, accordingly, dismiss the appeal of the European Communities from that ruling of the Panel.

XI. The Reading of Article 5.1 and 5.2 of the SPS Agreement Basing SPS Measures on a Risk Assessment [paras 178–209]

. . .

180. At the outset, two preliminary considerations need to be brought out. The first is that the Panel considered that Article 5.1 may be viewed as a specific application of the basic obligations contained in Article 2.2 of the *SPS Agreement*[160]. . . We agree with this general consideration and would also stress that Articles 2.2 and 5.1 should constantly be read together. Article 2.2 informs Article 5.1: the elements that define the basic obligation set out in Article 2.2 impart meaning to Article 5.1.

[160] US Panel Report, para 8.93; Canada Panel Report, para 8.96.

. . .

186. . . . In one part of its Reports, the Panel opposes a requirement of an "identifiable risk" to the uncertainty that theoretically always remains since science can *never* provide *absolute* certainty that a given substance will not *ever* have adverse health effects.[169] We agree with the Panel that this theoretical uncertainty is not the kind of risk which, under Article 5.1, is to be assessed. In another part of its Reports, however, the Panel appeared to be using the term "scientifically identified risk" to prescribe implicitly that a certain *magnitude* or threshold level of risk be demonstrated in a risk assessment if an SPS measure based thereon is to be regarded as consistent with Article 5.1.[170] To the extent that the Panel purported to require a risk assessment to establish a minimum magnitude of risk, we must note that imposition of such a quantitative requirement finds no basis in the *SPS Agreement*. A panel is authorized only to determine whether a given SPS measure is "based on" a risk assessment. As will be elaborated below, this means that a panel has to determine whether an SPS measure is sufficiently supported or reasonably warranted by the risk assessment.

[169] US Panel Report, paras 8.152–8.153; Canada Panel Report, paras 8.155–8.156.
[170] US Panel Report, footnote 331; Canada Panel Report, footnote 437.

. . .

187. To the extent that the Panel intended to refer to a process characterized by systematic, disciplined and objective enquiry and analysis, that is, a mode of studying and sorting out facts and opinions, the Panel's statement is unexceptionable.[173] However, to the extent that the Panel purports to exclude from the scope of a risk assessment in the sense of Article 5.1, all matters not susceptible of quantitative analysis by the empirical or experimental laboratory methods commonly associated with the physical sciences, we believe that the Panel is in error. Some of the kinds of factors listed in Article 5.2 such as "relevant processes and production methods" and "relevant inspection, sampling and testing methods" are not necessarily or wholly susceptible of investigation according to laboratory methods of, for example, biochemistry or pharmacology. Furthermore, there is nothing to indicate that the listing of factors that may be taken into account in a risk assessment of Article 5.2 was intended to be a closed list. It is essential to bear in mind that the risk that is to be evaluated in a risk assessment under Article 5.1 is not only risk ascertainable in a science laboratory operating under strictly controlled conditions, but also risk in human societies as they actually exist, in other words, the actual potential for adverse effects on human health in the real world where people live and work and die.

[173] "The ordinary meaning of 'scientific', as provided by dictionary definitions, includes 'of, relating to, or used in science', 'broadly, having or appearing to have an exact, objective, factual, systematic or methodological basis', 'of, relating to, or exhibiting the methods or principles of science' and 'of, pertaining to, using, or based on the methodology of science'. Dictionary definitions of 'science' include 'the observation, identification, description, experimental investigation, and theoretical explanation of natural phenomena', 'any methodological activity, discipline, or study', and 'knowledge attained through study or practice'" (footnotes omitted). *United States' Statement of Administrative Action, Uruguay Round Agreements Act,* 203d Congress, 2d Session, House Document 103–316, Vol. 1, 27 September 1994, p90.

. . .

190. Article 5.1 does not insist that a Member that adopts a sanitary measure shall have carried out its own risk assessment. It only requires that the SPS measures be "based on an assessment, as appropriate for the circumstances . . .". The SPS measure might well find its objective justification in a risk assessment carried out by another Member, or an international organization.

. . .

193. We consider that, in principle, the Panel's approach of examining the scientific conclusions implicit in the SPS measure under consideration and the scientific conclusion yielded by a risk assessment is a useful approach. The relationship between those two sets of conclusions is certainly relevant; they cannot, however, be assigned relevance to the exclusion of everything else. We believe that Article 5.1, when contextually read as it should be, in conjunction with and as informed by Article 2.2 of the SPS Agreement, requires that the results of the risk assessment must sufficiently warrant – that is to say, reasonably support – the SPS measure at stake. The requirement that an SPS measure be "based on" a risk assessment is a substantive requirement that there be a rational relationship between the measure and the risk assessment.

194. We do not believe that a risk assessment has to come to a monolithic conclusion that coincides with the scientific conclusion or view implicit in the SPS measure. The risk assessment could set out both the prevailing view representing the "mainstream" of scientific opinion, as well as the opinions of scientists taking a divergent view. Article 5.1 does not require that the risk assessment must necessarily embody only the view of a majority of the relevant scientific community. In some cases, the very existence of divergent views presented by qualified scientists who have investigated the particular issue at hand may indicate a state of scientific uncertainty. Sometimes the divergence may indicate a roughly equal balance of scientific opinion, which may itself be a form of scientific uncertainty. In most cases, responsible and representative governments tend to base their legislative and administrative measures on "mainstream" scientific opinion. In other cases, equally responsible and representative governments may act in good faith on the basis of what, at a given time, may be a divergent opinion coming from qualified and respected sources. By itself, this does not necessarily signal the absence of a reasonable relationship between the SPS measure and the risk assessment, especially where the risk involved is life-threatening in character and is perceived to constitute a clear and imminent threat to public health and safety. Determination of the presence or absence of that relationship can only be done on a case-to-case basis, after account is taken of all considerations rationally bearing upon the issue of potential adverse health effects.

. . .

XII. The Reading of Article 5.5 of the SPS Agreement: Consistency of Levels of Protection and Resulting Discrimination or Disguised Restriction on International Trade [paras 210–246]

213. The objective of Article 5.5 is formulated as the "achieving [of] consistency in the application of the concept of appropriate level of sanitary or phytosanitary protection". Clearly, the desired consistency is defined as a goal to be achieved in the future. To assist in the realization of that objective, the Committee on Sanitary and Phytosanitary Measures is to develop *guidelines for the practical implementation of Article 5.5*, bearing in mind, among other things, that ordinarily, people do not voluntarily expose themselves to health risks. Thus, we agree with the Panel's view that the statement of that goal does not establish a

legal obligation of consistency of appropriate levels of protection. We think, too, that the goal set is not absolute or perfect consistency, since governments establish their appropriate levels of protection frequently on an *ad hoc* basis and over time, as different risks present themselves at different times. It is only arbitrary or unjustifiable inconsistencies that are to be avoided.

214. Close inspection of Article 5.5 indicates that a complaint of violation of this Article must show the presence of three distinct elements. The first element is that the Member imposing the measure complained of has adopted its own appropriate levels of sanitary protection against risks to human life or health in several different situations. The second element to be shown is that those *levels of protection* exhibit arbitrary or unjustifiable differences ("distinctions" in the language of Article 5.5) in their treatment of different situations. The last element requires that the arbitrary or unjustifiable differences result in discrimination or a disguised restriction of international trade. We understand the last element to be referring to the *measure* embodying or implementing a particular level of protection as resulting, in its application, in discrimination or a disguised restriction on international trade.

215. We consider the above three elements of Article 5.5 to be cumulative in nature; all of them must be demonstrated to be present if violation of Article 5.5 is to be found. In particular, both the second and third elements must be found. The second element alone would not suffice. The third element must also be demonstrably present: the implementing measure must be shown to be applied in such a manner as to result in discrimination or a disguised restriction on international trade. The presence of the second element – the arbitrary or unjustifiable character of differences in *levels of protection* considered by a Member as appropriate in differing situations – may in practical effect operate as a "warning" signal that the implementing *measure* in its application *might* be a discriminatory measure or *might* be a restriction on international trade disguised as an SPS measure for the protection of human life or health. Nevertheless, the measure itself needs to be examined and appraised and, in the context of the differing levels of protection, shown to result in discrimination or a disguised restriction on international trade.

. . .

217 . . . Clearly, comparison of *several* levels of sanitary protection deemed appropriate by a Member is necessary if a panel's inquiry under Article 5.5 is to proceed at all. The situations exhibiting differing levels of protection cannot, of course, be compared unless they are comparable, that is, unless they present some common element or elements sufficient to render them comparable. If the situations proposed to be examined are *totally* different from one another, they would not be rationally comparable and the differences in levels of protection cannot be examined for arbitrariness.

. . .

240. In our view, the degree of difference, or the extent of the discrepancy, in the levels of protection, is only one kind of factor which, along with others, may cumulatively lead to the conclusion that discrimination or a disguised restriction on international trade in fact results from the application of a measure or measures embodying one or more of those different levels of protection. Thus, we do not think that the difference between a "no residues" level and "unlimited residues" level is, together with a finding of an arbitrary or unjustifiable difference, sufficient to demonstrate that the third, and most important, requirement of Article 5.5 has been met. It is well to bear in mind that, after all, the difference in levels of protection that is characterizable as arbitrary or unjustifiable is only an element of (indirect) proof that a Member may actually be applying an SPS measure in a manner that discriminates between Members or constitutes a disguised restriction on international trade, prohibited by the basic obligations set out in Article 2.3 of the *SPS Agreement*. Evidently, the answer to the question whether arbitrary or unjustifiable differences or distinctions in levels of protection established by a Member do in fact result in discrimination or a disguised restriction on international trade must be sought in the circumstances of each individual case.

Australia – Measures Affecting Importation of Salmon from Canada ('Australia – Salmon'), 1998

Short summary and commentary

Australia – Salmon involved a challenge by Canada against Australia's prohibition on the import of fresh, chilled or frozen salmon from Canada. Australia asserted that the prohibition was necessary to prevent the introduction of exotic diseases with the potential to severely damage the domestic salmon industry and threaten the survival of 25–30 species of native salmonids.

The panel found that Australia's measure was inconsistent with, among other provisions, the SPS Agreement's requirements that quarantine measures must be based on an assessment of risks and on scientific principles and that measures must not be maintained without sufficient scientific evidence pursuant to Articles 5.1 and 2.2, respectively. Australia appealed the panel's report.

The Appellate Body found that Australia's measure was inconsistent with Article 5.1 (and by implication, Article 2.2) and Article 5.5 (and by implication, Article 2.3). ' It held that Australia's import prohibition was not based on a valid risk assessment as required by Article 5.1. It found that the report, which Australia relied upon as the relevant risk assessment, failed to satisfy the requirements of a risk assessment as set out in paragraph 4 of Annex A of the SPS Agreement, in that it failed to evaluate the *likelihood* of entry, establishment or spread of the diseases of concern and the associated potential biological and economic consequences according to the SPS measures which might be applied.

In evaluating whether or not that report satisfied the requirements of a risk assessment under the SPS Agreement, the Appellate Body restated a number of the criteria it had established for risk assessment in *EC – Hormones*. It held that in the context of an assessment of the risk of entry, establishment or spread of a pest or disease within the territory of an importing Member, as opposed to an assessment of the risk of adverse effects from additives, contaminants, toxins or disease causing organisms, 'it is not sufficient that a risk assessment conclude that there is a *possibility* of entry, establishment or spread. . . A proper risk assessment . . . must evaluate the likelihood, i.e. the 'probability', of entry establishment or spread' (AB report, paragraph 123). The Appellate Body emphasized that 'only *some* evaluation of the likelihood' is insufficient (*Id.* at paragraph 124). Although this appears to be a very stringent requirement, the Appellate Body tempered it by holding that the likelihood or probability of a risk may be expressed either quantitatively or qualitatively (*Id.*).

The Appellate Body confirmed the panel's view that a violation of Article 5.1 gives rise by implication to a violation of Article 2.2, which provides that SPS measures must be based on scientific principles and not be maintained without sufficient scientific evidence (*Id.* at paragraphs 137–138). It should also be noted that the Appellate Body also found Australia to be in breach of Article 5.5 (and by implication Article 2.3) of the SPS Agreement, which relates to measures resulting in discrimination or a disguised restriction on international trade (*Id.* at paragraph 178).

Notably, in discussing the right of a Member to determine its own appropriate level of protection, the Appellate Body did not preclude the possibility of a Member adopting a level of protection equivalent to 'zero risk' (*Id.* at paragraph 125).

One year after the adoption of the Appellate Body report, Canada challenged Australia's implementation of the recommendations set forth in that report, pursuant to Article 21. 5 of the WTO Dispute Settlement Understanding, which allows a Member to take a case before the Dispute Settlement Body when there is a disagreement as to the existence or consistency of measures taken to comply with the recommendations and rulings of a previous panel or Appellate Body report (*Australia – Salmon* Recourse to Article 21.5 by Canada, Report of the Panel, WT/DS18/RW, 18 February 2000). Australia was found to have conducted a risk assessment as required by the SPS Agreement, but its revised SPS measure was found not to be based on that risk assessment as required by Article 5.1. Hence, the revised SPS measure was also found to be inconsistent with Article 5.1 and Article 2.2. The revised SPS measure was further found to be in violation of Article 5.6, which requires SPS measures to be no more trade restrictive than required to reach a Member's appropriate level of protection.

Excerpts

Report of the Appellate Body, *Australia – Measures Affecting Importation of Salmon*, WT/DS18/AB/R adopted on 6 November 1998.

V. The SPS Agreement

. . .

B. Article 5.1 of the SPS Agreement [paras 112–138]

. . .

120. Paragraph 4 of Annex A of the *SPS Agreement* defines two types of "risk assessment". We agree with the Panel that the type of risk assessment which is required in this case is the type defined in the first part of paragraph 4 of Annex A,[67] which reads as follows:

> Risk Assessment – *The evaluation of the likelihood of entry, establishment or spread of a pest or disease within the territory of an importing Member according to the sanitary or phytosanitary measures which might be applied, and of the associated potential biological and economic consequences.*

On the basis of this definition, we consider that, in this case, a risk assessment within the meaning of Article 5.1 must:

(1) *identify* the diseases whose entry, establishment or spread a Member wants to prevent within its territory, as well as the potential biological and economic consequences associated with the entry, establishment or spread of these diseases;
(2) *evaluate the likelihood* of entry, establishment or spread of these diseases, as well as the associated potential biological and economic consequences; and
(3) evaluate the likelihood of entry, establishment or spread of these diseases *according to the SPS measures which might be applied*.

[67] The SPS measure in dispute is a measure to protect animal life or health from risks arising from the entry, establishment or spread of diseases, rather than from risks arising from additives, contaminants, toxins or disease-causing organisms in foodstuffs. Therefore, the type of risk assessment required is the type defined in the first part, rather than the second part, of paragraph 4 of Annex A of the *SPS Agreement*.

. . .

123. . . . we maintain that for a risk assessment to fall within the meaning of Article 5.1 and the first definition in paragraph 4 of Annex A, it is not sufficient that a risk assessment conclude that there is a *possibility* of entry, establishment or spread of diseases and associated biological and economic consequences. A proper risk assessment of this type must evaluate the "likelihood", i.e., the "probability", of entry, establishment or spread of diseases and associated biological and economic consequences as well as the "likelihood", i.e., "probability", of entry, establishment or spread of diseases *according to the SPS measures which might be applied*.

124. . . . We do not agree with the Panel that a risk assessment of this type needs only *some* evaluation of the likelihood or probability. The definition of this type of risk assessment in paragraph 4 of Annex A refers to "the evaluation of the likelihood" and not to *some* evaluation of the likelihood. We agree, however, with the Panel's statements in paragraph 8.80 that the *SPS Agreement* does not require that the evaluation of the likelihood needs to be done quantitatively. The likelihood may be expressed either quantitatively or qualitatively. Furthermore, we recall, as does the Panel,[75] that we stated in *European Communities – Hormones* that there is no requirement for a risk assessment to establish a certain magnitude or threshold level of degree of risk.[76]

[75] Panel Report, para 8.80.
[76] Adopted 13 February 1998, WT/DS26/AB/R, WT/DS48/AB/R, para 186.

125. . . . we merely note that it is important to distinguish – perhaps more carefully than the Panel did – between the evaluation of "risk" in a risk assessment and the determination of the appropriate level of protection. As stated in our Report in *European Communities – Hormones*, the "risk" evaluated in a risk assessment must be an ascertainable risk; theoretical uncertainty is "not the kind of risk which, under Article 5.1, is to be assessed".[78] This does not mean, however, that a Member cannot determine its own appropriate level of protection to be "zero risk".

[78] Adopted 13 February 1998, WT/DS26/AB/R, WT/DS48/AB/R, para 186.

. . .

130. We might add that the existence of unknown and uncertain elements does not justify a departure from the requirements of Articles 5.1, 5.2 and 5.3, read together with paragraph 4 of Annex A, for a risk assessment. We recall that Article 5.2 requires that "in the assessment of risk, Members shall take into account available scientific evidence". We further recall that Article 2, entitled "Basic Rights and Obligations", requires in paragraph 2 that "Members shall ensure that any sanitary . . . measure . . . is based on scientific principles and is not maintained without sufficient scientific evidence, except as provided for in paragraph 7 of Article 5". As we stated in *European Communities – Hormones*, "Articles 2.2 and 5.1 should constantly be read together. Article 2.2 informs Article 5.1: the elements that define the basic obligation set out in Article 2.2 impart meaning to Article 5.1".[83]

[83] Adopted 13 February 1998, WT/DS26/AB/R, WT/DS48/AB/R, paragraph 180.

. . .

135. We conclude, on the basis of the factual findings made by the Panel and the requirements for a risk assessment as set forth above, that the 1996 Final Report meets neither the second nor the third requirement for the type of risk assessment applicable in this case, and, therefore, that the 1996 Final Report is *not* a proper risk assessment within the meaning of Article 5.1 and the first definition in paragraph 4 of Annex A.

. . .

137. We note that the Panel, after reiterating our statement on the relationship between Articles 2.3 and 5.5 in *European Communities – Hormones*, went on to say:

> *. . . Articles 5.1 and 5.2 . . . "may be seen to be marking out and elaborating a particular route leading to the same destination set out in" Article 2.2. Indeed, in the event a sanitary measure is not based on a risk assessment as required in Articles 5.1 and 5.2, this measure can be presumed, more generally, not to be based on scientific principles or to be maintained without sufficient scientific evidence. We conclude, therefore, that if we find a violation of the more specific Article 5.1 or 5.2 such finding can be presumed to imply a violation of the more general provisions of Article 2.2. We do recognize, at the same time, that given the more general character of Article 2.2 not all violations of Article 2.2 are covered by Articles 5.1 and 5.2.*[89]

[89] Panel Report, para 8.52

138. We agree with the Panel, and, therefore, conclude that, by maintaining an import prohibition on fresh, chilled or frozen ocean-caught Pacific salmon, in violation of Article 5.1, Australia has, by implication, also acted inconsistently with Article 2.2 of the *SPS Agreement*.

Japan – Measures Affecting Agricultural Products ('Japan – Varietals'), 1999

Short summary and commentary

In 1950, Japan prohibited the importation of certain fruits as potential hosts of the codling moth. Japan would lift the import prohibition if the exporting country proposed a quarantine treatment achieving the same level of protection as the import prohibition. The US proposed fumigation with methyl bromide, or a combination of methyl bromide fumigation and cold treatment. In 1987, Japan developed two guidelines on model test procedures to determine the efficacy of the quarantine procedures proposed. The guidelines set forth requirements for the initial lifting of the ban for a given product. Once such a ban was lifted, additional guidelines set forth requirements for the approval of additional varieties of the product in question. The US challenged the measure, claiming that the guidelines requiring varietal testing were inconsistent with Articles 2.2, 5.1, 5.2 and 5.6 (among others) of the SPS Agreement.

The panel found the Japanese measure inconsistent with the SPS Agreement, principally with Articles 2.2 and 5.6. Japan appealed the decision to the Appellate Body.

The Appellate Body upheld the panel's finding that Japan's measure (requiring separate approval for the importation of each variety of fruit) was inconsistent with Article 2.2, which prohibits measures from being maintained if they are not justified by sufficient scientific evidence. Additionally, the Appellate Body confirmed the panel's finding that Japan's measure on varietal testing did not fulfil the requirements of Article 5.7, which allows the adoption of provisional measures where scientific evidence is insufficient. With respect to Article 5.6, the Appellate Body upheld the reasoning of the panel, but overturned its conclusion that Japan had violated Article 5.6, finding that the panel improperly decided a burden of proof related issue.

Examining Article 2.2, the Appellate Body addressed the question of the meaning of the phrase, 'maintained without sufficient scientific evidence'. It concluded that Article 2.2 'requires that there be a rational or objective relationship between the SPS measure and the scientific evidence' (*Japan – Varietals* AB report, paragraph 84) and that the determination of whether such a relationship exists be made 'on a case-by-case basis and . . . depend[s] on the particular circumstances of the case, including the characteristics of the measure at issue and the quality and quantity of scientific evidence' (*Id.*). The Appellate Body also noted that 'maintained without sufficient scientific evidence' had to be considered in the context of Articles 5.1 (requiring a risk assessment), 3.3 (requiring scientific justification to maintain measures resulting in a higher level of SPS protection than would be achieved by international standards) and 5.7 (allowing the adoption of provisional measures in cases of insufficient scientific evidence). In the context of Article 2.2 and 5.7, the Appellate Body pointed out that the Article 5.7 'exemption' was a qualified exemption and that '[a]n overly broad and flexible interpretation of that obligation would render Article 5.7 meaningless' (*Id.* at paragraph 80).

In support of its varietal testing measure, Japan (in contrast to the European Communities in *EC – Hormones*) invoked Article 5.7. The Appellate Body agreed with the panel, holding that Japan had not fulfilled the requirements under Article 5.7. The Appellate Body listed four requirements under Article 5.7 that must be fulfilled cumulatively to adopt and maintain a provisional measure:

- a provisional SPS measure must be imposed only where 'relevant scientific information is insufficient';
- such a provision must be adopted 'on the basis of available pertinent information',
- the Member must 'seek to obtain the additional information necessary for a more objective assessment of risk'; and
- the Member must 'review the measure accordingly within a reasonable period of time' (*Id.* at paragraph 89).

The Appellate Body found that the third and fourth requirements were not fulfilled, and concurred with the panel that there was no need for an analysis of the first two requirements.

The Appellate Body's analysis of Article 5.6 is addressed in detail in Chapter 3: The Necessity Requirement.

Excerpts

Report of the Appellate Body, *Japan – Measures Affecting Agricultural Products*, WT/DS76/AB/R, adopted on 19 March 1999.

V. The *SPS Agreement*

A. Article 2.2 [paras 72–85]

. . .

73. Japan's appeal raises the issue of the meaning of the phrase "maintained without sufficient scientific evidence" in Article 2.2 and, in particular, the meaning of the word "sufficient". The ordinary meaning of "sufficient" is "of a quantity, extent, or scope adequate to a certain purpose or object". From this, we can conclude that "sufficiency" is a relational concept. "Sufficiency" requires the existence of a sufficient or adequate relationship between two elements, *in casu*, between the SPS measure and the scientific evidence.

74. The context of the word "sufficient" or, more generally, the phrase "maintained without sufficient scientific evidence" in Article 2.2, includes Article 5.1 as well as Articles 3.3 and 5.7 of the *SPS Agreement*.

75. Article 5.1 of the *SPS Agreement* requires that an SPS measure be based on a risk assessment. As we stated in our Report in *European Communities – Hormones*:

> *. . . Articles 2.2 and 5.1 should constantly be read together. Article 2.2 informs Article 5.1: the elements that define the basic obligation set out in Article 2.2 impart meaning to Article 5.1.*[25]

[25] *European Communities – Hormones, supra*, footnote 12, para 180.

76. In that Report, we found that:

> *. . . Article 5.1, when contextually read as it should be, in conjunction with and as informed by Article 2.2 of the SPS Agreement, requires that the results of the risk assessment must sufficiently warrant – that is to say, reasonably support – the SPS measure at stake. The requirement that an SPS measure be "based on" a risk assessment is a substantive requirement that there be a rational relationship between the measure and the risk assessment.*[26]

We agree with the Panel that this statement provides guidance for the interpretation of the obligation under Article 2.2 not to maintain an SPS measure without sufficient scientific evidence.[27]

[26] *European Communities – Hormones*, *supra,* footnote 12, para 193.
[27] Panel Report, para 8.29.

77. We also consider it useful in interpreting Article 2.2, and, in particular, the meaning of the word "sufficient", to recall the following statement on Article 5.1 in our Report in *European Communities – Hormones*:

> *Article 5.1 does not require that the risk assessment must necessarily embody only the view of a majority of the relevant scientific community. . . In most cases, responsible and representative governments tend to base their legislative and administrative measures on "mainstream" scientific opinion. In other cases, equally responsible and representative governments may act in good faith on the basis of what, at a given time, may be a divergent opinion coming from qualified and respected sources.*[28]

[28] *European Communities – Hormones· supra,* footnote 12, para 194.

78. Furthermore, in our Report in *Australia – Salmon*, we stated with regard to Article 5.1:

> *. . . it is not sufficient that a risk assessment conclude that there is a possibility of entry, establishment or spread. . . A proper risk assessment . . . must evaluate the "likelihood", i.e., the "probability", of entry, establishment or spread. . .*[29]

We also made it clear in that Report that *some* evaluation of the likelihood is not enough.[30]

[29] *Australia – Salmon, supra,* footnote 13, para 123.
[30] *Australia – Salmon, supra,* footnote 13, para 124.

. . .

80. Finally, it is clear that Article 5.7 of the *SPS Agreement*, to which Article 2.2 explicitly refers, is part of the context of the latter provision and should be considered in the interpretation of the obligation not to maintain an SPS measure without sufficient scientific evidence. Article 5.7 allows Members to adopt provisional SPS measures "[i]n cases where relevant scientific evidence is insufficient" and certain other requirements are fulfilled.[33] Article 5.7 operates as a *qualified* exemption from the obligation under Article 2.2 not to maintain SPS measures without sufficient scientific evidence. An overly broad and flexible interpretation of that obligation would render Article 5.7 meaningless.

[33] See *infra,* para 89.

81. We note Japan's argument that the requirement in Article 2.2 not to maintain an SPS measure without sufficient scientific evidence should be interpreted in light of the precautionary principle. In our Report in *European Communities – Hormones*,[34] we stated that the precautionary principle finds reflection in the preamble, Article 3.3 and Article 5.7 of the *SPS Agreement* and that this principle:

> *. . . has not been written into the* SPS Agreement *as a ground for justifying SPS measures that are otherwise inconsistent with the obligations of Members set out in particular provisions of that Agreement.*

[34] *European Communities – Hormones, supra,* footnote 12, para 124.

82. We do not agree with Japan's proposition that direct application of Article 2.2 of the *SPS Agreement* should be limited to situations in which the scientific evidence is "patently" insufficient, and that the issue raised in this dispute should have been dealt with under Article 5.1 of the *SPS Agreement*. There is nothing in the text of either Articles 2.2 or 5.1, or any other provision of the *SPS Agreement*, that requires or sanctions such limitation of the scope of Article 2.2. On the contrary, Article 2.2 sets out, as the title of Article 2 indicates, "Basic Rights and Obligations". In our Report *in European Communities – Hormones*, we agreed with a statement by the panel in that case that Article 5.1 may be viewed as a specific application of the basic obligations contained in Article 2.2.[35] This statement cannot possibly be interpreted as support for limiting the scope of Article 2.2 "in favour" of Article 5.1. Furthermore, we note that we said the following in our Report in *European Communities – Hormones*:

> *We are, of course, surprised by the fact that the Panel did not begin its analysis of this whole case by focusing on Article 2 that is captioned "Basic Rights and Obligations", an approach that appears logically attractive.*[36]

[35] *European Communities – Hormones, supra,* footnote 12, para 180.
[36] *European Communities – Hormones, supra,* footnote 12, para 250.

. . .

84. In the light of the above considerations based on the text and context of Article 2.2 of the *SPS Agreement*, we agree with the Panel that the obligation in Article 2.2 that an SPS measure not be maintained without sufficient scientific evidence requires that there be a rational or objective relationship between the SPS measure and the scientific evidence.[37] Whether there is a rational relationship between an SPS measure and the scientific evidence is to be determined on a case-by-case basis and will depend upon the particular circumstances of the case, including the characteristics of the measure at issue and the quality and quantity of the scientific evidence.

[37] Panel Report, paras 8.29 and 8.42.

. . .

B. article 5.7 [paras 86–94]

. . .

89. Article 5.7 of the *SPS Agreement* sets out four requirements which must be met in order to adopt and maintain a provisional SPS measure. Pursuant to the first sentence of Article 5.7, a Member may provisionally adopt an SPS measure if this measure is:

(1) imposed in respect of a situation where "relevant scientific information is insufficient"; and
(2) adopted "on the basis of available pertinent information".

Pursuant to the second sentence of Article 5.7, such a provisional measure may not be maintained unless the Member which adopted the measure:

(1) "seek[s] to obtain the additional information necessary for a more objective assessment of risk"; and
(2) "review[s] the . . . measure accordingly within a reasonable period of time".

These four requirements are clearly cumulative in nature and are equally important for the purpose of determining consistency with this provision. Whenever one of these four requirements is not met, the measure at issue is inconsistent with Article 5.7.

. . .

92. As to the question whether the Panel erred in finding that Japan has not acted consistently with the requirements of the second sentence of Article 5.7, we note that the first part of the second sentence stipulates that the Member adopting a provisional SPS measure "shall seek to obtain the additional information necessary for a more objective assessment of risk". Neither Article 5.7 nor any other provision of the *SPS Agreement* sets out explicit prerequisites regarding the additional information to be collected or a specific collection procedure. Furthermore, Article 5.7 does not specify what actual results must be achieved; the obligation is to "seek to obtain" additional information. However, Article 5.7 states that the additional information is to be sought in order to allow the Member to conduct "a more objective assessment of risk". Therefore, the information sought must be germane to conducting such a risk assessment, i.e., the evaluation of the likelihood of entry, establishment or spread of, *in casu*, a pest, according to the SPS measures which might be applied. We note that the Panel found that the information collected by Japan does not "examine the appropriateness" of the SPS measure at issue and does not address the core issue as to whether "varietal characteristics cause a divergency in quarantine efficacy".[40] In the light of this finding, we agree with the Panel that Japan did not seek to obtain the additional information necessary for a more objective risk assessment.

[40] Panel Report, para 8.56.

93. The second part of the second sentence of Article 5.7 stipulates that the Member adopting a provisional SPS measure shall "review the . . . measure accordingly within a reasonable period of time". In our view, what constitutes a "reasonable period of time" has to be established on a case-by-case basis and depends on the specific circumstances of each case, including the difficulty of obtaining the additional information necessary for the review *and* the characteristics of the provisional SPS measure. In the present case, the Panel found that collecting the necessary additional information would be relatively easy.[41] Although the obligation "to review" the varietal testing requirement has only been in existence since 1 January 1995, we agree with the Panel that Japan has not reviewed its varietal testing requirement "within a reasonable period of time".[42]

[41] *Ibid.*

[42] Panel Report, para 8.58.

Report of the Panel, *Japan – Measures Affecting Agricultural Products*, WT/DS76/R, adopted in conjunction with the Appellate Body Report on 19 March 1999

VIII. Findings

. . .

E. Matters not in dispute [paras 8.8–8.13]

. . .

8.13 Finally, with respect to the question of burden of proof under the SPS Agreement, we note that both parties refer to the Appellate Body Report on *EC – Measures Affecting Meat and Meat Products (Hormones)* (hereafter referred to as "*EC – Hormones*").[228] Reviewing this report, we agree with the parties that, in this dispute, it is for the United States to establish a *prima facie* case of inconsistency of the Japanese measure at issue with each of the provisions of the SPS Agreement the United States invokes. Once this is done, it is for Japan to counter or refute the claimed inconsistency. In other words, if "[the United States] adduces sufficient evidence to raise a presumption that what is claimed is true, the burden then shifts to [Japan], who will fail unless it adduces sufficient evidence to rebut the presumption".[229]

[228] Adopted 13 February 1998, WT/DS26/AB/R, stating as follows in paragraph 98: "The initial burden lies on the complaining party, which must establish a *prima facie* case of inconsistency with a particular provision of the *SPS Agreement* on the part of the defending party, or more precisely, of its SPS measure or measures complained about. When that *prima facie* case is made, the burden of proof moves to the defending party, which must in turn counter or refute the claimed inconsistency". See also the Panel Reports on *EC – Hormones,* op. cit., respectively, at paragraphs 8.51 and 8.54.

[229] Appellate Body Report on *United States – Measure Affecting Imports of Woven Wool Shirts and Blouses from India*, adopted 23 May 1997, WT/DS33/AB/R, p14.

. . .

F. Scientific basis and risk assessment (Articles 2.2, 5.1, 5.2 and 5.7) [paras 8.14–8.63]

. . .

8.58 On these grounds, we consider that there is no evidence before us which indicates that Japan sought to "obtain the information necessary for a more objective assessment of risk" and reviewed the varietal testing requirement accordingly "within a reasonable period of time". We consider, therefore, that the United States has established a presumption that Japan did not comply with the requirements in the second sentence of Article 5.7. We also consider that Japan has not been able to rebut this presumption.

8.59 Following the rules on burden of proof we set out earlier,[297] we thus find that even if the varietal testing requirement were considered as a provisional measure adopted in accordance with the first sentence of Article 5.7,[298] Japan has not fulfilled the requirements contained in the second sentence of Article 5.7.

[297] See para 8.13.

[298] See para 8.54.

Japan – Measures Affecting the Importation of Apples ('Japan – Apples'), 2003

Short summary and commentary

Japan – Apples involved a US challenge to Japan's phytosanitary measure restricting the import of American-grown apples to protect Japan from the introduction of 'fire blight', a disease affecting apple, pear, quince, loquat and several garden plants. The measure prohibited imports from orchards in or around which fire blight had been detected, and imposed geographical restrictions, periodic orchard inspections and treatment and transport requirements. Fire blight has spread from North America to other countries in the 200 years since its discovery. However, the risk of introduction and spread of fire blight varies considerably according to the host plant.

Both the panel and the Appellate Body found that Japan's measure:

- violated Article 2.2 of the SPS Agreement, which prohibits measures that are 'maintained without sufficient scientific evidence', except as provided for in Article 5.7;
- did not to comply with the Article 5.7 requirement that in order to justify the *provisional* adoption of a phytosanitary measure, relevant scientific evidence must be insufficient; and
- was not based on a risk assessment within the meaning of Article 5.1.

With regard to Article 2.2, the panel found as a matter of fact that the large amount of scientific evidence available suggested a negligible risk of possible transmission of fire blight through apple fruit. Therefore, the panel concluded that there was not sufficient scientific evidence to support the position that apples are likely to serve as a pathway for the entry, establishment or spread of fire blight to justify Japan's phytosanitary measure. The panel provisionally concluded (i.e. pending a decision on whether or not the measure fell under Article 5.7) that the Japanese measure was maintained without 'sufficient scientific evidence', and therefore violated Article 2.2., a conclusion upheld by the Appellate Body.

In the course of its decision, the panel discussed in detail the meaning of 'sufficient' and 'scientific evidence' within the context of Article 2.2. In analysing 'sufficient', the panel emphasized the need for a '"causal link" between the phytosanitary measure at issue and the scientific evidence establishing a phytosanitary risk'. The panel stated that the 'causal link' is established if, as the Appellate Body held in *Japan – Varietals,* there is 'a rational or objective relationship' between the measure and the relevant scientific evidence (AB Report, paragraph 162, referring panel report, paragraph 8.103). In this context it should be noted, to avoid confusion, that the panel and Appellate Body in *Japan – Apples* refer to the *Japan – Varietals* case as *Japan – Agricultural Products II*). Applying this analysis to the facts in *Japan – Apples,* the panel found that when the negligible risk identified on the basis of scientific evidence was compared to the elements of the challenged phytosanitary measure, the measure was 'on the face of it *disproportionate* to that risk'. As a result, the panel found that the measure at issue was maintained without 'sufficient scientific evidence', in violation of Article 2.2 (*Id.* at paragraph 163, referring panel report, paragraph 8.198). The panel's approach to interpreting Article 2.2 suggests some form of proportionality test between the scientific evidence and the measure taken.

The Appellate Body, while upholding the panel's 'proportionality test' in this context, emphasized that the appropriate approach or methodology to assess whether there is 'a rational or objective relationship' between the measure and the relevant scientific evidence depends on the circumstances of the case. It found that the methodology adopted by the panel was appropriate in this case, but stated that alternative approaches may be appropriate in other cases (AB report, at paragraph 164).

It is unclear how a proportionality test in the context of Article 2.2 relates to prior Appellate Body holdings that a risk assessment does not need to establish any minimum magnitude of risk, and that even a low level of risk can be a valid basis for phytosanitary measures.

Having provisionally found that the Japanese measure in issue violated Article 2.2, the panel next turned to consider Japan's argument that the measure was justified under Article 5.7. The panel noted that, if the measure was justified under Article 5.7, the preliminary finding of inconsistency with Article 2.2 would have to be reversed. However, if the measure was not justified under Article 5.7, the Article 2.2 finding would stand.

The panel restated the four cumulative requirements, identified by the Appellate Body in *Japan – Varietals*, which must be met for a measure to be justified under Article 5.7 (see above). The panel found that Japan's measure did not meet Article 5.7's first requirement for provisional measures because, in the opinion of the panel, the measure was not imposed in respect of a situation where 'relevant scientific evidence is insufficient' (Panel report, paragraphs 8.221–8.222). Based on the panel's findings, the Appellate Body came to the same conclusion.

The panel emphasized that a large amount of scientific evidence existed regarding the risk of fire blight transmission through apples, and concluded that Article 5.7 was not intended to address the type of situation in which a large quantity of high-quality scientific evidence was available. Rather, it found that Article 5.7 was directed to situations where little, or no, reliable evidence was available. Thus, as the first of the cumulative requirements under Article 5.7 was not met (i.e. that there was not, in fact, *insufficient* relevant scientific evidence), the panel found that the Japanese measure was not justified under Article 5.7.

In upholding the panel's reasoning on this point, the Appellate Body analysed 'relevance' and 'insufficiency' within the context of Article 5 as a whole. The Appellate Body concluded that:

> *'relevant scientific evidence' will be 'insufficient' within the meaning of Article 5.7 if the body of scientific evidence does not allow, in quantitative or qualitative terms, the performance of an adequate assessment of risks as required under Article 5.1. Thus . . . the question is whether the relevant evidence, be it 'general' or 'specific', in the Panel's parlance, is sufficient to permit the evaluation of the likelihood of entry, establishment or spread of, in this case, fireblight in Japan* (Japan – Apples *AB report, paragraph 179).*

The Appellate Body continued by stating that Article 5.7 is not 'triggered' by scientific uncertainty, but by the insufficiency of scientific evidence. (AB report, paragraph 184).

Nonetheless, the Appellate Body endorsed the panel's statement that Article 5.7 is intended to address situations where little, or no, reliable evidence is available, holding that this would cover situations where the available scientific evidence is more than minimal, but has not led to reliable or conclusive results (*Id.* at paragraph 185).

The Appellate Body's distinction between 'scientific uncertainty' and 'insufficient scientific evidence', in interpreting Article 5.7, leads to the question of how the precautionary principle as defined in international environmental instruments relates to Article 5.7. These instruments generally use the terms 'lack of full scientific certainty' or 'scientific uncertainty'. As explained earlier, the Appellate Body's *EC – Hormones,* found that the precautionary principle was reflected in Article 5.7, but if scientific uncertainty does not trigger Article 5.7, it is unclear how exactly the precautionary principle is reflected in that article.

The panel assigned the burden of proof to Japan to make a *prima facie* case in support of its position under Article 5.7 (a claim raised by Japan in the alternative). As the allocation of the burden of proof was not challenged on appeal – a point specifically raised by the Appellate Body in its report (AB Report, at paragraph 175 and footnote 316), the Appellate Body did not take position in this respect.

It would seem, however, that the panel's allocation of the burden of proof under Article 5.7 is inconsistent with the approach taken in *Japan – Varietals.* In that case, the panel appeared to take the view that the burden of proof under to Article 5.7 lay on the complaining party, although the issue was not explicitly addressed.

Additionally, the *Japan – Apples* panel also seemed to depart from the approach taken by the Appellate Body with respect to Articles 3.1 and 3.3 of the SPS Agreement (described above).

After considering Article 5.7, the panel addressed the US argument that Japan's measure was not based on a risk assessment as required by Article 5.1. The panel assessed whether or not Japan's risk assessment conformed to SPS requirements, drawing on the Appellate Body reports in *EC – Hormones* and *Australia – Salmon* (discussed above), and found that Japan:

- failed to evaluate the 'probability' of entry, establishment, or spread of fire blight sufficiently 'specifically' in relation to the pathway at issue, in this case apple fruit; and
- failed to evaluate this likelihood 'according to the SPS measures that might be applied', due to the fact that it failed to consider any SPS measure other than the one already in place.

The Appellate Body upheld the panel's decision, noting that while the SPS Agreement did not prescribe a particular methodology for risk assessments, it was still necessary for a risk assessment to satisfy the definition set forth in paragraph 4 of Annex A of the SPS Agreement.

Finally, Japan argued before the Appellate Body that the conformity of a risk assessment with Article 5.1 should be assessed only against information available at the time of the risk assessment and not against subsequently published scientific evidence. The Appellate Body, however, expressed no view on this interesting issue because it found that, in this case, the panel had not considered any information that became available after the completion of the risk assessment in evaluating its consistency with Article 5.1.

A year later, a panel established under Article 21.5 of the DSU found that the measures taken by Japan to comply with the recommendations still did not bring the measures into conformity with the SPS Agreement. In particular, the panel found that the measures were maintained without sufficient scientific evidence, not based on an appropriate risk assessment and were more trade restrictive than necessary to achieve Japan's level of SPS protection, in violation of Articles 2.2, 5.1 and 5.6 of the SPS Agreement. Once again it was recommended that the Dispute Settlement Body request that Japan bring the challenged phytosanitary measure into conformity with its obligations under the SPS Agreement.

Excerpts

Report of the Appellate Body, *Japan – Measures Affecting the Importation of Apples*, WT/DS245/AB/R26, adopted on 10 December 2003.

[NB: The Appellate Body in this report referred to *Japan – Measures Affecting Agricultural Products* by the short title, "*Japan – Agricultural Products II*"; however, the case is more commonly referred to as "*Japan – Varietals*". Except in the following excerpt, this book refers to *Japan – Measures Affecting Agricultural Products* as "*Japan – Varietals*".]

VII. Article 2.2 of the SPS Agreement [paras 143–168]

143. We proceed next to Japan's claim that the Panel erred in finding that the measure is maintained "without sufficient scientific evidence" within the meaning of Article 2.2 of the *SPS Agreement*.

. . .

162. We disagree with Japan. As the Panel correctly noted, the Appellate Body addressed, in *Japan – Agricultural Products II*, the meaning of the term "sufficient", in the context of the expression "sufficient scientific evidence" as found in Article 2.2.[293] The Panel stated that the term "sufficient" implies a "rational or objective relationship"[294] and referred to the Appellate Body's statement there that:

> *Whether there is a rational relationship between an SPS measure and the scientific evidence is to be determined on a case-by-case basis and will depend upon the particular circumstances of the case, including the characteristics of the measure at issue and the quality and quantity of the scientific evidence.*[295]

The Panel did not err in relying on this interpretation of Article 2.2 and in conducting its assessment of the scientific evidence on this basis.

[293] Panel Report, paras 8.101–8.103 and 8.180.
[294] *Ibid.*, paras 8.103 and 8.180.
[295] *Ibid.*, para 8.103, quoting Appellate Body Report, *Japan – Agricultural Products II,* para 84.

163. As we see it, the Panel examined the evidence adduced by the parties and considered the opinions of the experts. It concluded as a matter of fact that it is not likely that apple fruit would serve as a pathway for the entry, establishment or spread of fire blight in Japan.[296] The Panel then contrasted the extent of the risk and the nature of the elements composing the measure, and concluded that the measure was "clearly disproportionate to the risk identified on the basis of the scientific evidence available."[297] For the Panel, such "clear disproportion" implies that a "rational or objective relationship" does not exist between the measure and the relevant scientific evidence, and, therefore, the Panel concluded that the measure is maintained "without sufficient scientific evidence" within the meaning of Article 2.2 of the *SPS*

Agreement.[298] We note that the "clear disproportion" to which the Panel refers, relates to the application in this case of the requirement of a "rational or objective relationship between an SPS measure and the scientific evidence".

[296] Panel Report, para 8.176.
[297] *Ibid.*, para 8.198.
[298] *Ibid.*, para 8.199.

164. We emphasize, following the Appellate Body's statement in *Japan – Agricultural Products II*, that whether a given approach or methodology is appropriate in order to assess whether a measure is maintained "without sufficient scientific evidence", within the meaning of Article 2.2, depends on the "particular circumstances of the case", and must be "determined on a case-by-case basis".[299] Thus, the approach followed by the Panel in this case – disassembling the sequence of events to identify the risk and comparing it with the measure – does not exhaust the range of methodologies available to determine whether a measure is maintained "without sufficient scientific evidence" within the meaning of Article 2.2. Approaches different from that followed by the Panel in this case could also prove appropriate to evaluate whether a measure is maintained without sufficient scientific evidence within the meaning of Article 2.2. Whether or not a particular approach is appropriate will depend on the "particular circumstances of the case".[300] The methodology adopted by the Panel was appropriate to the particular circumstances of the case before it and, therefore, we see no error in the Panel's reliance on it.

[299] Appellate Body Report, para 84.
[300] *Ibid.*

. . .

VIII. Article 5.7 of the *SPS Agreement* [paras 169–188]

169. We turn to the issue whether the Panel erred in finding that Japan's phytosanitary measure was not imposed in respect of a situation where "relevant scientific evidence is insufficient" within the meaning of Article 5.7 of the *SPS Agreement*.

170. Article 2.2 of the *SPS Agreement* stipulates that Members shall not maintain sanitary or phytosanitary measures without sufficient scientific evidence "except as provided for in paragraph 7 of Article 5". Before the Panel, Japan contested that its phytosanitary measure is "maintained with~~out~~ [sic] sufficient scientific evidence" within the meaning of Article 2.2. Japan claimed, in the alternative, that its measure is a provisional measure consistent with Article 5.7.

. . .

172. The Panel found that Japan's measure is not a provisional measure justified under Article 5.7 of the *SPS Agreement* because the measure was not imposed in respect of a situation where "relevant scientific evidence is insufficient".[305]

[305] Panel Report, paras 8.221–8.222.

173. The Panel identified the "phytosanitary question at issue" as the risk of transmission of fire blight through apple fruit.[306] It observed that "scientific studies as well as practical experience have accumulated for the past 200 years"[307] on this question and that, in the course of its analysis under Article 2.2, it had come across an "important amount of relevant evidence".[308] The Panel observed that a large quantity of high quality scientific evidence on the risk of transmission of fire blight through apple fruit had been produced over the years, and noted that the experts had expressed strong and increasing confidence in this evidence. Stating that Article 5.7 was "designed to be invoked in situations where little, or no, reliable evidence was available on the subject matter at issue",[309] the Panel concluded that the measure was not

imposed in respect of a situation where relevant scientific evidence is insufficient.[310] The Panel added that, even if the term "relevant scientific evidence" in Article 5.7 referred to a *specific aspect* of a phytosanitary problem, as Japan claimed, its conclusion would remain the same. The Panel justified its view on the basis of the experts' indication that, not only is there a large volume of general evidence, but there is also a large volume of relevant scientific evidence on the specific scientific questions raised by Japan.[311]

[306] *Ibid.*, para 8.218.
[307] *Ibid.*, para 8.219.
[308] *Ibid.*, para 8.216.
[309] Panel Report, para 8.219.
[310] *Ibid.*
[311] *Ibid.*, para 8.220.

174. Japan challenges the Panel's finding that the measure is not imposed in respect of a situation where "relevant scientific evidence is insufficient" within the meaning of Article 5.7 of the *SPS Agreement*.[312] Moreover, Japan submits that its measure meets all the other requirements of Article 5.7.[313] Accordingly, Japan requests us to reverse the Panel's finding and to complete the analysis regarding the consistency of its measure with the other requirements set out in Article 5.7.[314]

[312] We note that Japan does not challenge the Panel's conclusion that in order to assess whether the measure was imposed in respect of a situation where "relevant scientific evidence is insufficient", the Panel had to consider "not only evidence supporting Japan's position, but also evidence supporting other views". (*Ibid.*, para 8.216.)
[313] Japan's appellant's submission, paras 117–120.
[314] *Ibid.*, paras 120–121.

A. The Insufficiency of Relevant Scientific Evidence

175. As noted above, Japan's claim under Article 5.7 was argued before the Panel in the alternative.[315] Japan relied on Article 5.7 only in the event that the Panel rejected Japan's view that "sufficient scientific evidence" exists to maintain the measure within the meaning of Article 2.2. It is in this particular context that the Panel assigned the burden of proof to Japan to make a *prima facie* case in support of its position under Article 5.7.[316]

[315] Panel Report, para 4.202.
[316] The Panel's assignment of the burden of proof to Japan to make a *prima facie* case of consistency with Article 5.7 is not challenged on appeal.

176. In *Japan – Agricultural Products II*, the Appellate Body stated that Article 5.7 sets out four requirements that must be satisfied in order to adopt and maintain a provisional phytosanitary measure.[317] These requirements are:

(i) the measure is imposed in respect of a situation where "relevant scientific evidence is insufficient";
(ii) the measure is adopted "on the basis of available pertinent information";
(iii) the Member which adopted the measure "seek[s] to obtain the additional information necessary for a more objective assessment of risk"; and
(iv) the Member which adopted the measure "review[s] the . . . measure accordingly within a reasonable period of time".[318]

These four requirements are "clearly cumulative in nature";[319] as the Appellate Body said in *Japan – Agricultural Products II*, "[w]henever *one* of these four requirements is not met, the measure at issue is inconsistent with Article 5.7."[320]

[317] Appellate Body Report, para 89.
[318] Appellate Body Report, *Japan – Agricultural Products II,* para 89. The third and fourth requirements relate to the maintenance of a provisional phytosanitary measure and highlight the provisional nature of measures adopted pursuant to Article 5.7.
[319] Appellate Body Report, *Japan – Agricultural Products II,* para 89.
[320] *Ibid.* (original italics).

177. The Panel's findings address exclusively the first requirement, which the Panel found Japan had not met.[321] The requirements being cumulative, the Panel found it unnecessary to address the other requirements to find an inconsistency with Article 5.7.

[321] Panel Report, para 8.222.

178. Japan's appeal also focuses on the first requirement of Article 5.7. Japan contends that the assessment as to whether relevant scientific evidence is insufficient should not be restricted to evidence "in general" on the phytosanitary question at issue, but should also cover a "particular situation" in relation to a "particular measure" or a "particular risk".[322] Hence, Japan submits that the phrase "[w]here relevant scientific evidence is insufficient", in Article 5.7, "should be interpreted to relate to a particular situation in respect of a particular *measure* to which Article 2.2 applies (or a particular risk), but not to a particular *subject matter* in general, which Article 2.2 does not address".[323] According to Japan, the Panel "erred by interpreting the applicability of [Article 5.7] too narrowly"[324] and too "rigid[ly]".[325]

[322] Japan's appellant's submission, para 102.
[323] *Ibid.* (original italics).
[324] *Ibid.,* para 96.
[325] *Ibid.,* paras 100–101.

179. It seems to us that Japan's reliance on the opposition between evidence "in general" and evidence relating to specific aspects of a particular subject matter is misplaced. The first requirement of Article 5.7 is that there must be insufficient scientific evidence. When a panel reviews a measure claimed by a Member to be provisional, that panel must assess whether "relevant scientific evidence is insufficient". This evaluation must be carried out, not in the abstract, but in the light of a particular inquiry. The notions of "relevance" and "insufficiency" in the introductory phrase of Article 5.7 imply a relationship between the scientific evidence and something else. Reading this introductory phrase in the broader context of Article 5 of the *SPS Agreement*, which is entitled "Assessment of Risk and Determination of the Appropriate Level of Sanitary or Phytosanitary Protection", is instructive in ascertaining the nature of the relationship to be established. Article 5.1 sets out a key discipline under Article 5, namely that "Members shall ensure that their sanitary or phytosanitary measures are based on an assessment . . . of the risks to human, animal or plant life or health".[326] This discipline informs the other provisions of Article 5, including Article 5.7. We note, as well, that the second sentence of Article 5.7 refers to a "more objective assessment of risks". These contextual elements militate in favour of a link or relationship between the first requirement under Article 5.7 and the obligation to perform a risk assessment under Article 5.1: "relevant scientific evidence" will be "insufficient" within the meaning of Article 5.7 if the body of available scientific evidence does not allow, in quantitative or qualitative terms, the performance of an adequate assessment of risks as required under Article 5.1 and as defined in Annex A to the *SPS Agreement*. Thus, the question is not whether there is sufficient evidence of a general nature or whether there is sufficient evidence related to a specific aspect of a phytosanitary problem, or a specific risk. The question is whether the relevant evidence, be it "general" or "specific", in the Panel's parlance, is sufficient to permit the evaluation of the likelihood of entry, establishment or spread of, in this case, fire blight in Japan.

[326] The risk assessment referred to in Article 5.1 is defined in Annex A to the *SPS Agreement.*

180. The Panel found that, with regard to the risk of transmission of fire blight through apples exported from the United States – "normally",[327] mature, symptomless apples – "not only a large quantity but a high quality of scientific evidence has been produced over the years that describes the risk of transmission of fire blight through apple fruit as negligible", and that "this is evidence in which the experts have expressed strong and increasing confidence".[328]

[327] Panel Report, paras 8.87 and 8.141.
[328] *Ibid.*, para 8.219.

. . .

182. These findings of fact by the Panel suggest that the body of available scientific evidence permitted, in quantitative and qualitative terms, the performance of an assessment of risks, as required under Article 5.1 and as defined in Annex A to the *SPS Agreement*, with respect to the risk of transmission of fire blight through apple fruit exported from the United States to Japan. In particular, according to these findings of fact by the Panel, the body of available scientific evidence would allow "[t]he evaluation of the likelihood of entry, establishment or spread"[332] of fire blight in Japan through apples exported from the United States. Accordingly, in the light of the findings of fact made by the Panel, we conclude that, with respect to the risk of transmission of fire blight through apple fruit exported from the United States to Japan ("normally", mature, symptomless apples), the "relevant scientific evidence" is not "insufficient" within the meaning of Article 5.7.

[332] Annex A to the *SPS Agreement,* paragraph 4.

B. Japan's Argument on "Scientific Uncertainty"

183. Japan challenges the Panel's statement that Article 5.7 is intended to address only "situations where little, or no, reliable evidence was available on the subject matter at issue"[333] because this does not provide for situations of "unresolved uncertainty". Japan draws a distinction between "new uncertainty" and "unresolved uncertainty"[334], arguing that both fall within Article 5.7. According to Japan, "new uncertainty" arises when a new risk is identified; Japan argues that the Panel's characterization that "little, or no, reliable evidence was available on the subject matter at issue" is relevant to a situation of "new uncertainty".[335] We understand that Japan defines "unresolved uncertainty" as uncertainty that the scientific evidence is not able to resolve, despite accumulated scientific evidence.[336] According to Japan, the risk of transmission of fire blight through apple fruit relates essentially to a situation of "unresolved uncertainty".[337] Thus, Japan maintains that, despite considerable scientific evidence regarding fire blight, there is still uncertainty about certain aspects of transmission of fire blight. Japan contends that the reasoning of the Panel is tantamount to restricting the applicability of Article 5.7 to situations of "new uncertainty" and to excluding situations of "unresolved uncertainty"; and that, by doing so, the Panel erred in law.[338]

[333] Panel Report, para 8.219.
[334] Japan's appellant's submission, para 101.
[335] *Ibid.*, footnote 76 to para 98.
[336] *Ibid.*, para 98.
[337] Japan's appellant's submission, paras 105–110.
[338] *Ibid.*, para 110.

184. We disagree with Japan. The application of Article 5.7 is triggered not by the existence of scientific uncertainty, but rather by the insufficiency of scientific evidence. The text of Article 5.7 is clear: it refers to "cases where relevant scientific evidence is insufficient", not to "scientific uncertainty". The two concepts are not interchangeable. Therefore, we are unable to endorse Japan's approach of interpreting Article 5.7 through the prism of "scientific uncertainty".

185. We also find no basis for Japan's argument that the Panel's interpretation of Article 5.7 is too narrow for the reason that it excludes cases where the quantity of evidence on a phytosanitary question is "more than little",[339] but the available scientific evidence has not resolved the question. The Panel's statement that Article 5.7 is intended to address "situations where little, or no, reliable evidence was available on the subject matter at issue", refers to the availability of *reliable* evidence. We do not read the Panel's interpretation as excluding cases where the available evidence is more than minimal in quantity, but has not led to reliable or conclusive results. Indeed, the Panel explicitly recognized that such cases fall within the scope of Article 5.7 when it observed, in the Interim Review section of its Report, that under its approach, Article 5.7 would be applicable to a situation where a lot of scientific research has been carried out on a particular issue without yielding reliable evidence.[340]

[339] Panel Report, para 7.8.
[340] *Ibid.,* para 7.9.

. . .

IX. Article 5.1 of the *SPS Agreement* [paras 189–216]

189. We turn now to Japan's allegations of error with respect to Article 5.1 of the *SPS Agreement*. The Panel began its evaluation of the United States' claim under Article 5.1 by noting that both parties effectively identified a document referred to as the "1999 PRA" as the risk assessment to be analyzed in this evaluation . . .[347]

[347] *Ibid.,* para 8.247. In response to questioning at the oral hearing, both participants reaffirmed the focus of the Panel's Article 5.1 analysis to be the 1999 PRA.

190. On the substance of the claim, the Panel noted first that the United States did not contest the fact that the 1999 PRA properly identified fire blight as the disease of concern.[349] The focus of the United States' claim was that (i) the risk assessment did not sufficiently evaluate the likelihood of entry, establishment or spread of fire blight, and (ii) this evaluation was not performed "according to the SPS measures which might be applied".[350]

[349] Panel Report, para 8.252.
[350] *Ibid.,* para 8.253.

191. As to the first element of the claim, the Panel said that a risk assessment must be sufficiently specific to the risk at issue. In this regard, the Panel observed that the 1999 PRA studied several possible hosts of fire blight, including apple fruit. Recognizing that the risk of transmission of fire blight could vary significantly from plant to plant, the Panel found that the risk assessment was not "sufficiently specific" because "the conclusion of the [1999] PRA [did] not purport to relate exclusively to the introduction of the disease through apple fruit, but rather more generally, apparently, through any susceptible host/vector".[351]

[351] *Ibid.,* para 8.271.

192. The Panel similarly found the discussion of possible pathways to have "intertwined" the risk of entry through apple fruit with that of other possible vectors, including vectors considered more likely to be potential sources of contamination than apple fruit.[352] The Panel also determined that those parts of the 1999 PRA that specifically addressed apple fruit, although noting the *possibility* of entry, establishment or spread of fire blight through this vector, did not properly evaluate the *probability* of the occurrence of such events. Finally, the Panel recalled the testimony of certain experts, identifying several steps in the evaluation of the probability of entry that had been "overlooked" by the 1999 PRA.[353] In the light of these shortcomings,

the Panel concluded that Japan's risk assessment did not properly evaluate the likelihood of entry, establishment or spread of fire blight through apple fruit.

[352] *Ibid.*, para 8.278.
[353] *Ibid.*, para 8.279.

193. With respect to the second element of the United States' claim, the Panel observed that a risk assessment, according to Annex A to the *SPS Agreement*, requires an evaluation "according to the sanitary or phytosanitary measures which might be applied". From this language, the Panel determined that a risk assessment must not only consider the particular measure already in place, but also other measures that "*might*" be applied.[354] Because the 1999 PRA did not consider other risk-mitigating measures, the Panel found the risk assessment inadequate for purposes of Article 5.1.

[354] *Ibid.*, para 8.283 (original italics).

194. Reviewing Japan's evaluation of the measure that was already in place, the Panel acknowledged that the 1999 PRA could be considered to have provided "some" evaluation of the likelihood of entry of the disease and possible mitigation through the existing measure. The Panel noted, however, that, in *Australia – Salmon*, the Appellate Body found that "some" evaluation was insufficient for purposes of Article 5.1 and that a comparison between Japan's evaluation and that of the importing Member in that case reveals the 1999 PRA to be "considerably less substantial".[355] The Panel also noted that the 1999 PRA assumes that the individual components of Japan's measure would be applied cumulatively, without consideration as to their individual effectiveness. The Panel found that the required consideration of alternative measures included an obligation to evaluate whether the independent elements needed to be applied cumulatively and to provide an explanation therefor.[356] As a result, the Panel concluded that, in the 1999 PRA, Japan did not sufficiently conduct its evaluation "according to the sanitary or phytosanitary measures which might be applied".

[355] Panel Report, para 8.287.
[356] *Ibid.*, para 8.288.

195. Japan challenges three specific aspects of the Panel's analysis of the 1999 PRA under Article 5.1. First, Japan contests the Panel's finding that the 1999 PRA is inconsistent with the requirements of Article 5.1 because it did not focus its analysis on the risk of fire blight entering through *apple fruit*, in particular. Japan contends that the Panel misinterpreted Article 5.1 and misunderstood the Appellate Body's decision in *EC – Hormones* with respect to the requirement of "specificity" of a risk assessment.[357] Secondly, Japan argues that Article 5.1, contrary to the Panel's interpretation, does not require a consideration of "alternative measures other than [the] existing measures."[358] Finally, Japan claims that its risk assessment should be assessed in the light of evidence available at the time of the assessment, not against evidence that has become available subsequently.[359]

[357] Japan's appellant's submission, paras 127–129.
[358] *Ibid.*, para 133, quoting Panel Report, para 8.285.
[359] Japan's appellant's submission, paras 135–138.

196. We begin our analysis with the text of the relevant provision at issue, Article 5.1 of the *SPS Agreement*:

> *Members shall ensure that their sanitary or phytosanitary measures are based on an assessment, as appropriate to the circumstances, of the risks to human, animal or plant life or health, taking into account risk assessment techniques developed by the relevant international organizations.*

The first clause of paragraph 4 of Annex A to the *SPS Agreement* defines the "risk assessment" for a measure designed to protect plant life or health from risks arising from the entry, establishment or spread of diseases as follows:

> Risk assessment – *The evaluation of the likelihood of entry, establishment or spread of a pest or disease within the territory of an importing Member according to the sanitary or phytosanitary measures which might be applied, and of the associated potential biological and economic consequences. . .*[360]

Based on this definition, the Appellate Body determined in *Australia – Salmon* that:

> *. . . a risk assessment within the meaning of Article 5.1 must:*
>
> *(1)* identify *the diseases whose entry, establishment or spread a Member wants to prevent within its territory, as well as the potential biological and economic consequences associated with the entry, establishment or spread of these diseases;*
> *(2)* evaluate the likelihood *of entry, establishment or spread of these diseases, as well as the associated potential biological and economic consequences; and*
> *(3) evaluate the likelihood of entry, establishment or spread of these diseases* according to the SPS measures which might be applied[361] *(original italics).*

[360] The second clause in paragraph 4 of Annex A to the SPS Agreement addresses risk assessments evaluating the "potential for adverse effects on human or animal health arising from the presence of additives, contaminants, toxins or disease-causing organisms in food, beverages or feedstuffs." As such, the second clause does not define the type of risk assessment relevant to this dispute involving the possibility of transmission of fire blight to plants in Japan (see Appellate Body Report, *Australia – Salmon,* footnote 67 to paragraph 120).
[361] *Ibid.,* para 121.

197. As the Panel noted, the United States does not claim that Japan's risk assessment failed to meet the first of these conditions.[362] The Panel therefore limited its analysis of Japan's risk assessment to the second and third conditions. The Panel found that the 1999 PRA did not constitute a "risk assessment", as that term is defined in the *SPS Agreement*, because it did not satisfy either of those conditions. Japan challenges aspects of the Panel's analysis with respect to both of these conditions. We consider each of these conditions before turning to Japan's argument regarding the evidence that may be relied upon by a panel when evaluating a risk assessment.

[362] Panel Report, para 8.252

A. Evaluating the Likelihood of Entry, Establishment or Spread of Fire Blight

198. Japan challenges first the Panel's finding that the 1999 PRA was not sufficiently specific to constitute a risk assessment under the *SPS Agreement* because it did not evaluate the risk in relation to *apple fruit*, in particular. In *EC – Hormones*, in the context of evaluating whether a measure was "based on" a risk assessment, the Appellate Body examined the specificity of the risk assessment relied upon by the importing Member. In that case, the importing Member had referred to certain scientific studies and articles as the risk assessment underlying its measures. In its Report, the Appellate Body described the panel's finding that these materials:

> *. . . relate[d] to the carcinogenic potential of entire* categories *of hormones, or of the hormones at issue* in general*. . . [They did] not evaluate] the carcinogenic potential of those hormones when used specifically* for growth promotion purposes*. Moreover, they [did] not evaluate the specific potential for carcinogenic effects arising from the presence* in "food", *more*

> *specifically, "meat or meat products" of residues of the hormones in dispute*[363] *(original emphasis).*

[363] Appellate Body Report, *EC – Hormones,* para 199.

199. The panel in *EC – Hormones* concluded, as a result, that the studies cited by the importing Member were insufficient to support the measures at issue. The Appellate Body upheld these findings, stating that, although the studies cited by the importing Member:

> *. . . [did] indeed show the existence of a general risk of cancer . . . they [did] not focus on and [did] not address the particular kind of risk [t]here at stake – the carcinogenic or genotoxic potential of the residues of those hormones found in meat derived from cattle to which the hormones had been administered for growth promotion purposes – as is required by paragraph 4 of Annex A of the* SPS Agreement.[364]

The Appellate Body therefore concluded that the risk assessment was not "sufficiently specific to the case at hand".[365]

[364] *Ibid.,* para 200.
[365] *Ibid.*

200. In this case, the Panel, relying on the Appellate Body's finding in *EC – Hormones*, concluded that the 1999 PRA was not sufficiently specific to constitute a "risk assessment" in accordance with the *SPS Agreement*.[366] The Panel based this conclusion on its finding that, although the 1999 PRA makes determinations as to the entry, establishment and spread of fire blight through a collection of various hosts (including apple fruit), it failed to evaluate the entry, establishment or spread of fire blight through apple fruit as a separate and distinct vector.[367] As the Panel stated in response to Japan's comments during the Interim Review, "Japan evaluated the risks associated with all possible hosts taken together, not sufficiently considering the risks specifically associated with the commodity at issue: US apple fruit exported to Japan."[368]

[366] Panel Report, paras 8.267 and 8.271.
[367] *Ibid.,* paras 8.268–8.271.
[368] *Panel Report,* para 7.14.

201. Japan does not contest the Panel's characterization of the risk assessment as one that did not analyze the risks of apple fruit separately from risks posed by other hosts.[369] Rather, Japan claims that the Panel's reasoning relates to a "matter of methodology", which lies within the discretion of the importing Member.[370] Japan contends that the requirement of "specificity" explained in *EC – Hormones* refers to the specificity of the risk and not to the methodology of the risk assessment.[371]

[369] Japan's appellant's submission, para 128; Japan's response to questioning at the oral hearing.
[370] Japan's appellant's submission, para 127.
[371] *Ibid.,* para 129.

202. We disagree with Japan. Under the *SPS Agreement*, the obligation to conduct an assessment of "risk" is not satisfied merely by a general discussion of the disease sought to be avoided by the imposition of a phytosanitary measure.[372] The Appellate Body found the risk assessment at issue in *EC – Hormones* not to be "sufficiently specific" even though the scientific articles cited by the importing Member had evaluated the "carcinogenic potential of entire *categories* of hormones, or of the hormones at issue *in general*."[373] In order to constitute a "risk assessment" as defined in the *SPS Agreement*, the Appellate

Body concluded, the risk assessment should have reviewed the carcinogenic potential, not of the relevant hormones in general, but of "residues of those hormones found in meat derived from cattle to which the hormones had been administered for growth promotion purposes".[374] Therefore, when discussing the risk to be specified in the risk assessment in *EC – Hormones*, the Appellate Body referred in general to the harm concerned (cancer or genetic damage) *as well as* to the precise agent that may possibly cause the harm (that is, the specific hormones when used in a specific manner and for specific purposes).

[372] Appellate Body Report, para 199 (original italics). In other words, the risk assessment proffered by the importing Member in *EC – Hormones* considered the relationship between the broad *grouping* of hormones that were the subject of the measure and cancer.
[373] *Ibid.,* para 200.
[374] Panel Report, para 8.270.

203. In this case, the Panel found that the conclusion of the 1999 PRA with respect to fire blight was "based on an overall assessment of possible modes of contamination, where apple fruit is only one of the possible hosts/vectors considered."[375] The Panel further found, on the basis of the scientific evidence, that the risk of entry, establishment or spread of the disease varies significantly depending on the vector, or specific host plant, being evaluated.[376] Given that the measure at issue relates to the risk of transmission of fire blight through apple fruit, in an evaluation of whether the risk assessment is "sufficiently specific to the case at hand",[377] the nature of the risk addressed by the measure at issue is a factor to be taken into account. In the light of these considerations, we are of the view that the Panel properly determined that the 1999 PRA "evaluat[ion of] the risks associated with all possible hosts taken together"[378] was not sufficiently specific to qualify as a "risk assessment" under the *SPS Agreement* for the evaluation of the likelihood of entry, establishment or spread of fire blight in Japan through apple fruit.[379]

[375] Panel Report, para 8.270.
[376] *Ibid.,* reads, in relevant part:

> The scientific evidence submitted by both parties leaves no doubt that the risk of introduction and spread of the disease varies considerably according to the host plant, with nursery stock and budding material identified as known sources for the spread of fire blight in some cases.

[377] Appellate Body Report, *EC – Hormones,* para 200.
[378] Panel Report, para 7.14.
[379] We note our understanding that the Panel did not base its finding on, nor make any reference to, whether the *SPS Agreement* requires a risk assessment to analyze the importation of products on a *country-specific* basis. Neither participant in this appeal has asked us to find that the definition of "risk assessment" in the *SPS Agreement* mandates an analysis of risk specific to *each country* of exportation. As a result, we make no findings with respect to whether such a *country-specific* analysis is required in order to satisfy a Member's obligations under Article 5.1 of the *SPS Agreement.*

204. Japan contends that the "methodology" of the risk assessment is not directly addressed by the *SPS Agreement*. In particular, Japan suggests that, whether to analyze the risk on the basis of the particular pest or disease, or on the basis of a particular commodity, is a "matter of methodology" not directly addressed by the *SPS Agreement*.[380] We agree. Contrary to Japan's submission, however, the Panel's reading of *EC – Hormones* does not suggest that there is an obligation to follow any particular methodology for conducting a risk assessment. In other words, even though, in a given context, a risk assessment must consider a specific agent or pathway through which contamination might occur, Members are not precluded from organizing their risk assessments along the lines of the disease or pest at issue, or of the commodity to be imported. Thus, Members are free to consider in their risk analysis multiple agents in relation to one disease, provided that the risk assessment attribute a likelihood of entry, establishment or spread of the disease to each agent specifically. Members are also free to follow the other "methodology" identified by Japan and focus on a particular commodity, subject to the same proviso.

[380] Japan's appellant's submission, paras 127–128.

205. Indeed, the relevant international standards, which, Japan claims, "adopt both methodologies",[381] expressly contemplate examining risk in relation to particular pathways.[382] Those standards call for that specific examination even when the risk analysis is initiated on the basis of the particular pest or disease at issue,[383] as was the 1999 PRA. Therefore, our conclusion that the Panel properly found Japan's risk assessment not to be sufficiently specific, does not limit an importing Member's right to adopt any appropriate "methodology", consistent with the definition of "risk assessment" in paragraph 4 of Annex A to the *SPS Agreement*.

[381] Japan's appellant's submission, para 128, quoting "Guidelines for Pest Risk Analysis", *International Standard for Phytosanitary Measures,* No. 2 (Rome, 1996), Food and Agriculture Organization of the United Nations; Exhibit JPN-30, submitted by Japan to the Panel; and "Pest Risk Analysis for Quarantine Pests", *International Standard for Phytosanitary Measures,* No. 11 (Rome, 2001), Food and Agriculture Organization of the United Nations; Exhibit USA-15, submitted by the United States to the Panel.

[382] For example, the *International Standard for Phytosanitary Measures,* No. 2, states at page 14:

> The final stage of assessment concerns the introduction potential which depends on the pathways from the exporting country to the destination, and the frequency and quantity of pests associated with them. . . . The following is a partial checklist that may be used to estimate the introduction potential divided into those factors which may affect the likelihood of entry and those factors which may affect the likelihood of establishment.

Entry:

- opportunity for contamination of commodities or conveyances by the pest

. . .

Establishment:

- number and frequency of consignments of the commodity

. . .

- intended use of the commodity

. . .

(Exhibit JPN-30, submitted by Japan to the Panel, *supra*, footnote 81.)

Similarly, the *International Standard for Phytosanitary Measures*, No 11, provides at pages 13–14:

> All relevant pathways should be considered. . . Consignments of plants and plant products moving in international trade are the principal pathways of concern and existing patterns of such trade will, to a substantial extent, determine which pathways are relevant. Other pathways such as other types of commodities . . . should be considered where appropriate. . .

. . .

Factors to consider are:

- dispersal mechanisms, including vectors to allow movement from the pathway to a suitable host
- whether the imported commodity is to be sent to a few or many destination points in the [pest risk analysis] area
  . . .
- intended use of the commodity
  . . .

(Exhibit USA-15, submitted by the United States to the Panel, *supra,* footnote 81.)

[383] See *supra,* footnote 82.

. . .

B. Evaluating the Likelihood of Entry, Establishment or Spread of Fire Blight "According to the Sanitary or Phytosanitary Measures Which Might Be Applied"

207. Japan also challenges the Panel's finding that Japan "has not . . . properly evaluated the likelihood of entry 'according to the SPS measures that might be applied'."[384] According to the Panel, the terms in the definition of "risk assessment" set out in paragraph 4 of Annex A to the *SPS Agreement* – more specifically, the phrase "according to the sanitary or phytosanitary measures which might be applied" – suggest that "consideration should be given not just to those specific measures which are currently in application, but at least to a potential range of relevant measures."[385] Japan acknowledged that it did not consider policies other than the measure already applied.[386] However, according to Japan, this "again relates to the matter of methodology", which is left to the discretion of the importing Member.[387]

[384] Panel Report, para 8.285. See Japan's appellant's submission, para 133.
[385] Panel Report, para 8.285.
[386] Japan's response to questioning at the oral hearing.
[387] Japan's appellant's submission, para 133.

208. The definition of "risk assessment" in the *SPS Agreement* requires that the evaluation of the entry, establishment or spread of a disease be conducted "according to the sanitary or phytosanitary measures which might be applied".[388] We agree with the Panel that this phrase "refers to the measures *which might* be applied, not merely to the measures which *are being* applied".[389] The phrase "which might be applied" is used in the conditional tense. In this sense, "might" means: "were or would be or have been able to, were or would be or have been allowed to, were or would perhaps".[390] We understand this phrase to imply that a risk assessment should not be limited to an examination of the measure already in place or favoured by the importing Member. In other words, the evaluation contemplated in paragraph 4 of Annex A to the *SPS Agreement* should not be distorted by preconceived views on the nature and the content of the measure to be taken; nor should it develop into an exercise tailored to and carried out for the purpose of justifying decisions *ex post facto*.

[388] Annex A to the *SPS Agreement,* para 4.
[389] Panel Report, para 8.283 (original italics).
[390] *Shorter Oxford English Dictionary,* 5th ed., W.R. Trumble, A. Stevenson (eds.) (Oxford University Press, 2002), Vol. I, p1725.

209. In this case, the Panel found that the 1999 PRA dealt exclusively with the "'plant quarantine measures against *E. amylovora* concerning US fresh apple fruit', which have been taken by Japan based on the proposal by the US government since 1994".[391] The Panel also found that, in the 1999 PRA, no attempts were made "to assess the 'relative effectiveness' of the various individual requirements applied, [that] the assessment appears to be based on the assumption from the outset that all these measures would apply cumulatively",[392] and that no analysis was made "of their relative effectiveness and whether and why all of them in combination are required in order to reduce or eliminate the possibility of entry, establishment or spread of the disease"[393] Moreover, the Panel referred to "the opinions of Dr Hale and Dr Smith that the 1999 PRA 'appeared to prejudge the outcome of its risk assessment' and that 'it was principally concerned to show that each of the measures already in place was effective in some respect, and concluded that all should therefore be applied'."[394] In our opinion, these findings of fact of the Panel leave no room for doubt that the 1999 PRA was designed and conducted in such a manner that *no* phytosanitary policy other than the regulatory scheme *already in place* was considered. Accordingly, we uphold the Panel's finding, in paragraph 8.285 of the Panel Report, that "Japan has not . . . properly evaluated the likelihood of entry 'according to the SPS measures that might be applied'."

[391] Panel Report, para 8.284, quoting 1999 PRA, § 3–1. Japan confirmed, in response to questioning at the oral hearing, that the 1999 PRA considered no phytosanitary measure other than the one in place.
[392] Panel Report, para 8.288.
[393] *Ibid.*
[394] *Ibid.*, para 8.289 (footnotes omitted).

C. Consideration of Scientific Evidence Arising Subsequent to the Risk Assessment at Issue

210. Finally, Japan argues that "Japan's PRA *was* consistent with Article 5.1 of the SPS Agreement at the time of the analysis, because conformity of a risk assessment with Article 5.1 should be assessed against the information available at the time of the risk assessment."[395] According to Japan, a risk assessment should be evaluated solely against the evidence available at the time of the risk assessment, such that a Member that fulfils the requirement of a risk assessment when adopting a measure is not held to have acted inconsistently with Article 5.1 upon the discovery of subsequently-published scientific evidence.[396]

[395] Japan's appellant's submission, para 135 (original italics).
[396] *Ibid.*, para 135.

. . .

215. As Japan failed to establish that the Panel utilized subsequent scientific evidence in evaluating the risk assessment at issue, it is not necessary for us to express views on the question whether the conformity of a risk assessment with Article 5.1 should be evaluated solely against the scientific evidence available at the time of the risk assessment, to the exclusion of subsequent information. Resolution of such hypothetical claims would not serve "to secure a positive solution" to this dispute.[404]

[404] Article 3.7 of the DSU.

European Communities – Measures Affecting Asbestos and Asbestos Containing Products ('EC – Asbestos'), 2001

Short summary and commentary

EC – Asbestos involved a claim by Canada that a French ban (subject to certain exceptions) on the manufacture, processing, sale and import of asbestos fibres and products containing asbestos fibres violated Article 2 of the TBT Agreement, and Articles III:4 (national treatment), XI (elimination of quantitative restrictions) and XXIII:1(b) (non-violation nullification or impairment) of the GATT. The stated purpose of the ban was to protect the health of workers and consumers from the carcinogenicity of asbestos fibres.

The panel concluded that the French ban was not a technical regulation and therefore did not fall within the scope of the TBT Agreement. It then turned to consider Article III:4 and held that asbestos fibres and products containing asbestos products were 'like' PVA, Cellulose and Glass (PCG) fibres (another type of fibre that could be used for similar purposes as asbestos fibres but did *not* have the associated known health risks) and products containing PCG fibres and, therefore, that the French ban violated Article III:4. In light of this finding the panel did not consider Canada's arguments under Article XI. Instead, it addressed the European Communities' argument that the ban fell within Article XX(b) of the GATT (the exception relating to the protection of human, animal and plant health) and held that the French ban was justified under this provision. Finally, the panel held that Canada had not established that it had suffered non-violation nullification or impairment of a benefit within the meaning of Article XXIII:1(b).

Canada appealed the panel's decision to the Appellate Body. The Appellate Body held that the French ban was a technical regulation under the TBT Agreement. However, in light of the panel's failure to address any of Canada's evidence regarding alleged TBT violations, the Appellate Body determined that it was not competent to decide whether or not the measure violated the TBT Agreement. The Appellate Body then overturned the panel's 'like product' finding under Article III:4, emphasizing that health risks could be taken into account in assessing 'likeness' (*see* Chapter 1: Like Products). Although the Appellate Body concluded that the French measure was not in violation of Article III:4, it went on to examine the panel's finding that the measure was justified under Article XX(b). The Appellate Body confirmed the panel's conclusion that the measure fell within the Article XX(b) exception (*see* Chapter 2: General Exceptions Clauses).

While the *EC – Asbestos* decision principally provided guidance on the concept of 'like products' under Article III:4 and on the 'necessity' requirement under Article XX(b) of the GATT, the Appellate Body also made three comments within its decision, which suggest that science-related jurisprudence under the SPS Agreement is cross-fertilizing jurisprudence under Article XX(b). Perhaps most importantly, the Appellate Body reiterated that Members have the right to determine their own appropriate levels of protection in relation to human, animal and plant health (AB report, paragraph 168). Additionally, in the context of the information required to justify a measure under Article XX(b), the Appellate Body noted that while some evaluation of the health risks was required, the evaluation could be either quantitative or qualitative (*Id.*). Finally, the Appellate Body restated that Members were entitled to rely not only on majority scientific opinions, but also on respected divergent scientific opinions in adopting measures to protect health (*Id.* at paragraph 178).

Excerpts

Report of the Appellate Body, *European Communities – Measures Affecting Asbestos and Asbestos Containing Products*, WT/DS135/AB/R, adopted on 5 April 2001.

VII. Article XX(b) of the GATT 1994 and Article 11 of the DSU

. . .

B. "Necessary' [paras 164–175]

. . .

167. As for Canada's second argument, relating to "quantification" of the risk, we consider that, as with the *SPS Agreement*, there is no requirement under Article XX(b) of the GATT 1994 to *quantify*, as such, the risk to human life or health.[156] A risk may be evaluated either in quantitative or qualitative terms. In this case, contrary to what is suggested by Canada, the Panel assessed the nature and the character of the risk posed by chrysotile cement products. The Panel found, on the basis of the scientific evidence, that "no minimum threshold of level of exposure or duration of exposure has been identified with regard to the risk of pathologies associated with chrysotile, except for asbestosis."[157] The pathologies which the Panel identified as being associated with chrysotile are of a very serious nature, namely lung cancer and

mesothelioma, which is also a form of cancer.[158] Therefore, we do not agree with Canada that the Panel merely relied on the French authorities' "hypotheses" of the risk.

[156] Appellate Body Report, *European Communities – Hormones, supra,* footnote 48, para 186.
[157] Panel Report, para 8.202.
[158] *Ibid.,* para 8.188. See Panel Report, para 5.29, for a description of mesothelioma given by Dr. Henderson.

168. As to Canada's third argument, relating to the level of protection, we note that it is undisputed that WTO Members have the right to determine the level of protection of health that they consider appropriate in a given situation. France has determined, and the Panel accepted,[159] that the chosen level of health protection by France is a "halt" to the spread of asbestos-related health risks. By prohibiting all forms of amphibole asbestos, and by severely restricting the use of chrysotile asbestos, the measure at issue is clearly designed and apt to achieve that level of health protection. Our conclusion is not altered by the fact that PCG fibres might pose a risk to health. The scientific evidence before the Panel indicated that the risk posed by the PCG fibres is, in any case, less than the risk posed by chrysotile asbestos fibres,[160] although that evidence did not indicate that the risk posed by PCG fibres is non-existent. Accordingly, it seems to us perfectly legitimate for a Member to seek to halt the spread of a highly risky product while allowing the use of a less risky product in its place. In short, we do not agree with Canada's third argument.

[159] *Ibid.*, para 8.204.
[160] *Ibid.*, para 8.220.

. . .

C. Article 11 of the DSU [paras 176–181]

. . .

178. In addition, in the context of the *SPS Agreement*, we have said previously, in *European Communities – Hormones*, that "responsible and representative governments may act in good faith on the basis of what, at a given time, may be a *divergent* opinion coming from qualified and respected sources"[126] (emphasis added). In justifying a measure under Article XX(b) of the GATT 1994, a Member may also rely, in good faith, on scientific sources which, at that time, may represent a divergent, but qualified and respected, opinion. A Member is not obliged, in setting health policy, automatically to follow what, at a given time, may constitute a majority scientific opinion. Therefore, a panel need not, necessarily, reach a decision under Article XX(b) of the GATT 1994 on the basis of the "preponderant" weight of the evidence.

[126] Supra*, footnote 48, para 194.*

Report of the Panel, *European Communities – Measures Affecting Asbestos and Asbestos Containing Products*, WT/DS135/R and WT/DS135/R/Add.1, adopted as modified on by the Appellate Body Report on 5 April 2001.

8.221. . . . In the opinion of the Panel, to make the adoption of health measures concerning a definite risk depend upon establishing with certainty a risk already assessed as being lower than that created by chrysotile would have the effect of preventing any possibility of legislating in the field of public health. In fact, it would mean waiting until scientific certainty, which is often difficult to achieve, had been established over the whole of a particular field before public health measures could be implemented.

CHAPTER 7

The Relationship between the TRIPS Agreement and the CBD

BACKGROUND

Introduction

The links between biodiversity and intellectual property, like many of the correlations between trade and environment, are complex and provide potential for both synergy and tension. As one of the main ways that societies decide who has the rights to control and benefit from information, intellectual property rights (IPRs) present both opportunities and obstacles for the conservation of the information encoded in genetic resources.

Intellectual property may act as an economic incentive for conserving biological diversity. The patenting of products and processes based on information encoded in genetic resources has enabled the commercialization of products developed on the basis of that information, including new crop and plant varieties, pharmaceuticals, herbicides and pesticides, as well as new biotechnological products and processes. Consequently, as acknowledgement of the significance of biodiversity has increased in the past decades, so too has its commercial value.

On the other hand, increasing pressure by commercial interests to gain intellectual property over genetic resources can also negatively affect the conservation of biodiversity. While intellectual property rights, as time limited privileges, were designed to balance private and public interests to maximize social welfare, international intellectual property rules have shifted the balance in favour of private interests. Economic and commercial rights such as intellectual property rights may be inadequate to protect the various facets of biodiversity and its numerous stakeholders and may in some cases even impair appropriate protection by other means.

At the international level, these issues have come to play out primarily in the context of two major multilateral agreements: the Convention on Biological Diversity (CBD) and the Agreement on Trade-Related Aspects of Intellectual Property Rights (TRIPS Agreement).

The CBD

The CBD was an important step taken by the international community to secure the conservation and sustainable use of biological diversity. It was agreed upon at the Earth Summit in 1992, came into force in 1993 and is today almost universally ratified (187 parties). The objectives of the CBD are the conservation of biological diversity, the sustainable use of its components, and the fair and equitable sharing of the benefits arising out of the utilization of genetic resources. To ensure that these objectives are met, the agreement establishes certain obligations for its parties, including facilitating access to genetic resources for environmentally sound uses and equitable sharing of the benefits arising from its use, respecting and preserving the biodiversity-related knowledge of indigenous and local communities, and facilitating the transfer of technology relevant to the conservation and sustainable use of biological diversity under fair and most favourable terms.

The implementation of the objectives of the CBD, therefore, relies on the protection and use of knowledge, including knowledge of genetic material, knowledge of technology and knowledge of indigenous and local communities regarding biological diversity (Walker, 2001). Many of the CBD's provisions are thus affected, directly or indirectly, by intellectual property. Accordingly, the CBD requires parties to cooperate to ensure that patents and other intellectual property rights 'are supportive of and do not run counter to' its objectives (Article 16.5 of the CBD).

The TRIPS Agreement

Just six months after the entry into force of the CBD, the TRIPS Agreement was adopted in the framework of the World Trade Organization (WTO). The insertion of intellectual property into the multilateral trading system reflects its growing importance in the international economy and the interest of certain countries in ensuring minimum standards of protection. The TRIPS Agreement brought the protection and enforcement of intellectual property under the WTO, including its binding dispute settlement mechanism. The framework of the TRIPS Agreement thus universalized the levels of intellectual property protection of industrialized countries (Correa, 2000). While the TRIPS Agreement explicitly recognizes, in its objectives and principles, the inherent balance of public and private interest in IPRs, the text has been criticized by many developing countries and much of civil society for not accomplishing such a balance. Moreover, the objectives and principles of the TRIPS Agreement have been treated as best endeavour clauses and have not been implemented.

Articles 7 and 8 of the TRIPS Agreement provide:

> *Article 7 – Objectives*
>
> *The protection and enforcement of intellectual property rights should contribute to the promotion of technological innovation and to the transfer and dissemination of technology, to the mutual advantage of producers and users of technological knowledge and in a manner conducive to social and economic welfare, and to a balance of rights and obligations.*

Article 8 – Principles

1. *Members may, in formulating or amending their laws and regulations, adopt measures necessary to protect public health and nutrition, and promote the public interest in sectors of vital importance to their socio-economic and technological development, provided that such measures are consistent with the provisions of this Agreement.*
2. *Appropriate measures, provided that they are consistent with the provisions of this Agreement, may be needed to prevent the abuse of intellectual property rights by right holders or the resort to practices which unreasonably restrain or adversely affect the international transfer of technology.*

Conflict or synergy?

An essential tenet of the TRIPS Agreement is thus that intellectual property consists of private rights. On the other hand, one of the basic principles of the CBD is that states have sovereign rights over their natural resources, thus subordinating private rights, such as intellectual property rights, to the public objectives of the agreement (CBD Preamble). As a result, there is much debate on the existence of an intrinsic conflict between the objectives of CBD and the objectives of the TRIPS Agreement.

In fact, the issue of the potential synergies and conflicts between the CBD and the TRIPS Agreement has achieved such significance that the Doha Declaration specifically provided for the examination of the relationship between the two agreements (Doha Declaration, paragraph 19). The subsequent discussions, however, as will be described below, have only had limited success, and the issue remains imperative and highly contentious.

Neither the CBD nor the TRIPS Agreement deal specifically with the legal consequences of a possible conflict between the two agreements. In the event that such a conflict was to arise, the rules of treaty conflict of public international law would come into play. Countries and commentators, however, do not concur on which of the rules of treaty conflict would be applicable. For some countries, the provisions of the later agreement (the TRIPS Agreement) prevail to the extent of the incompatibility (*lex posterior derogat lex anterior*). For others, the CBD provisions relating to IPRs in the specific context of conservation of biodiversity are more specialized and thus prevail over provisions in the TRIPS Agreement (*lex specialis derogat lex generalis*).

DISCUSSION OF RELEVANT PROVISIONS

Introduction

Four main clusters of issues have emerged in discussions on the relationship between the TRIPS Agreement and the CBD. These issues include: (i) patentability of life forms; (ii) access to and fair and equitable sharing of benefits arising from the use of genetic resources; (iii) preservation and respect for the knowledge, innovation and practices of indigenous and local communities; and (iv) transfer of technology.

Patenting of life forms (Article 27.3 (b) of the TRIPS Agreement)

Article 27.3(b) allows WTO Members to exclude plants, animals and processes that are essentially biological from patentability, but requires them to grant patents over micro-organisms, non-biological processes and micro-biological processes. These 'patents on life' allowed by the TRIPS Agreement raise a number of ethical, environmental, economic and social concerns.

Article 27.3(b) provides:

> *Members may also exclude from patentability:*
>
> *(b) plants and animals other than micro-organisms, and essentially biological processes for the production of plants or animals other than non-biological and microbiological processes. However, Members shall provide for the protection of plant varieties either by patents or by an effective* sui generis *system or by any combination thereof. The provisions of this subparagraph shall be reviewed four years after the date of entry into force of the WTO Agreement.*

For the conservation of biodiversity, the significance of Article 27 lies in the scope of the exclusions. Whether or not the TRIPS Agreement obliges Members to patent plant parts such as cells or genes, for instance, will directly impact the CBD's provisions on the access and benefit sharing of genetic resources. Moreover, the span of the Article 27.3(b) exclusions will affect the range of patent protection for biotechnology, with the potential risks to biodiversity.

Access to and fair and equitable sharing of benefits arising from the utilization of genetic resources (Article 15 of the CBD)

As mentioned, one of the basic principles of the CBD is that states have sovereign rights over their natural resources. The CBD thus recognizes the right of states to regulate access to resources such as genetic material. Access, where granted, must be on mutually agreed upon terms (Article 15.4), and subject to prior informed consent (Article 15.5). Moreover, the results of any benefit arising from commercial or other use of these resources must be shared on mutually agreed upon terms and as fairly and equitably as possible (Article 15.7).

The prior informed consent (PIC) requirement is a measure to prevent misappropriation and to facilitate fair benefit sharing. It requires collectors of biological resources or of related knowledge to provide sufficient information on the purpose and nature of their work, and to obtain permission from the holders of such resources or knowledge. Nothing in the TRIPS Agreement explicitly prevents the use of such a PIC mechanism, but the mere omission of the requirement within the TRIPS Agreement may effectively impede its utilization as required by the CBD. If the TRIPS Agreement does not recognize the rights of the community or country in which a biological resource originated, it may facilitate the submission of patent applications over such a resource in other countries without the knowledge or assent of the rightful owners. Such misappropriation has been dubbed 'bio-piracy'.

Likewise, the TRIPS Agreement does not require the intellectual property right holder of a biological resource or related knowledge to share the benefits of its use with the communities or countries of its origin. While that omission may leave open the possibility of negotiating benefit-sharing contracts or challenging cases of misappropriation of biological resources and traditional knowledge under the CBD, these are prohibitively complicated and expensive options that may not even ensure adequate protection.

Preservation of and respect for the knowledge, innovations, and practices of indigenous and local communities (Article 8(j) of the CBD)

The CBD provides for the preservation and promotion of traditional knowledge and innovation methods held by indigenous and local communities (Article 8(j)). Many indigenous and other local communities have cultivated and used biological diversity in a sustainable way for thousands of years and the CBD recognizes their skills and techniques as valuable for the conservation of biodiversity. While traditional knowledge also plays a vital role in the commercial development of numerous products and applications, the TRIPS Agreement does not expressly provide for its protection. As a regime developed to protect formal and systematic knowledge, the TRIPS Agreement emphasizes conventional intellectual property instruments and does not provide any specific mechanisms to grant traditional communities control over their knowledge and innovations.

The TRIPS Agreement, however, only sets minimum standards. Members are still able to adopt supplementary requirements, such as certification of origin or the combination of existing intellectual property instruments with benefit-sharing arrangements, which could adequately address the issue of traditional knowledge. Nevertheless, while these methods could result in financial benefits to indigenous and local communities, there is debate over whether they fulfil the CBD's requirement of respect for traditional knowledge, which might demand the recognition of the diverse and complex facets of the subject and the resort to non-intellectual property based solutions.

Transfer of technology (Article 16 of the CBD)

The CBD recognizes that 'both access to and transfer of technology, including biotechnology, among Contracting Parties are essential elements for the attainment of the objectives' of the agreement (Article 16). Although the TRIPS Agreement also refers to the transfer and dissemination of technology 'to the mutual advantage of producers and users of knowledge and in a manner conducive to social and economic welfare' as one of its objectives (Article 7), the implementation of these provisions, as mentioned above, has been limited. Moreover, some studies suggest that, in practice, the strength and scope of the intellectual property rights established in the TRIPS Agreement may be seriously undermining the transfer of technology between developed and developing countries (Commission on Intellectual Property Rights, 2002). As an issue high on the list of priorities of developing countries, technology transfer remains a key topic in the discussion of the relationship between the TRIPS Agreement and the CBD.

STATE OF PLAY AT THE WTO AND THE CBD

Developments at the WTO

Discussions on the relationship between the CBD and the TRIPS Agreements, as well as on the issues involved in that interface, have taken place in both the TRIPS Council and the Committee on Trade and Environment (CTE). Most of the issues raised, however, remain unresolved.

Developments at the TRIPS Council

The discussion of the relationship between the TRIPS Agreement and the CBD in the TRIPS Council has taken place primarily in the context of the review of Article 27.3(b) of the TRIPS Agreement. The views of the different Members on this issue can be loosely grouped in three broad categories. First, a number of developing countries have taken the position that there is inherent conflict between the two instruments. For instance, they point to Article 27.3(b) itself, which, as has been described, could eventually be interpreted in a way inconsistent with the sovereign rights recognized by the CBD. The second view, held by some developed countries, is that there is no conflict between the TRIPS Agreement and the CBD; they are two agreements with differing objects and purposes that do not prevent compliance with one another. Finally, some countries note that while there may be no inherent conflict between the two agreements as a matter of law, their considerable interaction creates a potential for conflict in their implementation.

Specific issues have been contentiously debated. For instance, the intrinsic inconsistency between patentability under the TRIPS Agreement with the CBD, sustained as mentioned by developing countries, has been strongly debated. Other countries feel that because life forms in their natural state do not satisfy patentability criteria in the TRIPS Agreement, as long as these criteria are properly applied, conflicts will be avoided. Moreover, a patent on isolated or modified genetic material would arguably not amount to ownership of the genetic material itself, and thus would not affect the source from which the gene was taken. However, some national legislation does in fact allow the patenting of naturally occurring matter that is 'discovered', and thus has led to patents on life forms found in their natural state.

Another critical issue discussed in the TRIPS Council has been access and benefit sharing. Some proposals have suggested that the TRIPS Agreement be amended to include provisions that, like the CBD, require prior informed consent and benefit sharing for the granting of patents for inventions that use genetic materials. However, the possibility of including such requirements has been rejected by other Members as inconsistent with the TRIPS Agreement, which limits disclosure rules to the determination of whether an invention meets the standards of patentability (Article 29). The alternate suggestion is that access should be regulated through contracts with the competent authorities. However, as has been previously noted, the negotiation of such contracts on equal terms would be extremely difficult.

The TRIPS Council has also discussed the topic of traditional knowledge. Countries have expressed the need for the TRIPS Agreement to provide defensive protection against traditional knowledge being patented and used without the authorization of the indigenous and local communities who developed it, and without proper sharing of the benefits resulting from such patents and use. Still, some countries resist discussions on traditional knowledge in the TRIPS Council, claiming that priority should be given to the work taking place in the World Intellectual Property Organization and other international fora. However, most Members recognize that the importance of the issue demands a systemic solution within the WTO. The issue of positive protection of traditional knowledge, however, has generally been avoided in the TRIPS Council. Many countries feel that although the existing IPR system may provide useful protection in certain situations, it is unable to comprehensively protect traditional knowledge, which is largely collective, intergenerational, and based on the use of trial and error methods over time.

The TRIPS Council's discussions on the transfer of technology as it relates to the CBD have been limited. A more general discussion on implementing the TRIPS Agreement in a way to achieve the transfer and dissemination of technology, though, has taken place in the framework of Articles 7 and 8, mentioned above. Moreover, Article 66.2 requires developed country Members to provide incentives to enterprises and institutions in their territories for the purpose of promoting and encouraging technology transfer to least-developed countries.

Developments at the Committee on Trade and Environment (CTE)

The CTE's mandate includes examining the relationship between the rules of the multilateral trading systems and the trade-related measures adopted by multilateral environmental agreements (MEAs). The CTE has looked at the relationship between the TRIPS agreement and the CBD under agenda item 8, which deals specifically with TRIPS provisions.

As in the TRIPS Council, three broad views have been expressed in the debate: that in at least some areas, the TRIPS Agreement and the CBD are incompatible; that there is no conflict between the two agreements; and that while there are no legal conflicts, potential conflicts exist as long as the implementation of the agreements is not mutually supportive. Specific issues such as traditional knowledge, access to genetic resources and the review of Article 27.3(b) have also been discussed.

Nevertheless, discussions of the TRIPS–CBD relationship in the CTE have always been limited due to the fact that deliberations on the subject were taking place in the TRIPS Council. In fact, several Members expressly recommended that the dialogue on this topic take place in that body, as it deals with intellectual property. After the Doha Declaration, which refers to the TRIPS–CBD relationship within its mandate for the

TRIPS Council, even more countries noted that work toward the clarification of the relationship between the two agreements should not continue in the CTE, which moreover has no negotiating mandate.

Jurisprudence relating to the TRIPS Agreement

No claim regarding the relationship between the TRIPS Agreement and the CBD has reached the WTO dispute settlement procedure. Notwithstanding, WTO jurisprudence has provided some initial guidance as to how such a case would potentially evolve.

An examination of some of the TRIPS-related cases, for instance, evidences the panels' and Appellate Body's approach to the interpretation of the Agreement's provisions, as well as their understanding of the general TRIPS exceptions in the patent and copyright areas. This is significant because the success or failure of any challenge to measures taken to implement CBD obligations (such as national legislation requiring patent holders to share their profits with the providers of genetic resources or providing for licences for the use and development of patented products) will largely depend on the interpretation of the scope of the exceptions within the TRIPS Agreement.

The *Canada – Patent Protection* case was the first time a panel was required to interpret one of the TRIPS Agreement's generally worded exception provisions. The case involved an EC challenge to a Canadian law that created exceptions to the exclusive rights of patent holders. To fall within the scope of Article 30 of the TRIPS Agreement, an exception must be 'limited', cannot 'unreasonably conflict with the normal exploitation of the patent', and cannot 'unreasonably prejudice the legitimate interests of the patent owner, taking account of the legitimate interests of third parties'. The panel stated that the first step in interpreting Article 30 was to examine its object and purpose, that is, to consider the goals and limitations established in Articles 7 and 8 of the TRIPS Agreement.

Despite the reference to Articles 7 and 8, however, the panel did not expressly consider these provisions when examining the meaning of Article 30, relying instead on the context provided by national patent laws and the negotiating history. As a result, some commentators believe that the decision sets a dangerous precedent by ignoring the public–private interest balance in TRIPS Agreement.

In the *US – Copyright* case, the European Communities challenged US limitations on certain exclusive rights in copyright works. The panel thus interpreted Article 13 of the TRIPS Agreement, which establishes limitations and exceptions for copyrights and related rights, but this time made no reference to Articles 7 and 8. A potential trend towards a limited interpretation of exceptions within the TRIPS Agreement raises the question of how this would affect measures taken by Members to implement the CBD, and whether it would increase tensions, rather than synergies, between the two agreements.

The TRIPS Agreement and Public Health

While unrelated to biodiversity, the 2001 Doha Declaration on the TRIPS Agreement and Public Health constitutes an important milestone. The Declaration recognized that the TRIPS Agreement 'does not and should not prevent Members from taking measures to protect public health' and that it 'can and should be interpreted and implemented in a manner supportive of WTO Members' right to protect public health'

(Doha Declaration on the TRIPS Agreement and Public Health, paragraph 4). In this regard, it is an important reaffirmation of existing flexibilities within the TRIPS Agreement and, as such, may provide a valuable precedent for the TRIPS–CBD relationship.

Developments at the CBD

Early on, the CBD recognized the multifaceted and complex correlation between the Convention and the TRIPS Agreement, and emphasized the need to liaise with the WTO in order to clarify tensions and increase synergies. For example, a document presented to the third Conference of the Parties recognized the varying perspectives on intellectual property under the CBD and the TRIPS Agreement. National measures to promote technology transfer under Article 16 of the CBD, for instance, might raise issues under the TRIPS Agreement if owners of proprietary technology were compelled to license technologies on grounds other than those explicitly prescribed. However, the Executive Secretary noted that both the CBD and the TRIPS Agreement allow a significant degree of flexibility in national implementation. Thus, certain legal or policy mechanisms could augment synergies and avoid conflicts between the two agreements. For example, mutually agreed-upon terms for access to genetic resources could allocate intellectual property rights as part of the benefits to be shared among parties to the agreement and such rights could be defined in a manner compatible with the TRIPS Agreement.

Over time, suggestions of the CBD decisions and documents have become even more specific, stressing the need to ensure consistency in the implementation of the two agreements and inviting the WTO to consider how to achieve mutual supportiveness in light of Article 16.5 of the CBD within the review of Article 27.3(b) of the TRIPS Agreement. In June 2002, the CBD presented a document to both the TRIPS Council and the CTE, examining the review of provisions of Article 27.3(b), the relationship between TRIPS and the CBD, and the protection of traditional knowledge and folklore.

SELECTED LITERATURE

Commission on Intellectual Property Rights, (2002) *Integrating Intellectual Property Rights and Development Policy*, CIPR, London

Correa, C. M. (2000) *Intellectual Property Rights, the WTO and Developing Countries: The TRIPS Agreement and Policy Options*, Zed Books and Third World Network, p5

Dutfield, G. (2000) *Intellectual Property Rights, Trade and Biodiversity: Seeds and Plant Varieties*, Earthscan, London

Walker, S. (2001) *The TRIPS Agreement, Sustainable Development and the Public Interest: Discussion Paper*, 32 IUCN and CIEL

SELECTED JURISPRUDENCE UNDER THE TRIPS AGREEMENT

Although no claim regarding the relationship between the TRIPS Agreement and the CBD has reached the WTO dispute settlement procedure, *Canada – Patent Protection and US – Copyright* provide some insight into TRIPS-related disputes at the WTO. Summaries, but not excerpts of these to cases are presented below.

Canada – Patent Protection of Pharmaceutical Products ('Canada – Patent Protection'), 2000

Short summary and commentary

The case involved an EC challenge to provisions of the Canadian patent law that created exceptions to the exclusive rights of patent holders. Canada argued these provisions were 'limited exceptions' to the exclusive rights conferred by a patent within the meaning of Article 30 of the TRIPS Agreement, particularly since the objective and principles of the TRIPS Agreement (Articles 7 and 8 of the TRIPS Agreement) allowed governments the necessary flexibility to adjust patent rights to maintain the desired balance with other important national policies.

One of the challenged exceptions was the regulatory review exception, which allows the use of patented product for the purpose of obtaining the relevant marketing approval. This exception, also known as the 'early working' or 'Bolar' exception, plays a fundamental role in national health policies by allowing the sale of lower priced generics as soon as the pharmaceutical patent expires. The panel upheld Canada's regulatory review exception, stating *inter alia* that 'the goals and the limitations stated in Articles 7 and 8.1', as well as other provisions of the TRIPS Agreement that indicate its object and purposes, 'must obviously be borne in mind' when determining the scope of exceptions to patent rights. The panel did not expressly consider, however, the way in which the objectives of the TRIPS Agreement played out in the circumstances or Canada's claim that general societal interests should be taken into account. No excerpts are thus included regarding this case. Because the panel did not fully consider the principles and objectives of the TRIPS Agreement in the case, some commentators believe that the decision ignores the public–private interest balance in the TRIPS Agreement and thus sets a dangerous precedent.

United States – Section 110(5) of the US Copyright Act ('US – Copyright'), 2000

Short summary and commentary

The European Communities challenged certain exemptions provided in the US Copyright Act as violating the US' obligations under the TRIPS Agreement. In particular, the European Communities alleged that the US measures could not be justified under any express or implied exception or limitation permissible under the TRIPS Agreement.

The US contended that the challenged provisions were permitted under Article 13 of the TRIPS Agreement, which establishes limitations and exceptions for copyrights and related rights. In interpreting these limitations and exceptions, the panel made no reference to the principles and objectives of the TRIPS Agreement, which has been seen by some commentators – when considered alongside the decision in the previous case – as a potential trend towards a limited interpretation of exceptions within the TRIPS Agreement. Nevertheless, the panel clarified that it interpreted Article 13 'in the light of the arguments made by the parties', neither of which had indeed raised the issue of the objective or purposes of the TRIPS Agreement. Consequently, no relevant excerpts from this case are included here.

CHAPTER 8

Participation in WTO Dispute Settlement: The Case of Amicus Briefs

BACKGROUND

Public participation in the creation and implementation of international law

Traditionally, only nation-states have had the right to participate in the creation and implementation of international law. This model led to non-transparent international negotiations and institutions managed behind closed doors. However, in the past decades, civil society and some governments have begun to demand more transparency and wider participation in international affairs. As a consequence, a number of intergovernmental organizations – including various bodies of the United Nations (UN) – international financial institutions and trade regimes are gradually moving toward more open and participatory governance.

In 1992, at the United Nations Conference on Environment and Development (UNCED) in Rio de Janeiro, the world community for the first time officially acknowledged public participation as a critical component to effective development. Principle 10 of the Rio Declaration on Environment and Development explicitly endorses the necessity of access to information, access to decision making, and access to justice in environmental decision making. In the decade since Rio, public involvement in domestic decision making has increased worldwide. Both countries and regions have undertaken initiatives to promote public involvement, as part of the recent emphasis on good governance. In short, people all over the world want to know what their governments are doing and to have a say in those decisions that affect their lives.

The same is increasingly true in the area of international policy making. The public has come to conceive international institutions as functioning under outdated models of governance and diplomacy. Addressing this concern, Agenda 21, a detailed action plan for realizing the Rio Declaration's goals, provides that the 'United Nations system, including international finance and development agencies, and all intergovernmental organizations and forums', should enhance or establish procedures to draw upon the expertise and views of civil society and to provide access to information.

This chapter examines how the emerging issues relating to public participation are addressed in the World Trade Organization's (WTO's) dispute settlement process, with a focus on amicus curiae submissions.

Public participation in the WTO's dispute settlement process

A fundamental characteristic of the WTO's dispute settlement system is that it is limited to claims brought by governments against other governments. Consequently, the submission of amicus briefs is currently the *only* means through which non-Members, including businesses, civil society groups and individuals, can present their views directly to the WTO's dispute settlement tribunals. An amicus brief is a written document, submitted by an amicus curiae (friend of the court), with the permission of the court, tribunal or dispute settlement body hearing the dispute in question. An amicus curiae is not a party to the dispute, but is instead an interested non-party – for example, an individual, corporation or non-governmental organization (NGO) – that wishes to bring certain matters of fact or law to the attention of the court (*see*, e.g. Shelton 1994). The notion that the WTO's dispute settlement tribunals should consider the views of non-Members when resolving disputes is controversial, sparking much debate both among WTO Members and within civil society. While some amicus briefs have involved purely business considerations, a number of briefs have been submitted in so-called 'trade and' cases that have aimed to integrate non-trade issues, such as environmental concerns, into the resolution of trade disputes. Thus, a major element of the trade and environment debate has involved the questions of whether and under what circumstances WTO tribunals should accept and consider amicus briefs.

At the Fourth WTO Ministerial Conference held in Doha in November 2001, Ministers agreed to improve and clarify the Dispute Settlement Understanding (DSU) based on work carried out in an earlier DSU Review and the various proposals submitted by Members. During the DSU negotiations some Members, including the US, advocated a 'more open and transparent process', which would include opening dispute settlement procedures to the public, providing timely access to submissions and reports, and formalizing the treatment of amicus briefs. However, this approach met resistance from many Members, primarily developing countries. Negotiators failed to meet a May 2003 deadline for the conclusion of DSU negotiations and, given the level of resistance, the issue of amicus briefs was dropped prior to the Cancun Ministerial meeting in the Fall of 2003. As of June 2005, the DSU negotiations have not resumed, and it is not clear what will happen when they do.

Although this chapter of the Guide broadly refers to 'amicus briefs', submissions by amicus curiae may take various forms. A submission may be a typical brief, such as the documents sent to the panel and Appellate Body by an environmental NGO in *US – Shrimp/Turtle.* Or, in other cases, such as *Australia – Salmon* and *US – Copyright,* the 'brief' may be simply a letter addressed or copied to the tribunal.

In addition to taking diverse forms, amicus briefs also come from diverse sources. For example, both public interest NGOs and businesses submitted briefs in *EC – Asbestos* and both an individual person and a WTO Member submitted amicus briefs in *EC – Sardines.* In the latter case, the Appellate Body concluded that it could accept and consider amicus submissions from both WTO Members and non-Members. Referring to its previous *US – Lead and Bismuth Carbon Steel* report, the Appellate Body noted that WTO Members had a legal right to participate as parties or third parties in a particular dispute, but that individuals and organizations, which are not Members of the WTO, had no such legal right (*US – Lead and Bismuth Carbon Steel* AB report, paragraphs 40–41). However, both WTO Members and non-Members could submit unsolicited amicus curiae briefs. In those cases, the Appellate Body stated that it had the power, but not the obligation, to accept and consider amicus submissions regardless of the source.

Finally, Amicus Briefs differ in the ways in which they are submitted to the WTO tribunals. Some, like the brief in *US – Shrimp/Turtle 21.5*, are attached as an exhibit to a party or third-party's submission. Others, like the brief submitted in *US – Softwood Lumber*, are stand-alone briefs, independent of party or third-party submissions.

Currently, it is clear that WTO panels and the Appellate Body claim the discretionary authority to accept and consider amicus briefs. (It is important to note that to 'accept' means to receive for the purpose of determining, at a later point, whether the arguments or evidence will actually be taken into account in resolving the dispute; to 'consider' means taking the arguments or evidence into account.) Still, many issues remain unresolved. One such issue relates to the fact that dispute settlement proceedings are closed, and access to documents remains limited, making it more difficult to produce relevant and on-the-point amicus briefs. Access to basic information is fundamental for the drafting of quality briefs.

In addition to the developments regarding amicus briefs, recent developments have taken place that have opened the door to public observation of panel hearings in two cases filed by the European Communities: *US – Continued Suspension of Obligations in the EC – Hormones Dispute*, and *Canada – Continued Suspension of Obligations in the EC – Hormones Dispute*. On 12–15 September 2005, for the first time in GATT/WTO history, the public was invited to observe the panel hearing via closed circuit television in a separate room. However, transparency in WTO proceedings has not been institutionalized. Panel hearings are currently only open at the request of the disputing parties.

DISCUSSION OF RELEVANT WTO PROVISIONS

Article 13 of the DSU: Legal authority of panels to accept and consider amicus briefs

The legal authority of panels to accept and consider amicus briefs came into sharp focus in the *Shrimp/Turtle* cases, where the panel and the Appellate Body authoritatively expounded their readings of Article 13 of the DSU.

The *US – Shrimp/Turtle* panel first declared that parties could *attach* amicus briefs to their own submissions (*US – Shrimp/Turtle I* panel report, paragraph 8). It then proceeded to address the more interesting question of whether panels could accept and consider amicus briefs submitted *independently* of parties' or third parties' submissions. In this context, the panel examined Article 13 of the DSU, which reads:

Right to seek information

1 Each panel shall have the right to seek information and technical advice from any individual or body which it deems appropriate. However, before a panel seeks such information or advice from any individual or body within the jurisdiction of a Member it shall inform the authorities of that Member. A Member should respond promptly and fully to any request by a panel for such information as the panel considers necessary and appropriate. Confidential information which is provided shall not be revealed without formal authorization from the individual, body or authorities of the Member providing the information.

2 Panels may seek information from any relevant source and may consult experts to obtain their opinion on certain aspects of the matter. With respect to a factual issue concerning a scientific or other technical matter raised by a party to a dispute, a panel may request an advisory report in writing from an expert review group. Rules for the establishment of such a group and its procedures are set forth in Appendix 4.

Based on a technical reading of the word 'seek' in Article 13, the panel concluded that it did not have the authority to accept or consider such unsolicited, stand-alone amicus briefs. It reasoned that Article 13 of the DSU allowed a panel to consider only the information it had actually 'sought'. The Appellate Body subsequently overruled the panel's interpretation of Article 13 of the DSU. It found that the authority to 'seek' information could not be equated with a prohibition on accepting unsolicited information and that a panel had 'the discretionary authority either to accept and consider or to reject information and advice submitted to it, *whether requested by a panel or not*' (*US – Shrimp/Turtle* AB report, paragraph 108, emphasis added). Thus, the Appellate Body established the principle that Article 13 of the DSU confers upon panels a broad grant of discretionary authority to accept and consider unsolicited, independently submitted amicus briefs.

However, Article 13 of the DSU governs only WTO panels, not the Appellate Body. Thus, although the Appellate Body in its *US – Shrimp/Turtle* decision indicated that it too had the authority to accept and consider unsolicited stand-alone amicus briefs, it did not address the question of what provision, if any, in the DSU conferred upon it this power.

Article 17.9 of the DSU and Rule 16(1) of the working procedures: Authority of the Appellate Body to accept and consider amicus briefs

In *US – Lead and Bismuth Carbon Steel*, the Appellate Body explained the legal foundation for its discretionary authority to accept and consider amicus briefs. In that case, the Appellate Body pointed to Article 17.9 of the DSU, the provision setting out the development of Appellate Body working procedures, as evidence that it has 'broad authority to adopt procedural rules which do not conflict with any rules and procedures in the DSU or the other covered agreements' (*US – Lead and Bismuth Carbon Steel* AB report, paragraph 39). Consequently, the Appellate Body reasoned, it was free to choose 'whether or not to accept and consider any information [in an amicus brief] that is pertinent and useful in an appeal' (*Id.*).

However, some have questioned whether Article 17.9 of the DSU truly grants the Appellate Body the power it claimed. Article 17.9 of the DSU obligates the Appellate Body to develop working procedures in consultation with the chairman of the Dispute Settlement Body and the Director General, and then to communicate those procedures to the Members for their information. In 1997, the Appellate Body adopted Working Procedures for Appellate Review pursuant to that process. While the Working Procedures do not directly address the amicus question, they set forth a process for answering procedural questions not addressed in the DSU or in the procedures themselves. That relevant process, which is explained in Rule 16(1), provides that 'where a procedural question arises that is not covered by these Rules, a division *may* adopt an appropriate procedure for the purposes of that appeal only, provided that it is not inconsistent with the DSU, the other covered agreements, and these Rules' (emphasis added). Thus, on one hand, Article 17.9 of the DSU creates a process for rule making, which sets limits on the Appellate Body's power and ensures the sovereignty of the Members. But on the other hand, Rule 16(1) of the Working Procedures takes a subset of rules out of that process, in order to ensure procedural efficiency, by granting the Appellate Body the discretion to take necessary housekeeping measures. It could be argued that the two provisions cannot be reconciled and that Article 16(1) must be seen as an abuse of the Appellate Body's Article 17.9 discretion.

In *US – Lead and Bismuth Carbon Steel*, the Appellate Body did not explicitly cite Rule 16(1) as its basis for declaring it had the authority to accept and consider amicus briefs. Some have argued that this failure to explicitly employ the gap-filling procedure set forth in Rule 16(1) leaves the Appellate Body's *US – Lead and Bismuth Carbon Steel* actions on shaky legal ground. However, that argument can be countered by the argument that because Rule 16(1) states that the Appellate Body 'may' adopt an appropriate procedure, it *need* not follow the Rule 16(1) process. Consequently, although the Appellate Body did not employ the Rule 16(1) process in *US – Lead and Bismuth Carbon Steel*, it did not necessarily exceed the bounds of its Article 17.9 discretion.

Subsequent to the *US – Lead and Bismuth Carbon Steel* decision, the Appellate Body did specifically employ Rule 16(1) to govern the submission of amicus briefs. In *EC – Asbestos*, the Appellate Body drafted procedural rules, which were subsequently posted and disseminated via the WTO's website, for potential amicus curiae to follow in requesting leave to file amicus briefs. This action sparked much criticism from WTO Members who believed the Appellate Body had overstepped its authority. Perhaps because of the political controversy caused by *EC – Asbestos*, the Appellate Body has not again attempted to use Rule 16(1) to impose procedural order on the submission of amicus briefs.

AUTHORITY OF PANELS AND THE APPELLATE BODY TO ACCEPT AND CONSIDER LEGAL AND/OR FACTUAL INFORMATION

Although some may still question the exact source and nature of the panels' and the Appellate Body's authority to accept and consider unsolicited, independently submitted amicus briefs, it is clear that the tribunals consider themselves to possess such power. This power, however, is not unbounded, and the scope of this power differs between the panel and the Appellate Body level.

With respect to panels, WTO jurisprudence suggests that they have the authority to accept and consider amicus briefs presenting both legal arguments and factual information. In *Shrimp/Turtle I*, the Appellate Body, in interpreting the DSU, held that a panel had 'ample and extensive authority to undertake and to control the process by which it informs itself both of the *relevant facts* of the dispute and of the *legal norms and principles* applicable to such facts' (*US – Shrimp/Turtle I* AB report, paragraph 106, emphasis added).

Jurisprudence seems to indicate that panels can consider legal arguments made in amicus briefs even if such arguments have not been raised by the parties or third parties to the case. In *EC – Hormones*, while not specifically addressing amicus submissions, the Appellate Body clarified that panels could consider arguments and reasoning not raised by the parties (*EC – Hormones* AB report, paragraph 156). It commented that a panel might not be able 'to carry out an objective assessment of the matter, as mandated by Article 11 of the DSU, if in its reasoning it had to restrict itself solely to arguments presented by the parties to the dispute' (*Id.*).

Although panels seem to have unbounded discretion to consider any *legal* argument raised by amicus curiae, there does appear to be some limit on the ability of panels to accept and consider *factual* evidence and information submitted in amicus briefs: in *Japan – Varietals*, the Appellate Body concluded that panels cannot allow factual evidence submitted by non-parties to 'make the case' for a party (*Japan – Varietals* AB report, paragraph 129). While that case did not specifically address information submitted by amicus curiae, it examined the extent to which panels can rely on information from non-parties – a category which arguably includes amicus curiae. In addition, there are due process and evidentiary difficulties involved in establishing facts asserted by amici curiae.

In contrast to the panels, the Appellate Body appears to possess a more limited power in the amicus context. While the mandate of panels under the DSU is to consider issues of fact and law, Article 17.6 of the DSU limits appeals to issues of law and legal interpretations developed by the panels. Consequently, the Appellate Body can only accept and consider those elements of amicus briefs dealing with legal issues, as opposed to factual ones. The Appellate Body explicitly confirmed this view in *EC – Sardines*, in which it rejected as irrelevant those aspects in the amicus brief that presented factual information (*EC – Sardines* AB report, paragraph 169).

A related and apparently open question is whether the Appellate Body can only consider arguments made in amicus briefs that address legal interpretations and findings made by the panel, or whether it can also consider *new* arguments introduced in amicus briefs at the appellate level. A strict reading of Article 17.6 seems to suggest that the Appellate Body would be restricted to considering only arguments that address the legal interpretations and findings developed by the panel. Nevertheless, the Appellate Body has not issued any rulings explicitly setting forth its position on this issue.

APPLICATION OF DISCRETIONARY POWER

The fact that WTO tribunals *can* accept and consider amicus briefs (subject to constraints related to the legal or factual contents of the briefs) does not mean that they *will* accept and consider such submissions. Instead, the panels' and Appellate Body's authority to accept and consider amicus briefs is discretionary. Furthermore, it is important to keep in mind that the tribunals may exercise that discretionary authority at two stages: first, in deciding whether to accept an amicus brief, and second, in deciding whether to actually consider the submission.

The tribunals are technically at liberty to completely ignore any unsolicited submissions from non-parties or non-third parties. Yet, in practice, WTO tribunals have not completely ignored all such submissions. Thus, it becomes important to attempt to identify what factors might influence a tribunal's choice to reject, accept or consider an amicus brief. When looking at how the WTO tribunals have actually used their discretion in the amicus arena, it becomes apparent that certain considerations, such as the form of submission or due process, might guide the panels' and Appellate Body's decisions regarding how to treat particular amicus submissions.

The brief as an attachment to the party or third-party submission

A prime distinguishing feature between those briefs that are accepted and/or considered by the tribunals and those which are not, is whether the briefs are attached to or incorporated by reference in a party or third-party's submission. WTO panels and the Appellate Body rarely take into account or consider those briefs that are not attached to a party or third-party's submission. On the other hand, seemingly without exception, WTO panels and the Appellate Body allow participants to attach for consideration submissions from amicus curiae. In *US – Shrimp/Turtle I*, for example, the Appellate Body accepted for consideration three briefs from non-governmental organizations that the US had attached to its appellate submission (*US – Shrimp/Turtle I* AB report, paragraph 91). Similarly, in *US – Shrimp/Turtle 21.5*, both the panel and the Appellate Body accepted and considered the attached amicus briefs, but neglected to do the same with briefs that were not attached (*US – Shrimp/Turtle 21.5* panel report, paragraph 5.16; *US – Shrimp/Turtle 21.5* AB report, paragraphs 75–76, 78).

The Appellate Body in *US – Shrimp/Turtle I* explained that by attaching the briefs, those documents became 'at least prima facie an integral part of that participant's submission' (*US – Shrimp/Turtle I* AB report, paragraph 89). Given that parties and third parties have a legal right to have their submissions considered, this characterization of attached briefs as *prima facie* integral parts of a participant's submission suggests that, at least in some cases, such attached briefs *must* be considered. In *US – Shrimp/Turtle I*, however, the US attached the amicus briefs with the caveat that it only supported the arguments made in the briefs to the extent those arguments concurred with the ones made in the US' main submission. In light of that disclaimer, the Appellate Body clarified that it would focus its analysis on those arguments made in the US' main submission (*Id.* at paragraph 91). Thus, to the extent that certain elements were addressed in the US' own submission, the Appellate Body also considered the corresponding elements set forth in the attached amicus briefs. The text of the report, however, does not indicate whether the Appellate Body also considered other arguments independently raised in those amicus briefs.

In *US – Shrimp/Turtle 21.5*, the US attached a brief to its submission without agreeing with all of the legal arguments it set forth. Because the US chose to attach the brief, the panel concluded that the brief was part of the record (*US – Shrimp/Turtle 21.5* panel report, paragraph 5.16). The panel did not specify, however, whether it would consider only those arguments made in the amicus brief which were also endorsed by the US. In the same dispute, the US attached another brief as an exhibit to its submission filed in the appeals process. The Appellate Body, noting that the US adopted the views expressed in the amicus brief only to the extent they were the same as the US view, decided to 'focus [its] attention on the legal arguments in the appellee's submission of the United States' (*US – Shrimp/Turtle 21.5* AB report, paragraph 77).

In sum, the general practice of the WTO tribunals suggests that if a party or third party attaches or incorporates the brief by reference, the tribunals will likely consider that amicus brief. If a brief is not attached, however, WTO jurisprudence indicates that it likely will not be considered. Where briefs are attached, panels and the Appellate Body will tend to 'focus' on the views expressed in the brief only to the extent that parties or third parties have explicitly adopted them.

Due process considerations

A second distinguishing feature between briefs that are accepted and/or considered, and those that are not, is whether or not the briefs' submission raises due process concerns. Taking due process into account, both panels and the Appellate Body have declined to accept or consider briefs that were submitted late in the proceedings, in order to ensure that parties and third parties have sufficient time to adequately respond to amicus briefs. In *EC – Sardines*, the Appellate Body explained that it 'could exercise [its] discretion to reject an amicus curiae brief if, by accepting it, this would interfere with the "fair, prompt and effective resolution of trade disputes"' (*EC – Sardines* AB report, paragraph 167). It noted that '[t]his could arise, for example, if a WTO Member were to seek to submit an amicus curiae brief at a very late stage in the appellate proceedings, with the result that accepting the brief would impose an undue burden on other participants' (*Id.*).

Yet, while timely submission currently seems to be a prerequisite for a brief to be accepted and/or considered, the WTO tribunals have not set forth any specific guidelines as to what constitutes 'timely' submission. In fact, except for the procedures established solely for the *EC – Asbestos* appeal, tribunals have not set forth any specific guidelines governing the submission of amicus briefs in general.

In *EC – Asbestos*, the Appellate Body drafted certain guidelines for would-be amici to follow when requesting leave to file amicus briefs, and subsequently, when submitting such a brief (*EC – Asbestos* AB report, paragraph 51). The guidelines mandated that applicants submit, by a certain date, a request setting forth such elements as the interests, motivations and nature of the amicus curiae, the purpose of the brief, and the way in which the brief could contribute to the settlement of the dispute (*Id.* at paragraph 52). With respect to the actual brief itself, the guidelines stated the document could not be longer than 20 pages, and mandated that it address only those legal issues the applicant had been granted leave to address (*Id.*). In issuing those guidelines, the Appellate Body was likely only attempting to impose some order on the ad hoc process that had governed the acceptance of amicus briefs in previous cases. Nevertheless, the Appellate Body's move drew much criticism from WTO Members, and sparked tension between the legislative and judicial arms of the WTO. After that single controversial experiment in producing procedural rules, WTO tribunals have since refrained from issuing any guidelines governing the submission of amicus briefs.

State-of-play

Overall, the practices of WTO panels and the Appellate Body with respect to amicus briefs seem to try to strike a balance between two opposing forces: on one side the Members hostile to allowing non-Member or non-purely trade concerns to have a voice in WTO dispute settlement, and on the other, civil society groups, businesses and industries affected by the interpretation and application of WTO law, and Members that support them. Attempting to please the latter, tribunals have accepted and considered some submissions. At the same time, trying to please the sceptical Members, tribunals generally only consider amicus briefs attached, in whole or in part, to parties or third-parties' submissions. They also try to ensure that parties and third parties do not feel unduly burdened when having to respond to the contents of amicus briefs.

SELECTED LITERATURE

Appleton, A. (2001) 'Amicus curiae submissions in the carbon steel case: Another rabbit from the Appellate Body's hat?', *Journal of International Economic Law*, vol 3, p697

Charnovitz, S. (1997) 'Two centuries of participation: NGOs and international governance', *Michigan Journal of International Law*, vol 18, p183

Charnovitz, S. (2001) 'International Law Weekend Proceedings: Economic and social actors in the World Trade Organization', *ILSA Journal of International and Comparative Law*, vol 7, p259

Covelli, N. (2003) 'Dispute settlement proceedings after *EC – Sardines*: The rules, jurisprudence, and controversy', *World Trade*, vol 37, p676

Dunnoff, J. (1998) 'The misguided debate over NGO participation in the WTO', *Journal of International Economic Law*, vol 1, p433

Hernández-López, E. (2001) 'Recent trends and perspectives for non-state actor participation in World Trade Organization disputes', *Journal of World Trade*, vol 35, p469

Marceau, G. and Stilwell, M. (2001) 'Practical suggestions for amicus curiae briefs before WTO adjudicating bodies', *Journal of International Economic Law*, vol 4, p155

Shelton, D. (1994) 'The Participation of Nongovernmental Organizations in International Judicial Proceedings', *American Journal of International Law*, vol 88, p611

SELECTED JURISPRUDENCE RELATING TO AMICUS BRIEFS

The following are excerpts of WTO cases that are relevant for a discussion of the acceptance and consideration of amicus briefs. The excerpts are preceded by a short summary and commentary of the corresponding case, aiming to put the excerpts into context. Not all of the cases below specifically involve amicus briefs. Rather, some cases, such as *Japan – Varietals* and *EC – Hormones*, are included in this chapter because they examine the extent to which WTO tribunals can use, or base their decisions on, factual information or legal arguments submitted by non-parties or non-third parties. Because amicus curiae fall within this broader category of non-parties and non-third parties, these cases are arguably relevant to the amicus issue. The cases are listed in chronological order, and the summaries do not encompass all the issues raised in the cases, but focus primarily on issues regarding public participation, and thus are not comprehensive for other purposes.

European Communities – Measures Concerning Meat and Meat Products ('EC – Hormones'), 1998

Short summary and commentary

The US and Canada initiated dispute settlement proceedings to challenge the European Communities' ban on meat and meat products from animals to which certain growth hormones had been administered. One panel was established to resolve Canada's claim, another to resolve the US' claim. Both panels comprised the same members. Each of the panel reports found that the European Communities' ban was inconsistent with several provisions of the SPS Agreement. The European Communities appealed; the US and Canada cross-appealed.

The excerpt in this case does not address WTO tribunals' acceptance or consideration of amicus briefs, per se. Rather, it addresses a claim by the European Communities that the panel had erred by not limiting its analysis to a consideration of solely those arguments advanced by the parties. The Appellate Body disagreed with the European Communities' position; it held that although panels were limited to addressing only those claims specified in their terms of reference, they were not limited with respect to the arguments or reasoning they could use to resolve those claims (AB report, paragraph 156). According to the Appellate Body, any such limit on a panel's ability to make an 'objective assessment of the matter' before it would be inconsistent with the panels' mandate under the DSU (*Id.*).

Thus, although this decision does not address amicus submissions directly, it is relevant to the amicus issue in that it examines the broader question of whether panels can employ legal arguments from non-parties and non-third parties.

Excerpts

Report of the Appellate Body, *European Communities – Measures Concerning Meat and Meat Products (Hormones)*, WT/DS26/AB/R, WT/DS48/AB/R, adopted on 13 February 1998.

IX. Certain Procedures Adopted by the Panel

. . .

C. The Difference Between Legal Claims and Arguments [paras 155–156]

155. Arguing that panels are not entitled to make findings beyond what has been requested by the parties, the European Communities asserts that the Panel has erred by basing the main part of its reasoning on Article 5.5 of the *SPS Agreement* on a claim that the complainants had not made.[144] According to the European Communities, the complainants did not complain of a supposed difference of treatment between artificially added or exogenous natural and synthetic hormones when used for growth promotion purposes compared with the naturally present endogenous hormones in untreated meat and other foods (such as milk, cabbage, broccoli or eggs). The European Communities states that nowhere in the sections of the Panel Reports summarising the arguments on Article 5.5 is there any mention of such an argument.

[144] EC's appellant's submission, paras 495 and 594.

156. Considering that in the request for the establishment of a panel in the proceeding initiated by the United States,[145] as well as in the proceeding started by Canada,[146] both complainants have included a claim that the EC ban is inconsistent with Article 5 of the *SPS Agreement*, we believe that the objection of the European Communities overlooks the distinction between legal claims made by the complainant and arguments used by that complainant to sustain its legal claims. In *India – Patent Protection for Pharmaceutical and Agricultural Chemical Products* we said:

> *We stated . . . in* Brazil – Desiccated Coconut *that all claims must be included in the request for establishment of a panel in order to come within the panel's terms of reference, based on the practice of panels under the GATT 1947 and the Tokyo Round Codes. That past practice required that a claim had to be included in the documents referred to, or contained in, in the terms of reference in order to form part of the "matter" referred to a panel for consideration. Following both this past practice and the provisions of the DSU, in* European Communities – Bananas, *we observed that there is a significant difference between the* claims *identified in the request for the establishment of a panel, which establish the panel's terms of reference under Article 7 of the DSU, and the* arguments *supporting those claims, which are set out and progressively clarified in the first written submissions, the rebuttal submissions and the first and second panel meetings with the parties as a case proceeds*[147] *(footnotes omitted).*

Panels are inhibited from addressing legal claims falling outside their terms of reference. However, nothing in the DSU limits the faculty of a panel freely to use arguments submitted by any of the parties – or to develop its own legal reasoning – to support its own findings and conclusions on the matter under its consideration. A panel might well be unable to carry out an objective assessment of the matter, as mandated by Article 11 of the DSU, if in its reasoning it had to restrict itself solely to arguments presented by the parties to the dispute. Given that in this particular case both complainants claimed that the EC measures were inconsistent with Article 5.5 of the *SPS Agreement*, we conclude that the Panel did not make any legal finding beyond those requested by the parties.

[145] *WT/DS26/6, 25 April 1996.*
[146] *WT/DS48/5, 17 September 1996.*
[147] *Adopted 16 January 1998, WT/DS50/AB/R, para 88.*

United States – Import Prohibition of Certain Shrimp and Shrimp Products ('US – Shrimp/Turtle I'), 1998

Short summary and commentary

This dispute involved a claim brought by Malaysia, Thailand, Pakistan and India, challenging a US import ban on certain shrimp and shrimp products that were harvested in a manner resulting in the incidental deaths of a relatively large number of sea turtles. The US defended its measure on environmental grounds. Several environmental NGOs independently submitted amicus briefs to the panel, presenting both factual information and legal arguments in support of the US' ban.

As a preliminary matter, the NGOs argued that Article 13 of the DSU grants panels the authority to accept and consider such briefs. The panel, however, produced a different reading of Article 13. Article 13, it concluded, allowed a panel only to consider information it had actually 'sought' (Panel report, paragraph 8). Because the amicus briefs submitted to the panel in that case were unsolicited, the panel determined that it did not have the authority to consider the briefs (*Id.*). Nevertheless, the panel concluded that the parties could append or attach the amicus briefs to their own submissions (*Id.*). The US elected to follow this approach (*Id.*).

After the panel concluded that the US ban on certain shrimp and shrimp products was inconsistent with the GATT, the US appealed. As part of its appeal, the US alleged that the panel had erred in concluding it did not have the authority to accept or consider unsolicited, independently submitted information from amici curiae. The Appellate Body agreed with the US; it declared that panels have broad discretionary authority to accept and consider amicus briefs, irrespective of whether those briefs contain solicited or unsolicited information (AB report, paragraphs 104–110). Thus, the Appellate Body's decision overturned the *US – Shrimp/Turtle* panel's interpretation of Article 13, finding that interpretation to have been unnecessarily formal and technical (*Id.* at paragraph 107). The Appellate Body also took care to emphasize that a panels' *discretionary power* to accept and consider amicus briefs had to be distinguished from their *obligation* to consider submissions from actual participants in the case (*Id.* at paragraph 101).

Another issue addressed in this appeal was whether or not the Appellate Body could consider the NGO briefs the US had attached to its submission. Malaysia, Thailand, Pakistan and India argued that the Appellate Body could not take those attached briefs into account. The Appellate Body, however, disagreed and concluded that participants may attach amicus submissions (either in whole or in part) to their own submissions, and that, when they do so, the amicus submissions become *prima facie* integral parts of the participants' submissions (*Id.* at paragraph 89).

Excerpts

Report of the Panel, *United States – Import Prohibition of Certain Shrimp and Shrimp Products*, WT/DS58/R, adopted as modified by WT/DS58/AB/R on 6 November 1998.

VII. FINDINGS

. . .

B. Rulings made by the Panel in the course of the proceedings [paras 7–10]

7. In the course of the proceedings, we received two documents called amicus briefs and submitted by non-governmental organizations. These documents were also communicated by their authors to the parties to the dispute. In a letter dated 1 August 1997 and at the second substantive meeting of the Panel, India, Malaysia, Pakistan and Thailand requested us not to consider the content of these documents in our examination of the matter under dispute. At the second substantive meeting of the Panel, the United States, stressing that the Panel could seek information from any relevant source under Article 13 of the Understanding on Rules and Procedures Governing the Settlement of Disputes (hereafter "DSU"), urged us to avail ourselves of any relevant information in the two documents, as well as in any other similar communications.

8. We had not requested such information as was contained in the above-mentioned documents. We note that, pursuant to Article 13 of the DSU, the initiative to seek information and to select the source of information rests with the Panel. In any other situations, only parties and third parties are allowed to submit information directly to the Panel. Accepting non-requested information from non-governmental sources would be, in our opinion, incompatible with the provisions of the DSU as currently applied. We therefore informed the parties that we did not intend to take these documents into consideration. We observed, moreover, that it was usual practice for parties to put forward whatever documents they considered relevant to support their case and that, if any party in the present dispute wanted to put forward these documents, or parts of them, as part of their own submissions to the Panel, they were free to do so. If this were the case, the other parties would have two weeks to respond to the additional material. We noted that the United States availed themselves of this opportunity by designating Section III of the document submitted by the Center for Marine Conservation and the Center for International Environmental Law as an annex to its second submission to the Panel.

Report of the Appellate Body, *United States – Import Prohibition of Certain Shrimp and Shrimp Products*, WT/DS58/AB/R, adopted on 6 November 1998.

III. Procedural Matters and Rulings

A. Admissibility of the Briefs by Non-governmental Organizations Appended to the United States Appellant's Submission [paras 79–91]

79. The United States attached to its appellant's submission, filed on 23 July 1998, three Exhibits, containing comments by, or "*amicus curiae* briefs" submitted by, the following three groups of non-governmental organizations:[66] 1. the Earth Island Institute; the Humane Society of the United States; and the Sierra Club; 2. the Center for International Environmental Law ("CIEL"); the Centre for Marine Conservation; the Environmental Foundation Ltd.; the Mangrove Action Project; the Philippine Ecological Network; Red Nacional de Accion Ecologica; and Sobrevivencia; and 3. the Worldwide Fund for Nature and the Foundation for International Environmental Law and Development. On 3 August 1998, CIEL et al. submitted a slightly revised version of their brief.

[66] In respect of these Exhibits, the United States stated the following: "Encouraging the use of TEDs in order to promote sea turtle conservation is a matter of great importance to a number of nongovernmental environmental organizations. Three groups of these organizations – each with specialized expertise in conservation of sea turtles and other endangered species – have prepared submissions reflecting their respective independent views with respect to the use of TEDs and other issues. The United States is submitting these materials to the Appellate Body for its information attached hereto as U.S. Appellant Exhibits 1–3" (United States appellant's submission, para 2, footnote 1).

80. In their joint appellees' submission, filed on 7 August 1998, Joint Appellees object to these briefs appended to the appellant's submission, and request that the Appellate Body not consider these briefs. Joint Appellees argue that the appellant's submission, including its three Exhibits, is not in conformity with the stipulation in Article 17.6 of the DSU that an appeal "shall be limited to issues of law covered in the panel report and legal interpretations developed by the panel", nor with Rule 21(2) of the *Working Procedures for Appellate Review*. They ask the Appellate Body to reject as irrelevant the factual assertions made in certain paragraphs of the appellant's submission, as well as the factual information presented in the Exhibits. In their view, because of the incorporation of unauthorized material through the attachment of the Exhibits, the appellant's submission could no longer be considered a "precise statement" as required by Rule 21(2) of the *Working Procedures for Appellate Review*. Rather, a number of the factual and legal assertions contained in the Exhibits go beyond the position taken by the appellant, resulting in confusion concerning the exact nature and linkage between the appeal and the three Exhibits.

81. Joint Appellees state further that the submission of Exhibits that present the views of non-governmental organizations, as opposed to the views of the appellant Member, is not contemplated in, or authorized by, the DSU or the *Working Procedures for Appellate Review*. Such submissions were not in conformity with Article 17.4 of the DSU, nor with Rule 28(1) of the *Working Procedures for Appellate Review*, which vests the discretion to request additional submissions with the Appellate Body. According to Joint Appellees, the decision of the appellant to attach the Exhibits to its submission gives rise both to contradictions and internal inconsistencies, and raises serious procedural and systemic problems. Joint Appellees maintain that by virtue of their incorporation into the appellant's submission, these pleadings are no longer "*amicus curiae* briefs", but instead have become a portion of the appellant's submission, and thus have also become what would appear to be the official United States position.

82. In its appellee's submission, also filed on 7 August 1998, Malaysia similarly urges the Appellate Body to rule that the three Exhibits appended to the United States appellant's submission are inadmissible in this appeal. Malaysia refers to its argument before the Panel that briefs from non-governmental organizations do not fall within Article 13 of the DSU. In addition, according to Malaysia, admission of the Exhibits would not be consonant with Article 17.6 of the DSU, or with Rule 21(2) of the *Working Procedures for Appellate Review*, as the United States appellant's submission and Exhibit 2 contain statements of facts. Moreover, Article 17.4 of the DSU only grants the right to make written and oral submissions to third parties. Articles 11 and 17.12 of the DSU are significant and serve to safeguard the admissibility of evidence before the Appellate Body. In the alternative, in the event the Appellate Body ruled that Exhibits 1–3 of the appellant's submission should be admitted, Malaysia submits rebuttals to each of the Exhibits.

83. On 11 August 1998, we issued a ruling on this preliminary procedural matter addressed to the participants and third participants, as follows:

> *We have decided to accept for consideration, insofar as they may be pertinent, the legal arguments made by the various non-governmental organizations in the three briefs attached as exhibits to the appellant's submission of the United States, as well as the revised version of the brief by the Center for International Environmental Law et al., which was submitted to us on 3 August 1998. The reasons for our ruling will be given in the Appellate Body Report.*

84. In the same ruling, we addressed the following questions to the appellant, the United States:

> *to what extent do you agree with or adopt any one or more of the legal arguments set out in the three briefs prepared by the non-governmental organizations and appended as exhibits to your appellant's submission? In particular, do you adopt the legal arguments stated therein relating to paragraphs (b) and (g) and the chapeau of Article XX of the GATT 1994?*

85. We asked the United States to respond in writing to these questions by 13 August 1998, and offered an opportunity to the appellees and the third participants to respond, by 17 August 1998, to the answer filed by the United States concerning which aspects of these briefs it accepted and endorsed as part of

its appeal as well as to the legal arguments made in the briefs by the non-governmental organizations. We noted at the time that Malaysia had already done the latter in Exhibits 1 through 3 attached to its appellee's submission.

86. On 13 August 1998, the United States replied as follows:

> *The main US submission reflects the views of the United States on the legal issues in this appeal. As explained in our appellant's submission, the three submissions prepared by non-governmental organizations reflect the independent views of those organizations. . . These non-governmental organizations have a great interest, and specialized expertise, in sea turtle conservation and related matters. It is appropriate therefore that the Appellate Body be informed of those organizations' views. The United States is not adopting these views as separate matters to which the Appellate Body must respond.*

The United States agrees with the legal arguments in the submissions of the non-governmental organizations to the extent those arguments concur with the U.S. arguments set out in our main submission . . .

87. On 17 August 1998, Joint Appellees filed a joint response, and Malaysia filed a separate one, to the matters raised in the reply of the United States, as well as in the Exhibits. Without prejudice to their view that the receipt and consideration by the Appellate Body of the briefs of non-governmental organizations attached to the appellant's submission is not authorized by the DSU or the *Working Procedures for Appellate Review*, Joint Appellees responded to certain legal arguments made in the briefs. Malaysia incorporated by reference its rebuttals to the briefs contained in its appellee's submission of 7 August 1998, and made certain additional comments in respect of each of the briefs. Also, on 17 August 1998, Hong Kong, China and Mexico filed statements in respect of the same matters. Hong Kong and China stated that the reply by the United States was unclear and that it was not possible, at that stage, to comment further on the legal arguments. For its part, Mexico stated that if the Appellate Body were to make use of arguments which are outside the terms of Article 17.6 of the DSU and which are not clearly and explicitly attributable to a Member that is a party to the dispute, the Appellate Body would exceed its powers under the DSU.

88. The admissibility of the briefs by certain non-governmental organizations which have been appended to the appellant's submission of the United States is a legal question raised by the appellees. This is a legal issue which does not relate to a finding of law made, or a legal interpretation developed, by the Panel in the Panel Report. For this reason, it has seemed appropriate to us to deal with this issue separately from the issues raised by the appellant and addressed in the succeeding portions of this Appellate Body Report.

89. We consider that the attaching of a brief or other material to the submission of either appellant or appellee, no matter how or where such material may have originated, renders that material at least *prima facie* an integral part of that participant's submission. On the one hand, it is of course for a participant in an appeal to determine for itself what to include in its submission. On the other hand, a participant filing a submission is properly regarded as assuming responsibility for the contents of that submission, including any annexes or other attachments.

90. In the present appeal, the United States has made it clear that its views "on the legal issues in this appeal" are found in "the main U.S. submission". The United States has confirmed its agreement with the legal arguments in the attached submissions of the non-governmental organizations, to the extent that those arguments "concur with the U.S. arguments set out in [its] main submission".

91. We admit, therefore, the briefs attached to the appellant's submission of the United States as part of that appellant's submission. At the same time, considering that the United States has itself accepted the briefs in a tentative and qualified manner only, we focus in the succeeding sections below on the legal arguments in the main U.S. appellant's submission.

. . .

V. Panel Proceedings and Non-requested Information [paras. 99–110]

99. In the course of the proceedings before the Panel, on 28 July 1997, the Panel received a brief from the Center for Marine Conservation ("CMC") and the Center for International Environmental Law ("CIEL"). Both are non-governmental organizations. On 16 September 1997, the Panel received another brief, this time from the World Wide Fund for Nature. The Panel acknowledged receipt of the two briefs, which the non-governmental organizations also sent directly to the parties to this dispute. The complaining parties – India, Malaysia, Pakistan and Thailand – requested the Panel not to consider the contents of the briefs in dealing with the dispute. In contrast, the United States urged the Panel to avail itself of any relevant information in the two briefs, as well as in any other similar communications.[68] The Panel disposed of this matter in the following manner:

> We had not requested such information *as was contained in the above-mentioned documents. We note that, pursuant to Article 13 of the DSU, the initiative to seek information and to select the source of information rests with the Panel. In any other situations, only parties and third parties are allowed to submit information directly to the Panel.* Accepting non-requested information from non-governmental sources would be, in our opinion, incompatible with the provisions of the DSU as currently applied. We therefore informed the parties that we did not intend to take these documents into consideration. *We observed, moreover, that it was usual practice for parties to put forward whatever documents they considered relevant to support their case and that,* if any party in the present dispute wanted to put forward these documents, or parts of them, as part of their own submissions to the Panel, they were free to do so. If this were the case, the other parties would have two weeks to respond to the additional material. *We noted that the United States availed themselves of this opportunity by designating Section III of the document submitted by the Center for Marine Conservation and the Center for International Environmental Law as an annex to its second submission to the Panel*[69] *(emphasis added).*

[68] Panel Report, para 3.129.
[69] Panel Report, para 7.8.

100. We note that the Panel did two things. First, the Panel declared a legal interpretation of certain provisions of the DSU: i.e., that accepting non-requested information from non-governmental sources would be "incompatible with the provisions of the DSU as currently applied". Evidently as a result of this legal interpretation, the Panel announced that it would not take the briefs submitted by non-governmental organizations into consideration. Second, the Panel nevertheless allowed any party to the dispute to put forward the briefs, or any part thereof, as part of its own submissions to the Panel, giving the other party or parties, in such case, two additional weeks to respond to the additional material. The United States appeals from this legal interpretation of the Panel.

101. It may be well to stress at the outset that access to the dispute settlement process of the WTO is limited to Members of the WTO. This access is not available, under the *WTO Agreement* and the covered agreements as they currently exist, to individuals or international organizations, whether governmental or non-governmental. Only Members may become parties to a dispute of which a panel may be seized, and only Members "having a substantial interest in a matter before a panel" may become third parties in the proceedings before that panel.[70] Thus, under the DSU, only Members who are parties to a dispute, or who have notified their interest in becoming third parties in such a dispute to the DSB, have a *legal right* to make submissions to, and have a *legal right* to have those submissions considered by, a panel.[71] Correlatively, a panel is *obliged* in law to accept and give due consideration only to submissions made by the parties and the third parties in a panel proceeding. These are basic legal propositions; they do not, however, dispose of the issue here presented by the appellant's first claim of error. We believe this interpretative issue is most appropriately addressed by examining what a panel is *authorized* to do under the DSU.

[70] See Articles 4, 6, 9 and 10 of the DSU.
[71] Articles 10 and 12, and Appendix 3 of the DSU. We note that Article 17.4 of the DSU limits the right to appeal a panel report to parties to a dispute, and permits third parties which have notified the DSB of their substantial interest in the matter to make written submissions to, and be given an opportunity to be heard by, the Appellate Body.

. . .

103. In *EC Measures Affecting Meat and Meat Products (Hormones)*, we observed that Article 13 of the DSU[72] "enable[s] panels to seek information and advice as they deem appropriate in a particular case."[73] Also, in *Argentina – Measures Affecting Imports of Footwear, Textiles, Apparel and Other Items*, we ruled that:

> *Pursuant to Article 13.2 of the DSU, a panel may seek information from any relevant source and may consult experts to obtain their opinions on certain aspects of the matter at issue.* This is a grant of discretionary authority: a panel is not duty-bound to seek information in each and every case or to consult particular experts under this provision. *We recall our statement in* EC Measures Concerning Meat and Meat Products (Hormones) *that Article 13 of the DSU enables a panel to seek information and technical advice as it deems appropriate in a particular case, and that the DSU leaves "to the sound discretion of a panel the determination of whether the establishment of an expert review group is necessary or appropriate".* Just as a panel has the discretion to determine how to seek expert advice, so also does a panel have the discretion to determine whether to seek information or expert advice at all.

. . .

In this case, we find that the *Panel acted within the bounds of its discretionary authority under Articles 11 and 13 of the DSU in deciding not to seek information from, nor to consult with, the IMF*[74] (emphasis added).

[72] As well as Article 11.2 of the *Agreement on the Application of Sanitary and Phytosanitary Measures*.
[73] Adopted 13 February 1998, WT/DS26/AB/R, WT/DS48/AB/R, para 147.
[74] Adopted 22 April 1998, WT/DS56/AB/R, paras 84–86.

104. The comprehensive nature of the authority of a panel to "seek" information and technical advice from "any individual or body" it may consider appropriate, or from "any relevant source", should be underscored. This authority embraces more than merely the choice and evaluation of the *source* of the information or advice which it may seek. A panel's authority includes the authority to decide *not to seek* such information or advice at all. We consider that a panel also has the authority to *accept or reject* any information or advice which it may have sought and received, or to *make some other appropriate disposition* thereof. It is particularly within the province and the authority of a panel to determine *the need for information and advice* in a specific case, to ascertain the *acceptability* and *relevancy* of information or advice received, and to decide *what weight to ascribe to that information or advice* or to conclude that no weight at all should be given to what has been received.

105. It is also pertinent to note that Article 12.1 of the DSU authorizes panels to depart from, or to add to, the Working Procedures set forth in Appendix 3 of the DSU, and in effect to develop their own Working Procedures, after consultation with the parties to the dispute. Article 12.2 goes on to direct that "[p]anel procedures should provide *sufficient flexibility* so as to *ensure high-quality panel reports* while *not unduly delaying the panel process*" (emphasis added).

106. The thrust of Articles 12 and 13, taken together, is that the DSU accords to a panel established by the DSB, and engaged in a dispute settlement proceeding, ample and extensive authority to undertake and to control the process by which it informs itself both of the relevant facts of the dispute and of the legal norms and principles applicable to such facts. That authority, and the breadth thereof, is indispensably necessary to enable a panel to discharge its duty imposed by Article 11 of the DSU to "make an objective

assessment of the matter before it, including an *objective assessment of the facts of the case* and the *applicability of and conformity with the relevant covered agreements* . . ." (emphasis added).

107. Against this context of broad authority vested in panels by the DSU, and given the object and purpose of the Panel's mandate as revealed in Article 11, we do not believe that the word "seek" must necessarily be read, as apparently the Panel read it, in too literal a manner. That the Panel's reading of the word "seek" is unnecessarily formal and technical in nature becomes clear should an "individual or body" first ask a panel for permission to file a statement or a brief. In such an event, a panel may decline to grant the leave requested. If, in the exercise of its sound discretion in a particular case, a panel concludes *inter alia* that it could do so without "unduly delaying the panel process", it could grant permission to file a statement or a brief, subject to such conditions as it deems appropriate. The exercise of the panel's discretion could, of course, and perhaps should, include consultation with the parties to the dispute. In this kind of situation, for all practical and pertinent purposes, the distinction between "requested" and "non-requested" information vanishes.

108. In the present context, authority to *seek* information is not properly equated with a *prohibition* on accepting information which has been submitted without having been requested by a panel. A panel has the discretionary authority either to accept and consider or to reject information and advice submitted to it, *whether requested by a panel or not*. The fact that a panel may *motu proprio* have initiated the request for information does not, by itself, bind the panel to accept and consider the information which is actually submitted. The amplitude of the authority vested in panels to shape the processes of fact-finding and legal interpretation makes clear that a panel will *not* be deluged, as it were, with non-requested material, *unless that panel allows itself to be so deluged*.

109. Moreover, acceptance and rejection of the information and advice of the kind here submitted to the Panel need not exhaust the universe of possible appropriate dispositions thereof. In the present case, the Panel did not reject the information outright. The Panel suggested instead, that, if any of the parties wanted "to put forward these documents, or parts of them, as part of their own submissions to the Panel, they were free to do so". [75] In response, the United States then designated Section III of the document submitted by CIEL/CMC as an annex to its second submission to the Panel, and the Panel gave the appellees two weeks to respond. We believe that this practical disposition of the matter by the Panel in this dispute may be detached, as it were, from the legal interpretation adopted by the Panel of the word "seek" in Article 13.1 of the DSU. When so viewed, we conclude that the actual disposition of these briefs by the Panel does not constitute either legal error or abuse of its discretionary authority in respect of this matter. The Panel was, accordingly, entitled to treat and take into consideration the section of the brief that the United States appended to its second submission to the Panel, just like any other part of the United States pleading.

[75] Panel Report, para 7.8.

110. We find, and so hold, that the Panel erred in its legal interpretation that accepting non-requested information from non-governmental sources is incompatible with the provisions of the DSU. At the same time, we consider that the Panel acted within the scope of its authority under Articles 12 and 13 of the DSU in allowing any party to the dispute to attach the briefs by non-governmental organizations, or any portion thereof, to its own submissions.

Japan – Measures Affecting Agricultural Products ('Japan – Varietals'), 1999

Short summary and commentary

This case involved a challenge by the US that Japan's method of testing and confirming the efficacy of quarantine treatment for various agricultural products was inconsistent with the SPS Agreement. As part of the appeal, Japan alleged that the panel had erred by basing a finding on information from experts, gathered pursuant to Article 13 of the DSU and Article 11.2 of the SPS Agreement.

This case, like *EC – Hormones* discussed above, did not directly discuss the issue of amicus briefs in the WTO context. Yet, it shed light on the role an amicus brief can play in WTO dispute settlements by addressing the extent to which information from non-parties and non-third parties can be used by panels as a basis upon which to make their findings.

The Appellate Body first explained that panels have significant investigative authority under the DSU and the SPS Agreement (AB report, paragraph 129). However, it then concluded that when making their findings, panels may not *rely* on information from non-party and non-third party sources if in so doing it effectively alters the parties' respective burdens of proof (*Id.* at paragraphs 130–131).

Excerpts

Report of the Appellate Body, *Japan – Measures Affecting Agricultural Products*, WT/DS76/AB/R, adopted on 19 March 1999.

VI. General Issues

A. Burden of Proof [paras 118–131]

. . .

129. Article 13 of the DSU and Article 11.2 of the *SPS Agreement* suggest that panels have a significant investigative authority. However, this authority cannot be used by a panel to rule in favour of a complaining party which has not established a *prima facie* case of inconsistency based on specific legal claims asserted by it. A panel is entitled to seek information and advice from experts and from any other relevant source it chooses, pursuant to Article 13 of the DSU and, in an SPS case, Article 11.2 of the *SPS Agreement*, to help it to understand and evaluate the evidence submitted and the arguments made by the parties, but not to make the case for a complaining party.

130. In the present case, the Panel was correct to seek information and advice from experts to help it to understand and evaluate the evidence submitted and the arguments made by the United States and Japan with regard to the alleged violation of Article 5.6. The Panel erred, however, when it used that expert information and advice as the basis for a finding of inconsistency with Article 5.6, since the United States did not establish a *prima facie* case of inconsistency with Article 5.6 based on claims relating to the "determination of sorption levels". The United States did not even *argue* that the "determination of sorption levels" is an alternative measure which meets the three elements under Article 5.6.

131. We, therefore, reverse the Panel's finding that it can be presumed that the "determination of sorption levels" is an alternative SPS measure which meets the three elements under Article 5.6, because this finding was reached in a manner inconsistent with the rules on burden of proof.

Australia – Measures Affecting Importation of Salmon ('Australia – Salmon 21.5'), 2000

Short summary and commentary

In this case, Canada alleged that Australia had not implemented the decision of the Appellate Body holding that an import ban Australia imposed on untreated fresh, chilled or frozen salmon violated provisions of the GATT and the SPS Agreement. 'Concerned

Fisherman and Processors in South Australia' submitted a letter to the panel, in which they explained a certain factual aspect of one of the claims made by Canada. The panel decided to accept the letter as part of the record of the case (Panel report, paragraph 7.8). In explaining its reasons for doing so, the panel seemed to place particular importance on the fact that the unsolicited material had a 'direct bearing' on Canada's claim (*Id.* at paragraph 7.9). The panel's final report did not clearly indicate whether the information contained in the fishermen's letter ultimately had any influence on the panel's decision making.

Excerpts

Implementation Panel, *Australia – Measures Affecting Importation of Salmon*, WT/DS18/RW, adopted on 17 April 2000.

VII. FINDINGS

. . .

B. Preliminary issues

. . .

3. Non-requested information submitted to the Panel [paras 7.8–7.9]

7.8. On 29 November 1999 the Panel sent the following letter to the parties:

> *On 25 November 1999, the Panel received a letter from "Concerned Fishermen and Processors" in South Australia. The letter addresses the treatment by Australia of, on the one hand, imports of pilchards for use as bait or fish feed and, on the other hand, imports of salmon. The Panel considered the information submitted in the letter as relevant to its procedures and has accepted this information as part of the record. It did so pursuant to the authority granted to the Panel under Article 13.1 of the DSU.*

7.9. We confirm this ruling recalling, in particular, that the information submitted in the letter has a direct bearing on a claim that was already raised by Canada, namely inconsistency in the sense of Article 5.5 of the *SPS Agreement* in the treatment by Australia of pilchard *versus* salmon imports. We refer in this respect to the Appellate Body report on *US – Import Prohibition of Certain Shrimp and Shrimp Products*,[136] in particular, where it states that a panel's

> *"authority to* seek *information is not properly equated with a* prohibition *on accepting information which has been submitted without having been requested by a panel. A panel has the discretionary authority either to accept and consider or to reject information and advice submitted to it,* whether requested by a panel or not. . . *The amplitude of the authority vested in panels to shape the processes of fact-finding and legal interpretation makes clear that a panel will* not *be deluged, as it were, with non-requested material,* unless that panel allows itself to be so deluged.*"*[137]

[136] Adopted 6 November 1998, WT/DS58/AB/R, paras 99–110.
[137] *Ibid.*, para 108, emphasis in the original.

United States – Imposition of Countervailing Duties on Certain Hot-Rolled Lead and Bismuth Carbon Steel Products Originating in the United Kingdom ('US – Lead and Bismuth Carbon Steel'), 2000

Short summary and commentary

This case involved a claim by the European Communities that the US had imposed countervailing duties on certain steel products in violation of provisions of the GATT and the Subsidies and Countervailing Measures (SCM) Agreement. An industry association, the American Iron and Steel Institute, submitted an amicus brief to the panel. However, sensitivity to due process concerns led the panel to refrain from accepting that brief (Panel report, paragraph 6.3). The panel clarified that it could have eased those due process concerns by delaying the panel proceedings to give the parties time to respond to the contents of the brief (*Id.*). Nevertheless, the panel determined (for unspecified reasons) that such a delay would not be justified in this case (*Id.*). The finding was not appealed.

However, the US appealed the panel's findings that it had violated the SCM Agreement. Two industry associations sought to support the US' position by submitting amicus briefs to the Appellate Body. Those submissions provided the Appellate Body with an opportunity to address unanswered questions regarding the acceptance and consideration of amicus briefs. While the Appellate Body decision in *US – Shrimp/ Turtle* set forth the legal foundations for WTO *panels'* discretionary authority to accept and consider independently submitted amicus briefs, it had not yet recognized the *Appellate Body's* authority to do the same. The *US – Lead and Bismuth Carbon Steel* decision explained why the DSU also enables the Appellate Body to accept and consider such briefs.

The Appellate Body first noted that nothing in the DSU explicitly conferred upon the Appellate Body any authority to accept information from non-parties or non-third parties (AB report, paragraph 39). It subsequently looked to Article 17.9 of the DSU and found that that provision granted the Appellate Body broad authority to adopt its own procedures, provided that those procedures did not violate the DSU or other covered agreements (*Id.*). Based on this finding, the Appellate Body concluded that, as long as it acted consistently with provisions in the DSU and other covered agreements, it had the legal authority to decide whether or not to accept or consider any information pertinent and useful in an appeal (*Id.*). If, therefore, amicus briefs were pertinent and useful in an appeal, it would be within the Appellate Body's power to accept and consider those documents. In this particular case, the Appellate Body, however, did not find it necessary to 'take the two amicus curiae briefs filed into account' in rendering its decision (*Id.* at paragraph 42).

Excerpts

Report of the Panel, *United States – Imposition of Countervailing Duties on Certain Hot-Rolled Lead and Bismuth Carbon Steel Products Originating in the United Kingdom*, WT/DS138/R, adopted as amended by WT/DS138/AB/R on 7 June 2000.

VI. Findings

. . .

B. Preliminary ISSUES

. . .

2. Amicus curiae brief [para 6.3]

6.3. On 19 July 1999, we received a brief from the American Iron and Steel Institute ("AISI") dated 13 July 1999. We note that, by virtue of Articles 12 and 13 of the DSU, a panel "has the discretionary authority either to accept and consider or to reject information and advice submitted to it, *whether requested by a panel or not*."[38] While we clearly have the discretionary authority to accept the AISI brief, in this case we chose not to exercise that authority as a result of the late submission of the brief. The AISI brief was submitted after the deadline for the parties' rebuttal submissions, and after the second substantive meeting of the Panel with the parties. Thus, the parties have not, as a practical matter, had adequate opportunity to present their comments on the AISI brief to the Panel. In our view, the inability of the parties to present their comments on the AISI brief raises serious due process concerns as to the extent to which the Panel could consider the brief. In accordance with Article 12.1 of the DSU, the Panel may have been entitled to delay its proceedings in order to provide the parties sufficient opportunity to comment on the AISI brief. However, we considered that any such delay could not be justified in the present case.

[38] *United States – Import Prohibition of Certain Shrimp and Shrimp Products* (hereinafter "*United States – Shrimp*"), WT/DS58/AB/R, adopted 6 November 1998, para 108.

Report of the Appellate Body, *United States – Imposition of Countervailing Duties on Certain Hot-Rolled Lead and Bismuth Carbon Steel Products Originating in the United Kingdom*, WT/DS138/AB/R, adopted on 7 June 2000.

III. Preliminary Procedural Matter [paras. 36–42]

36. On 7 February 2000, we received two documents, described in their respective covering letters as "*amicus curiae* briefs", from the American Iron and Steel Institute and the Specialty Steel Industry of North America. On 15 February 2000, the European Communities filed a letter arguing that these *amicus curiae* briefs are "inadmissible" in appellate review proceedings, and stating that it did not intend to respond to the content of the briefs. According to the European Communities, the basis for allowing *amicus curiae* briefs in *panel* proceedings is Article 13 of the DSU, as explained in *United States – Shrimp*. The European Communities notes that Article 13 of the DSU does not apply to the Appellate Body and that, in any case, that provision is limited to *factual information and technical advice*, and would not include *legal arguments or legal interpretations* received from non-Members. Furthermore, the European Communities contends, neither the DSU nor the *Working Procedures* allow *amicus curiae* briefs to be admitted in Appellate Body proceedings, given that Article 17.4 of the DSU and Rules 21, 22 and 28.1 of the *Working Procedures* confine participation in an appeal to participants and third participants, and that Article 17.10 of the DSU provides for the confidentiality of Appellate Body proceedings.

37. By letter dated 16 February 2000, we requested the *United States*, Brazil and Mexico to comment on the arguments made by the European Communities. Brazil, in its third participant's submission, and Mexico, in a letter submitted to us on 23 February 2000, agree with the European Communities that the Appellate Body does not have the authority to accept *amicus curiae* briefs. Brazil and Mexico emphasize that neither the DSU nor the *Working Procedures* allow the Appellate Body to receive factual information of the type contemplated by Article 13 of the DSU, much less briefs from private entities containing legal arguments on the issues under appeal. Mexico underlines that the DSU and the *Working Procedures*

limit participation in appellate proceedings and require those proceedings to be confidential. Brazil adds that Members of the WTO and, in particular, parties and third parties to a dispute, are uniquely qualified to make legal arguments regarding panel reports and the parameters of WTO obligations.

38. In a letter submitted on 23 February 2000, the United States argues that the Appellate Body has the authority to accept *amicus curiae* briefs, and urges us to accept the briefs submitted by the steel industry associations. The United States notes that, in *United States – Shrimp*, the Appellate Body explained that the authority to accept unsolicited submissions is found in the DSU's grant to a panel of "*ample and extensive authority to undertake and to control the process* by which it informs itself both of the relevant facts of the dispute and of the legal norms and principles applicable to such facts".[32] To the United States, it is clear that the Appellate Body also has such authority, given that Article 17.9 of the DSU authorizes the Appellate Body to draw up its own working procedures, and Rule 16(1) of the *Working Procedures* authorizes a division to create an appropriate procedure when a question arises that is not covered by the *Working Procedures*. The United States does not agree that acceptance of an unsolicited *amicus curiae* brief would compromise the confidentiality of the Appellate Body proceedings, or give greater rights to a non-WTO Member than to WTO Members that are not participants or third participants in an appeal.

[32] Appellate Body Report, *supra,* footnote 29, para 106 (emphasis added by the United States).

39. In considering this matter, we first note that nothing in the DSU or the *Working Procedures* specifically provides that the Appellate Body may accept and consider submissions or briefs from sources other than the participants and third participants in an appeal. On the other hand, neither the DSU nor the *Working Procedures* explicitly prohibit acceptance or consideration of such briefs. However, Article 17.9 of the DSU provides:

> *Working procedures shall be drawn up by the Appellate Body in consultation with the Chairman of the DSB and the Director-General, and communicated to the Members for their information.*

This provision makes clear that the Appellate Body has broad authority to adopt procedural rules which do not conflict with any rules and procedures in the DSU or the covered agreements.[33] Therefore, we are of the opinion that as long as we act consistently with the provisions of the DSU and the covered agreements, we have the legal authority to decide whether or not to accept and consider any information that we believe is pertinent and useful in an appeal.

[33] In addition, Rule 16(1) of the *Working Procedures* allows a division hearing an appeal to develop an appropriate procedure in certain specified circumstances where a procedural question arises that is not covered by the *Working Procedures*.

40. We wish to emphasize that in the dispute settlement system of the WTO, the DSU envisages *participation* in panel or Appellate Body proceedings, as a matter of legal right, *only* by parties and third parties to a dispute. And, under the DSU, *only* Members of the WTO have a legal right to participate as parties or third parties in a particular dispute. As we clearly stated in *United States – Shrimp*:

> *. . . access to the dispute settlement process of the WTO is limited to Members of the WTO. This access is not available, under the WTO Agreement and the covered agreements as they currently exist, to individuals or international organizations, whether governmental or non-governmental.*[34]

We also highlighted in *United States – Shrimp* that:

> *. . . under the DSU, only Members who are parties to a dispute, or who have notified their interest in becoming third parties in such a dispute to the DSB, have a* legal right *to make submissions to, and have a* legal right *to have those submissions considered by, a panel. Correlatively, a panel is* obliged *in law to accept and give due consideration only to submissions made by the parties and the third parties in a panel proceeding.*[35]

[34] Appellate Body Report, *supra*, footnote 29, para 101.
[35] Appellate Body Report, *supra,* footnote 29, para 101.

41. Individuals and organizations, which are not Members of the WTO, have no legal *right* to make submissions to or to be heard by the Appellate Body. The Appellate Body has no legal *duty* to accept or consider unsolicited *amicus curiae* briefs submitted by individuals or organizations, not Members of the WTO. The Appellate Body has a legal *duty* to accept and consider *only* submissions from WTO Members which are parties or third parties in a particular dispute.[36]

[36] Article 17.4 of the DSU and Rules 21 to 24 of the *Working Procedures.*

42. We are of the opinion that we have the legal authority under the DSU to accept and consider *amicus curiae* briefs in an appeal in which we find it pertinent and useful to do so. In this appeal, we have not found it necessary to take the two *amicus curiae* briefs filed into account in rendering our decision.

United States – Section 110(5) of the US Copyright Act ('US – Copyright'), 2000

Short summary and commentary

This case, in which the European Communities claimed that a US law was inconsistent with the TRIPS Agreement, illustrates the different forms that an 'amicus' submission might take. A law firm representing the American Society of Composers, Authors, and Publishers sent a letter to the US Trade Representative (USTR), copying the panel on that letter. Thus, the letter was neither a typical amicus brief, nor was it addressed directly to the panel.

Both the parties and the panel noted that the letter essentially duplicated the factual information already submitted by the participants (Panel report, paragraph 6.8). The panel also noted that it was only copied on the letter (*Id.*). For these reasons, while not rejecting the letter, the panel ultimately chose not to rely on it in conducting its analysis and in its findings (*Id.*).

The panel also refrained from explicitly addressing whether, as argued by the European Communities, panels can only accept non-participant submissions related to factual information and analysis, and do not have the authority to consider legal arguments not raised by the parties. While the *US – Section 110(5)* panel did not resolve this issue, it is worth recalling *EC – Hormones*, described above. In *EC – Hormones*, the Appellate Body explained that the DSU does not obligate panels to 'restrict [themselves] solely to arguments presented by the parties to the dispute' (*EC – Hormones* AB report, paragraph 156). However, the Appellate Body issued that statement in the context of its discussion of whether or not panels could develop their own legal reasoning when resolving disputes. Thus, *EC – Hormones* did not specifically address the question of whether and to what extent the DSU limits panels' ability to use arguments submitted by amici curiae.

Excerpts

Report of the Panel, *United States – Section 110(5) of the US Copyright Act*, WT/DS/160, adopted on 27 July 2000.

VI. Findings

. . .

B. Preliminary issue [paras 6.3–6.8]

6.3. Before examining the substantive aspects of this dispute, we discuss how we treat a letter from a law firm representing ASCAP to the United States Trade Representative ("USTR") that was copied to the Panel.

6.4. By means of a letter addressed to a law firm representing ASCAP, dated 16 November 1999,[22] the USTR requested information from ASCAP in relation to questions 9–11 from the Panel to the United States, which were reproduced in the letter.[23] The law firm responded to the USTR by means of a letter, dated 3 December 1999. It forwarded a copy of this letter, addressed to the USTR, to the Panel. The Panel received this copy on 8 December 1999. The Panel transmitted the letter forthwith to both parties and invited them to comment on it if they so wished.

[22] Exhibit US-19(a). The USTR sent a similar letter to the BMI, Exhibit US-19(b).
[23] These questions and the responses thereto by the United States are contained in Attachment 2.3 to the report.

6.5. In a letter, dated 17 December 1999, the United States, *inter alia*, distanced itself from positions expressed in the letter by that law firm and emphasized that in its view the letter was of little probative value for the Panel because it provided essentially no factual data not already provided by either party. But the United States supported in general the right of private parties to make their views known to WTO dispute settlement panels.

6.6. In a letter, dated 12 January 2000, the European Communities stated that it did not have substantive comments on the letter. While it appreciated ASCAP's contribution to the current case, it considered that the letter did not add any new element to what was already submitted by the parties. In referring to the Appellate Body's interpretation of Article 13 of the DSU in its report in the dispute *United States – Import Prohibition of Certain Shrimp and Shrimp Products*,[24] the European Communities also remarked that in its view, the authority of panels is limited to the consideration of factual information and technical advice by individuals or bodies alien to the dispute and thus did not include the possibility for a panel to accept any legal argument or legal interpretation from such individuals or bodies.

[24] Appellate Body Report on *United States – Import Prohibition on Certain Shrimp and Shrimp Products,* adopted on 6 November 1998, WT/DS58/AB/R, paragraphs 99–110.

6.7. According to Article 13 of the DSU, "each panel shall have the right to seek information and technical advice from any individual or body which it deems appropriate. . ." We recall that in the *United States – Shrimps* dispute the Appellate Body reasoned with respect to the treatment by a panel of non-requested information that the "authority to seek information is not properly equated with a prohibition on accepting information which has been submitted without having been requested by a panel. A panel has discretionary authority to accept and consider or to reject information and advice submitted to it, whether requested by a panel or not. . ."[25]

[25] Appellate Body Report on *United States – Shrimps,* op. cit., paragraph 108.

6.8. In this dispute, we do not reject outright the information contained in the letter from the law firm representing ASCAP to the USTR that was copied to the Panel. We recall that the Appellate Body has recognized the authority of panels to accept non-requested information. However, we share the view expressed by the parties that this letter essentially duplicates information already submitted by the parties. We also emphasize that the letter was not addressed to the Panel but only copied to it. Therefore, while not having refused the copy of the letter, we have not relied on it for our reasoning or our findings.

European Communities – Measures Affecting Asbestos and Asbestos Containing Products ('EC – Asbestos'), 2001

Short summary and commentary

Canada initiated this case to challenge a French import ban on asbestos fibres and products containing asbestos fibres. France defended its measure on public health grounds. The panel received five amicus briefs: three from public interest groups and two from industry-related groups. During the proceedings, the European Communities incorporated one of the public interest and one of the industry briefs into its submission by reference. The panel concluded that it would only consider the briefs included in the EC submission, thereby demonstrating the importance of attachment of a brief to parties' submissions (Panel report, paragraph 6.3). Although the panel specified that it based its decision to reject one of the other three briefs on the fact that the brief was submitted late in the proceedings, it did not provide much insight into its reasoning for rejecting the other two submissions (*Id.* at paragraphs 6.3–6.4).

The decision was appealed for reasons other than the panel's treatment of the amicus submissions.

Both public interest NGOs and business groups were expected to add their voices to the resolution of this dispute through the submission of amicus briefs. In an attempt to regulate the procedures for such submissions to be made, the Appellate Body drafted a set of guidelines for amici to request leave to file an amicus brief (AB report, paragraphs 51–52). Subsequently, these guidelines were posted on the WTO's website (*Id.* at paragraph 51). The Appellate Body based the drafting of these guidelines on Article 17.9 of the DSU and Rule 16(1) of its Working Procedures (*Id.*). Those guidelines were not permanent, but rather applied solely to the *EC – Asbestos* appeal (*Id.*). The Appellate Body's action drew much criticism from WTO Members hostile to the idea that non-Members could play a role or provide a voice in WTO dispute settlement.

The Appellate Body ultimately received 17 applications for leave to file an amicus brief. It rejected six of those applications because they were untimely, but rejected the remaining 11 for unspecified reasons (*Id.* at paragraphs 55–56). Some speculate that the political tension generated by the drafting and posting of the guidelines motivated the Appellate Body to refrain from granting any of the applications to file briefs. While this action might have placated Members, it inspired NGOs and interested persons to criticize the lack of transparency and predictability in WTO procedures.

Excerpts

Report of the Panel, *European Communities – Measures Affecting Asbestos and Asbestos Containing Products*, WT/DS135/R, adopted as modified by WT/DS/135/AB/R on 5 April 2001.

VI. Submissions from non-governmental organizations [paras 6.1–6.4]

6.1. The Panel received four *amicus briefs* from the following non-governmental organizations:
Collegium Ramazzini, dated 7 May 1999
Ban Asbestos Network, dated 22 July 1999
Instituto Mexicano de Fibro-Industrias AC, dated 26 July 1999
American Federation of Labor and Congress of Industrial Organizations, dated 28 July 1999

6.2. These *amicus briefs* were transmitted to the parties for their information. In their written rebuttals of 30 June 1999, the EC incorporated by reference the submission of the *Collegium Ramazzini*. In a letter dated 18 August 1999, Canada notified the Panel that, bearing in mind the general nature of the opinions expressed by the non-governmental organizations in those submissions, they would not be useful to the Panel at this advanced stage of the proceedings. Should the Panel nonetheless accept the submissions as *amicus briefs*, Canada believed that the parties should be given the possibility to respond to the factual and legal arguments set out in them. In a letter dated 3 November 1999, the EC informed the Panel that it was incorporating by reference the *amicus brief* submitted by the *American Federation of Labor and Congress of Industrial Organizations*, as that body supported the EC's scientific and legal arguments in this dispute. The EC also proposed to the Panel that it reject the submissions from the *Ban Asbestos Network* and the *Insituto Mexicano de Fibro-Industrias AC*, as those documents contained no information of relevance to the dispute. In a letter dated 10 November 1999, Canada again urged the Panel to reject the four *amicus briefs* as it was inappropriate to admit them at this stage in the proceedings. Should the Panel nevertheless consider these submissions, Canada considered that, for the sake of procedural fairness, the parties should have an opportunity to comment on their content.

6.3. In a letter dated 12 November 1999, the Panel informed the parties that, in the light of the EC's decision to incorporate into its own submissions the *amicus briefs* submitted by the *Collegium Ramazzini* and the *American Federation of Labor and Congress of Industrial Organizations*, the Panel would consider these two documents on the same basis as the other documents furnished by the EC in this dispute. It was also on that basis that the Panel submitted those two submissions to the scientific experts for their information. At the second substantive meeting of the Panel with the parties, the Panel gave Canada the opportunity to reply, in writing or orally, to the arguments set forth in these two *amicus briefs*. At that same meeting, the Panel also informed the parties that it had decided not to take into consideration the *amicus briefs* submitted by the *Ban Asbestos Network* and by the *Instituto Mexicano de Fibro-Industrias AC*

6.4. On 27 June 2000, the Panel received a written brief from the non-governmental organization *ONE* ("*Only Nature Endures*") situated in Mumbai, India. The Panel considered that this brief had been submitted at a stage in the procedure when it could no longer be taken into account. It therefore decided not to accept the request of *ONE* and informed the organization accordingly. The Panel transmitted a copy of the documents received from *ONE* to the parties for information and notified them of the decision it had taken. At the same time, it also informed the parties that the same decision would apply to any briefs received from non-governmental organizations between that point and the end of the procedure.

. . .

VIII. Findings

. . .

B. Issues on which the panel had to take a position during the procedure

. . .

3. Amicus curiae briefs [paras 8.12–8.14]

8.12. In the course of the procedure, the Panel received written submissions or "*amicus curiae*" briefs from four sources other than Members of the WTO.[13] Referring to the position taken by the Appellate Body in *United States – Import Prohibition of Certain Shrimp and Shrimp Products*[14] on the interpretation of Article 13 of the Understanding concerning *amicus curiae* briefs, the Panel informed the parties accordingly and transmitted the submissions to them. The EC included two of these submissions in their own submission. Having examined each of the *amicus curiae* briefs, the Panel decided to take into account the submissions by the *Collegium Ramazzini* and the *American Federation of Labor and Congress of Industrial Organizations*, as they had been included by the EC in their own submissions on an equal footing. At the second meeting with the parties, Canada was given an opportunity to respond in writing and orally to the arguments in the two *amicus curiae* briefs.

[13] See paras 6.1–6.3 above.

[14] Adopted on 20 September 1999, WT/DS58/AB/R (hereinafter *"United States – Shrimp"),* paras 101–109. See also the report of the Appellate Body in *United States – Imposition of Countervailing Duties on Certain Hot-Rolled Lead and Bismuth Carbon Steel Products Originating in the United Kingdom,* adopted on 7 June 2000, WT/DS/138/AB/R, paras 40–42.

8.13. On the other hand, the Panel decided not to take into account the *amicus curiae* briefs submitted respectively by the *Ban Asbestos Network* and by the *Instituto Mexicano de Fibro-Industrias AC* and informed Canada and the EC accordingly at the second meeting with the parties held on 21 January 2000.

8.14. On 27 June 2000, the Panel received a written brief from the non-governmental organization *ONE* ("*Only Nature Endures*") situated in Mumbai, India. In view of the provisions in the Understanding on the interim review, the Panel considered that this brief had been submitted at a stage in the procedure when it could no longer be taken into account. It therefore decided not to accept the request of *ONE* and informed the organization accordingly. The Panel transmitted a copy of the documents received from *ONE* to the parties for information and notified them of the decision it had taken. At the same time, it also informed the parties that the same decision would apply to any briefs received from non-governmental organizations between that point and the end of the procedure.

Report of the Appellate Body, *European Communities – Measures Affecting Asbestos and Asbestos Containing Products*, WT/DS135/AB/R, adopted on 5 April 2001.

III. Preliminary Procedural Matter [paras 50–57]

50. On 27 October 2000, we wrote to the parties and the third parties indicating that we were mindful that, in the proceedings before the Panel in this case, the Panel received five written submissions from non-governmental organizations, two of which the Panel decided to take into account.[28] In our letter, we recognized the possibility that we might receive submissions in this appeal from persons other than the parties and the third parties to this dispute, and stated that we were of the view that the fair and orderly conduct of this appeal could be facilitated by the adoption of appropriate procedures, for the purposes of this appeal only, pursuant to Rule 16(1) of the *Working Procedures*, to deal with any possible submissions

received from such persons. To this end, we invited the parties and the third parties in this appeal to submit their comments on a number of questions. These related to: whether we should adopt a "request for leave" procedure; what procedures would be needed to ensure that the parties and third parties would have a full and adequate opportunity to respond to submissions that might be received; and whether we should take any other points into consideration if we decided to adopt a "request for leave" procedure. On 3 November 2000, all of the parties and third parties responded in writing to our letter of 27 October. Canada, the European Communities and Brazil considered that issues pertaining to any such procedure should be dealt with by the WTO Members themselves. The United States welcomed adoption of a request for leave procedure, and Zimbabwe indicated that it had no specific reasons to oppose adoption of a request for leave procedure. Without prejudice to their positions, Canada, the European Communities and the United States each made a number of suggestions regarding any such procedure that might be adopted.

[28] Panel Report, paras 6.1–6.4 and 8.12–8.14.

51. On 7 November 2000, and after consultations among all seven Members of the Appellate Body, we adopted, pursuant to Rule 16(1) of the *Working Procedures*, an additional procedure, *for the purposes of this appeal only*, to deal with written submissions received from persons other than the parties and third parties to this dispute (the "Additional Procedure"). The Additional Procedure was communicated to the parties and third parties in this appeal on 7 November 2000. On 8 November 2000, the Chairman of the Appellate Body informed the Chairman of the Dispute Settlement Body, in writing, of the Additional Procedure adopted, and this letter was circulated, for information, as a dispute settlement document to the Members of the WTO.[29] In that communication, the Chairman of the Appellate Body stated that:

> ... *This additional procedure has been adopted by the Division hearing this appeal for the purposes of this appeal only pursuant to Rule 16(1) of the* Working Procedures for Appellate Review, *and is* not *a new working procedure drawn up by the Appellate Body pursuant to paragraph 9 of Article 17 of the* Understanding on Rules and Procedures Governing the Settlement of Disputes *(original emphasis).*

The Additional Procedure was posted on the WTO website on 8 November 2000.

[29] WT/DS135/9, 8 November 2000.

52. The Additional Procedure provided:

1. In the interests of fairness and orderly procedure in the conduct of this appeal, the Division hearing this appeal has decided to adopt, pursuant to Rule 16(1) of the *Working Procedures for Appellate Review*, and after consultations with the parties and third parties to this dispute, the following additional procedure for purposes of this appeal only.
2. Any person, whether natural or legal, other than a party or a third party to this dispute, wishing to file a written brief with the Appellate Body, must apply for leave to file such a brief from the Appellate Body *by noon* on *Thursday, 16 November 2000*.
3. An application for leave to file such a written brief shall:
   (a) be made in writing, be dated and signed by the applicant, and include the address and other contact details of the applicant;
   (b) be in no case longer than three typed pages;
   (c) contain a description of the applicant, including a statement of the membership and legal status of the applicant, the general objectives pursued by the applicant, the nature of the activities of the applicant, and the sources of financing of the applicant;
   (d) specify the nature of the interest the applicant has in this appeal;

(e) identify the specific issues of law covered in the Panel Report and legal interpretations developed by the Panel that are the subject of this appeal, as set forth in the Notice of Appeal (WT/DS135/8) dated 23 October 2000, which the applicant intends to address in its written brief;
(f) state why it would be desirable, in the interests of achieving a satisfactory settlement of the matter at issue, in accordance with the rights and obligations of WTO Members under the DSU and the other covered agreements, for the Appellate Body to grant the applicant leave to file a written brief in this appeal; and indicate, in particular, in what way the applicant will make a contribution to the resolution of this dispute that is not likely to be repetitive of what has been already submitted by a party or third party to this dispute; and
(g) contain a statement disclosing whether the applicant has any relationship, direct or indirect, with any party or any third party to this dispute, as well as whether it has, or will, receive any assistance, financial or otherwise, from a party or a third party to this dispute in the preparation of its application for leave or its written brief.

4. The Appellate Body will review and consider each application for leave to file a written brief and will, without delay, render a decision whether to grant or deny such leave.
5. The grant of leave to file a brief by the Appellate Body does not imply that the Appellate Body will address, in its Report, the legal arguments made in such a brief.
6. Any person, other than a party or a third party to this dispute, granted leave to file a written brief with the Appellate Body, must file its brief with the Appellate Body Secretariat *by noon* on *Monday, 27 November 2000*.
7. A written brief filed with the Appellate Body by an applicant granted leave to file such a brief shall:
   (a) be dated and signed by the person filing the brief;
   (b) be concise and in no case longer than 20 typed pages, including any appendices; and
   (c) set out a precise statement, strictly limited to legal arguments, supporting the applicant's legal position on the issues of law or legal interpretations in the Panel Report with respect to which the applicant has been granted leave to file a written brief.
8. An applicant granted leave shall, in addition to filing its written brief with the Appellate Body Secretariat, also serve a copy of its brief on all the parties and third parties to the dispute *by noon* on *Monday, 27 November 2000.*
9. The parties and the third parties to this dispute will be given a full and adequate opportunity by the Appellate Body to comment on and respond to any written brief filed with the Appellate Body by an applicant granted leave under this procedure (original emphasis).

53. The Appellate Body received 13 written submissions from non-governmental organizations relating to this appeal that were not submitted in accordance with the Additional Procedure.[30] Several of these were received while we were considering the possible adoption of an additional procedure. After the adoption of the Additional Procedure, each of these 13 submissions was returned to its sender, along with a letter informing the sender of the procedure adopted by the Division hearing this appeal and a copy of the Additional Procedure. Only one of these associations, the Korea Asbestos Association, subsequently submitted a request for leave in accordance with the Additional Procedure.

[30] Such submissions were received from: Asbestos Information Association (United States); HVL Asbestos (Swaziland) Limited (Bulembu Mine); South African Asbestos Producers Advisory Committee (South Africa); J & S Bridle Associates (United Kingdom); Associação das Indústrias de Produtos de Amianio Crisótilo (Portugal); Asbestos Cement Industries Limited (Sri Lanka); The Federation of Thai Industries, Roofing and Accessories Club (Thailand); Korea Asbestos Association (Korea); Senac (Senegal); Syndicat des Métallos (Canada); Duralita de Centroamerica, S.A. de C.V. (El Salvador); Asociación Colombiana de Fibras (Colombia); and Japan Asbestos Association (Japan).

54. By letter dated 15 November 2000, Canada and the European Communities jointly requested that they be provided with copies of all applications filed pursuant to the Additional Procedure, and of the decision taken by the Appellate Body in respect of each such application. All such documents were subsequently provided to the parties and third parties in this dispute.

55. Pursuant to the Additional Procedure, the Appellate Body received 17 applications requesting leave to file a written brief in this appeal. Six of these 17 applications were received after the deadline specified in paragraph 2 of the Additional Procedure and, for this reason, leave to file a written brief was denied to these six applicants.[31] Each such applicant was sent a copy of our decision denying its application for leave because the application was not filed in a timely manner.

[31] Applications from the following persons were received by the Division after the deadline specified in the Additional Procedure for receipt of such applications: Association of Personal Injury Lawyers (United Kingdom); All India A.C. Pressure Pipe Manufacturer's Association (India); International Confederation of Free Trade Unions/European Trade Union Confederation (Belgium); Maharashtra Asbestos Cement Pipe Manufacturers' Association (India); Roofit Industries Ltd. (India); and Society for Occupational and Environmental Health (United States).

56. The Appellate Body received 11 applications for leave to file a written brief in this appeal within the time limits specified in paragraph 2 of the Additional Procedure.[32] We carefully reviewed and considered each of these applications in accordance with the Additional Procedure and, in each case, decided to deny leave to file a written brief. Each applicant was sent a copy of our decision denying its application for leave for failure to comply sufficiently with all the requirements set forth in paragraph 3 of the Additional Procedure.

[32] Applications from the following persons were received by the Division within the deadline specified in the Additional Procedure for receipt of such applications: Professor Robert Lloyd Howse (United States); Occupational & Environmental Diseases Association (United Kingdom); American Public Health Association (United States); Centro de Estudios Comunitarios de la Universidad Nacional de Rosario (Argentina); Only Nature Endures (India); Korea Asbestos Association (Korea); International Council on Metals and the Environment and American Chemistry Council (United States); European Chemical Industry Council (Belgium); Australian Centre for Environmental Law at the Australian National University (Australia); Associate Professor Jan McDonald and Mr. Don Anton (Australia); and a joint application from Foundation for Environmental Law and Development (United Kingdom), Center for International Environmental Law (Switzerland), International Ban Asbestos Secretariat (United Kingdom), Ban Asbestos International and Virtual Network (France), Greenpeace International (The Netherlands), World Wide Fund for Nature, International (Switzerland), and Lutheran World Federation (Switzerland).

57. We received a written brief from the Foundation for International Environmental Law and Development, on its behalf and on behalf of Ban Asbestos (International and Virtual) Network, Greenpeace International, International Ban Asbestos Secretariat, and World Wide Fund for Nature, International, dated 6 February 2001. As we had already denied, in accordance with the Additional Procedure, an application from these organizations for leave to file a written brief in this appeal,[33] we did not accept this brief.

[33] These organizations, together with the Center for International Environmental Law and the Lutheran World Federation, filed a joint application for leave to file a written brief. We decided to deny leave to these applicants to file a written brief. See *supra*, para 56 and footnote 32.

European Communities – Anti-dumping Duties on Imports of Cotton-type Bed Linen from India ('EC – Cotton from India'), 2001

Short summary and commentary

In this case, India alleged that the EC violated numerous provisions of the GATT when it imposed anti-dumping duties on imports of certain bed linen from India. Dr Konrad Neundörfer submitted an amicus brief on behalf of a trade association and in support of India. The panel merely mentioned the amicus submission in a footnote to its report, stating that it made copies available to the parties for comment (Panel report, section VI:A, footnote 10). Perhaps because no party made any substantive comments regarding the submission, the panel found it unnecessary to take the brief into account (*Id.*). It did not give any reasoning for this action. This case provides an example of the cursory explanations given by WTO tribunals regarding their treatment of amicus briefs and the reliance on the reactions of the parties.

Excerpts

Report of the Panel, *European Communities – Anti-dumping Duties on Imports of Cotton-type Bed Linen from India*, WT/DS141/R, adopted as amended by WT/DS141/AB/R on 12 March 2001.

VI. Findings

. . .

A. Requests for preliminary rulings

. . .

[10] *On Tuesday, 9 May 2000, the day before our first meeting with the parties, the Panel received an unsolicited* amicus curiae *brief in support of the complaint by India in this dispute, submitted on behalf of the Foreign Trade Association by Dr Konrad Neundörfer. We made copies available to the parties for comment. No party made any substantive comments regarding that submission. We did not find it necessary to take the submission into account in reaching our decision in this dispute.*

Thailand – Anti-dumping Duties on Angles, Shapes and Sections of Iron or Non-alloy Steel and H-beams from Poland ('Thailand – Anti-dumping Duties'), 2001

Short summary and commentary

Poland initiated this action to challenge certain Thai anti-dumping actions. A coalition of trade industries and associations submitted a brief in support of Poland. During the proceedings, Thailand alleged that this brief contained information that should only have been accessible to the parties and third parties to the case (i.e. that the author of the brief should not have had access to the Thai submission in the appellate proceedings). The Appellate Body agreed that the brief's contents suggested there had indeed been an improper leak of confidential information contained in Thailand's submission (AB report, paragraph 74). The Appellate Body ultimately explained that it rejected the amicus brief because it found it irrelevant to the task of deciding the appeal, without commenting further on the allegedly confidential information.

The events of this case help to highlight an important issue in the *amicus* context. Because the DSU's confidentiality rules essentially prevent non-parties and non-third parties from having any right of access to parties' and third parties' submissions in dispute settlement proceedings, it is difficult for any amicus curiae to identify the crucial issues and arguments at play in a given dispute. Without the ability to identify those issues and arguments, amici face a high hurdle when attempting to tailor their briefs so that they are relevant to and useful in the dispute settlement proceedings.

Excerpts

Report of the Appellate Body, *Thailand – Anti-dumping Duties on Angles, Shapes and Sections of Iron or Non-alloy Steel and H-beams from Poland*, WT/DS122/AB/R, adopted on 5 April 2001.

IV. Preliminary procedural matter and ruling [paras 62–78]

62. On 1 December 2000, the Appellate Body received a written brief from the Consuming Industries Trade Action Coalition ("CITAC"), a coalition of United States companies and trade associations. In its brief, CITAC addressed some of the legal issues raised in this appeal. On the same day, CITAC sent copies of its brief to Thailand and Poland, the participants in this appeal, as well as to the European Communities, Japan and the United States, the third participants in this appeal.

63. On 6 December 2000, Thailand wrote to us requesting that we reject this brief, as well as any other such briefs that might be submitted in this appeal. Thailand said it considered that the Appellate Body lacked the authority to consider *amicus curiae* briefs in this dispute. Thailand added that aside from the acceptance of such briefs by the Appellate Body, a potentially more serious issue had arisen with respect to the brief submitted by CITAC.

64. Thailand stated that it appeared on the face of the CITAC brief that this organization had had access to the appellant's submission in this appeal. Thailand stated that, in the CITAC brief, certain references to the specific arguments of Thailand use the format set out in Thailand's appellant's submission. In particular, Thailand noted that in paragraph 2 of the brief submitted by CITAC, there is an explicit reference to "Section III.C.5 of the Thailand Submission". Thailand also stated that certain arguments made in the brief showed a level of knowledge of Thailand's arguments that "goes beyond what could be divined in the Notice of Appeal". Thailand stated that there was no plausible explanation for CITAC, a United States private sector association, to have learned the precise format of Thailand's appellant' submission, other than that Poland or a third participant in this appeal had failed to treat Thailand's submission as confidential and had disclosed it to CITAC, in violation of Articles 17.10 and 18.2 of the DSU.

. . .

74. In our preliminary ruling of 14 December 2000, we stated:

> *The terms of Article 17.10 of the DSU are clear and unequivocal: "[t]he proceedings of the Appellate Body shall be confidential". Like all obligations under the DSU, this is an obligation that all Members of the WTO, as well as the Appellate Body and its staff, must respect.*

. . .

We note that Poland has made substantial efforts to investigate this matter, and to gather information from its legal counsel, Hogan & Hartson L.L.P. We note as well the responses from the third participants, the European Communities, Japan and the United States. Furthermore, Poland has accepted the proposal made by Hogan & Hartson L.L.P. to withdraw as Poland's legal counsel in this appeal. On the basis of the responses we have received from Poland and from the third participants, and on the basis of our own examination of the facts on the record in this appeal, we believe that there is *prima facie* evidence that CITAC received, or had access to, Thailand's appellant's submission in this appeal.

We see no reason to accept the written brief submitted by CITAC in this appeal. Accordingly, we have returned this brief to CITAC.

75. On 20 December 2000, Thailand sent us a letter in response to this ruling. In this letter, Thailand stated that Poland had not provided any explanation of how the breach came to occur, and requested that we take further action in this connection. Thailand suggested that we ask CITAC how it came to be in possession of the information in its brief. Thailand also asked that we consider what further steps we should take to deter violations by WTO Members in future cases. Thailand also asked that we clarify the meaning of Poland's explanation that it had accepted the proposal made by Hogan & Hartson L.L.P. to

withdraw as Poland's legal counsel in this appeal. Thailand also requested that we clarify our reasons for rejecting the written brief submitted by CITAC. Finally, Thailand asked that we reflect a full record of this issue in our Report in this appeal.

76. As we indicated in our ruling of 14 December 2000, we have noted Thailand's concerns with respect to the confidentiality of these proceedings. Accordingly, we have, as we indicated in our ruling, provided a full account of all the aspects pertaining to this issue. We also noted these concerns at the oral hearing in this appeal. We believe that we have done all that is possible within our mandate under the DSU to address Thailand's concerns. With respect to Thailand's suggestion that we seek an explanation from CITAC, we note that we have rejected the written brief filed by this organization. Under these circumstances, it would not be appropriate for the Appellate Body to communicate with this organization.

. . .

78. With respect to a clarification of the reasons for rejecting the brief from CITAC, we would only add that we did not find the brief filed by CITAC to be relevant to our task.

United States – Import Prohibition of Certain Shrimp and Shrimp Products ('US – Shrimp/Turtle 21.5'), 2001

Short summary and commentary

US – Shrimp/Turtle 21.5 involved the implementation of the panel and Appellate Body reports in *Shrimp /Turtle I,* described above. After the Appellate Body in *US – Shrimp/ Turtle I* upheld the panel's finding that the ban was inconsistent with the GATT, the US took several steps to bring its ban into compliance with its obligations under that agreement as specified in the panel and Appellate Body reports. Malaysia, nevertheless, did not view the steps taken by the US as sufficient, and, consequently, sought a second review of the GATT-consistency of the US import ban pursuant to Article 21.5 of the DSU.

Public interest NGOs submitted two amicus briefs to the panel in this case. The US attached one of the briefs to its submission, with the caveat that it did not agree with all of the legal arguments it set forth. Because the US chose to attach the brief, the panel concluded that the brief was part of the record (Panel report, paragraph 5.16). The panel did not specify, however, whether it would consider only those arguments made in the amicus brief that were also endorsed by the US.

Neither of the parties attached the second brief to their submissions. The US argued that it was not especially relevant to the dispute, and Malaysia argued that the panel had no authority under the DSU to accept or consider the brief. Taking note of the positions taken by the parties, the panel declined to include the brief in the case's record (*Id.*).

The panel's findings regarding amicus briefs were not appealed, but Malaysia appealed the panel's decision that the US had fulfilled the requirements set in the *US – Shrimp/Turtle* reports.

In the appeal, the Appellate Body received two amicus briefs, both supporting the US import ban on certain shrimp and shrimp products. One of those briefs, which had been submitted jointly by two public interest NGOs, was also attached as an exhibit to the US submission. The Appellate Body cited its decision in *US – Shrimp/Turtle I* when holding that it would consider the attached brief (AB report, paragraph 76). Although it then stated that it would focus on those arguments in the brief which the US supported, it is not clear whether the Appellate Body meant that it would *only* focus on those particular arguments endorsed by the US (*Id.* at paragraph 77).

The second brief received by the Appellate Body was submitted by a law professor. The US did not attach this brief as an exhibit to its submission. Without elaboration, the Appellate Body simply stated that it found it unnecessary to take the unattached brief into account (*Id.* at paragraph 78).

Excerpts

Implementation Report of the Panel, *United States – Import Prohibition of Certain Shrimp and Shrimp Products*, WT/DS58/RW, adopted as amended by WT/DS58/AB/RW on 21 November 2001.

V. Findings

. . .

B. Preliminary issues

. . .

3. Admissibility of submissions from non-governmental organizations [paras 5.14–5.16]

5.14. In the course of the proceedings, the Panel received two unsolicited submissions from non-governmental organizations. One was submitted by *Earthjustice Legal Defense Fund* on behalf of *Turtle Island Restoration Network*, *The Humane Society of the United States*, *The American Society for the Prevention of Cruelty to Animals*, *Defenders of Wildlife* and *Fiscalia del Medio Ambiente (Chile)*.[167] The other submission was filed by the *National Wildlife Federation* on behalf of the *Center for Marine Conservation*, *Centro Ecoceanos*, *Defenders of Wildlife*, *Friends of the Earth*, *Kenya Sea Turtle Committee*, *Marine Turtle Preservation Group of India*, *National Wildlife Federation*, *Natural Resources Defense Council*, *Operation Kachhapa*, *Project Swarajya*, *Visakha Society for Prevention of Cruelty to Animals*.[168] Those submissions were respectively communicated to the parties on 15 and 18 December 2000. In a letter accompanying these submissions, the Panel informed the parties that they were free to comment in their rebuttals on the admissibility and relevance of these submissions. The Panel also informed the parties that it would set out in its report its decision as to how it would address these submissions.

[167] Hereafter the "Earthjustice Submission".
[168] Hereafter the "National Wildlife Federation Submission".

5.15. The parties discussed the above-mentioned submissions in their rebuttals, at the hearing and in replies to questions of the Panel.[169] The Panel notes that Malaysia considers in substance that the Panel has no right under the DSU to accept or consider any unsolicited briefs, whereas the United States argues that the Earthjustice Submission, which addresses a hypothetical question not before the Panel, does not appear to be as relevant to the issue in this dispute as the National Wildlife Federation Submission. As far as the National Wildlife Federation Submission is concerned, the United States considers that it raises issues directly relevant to the matter before the Panel and decided to attach it as an exhibit to its submissions "to ensure that a relevant and informative document [would be] before the Panel, regardless of whether the Panel decid[ed] to exercise its discretion to accept [that submission] directly from the submitters". However, we take note of the fact that the United States does not endorse some of the legal arguments contained in the "amicus brief" submitted by the National Wildlife Federation.[170]

[169] See paras 3.5–3.15 above.
[170] The United States specified that "[t]he amicus brief attached to the US rebuttal submission reflects the independent views of the organizations that signed on to the amicus brief. [. . .] We would note, however, that the amicus brief includes certain procedural and substantive defences not advanced in the US submission [. . .], and thus that these matters are not before the Panel."

5.16. As far as the Earthjustice Submission is concerned, the Panel takes note of the arguments of the parties and decides not to include it in the record of this case. Regarding the National Wildlife Federation Submission, the Panel notes that it is part of the submissions of the United States in this case and, as a result, is already part of the record.

Implementation Report of the Appellate Body, *United States – Import Prohibition of Certain Shrimp and Shrimp Products*, WT/DS58/AB/RW, adopted on 21 November 2001.

III. Preliminary Procedural Matter [paras 75–78]

75. On 13 August 2001, we received a brief from the American Humane Society and Humane Society International (the "Humane Society brief"). This brief was also attached as an exhibit to the appellee's submission filed by the United States in this appeal.

76. As we have previously stated in our Report in *United States – Import Prohibition of Certain Shrimp and Shrimp Products* ("*United States – Shrimp*"), attaching a brief or other material to the submission of either an appellant or an appellee, no matter how or where such material may have originated, renders that material at least *prima facie* an integral part of that participant's submission.[24] In that Report, we stated further that it is for a participant in an appeal to determine for itself what to include in its submission.[25]

[24] Appellate Body Report, WT/DS58/AB/R, adopted 6 November 1998, para 89.
[25] *Ibid*.

77. At the oral hearing in this appeal, held on 4 September 2001, we asked the United States to clarify the extent to which it adopted the arguments set out in the Humane Society brief. The United States stated: "[t]hose are the independent views of that organization. We adopt them to the extent they are the same as ours but otherwise they are their independent views. We submit them for your consideration but not like our arguments where, for example, the panel is expected to address each one." Accordingly, we focus our attention on the legal arguments in the appellee's submission of the United States.

78. On 20 August 2001, we received a brief from Professor Robert Howse, a professor of international trade law at the University of Michigan Law School in Ann Arbor, Michigan, in the United States. In rendering our decision in this appeal, we have not found it necessary to take into account the brief submitted by Professor Howse.

European Communities – Trade Description of Sardines ('EC – Sardines'), 2002

Short summary and commentary

This case involved a claim by Peru that certain marketing regulations imposed by the European Communities were inconsistent with the Agreement on Technical Barriers to Trade (TBT) and with the GATT. During the proceedings the Appellate Body received two amicus briefs: one from a private citizen and the other from a WTO Member. In explaining how it would treat those submissions, the Appellate Body clarified several issues with respect to its power to accept and consider amicus briefs.

First, the Appellate Body concluded that it could accept and consider amicus submissions from WTO Members (AB report, paragraphs 162–167). Some commentators have questioned whether this decision effectively allows Members to sidestep the DSU's rules governing their participation in dispute settlement procedures as parties or third parties. However, others have argued that even if the ruling is technically inconsistent with the procedures set forth in the DSU, it was likely the only politically feasible decision for the Appellate Body to reach; arguably, the Appellate Body would have faced much criticism if, after having granted non-Members the right to submit amicus briefs (though not the right to have those briefs considered), it denied Members that same right of submission.

Another significant aspect of this decision is that the Appellate Body highlighted what it deemed to be appropriate content for an amicus brief at the appellate stage. Because Article 17.6 of the DSU limits appeals to issues of law and legal interpretations developed by the panel, the Appellate Body rejected as irrelevant those aspects of Morocco's amicus brief that presented factual information (*Id.* at paragraph 169).

With respect to procedural matters, Canada wanted the Appellate Body to make its decision regarding whether or not to accept the briefs prior to the oral hearing in the case. The procedural approach advocated by Canada arguably could have eased the burden on parties and third parties by narrowing the issues to be addressed at the oral hearing. Nevertheless, the Appellate Body chose to postpone its decision on how to treat the briefs until after giving the parties an opportunity to address the amicus issue during the oral hearing.

Excerpts

Report of the Appellate Body, *European Communities – Trade Description of Sardines*, WT/DS231/AB/R, adopted on 23 October 2002.

I. Introduction [paras 1–21]

. . .

19. An *amicus curiae* brief was received, on 18 July 2002, from a private individual. The Kingdom of Morocco also filed an *amicus curiae* brief on 22 July 2002. In a letter dated 26 July 2002, Peru objected to the acceptance and consideration of both *amicus curiae* briefs. Ecuador expressed similar objections in a letter received on 2 August 2002. Canada submitted a letter, on 26 July 2002, requesting that we decide whether or not to accept the briefs in advance of the oral hearing.

20. By letter of 31 July 2002, the participants and third participants were informed that they would have an opportunity to address the issues relating to the *amicus curiae* briefs during the oral hearing, without prejudice to their legal status or to any action th[at] we might take in connection with these briefs.

. . .

IV. Procedural Issues

. . .

B. Amicus curiae briefs [paras 153–170]

153. We turn next to the second procedural issue in this case, namely whether we may accept and consider the *amicus curiae* briefs that have been submitted to us. One brief was filed by a private individual, and the other by the Kingdom of Morocco ("Morocco"), a Member of the WTO that did not exercise its third party rights at the panel stage of these proceedings.

154. Peru objects to our acceptance and consideration of these unsolicited submissions. Peru argues that, although it "welcomes non-Member submissions where they are attached to the submission of a WTO Member engaged in dispute settlement proceedings, the DSU makes clear that only WTO Members can make independent submissions to panels and to the Appellate Body".[52] As for the brief submitted by Morocco, a WTO Member, Peru contends that accepting such a brief "would be to allow a

WTO Member impermissibly to circumvent the DSU", which "establishes the conditions under which WTO Members can participate as third parties in dispute settlement proceedings".[53] On this basis, Peru requests us to reject both of these briefs.

[52] Peru's letter dated 26 July 2002.
[53] Peru's letter dated 26 July 2002.

155. The European Communities does not address this issue in its written submission. In response to our questioning at the oral hearing, however, the European Communities stated that the *amicus curiae* briefs are pertinent, and that we have the discretion to accept them. Among the third participants, Canada argues that there is a lack of clear agreement among WTO Members as to the role of *amicus curiae* briefs in dispute settlement, and contends that WTO Members have a legal right to participate in dispute settlement proceedings only if they reserve their third party rights at the outset of the dispute settlement process. Moreover, Canada asserts that both *amicus curiae* briefs should be rejected because they are not pertinent or useful. Chile and Ecuador also ask us to reject the *amicus curiae* briefs, alleging that the DSU does not permit participation by *amici*. The United States is of the view that we have the authority to accept both briefs, but believes we should not consider either of them because they are not pertinent or useful.

156. We recall that, in *US – Shrimp*,[54] we admitted three *amicus curiae* briefs that were attached as exhibits to the appellant's submission in that appeal. We concluded that those briefs formed part of the appellant's submission, and observed that it is for a participant in an appeal to determine for itself what to include in its submission.[55] We followed this approach in *Thailand – Anti-Dumping Duties on Angles, Shapes and Sections of Iron or Non-Alloy Steel and H-Beams from Poland* ("*Thailand – H-Beams*"),[56] and in *United States – Import Prohibition of Certain Shrimp and Shrimp Products – Recourse to Article 21.5 of the DSU by Malaysia* ("*US – Shrimp (Article 21.5 – Malaysia)*").[57] In subsequent cases, *amicus curiae* briefs were submitted by private individuals or organizations separately from participants' submissions. We admitted those briefs as well.[58]

[54] Appellate Body Report, *supra,* footnote 50.
[55] *Ibid.,* para 91.
[56] Appellate Body Report, *Thailand – Anti-Dumping Duties on Angles, Shapes and Sections of Iron or Non-Alloy Steel and H-Beams from Poland ("Thailand – H-Beams"),* WT/DS122/AB/R, adopted 5 April 2001.
[57] Appellate Body Report, *United States – Import Prohibition of Certain Shrimp and Shrimp Products – Recourse to Article 21.5 of the DSU by Malaysia ("US – Shrimp (Article 21.5 – Malaysia)"),* WT/DS58/AB/RW, adopted 21 November 2001.
[58] Appellate Body Report, *EC – Asbestos, supra,* footnote 15, Appellate Body Report, *Thailand – H-Beams, supra,* footnote 56, Appellate Body Report, *US – Lead and Bismuth II,* WT/DS138/AB/R, adopted 7 June 2000, DSR 2000:V, 2601.

157. We have the authority to accept *amicus curiae* briefs. We enunciated this authority for the first time in our Report in *United States – Imposition of Countervailing Duties on Certain Hot-Rolled Lead and Bismuth Carbon Steel Products Originating in the United Kingdom* ("*US – Lead and Bismuth II*"), where we reasoned:

> *In considering this matter, we first note that nothing in the DSU or the* Working Procedures *specifically provides that the Appellate Body may accept and consider submissions or briefs from sources other than the participants and third participants in an appeal. On the other hand, neither the DSU nor the* Working Procedures *explicitly prohibit[s] acceptance or consideration of such briefs. . . [Article 17.9*[59]*] makes clear that the Appellate Body has broad authority to adopt procedural rules which do not conflict with any rules and procedures in the DSU or the covered agreements. Therefore, we are of the opinion that as long as we act consistently with the provisions of the DSU and the covered agreements, we have the legal authority to decide whether or not to accept and consider any information that we believe is pertinent and useful in an appeal.*[60] *(footnote omitted)*

[59] Article 17.9 of the DSU provides as follows:
Procedures for Appellate Review
9. Working procedures shall be drawn up by the Appellate Body in consultation with the Chairman of the DSB and the Director-General, and communicated to the Members for their information.
[60] Appellate Body Report, *supra,* footnote 58, para 39.

158. In that finding, we drew a distinction between, on the one hand, parties and third parties to a dispute, which have a *legal right* to participate in panel and Appellate Body proceedings, and, on the other hand, private individuals and organizations, which are not Members of the WTO, and which, therefore, do not have a *legal right* to participate in dispute settlement proceedings. We said there:

> *We wish to emphasize that in the dispute settlement system of the WTO, the DSU envisages* participation *in panel or Appellate Body proceedings, as a matter of legal right,* only *by parties and third parties to a dispute. And, under the DSU,* only *Members of the WTO have a legal right to participate as parties or third parties in a particular dispute. . .*

Individuals and organizations, which are not Members of the WTO, have no legal *right* to make submissions to or to be heard by the Appellate Body. The Appellate Body has no legal *duty* to accept or consider unsolicited *amicus curiae* briefs submitted by individuals or organizations, not Members of the WTO. The Appellate Body has a legal *duty* to accept and consider *only* submissions from WTO Members which are parties or third parties in a particular dispute.[61] (original emphasis; underlining added; footnotes omitted)

[61] *Ibid.,* paras 40–41.

159. We explained further in that appeal that participation by private individuals and organizations is dependent upon our permitting such participation if we find it useful to do so. We observed that:

> *. . . we have the legal authority under the DSU to accept and consider* amicus curiae *briefs in an appeal in which we find it pertinent and useful to do so. In this appeal, we have not found it necessary to take the two* amicus curiae *briefs filed into account in rendering our decision.*[62]

We have followed this same approach in a number of subsequent appeals.[63]

[62] Appellate Body Report, *US – Lead and Bismuth II, supra,* footnote 58, para 42.
[63] The issue of unsolicited *amicus curiae* briefs submitted to us by private individuals also arose in *EC – Asbestos, supra,* footnote 15; *Thailand – H-Beams, supra,* footnote 56; and *US – Shrimp (Article 21.5 – Malaysia), supra,* footnote 57.

160. Peru conceded at the oral hearing that its "position is not exactly supported by the case law of the Appellate Body".[64] On this, Peru is correct. Accordingly, we believe that the objections of Peru with regard to the *amicus curiae* brief submitted by a private individual are unfounded. We find that we have the authority to accept the brief filed by a private individual, and to consider it. We also find that the brief submitted by a private individual does not assist us in this appeal.

[64] Peru's response to questioning at the oral hearing.

161. We turn now to the issue of the *amicus curiae* brief filed by Morocco, which raises a novel issue, as this is the first time that a WTO Member has submitted such a brief in any WTO dispute settlement proceeding. The European Communities is of the view that we should not treat *amicus curiae* briefs submitted by private individuals differently from *amicus curiae* briefs submitted by WTO Members.[65] Peru objects to our accepting Morocco's brief, arguing that such acceptance would circumvent the rules in

the DSU setting out the conditions under which WTO Members can participate as third parties in dispute settlement proceedings.[66] Peru refers specifically to Articles 10.2 and 17.4 of the DSU, which provide, respectively:

Article 10

2. Any Member having a substantial interest in a matter before a panel and having notified its interest to the DSB (referred to in this Understanding as a "third party") shall have an opportunity to be heard by the panel and to make written submissions to the panel. These submissions shall also be given to the parties to the dispute and shall be reflected in the panel report.

Article 17

4. Only parties to the dispute, not third parties, may appeal a panel report. Third parties which have notified the DSB of a substantial interest in the matter pursuant to paragraph 2 of Article 10 may make written submissions to, and be given an opportunity to be heard by, the Appellate Body.

Peru asserts that, because Morocco did not notify its interest to the DSB in accordance with these provisions, Morocco cannot be given an opportunity to be heard by us.

[65] European Communities' response to questioning at the oral hearing.
[66] Peru's letter dated 26 July 2002.

162. We do not agree. As we said earlier, we found in *US – Lead and Bismuth II* that "nothing in the DSU or the *Working Procedures* specifically provides that we may accept and consider submissions or briefs from sources other than the participants and third participants in an appeal."[67] We also stated in that appeal that "neither the DSU nor the *Working Procedures* explicitly prohibit acceptance or consideration of such briefs."[68] In so ruling, we did *not* distinguish between, on the one hand, submissions from WTO Members that are not participants or third participants in a particular appeal, and, on the other hand, submissions from *non*-WTO Members.

[67] Appellate Body Report, *supra*, footnote 58, para 39.
[68] *Ibid*.

163. It is true that, unlike private individuals or organizations, WTO Members are given an explicit right, under Articles 10.2 and 17.4 of the DSU, to participate in dispute settlement proceedings as third parties. Thus, the question arises whether the existence of this explicit right, which is not accorded to non-Members, justifies treating WTO Members differently from non-WTO Members in the exercise of our authority to receive *amicus curiae* briefs. We do not believe that it does.

164. We have been urged by the parties to this dispute not to treat Members less favourably than non-Members with regard to participation as *amicus curiae*.[69] We agree. We have not. And we will not. As we have already determined that we have the authority to receive an *amicus curiae* brief from a private individual or an organization, *a fortiori* we are entitled to accept such a brief from a WTO Member, provided there is no prohibition on doing so in the DSU. We find no such prohibition.

[69] European Communities' response to questioning at the oral hearing; Peru's response to questioning at the oral hearing. Ecuador and Chile argued that if we were to accept and consider an amicus curiae brief submitted by a WTO Member that had not followed the procedures for participation as a third party or third participant, we would be according such Member greater rights than we would a WTO Member which had followed those procedures, but had not filed a written submission on appeal as specified in Rule 27(3) of our *Working Procedures*. According to Chile and Ecuador, the Member that had not filed a written submission on appeal would have an opportunity only to participate as a passive observer at the oral hearing, but would not be permitted to make its views known at that hearing. Chile

and Ecuador argue that, by contrast, the Member which had filed an *amicus curiae* brief would have greater rights because its views would be before us. We do not agree. A Member that has participated as a third party at the panel stage has a right to file a written submission on appeal in accordance with Rule 24, and if it does so we would have a duty to consider it. If such Member chooses for its own reasons not to file a written submission on appeal, our practice is to permit such Member to attend the oral hearing. By contrast, a Member which files an *amicus curiae* brief is not guaranteed that we will accept or consider the brief, and the Member will not be entitled to attend the oral hearing in any capacity.

165. None of the participants in this appeal has pointed to any provision of the DSU that can be understood as prohibiting WTO Members from participating in panel or appellate proceedings as an *amicus curiae*. Nor has any participant in this appeal demonstrated how such participation would contravene the DSU. Peru states only that the DSU provides that participation as a third party is governed by Articles 10.2 and 17.4, and appears to draw from this a negative inference such that Members may participate pursuant to those rules, or not at all. We have examined Articles 10.2 and 17.4, and we do not share Peru's view. Just because those provisions stipulate when a Member may participate in a dispute settlement proceeding as a third party or third participant, does not, in our view, lead inevitably to the conclusion that participation by a Member as an *amicus curiae* is prohibited.

166. As we explained in *US – Lead and Bismuth II*, the DSU gives WTO Members that are participants and third participants a legal *right* to participate in appellate proceedings.[70] In particular, WTO Members that are third participants in an appeal have the *right* to make written and oral submissions. The corollary is that we have a *duty*, by virtue of the DSU, to accept and consider these submissions from WTO Members. By contrast, participation as *amici* in WTO appellate proceedings is not a legal *right*, and we have no duty to accept any *amicus curiae* brief. We may do so, however, based on our legal authority to regulate our own procedures as stipulated in Article 17.9 of the DSU. The fact that Morocco, as a sovereign State, has chosen not to exercise its *right* to participate in this dispute by availing itself of its third-party rights at the panel stage does not, in our opinion, undermine our *legal authority* under the DSU and our *Working Procedures* to accept and consider the *amicus curiae* brief submitted by Morocco.

[70] Appellate Body Report, *supra,* footnote 58, para 40. This is subject to meeting the requirements in Rule 27(3) of the *Working Procedures*, which provides that "[a]ny third participant who has filed a submission pursuant to Rule 24 may appear to make oral arguments or presentations at the oral hearing." However, we have on several occasions permitted third parties who have not filed a submission to attend the oral hearing as passive observers.

167. Therefore, we find that we are entitled to accept the *amicus curiae* brief submitted by Morocco, and to consider it. We wish to emphasize, however, that, in accepting the brief filed by Morocco in this appeal, we are not suggesting that each time a Member files such a brief we are required to accept and consider it. To the contrary, acceptance of any *amicus curiae* brief is a matter of discretion, which we must exercise on a case-by-case basis. We recall our statement that:

> *The procedural rules of WTO dispute settlement are designed to promote . . . the fair, prompt and effective resolution of trade disputes.*[71]

Therefore, we could exercise our discretion to reject an *amicus curiae* brief if, by accepting it, this would interfere with the "fair, prompt and effective resolution of trade disputes". This could arise, for example, if a WTO Member were to seek to submit an *amicus curiae* brief at a very late stage in the appellate proceedings, with the result that accepting the brief would impose an undue burden on other participants.

[71] Appellate Body Report, *US – FSC, supra,* footnote 20, para 166. In that appeal, we were not referring in the quoted excerpt to the issue of amicus curiae briefs. The issue there related to the exercise of the right of appeal. We nevertheless believe that our views on how to interpret the *Working Procedures* are of general application and are thus pertinent to the *amicus curiae* issue as it arises in this case.

168. Having concluded that we have the legal authority to accept the *amicus curiae* brief submitted by Morocco, we now consider whether Morocco's brief assists us in this appeal.

169. Morocco's *amicus curiae* brief provides mainly factual information. It refers to the scientific differences between *Sardina pilchardus* Walbaum ("*Sardina pilchardus*") and *Sardinops sagax sagax* ("*Sardinops sagax*"), and it also provides economic information about the Moroccan fishing and canning industries. As Article 17.6 of the DSU limits an appeal to issues of law and legal interpretations developed by the panel, the factual information provided in Morocco's *amicus curiae* brief is not pertinent in this appeal. In addition, Morocco has alleged in its *amicus curiae* brief that the measure at issue in this appeal is consistent with relevant international standards, including those of the Codex Alimentarius Commission (the "Codex Commission"). Morocco does not elaborate on this allegation, and provides no support for this position. Therefore, this, too, fails to assist us in this appeal. However, some of the legal arguments put forward by Morocco relate to Article 2.1 of the *TBT Agreement* and to the GATT 1994. Therefore, we will consider whether these arguments are of assistance when we consider Article 2.1 and the GATT 1994 later in this Report.

170. In sum, with the exception of the arguments relating to Article 2.1 of the *TBT Agreement* and the GATT 1994, to which we will return later, we find that Morocco's *amicus curiae* brief does not assist us in this appeal.

United States – Preliminary Determinations with Respect to Certain Softwood Lumber from Canada ('US – Softwood Lumber (Preliminary Determinations)'), 2002

Short summary and commentary

In this case (one in a series of cases on softwood lumber from Canada), Canada challenged certain preliminary countervailing duty determinations that the US had made with respect to softwood lumber. Canada argued that those determinations were inconsistent with the GATT and the SCM Agreement. During the proceedings, the panel received four amicus briefs. Although the panel report indicates that one of the briefs was from a public interest NGO (the Interior Alliance) it does not reveal the source of the other three submissions, nor indicate which party those submissions supported (Panel report, paragraph 7.2).

This case illustrates how the timing of the amicus submissions can affect their fate. The one brief that was accepted for consideration in this case was submitted prior to the first substantive meeting of the panel. The panel cited the late timing of three other submissions as its reason for rejecting those briefs (*Id.*).

Excerpts

Report of the Panel, *United States – Preliminary Determinations with Respect to Certain Softwood Lumber from Canada*, WT/DS236/R, adopted on 1 November 2002.

VII. Findings [paras 7.1–7.2]

. . .

7.2. As a preliminary matter, we note that in the course of these proceedings, we decided to accept for consideration one unsolicited *amicus curiae* brief from a Canadian non-governmental organization, the *Interior Alliance*. This brief was submitted to us prior to the first substantive meeting of the Panel with the parties and the parties and third parties were given an opportunity to comment on this *amicus curiae* brief. After this meeting, we received three additional unsolicited *amicus curiae* briefs. For reasons relating to the timing of these submissions, we decided not to accept any of these later briefs.

United States – Countervailing Measures Concerning Certain Products from the European Communities ('US – Countervailing Measures on Certain EC Products'), 2003

Short summary and commentary

The central issue in this dispute was whether the US, when applying countervailing duties to certain products from the European Communities, had acted inconsistently with its obligations under the SCM Agreement and the WTO Agreement. The panel found that it had, and the US appealed. During the appellate proceedings, the Appellate Body received an amicus brief supporting the US position.

The Appellate Body made its decision regarding how it would treat the amicus brief after giving the parties and third parties the opportunity to comment – both in writing and orally – on the submission (AB report, paragraph 10). The Appellate Body concluded that it accepted the brief (in accordance with the parties' views) but would not take the brief into account as it was not 'of assistance' in the appeal (*Id.* at paragraph 76). It did not provide any elaboration on just why the brief was not 'of assistance'. While the dispute gives little guidance in this respect, it does, to some extent, illustrate a procedural route that WTO tribunals might take when considering whether and to what extent to consider the contents of amicus briefs. It also confirms the approach taken in previous cases, not to consider briefs that are not part of a party's official submission.

Excerpts

Report of the Appellate Body, *United States – Countervailing Measures Concerning Certain Products from the European Communities*, WT/DS212/AB/R, adopted on 8 January 2003.

I. Introduction [paras 1–11]

. . .

10. The Appellate Body responded to the request of the European Communities on 27 September 2002, stating that a decision on the admissibility or relevance of the *amicus submission* would not be made until the written and oral submissions of all the participants had been considered.[20] The Appellate Body therefore invited all the participants "to address the [*amicus curiae*] brief in the further course of this appeal".[21]

[20] Letter dated 27 September 2002, from the Director of the Appellate Body Secretariat to the Minister-Counsellor, Permanent Delegation of the European Communities to the WTO.
[21] *Ibid.*

. . .

V. Procedural Issues

. . .

B. The *Amicus Curiae* Brief [para 76]

76. We turn next to the issue of the *amicus curiae* brief that we received from an industry association[151] in the course of this appeal. Both the United States and the European Communities agreed that we have the authority to accept the brief.[152] The United States confirmed that the brief was not a part of the official submission of the United States, but that the United States agreed with much, although not all, of the brief.[153] The European Communities said that it disagreed with a number of aspects of the brief, and argued that there was no reason for the Appellate Body to take the brief into account in this appeal.[154] We have considered the arguments of the participants and the third participants. The brief has not been taken into account by us as we do not find it to be of assistance in this appeal.

[151] American Iron and Steel Institute.

[152] United States' and European Communities' responses to questioning at the oral hearing. The third participants disagreed.

[153] United States' responses to questioning at the oral hearing.

[154] European Communities' responses to questioning at the oral hearing.

United States – Final Countervailing Duty Determination with Respect to Certain Softwood Lumber from Canada ('US – Softwood Lumber (Final Determinations)'), 2004

Short summary and commentary

In this case, Canada challenged the US-imposed final countervailing duties on certain softwood lumber from Canada under the SCM Agreement and the GATT. (The final countervailing duties at issue in this case were different from the preliminary countervailing duty determinations at issue in *US – Preliminary Determinations with Respect to Certain Softwood Lumber from Canada,* discussed above). The dispute drew attention from, among others, environmental NGOs who saw the case as providing an important opportunity to address the relationship between the WTO's disciplines and environmentally harmful subsidies.

A footnote in the panel's report reveals that the panel received three amicus submissions relating to the dispute (Panel report, footnote 75). It does not, however, provide other details regarding the source or content of those briefs. In addressing the three submissions, the panel declared that it would only consider arguments raised in amicus briefs if those arguments were also taken up by the parties or third parties.

The approach taken by the panel in this case seems to be an attempt to minimize controversy; by leaving open the possibility that it will accept amicus briefs, the panel could appease interested submitters. Yet, by so limiting the types of arguments it would consider, the panel could also placate those parties or third parties who would otherwise argue that the consideration of amicus briefs places upon them the additional burden of having to respond to the contents of those submissions.

At the same time, however, the third party oral statement of India indicates that even this approach goes too far for certain Members. In its statement reproduced below, India expressed its 'systemic concern' that the panel accept or consider any submission other than from parties and third parties to the dispute.

In the appellate process of *US – Softwood Lumber (Final Determinations)*, the Appellate Body also received two amicus briefs. Like the panel, the Appellate Body gave the parties and third parties a chance to address issues raised in the brief. Because the 'briefs dealt with some questions not addressed in the submissions' and given that none of the parties adopted the arguments made by the amici, the Appellate Body found it unnecessary to take the briefs into account (AB report, paragraph 9).

India, again, took the occasion at the oral hearing to vehemently contest the admissibility of unsolicited *amicus curiae* briefs in WTO dispute settlement proceedings.

The excerpts reproduced below include excerpts from both the panel and the Appellate Body reports.

Excerpts

Report of the Panel, *United States – Final Countervailing Duty Determination with Respect to Certain Softwood Lumber from Canada*, WT/DS257/R, adopted as modified by the Appellate Body Report on 17 February 2004.

V. Arguments of the third parties

. . .

C. Third party oral statement of India [paras 5.53–5.56]

. . .

5.54 More importantly, India has systemic concern about the Panel's decision to accept amicus curiae briefs and consider their arguments to the extent that such arguments raised by the parties and third parties to the dispute.

5.55. India considers that the WTO panels and the Appellate Body do not have a right to accept and consider any briefs or arguments submitted by anyone other than the parties or third parties to the dispute. WTO panels, however, under Article 13 of the DSU, could seek information or technical advice or opinion of any individual or body on certain aspects of the matter or factual issues concerning scientific or technical matter raised in a dispute. We do not consider that 'arguments' of uninvited bodies or individuals would fall into such category.

5.56. India is aware of the Appellate Body's view on amicus curiae briefs and the so-called "case law" developed by it. India does not agree with the Appellate Body's view that whatever is not prohibited by the DSU or other covered agreements is permissible and, therefore, the Appellate Body and the panels have authority to accept amicus briefs. There is no textual or other legal basis for such assertions. Therefore, India requests the panel refrain from accepting or considering the unsolicited amicus curiae briefs submitted to it.

. . .

[75] In addition to these seven claims, we note that Canada's request for establishment of a Panel also included a claim relating to expedited and administrative reviews. Canada did not advance any arguments in respect of this claim, and therefore we will not address this undeveloped claim.

WT/DS257/R/Corr.1: The following text should be added to the end of footnote 75 in document WT/DS257/R:

"In addition, prior to the first substantive meeting we ruled, in respect of three unsolicited *amicus curiae* briefs that were sent to us, that we would consider any arguments raised by *amici curiae* only to the extent that those arguments were taken up in the written submissions and/or oral statements of any party or third party."

Report of the Appellate Body, *United States – Final Countervailing Duty Determination with Respect to Certain Softwood Lumber from Canada*, WT/DS257/AB/R, adopted on 19 January 2004.

I. Introduction [paras 1–11]

. . .

9. The Appellate Body received two *amicus curiae* briefs during the course of these proceedings. The first, dated 21 October 2003, was received from the Indigenous Network on Economies and Trade (based in Vancouver, British Columbia, Canada).[21] The second, dated 7 November 2003, was a joint brief filed by Defenders of Wildlife (based in Washington, D.C., United States), Natural Resources Defense Council (based in Washington, D.C., United States) and Northwest Ecosystem Alliance (based in Bellingham, state of Washington, United States).[22] These briefs dealt with some questions not addressed in the submissions of the participants or third participants. No participant or third participant adopted the arguments made in these briefs.[23] Ultimately, in this appeal, the Division did not find it necessary to take the two *amicus curiae* briefs into account in rendering its decision.

[21] This brief purported to add an indigenous dimension to the issues raised by this appeal.
[22] The organizations filing this brief commented on the environmental implications of the issues raised by this appeal.
[23] Responses to questioning at the oral hearing.

. . .

II. Arguments of the Participants and the Third Participants

. . .

E. Arguments of the Third Participants

. . .

2. India [para 42]

42. Pursuant to Rule 24 of the *Working Procedures*, India chose not to submit a third participant's submission. In its statement at the oral hearing, India addressed the issue of calculation of benefit and contested the admissibility of unsolicited *amicus curiae* briefs in WTO dispute settlement proceedings.

Index